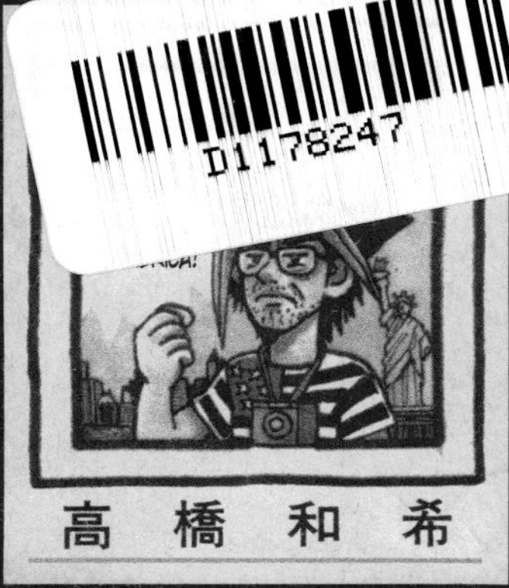
高橋和希

YU-GI-OH! IS FINISHED IN THE
AZINE, AND I THINK I'VE MAN-
D TO CONVEY THE THEMES I
TED TO. THE CARDS PLAYED A
ROLE IN THE STORY, BUT MORE
IMPORTANTLY, THE CHARACTERS' HEARTS SWUNG LIKE A PENDULUM BETWEEN THE TWO SIDES WHICH EXIST IN EVERYONE...LIGHT AND DARK, GOOD AND EVIL, KINDNESS AND ANGER. THE CARDS EXPRESSED THE PAIN AND SORROW OF THIS BACK-AND-FORTH CONFLICT, IN THE FORM OF DUELS.

BUT WHEN A PENDULUM SWINGS ALL THE WAY AROUND, IT DRAWS A CIRCLE, AND THAT IS THE STRENGTH OF THE MAIN CHARACTER.

—KAZUKI TAKAHASHI, 2004

Artist/author Kazuki Takahashi first tried to break into the manga business in 1982, but success eluded him until **Yu-Gi-Oh!** debuted in the Japanese **Weekly Shonen Jump** magazine in 1996. **Yu-Gi-Oh!**'s themes of friendship and fighting, together with Takahashi's weird and wonderful art, soon became enormously successful, spawning a real-world card game, video games, and two anime series. A lifelong gamer, Takahashi enjoys Shogi (Japanese chess), Mahjong, card games, and tabletop RPGs, among other games.

Yu-Gi-Oh!
2-in-1 Edition
Volume 13

SHONEN JUMP Manga Omnibus Edition

A compilation of the graphic novel volumes 37 & 38

STORY AND ART BY Kazuki Takahashi

Translation & English Adaptation/Anita Sengupta
Touch-up Art & Lettering/Kelle Han
Design/Sean Lee (Manga Edition)
Design/Sam Elzway (Omnibus Edition)
Editor/Jason Thompson (Manga Edition)
Editor/Erica Yee (Omnibus Edition)

Printed in the U.S.A.

Published by VIZ Media, LLC
P.O. Box 77010
San Francisco, CA 94107

10 9 8 7 6 5 4 3 2 1
Omnibus edition first printing, February 2018

www.shonenjump.com

VIZ media
www.viz.com

SHONEN JUMP MANGA

YU-GI-OH! Millennium World

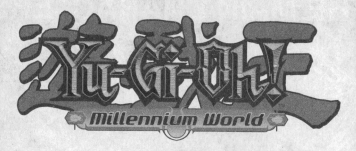

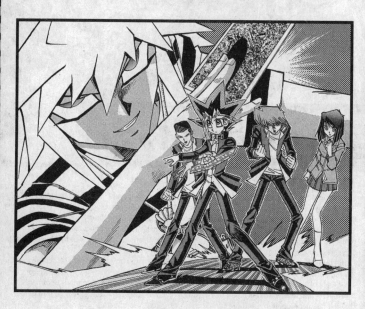

Vol. 37

THE NAME OF THE PHARAOH

STORY AND ART BY

KAZUKI TAKAHASHI

THE MAIN CHARACTERS

KATSUYA JONOUCHI

HASAN **ANZU MAZAKI** **HIROTO HONDA**

YUGI MUTOU

THE STORY SO FAR...

Shy 10th-grader Yugi spent most of his time alone playing games…until he solved the Millennium Puzzle, a mysterious Egyptian artifact. Possessed by the puzzle, Yugi developed an alter ego: Yu-Gi-Oh, the King of Games, the soul of a pharaoh from ancient Egypt! Using the three Egyptian God Cards, Yu-Gi-Oh traveled into the "world of memories" of his own life 3,000 years ago. There, he found himself on the throne, served by six priests who used the Millennium Items, which had been created 15 years ago to save Egypt from invaders.

But unbeknownst even to the pharaoh, the Millennium Items were stained with blood. Created by the high priest Akhenaden, the Millennium Items were powered by human souls—the souls of the village of Kul Elna, which had been ritually slaughtered by troops under Akhenaden's command! Bakura, the sole survivor of Kul Elna, grew up into a revenge-obsessed madman. His goal: to gather the seven Millennium Items and summon the dark god Zorc Necrophades!

After many battles, the pharaoh's forces pursued Bakura to a shrine beneath the village of Kul Elna. But just when the Ancient Egyptian Bakura was defeated, the modern-day Bakura suddenly appeared. Bakura told Yu-Gi-Oh the shocking truth: he really hadn't gone back in time. The "world of memories" is a simulation, a shadow role-playing game based on Yugi's memories of the past. And if Bakura wins the game, then the soul of Zorc Necrophades will be reborn in the modern world!

Before Yu-Gi-Oh's eyes, the corrupt priest Akhenaden switches sides and summons the dark god, Zorc Necrophades. Now the only thing that can save Yu-Gi-Oh is his friends—Yugi, Honda, Anzu and Jonouchi—who have followed him into the "world of memories." As Yu-Gi-Oh fights the last battle, his friends explore the pharaoh's tomb to find the most powerful magic in the "world of memories": the pharaoh's forgotten name!

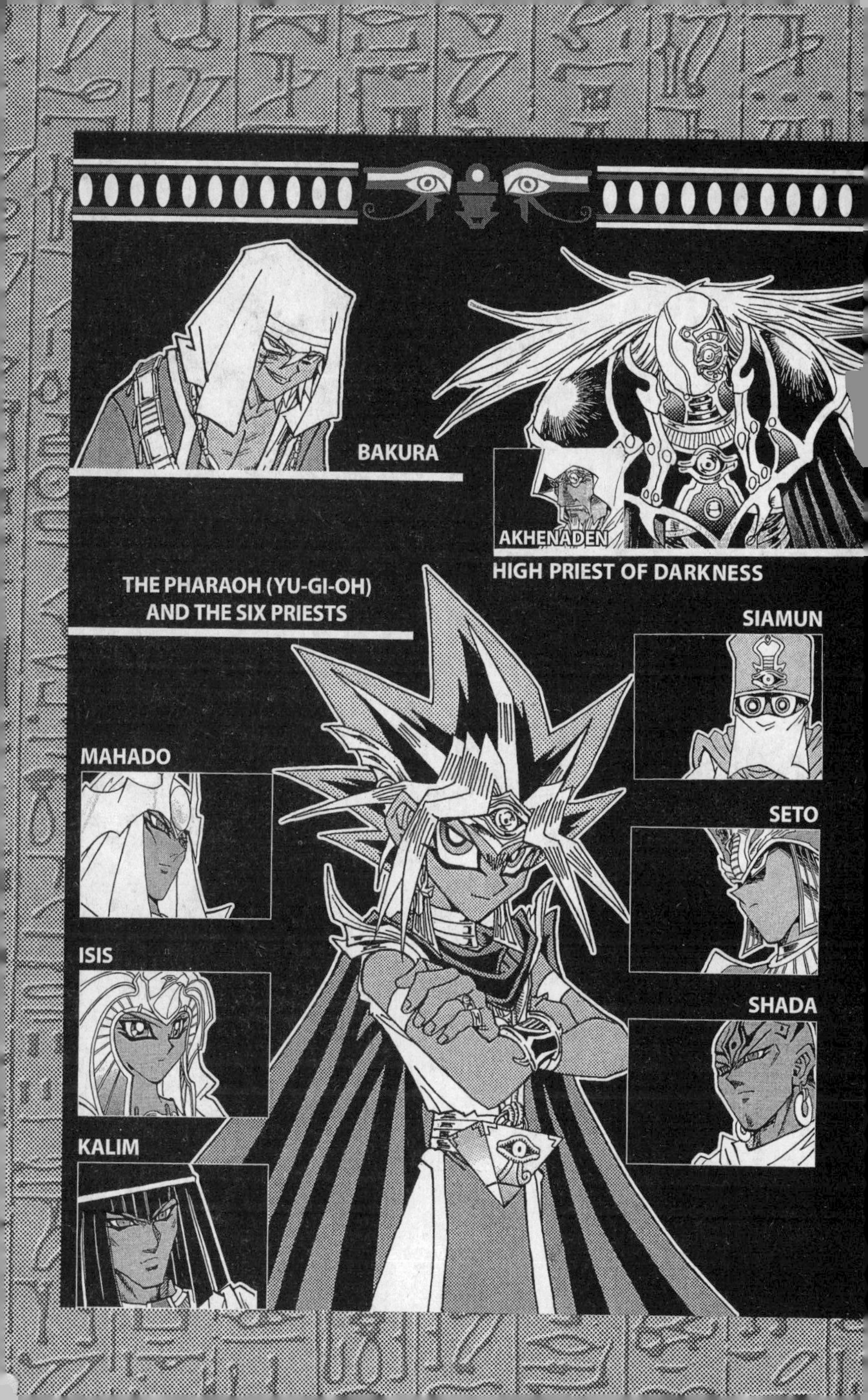
BAKURA
AKHENADEN
HIGH PRIEST OF DARKNESS
THE PHARAOH (YU-GI-OH)
AND THE SIX PRIESTS
SIAMUN
MAHADO
SETO
ISIS
SHADA
KALIM

Vol. 37

CONTENTS

Duel 324	Battle in the Shrine!	7
Duel 325	The Silent Duelist!!	27
Duel 326	Gather, Ghosts!	47
Duel 327	I Won't Give Up!!	67
Duel 328	The End of the World!!	87
Duel 329	Until Our *Ba* Runs Out!	107
Duel 330	The Guardian God!	127
Duel 331	The Light of the Soul!	147
Duel 332	The Stone Slabs of the Modern World!	165
Duel 333	In the Name of the Pharaoh	183

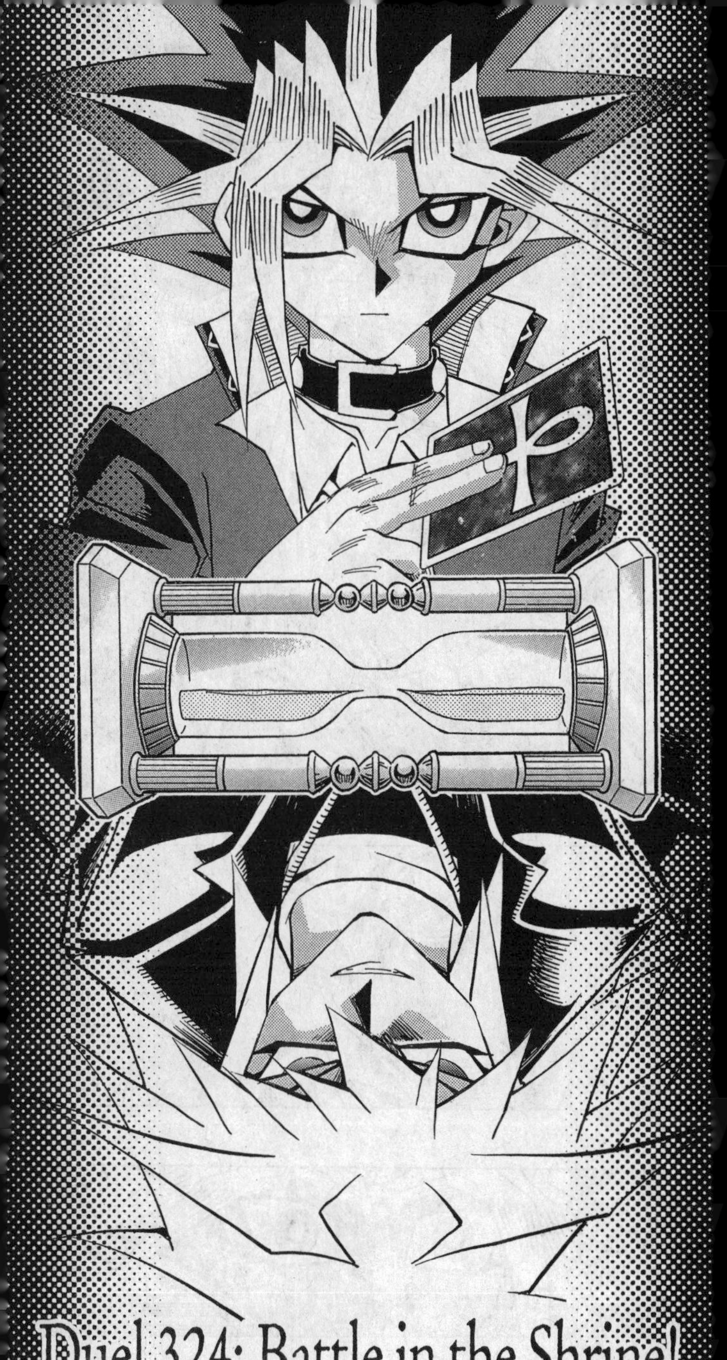

Duel 324: Battle in the Shrine!

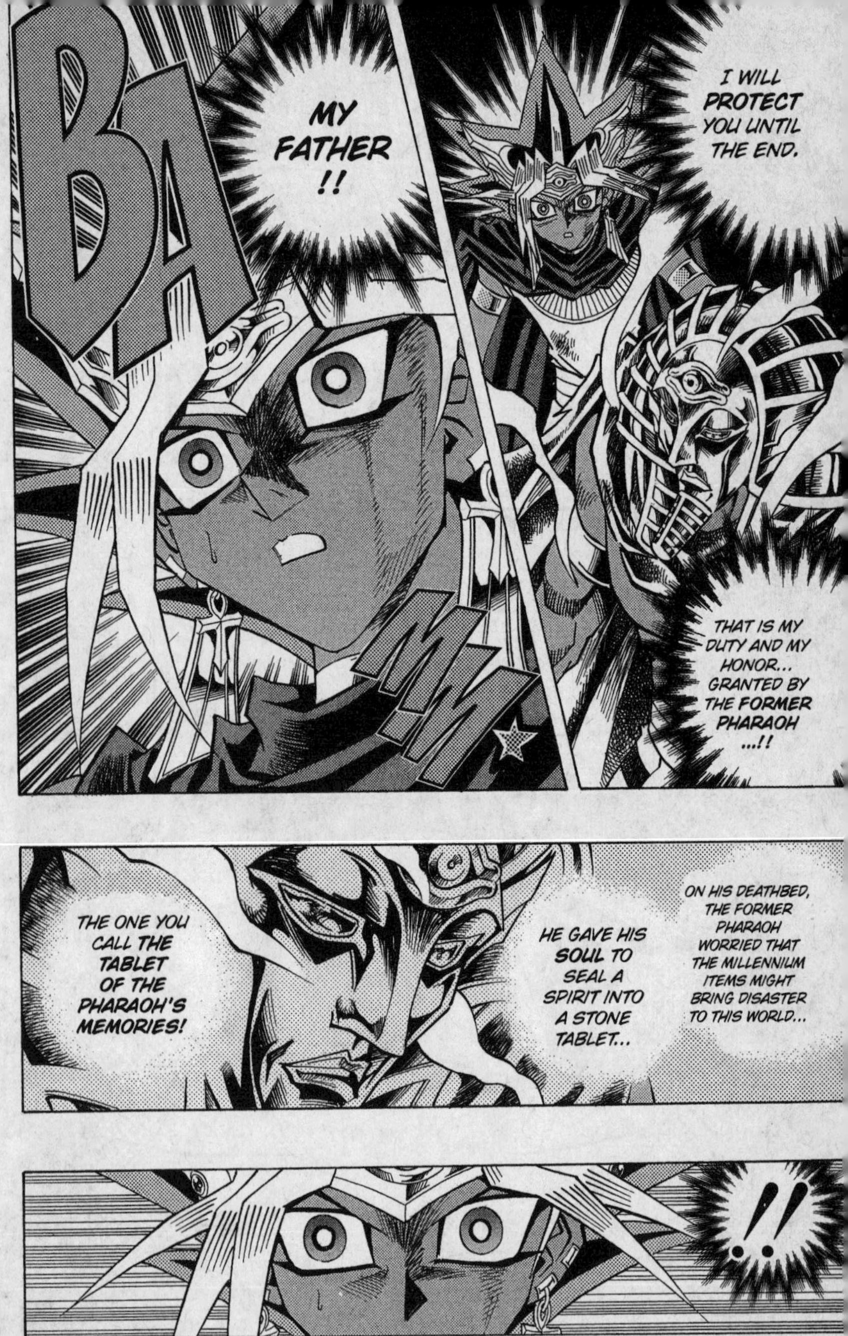
I WILL PROTECT YOU UNTIL THE END.
THAT IS MY DUTY AND MY HONOR... GRANTED BY THE FORMER PHARAOH ...!!
MY FATHER !!
BA
MM
ON HIS DEATHBED, THE FORMER PHARAOH WORRIED THAT THE MILLENNIUM ITEMS MIGHT BRING DISASTER TO THIS WORLD...
HE GAVE HIS SOUL TO SEAL A SPIRIT INTO A STONE TABLET...
THE ONE YOU CALL THE TABLET OF THE PHARAOH'S MEMORIES!
!!

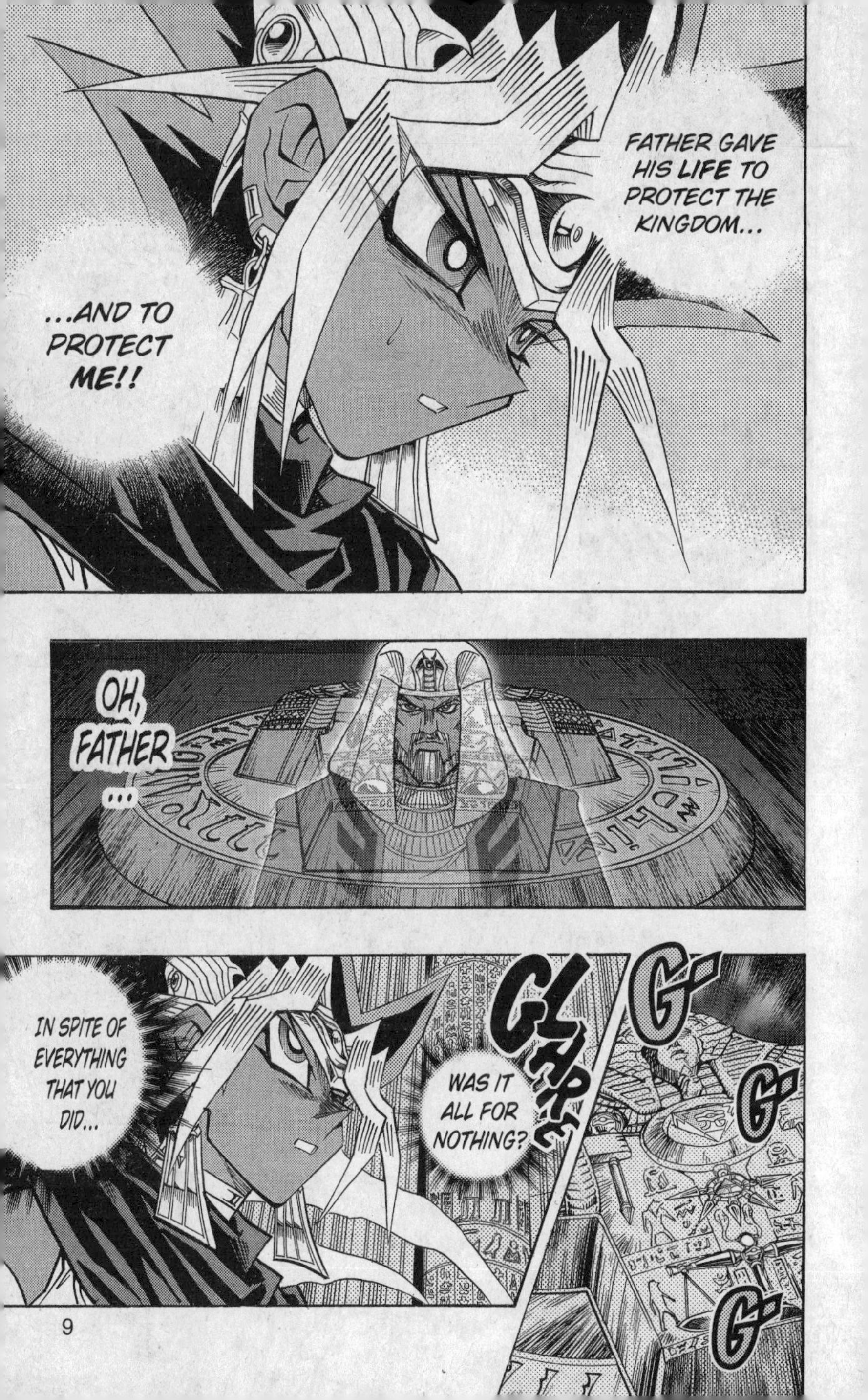
FATHER GAVE HIS LIFE TO PROTECT THE KINGDOM...
...AND TO PROTECT ME!!
OH, FATHER...
G-
G-
G-
GLARE
IN SPITE OF EVERYTHING THAT YOU DID...
WAS IT ALL FOR NOTHING?

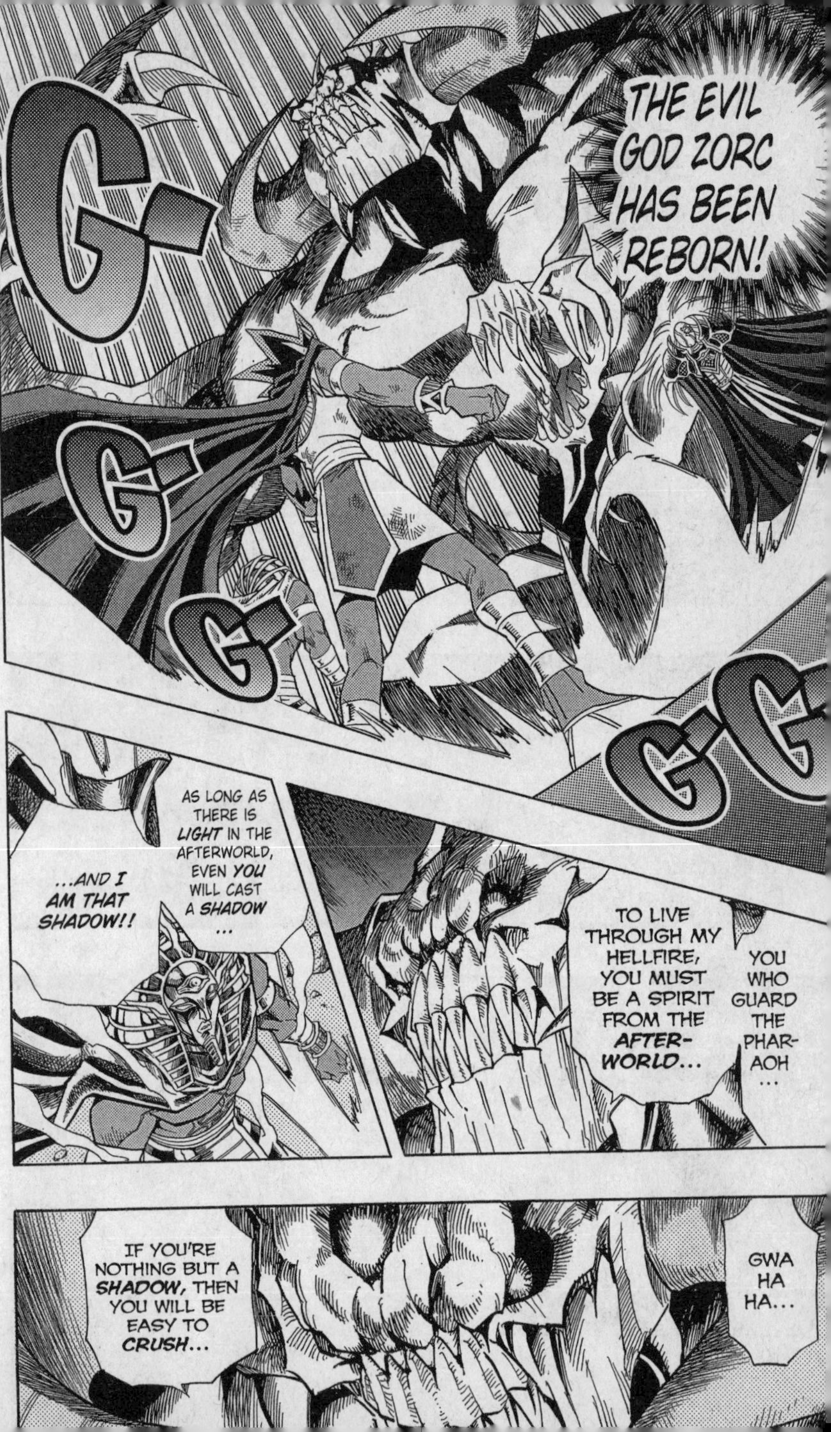
THE EVIL GOD ZORC HAS BEEN REBORN!
G-
G-
G
G-G-
YOU WHO GUARD THE PHARAOH...
TO LIVE THROUGH MY HELLFIRE, YOU MUST BE A SPIRIT FROM THE AFTERWORLD...
AS LONG AS THERE IS LIGHT IN THE AFTERWORLD, EVEN YOU WILL CAST A SHADOW...
...AND I AM THAT SHADOW!!
GWA HA HA...
IF YOU'RE NOTHING BUT A SHADOW, THEN YOU WILL BE EASY TO CRUSH...

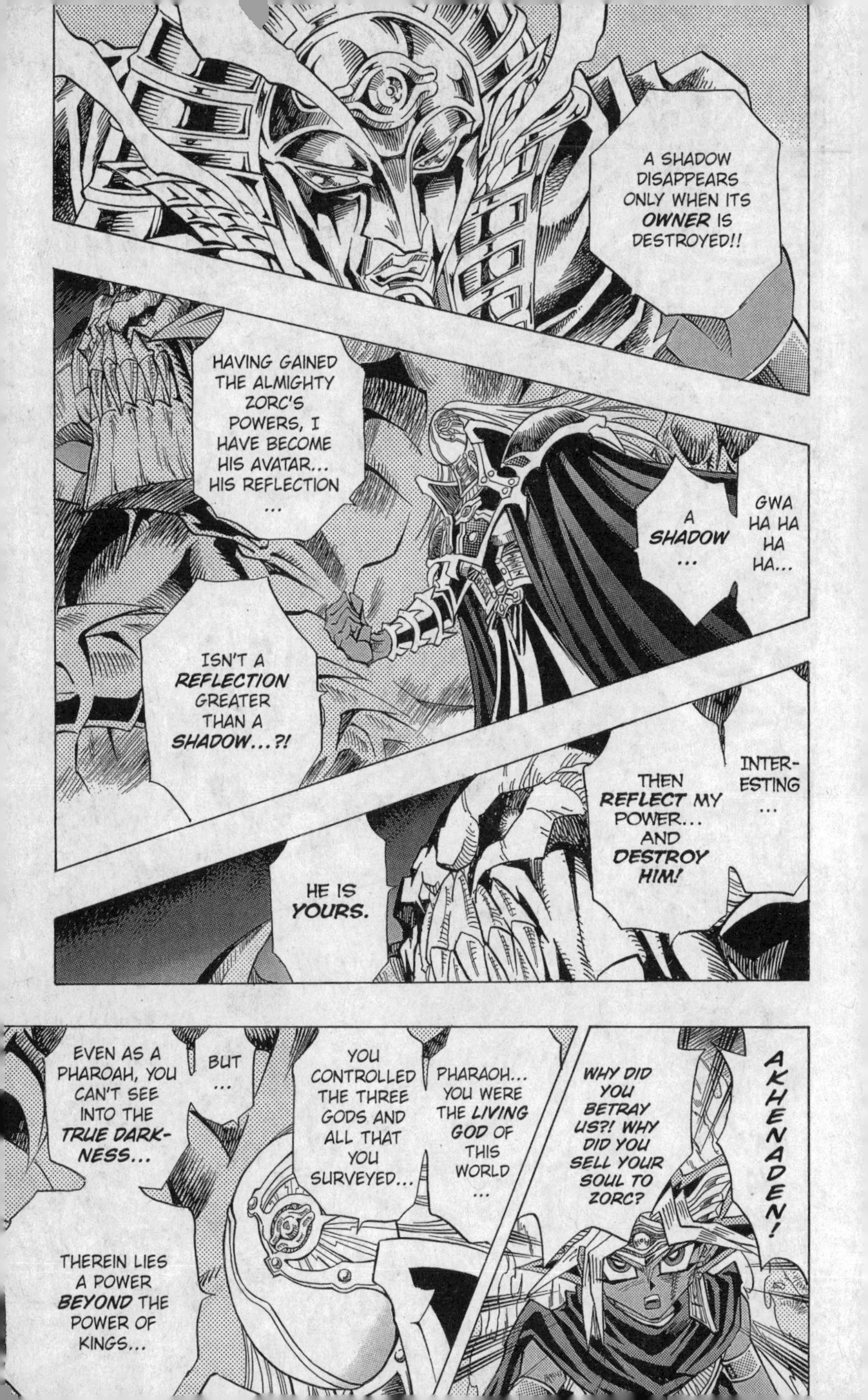
A SHADOW DISAPPEARS ONLY WHEN ITS OWNER IS DESTROYED!!
GWA HA HA HA HA...
A SHADOW...
HAVING GAINED THE ALMIGHTY ZORC'S POWERS, I HAVE BECOME HIS AVATAR... HIS REFLECTION...
ISN'T A REFLECTION GREATER THAN A SHADOW...?!
INTER-ESTING...
THEN REFLECT MY POWER... AND DESTROY HIM!
HE IS YOURS.
AKHENADEN!
WHY DID YOU BETRAY US?! WHY DID YOU SELL YOUR SOUL TO ZORC?
PHARAOH... YOU WERE THE LIVING GOD OF THIS WORLD...
YOU CONTROLLED THE THREE GODS AND ALL THAT YOU SURVEYED...
BUT...
EVEN AS A PHARAOH, YOU CAN'T SEE INTO THE TRUE DARK-NESS...
THEREIN LIES A POWER BEYOND THE POWER OF KINGS...

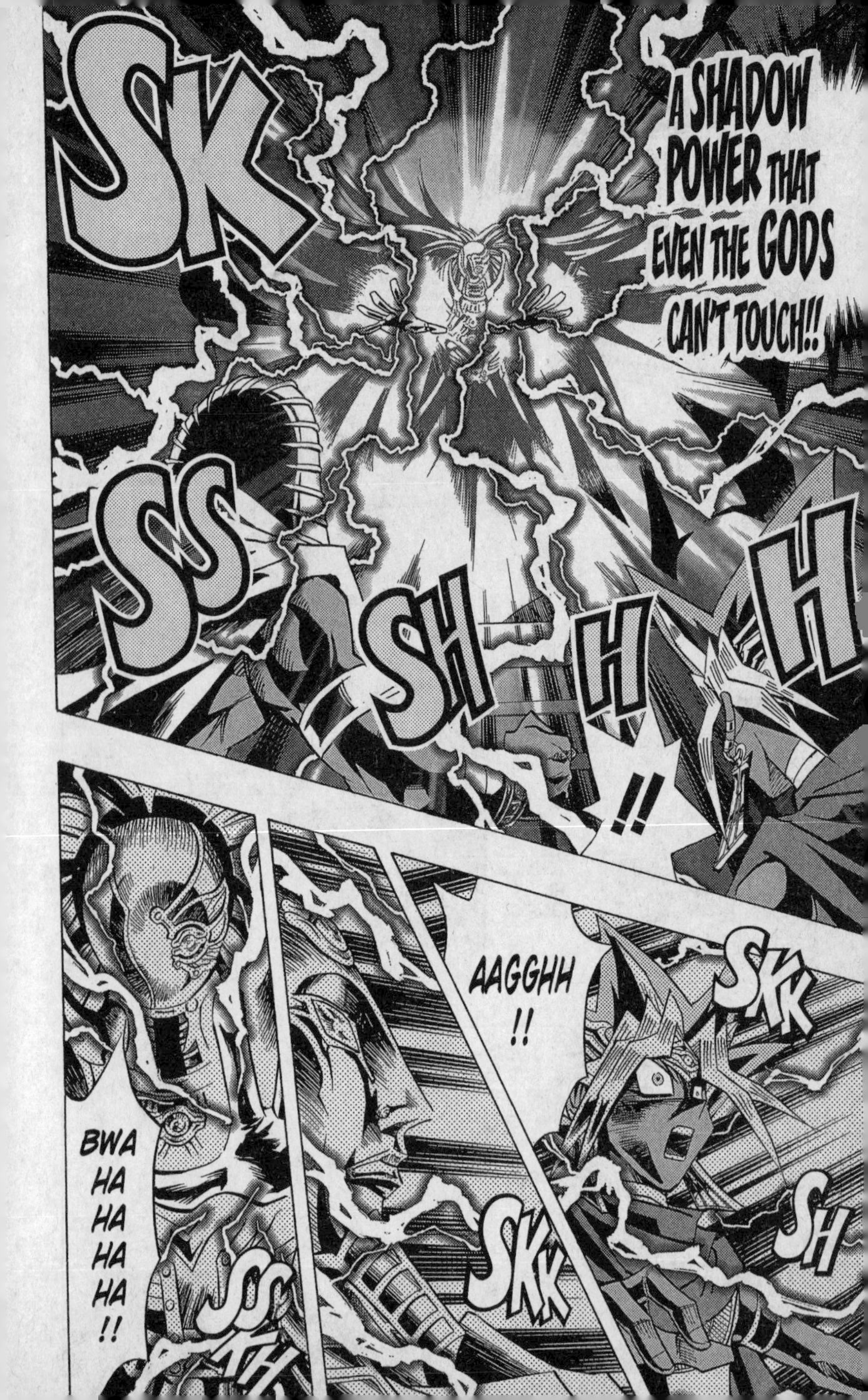
A SHADOW POWER THAT EVEN THE GODS CAN'T TOUCH!!
SK
SS
SH
H
H
!!
SKK
SH
AAGGHH!!
SKK
BWA HA HA HA HA!!
SS

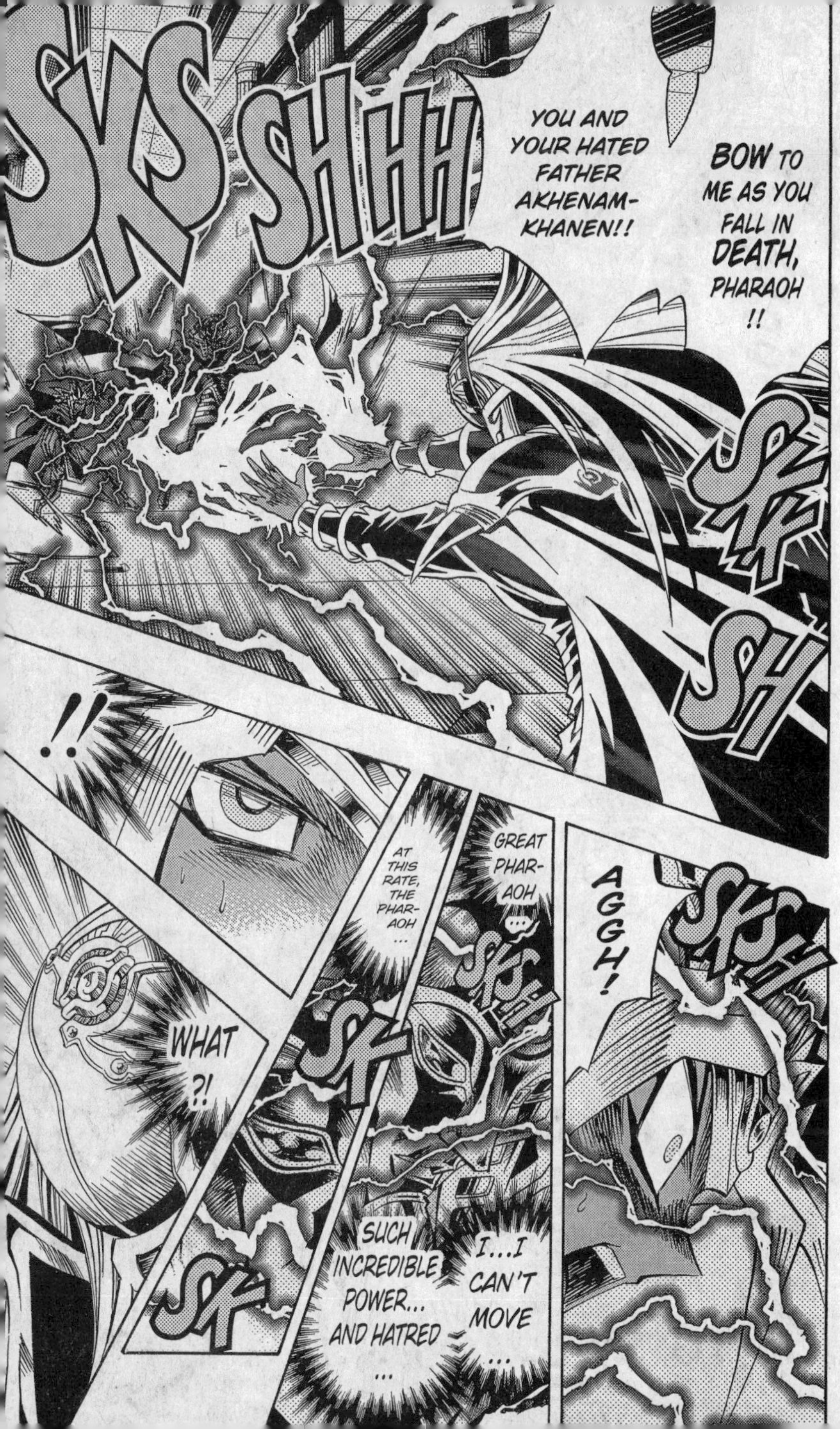
BOW TO ME AS YOU FALL IN DEATH, PHARAOH!!
YOU AND YOUR HATED FATHER AKHENAMKHANEN!!
SKS SHHH
SK
SH
!!
SKSH
AGGH!
GREAT PHARAOH...
AT THIS RATE, THE PHARAOH...
SKSH
SK
I...I CAN'T MOVE...
SUCH INCREDIBLE POWER... AND HATRED...
WHAT?!
SK

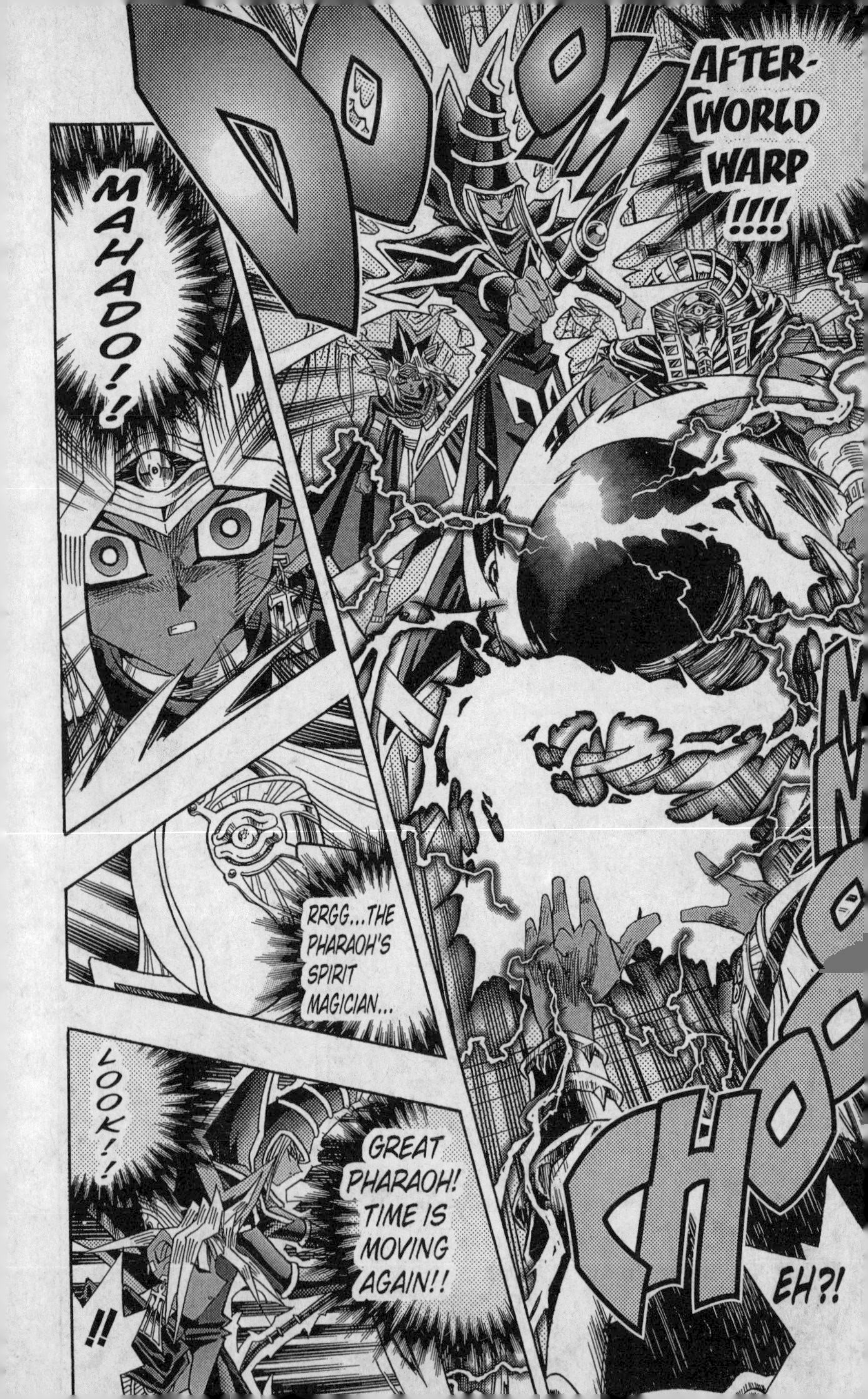
AFTER-WORLD WARP!!!!
EH?!
MAHADO!!
RRGG...THE PHARAOH'S SPIRIT MAGICIAN...
LOOK!!
GREAT PHARAOH! TIME IS MOVING AGAIN!!
!!

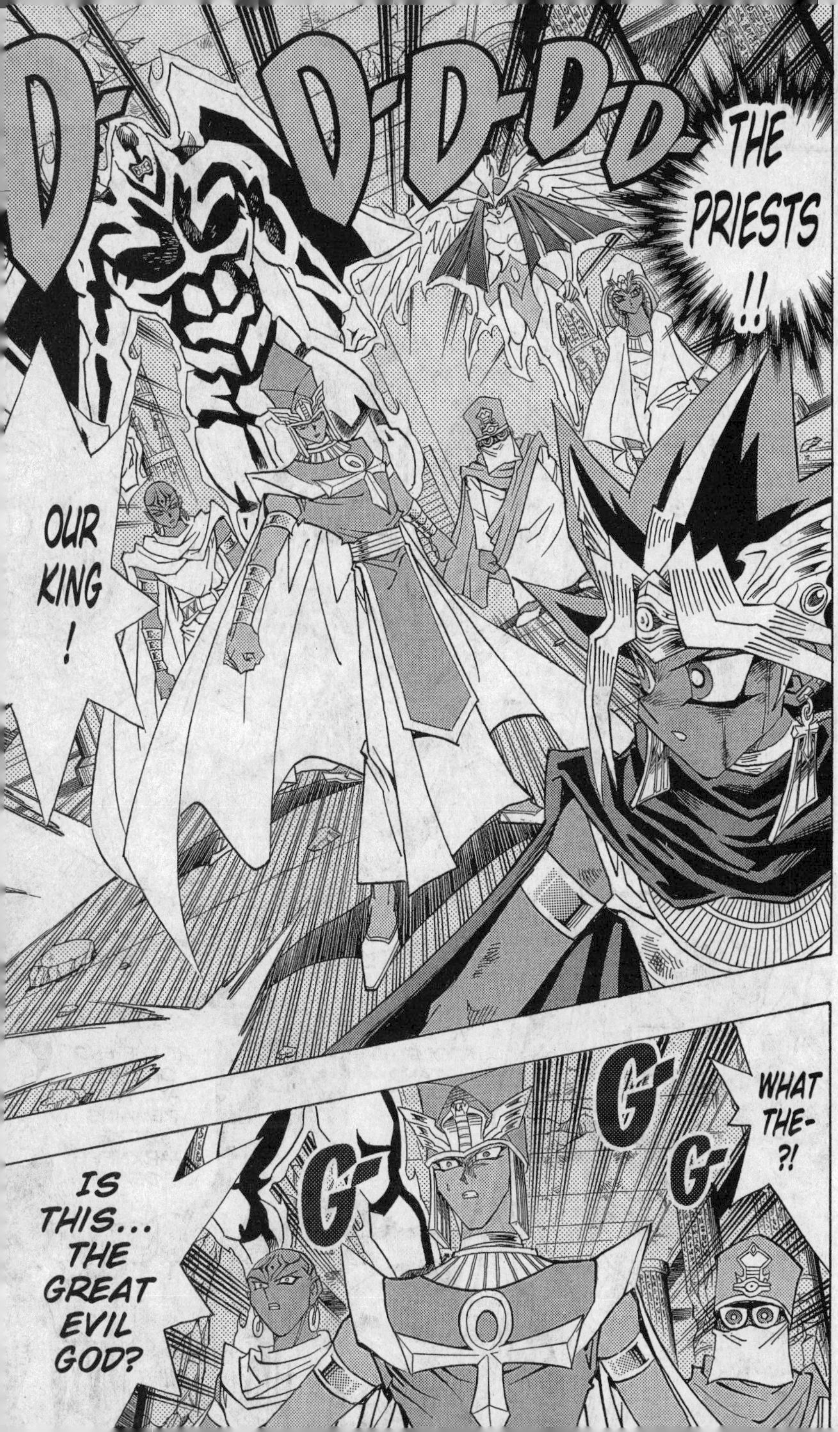
THE PRIESTS!!
D-D-D-D-D
OUR KING!
WHAT THE-?!
G-G-G-G
IS THIS... THE GREAT EVIL GOD?

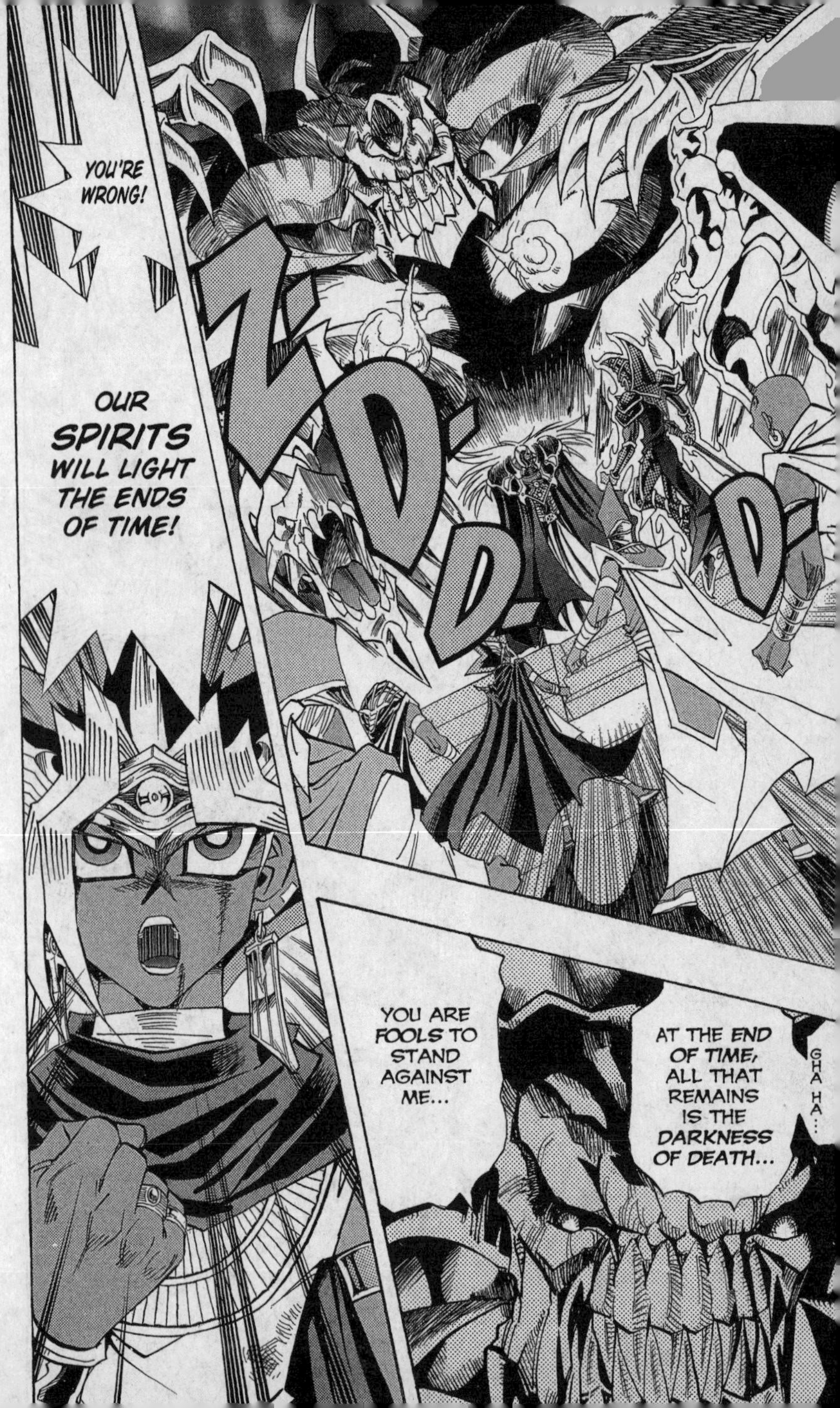
ZDDD
GHA HA...
AT THE END OF TIME, ALL THAT REMAINS IS THE DARKNESS OF DEATH...
YOU ARE FOOLS TO STAND AGAINST ME...
YOU'RE WRONG!
OUR SPIRITS WILL LIGHT THE ENDS OF TIME!

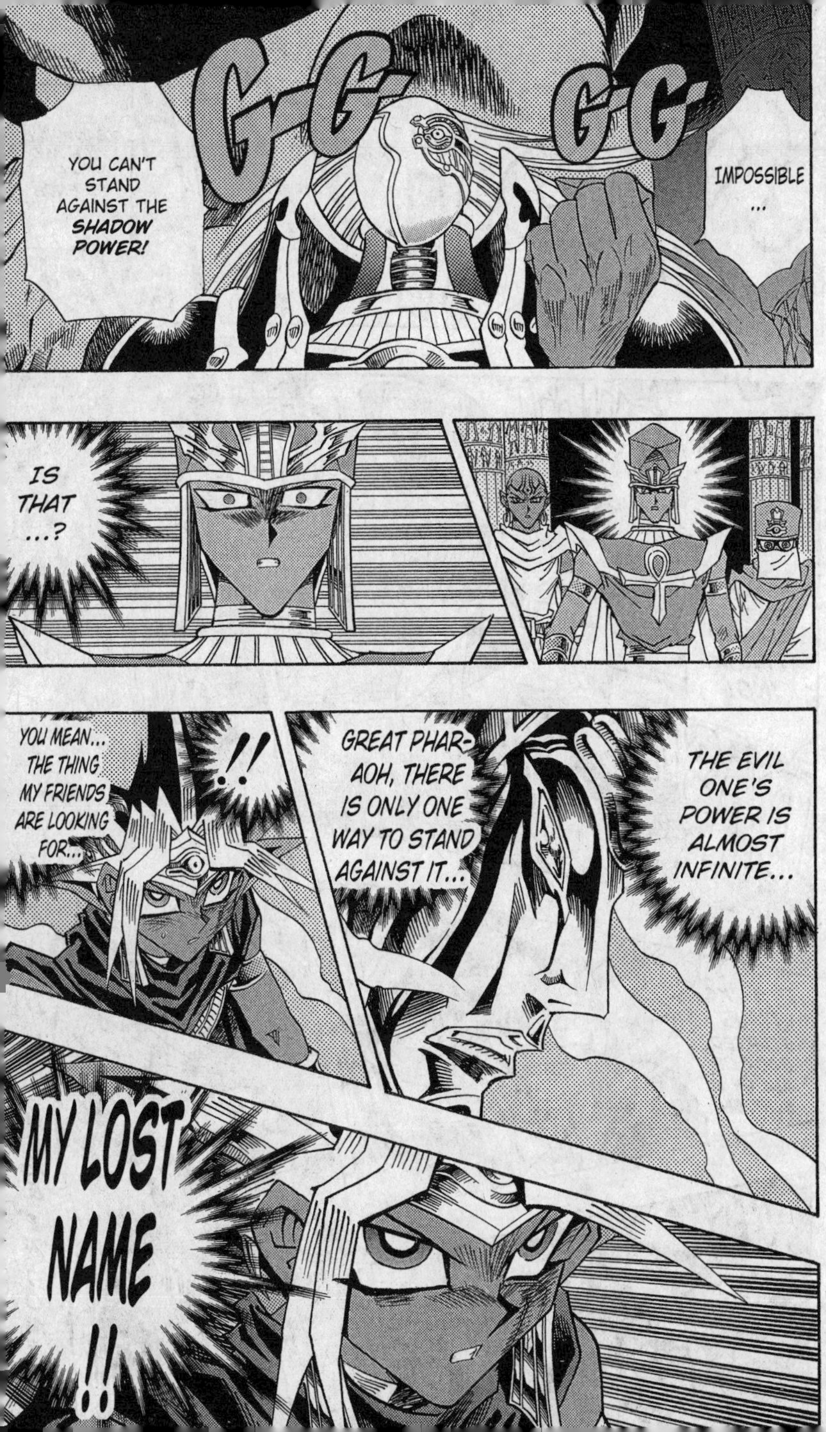
G-G
IMPOSSIBLE ...
G-G
YOU CAN'T STAND AGAINST THE SHADOW POWER!
IS THAT ...?
THE EVIL ONE'S POWER IS ALMOST INFINITE...
GREAT PHAR-AOH, THERE IS ONLY ONE WAY TO STAND AGAINST IT...
!!
YOU MEAN... THE THING MY FRIENDS ARE LOOKING FOR...
MY LOST NAME !!

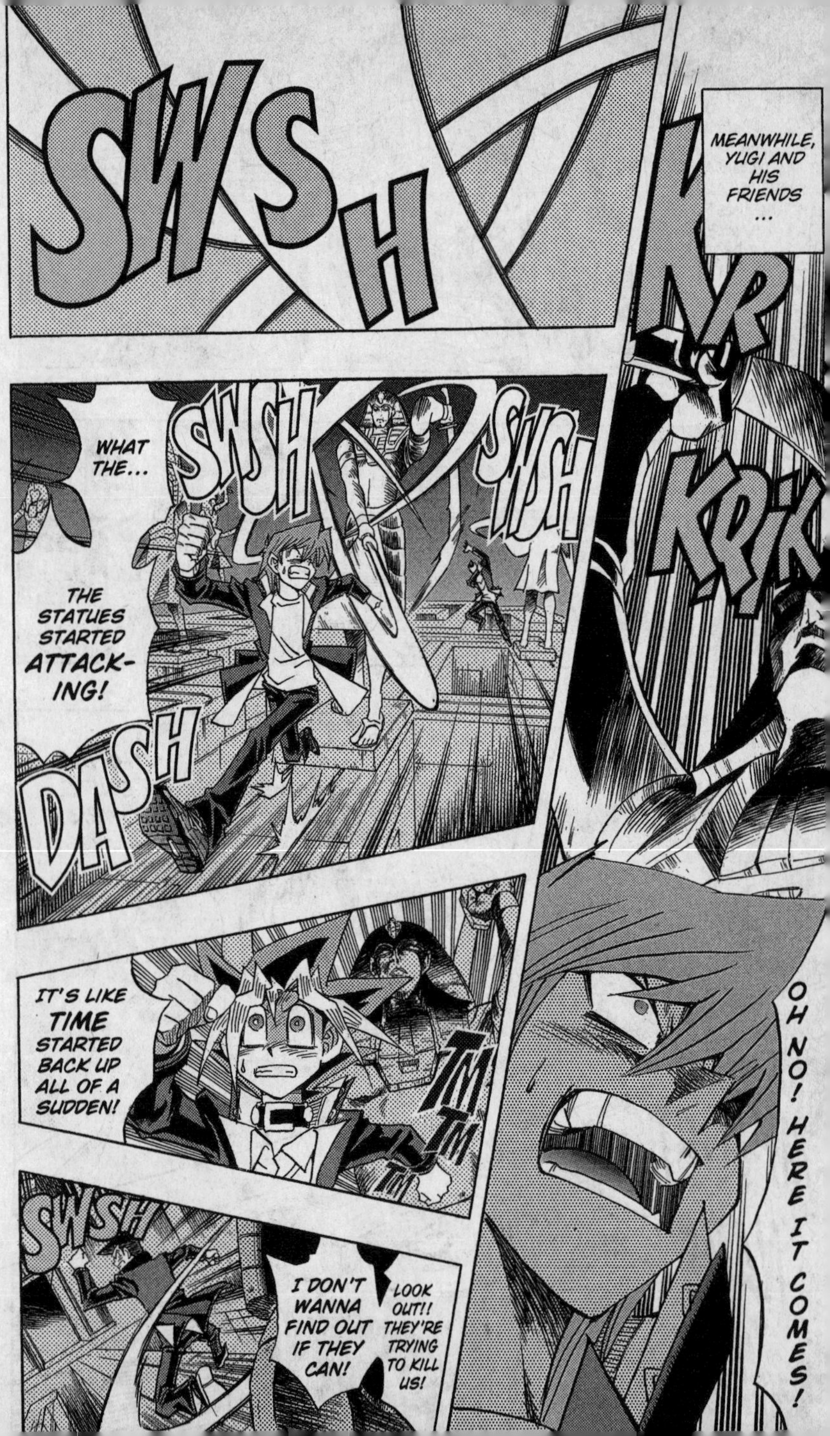
MEANWHILE, YUGI AND HIS FRIENDS ...
KR
KRIK
OH NO! HERE IT COMES!
SWSH
SWSH
SWSH
WHAT THE...
THE STATUES STARTED ATTACKING!
DASH
TM TM TM
IT'S LIKE TIME STARTED BACK UP ALL OF A SUDDEN!
SWSH
LOOK OUT!! THEY'RE TRYING TO KILL US!
I DON'T WANNA FIND OUT IF THEY CAN!

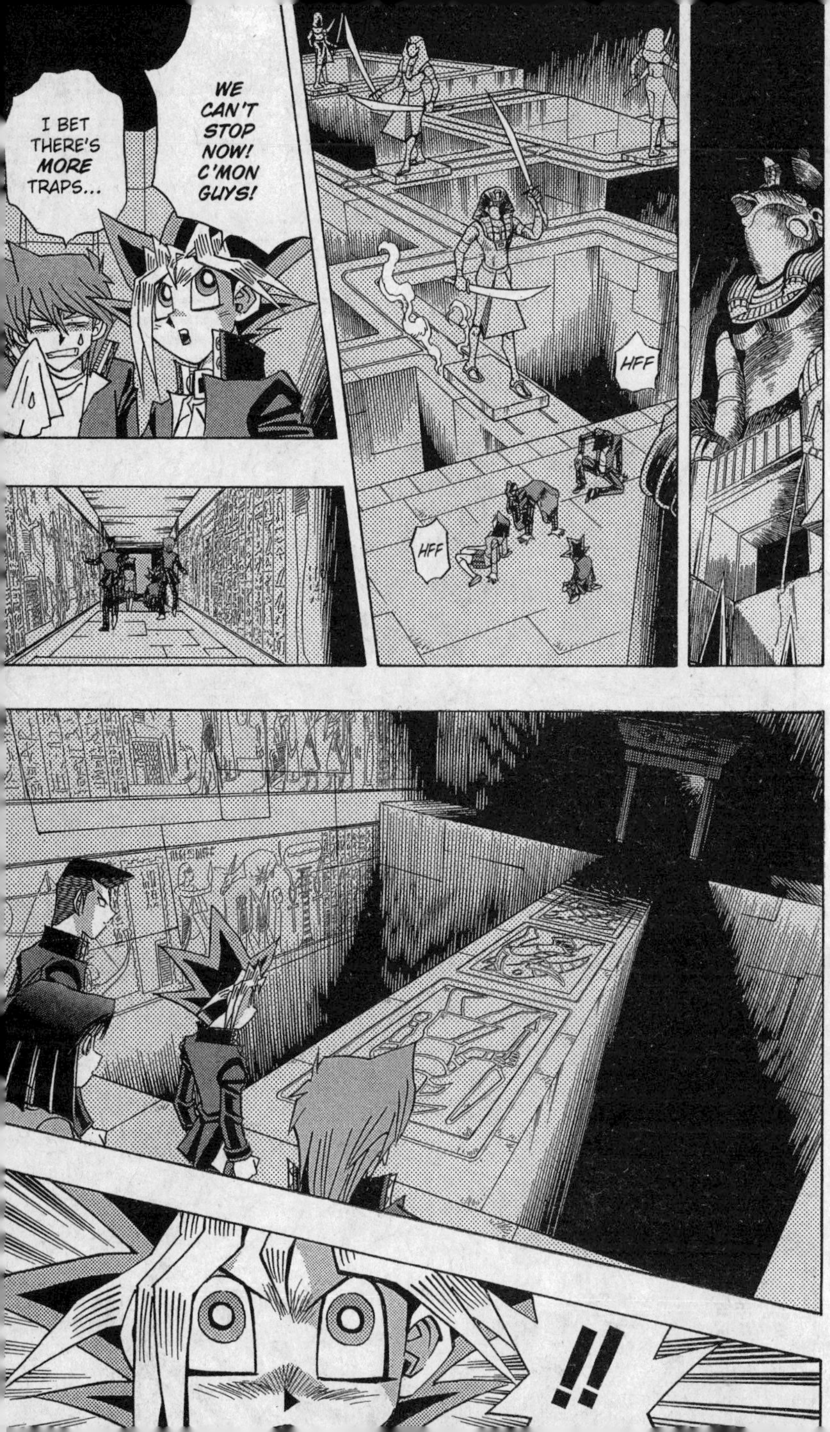
HFF
HFF
WE CAN'T STOP NOW! C'MON GUYS!
I BET THERE'S MORE TRAPS...
!!

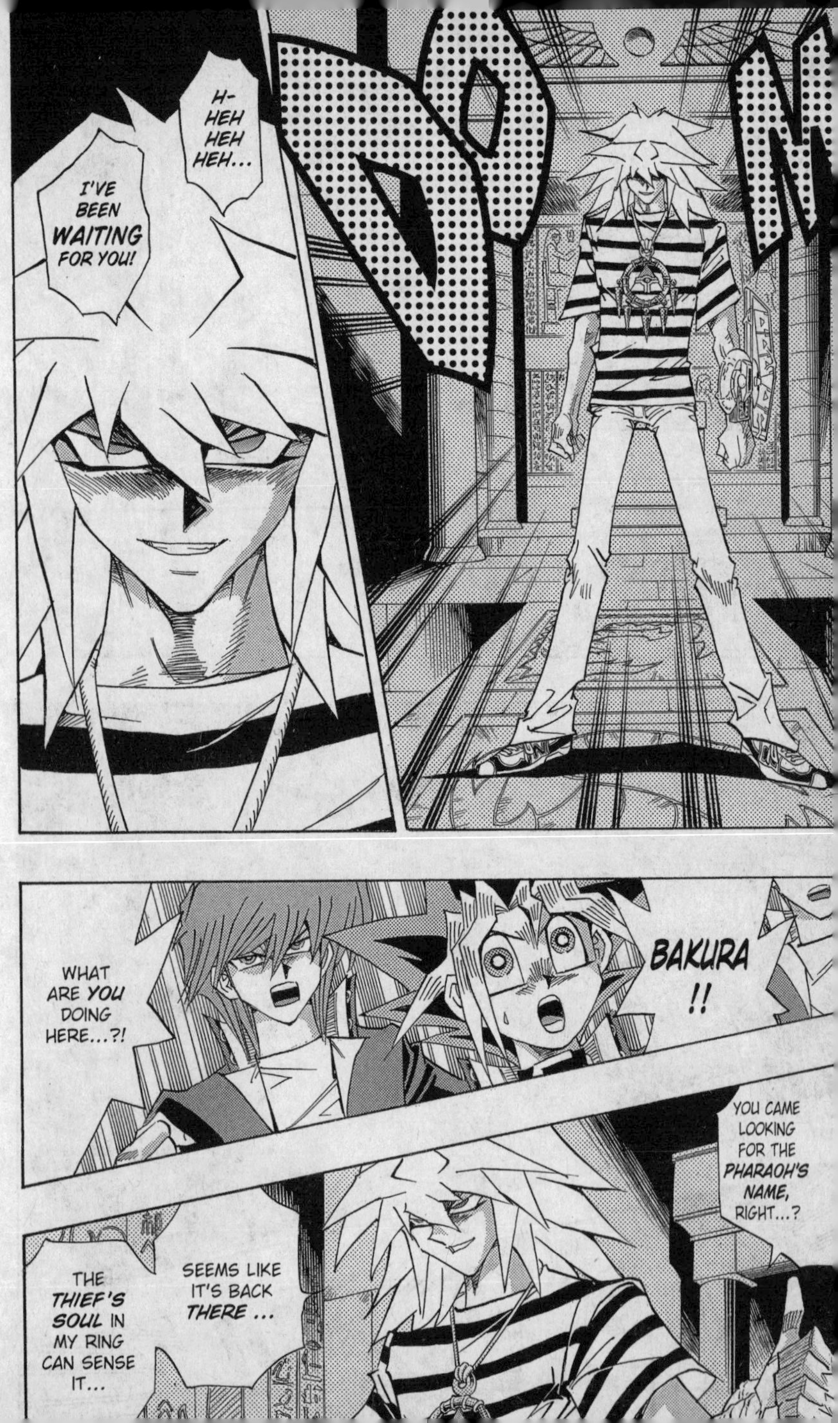
H-HEH HEH HEH...
I'VE BEEN WAITING FOR YOU!
BAKURA!!
WHAT ARE YOU DOING HERE...?!
YOU CAME LOOKING FOR THE PHARAOH'S NAME, RIGHT...?
SEEMS LIKE IT'S BACK THERE...
THE THIEF'S SOUL IN MY RING CAN SENSE IT...

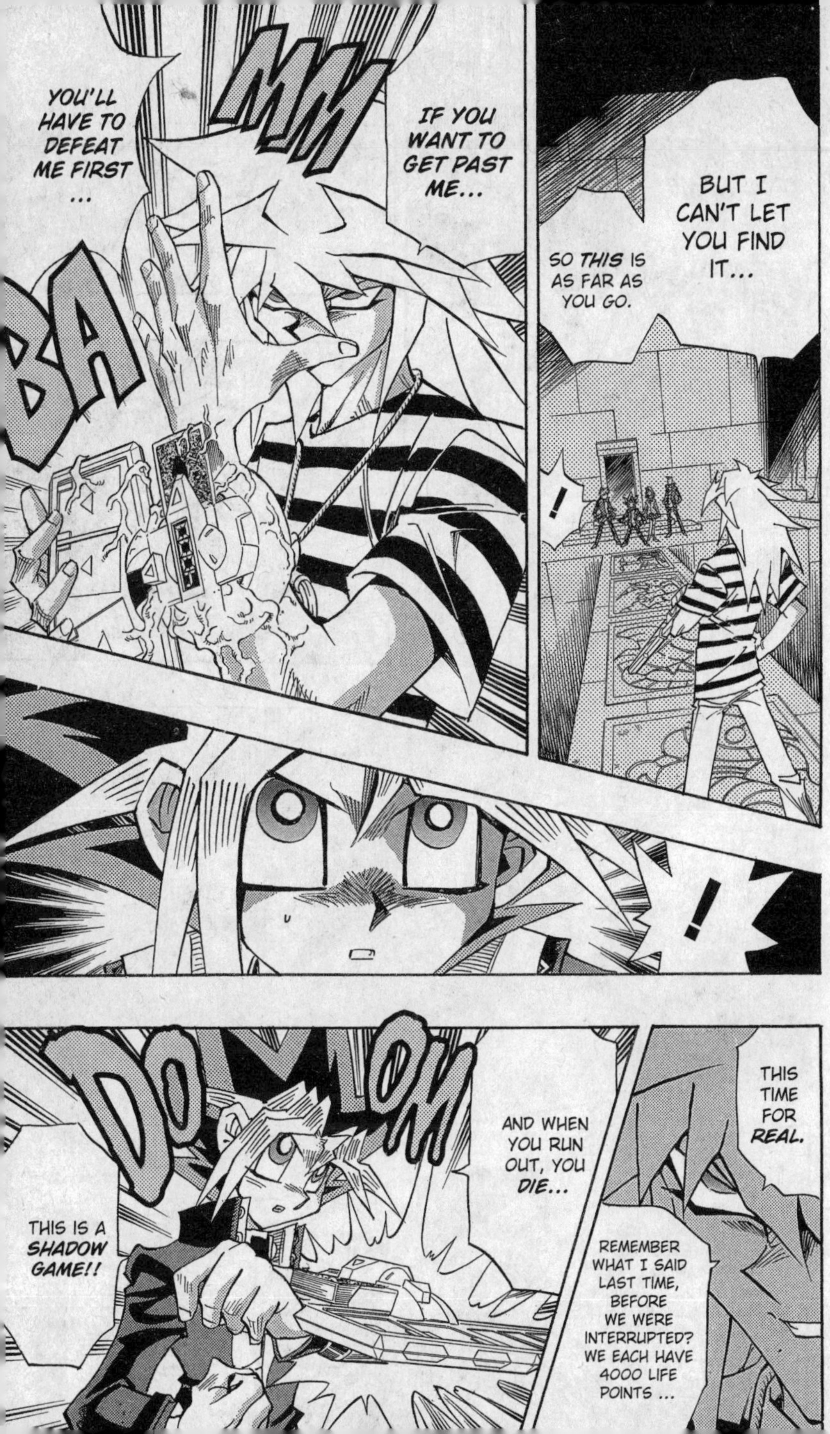
BUT I CAN'T LET YOU FIND IT...
SO THIS IS AS FAR AS YOU GO.
!
IF YOU WANT TO GET PAST ME...
MM
YOU'LL HAVE TO DEFEAT ME FIRST...
BA
!
THIS TIME FOR REAL.
REMEMBER WHAT I SAID LAST TIME, BEFORE WE WERE INTERRUPTED? WE EACH HAVE 4000 LIFE POINTS...
AND WHEN YOU RUN OUT, YOU DIE...
DO
OM
THIS IS A SHADOW GAME!!

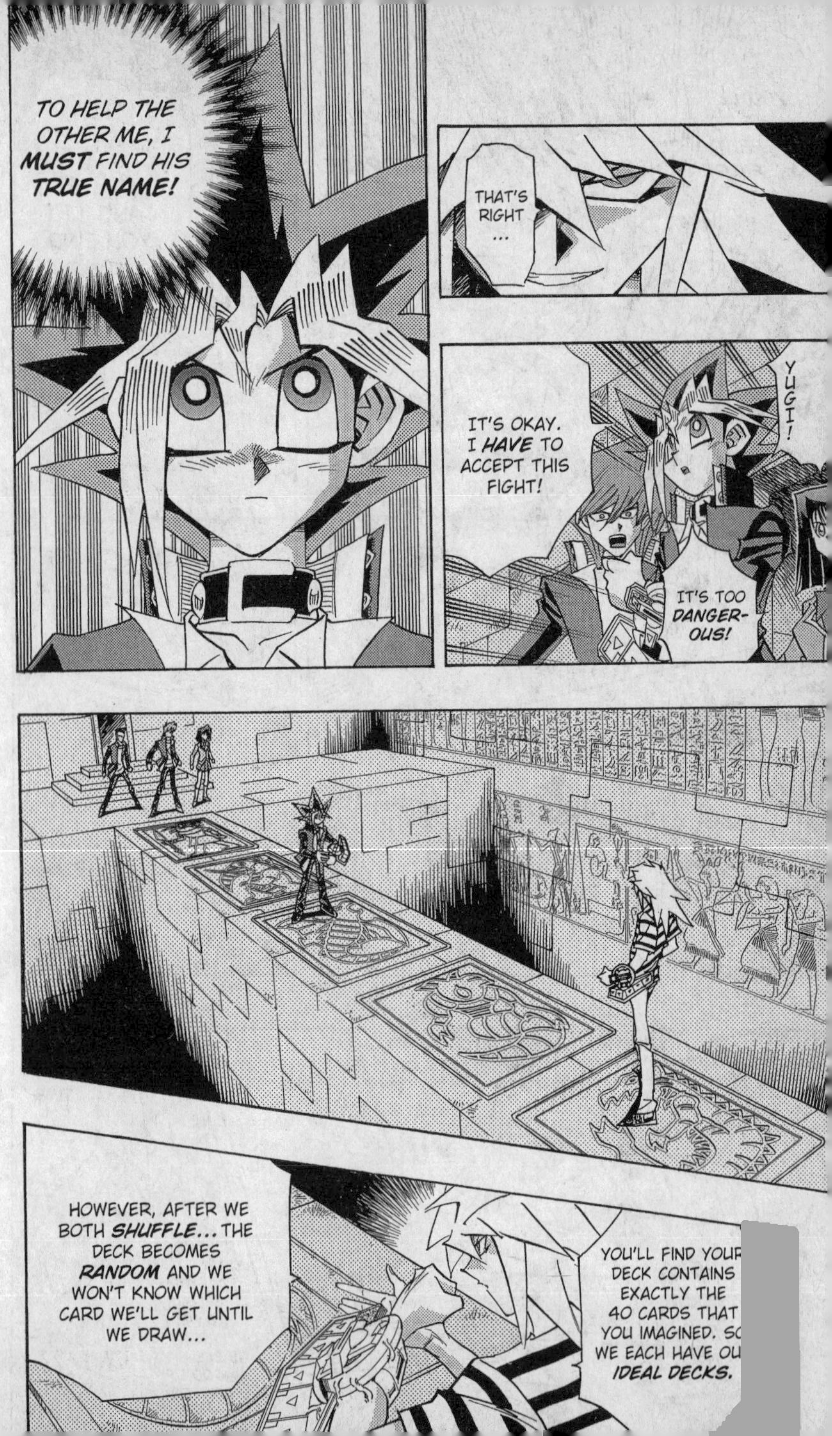
THAT'S RIGHT ...
YUGI!
IT'S OKAY. I HAVE TO ACCEPT THIS FIGHT!
IT'S TOO DANGER-OUS!
TO HELP THE OTHER ME, I MUST FIND HIS TRUE NAME!
YOU'LL FIND YOUR DECK CONTAINS EXACTLY THE 40 CARDS THAT YOU IMAGINED. SO WE EACH HAVE OU IDEAL DECKS.
HOWEVER, AFTER WE BOTH SHUFFLE... THE DECK BECOMES RANDOM AND WE WON'T KNOW WHICH CARD WE'LL GET UNTIL WE DRAW...

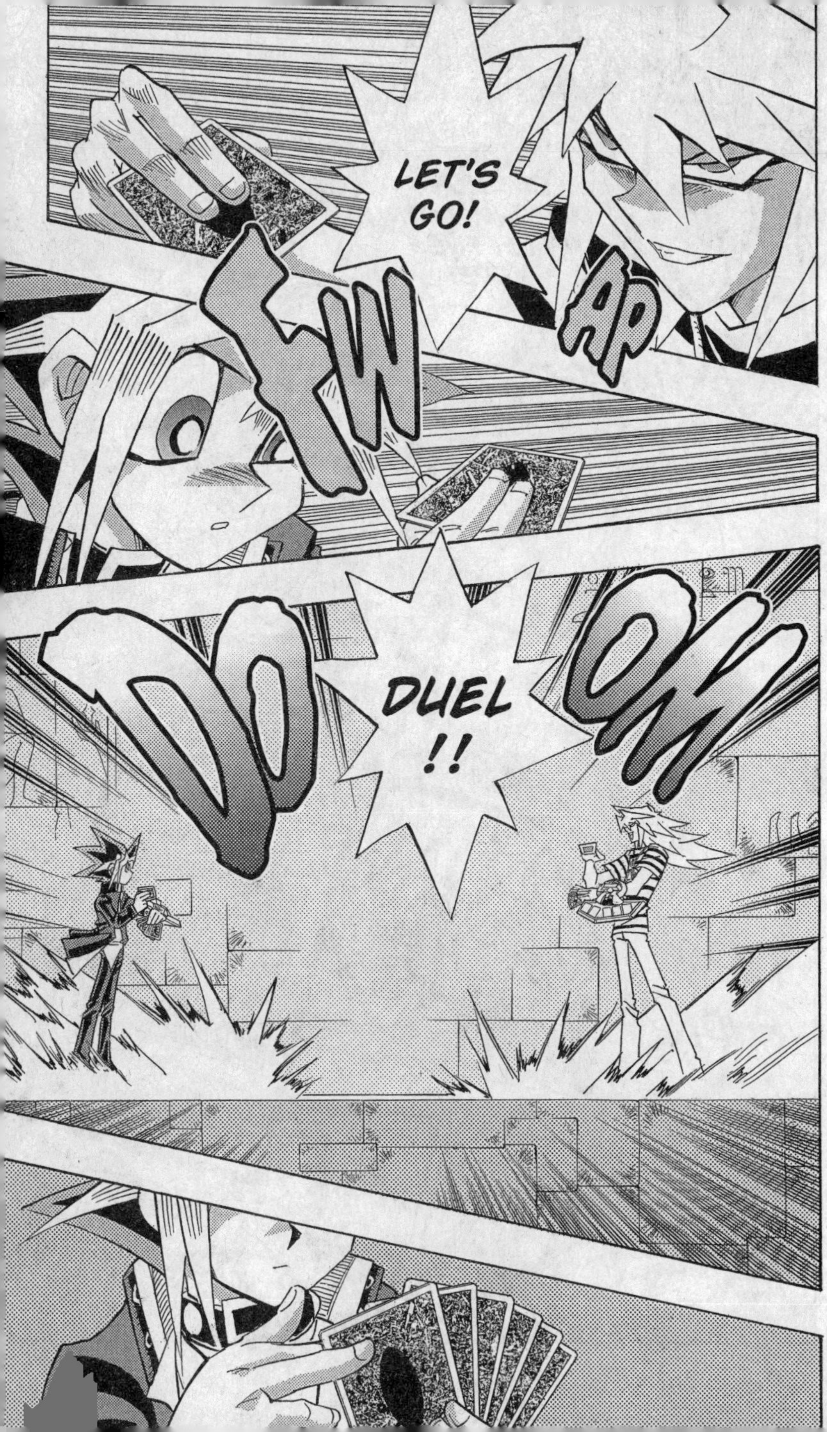
LET'S GO!
FWAP
DOOM
DUEL !!

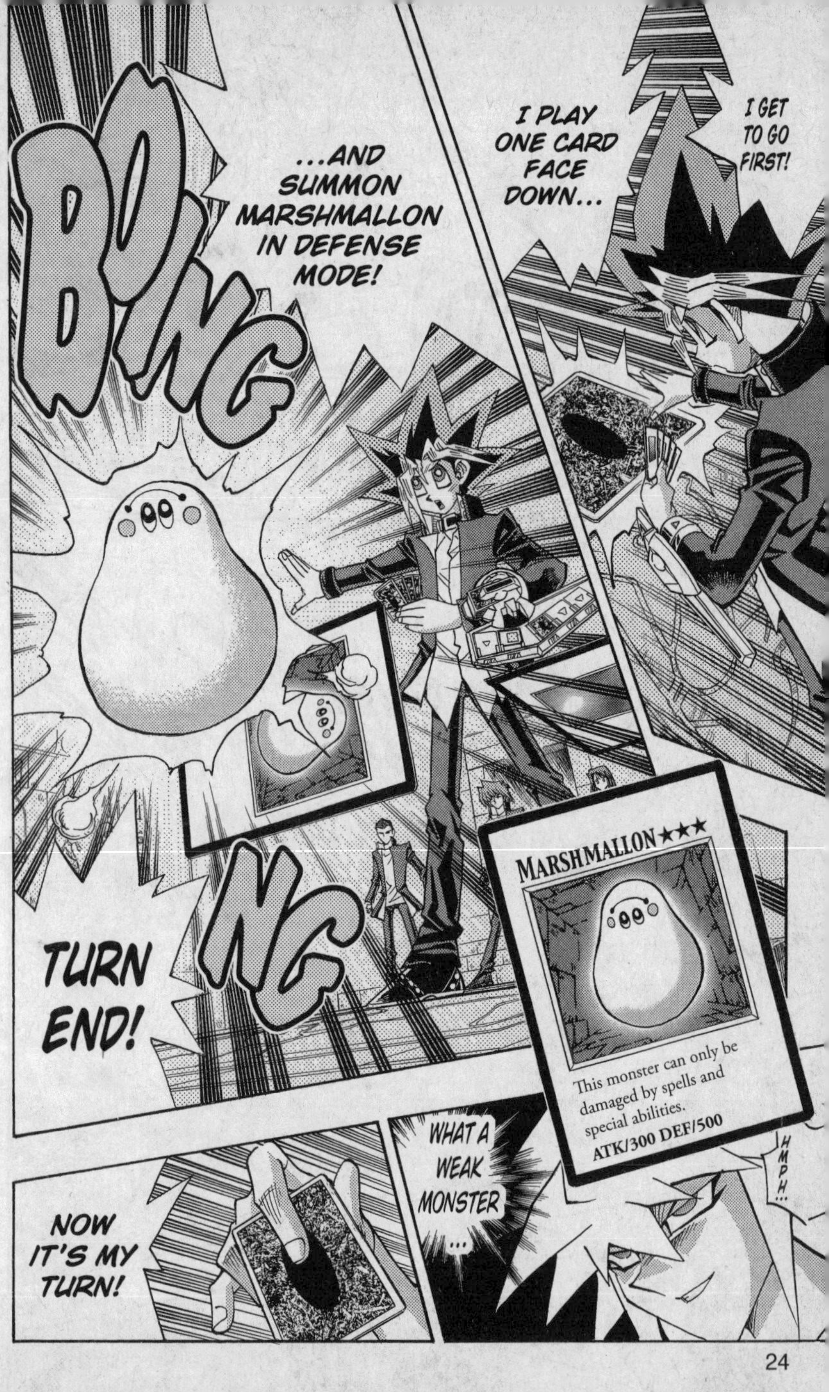
I GET TO GO FIRST!
I PLAY ONE CARD FACE DOWN...
...AND SUMMON MARSHMALLON IN DEFENSE MODE!
BOING
NG
TURN END!
MARSHMALLON ★★★
This monster can only be damaged by spells and special abilities.
ATK/300 DEF/500
HMPH...
WHAT A WEAK MONSTER...
NOW IT'S MY TURN!

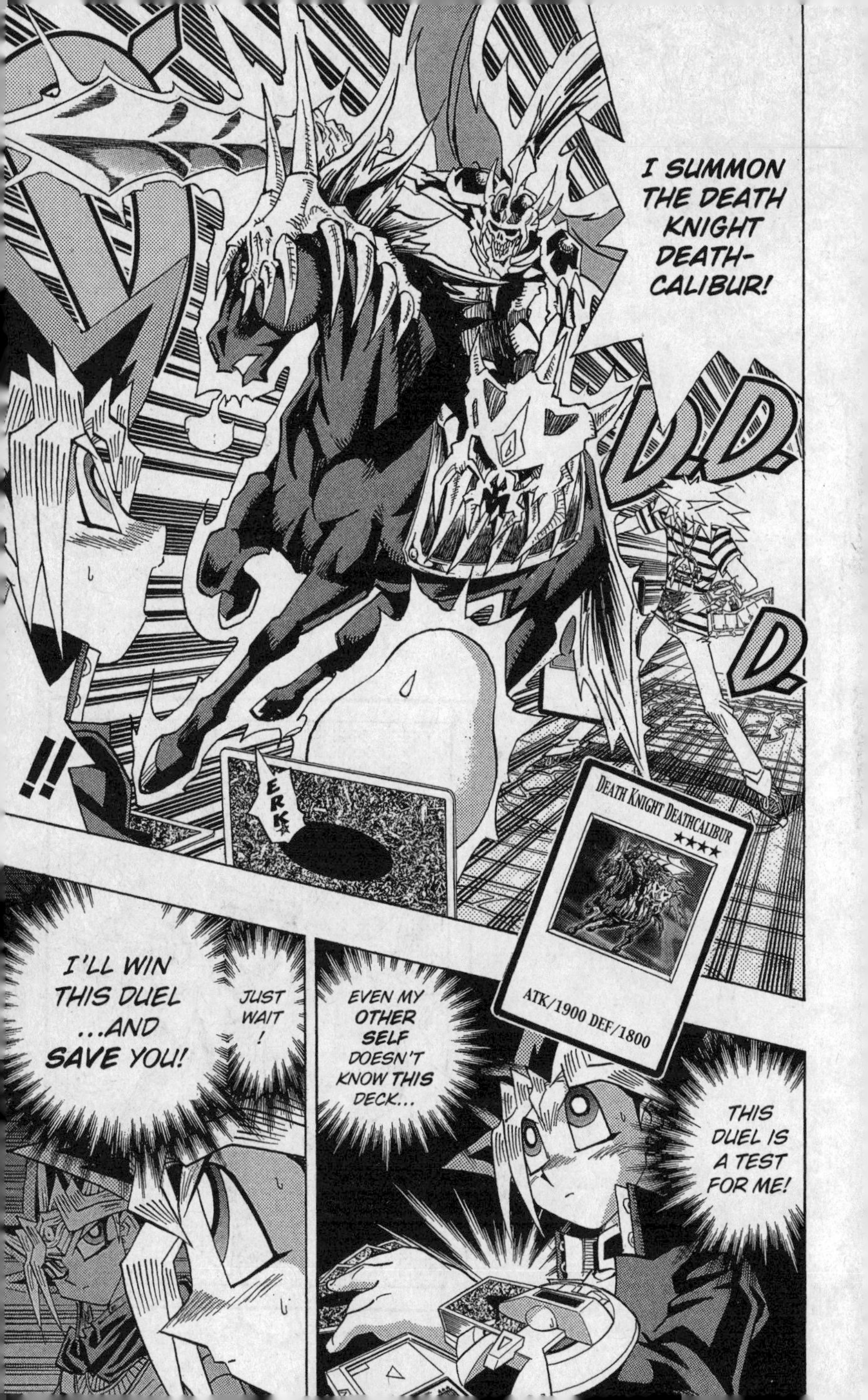
I SUMMON THE DEATH KNIGHT DEATH-CALIBUR!
D.D. D.
!!
ERK
DEATH KNIGHT DEATHCALIBUR
ATK/1900 DEF/1800
THIS DUEL IS A TEST FOR ME!
EVEN MY OTHER SELF DOESN'T KNOW THIS DECK...
JUST WAIT!
I'LL WIN THIS DUEL ...AND SAVE YOU!

Duel 325: The Silent Duelist!!

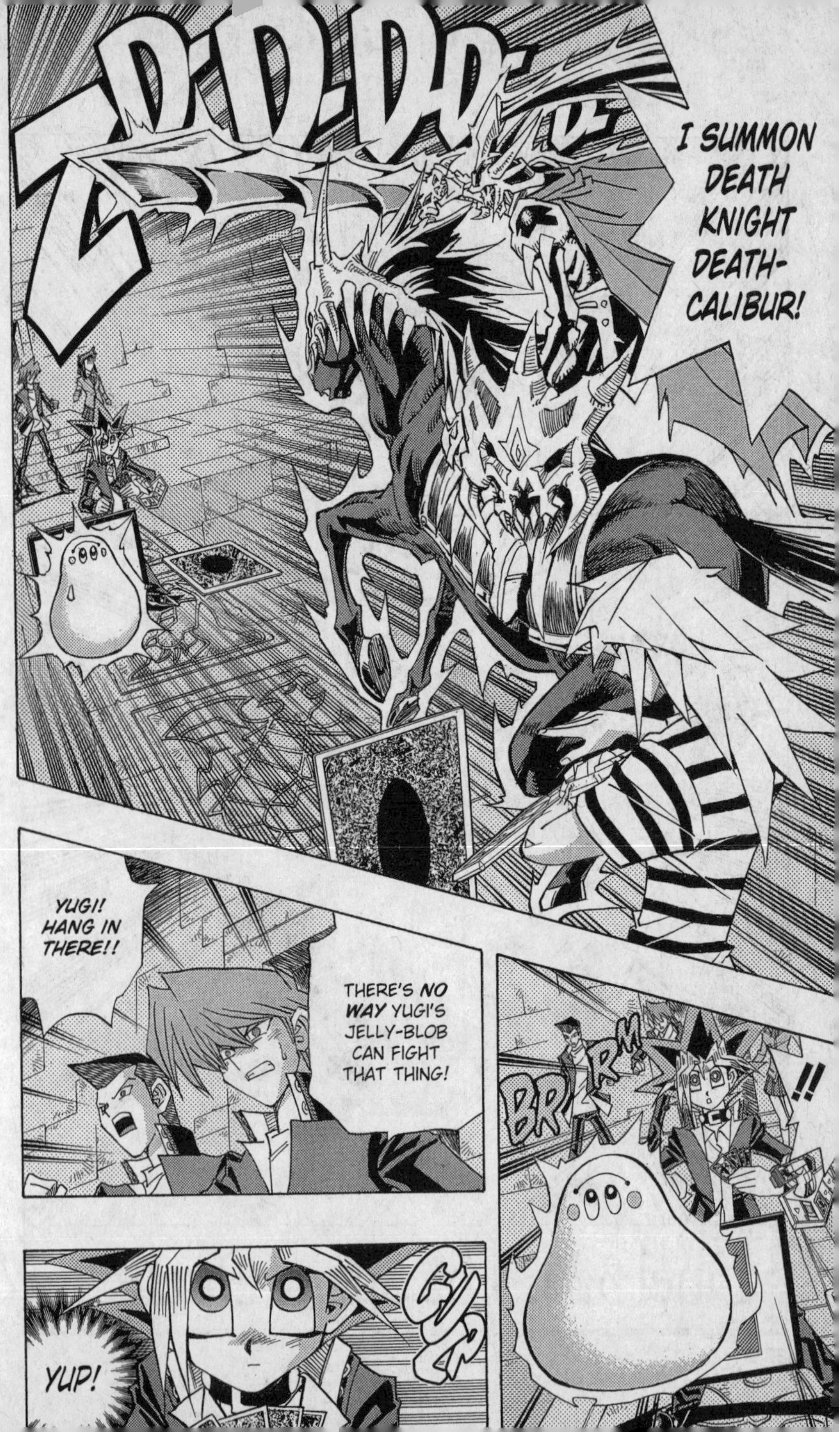
I SUMMON DEATH KNIGHT DEATH-CALIBUR!
BRRM
!!
YUGI! HANG IN THERE!!
THERE'S NO WAY YUGI'S JELLY-BLOB CAN FIGHT THAT THING!
GLP
YUP!

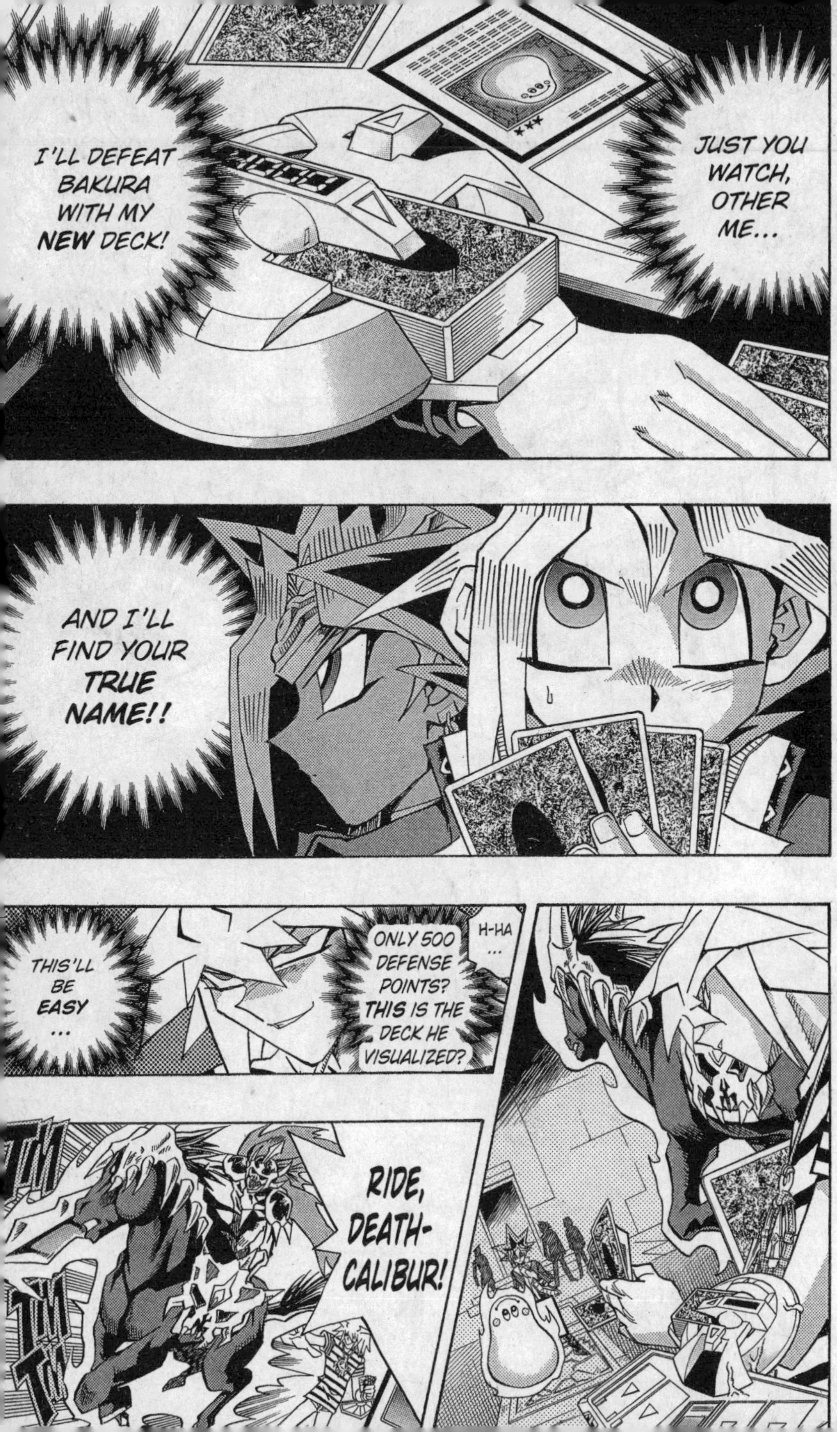
JUST YOU WATCH, OTHER ME...
I'LL DEFEAT BAKURA WITH MY NEW DECK!
AND I'LL FIND YOUR TRUE NAME!!
H-HA ...
ONLY 500 DEFENSE POINTS? THIS IS THE DECK HE VISUALIZED?
THIS'LL BE EASY ...
RIDE, DEATH-CALIBUR!

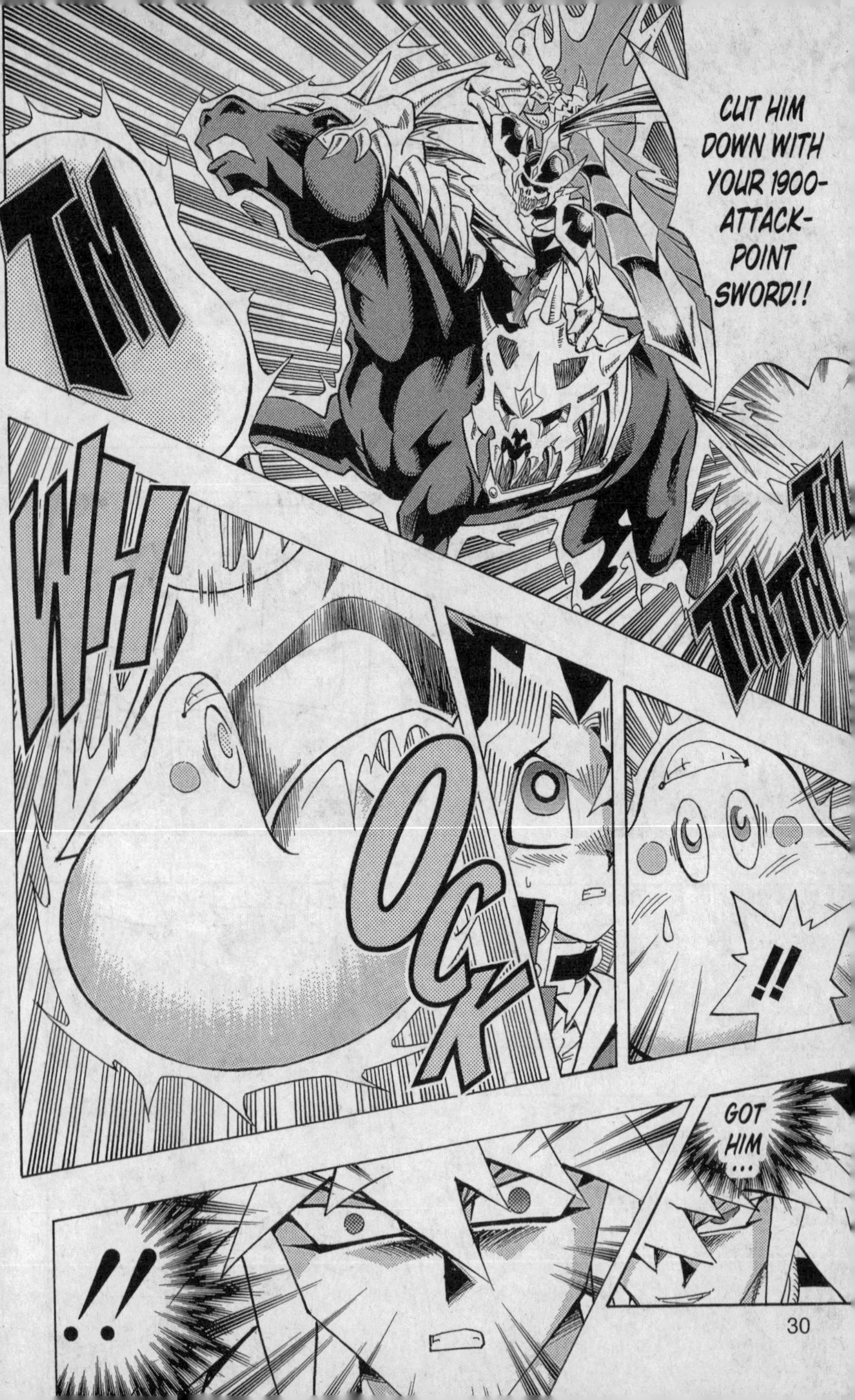
CUT HIM DOWN WITH YOUR 1900-ATTACK-POINT SWORD!!
TM TM TM
TM
WH
OOCK
!!
GOT HIM...
!!

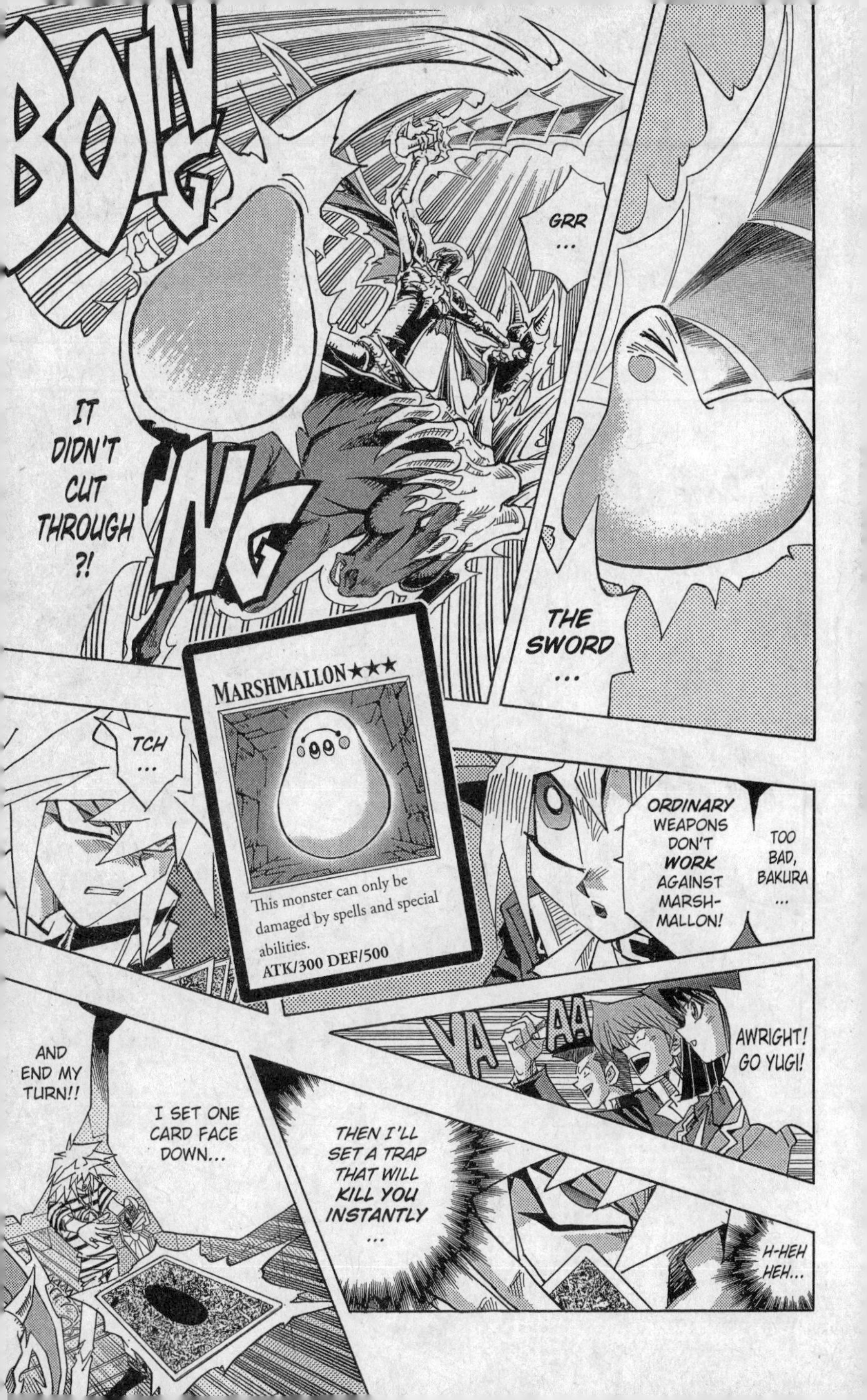

GRR ...
THE SWORD ...
BOING
IT DIDN'T CUT THROUGH ?!
NG
TOO BAD, BAKURA ...
ORDINARY WEAPONS DON'T WORK AGAINST MARSH-MALLON!
MARSHMALLON★★★
This monster can only be damaged by spells and special abilities.
ATK/300 DEF/500
TCH ...
AWRIGHT! GO YUGI!
YAAA
H-HEH HEH...
THEN I'LL SET A TRAP THAT WILL KILL YOU INSTANTLY ...
I SET ONE CARD FACE DOWN...
AND END MY TURN!!

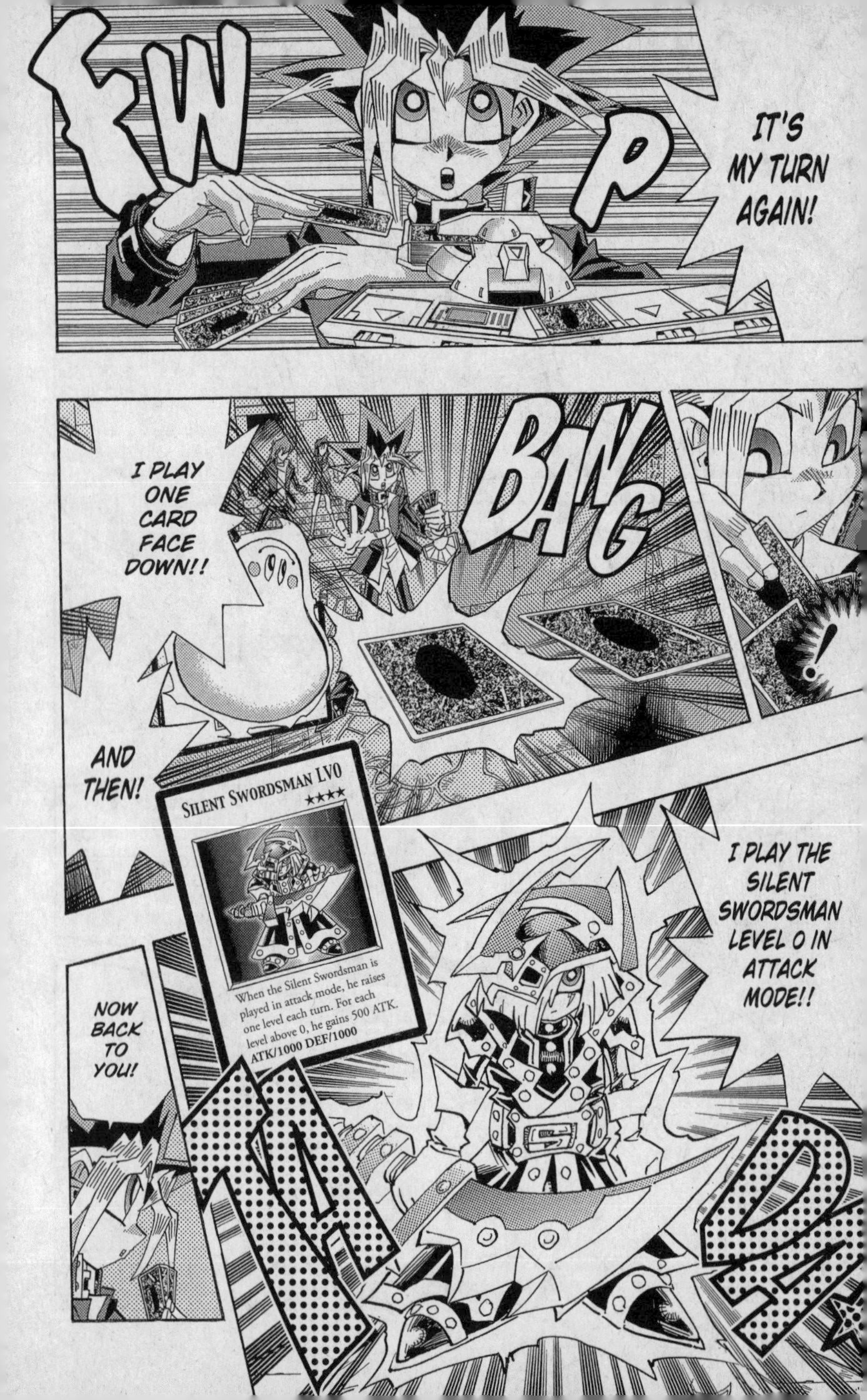
FWP
IT'S MY TURN AGAIN!
!
BANG
I PLAY ONE CARD FACE DOWN!!
AND THEN!
I PLAY THE SILENT SWORDSMAN LEVEL 0 IN ATTACK MODE!!
SILENT SWORDSMAN LV0 ★★★★
When the Silent Swordsman is played in attack mode, he raises one level each turn. For each level above 0, he gains 500 ATK.
ATK/1000 DEF/1000
NOW BACK TO YOU!

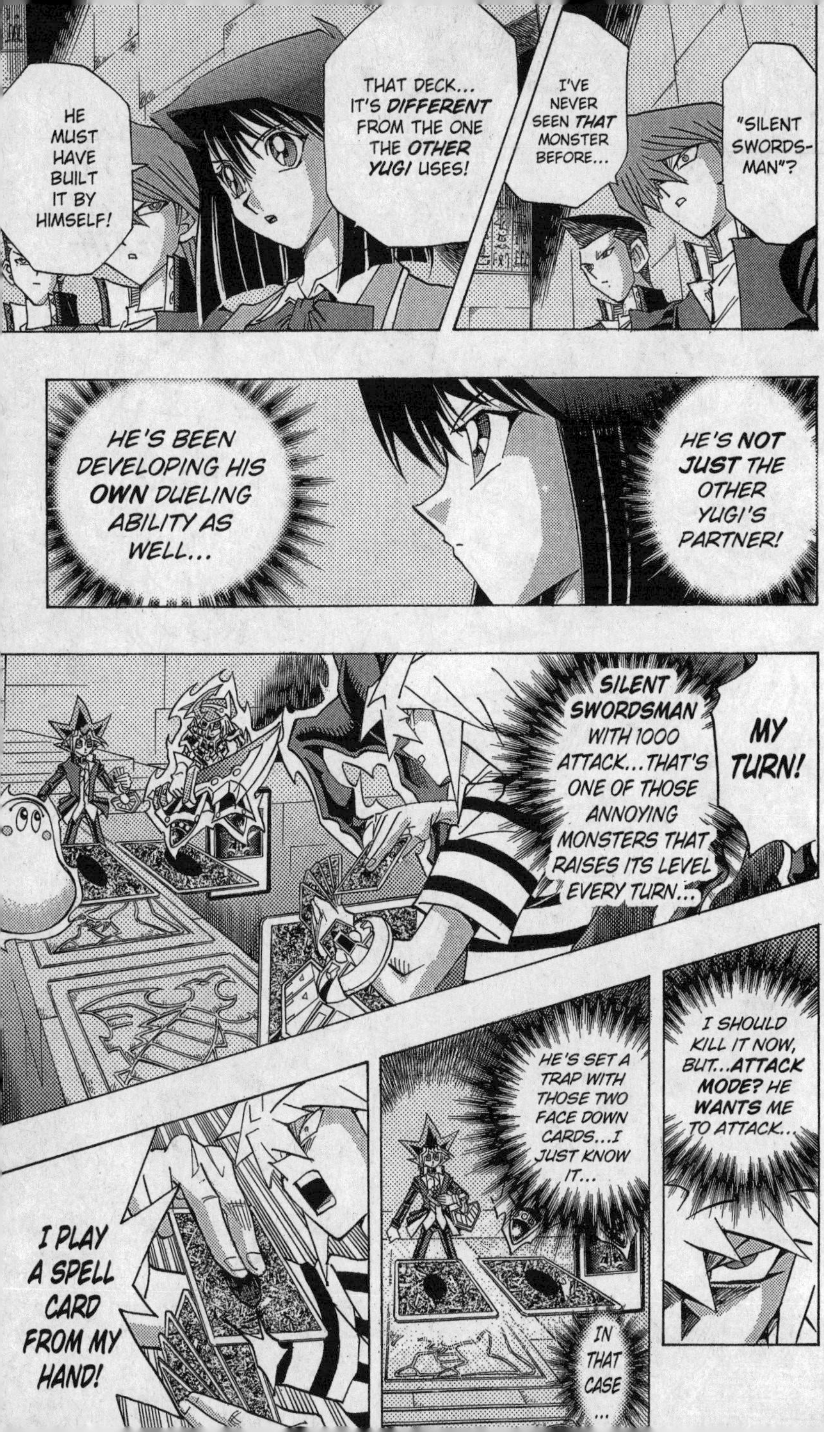

"SILENT SWORDSMAN"?
I'VE NEVER SEEN THAT MONSTER BEFORE...
THAT DECK... IT'S DIFFERENT FROM THE ONE THE OTHER YUGI USES!
HE MUST HAVE BUILT IT BY HIMSELF!
HE'S NOT JUST THE OTHER YUGI'S PARTNER!
HE'S BEEN DEVELOPING HIS OWN DUELING ABILITY AS WELL...
MY TURN!
SILENT SWORDSMAN WITH 1000 ATTACK...THAT'S ONE OF THOSE ANNOYING MONSTERS THAT RAISES ITS LEVEL EVERY TURN...
I SHOULD KILL IT NOW, BUT...ATTACK MODE? HE WANTS ME TO ATTACK...
HE'S SET A TRAP WITH THOSE TWO FACE DOWN CARDS...I JUST KNOW IT...
IN THAT CASE...
I PLAY A SPELL CARD FROM MY HAND!

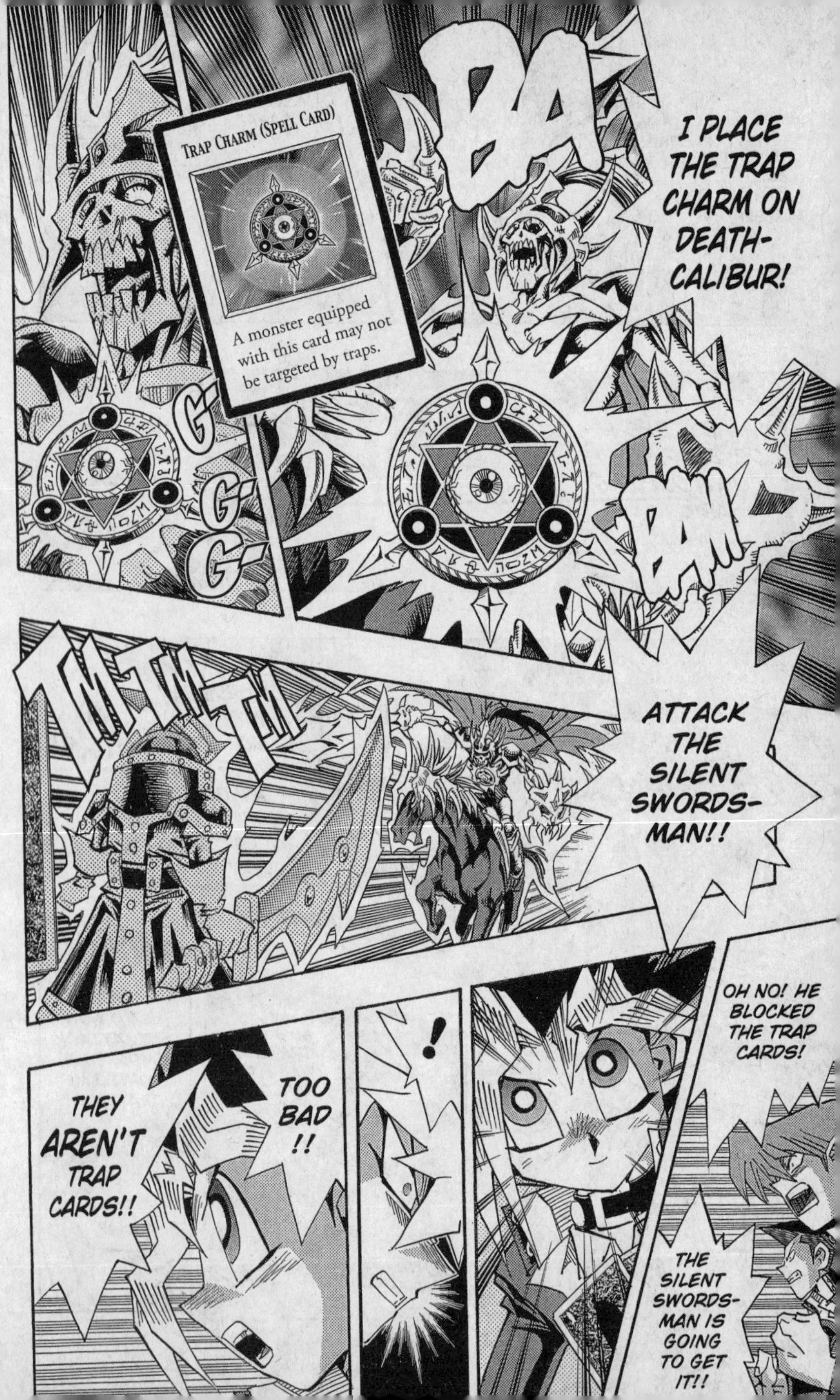
BA
I PLACE THE TRAP CHARM ON DEATH-CALIBUR!
BAM
TRAP CHARM (SPELL CARD)
A monster equipped with this card may not be targeted by traps.
G- G- G-
ATTACK THE SILENT SWORDS-MAN!!
TM TM TM TM
OH NO! HE BLOCKED THE TRAP CARDS!
THE SILENT SWORDS-MAN IS GOING TO GET IT!!
!
TOO BAD!!
THEY AREN'T TRAP CARDS!!

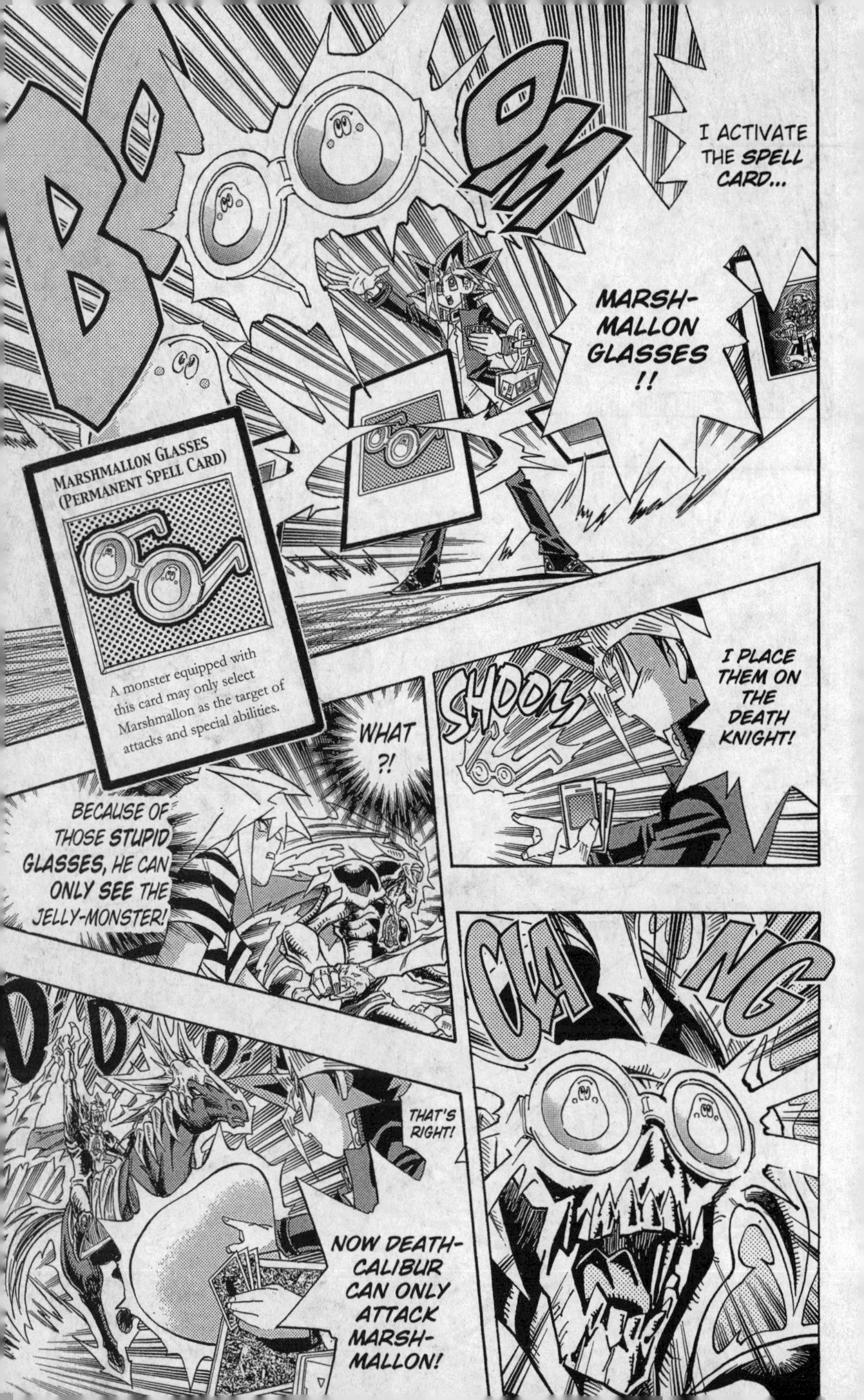
BOOM
I ACTIVATE THE SPELL CARD...
MARSH-MALLON GLASSES!!
Marshmallon Glasses (Permanent Spell Card)
A monster equipped with this card may only select Marshmallon as the target of attacks and special abilities.
SHOOM
I PLACE THEM ON THE DEATH KNIGHT!
WHAT?!
BECAUSE OF THOSE STUPID GLASSES, HE CAN ONLY SEE THE JELLY-MONSTER!
CLANG
THAT'S RIGHT!
NOW DEATH-CALIBUR CAN ONLY ATTACK MARSH-MALLON!

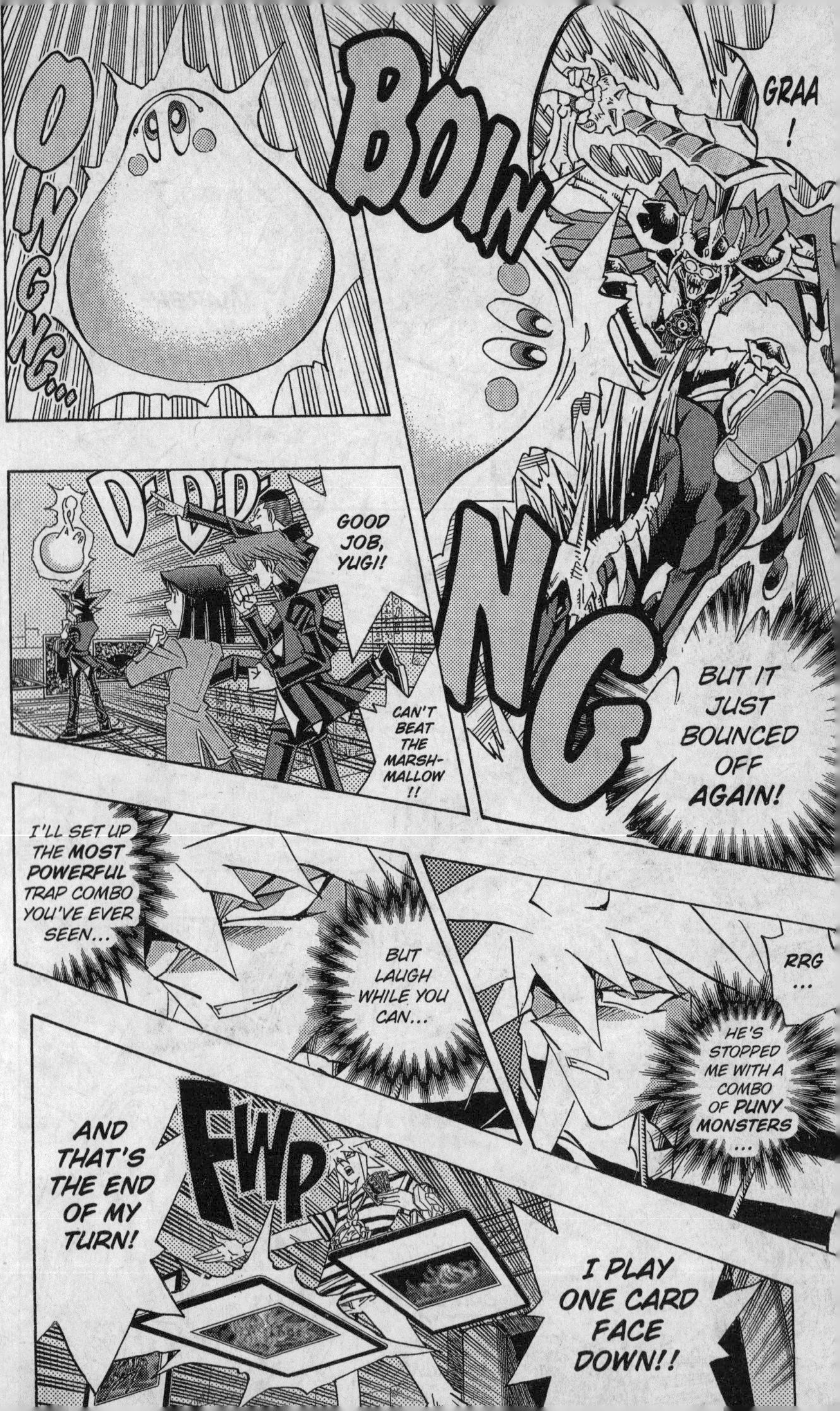
BOIN
GRAA!
NG
BUT IT JUST BOUNCED OFF AGAIN!
OINGNG...
D-D-D
GOOD JOB, YUGI!
CAN'T BEAT THE MARSH-MALLOW!!
RRG...
HE'S STOPPED ME WITH A COMBO OF PUNY MONSTERS...
I'LL SET UP THE MOST POWERFUL TRAP COMBO YOU'VE EVER SEEN...
BUT LAUGH WHILE YOU CAN...
I PLAY ONE CARD FACE DOWN!!
FWP
AND THAT'S THE END OF MY TURN!

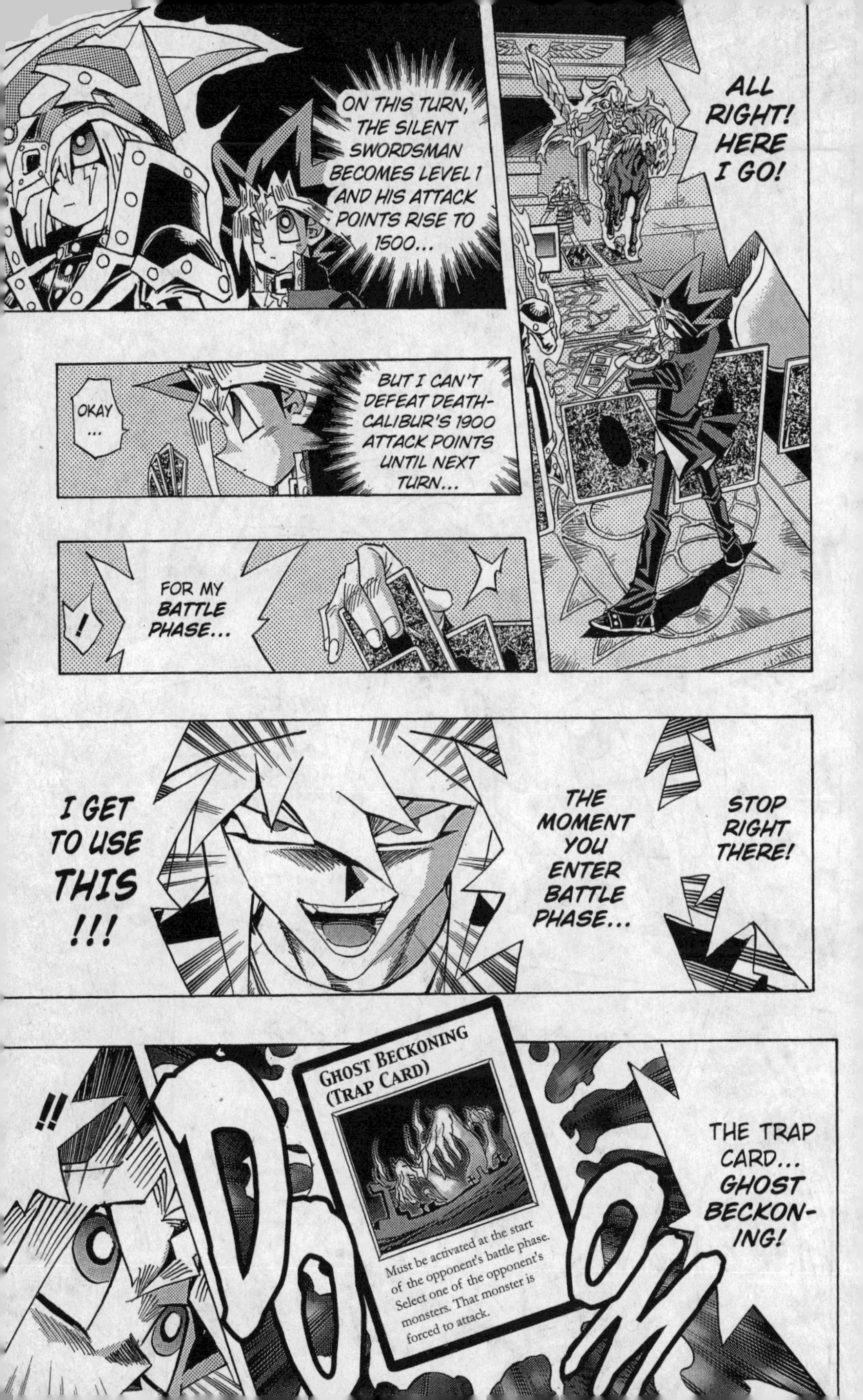
ALL RIGHT! HERE I GO!
ON THIS TURN, THE SILENT SWORDSMAN BECOMES LEVEL 1 AND HIS ATTACK POINTS RISE TO 1500...
BUT I CAN'T DEFEAT DEATH-CALIBUR'S 1900 ATTACK POINTS UNTIL NEXT TURN...
OKAY...
FOR MY BATTLE PHASE...
!
STOP RIGHT THERE!
THE MOMENT YOU ENTER BATTLE PHASE...
I GET TO USE THIS!!!
THE TRAP CARD... GHOST BECKON-ING!
GHOST BECKONING (TRAP CARD)
Must be activated at the start of the opponent's battle phase. Select one of the opponent's monsters. That monster is forced to attack.
!!

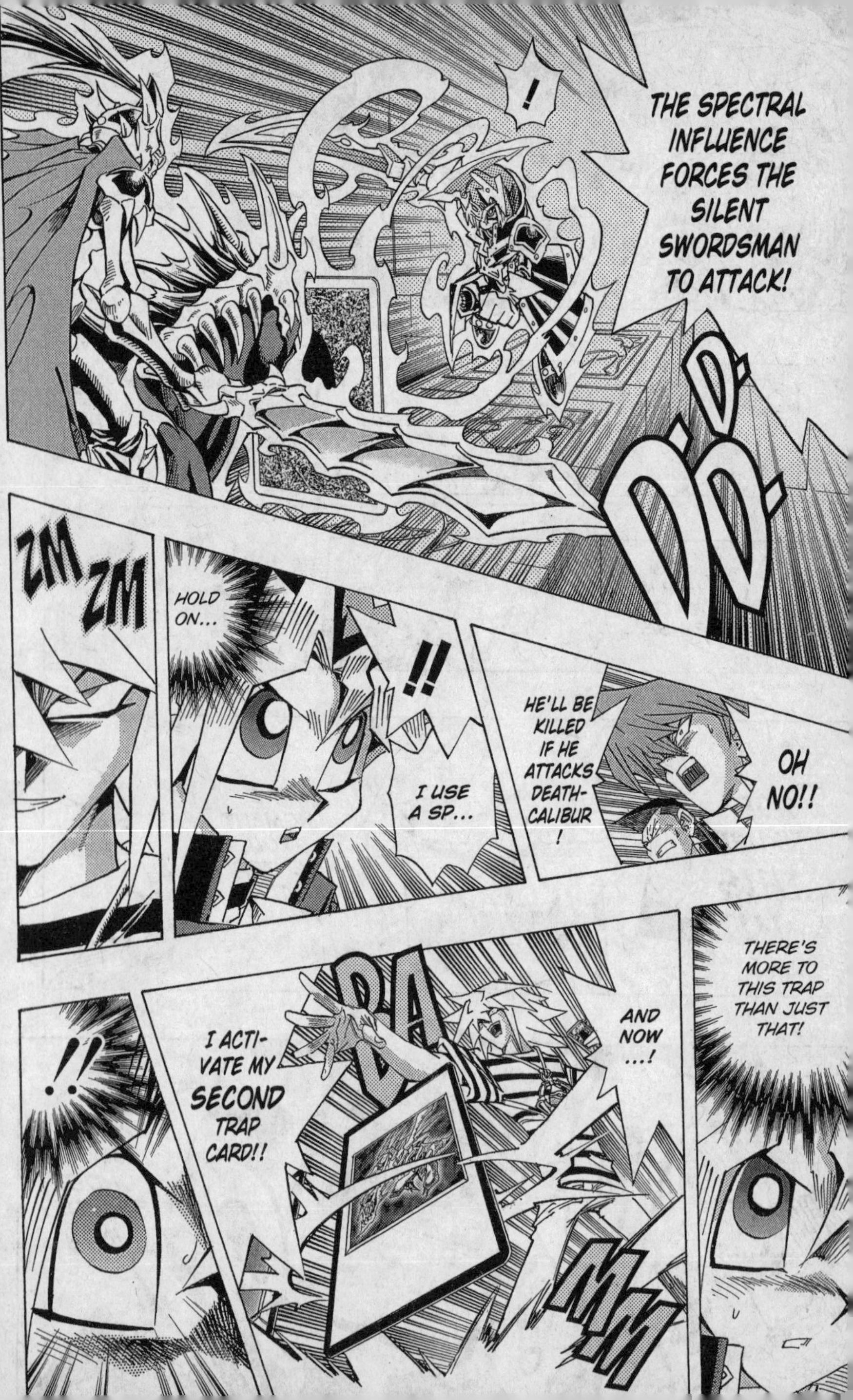
THE SPECTRAL INFLUENCE FORCES THE SILENT SWORDSMAN TO ATTACK!
!
D D D
OH NO!!
HE'LL BE KILLED IF HE ATTACKS DEATH-CALIBUR!
!!
I USE A SP...
HOLD ON...
ZM ZM
THERE'S MORE TO THIS TRAP THAN JUST THAT!
AND NOW ...!
BA
I ACTI-VATE MY SECOND TRAP CARD!!
!!

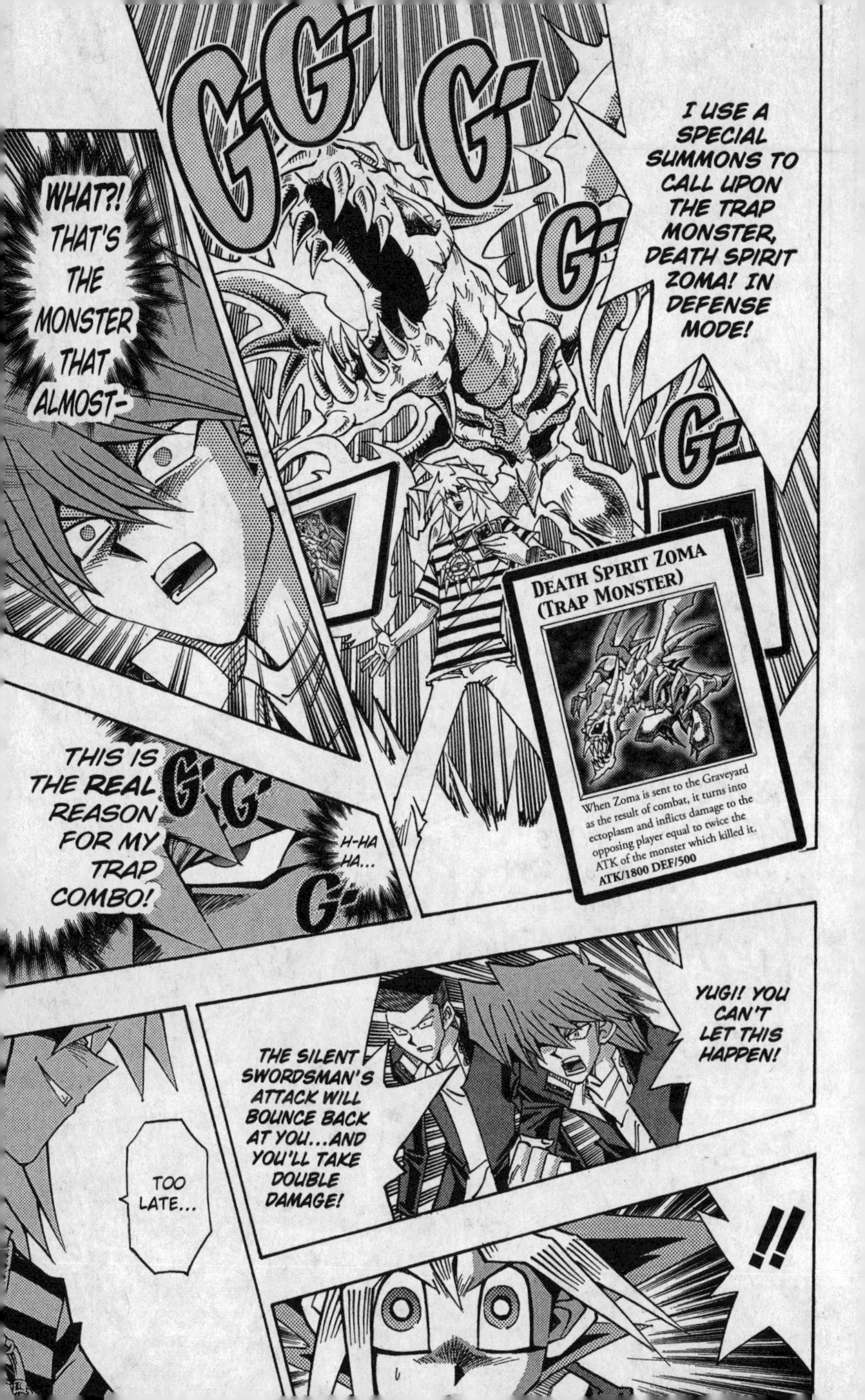
I USE A SPECIAL SUMMONS TO CALL UPON THE TRAP MONSTER, DEATH SPIRIT ZOMA! IN DEFENSE MODE!
G-G-G-G-G-
DEATH SPIRIT ZOMA (TRAP MONSTER)
When Zoma is sent to the Graveyard as the result of combat, it turns into ectoplasm and inflicts damage to the opposing player equal to twice the ATK of the monster which killed it.
ATK/1800 DEF/500
WHAT?! THAT'S THE MONSTER THAT ALMOST-
THIS IS THE REAL REASON FOR MY TRAP COMBO!
G-G-G-
H-HA HA...
YUGI! YOU CAN'T LET THIS HAPPEN!
THE SILENT SWORDSMAN'S ATTACK WILL BOUNCE BACK AT YOU...AND YOU'LL TAKE DOUBLE DAMAGE!
TOO LATE...
!!

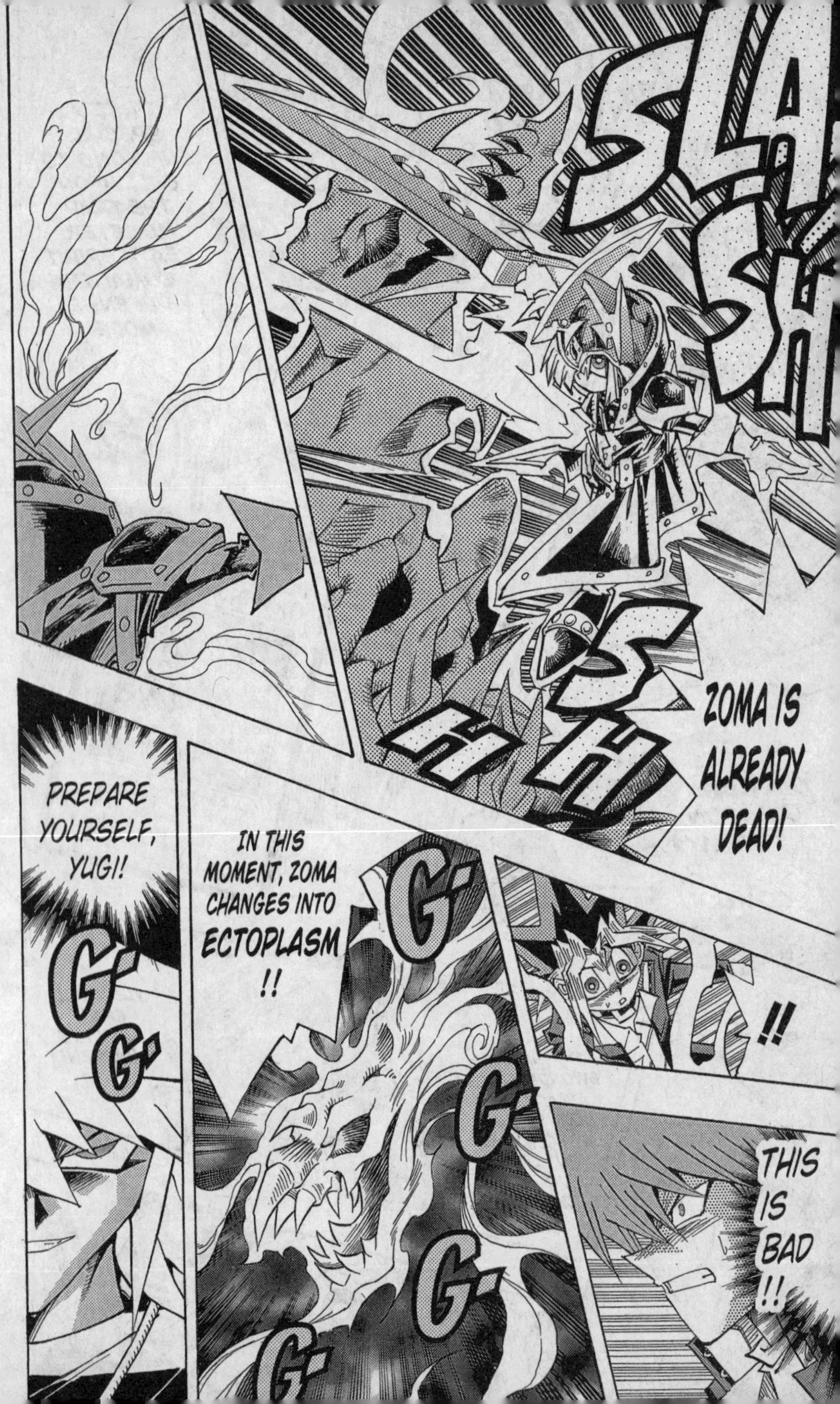
SLA
SH
SHH
ZOMA IS ALREADY DEAD!
!!
THIS IS BAD!!
G-
IN THIS MOMENT, ZOMA CHANGES INTO ECTOPLASM!!
G-
G-
G-
PREPARE YOURSELF, YUGI!
G-
G-

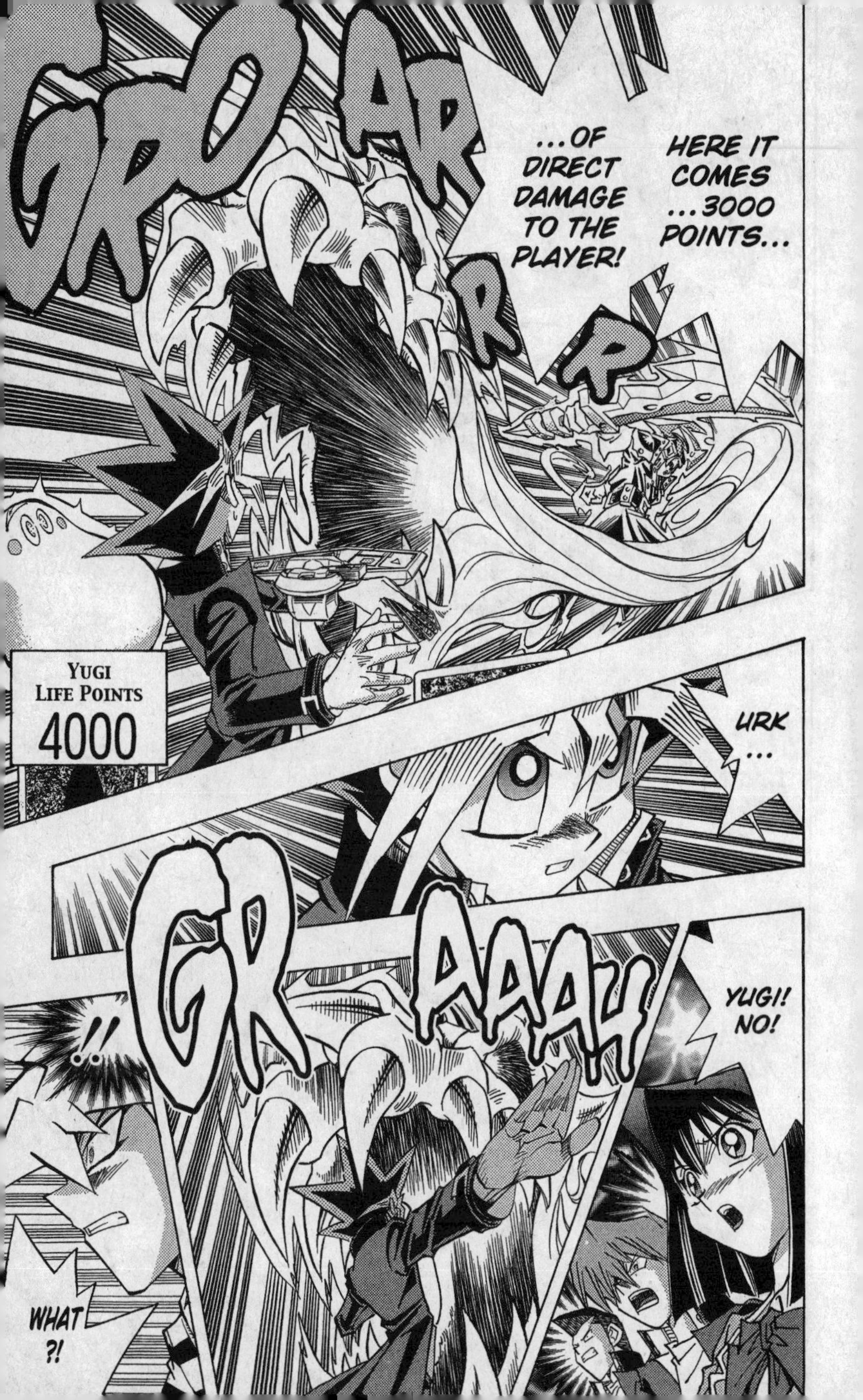
HERE IT COMES ...3000 POINTS...
...OF DIRECT DAMAGE TO THE PLAYER!
GROARRR
YUGI LIFE POINTS 4000
URK ...
GRAAAH
YUGI! NO!
!!
WHAT ?!

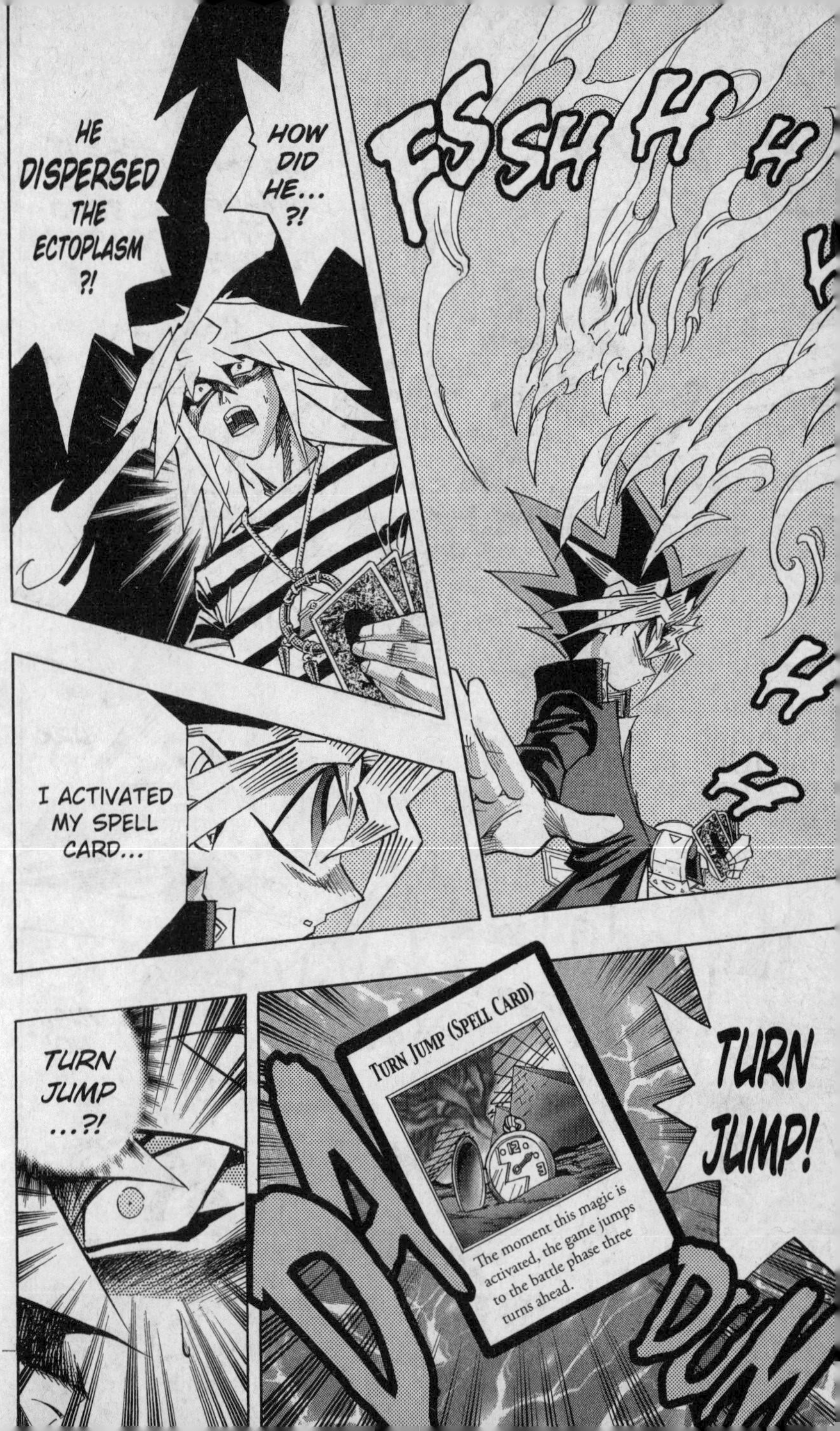

FSSH H H H H H
HOW DID HE... ?!
HE DISPERSED THE ECTOPLASM ?!
I ACTIVATED MY SPELL CARD...
TURN JUMP (SPELL CARD)
The moment this magic is activated, the game jumps to the battle phase three turns ahead.
TURN JUMP!
TURN JUMP ...?!

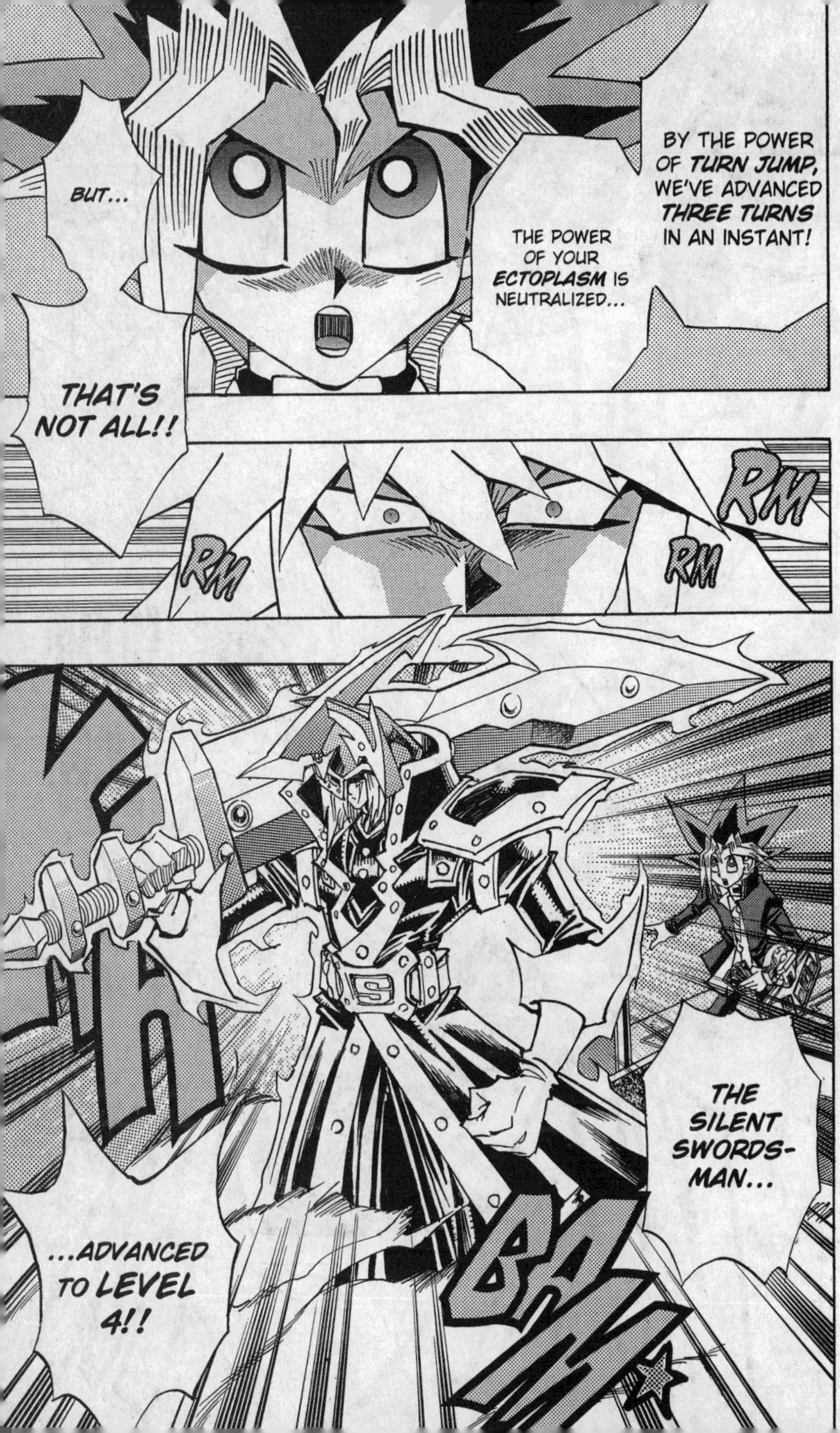
BY THE POWER OF TURN JUMP, WE'VE ADVANCED THREE TURNS IN AN INSTANT!
THE POWER OF YOUR ECTOPLASM IS NEUTRALIZED...
BUT...
THAT'S NOT ALL!!
RM
RM
RM
THE SILENT SWORDS-MAN...
...ADVANCED TO LEVEL 4!!

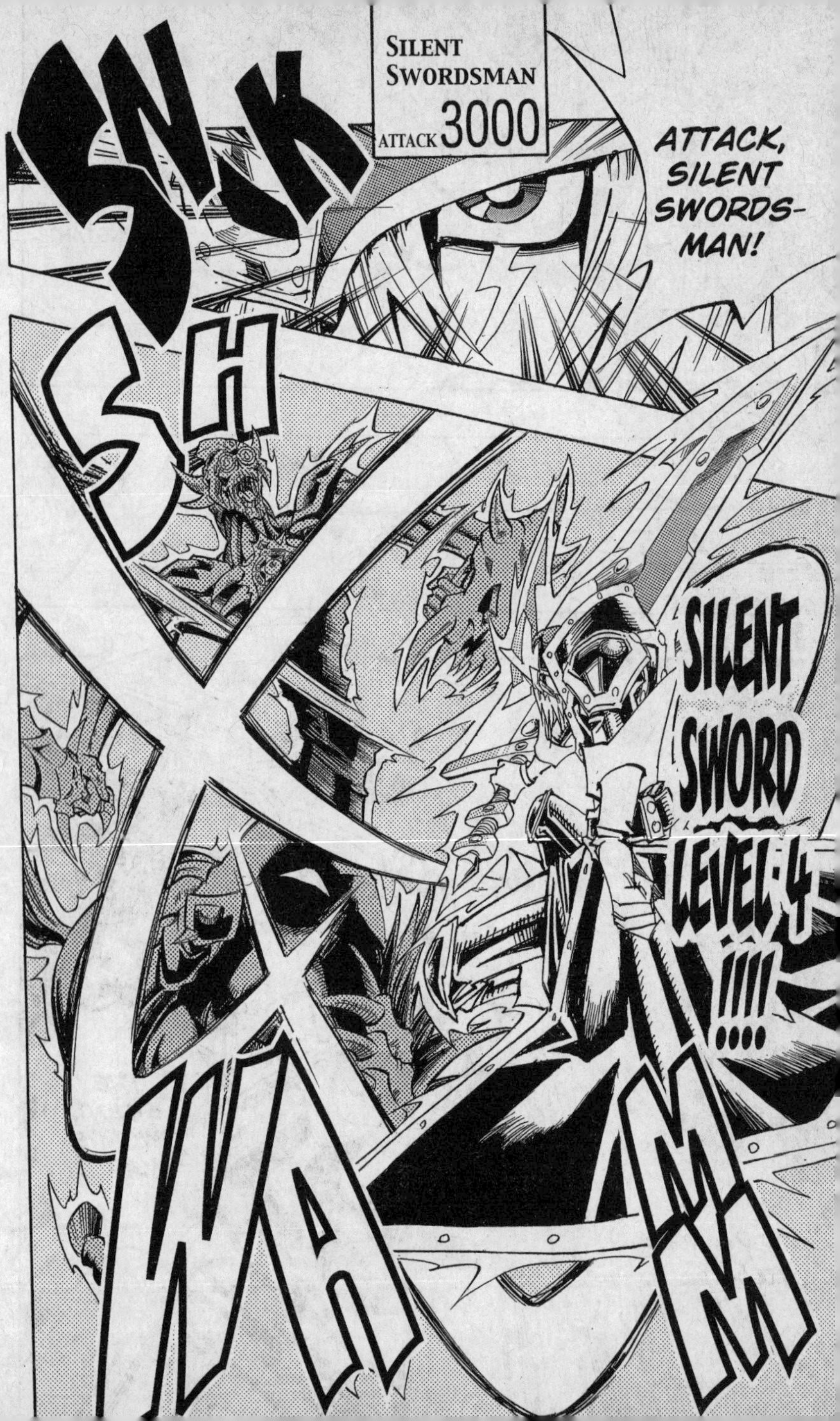
SILENT SWORDSMAN ATTACK 3000
ATTACK, SILENT SWORDS-MAN!
SILENT SWORD LEVEL 4!!!!

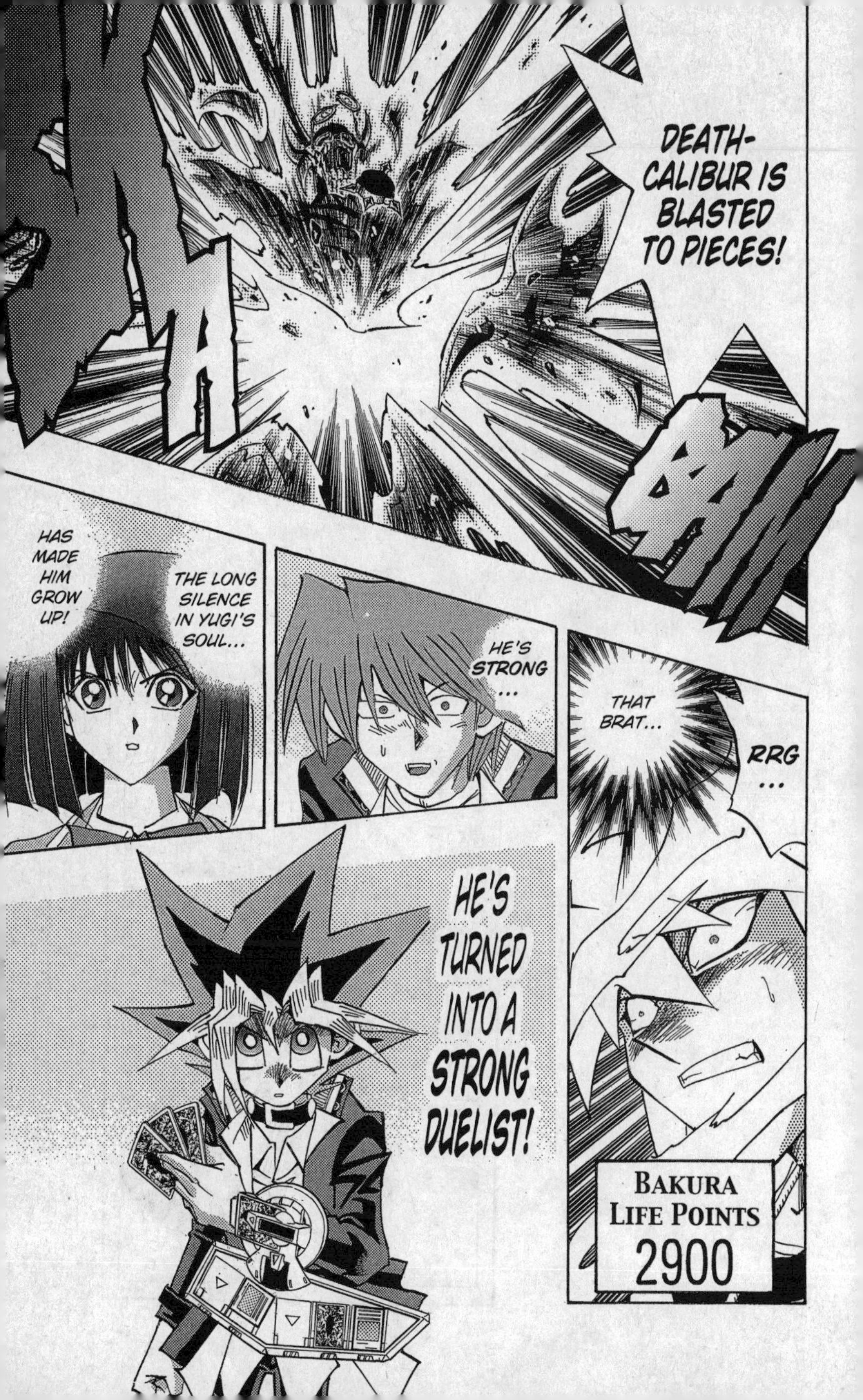
DEATH-CALIBUR IS BLASTED TO PIECES!
RRG...
THAT BRAT...
BAKURA LIFE POINTS 2900
HE'S STRONG...
THE LONG SILENCE IN YUGI'S SOUL...
HAS MADE HIM GROW UP!
HE'S TURNED INTO A STRONG DUELIST!

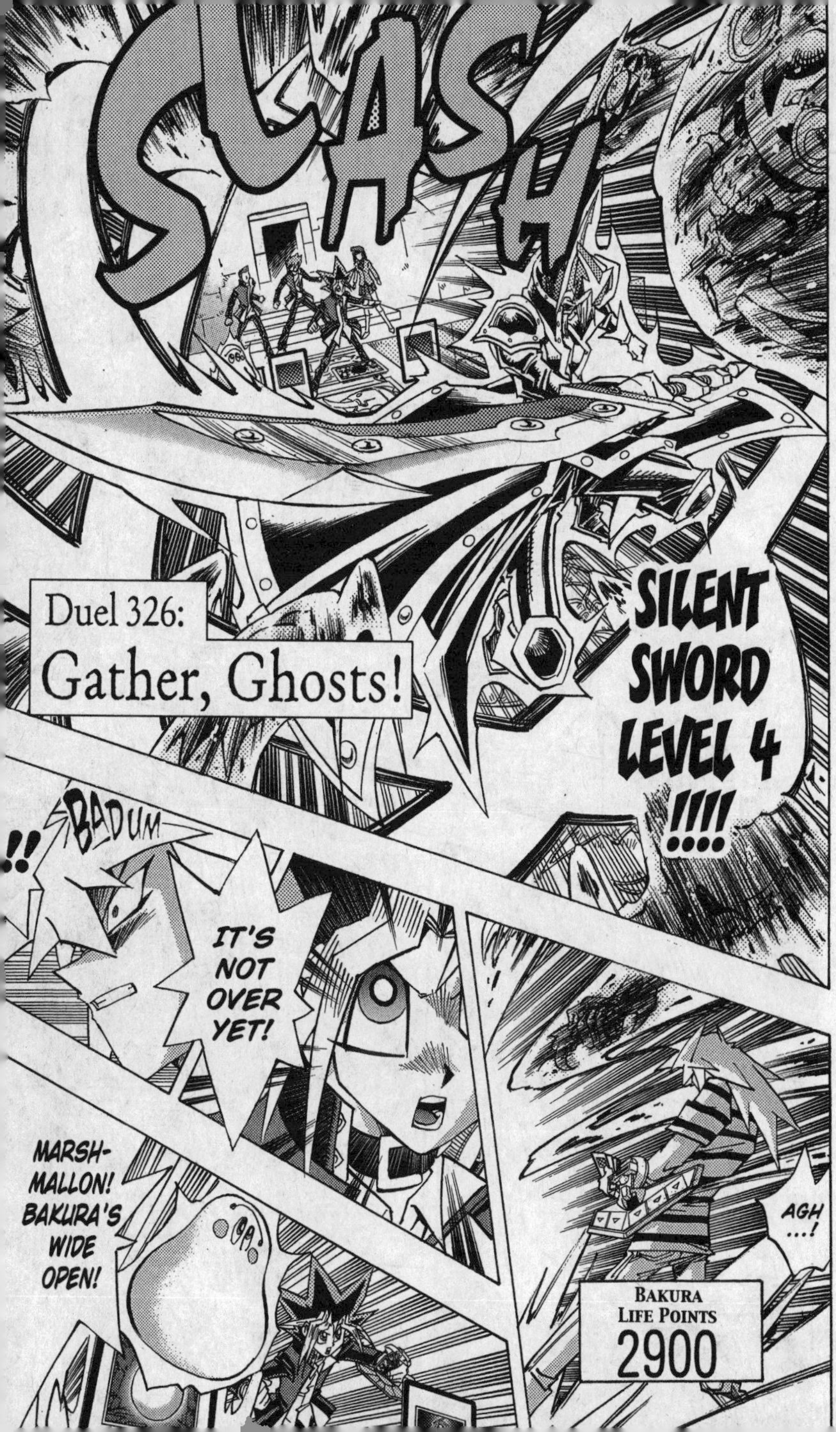
SLASH
SILENT SWORD LEVEL 4 !!!!
Duel 326:
Gather, Ghosts!
AGH ...!
BAKURA LIFE POINTS 2900
BADUM
!!
IT'S NOT OVER YET!
MARSH-MALLON! BAKURA'S WIDE OPEN!

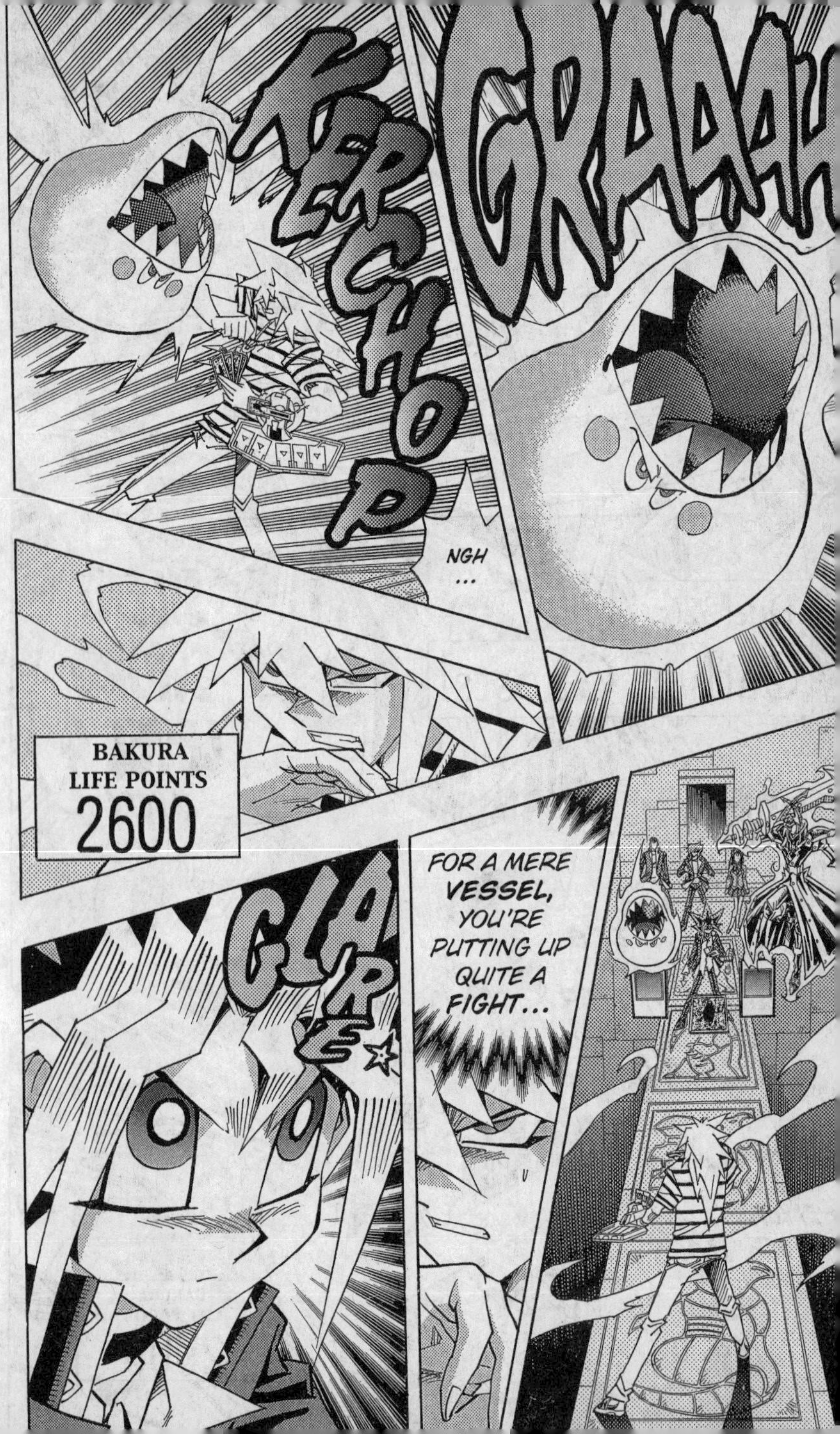
GRAAAH
NGH...
KERCHOP
BAKURA LIFE POINTS 2600
FOR A MERE VESSEL, YOU'RE PUTTING UP QUITE A FIGHT...
GLARE

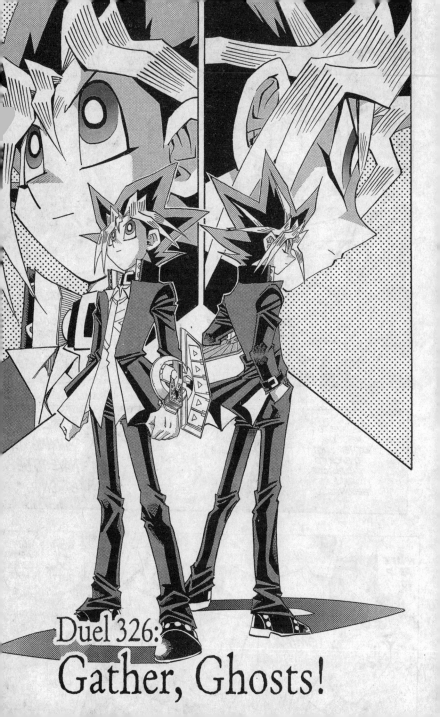

Duel 326:
Gather, Ghosts!

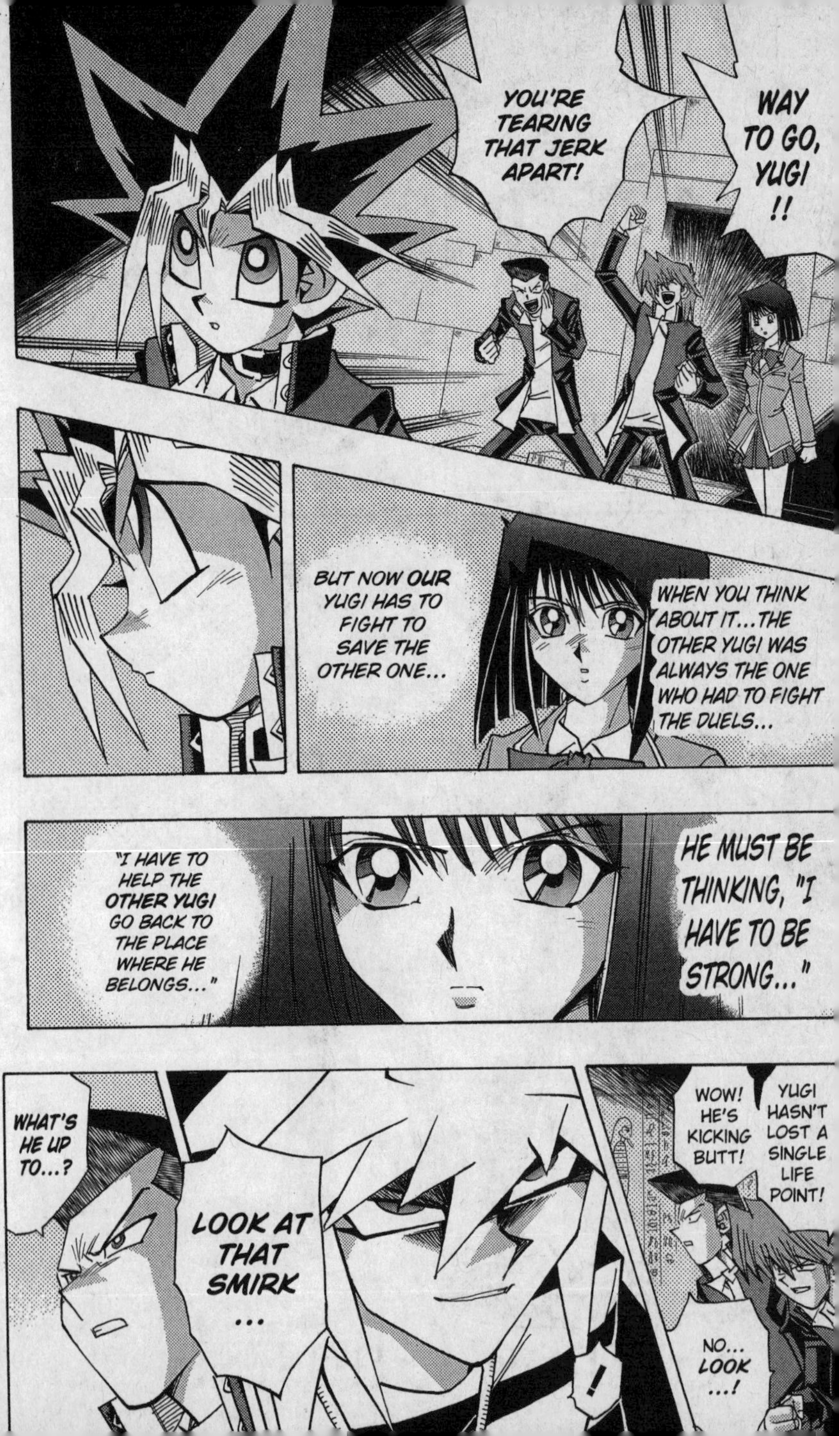
WAY TO GO, YUGI!!
YOU'RE TEARING THAT JERK APART!
WHEN YOU THINK ABOUT IT...THE OTHER YUGI WAS ALWAYS THE ONE WHO HAD TO FIGHT THE DUELS...
BUT NOW OUR YUGI HAS TO FIGHT TO SAVE THE OTHER ONE...
HE MUST BE THINKING, "I HAVE TO BE STRONG..."
"I HAVE TO HELP THE OTHER YUGI GO BACK TO THE PLACE WHERE HE BELONGS..."
YUGI HASN'T LOST A SINGLE LIFE POINT!
WOW! HE'S KICKING BUTT!
NO... LOOK...!
!
LOOK AT THAT SMIRK...
WHAT'S HE UP TO...?

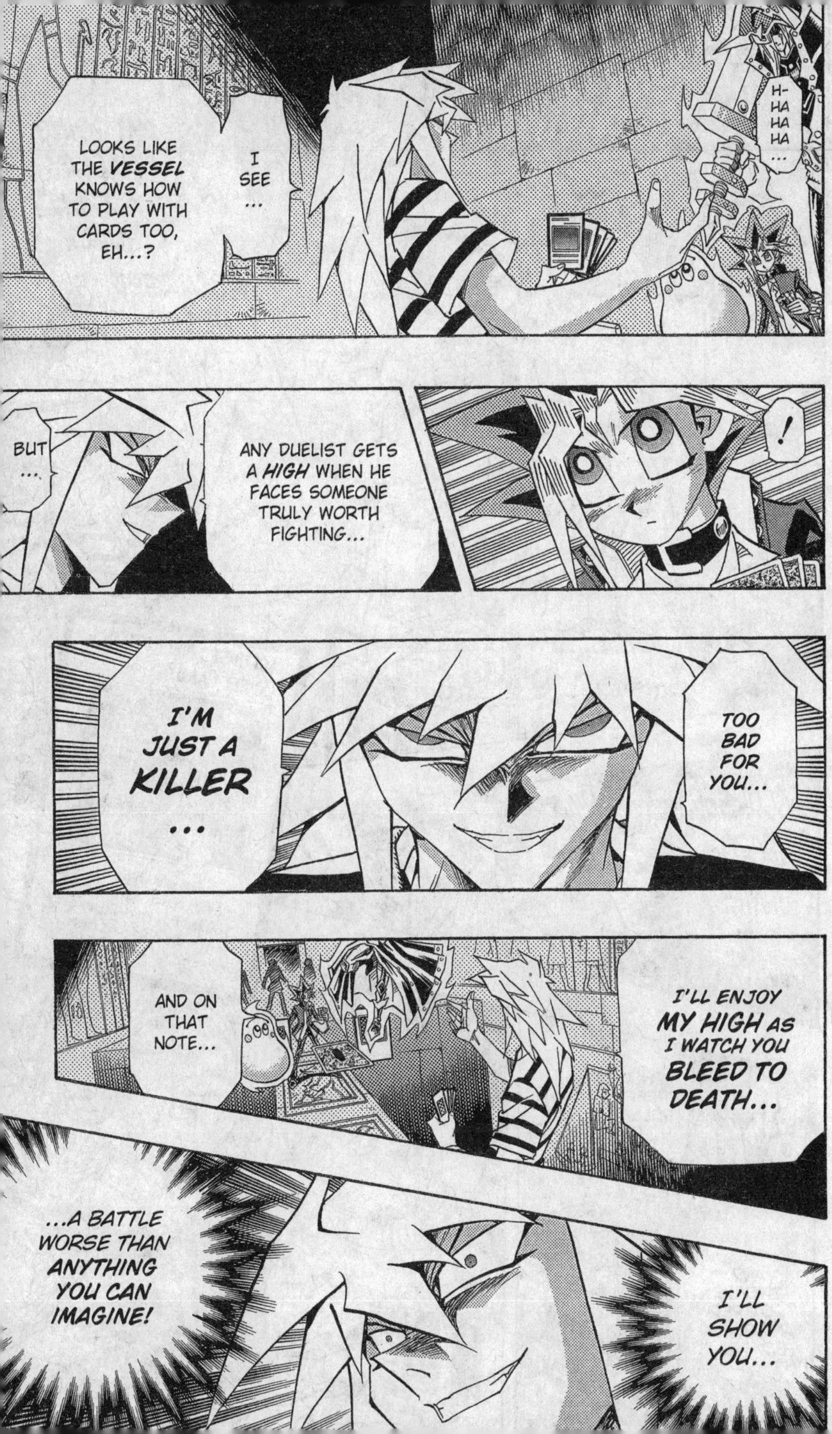
H-HA HA HA...
I SEE...
LOOKS LIKE THE VESSEL KNOWS HOW TO PLAY WITH CARDS TOO, EH...?
!
ANY DUELIST GETS A HIGH WHEN HE FACES SOMEONE TRULY WORTH FIGHTING...
BUT...
TOO BAD FOR YOU...
I'M JUST A KILLER...
I'LL ENJOY MY HIGH AS I WATCH YOU BLEED TO DEATH...
AND ON THAT NOTE...
I'LL SHOW YOU...
...A BATTLE WORSE THAN ANYTHING YOU CAN IMAGINE!

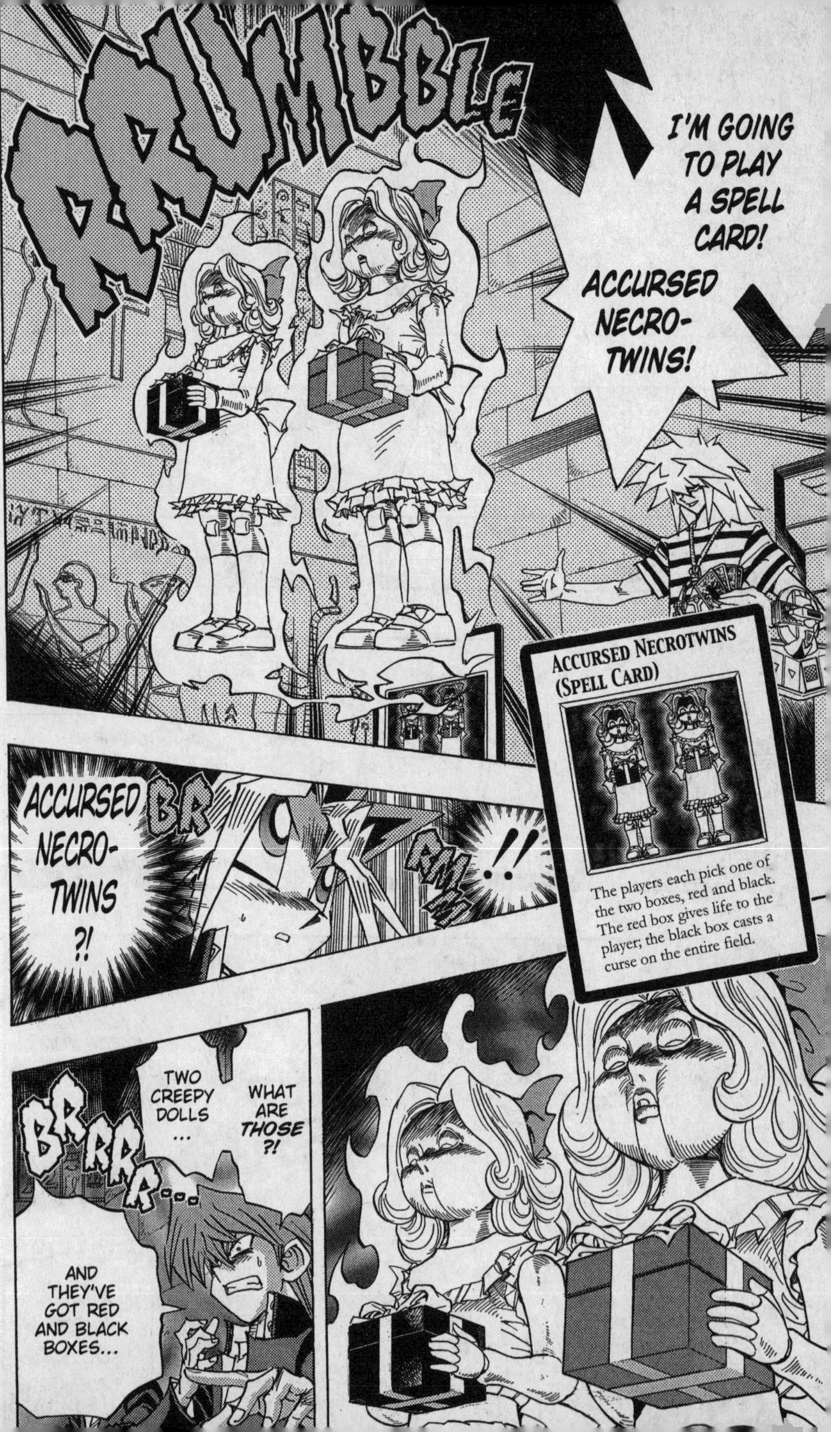

I'M GOING TO PLAY A SPELL CARD!
ACCURSED NECRO-TWINS!
RRUMBBLE
ACCURSED NECROTWINS (SPELL CARD)
The players each pick one of the two boxes, red and black. The red box gives life to the player; the black box casts a curse on the entire field.
!!
BRRMM
ACCURSED NECRO-TWINS?!
WHAT ARE THOSE?!
TWO CREEPY DOLLS...
BRRRR...
AND THEY'VE GOT RED AND BLACK BOXES...

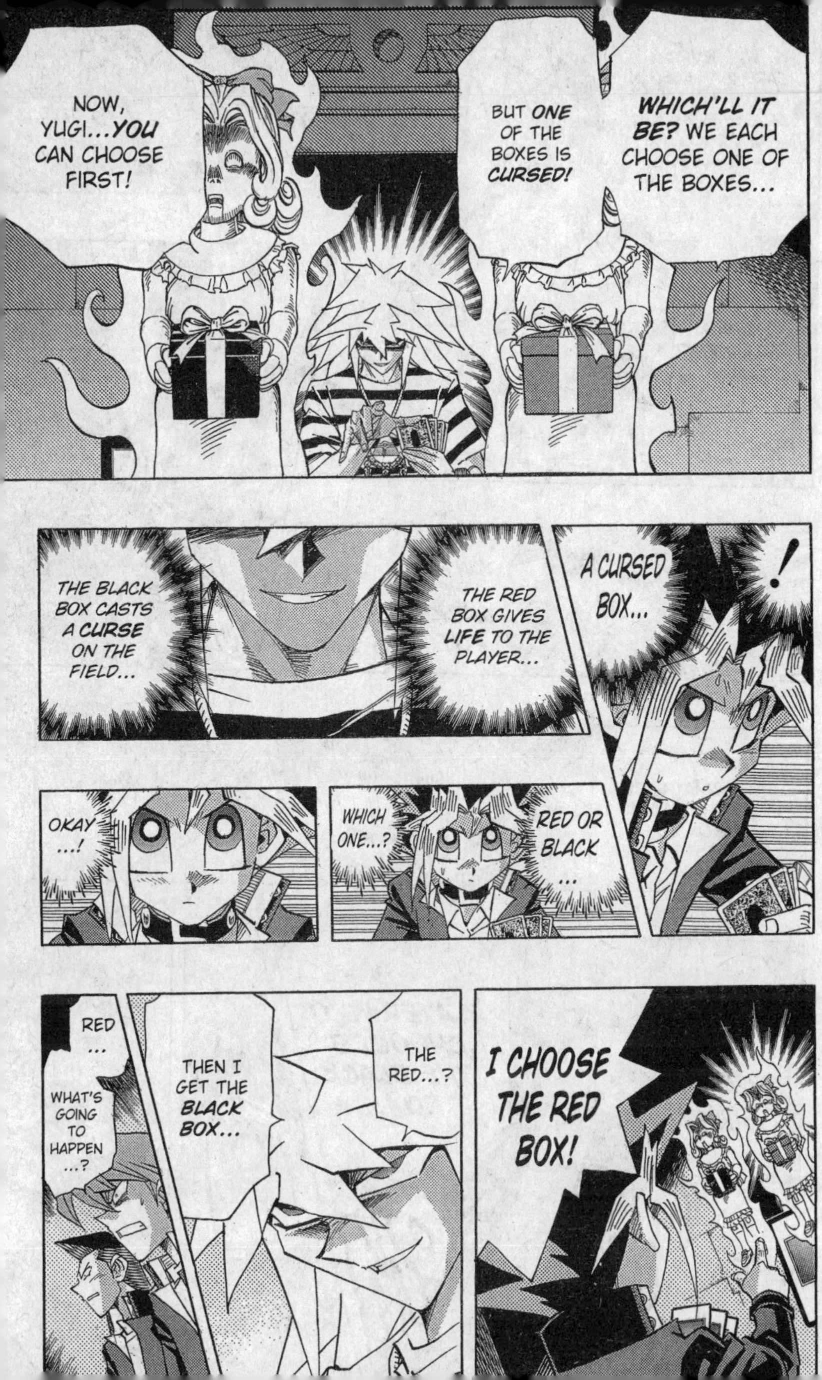
WHICH'LL IT BE? WE EACH CHOOSE ONE OF THE BOXES...
BUT ONE OF THE BOXES IS CURSED!
NOW, YUGI...YOU CAN CHOOSE FIRST!
!
A CURSED BOX...
THE RED BOX GIVES LIFE TO THE PLAYER...
THE BLACK BOX CASTS A CURSE ON THE FIELD...
RED OR BLACK...
WHICH ONE...?
OKAY...!
I CHOOSE THE RED BOX!
THE RED...?
THEN I GET THE BLACK BOX...
RED...
WHAT'S GOING TO HAPPEN...?

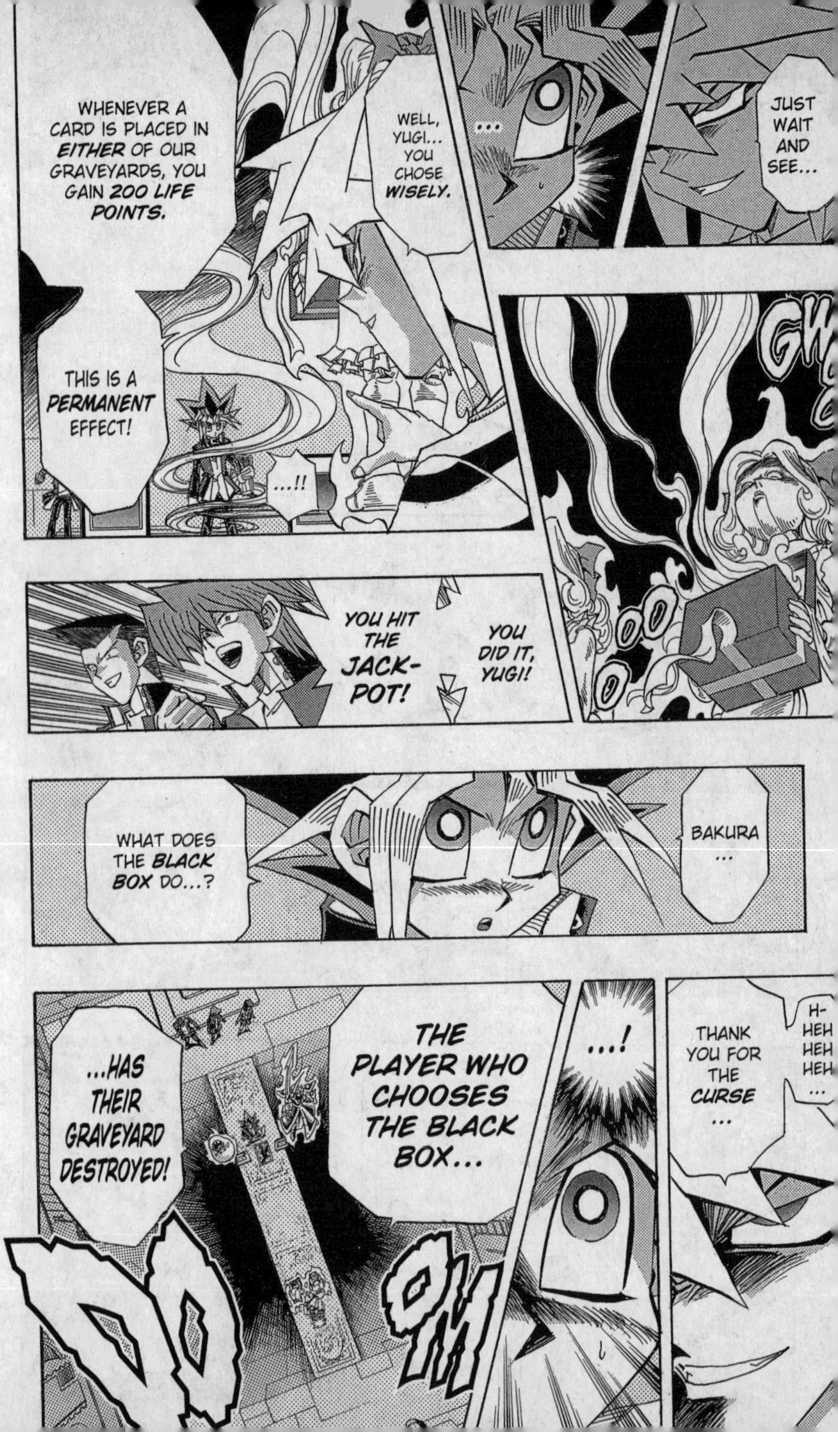

JUST WAIT AND SEE...
...
WELL, YUGI... YOU CHOSE WISELY.
WHENEVER A CARD IS PLACED IN EITHER OF OUR GRAVEYARDS, YOU GAIN 200 LIFE POINTS.
THIS IS A PERMANENT EFFECT!
...!!
GW
YOU DID IT, YUGI!
YOU HIT THE JACK-POT!
BAKURA...
WHAT DOES THE BLACK BOX DO...?
H-HEH HEH HEH...
THANK YOU FOR THE CURSE...
...!
THE PLAYER WHO CHOOSES THE BLACK BOX...
...HAS THEIR GRAVEYARD DESTROYED!
DOOM

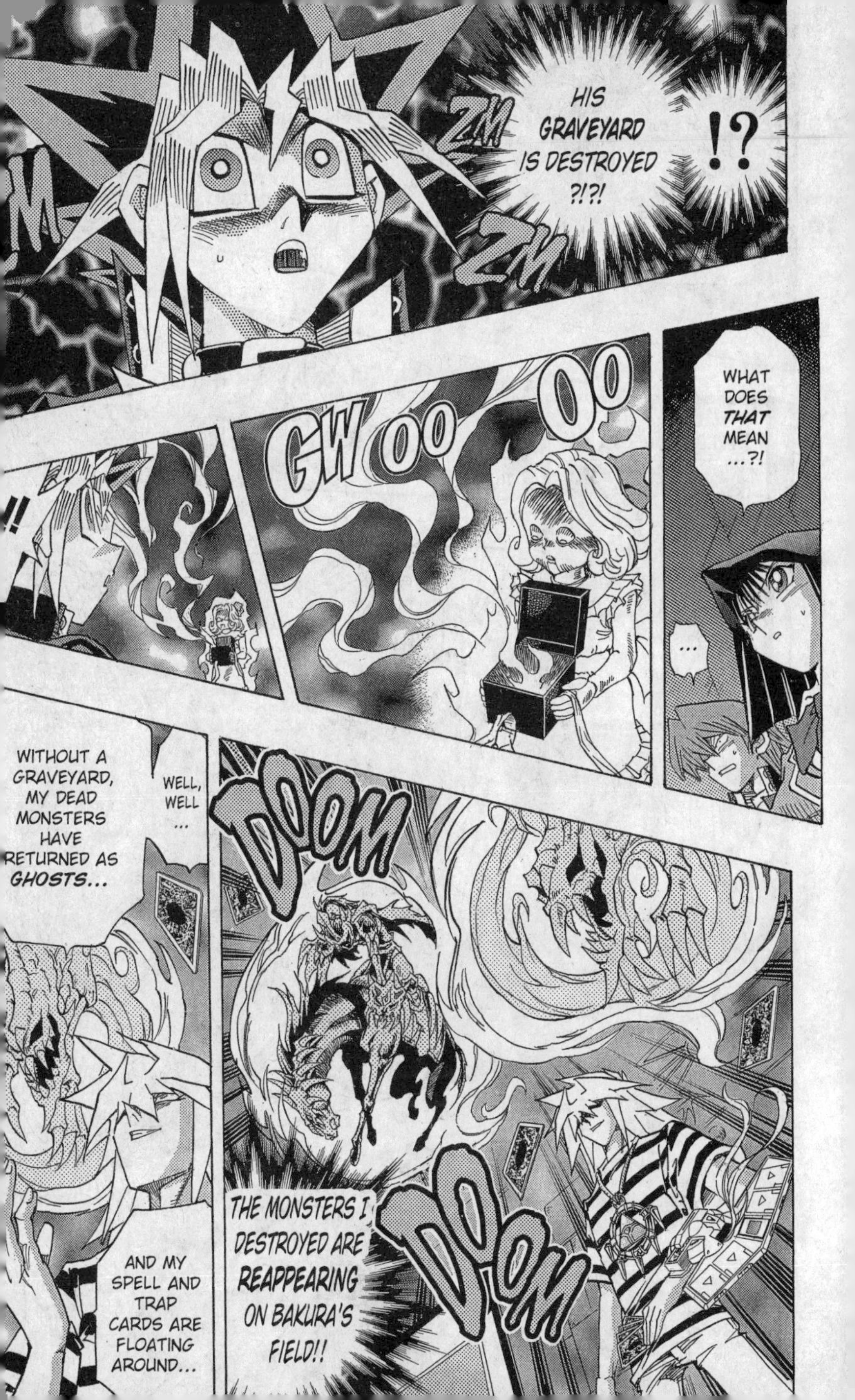
ZM
HIS GRAVEYARD IS DESTROYED ?!?!
!?
ZM
WHAT DOES THAT MEAN ...?!
...
GWOOOO
!!
DOOM
THE MONSTERS I DESTROYED ARE REAPPEARING ON BAKURA'S FIELD!!
DOOM
WELL, WELL ...
WITHOUT A GRAVEYARD, MY DEAD MONSTERS HAVE RETURNED AS GHOSTS...
AND MY SPELL AND TRAP CARDS ARE FLOATING AROUND...

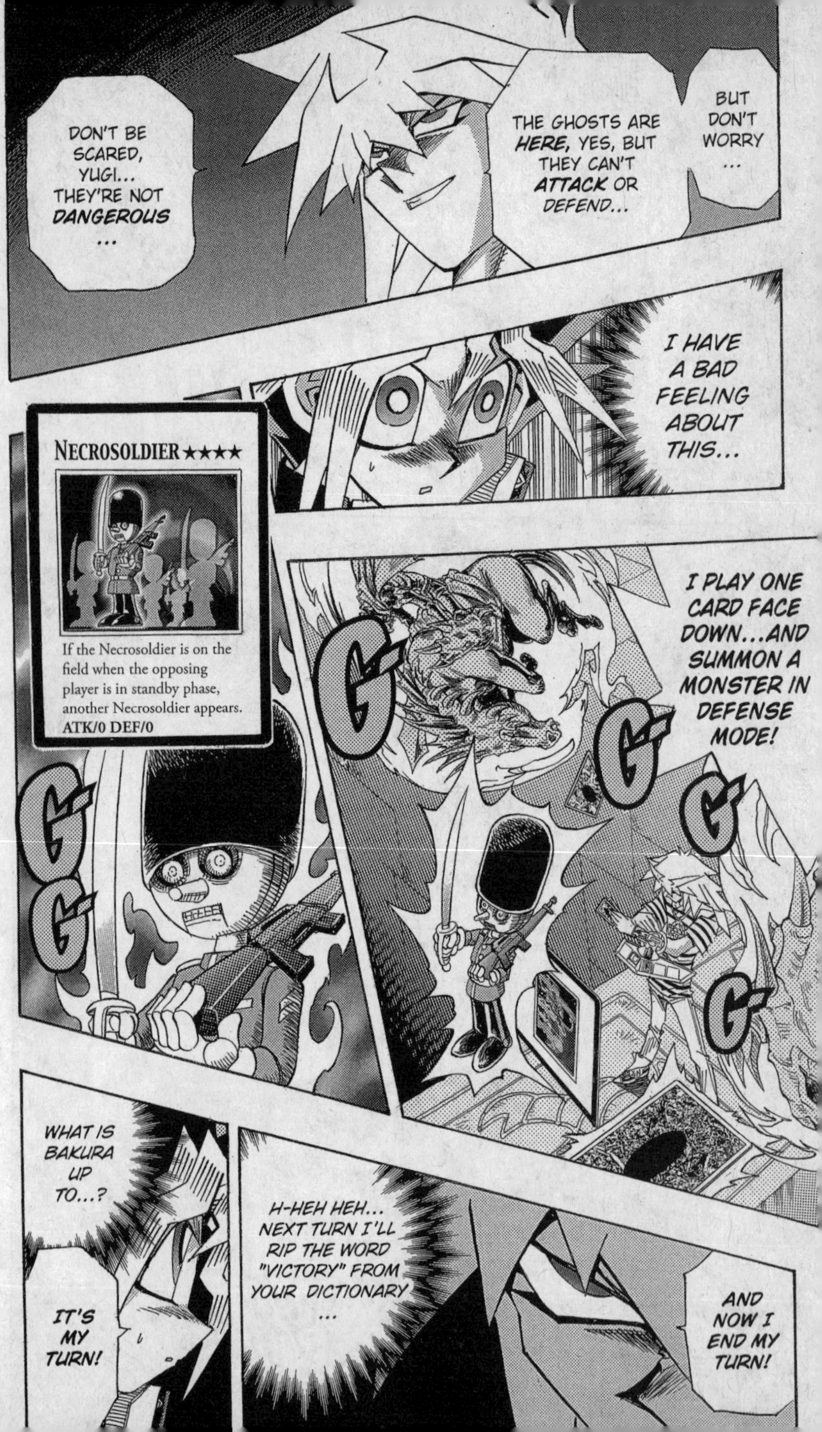
BUT DON'T WORRY...
THE GHOSTS ARE HERE, YES, BUT THEY CAN'T ATTACK OR DEFEND...
DON'T BE SCARED, YUGI... THEY'RE NOT DANGEROUS...
I HAVE A BAD FEELING ABOUT THIS...
I PLAY ONE CARD FACE DOWN...AND SUMMON A MONSTER IN DEFENSE MODE!
G
G
G
G
G
NECROSOLDIER ★★★★
If the Necrosoldier is on the field when the opposing player is in standby phase, another Necrosoldier appears.
ATK/0 DEF/0
G
G
AND NOW I END MY TURN!
H-HEH HEH... NEXT TURN I'LL RIP THE WORD "VICTORY" FROM YOUR DICTIONARY...
WHAT IS BAKURA UP TO...?
IT'S MY TURN!

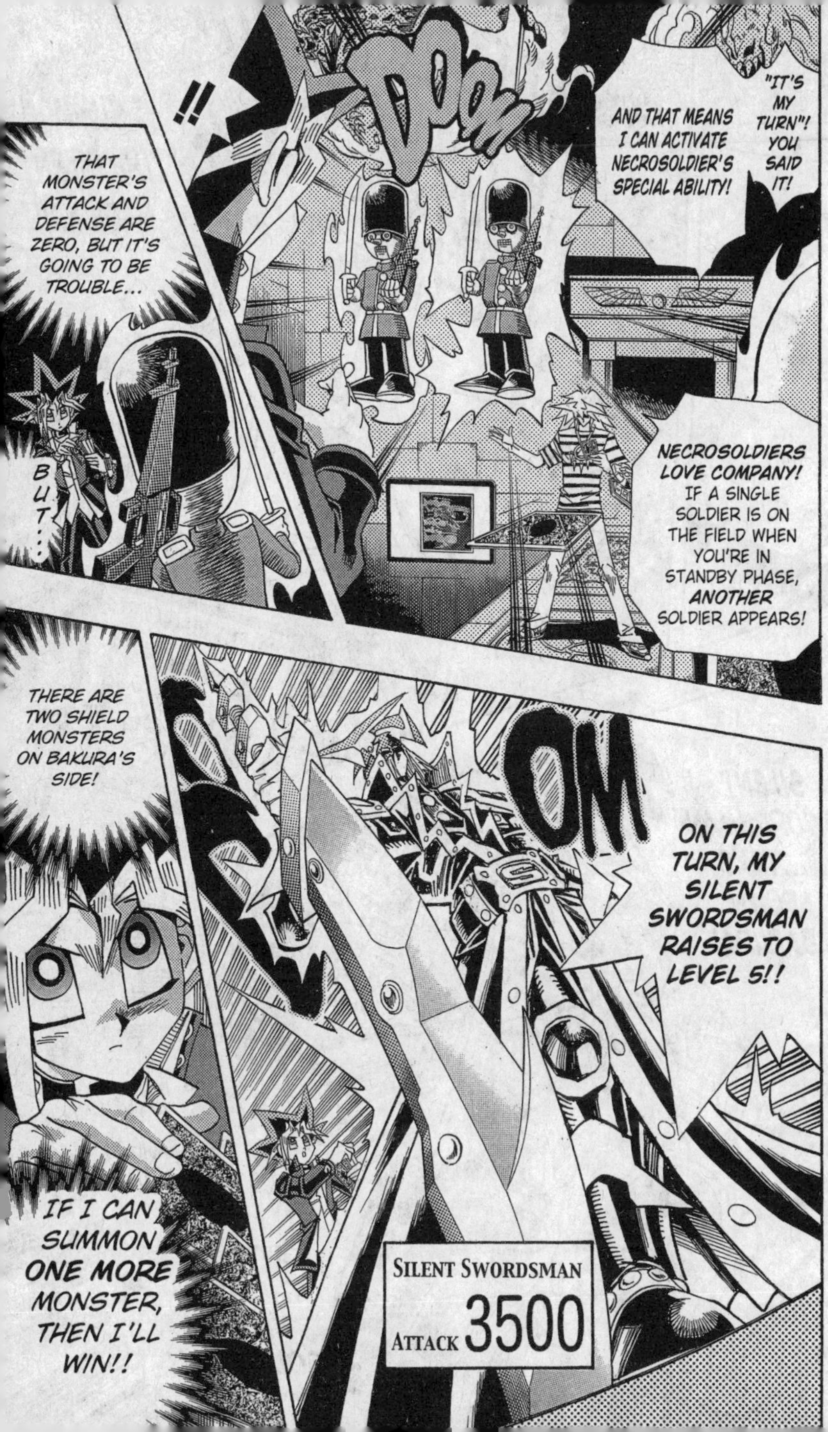
"IT'S MY TURN"! YOU SAID IT!
AND THAT MEANS I CAN ACTIVATE NECROSOLDIER'S SPECIAL ABILITY!
DOOM
!!
NECROSOLDIERS LOVE COMPANY! IF A SINGLE SOLDIER IS ON THE FIELD WHEN YOU'RE IN STANDBY PHASE, ANOTHER SOLDIER APPEARS!
THAT MONSTER'S ATTACK AND DEFENSE ARE ZERO, BUT IT'S GOING TO BE TROUBLE...
BUT...
ON THIS TURN, MY SILENT SWORDSMAN RAISES TO LEVEL 5!!
OM
SILENT SWORDSMAN
ATTACK 3500
THERE ARE TWO SHIELD MONSTERS ON BAKURA'S SIDE!
IF I CAN SUMMON ONE MORE MONSTER, THEN I'LL WIN!!

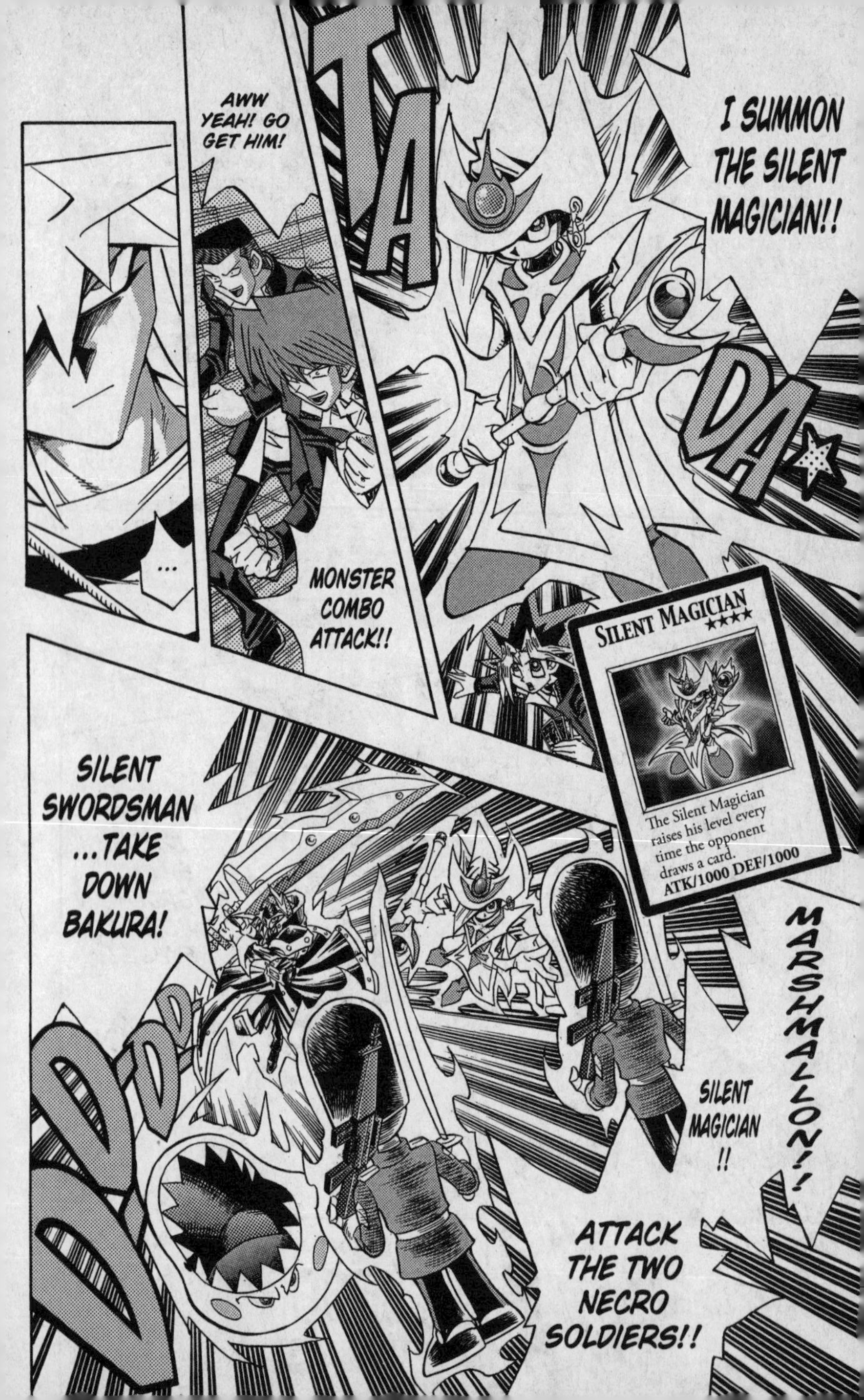
TA
I SUMMON THE SILENT MAGICIAN!!
DA
SILENT MAGICIAN ★★★★
The Silent Magician raises his level every time the opponent draws a card.
ATK/1000 DEF/1000
AWW YEAH! GO GET HIM!
MONSTER COMBO ATTACK!!
...
MARSHMALLON!!
SILENT MAGICIAN!!
ATTACK THE TWO NECRO SOLDIERS!!
SILENT SWORDSMAN ...TAKE DOWN BAKURA!
DODODO

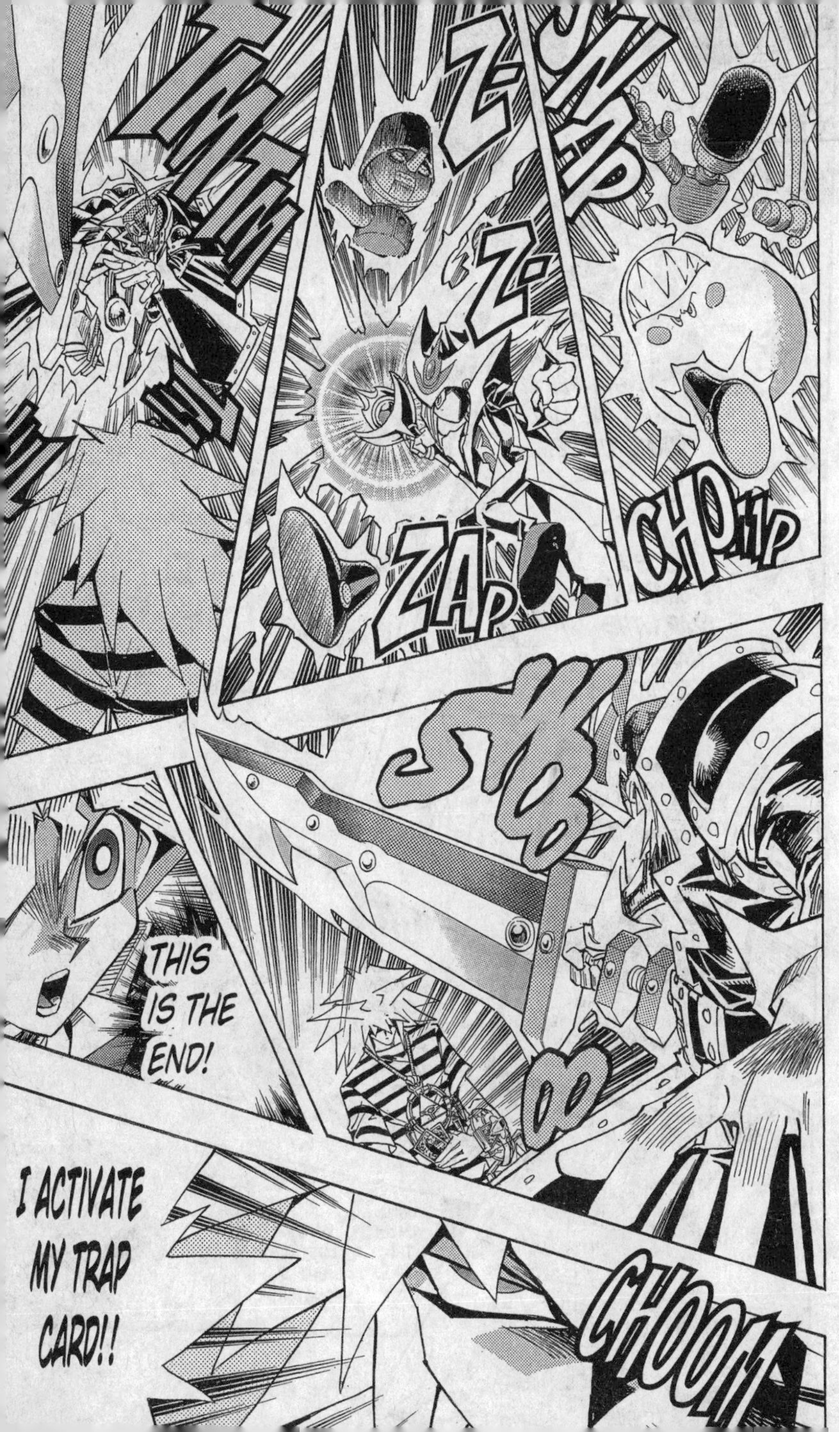
Z-
Z-
ZAP
THIS IS THE END!
I ACTIVATE MY TRAP CARD!!

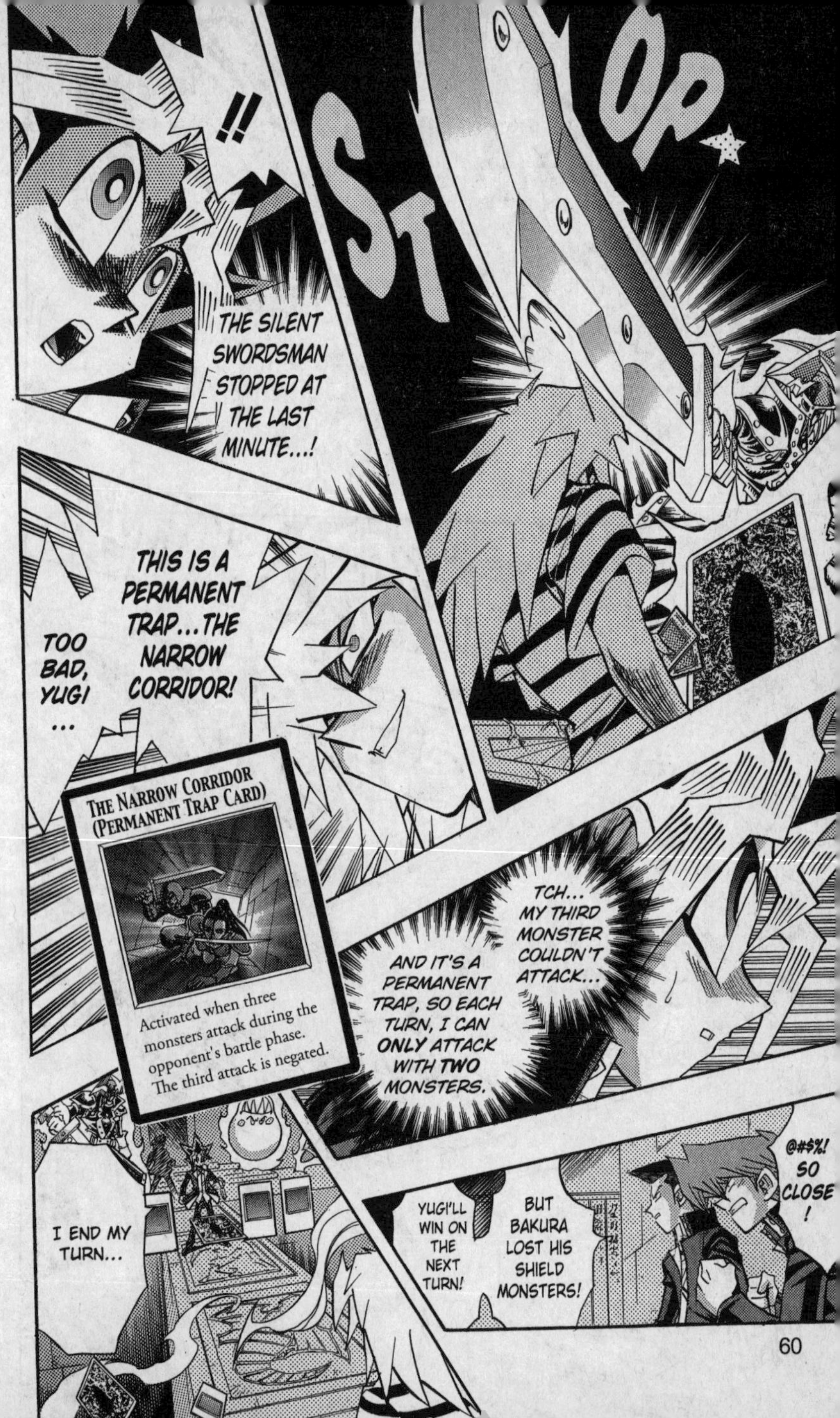

STOP★
!!
THE SILENT SWORDSMAN STOPPED AT THE LAST MINUTE...!
THIS IS A PERMANENT TRAP...THE NARROW CORRIDOR!
TOO BAD, YUGI...
THE NARROW CORRIDOR (PERMANENT TRAP CARD)
Activated when three monsters attack during the opponent's battle phase. The third attack is negated.
TCH... MY THIRD MONSTER COULDN'T ATTACK...
AND IT'S A PERMANENT TRAP, SO EACH TURN, I CAN ONLY ATTACK WITH TWO MONSTERS.
@#$%! SO CLOSE!
BUT BAKURA LOST HIS SHIELD MONSTERS!
YUGI'LL WIN ON THE NEXT TURN!
I END MY TURN...

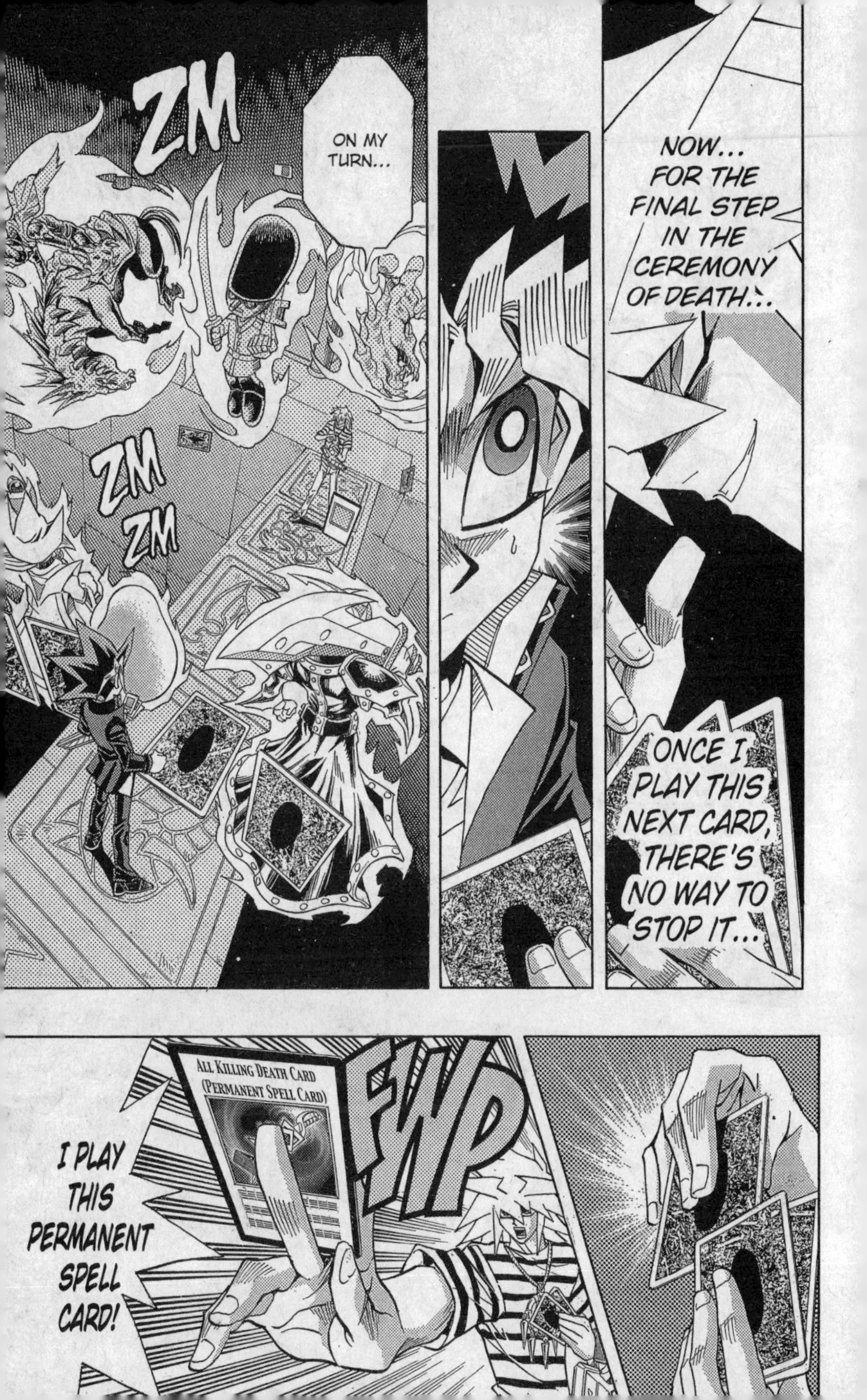
NOW... FOR THE FINAL STEP IN THE CEREMONY OF DEATH...
ONCE I PLAY THIS NEXT CARD, THERE'S NO WAY TO STOP IT...
ON MY TURN...
ZM
ZM
ZM
FWP
ALL KILLING DEATH CARD
(PERMANENT SPELL CARD)
I PLAY THIS PERMANENT SPELL CARD!

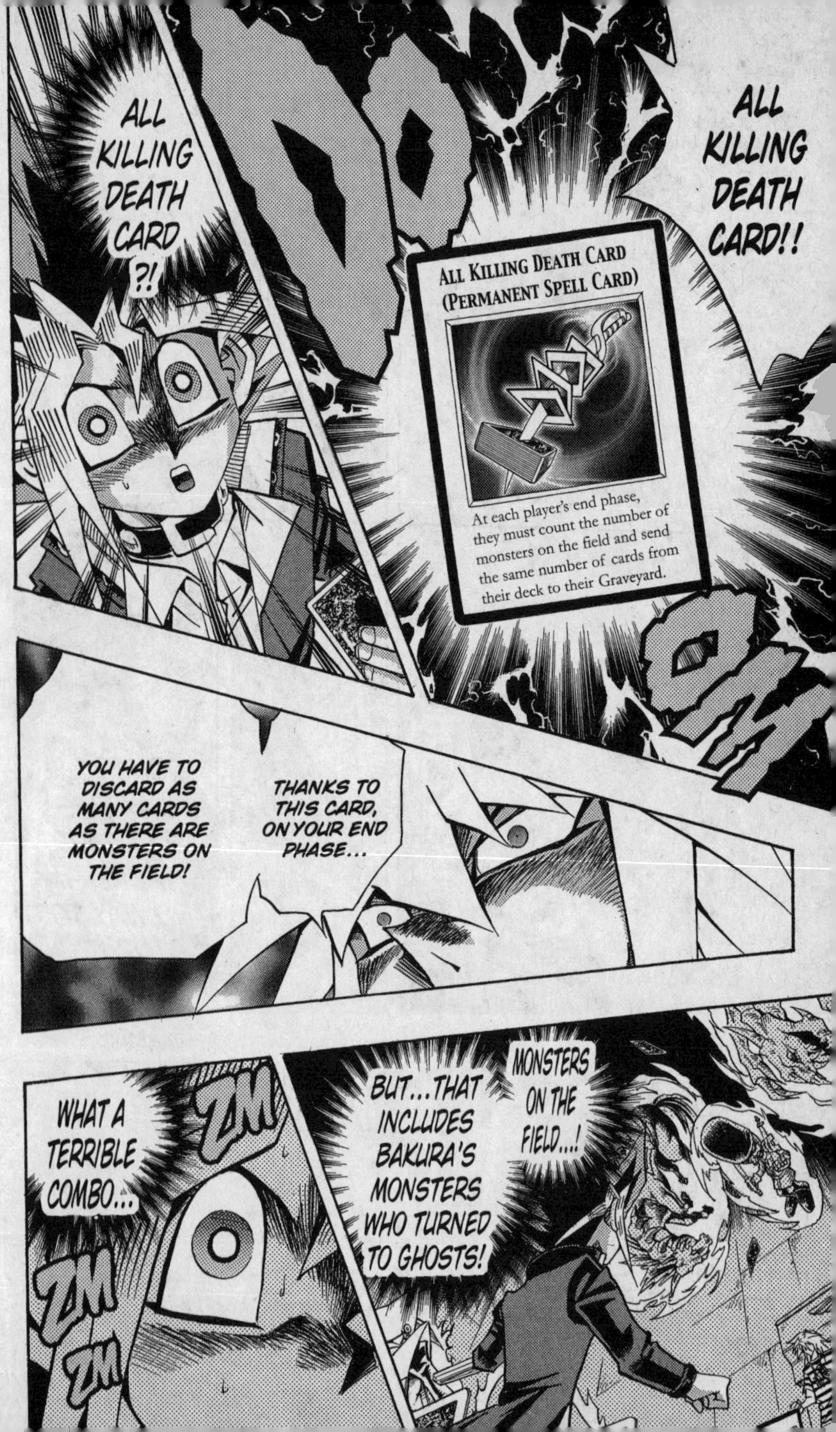
ALL KILLING DEATH CARD!!
ALL KILLING DEATH CARD (PERMANENT SPELL CARD)
At each player's end phase, they must count the number of monsters on the field and send the same number of cards from their deck to their Graveyard.
DO
OM
ALL KILLING DEATH CARD ?!
THANKS TO THIS CARD, ON YOUR END PHASE...
YOU HAVE TO DISCARD AS MANY CARDS AS THERE ARE MONSTERS ON THE FIELD!
MONSTERS ON THE FIELD...!
BUT...THAT INCLUDES BAKURA'S MONSTERS WHO TURNED TO GHOSTS!
ZM
WHAT A TERRIBLE COMBO...
ZM
ZM

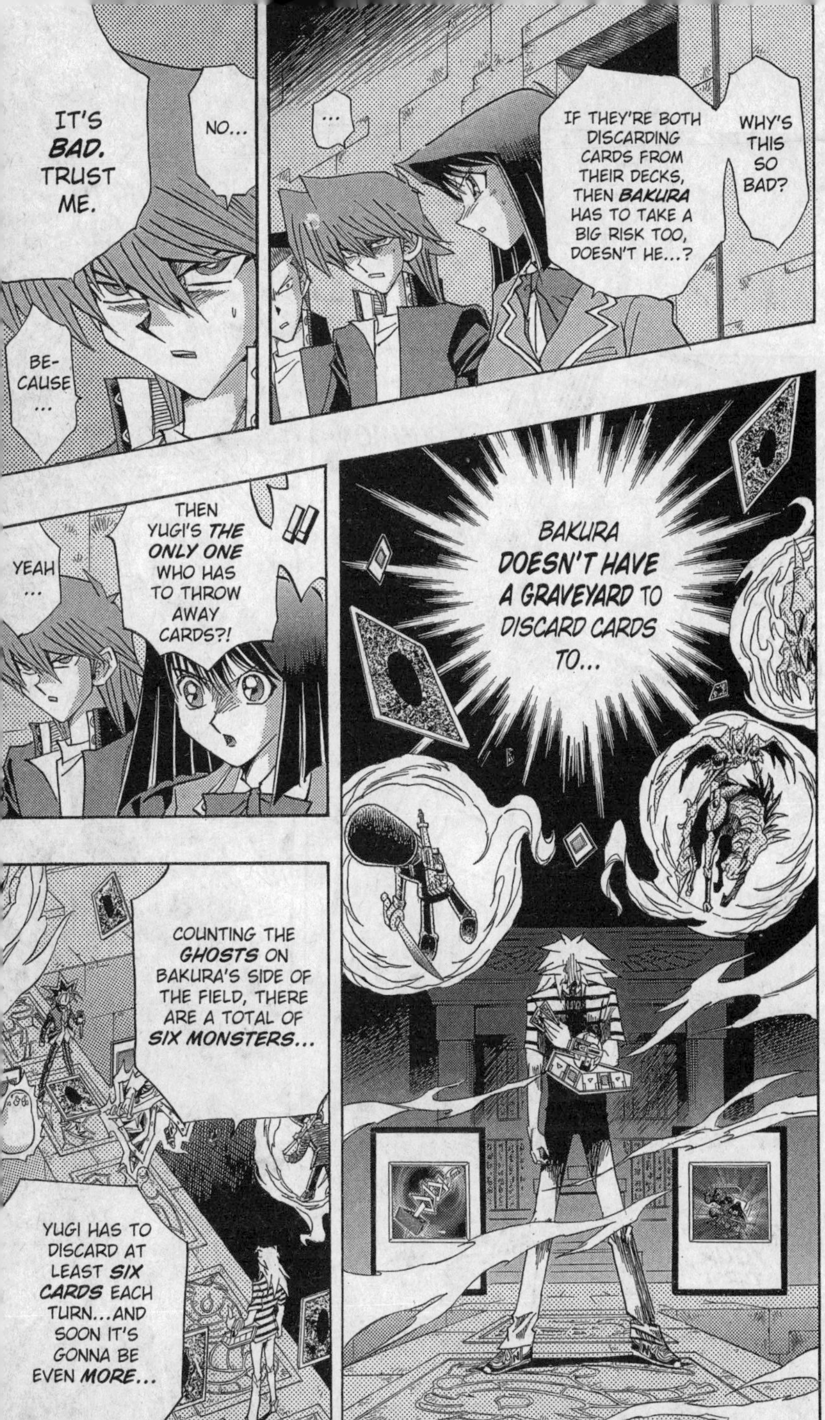
WHY'S THIS SO BAD?
IF THEY'RE BOTH DISCARDING CARDS FROM THEIR DECKS, THEN BAKURA HAS TO TAKE A BIG RISK TOO, DOESN'T HE...?
...
NO...
IT'S BAD. TRUST ME.
BE-CAUSE ...
BAKURA DOESN'T HAVE A GRAVEYARD TO DISCARD CARDS TO...
THEN YUGI'S THE ONLY ONE WHO HAS TO THROW AWAY CARDS?!
YEAH ...
COUNTING THE GHOSTS ON BAKURA'S SIDE OF THE FIELD, THERE ARE A TOTAL OF SIX MONSTERS...
YUGI HAS TO DISCARD AT LEAST SIX CARDS EACH TURN...AND SOON IT'S GONNA BE EVEN MORE...

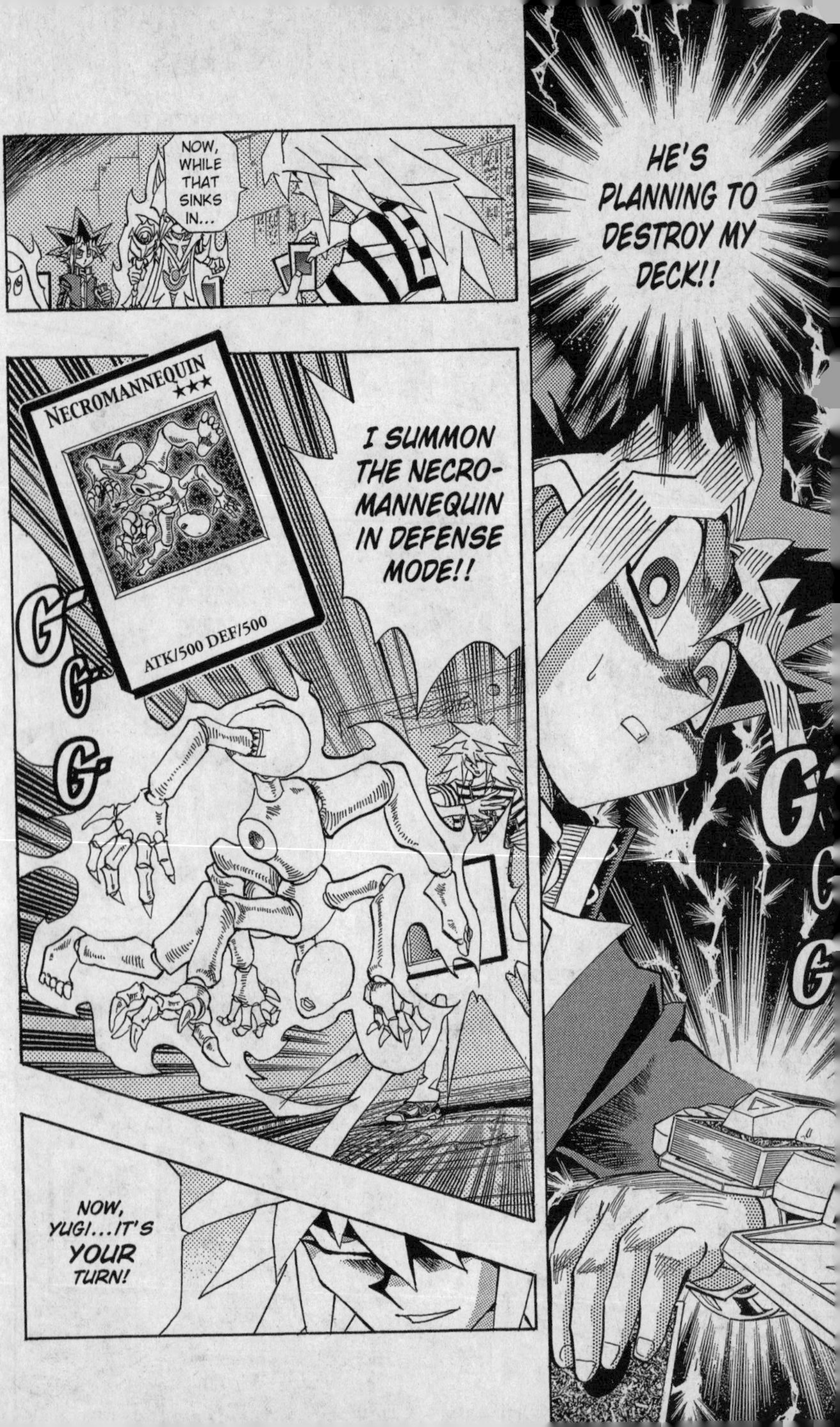
HE'S PLANNING TO DESTROY MY DECK!!
G- G- G
NOW, WHILE THAT SINKS IN...
NECROMANNEQUIN ★★★
ATK/500 DEF/500
I SUMMON THE NECRO-MANNEQUIN IN DEFENSE MODE!!
G- G- G-
NOW, YUGI...IT'S YOUR TURN!

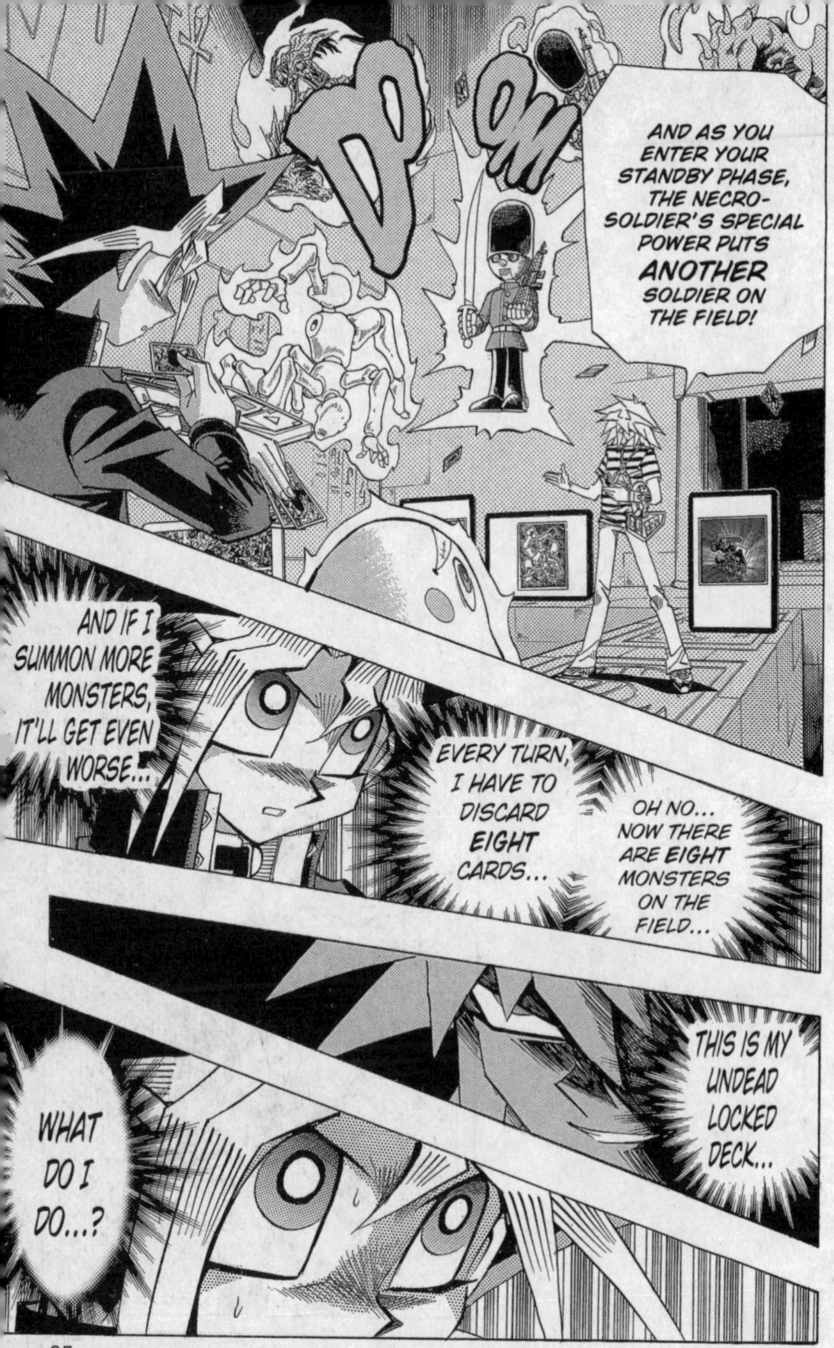

BOOM
AND AS YOU ENTER YOUR STANDBY PHASE, THE NECRO-SOLDIER'S SPECIAL POWER PUTS ANOTHER SOLDIER ON THE FIELD!
OH NO... NOW THERE ARE EIGHT MONSTERS ON THE FIELD...
EVERY TURN, I HAVE TO DISCARD EIGHT CARDS...
AND IF I SUMMON MORE MONSTERS, IT'LL GET EVEN WORSE...
THIS IS MY UNDEAD LOCKED DECK...
WHAT DO I DO...?

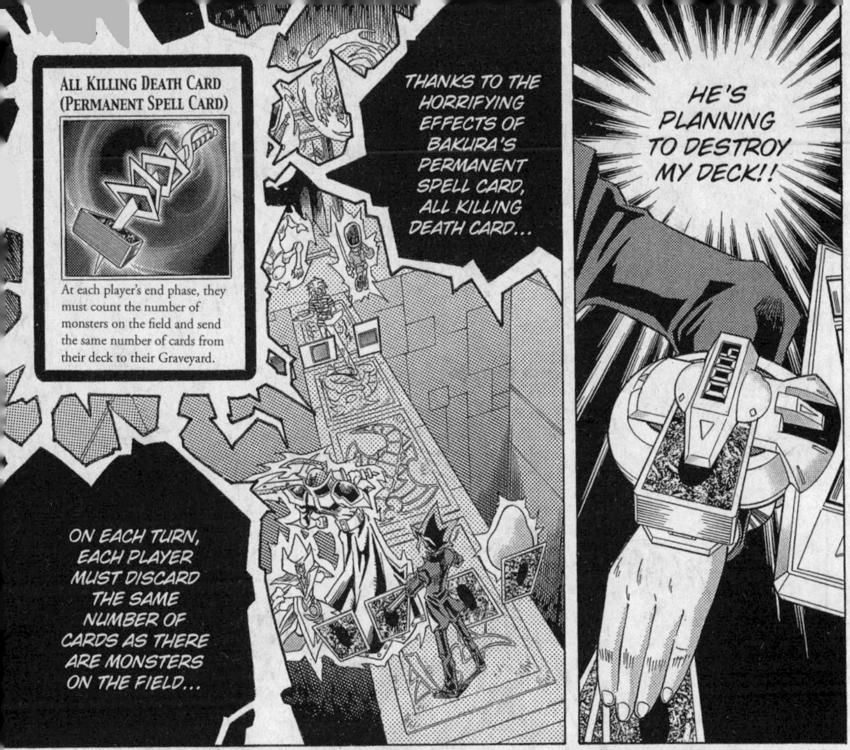
HE'S PLANNING TO DESTROY MY DECK!!
THANKS TO THE HORRIFYING EFFECTS OF BAKURA'S PERMANENT SPELL CARD, ALL KILLING DEATH CARD...
ALL KILLING DEATH CARD (PERMANENT SPELL CARD)
At each player's end phase, they must count the number of monsters on the field and send the same number of cards from their deck to their Graveyard.
ON EACH TURN, EACH PLAYER MUST DISCARD THE SAME NUMBER OF CARDS AS THERE ARE MONSTERS ON THE FIELD...

Duel 327: I Won't Give Up!!

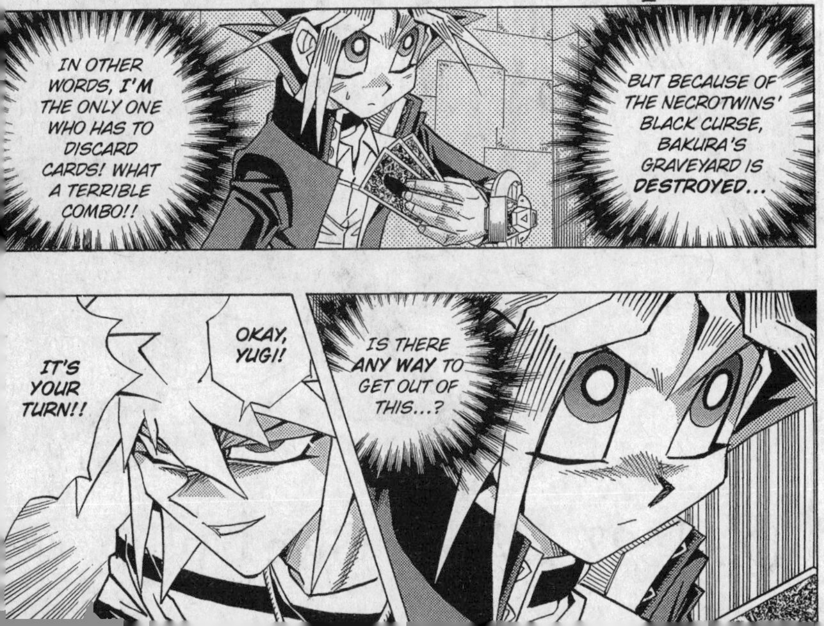
BUT BECAUSE OF THE NECROTWINS' BLACK CURSE, BAKURA'S GRAVEYARD IS **DESTROYED**...
IN OTHER WORDS, **I'M** THE ONLY ONE WHO HAS TO DISCARD CARDS! WHAT A TERRIBLE COMBO!!
IS THERE **ANY WAY** TO GET OUT OF THIS...?
OKAY, YUGI!
IT'S YOUR TURN!!

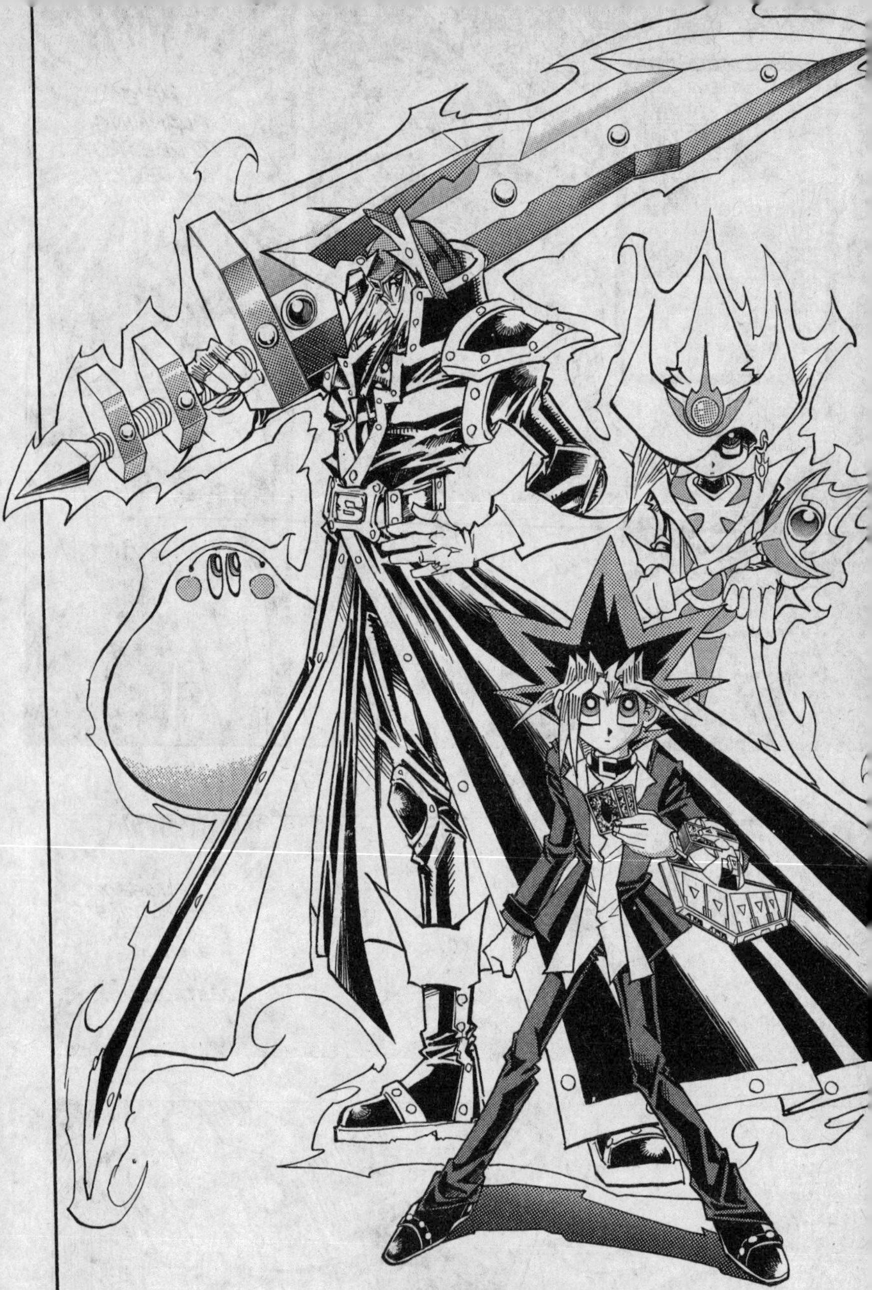

Duel 327: I Won't Give Up!!

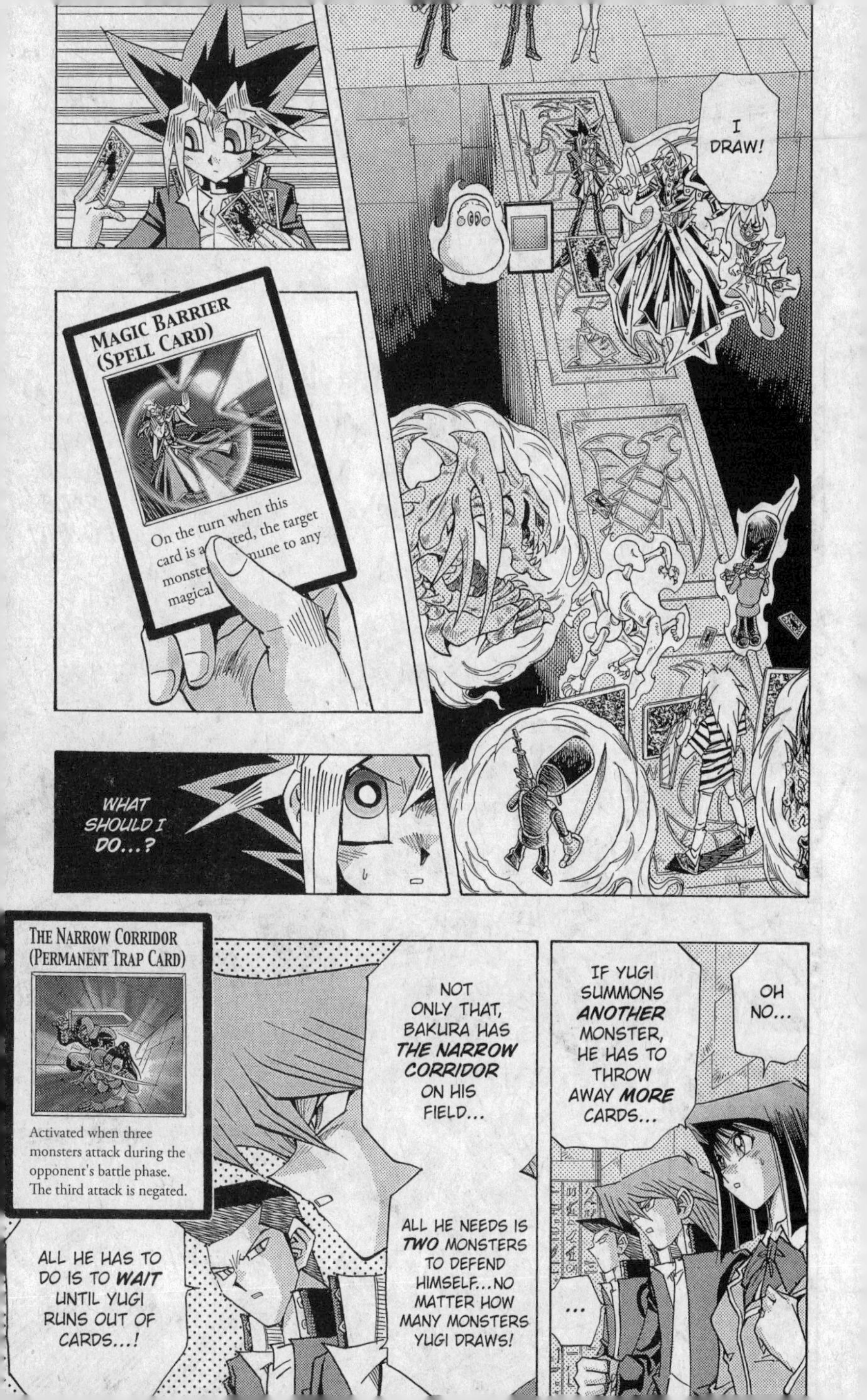
I DRAW!
MAGIC BARRIER (SPELL CARD)
On the turn when this card is a ted, the target card is mune to any monster magical
WHAT SHOULD I DO...?
OH NO...
IF YUGI SUMMONS ANOTHER MONSTER, HE HAS TO THROW AWAY MORE CARDS...
...
NOT ONLY THAT, BAKURA HAS THE NARROW CORRIDOR ON HIS FIELD...
ALL HE NEEDS IS TWO MONSTERS TO DEFEND HIMSELF...NO MATTER HOW MANY MONSTERS YUGI DRAWS!
THE NARROW CORRIDOR (PERMANENT TRAP CARD)
Activated when three monsters attack during the opponent's battle phase. The third attack is negated.
ALL HE HAS TO DO IS TO WAIT UNTIL YUGI RUNS OUT OF CARDS...!

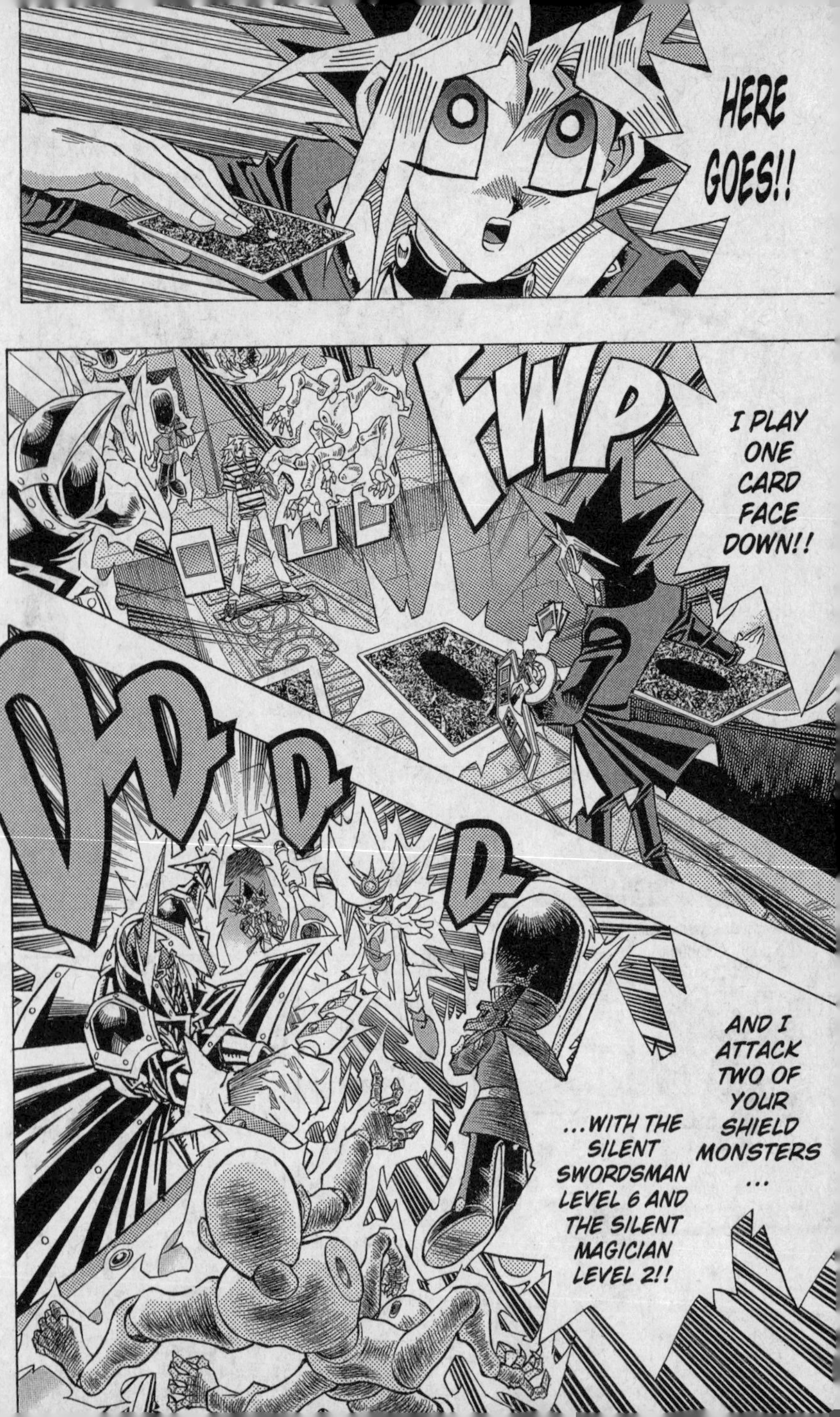
HERE GOES!!
FWP
I PLAY ONE CARD FACE DOWN!!
DDDD
AND I ATTACK TWO OF YOUR SHIELD MONSTERS...
...WITH THE SILENT SWORDSMAN LEVEL 6 AND THE SILENT MAGICIAN LEVEL 2!!

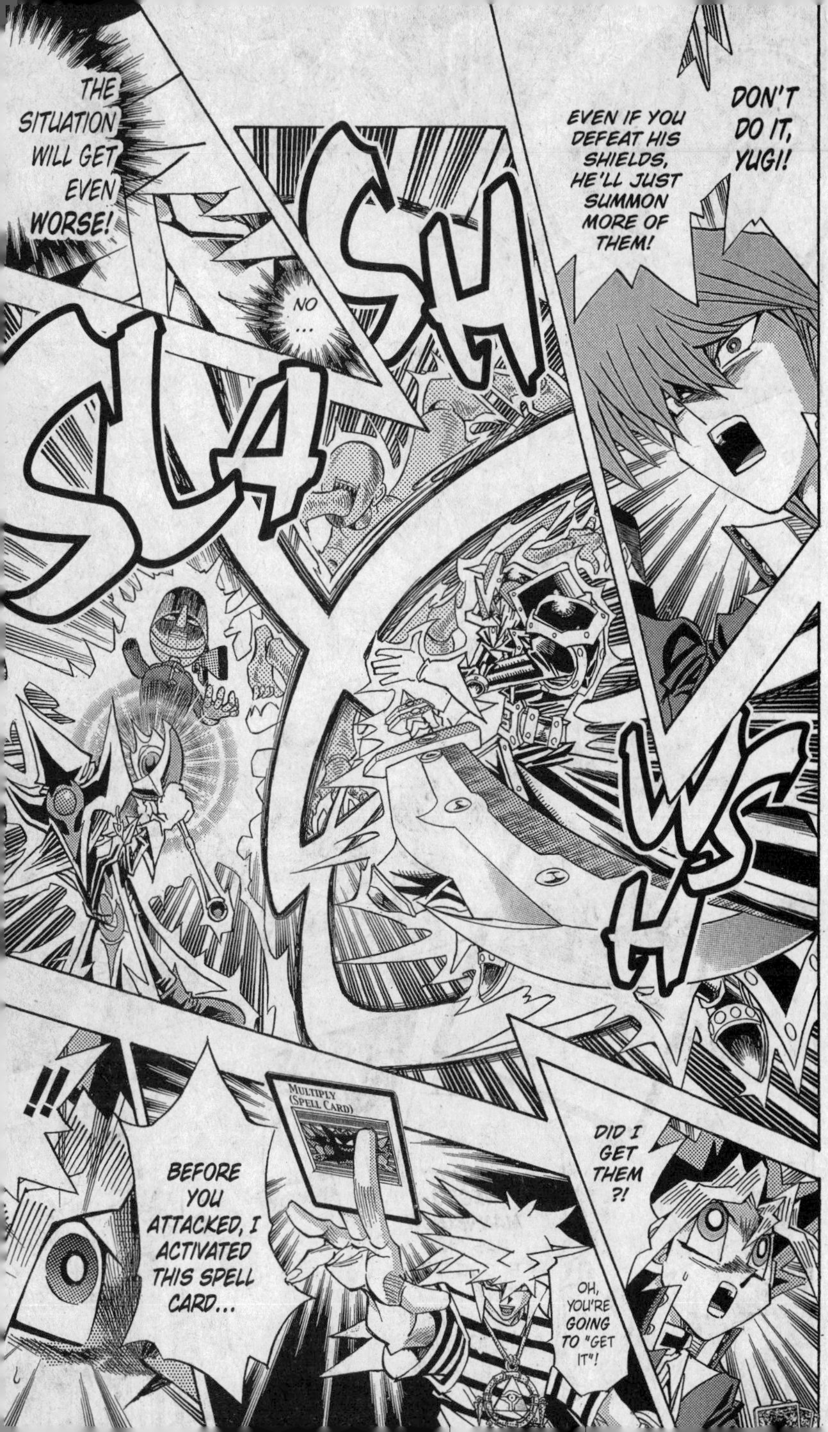
DON'T DO IT, YUGI!
EVEN IF YOU DEFEAT HIS SHIELDS, HE'LL JUST SUMMON MORE OF THEM!
THE SITUATION WILL GET EVEN WORSE!
NO ...
SLASH
DID I GET THEM?!
OH, YOU'RE GOING TO "GET IT"!
MULTIPLY (SPELL CARD)
BEFORE YOU ATTACKED, I ACTIVATED THIS SPELL CARD...
!!

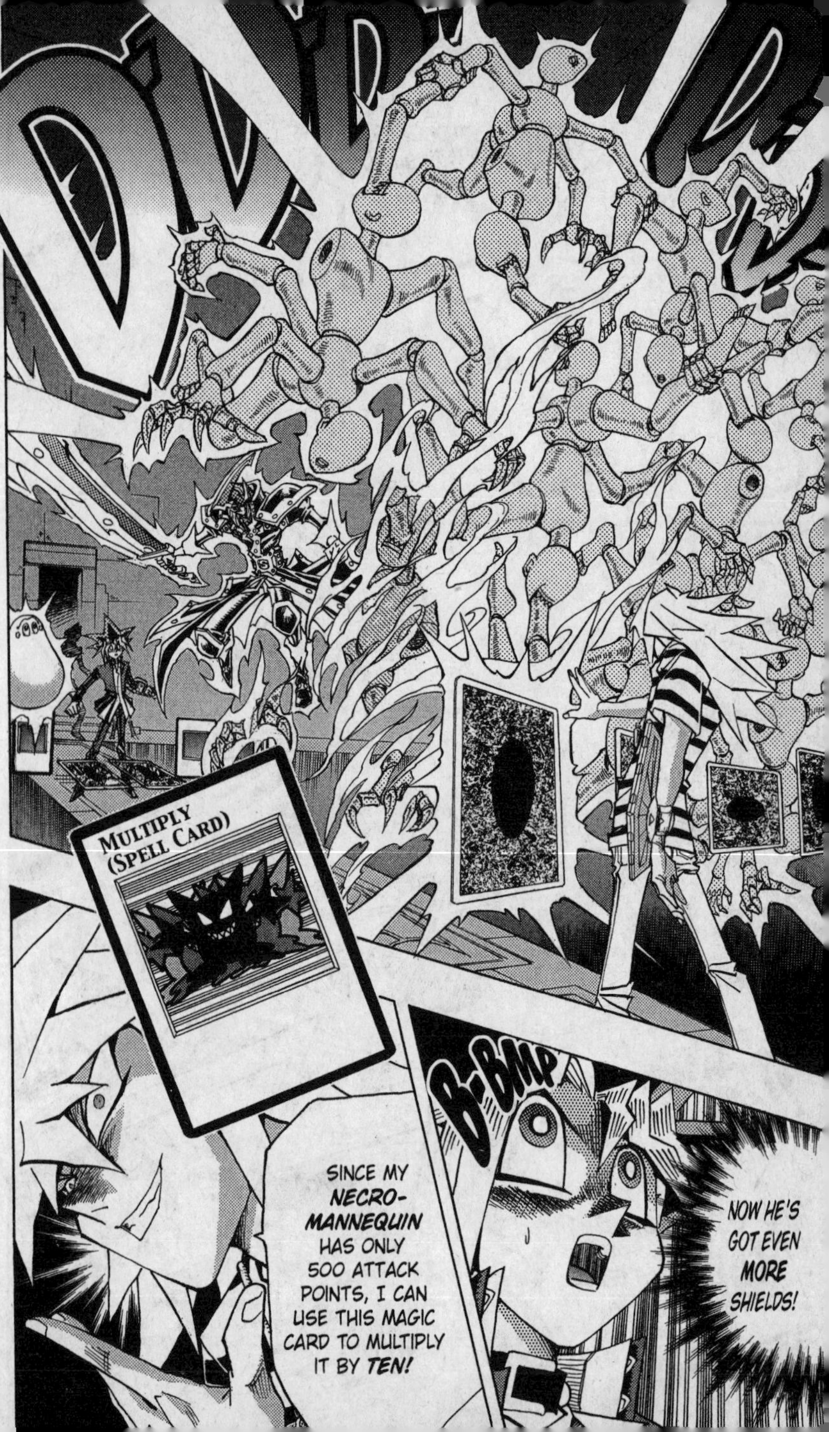
MULTIPLY
(SPELL CARD)
B-BMP
NOW HE'S GOT EVEN MORE SHIELDS!
SINCE MY NECRO-MANNEQUIN HAS ONLY 500 ATTACK POINTS, I CAN USE THIS MAGIC CARD TO MULTIPLY IT BY TEN!

READ THIS WAY

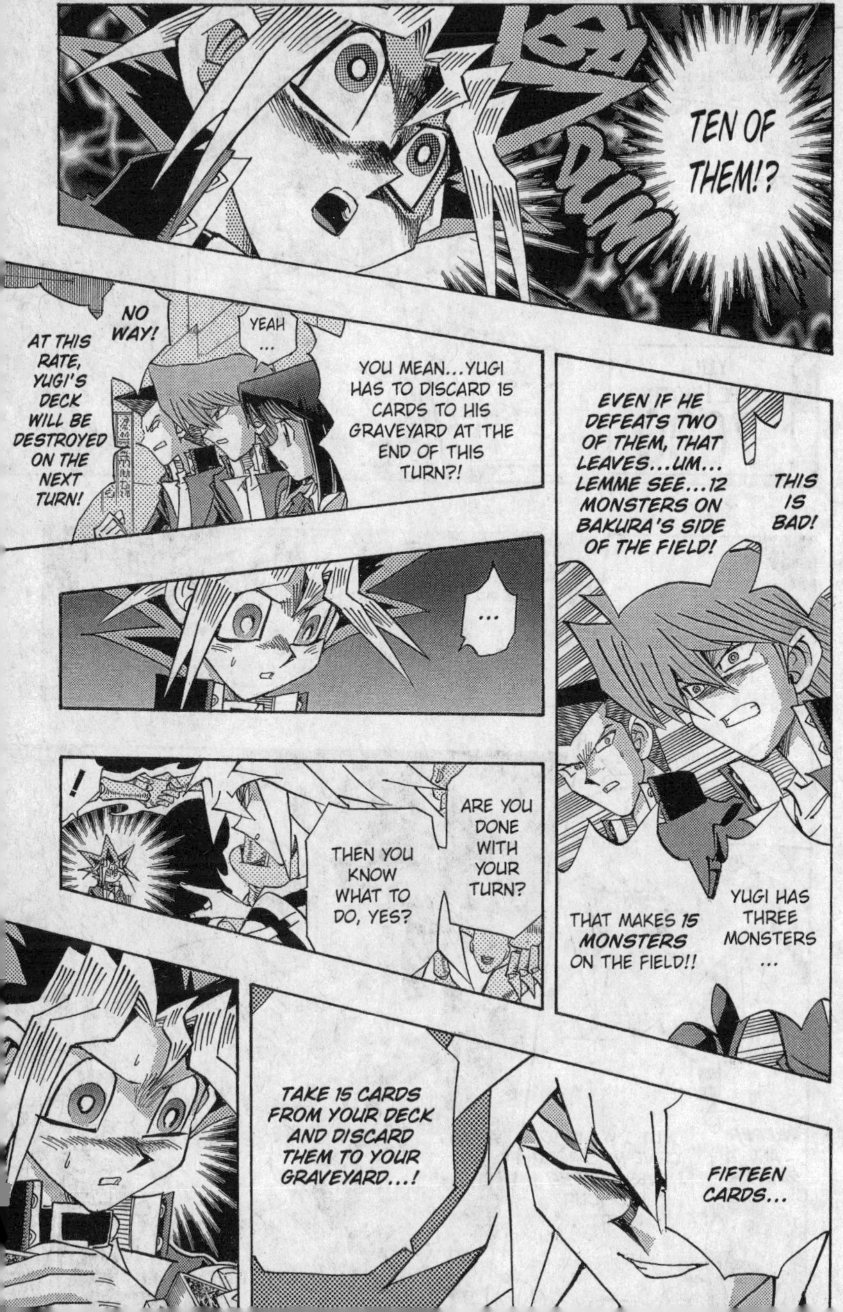
TEN OF THEM!?
THIS IS BAD!
EVEN IF HE DEFEATS TWO OF THEM, THAT LEAVES...UM... LEMME SEE...12 MONSTERS ON BAKURA'S SIDE OF THE FIELD!
YUGI HAS THREE MONSTERS...
THAT MAKES 15 MONSTERS ON THE FIELD!!
YOU MEAN...YUGI HAS TO DISCARD 15 CARDS TO HIS GRAVEYARD AT THE END OF THIS TURN?!
YEAH...
NO WAY!
AT THIS RATE, YUGI'S DECK WILL BE DESTROYED ON THE NEXT TURN!
...
ARE YOU DONE WITH YOUR TURN?
THEN YOU KNOW WHAT TO DO, YES?
!
FIFTEEN CARDS...
TAKE 15 CARDS FROM YOUR DECK AND DISCARD THEM TO YOUR GRAVEYARD...!

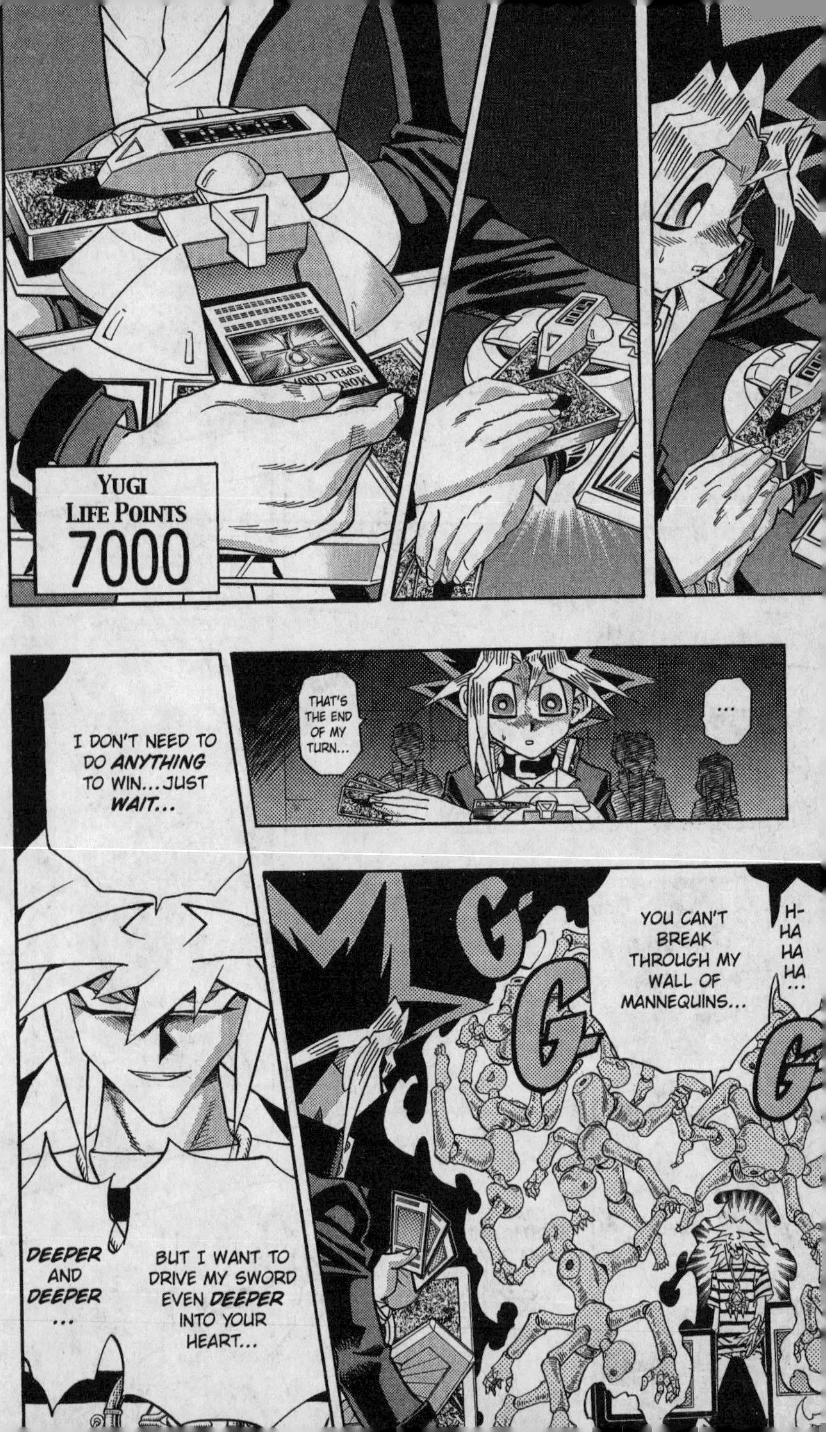
YUGI LIFE POINTS 7000
...
THAT'S THE END OF MY TURN...
H-HA HA HA...
YOU CAN'T BREAK THROUGH MY WALL OF MANNEQUINS...
I DON'T NEED TO DO ANYTHING TO WIN... JUST WAIT...
BUT I WANT TO DRIVE MY SWORD EVEN DEEPER INTO YOUR HEART...
DEEPER AND DEEPER...

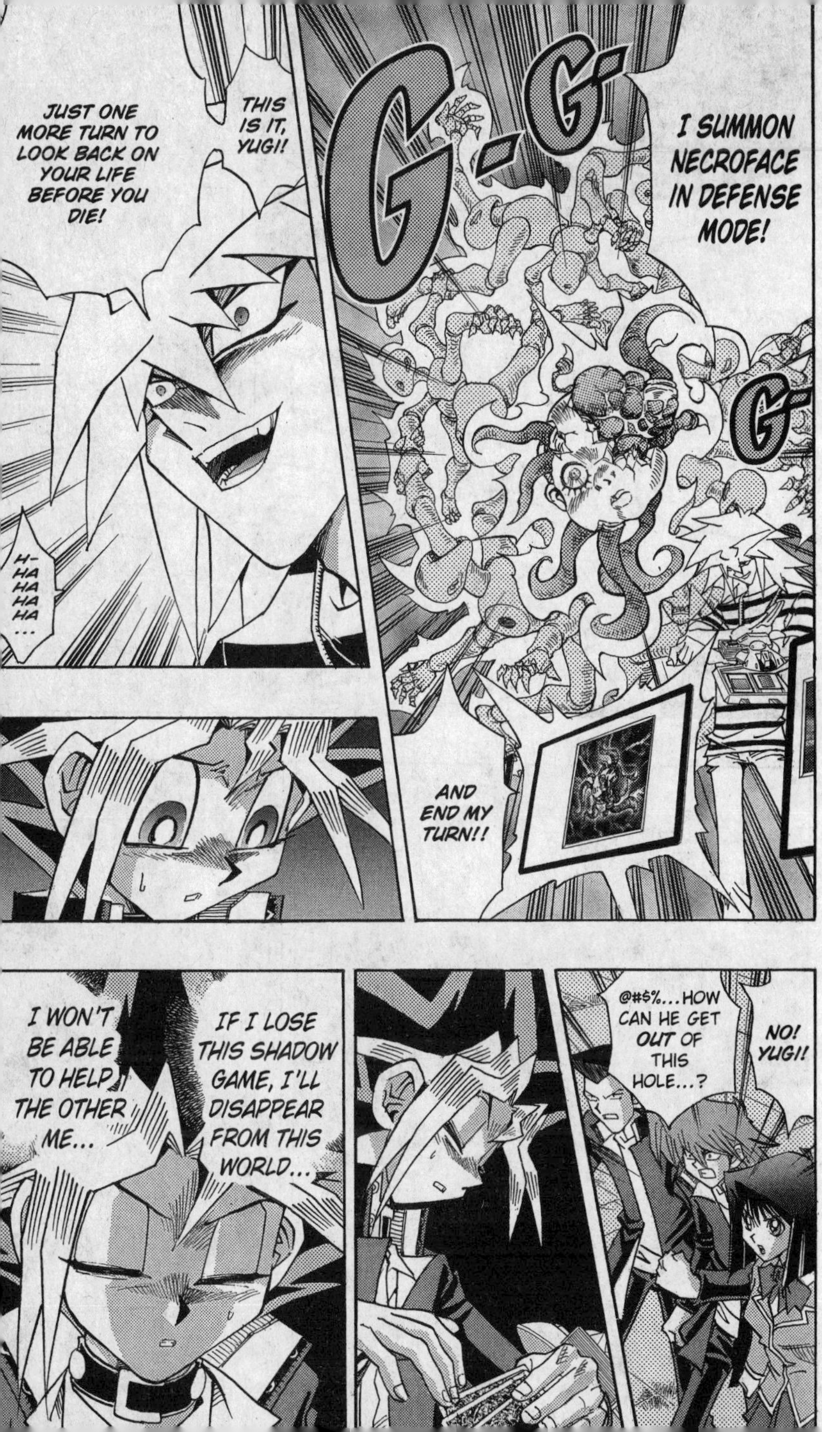
G-G-
I SUMMON NECROFACE IN DEFENSE MODE!
G-
AND END MY TURN!!
THIS IS IT, YUGI!
JUST ONE MORE TURN TO LOOK BACK ON YOUR LIFE BEFORE YOU DIE!
H-HAHAHAHAHA...
NO! YUGI!
@#$%... HOW CAN HE GET OUT OF THIS HOLE...?
IF I LOSE THIS SHADOW GAME, I'LL DISAPPEAR FROM THIS WORLD...
I WON'T BE ABLE TO HELP THE OTHER ME...

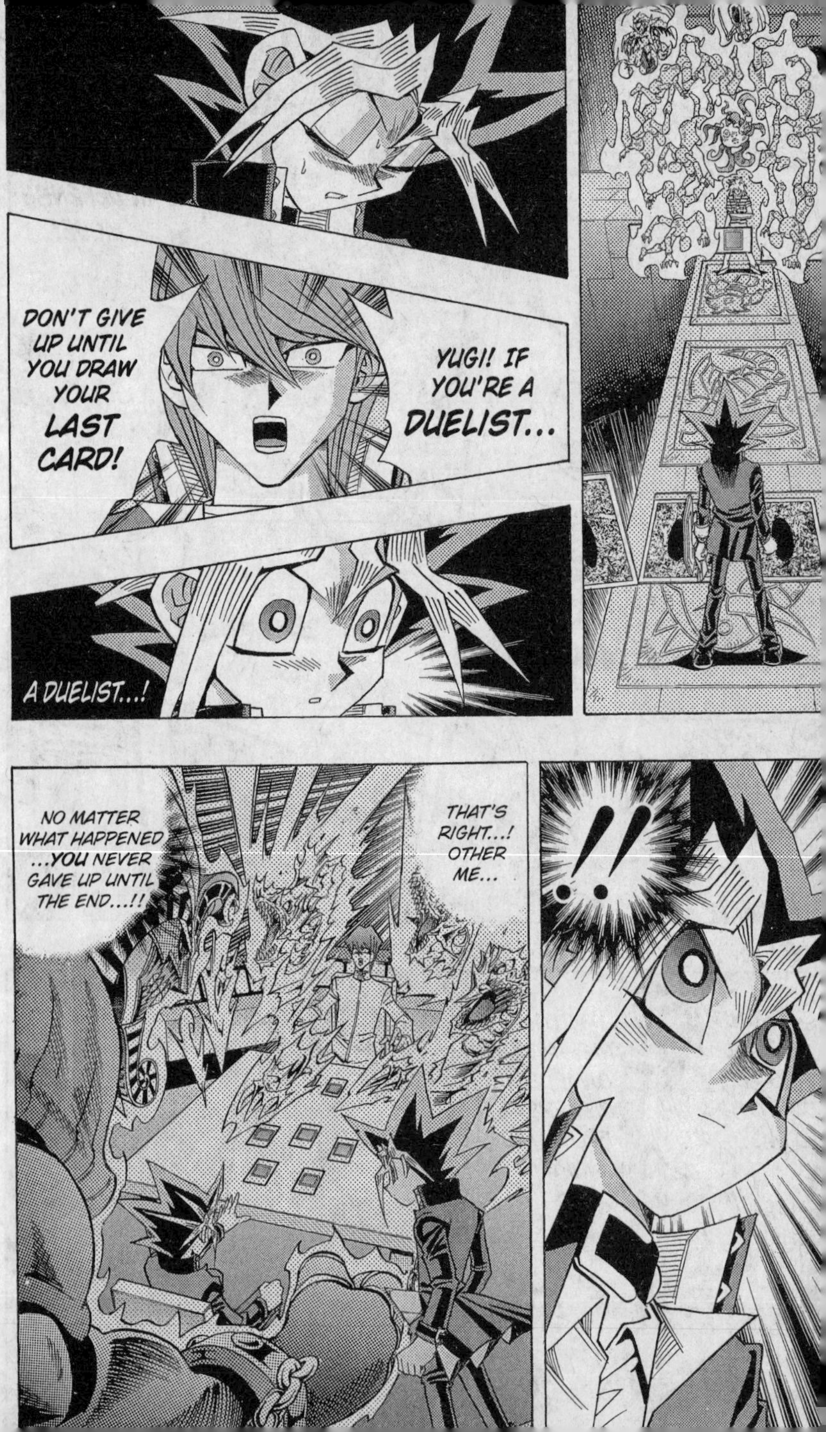
YUGI! IF YOU'RE A DUELIST...
DON'T GIVE UP UNTIL YOU DRAW YOUR LAST CARD!
A DUELIST...!
!!
THAT'S RIGHT...! OTHER ME...
NO MATTER WHAT HAPPENED ...YOU NEVER GAVE UP UNTIL THE END...!!

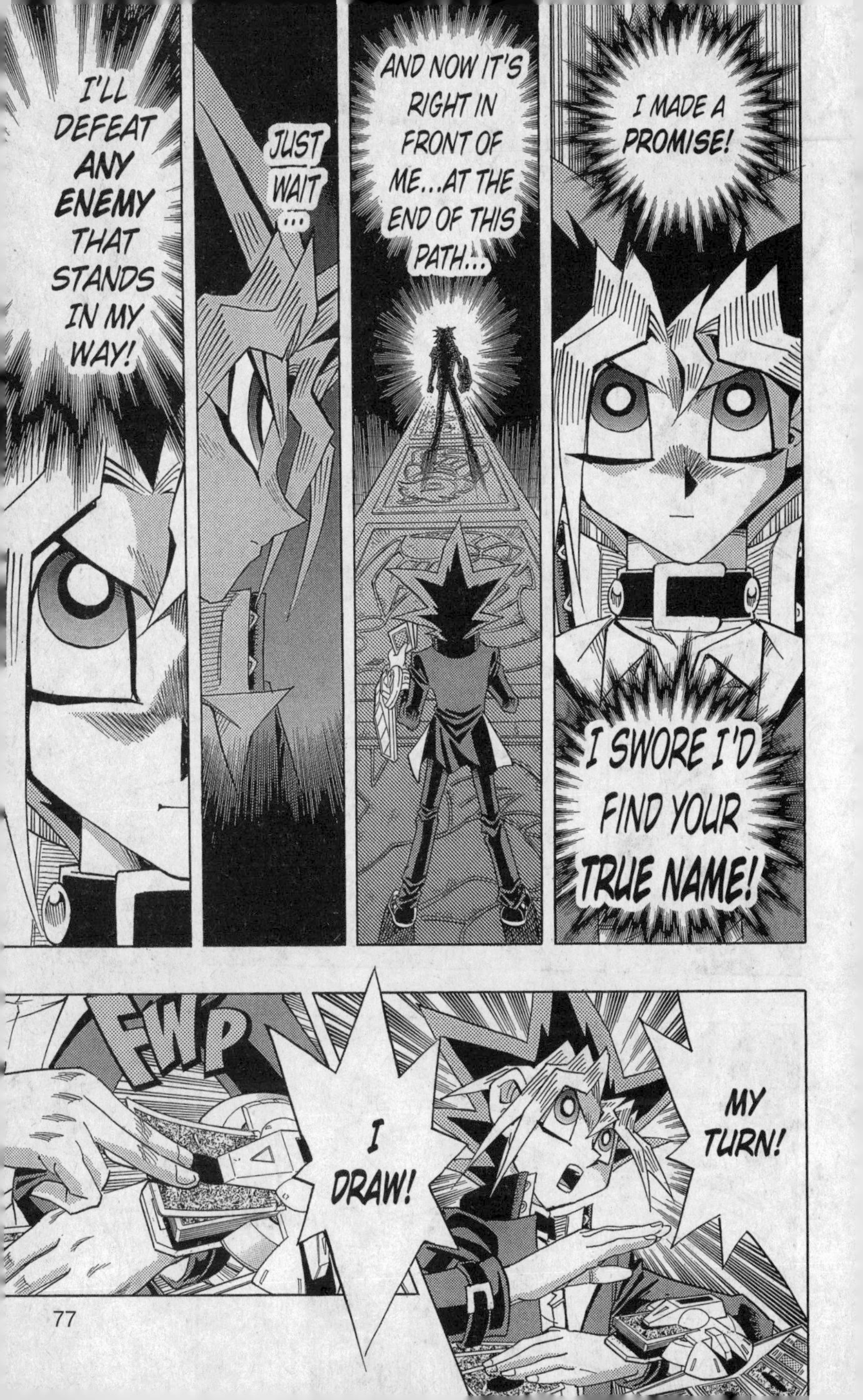
I MADE A PROMISE!
I SWORE I'D FIND YOUR TRUE NAME!
AND NOW IT'S RIGHT IN FRONT OF ME...AT THE END OF THIS PATH...
JUST WAIT...
I'LL DEFEAT ANY ENEMY THAT STANDS IN MY WAY!
MY TURN!
I DRAW!
FWP

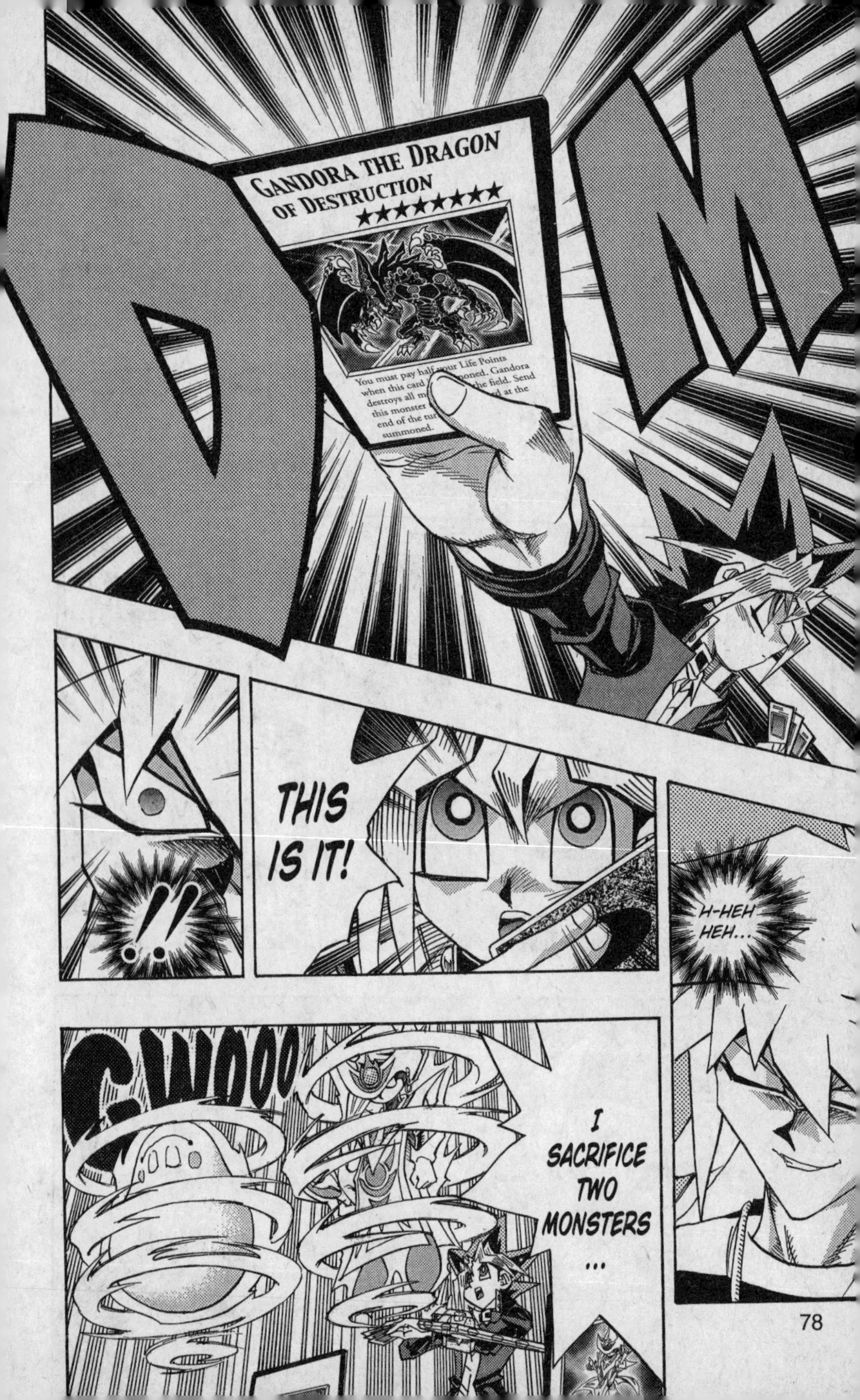
GANDORA THE DRAGON OF DESTRUCTION
H-HEH HEH...
THIS IS IT!
!!
I SACRIFICE TWO MONSTERS ...
GWOOO

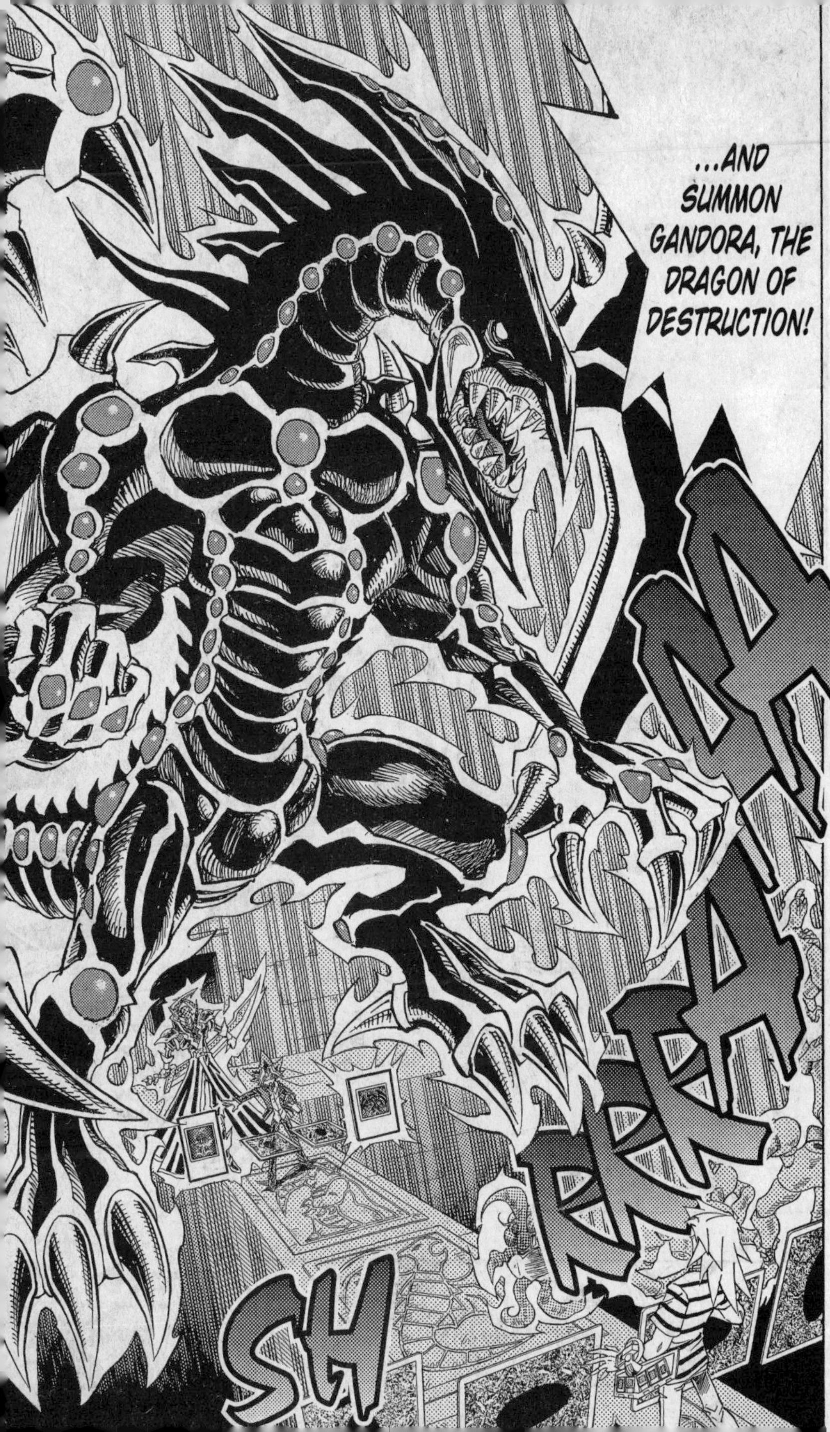
...AND SUMMON GANDORA, THE DRAGON OF DESTRUCTION!
SHAAAA

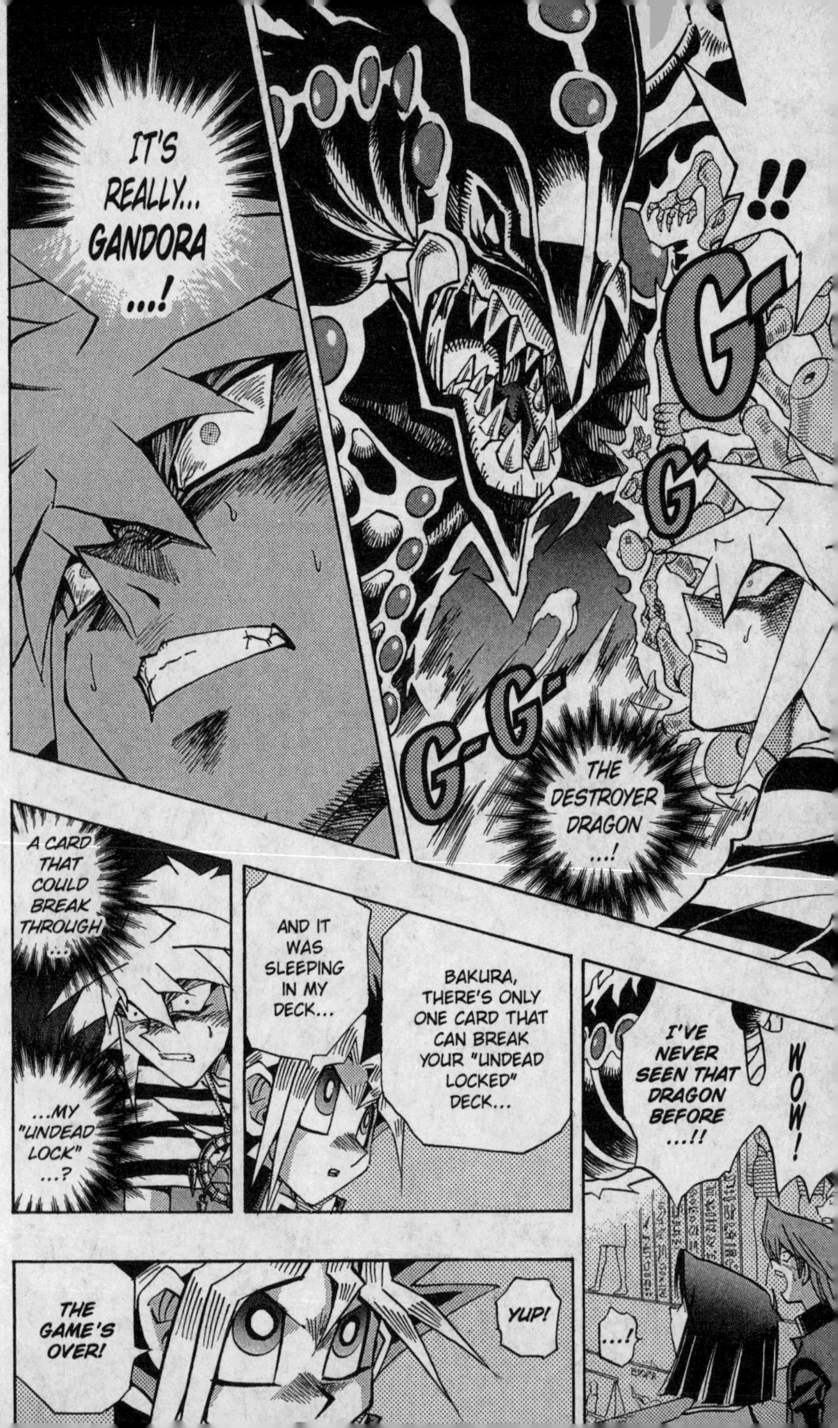
!!
G-
G-
G-G-
THE DESTROYER DRAGON ...!
IT'S REALLY... GANDORA ...!
WOW!
I'VE NEVER SEEN THAT DRAGON BEFORE ...!!
BAKURA, THERE'S ONLY ONE CARD THAT CAN BREAK YOUR "UNDEAD LOCKED" DECK...
AND IT WAS SLEEPING IN MY DECK...
A CARD THAT COULD BREAK THROUGH ...
...MY "UNDEAD LOCK" ...?
...!
YUP!
THE GAME'S OVER!

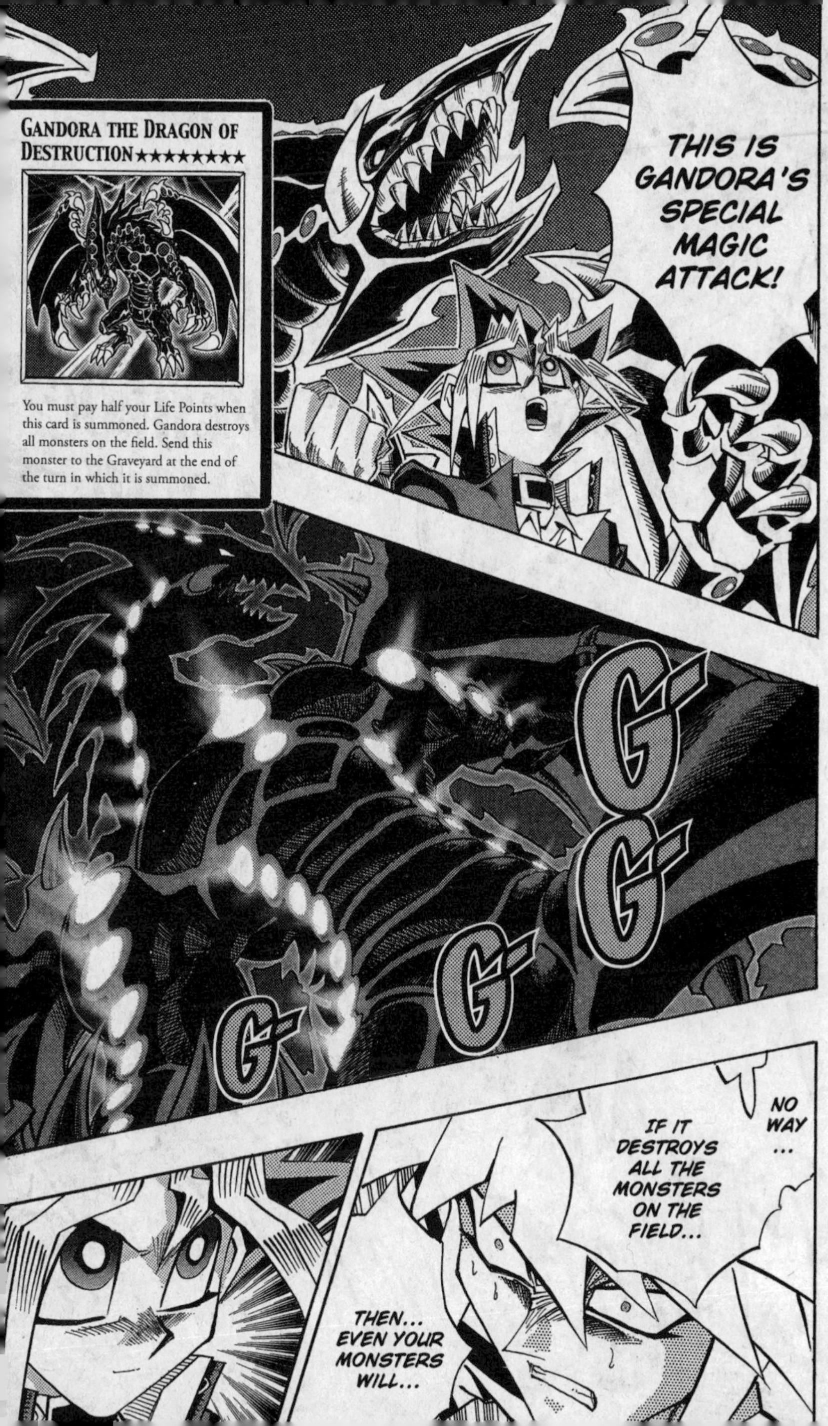
THIS IS GANDORA'S SPECIAL MAGIC ATTACK!
GANDORA THE DRAGON OF DESTRUCTION★★★★★★★★
You must pay half your Life Points when this card is summoned. Gandora destroys all monsters on the field. Send this monster to the Graveyard at the end of the turn in which it is summoned.
G- G- G- G-
NO WAY...
IF IT DESTROYS ALL THE MONSTERS ON THE FIELD...
THEN... EVEN YOUR MONSTERS WILL...

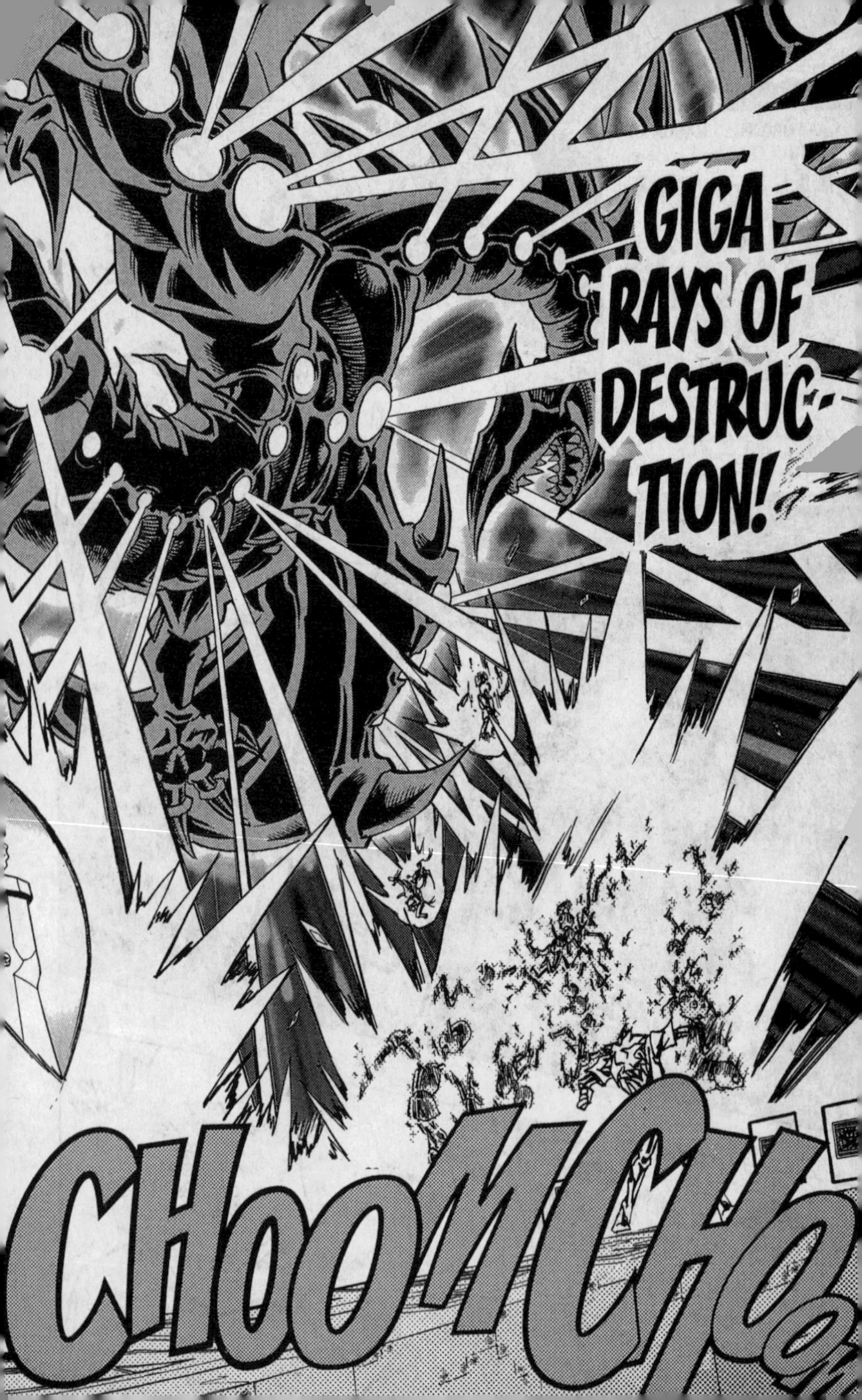
GIGA RAYS OF DESTRUCTION!
CHOOMCHOO

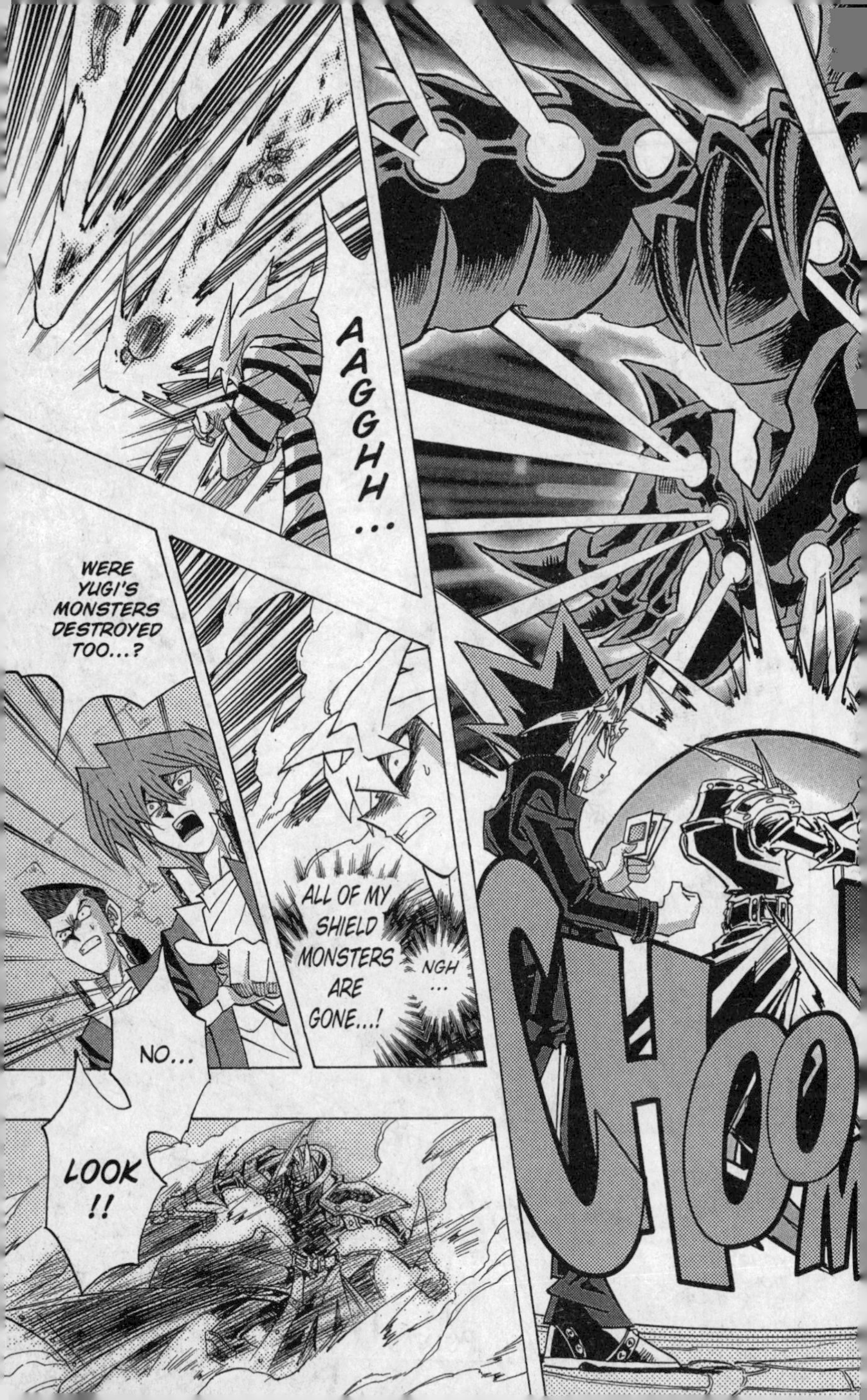
CHOO
AAGGHH...
NGH...
ALL OF MY SHIELD MONSTERS ARE GONE...!
WERE YUGI'S MONSTERS DESTROYED TOO...?
NO...
LOOK!!

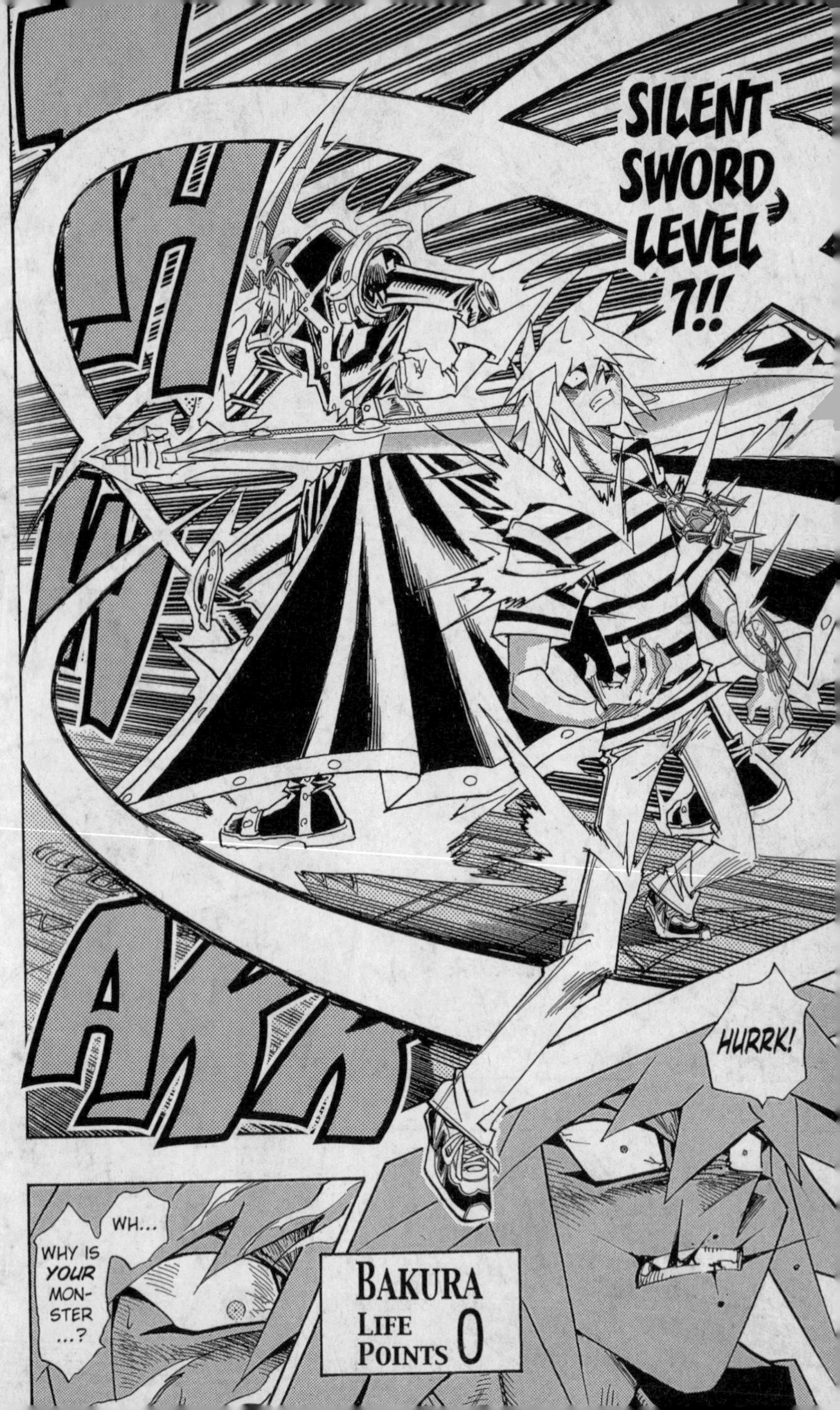
SILENT SWORD, LEVEL 7!!
HURRK!
BAKURA LIFE POINTS 0
WH...
WHY IS YOUR MONSTER ...?

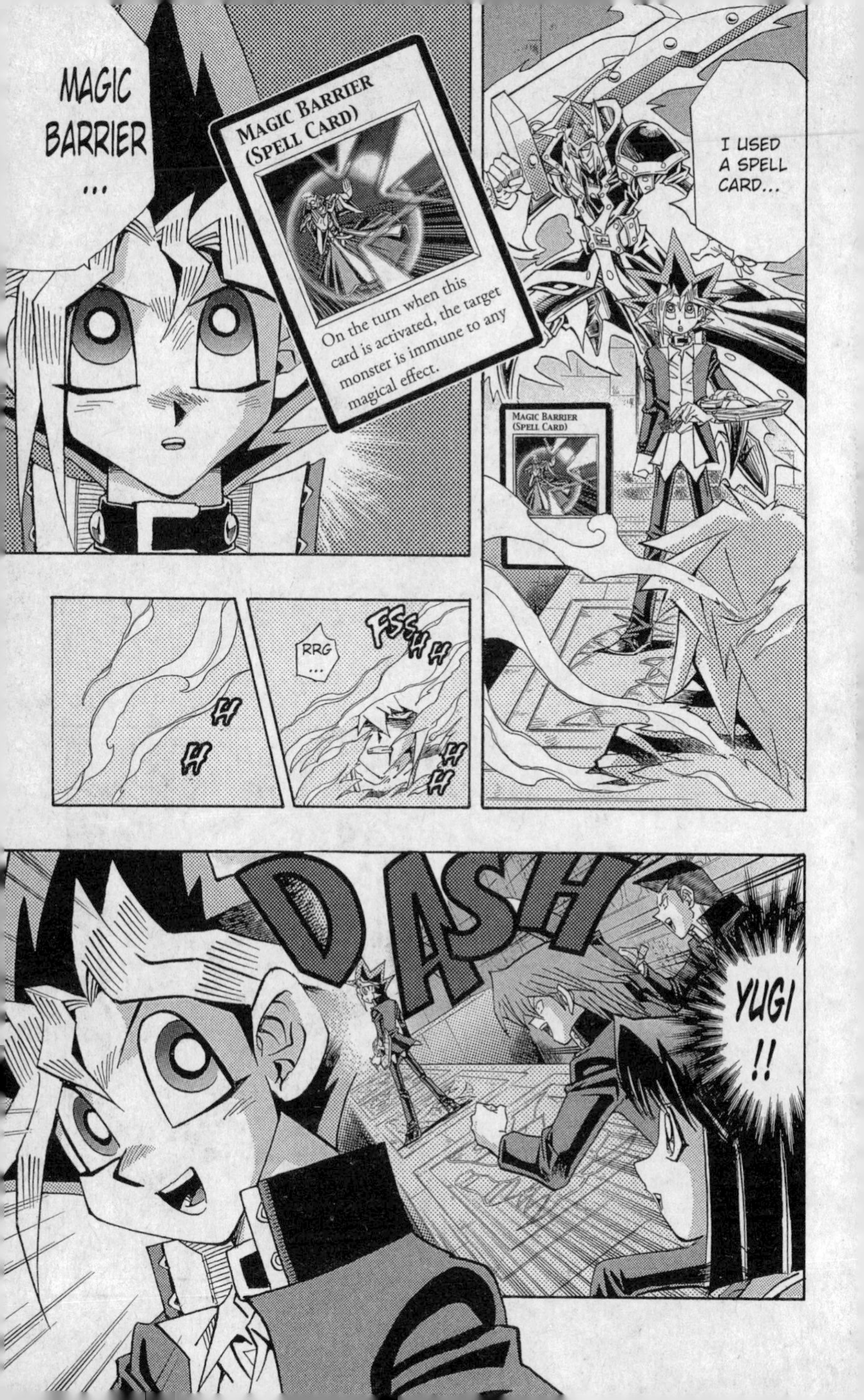
I USED A SPELL CARD...
MAGIC BARRIER (SPELL CARD)
MAGIC BARRIER (SPELL CARD)
On the turn when this card is activated, the target monster is immune to any magical effect.
MAGIC BARRIER ...
RRG ...
FSSHH
HH
HH
HH
DASH
YUGI !!

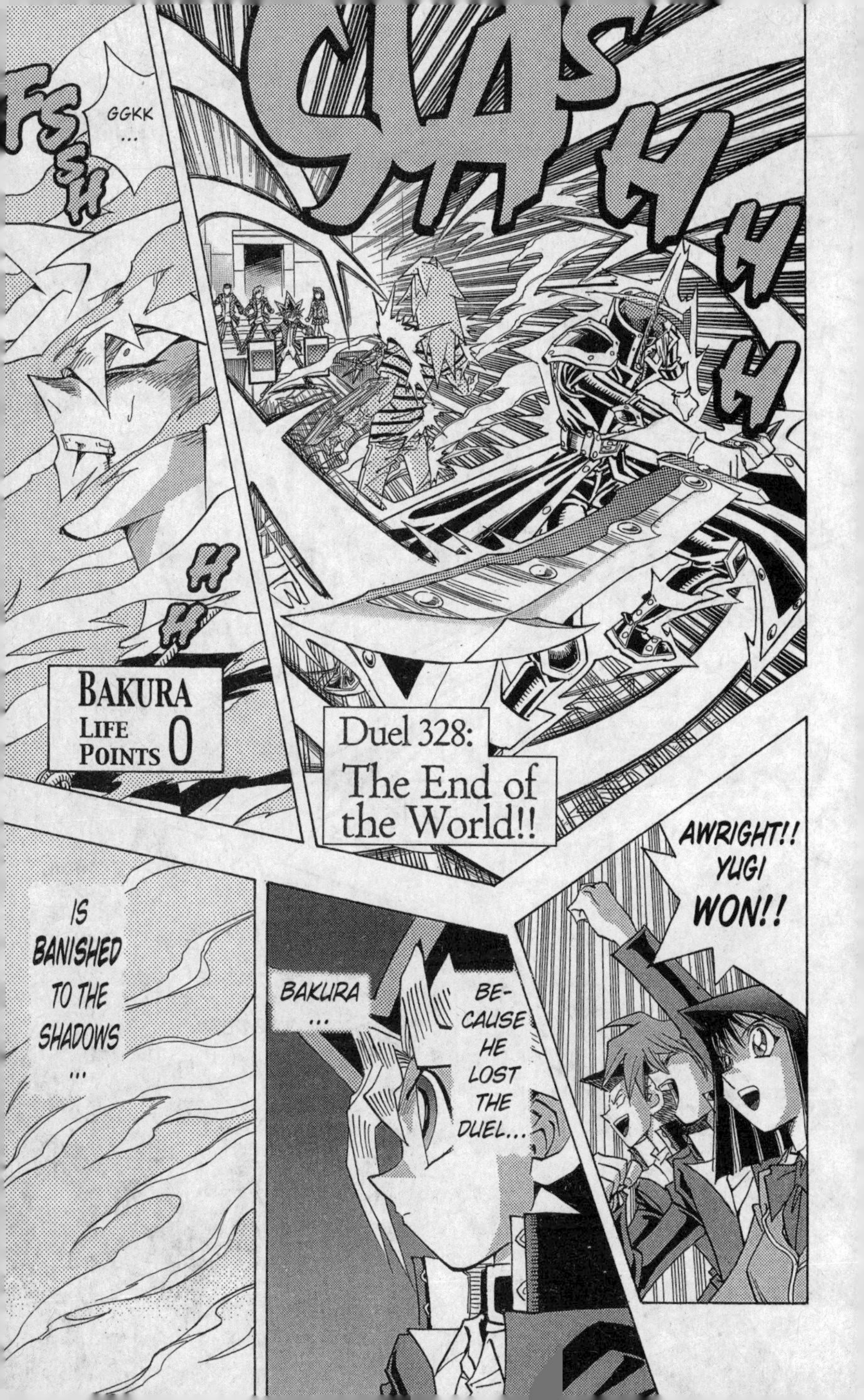
CLASHHHH
Duel 328:
The End of the World!!
FSSH
GGKK ...
HH
BAKURA
LIFE POINTS 0
AWRIGHT!! YUGI WON!!
BE-CAUSE HE LOST THE DUEL...
BAKURA ...
IS BANISHED TO THE SHADOWS ...

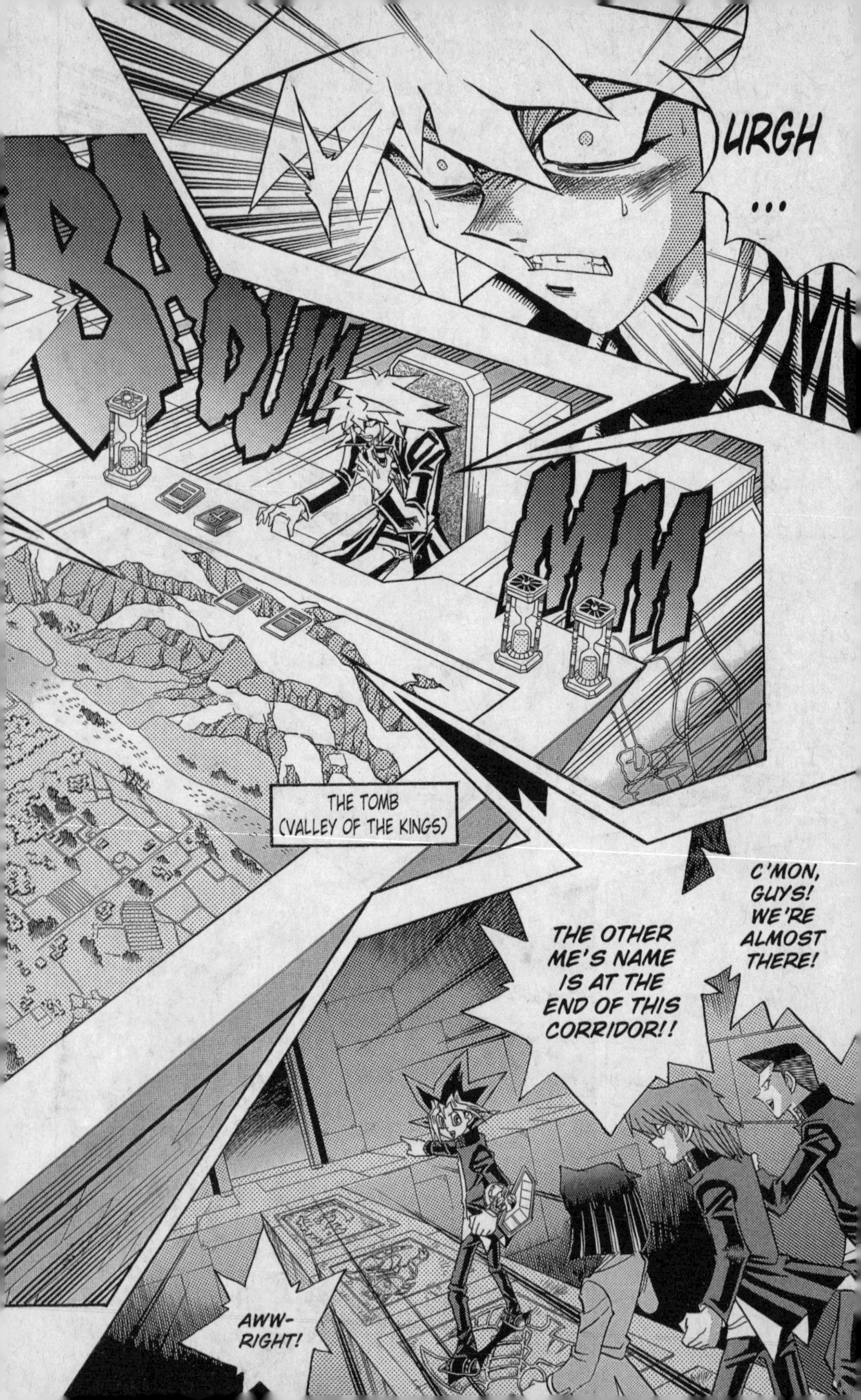

URGH...
BA DUM
MM
THE TOMB (VALLEY OF THE KINGS)
C'MON, GUYS! WE'RE ALMOST THERE!
THE OTHER ME'S NAME IS AT THE END OF THIS CORRIDOR!!
AWW-RIGHT!

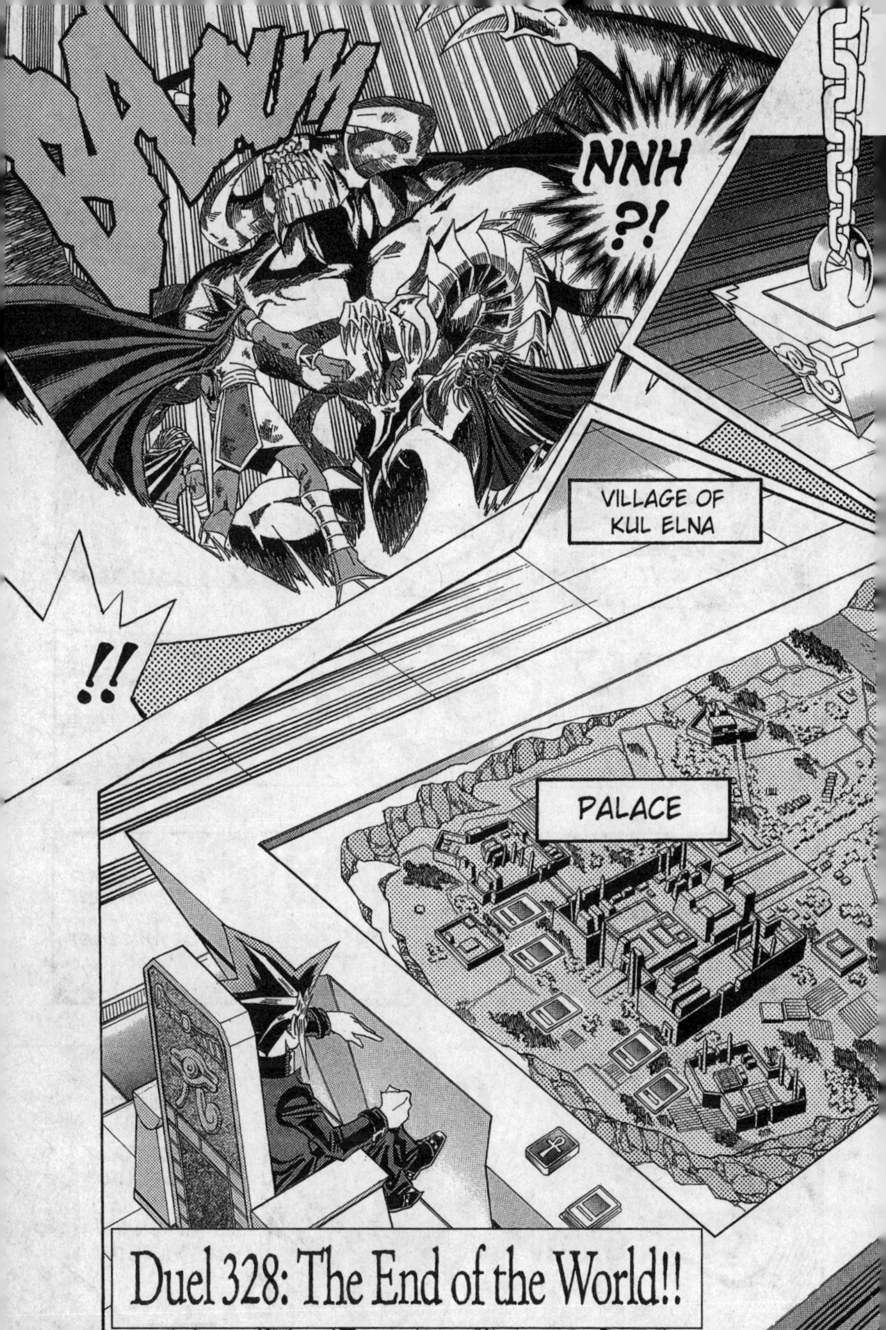
VILLAGE OF KUL ELNA
BADUM
NNH ?!
!!
PALACE
Duel 328: The End of the World!!

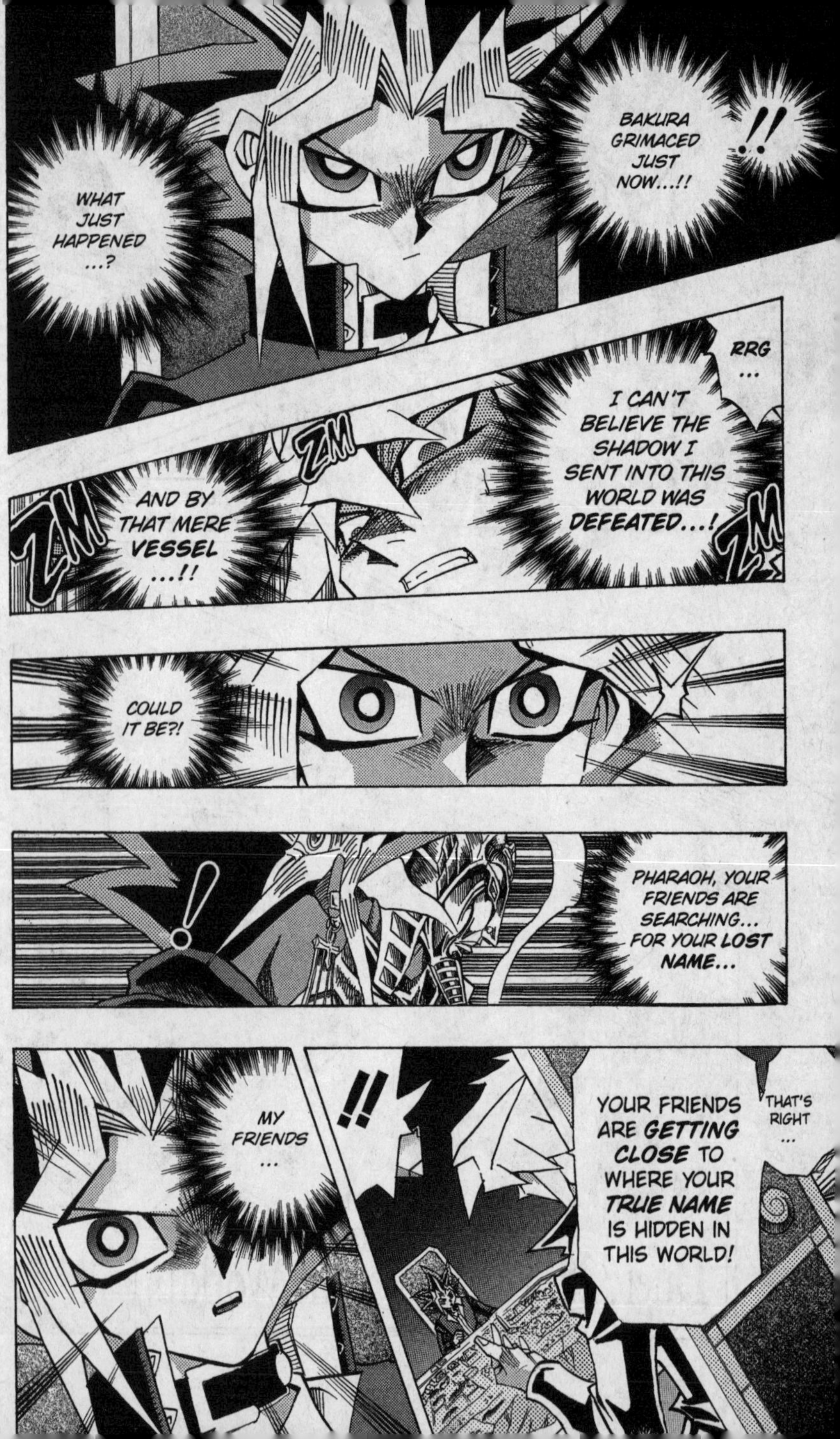
!!
BAKURA GRIMACED JUST NOW...!!
WHAT JUST HAPPENED...?
RRG...
I CAN'T BELIEVE THE SHADOW I SENT INTO THIS WORLD WAS **DEFEATED**...!
ZM
ZM
AND BY THAT MERE **VESSEL**...!!
ZM
COULD IT BE?!
PHARAOH, YOUR FRIENDS ARE SEARCHING... FOR YOUR **LOST NAME**...
!
THAT'S RIGHT...
YOUR FRIENDS ARE ***GETTING CLOSE*** TO WHERE YOUR ***TRUE NAME*** IS HIDDEN IN THIS WORLD!
!!
MY FRIENDS...

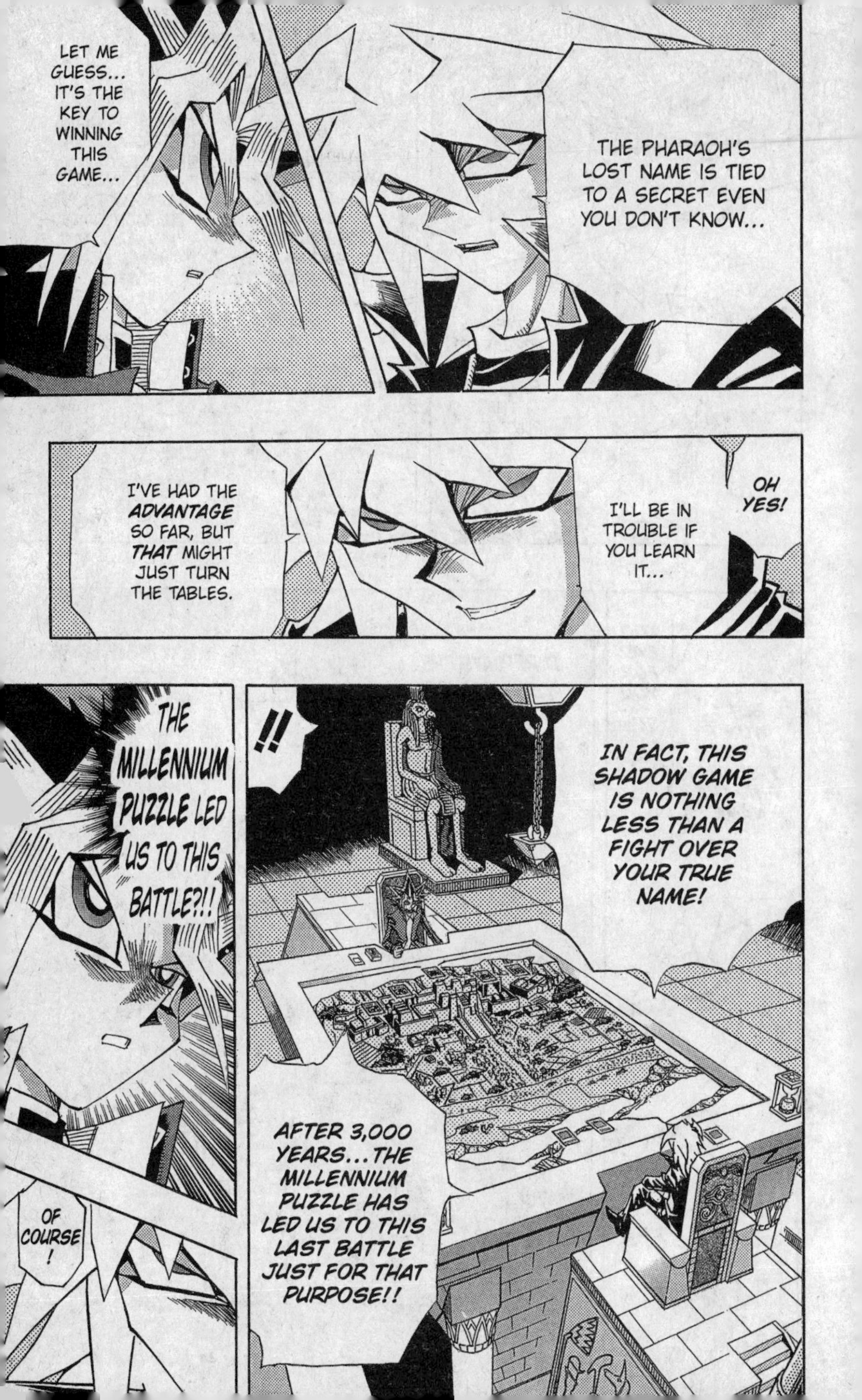
THE PHARAOH'S LOST NAME IS TIED TO A SECRET EVEN YOU DON'T KNOW...
LET ME GUESS... IT'S THE KEY TO WINNING THIS GAME...
OH YES!
I'LL BE IN TROUBLE IF YOU LEARN IT...
I'VE HAD THE *ADVANTAGE* SO FAR, BUT *THAT* MIGHT JUST TURN THE TABLES.
!!
IN FACT, THIS SHADOW GAME IS NOTHING LESS THAN A FIGHT OVER YOUR TRUE NAME!
AFTER 3,000 YEARS...THE MILLENNIUM PUZZLE HAS LED US TO THIS LAST BATTLE JUST FOR THAT PURPOSE!!
THE MILLENNIUM PUZZLE LED US TO THIS BATTLE?!!
OF COURSE!

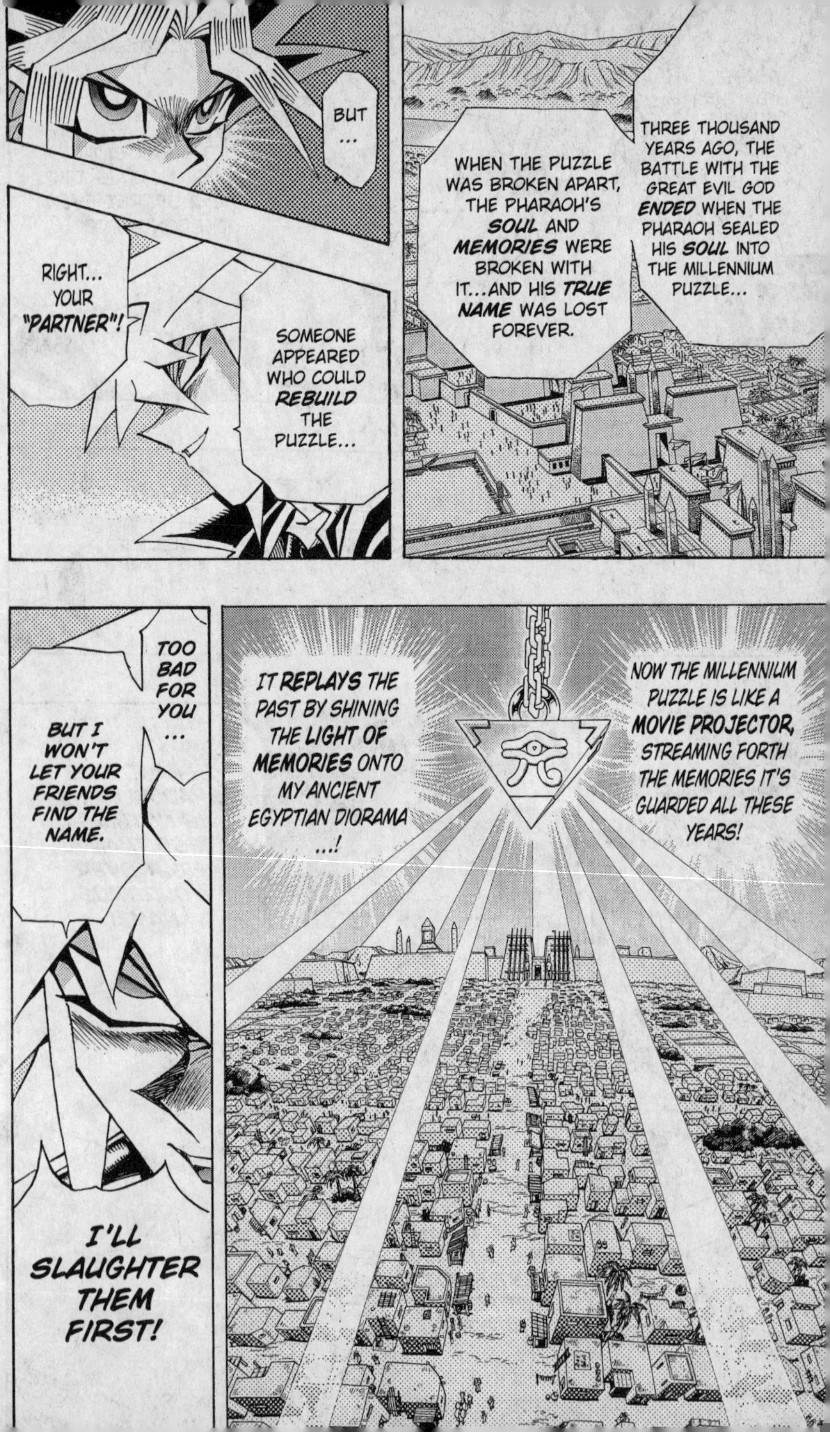
THREE THOUSAND YEARS AGO, THE BATTLE WITH THE GREAT EVIL GOD ENDED WHEN THE PHARAOH SEALED HIS SOUL INTO THE MILLENNIUM PUZZLE...
WHEN THE PUZZLE WAS BROKEN APART, THE PHARAOH'S SOUL AND MEMORIES WERE BROKEN WITH IT...AND HIS TRUE NAME WAS LOST FOREVER.
BUT ...
SOMEONE APPEARED WHO COULD REBUILD THE PUZZLE...
RIGHT... YOUR "PARTNER"!
NOW THE MILLENNIUM PUZZLE IS LIKE A MOVIE PROJECTOR, STREAMING FORTH THE MEMORIES IT'S GUARDED ALL THESE YEARS!
IT REPLAYS THE PAST BY SHINING THE LIGHT OF MEMORIES ONTO MY ANCIENT EGYPTIAN DIORAMA ...!
TOO BAD FOR YOU ...
BUT I WON'T LET YOUR FRIENDS FIND THE NAME.
I'LL SLAUGHTER THEM FIRST!

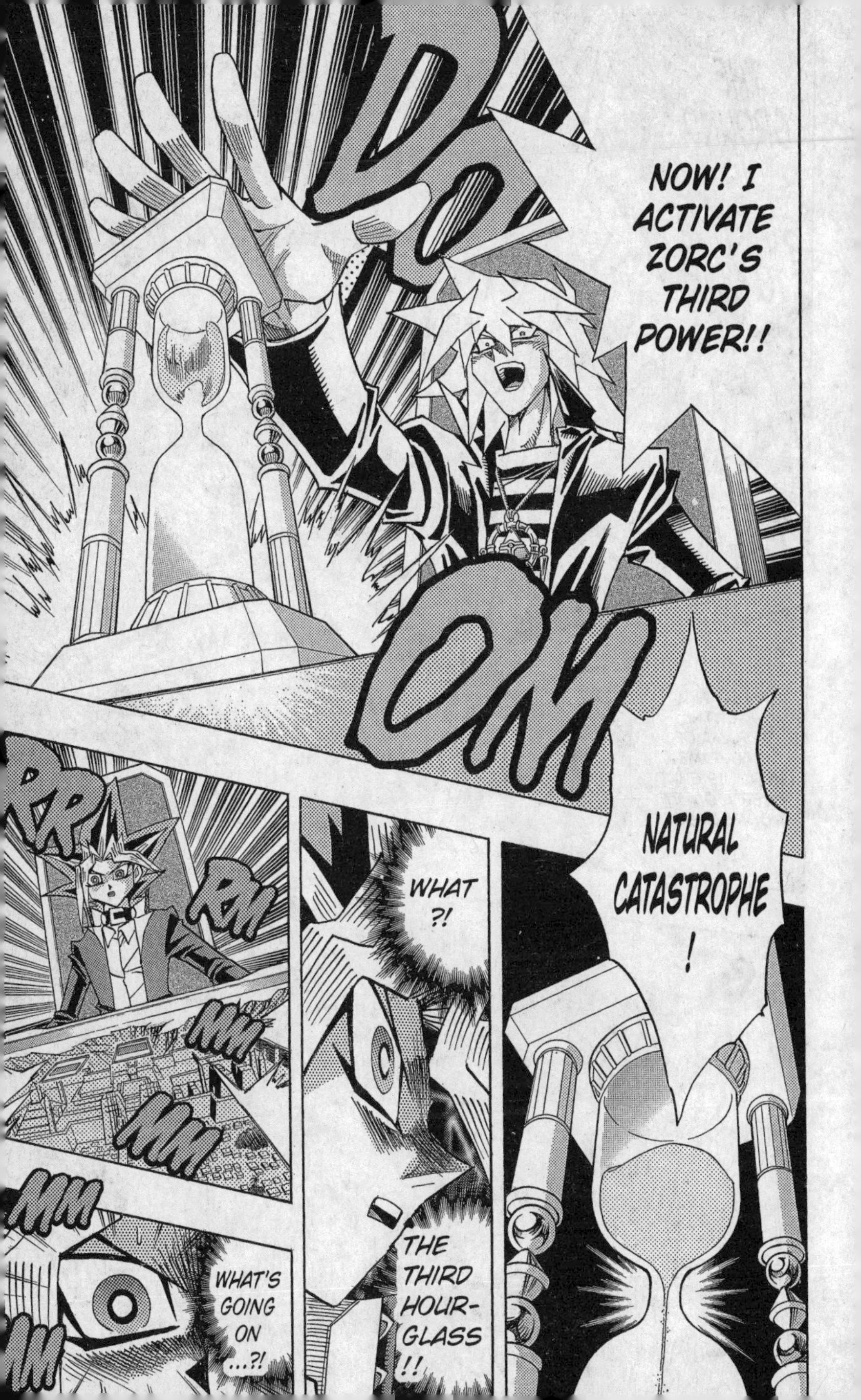
DO
OM
NOW! I ACTIVATE ZORC'S THIRD POWER!!
NATURAL CATASTROPHE!
WHAT ?!
THE THIRD HOUR-GLASS!!
RR
RM
MM
MM
MM
WHAT'S GOING ON ...?!

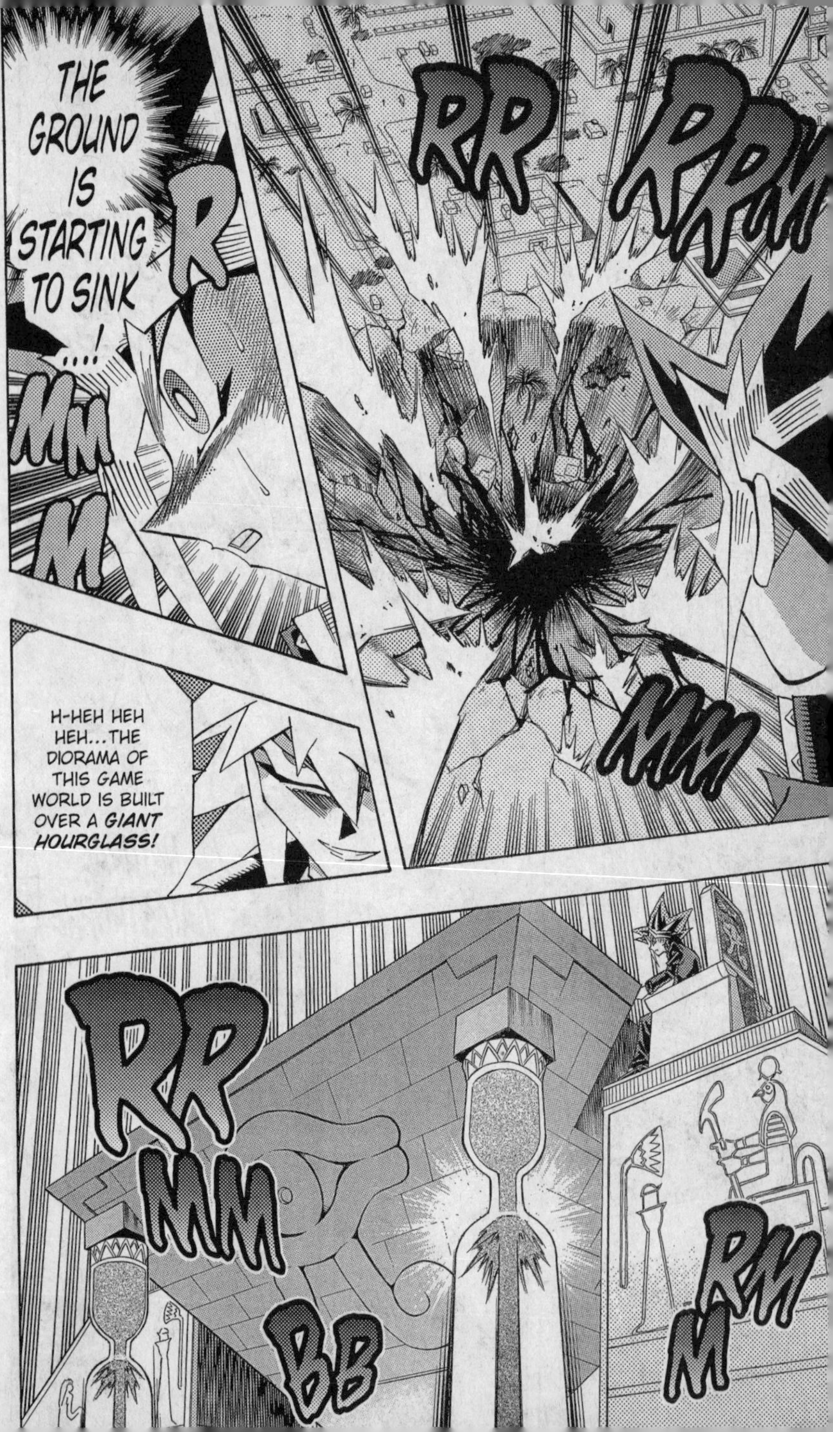
RR
RRRM
MM
R
THE GROUND IS STARTING TO SINK ...!
MM
M
H-HEH HEH HEH...THE DIORAMA OF THIS GAME WORLD IS BUILT OVER A *GIANT HOURGLASS!*
RM
M
RR
MM
BB

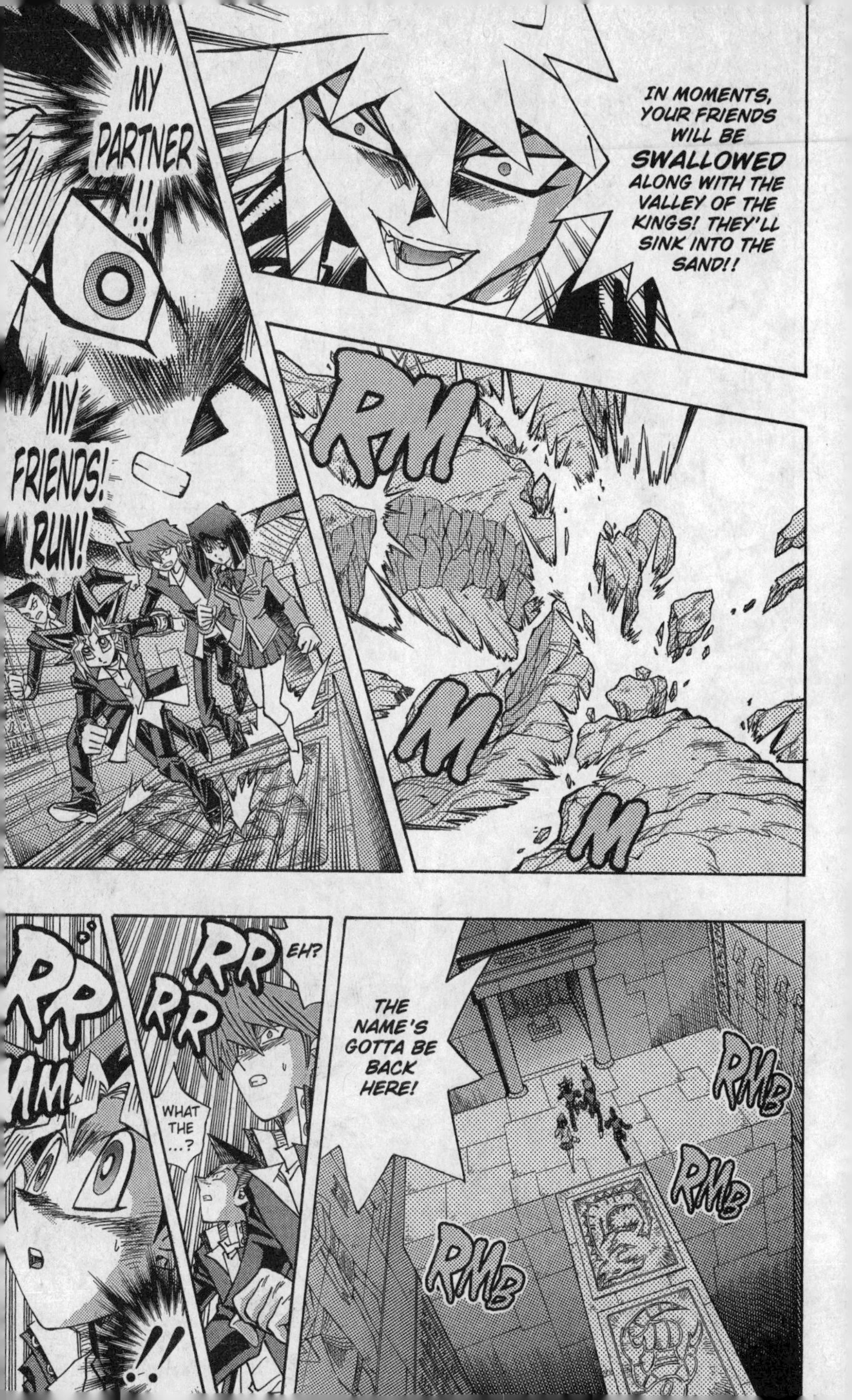
IN MOMENTS, YOUR FRIENDS WILL BE SWALLOWED ALONG WITH THE VALLEY OF THE KINGS! THEY'LL SINK INTO THE SAND!!
RMMM
MY PARTNER!!
MY FRIENDS! RUN!
THE NAME'S GOTTA BE BACK HERE!
RMB
RMB
RMB
RRRR
EH?
WHAT THE...?
RRMM
!!

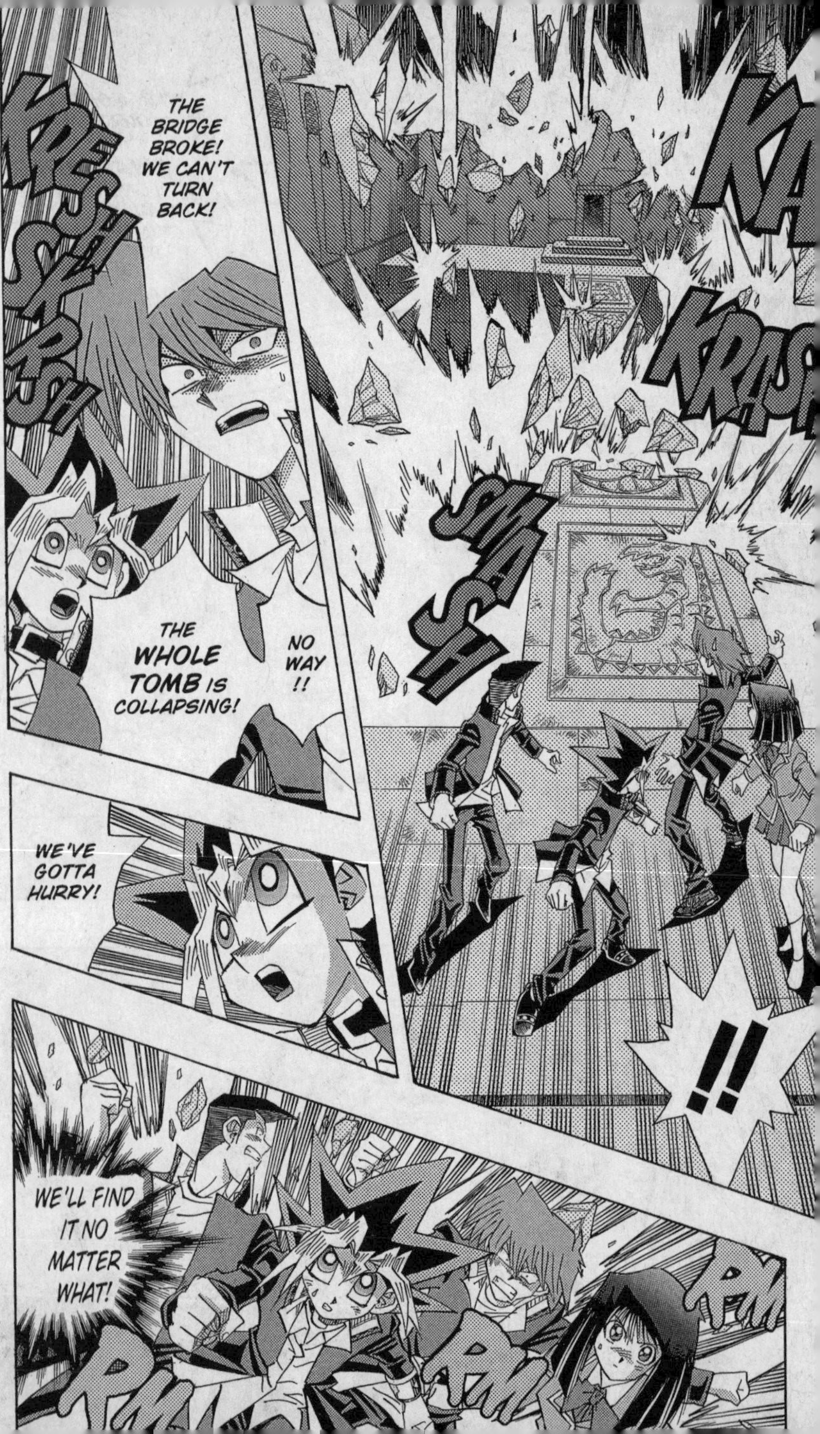
SMASH
!!
KRESH
SKRSH!!
THE BRIDGE BROKE! WE CAN'T TURN BACK!
NO WAY!!
THE WHOLE TOMB IS COLLAPSING!
WE'VE GOTTA HURRY!
WE'LL FIND IT NO MATTER WHAT!

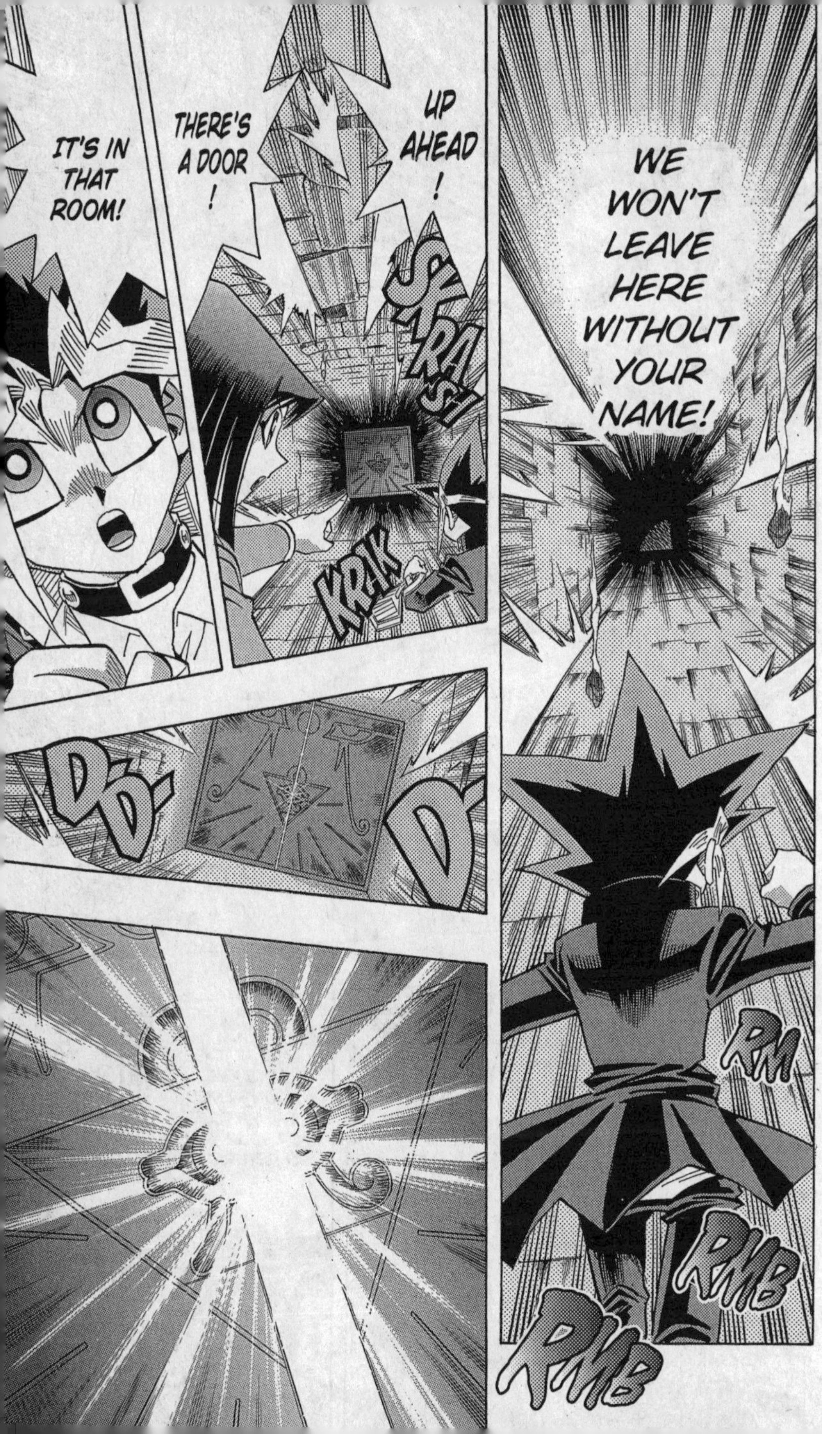
WE WON'T LEAVE HERE WITHOUT YOUR NAME!
RM
RMB
RMB
UP AHEAD!
SKRASH!
THERE'S A DOOR!
KRAK
IT'S IN THAT ROOM!
DOD
D

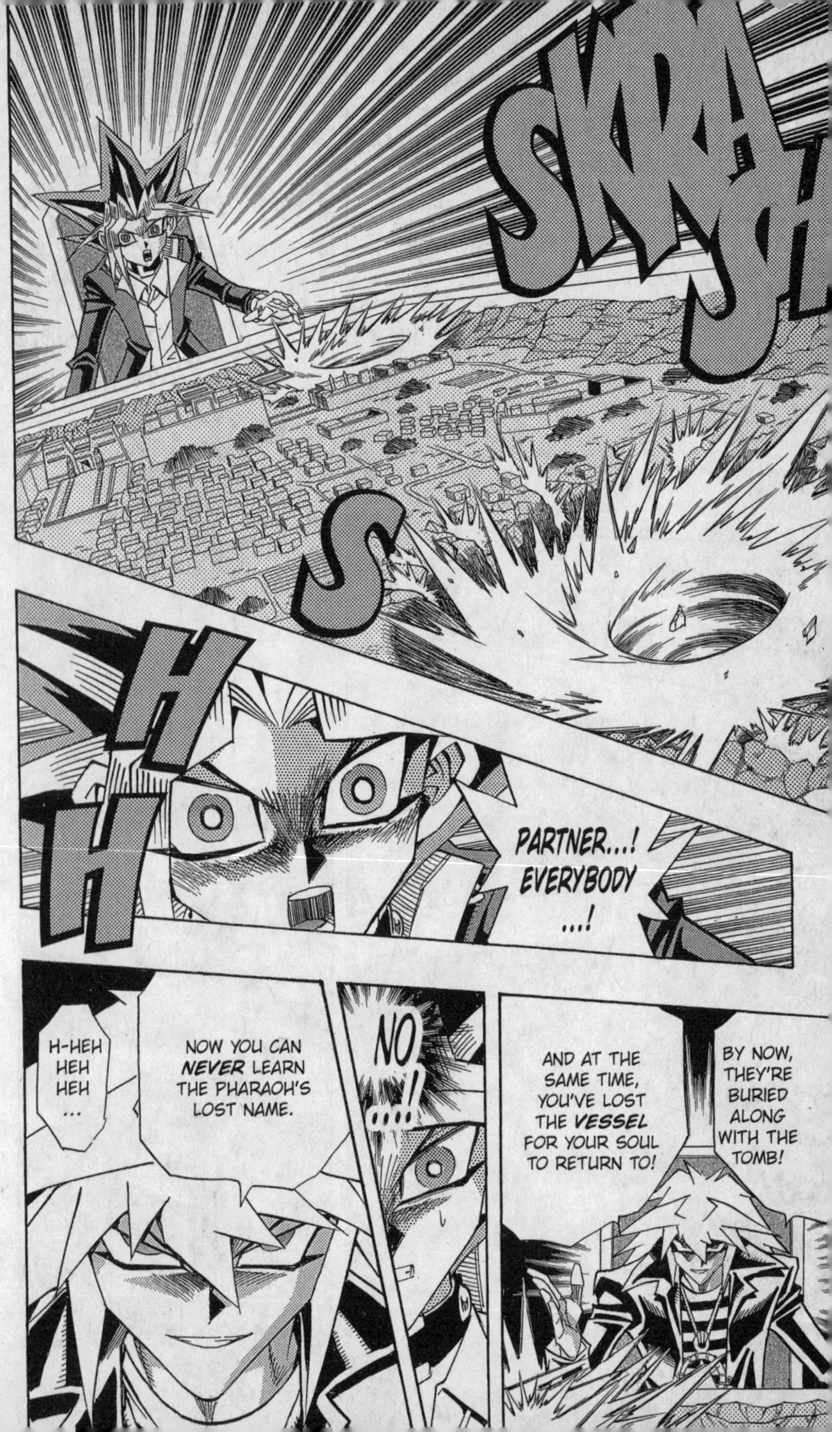
SKRA
SH
S
H
H
PARTNER...! EVERYBODY ...!
BY NOW, THEY'RE BURIED ALONG WITH THE TOMB!
AND AT THE SAME TIME, YOU'VE LOST THE *VESSEL* FOR YOUR SOUL TO RETURN TO!
NO ...!!
NOW YOU CAN *NEVER* LEARN THE PHARAOH'S LOST NAME.
H-HEH HEH HEH ...

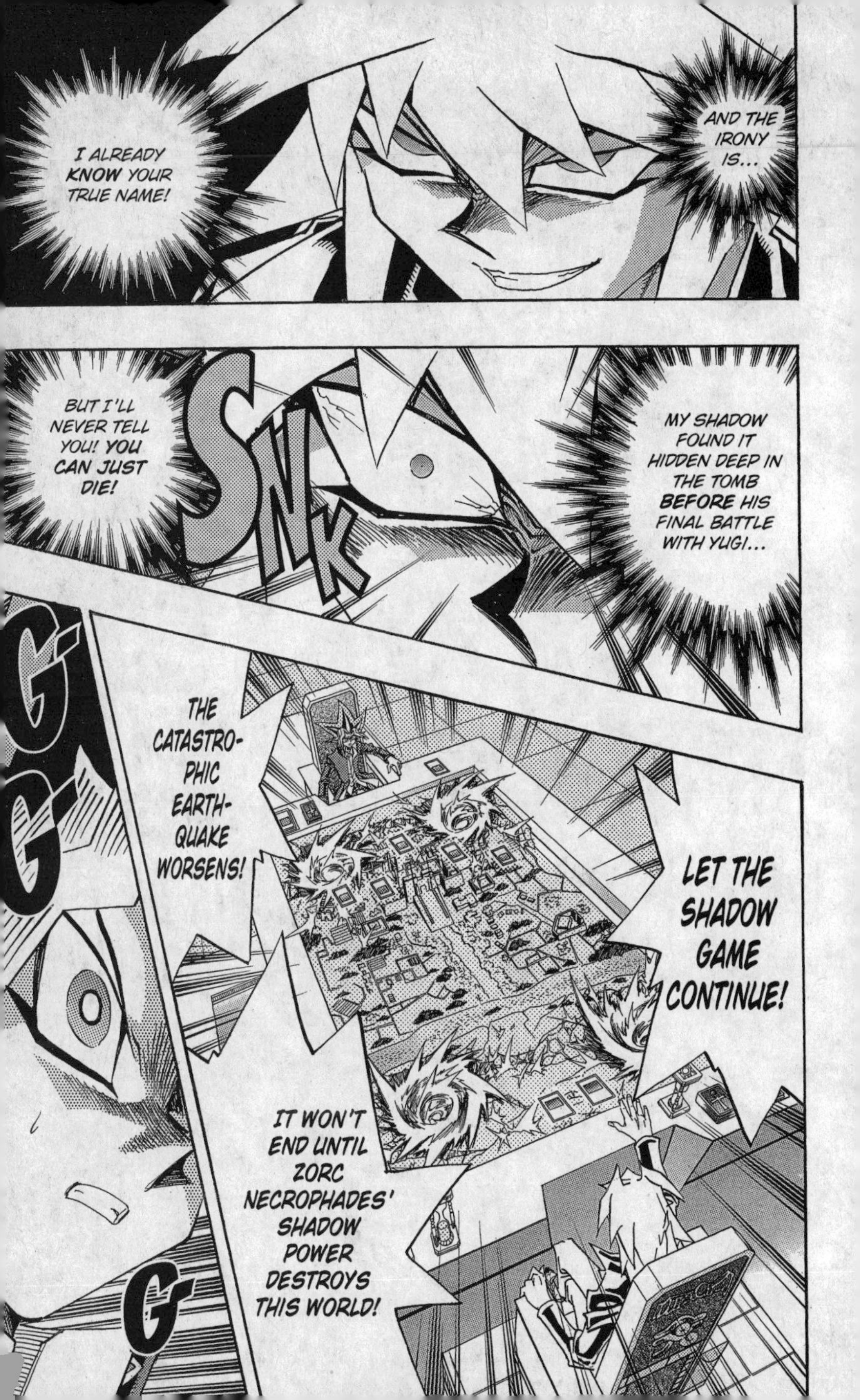
AND THE IRONY IS...
I ALREADY KNOW YOUR TRUE NAME!
MY SHADOW FOUND IT HIDDEN DEEP IN THE TOMB BEFORE HIS FINAL BATTLE WITH YUGI...
SNK
BUT I'LL NEVER TELL YOU! YOU CAN JUST DIE!
THE CATASTROPHIC EARTHQUAKE WORSENS!
LET THE SHADOW GAME CONTINUE!
IT WON'T END UNTIL ZORC NECROPHADES' SHADOW POWER DESTROYS THIS WORLD!
GGGG

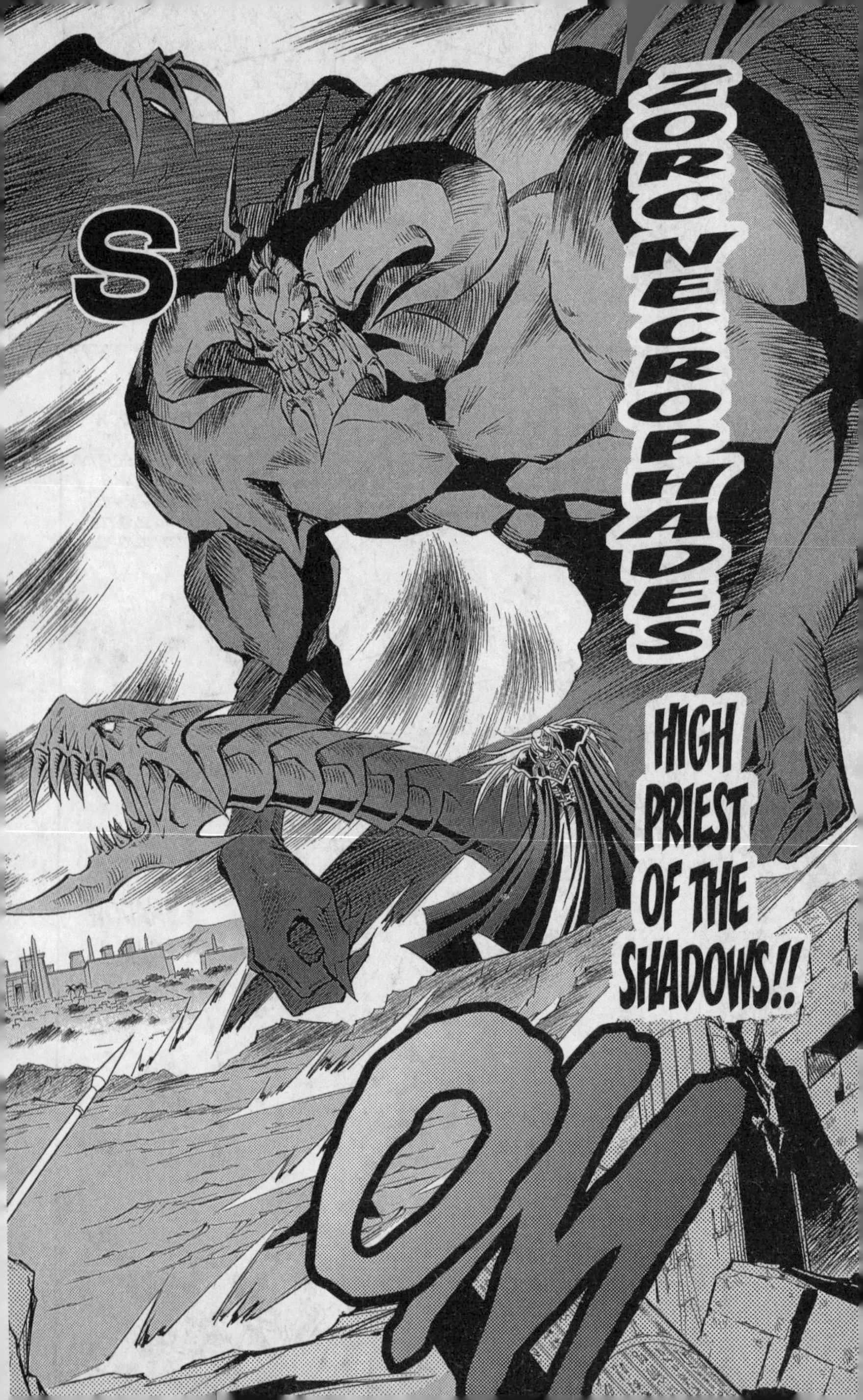
ZORC NECROPHADES
HIGH PRIEST OF THE SHADOWS!!
S

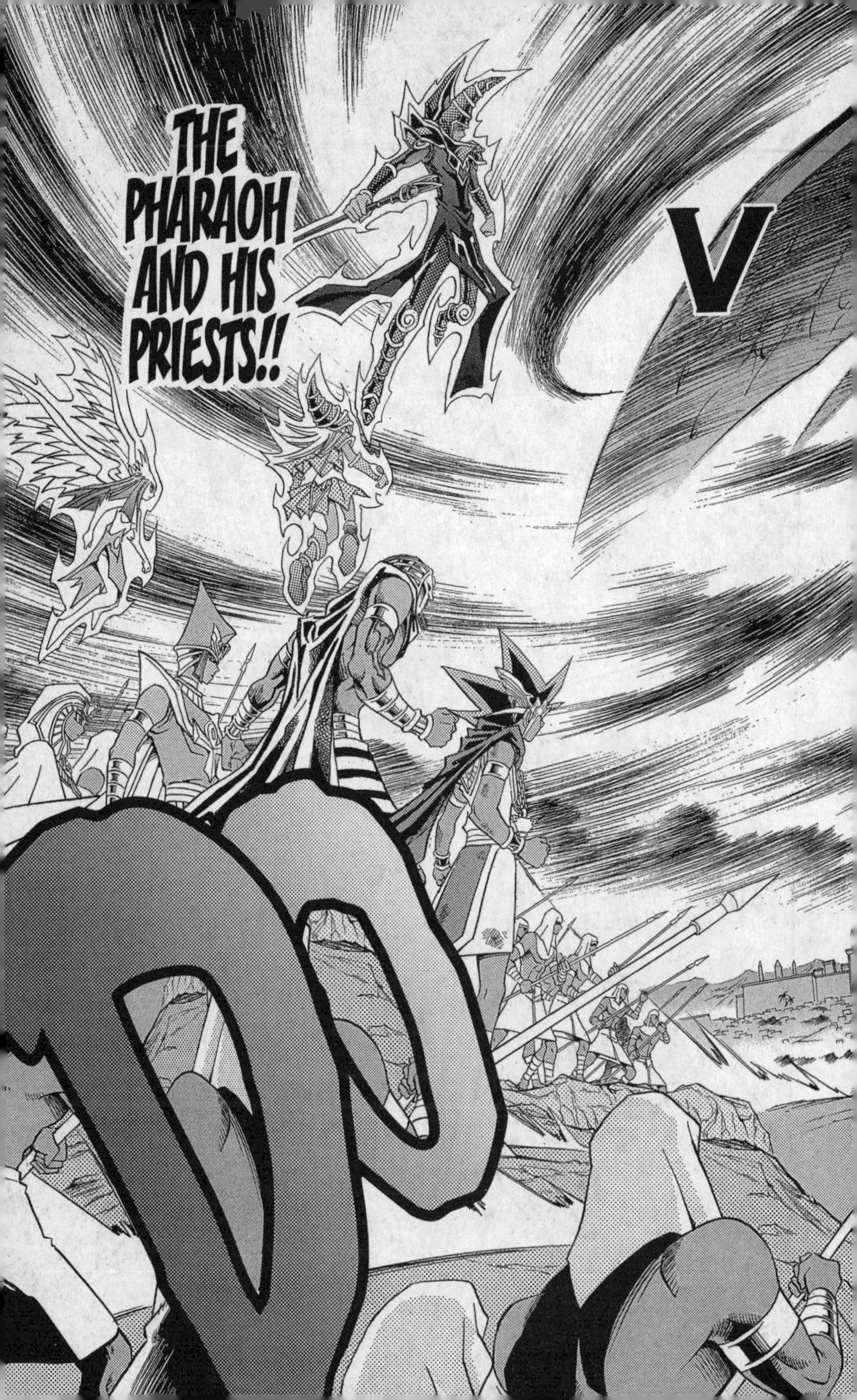
THE PHARAOH AND HIS PRIESTS!!
V

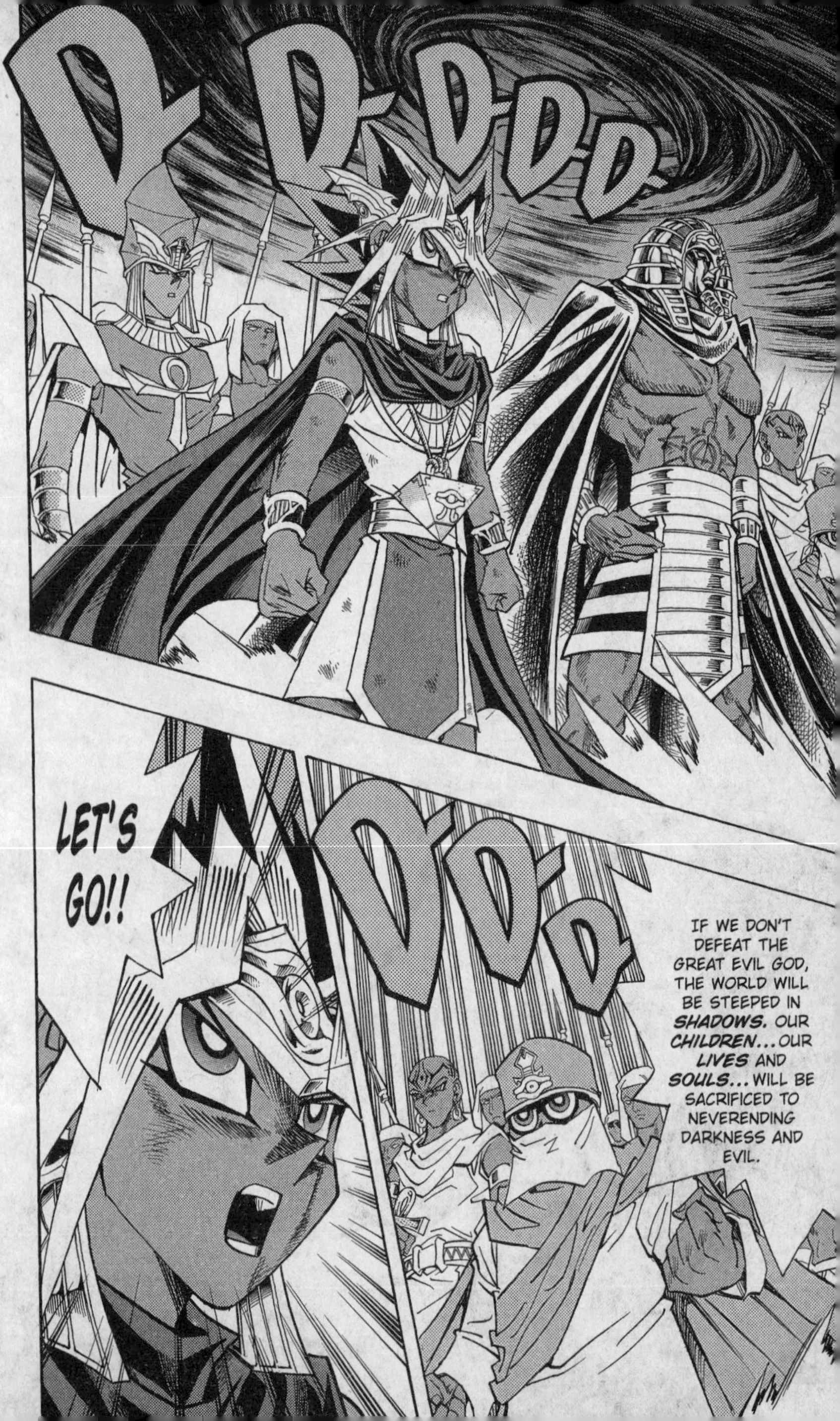
DDDDDD
IF WE DON'T DEFEAT THE GREAT EVIL GOD, THE WORLD WILL BE STEEPED IN SHADOWS. OUR CHILDREN...OUR LIVES AND SOULS...WILL BE SACRIFICED TO NEVERENDING DARKNESS AND EVIL.
DDD
LET'S GO!!

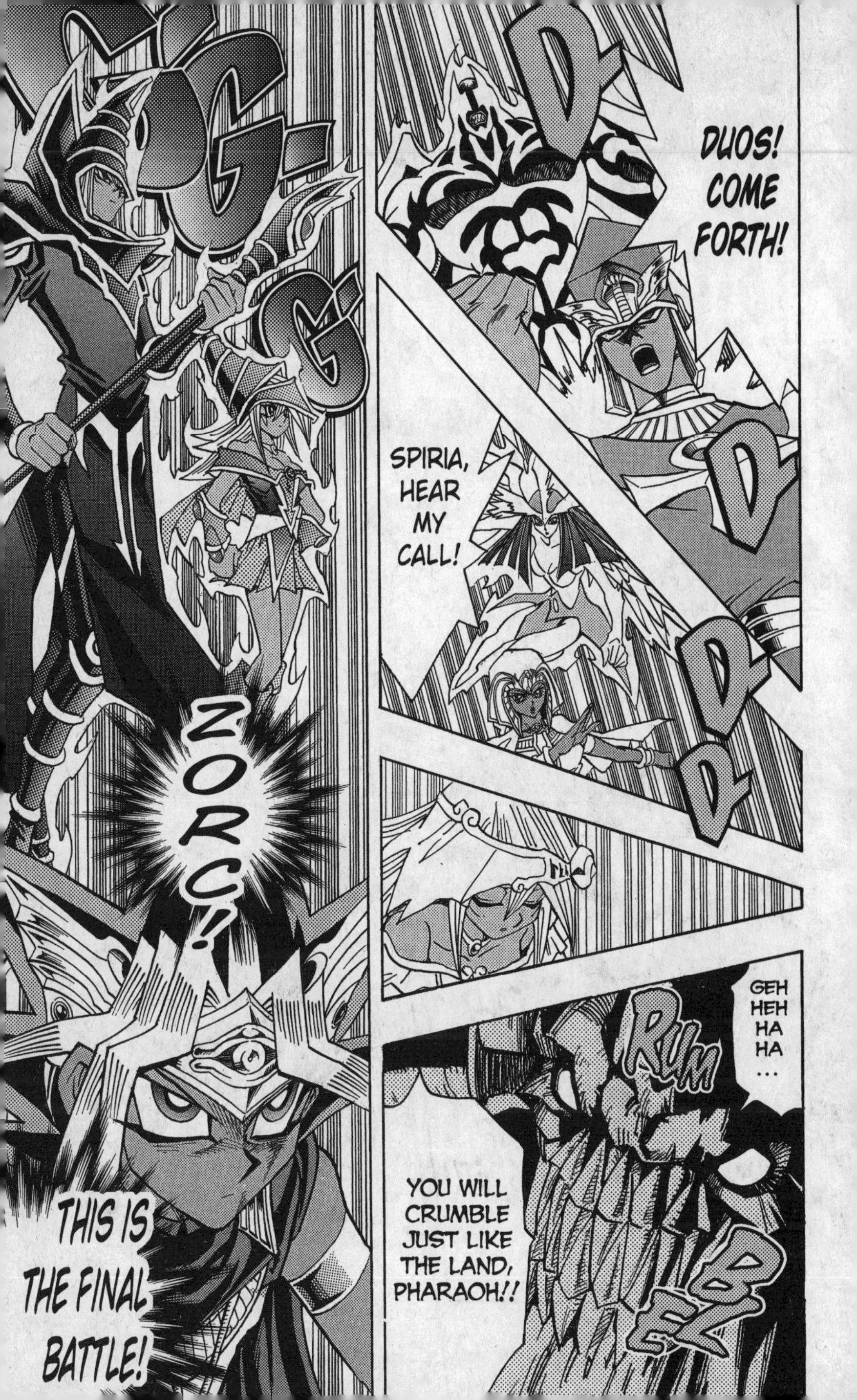
DUOS! COME FORTH!
SPIRIA, HEAR MY CALL!
GEH HEH HA HA...
RUMBLE
YOU WILL CRUMBLE JUST LIKE THE LAND, PHARAOH!!
ZORC!!
THIS IS THE FINAL BATTLE!

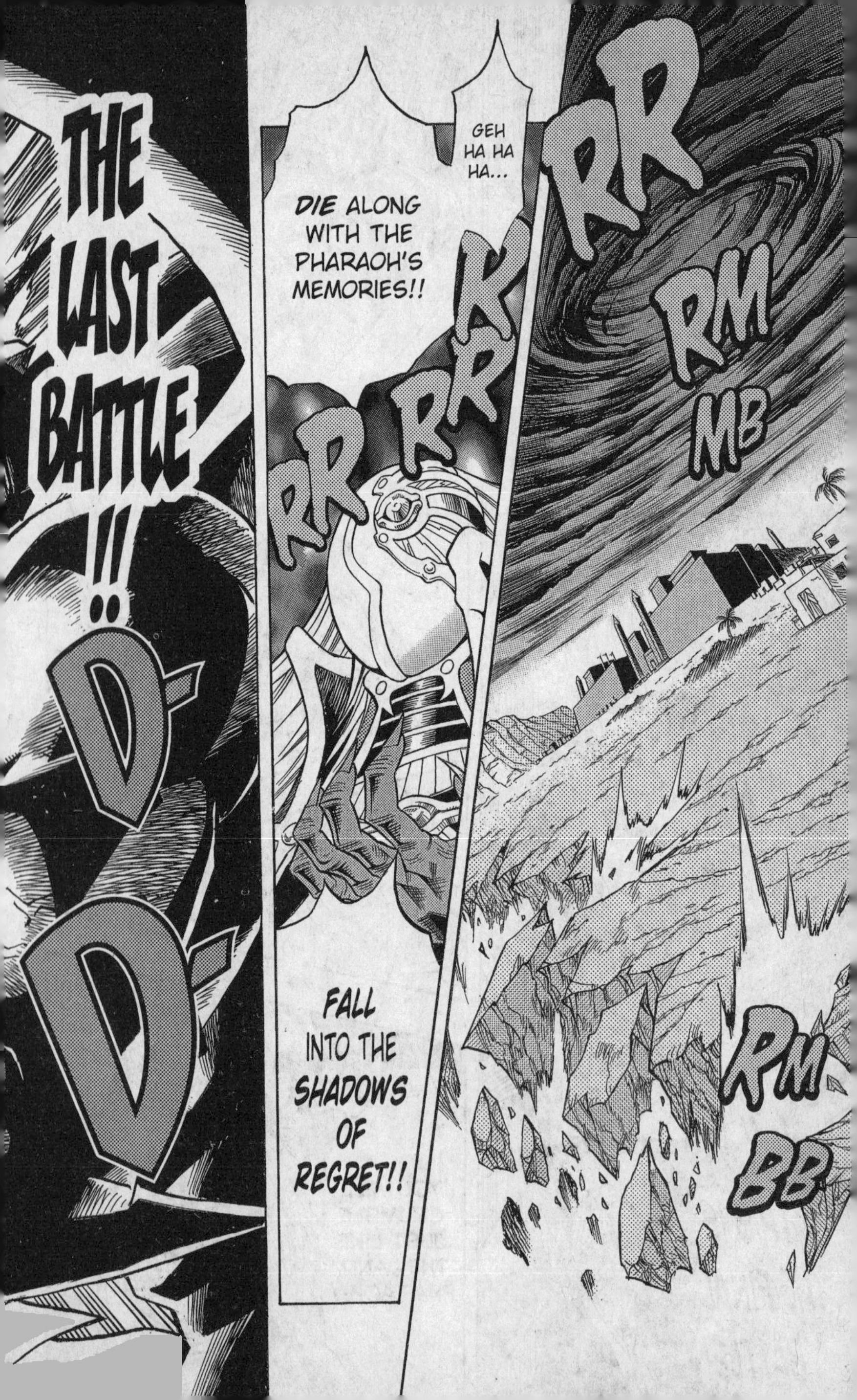

RR
RM
MB
RM
BB
GEH HA HA HA...
DIE ALONG WITH THE PHARAOH'S MEMORIES!!
RR RR K
FALL INTO THE SHADOWS OF REGRET!!
THE LAST BATTLE!!
D
D

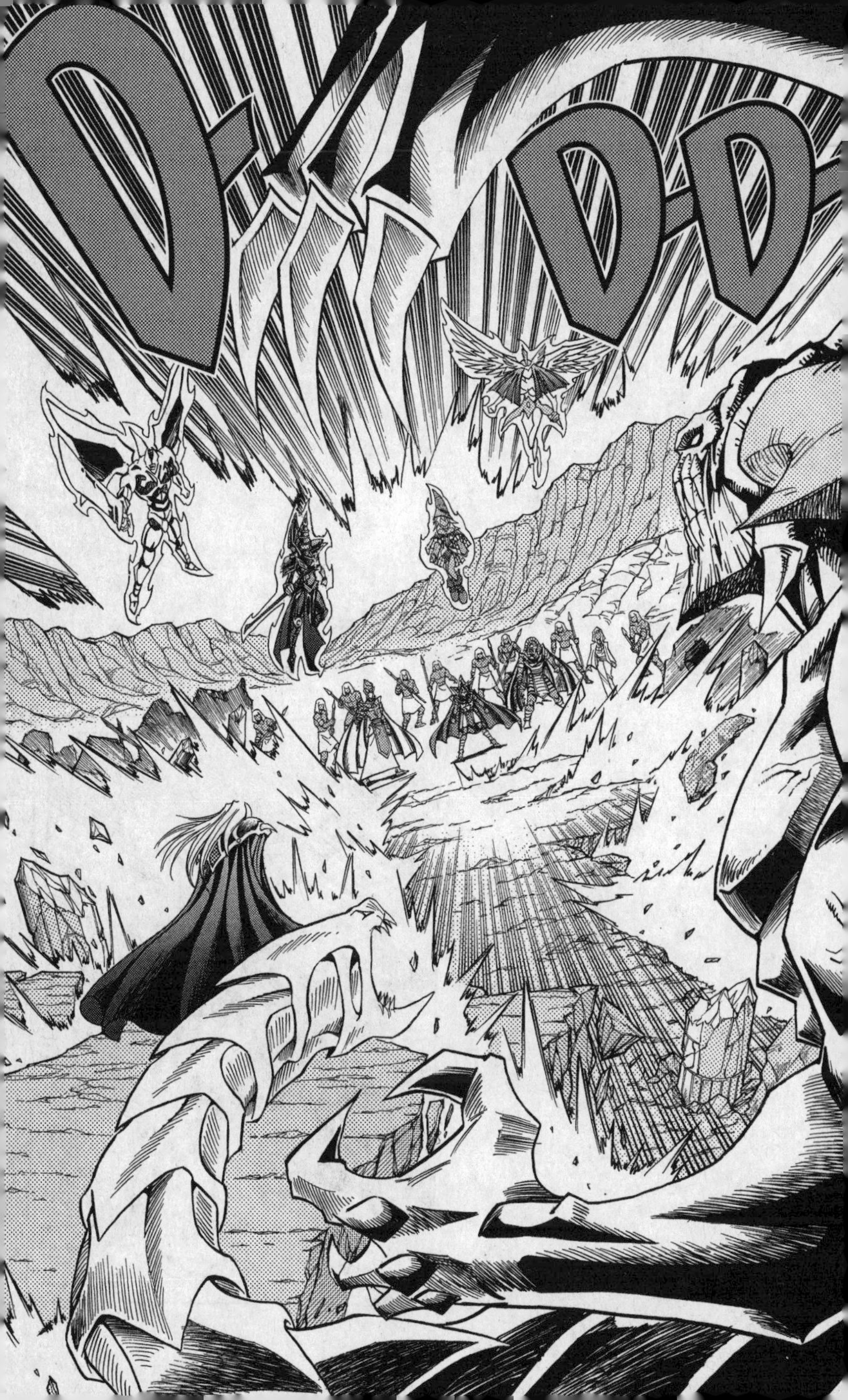

Duel 329: Until Our *Ba* Runs Out!

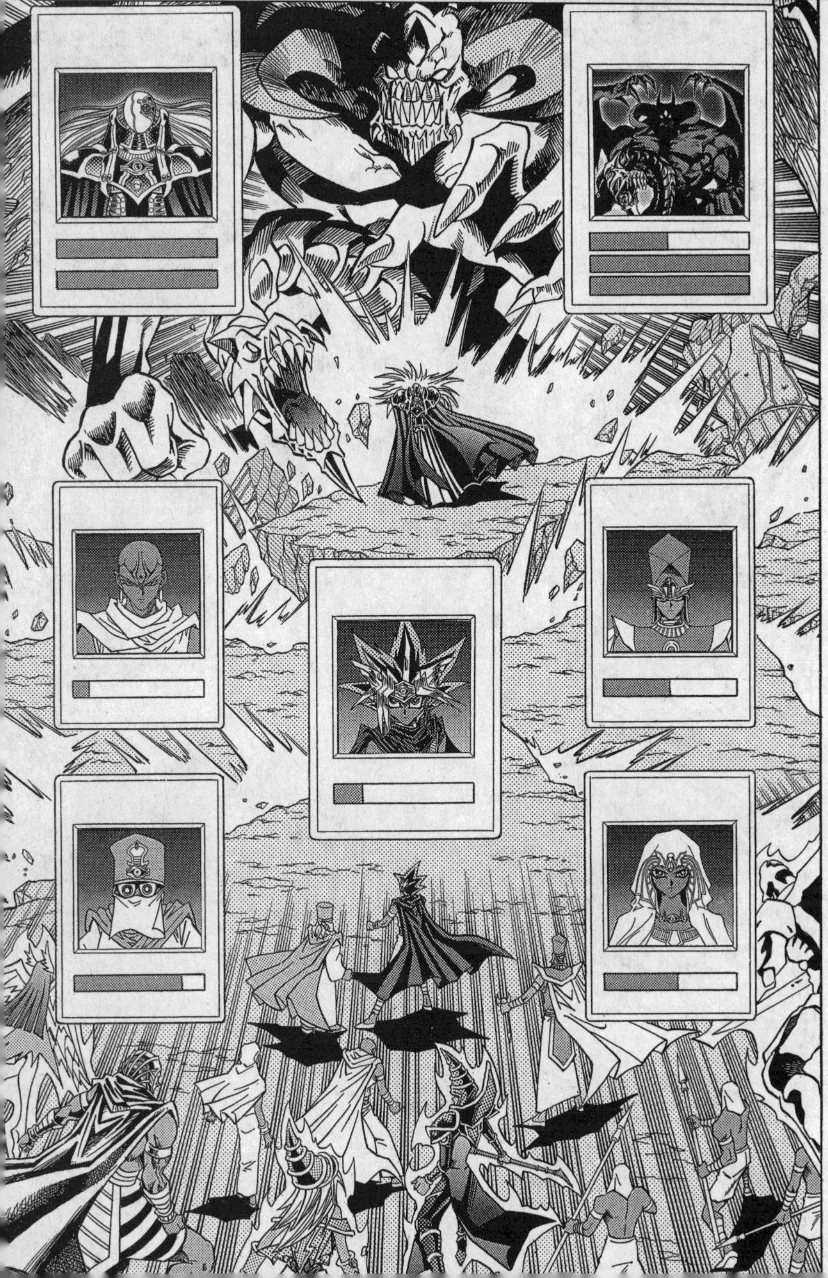

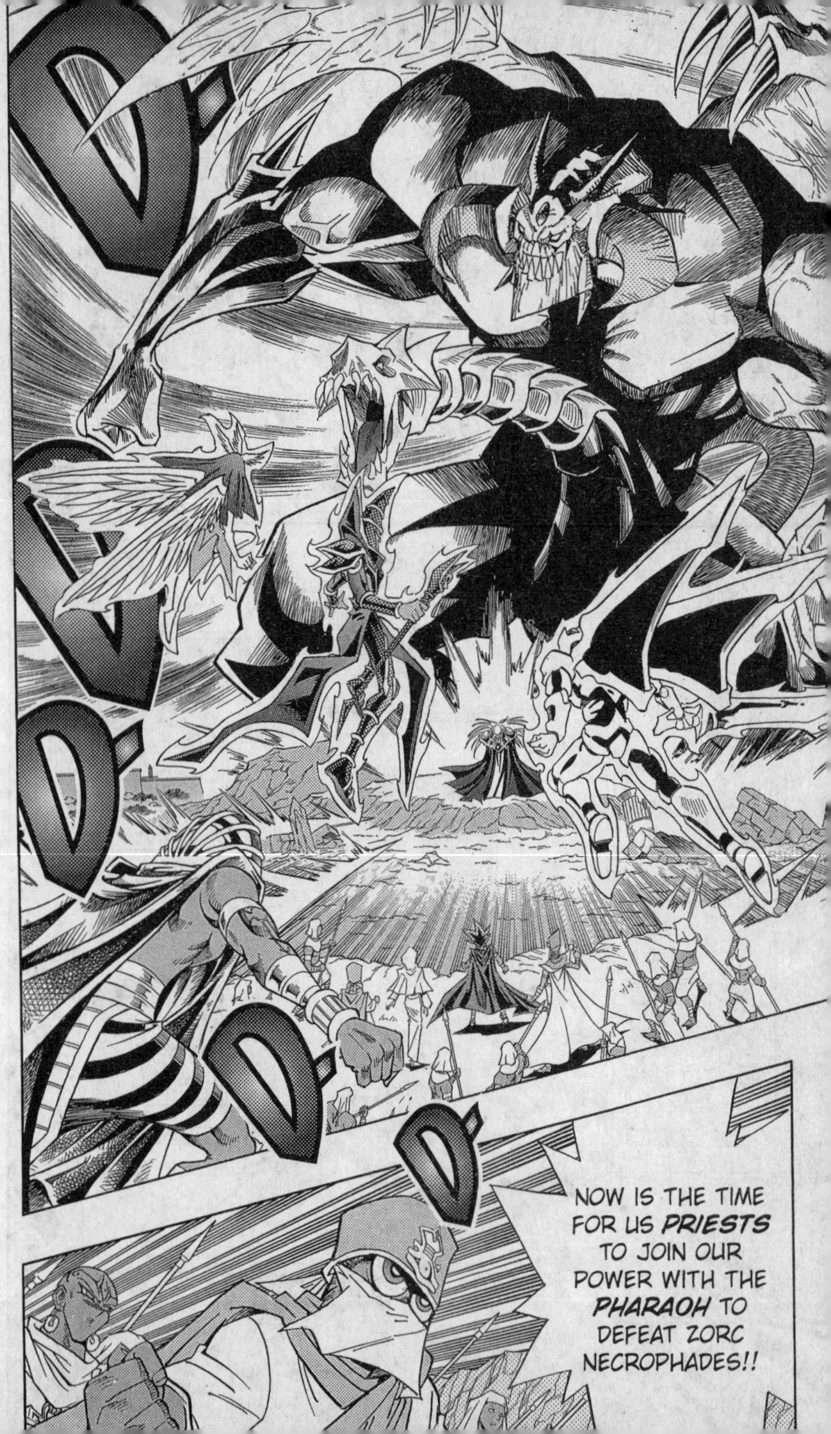
NOW IS THE TIME FOR US PRIESTS TO JOIN OUR POWER WITH THE PHARAOH TO DEFEAT ZORC NECROPHADES!!

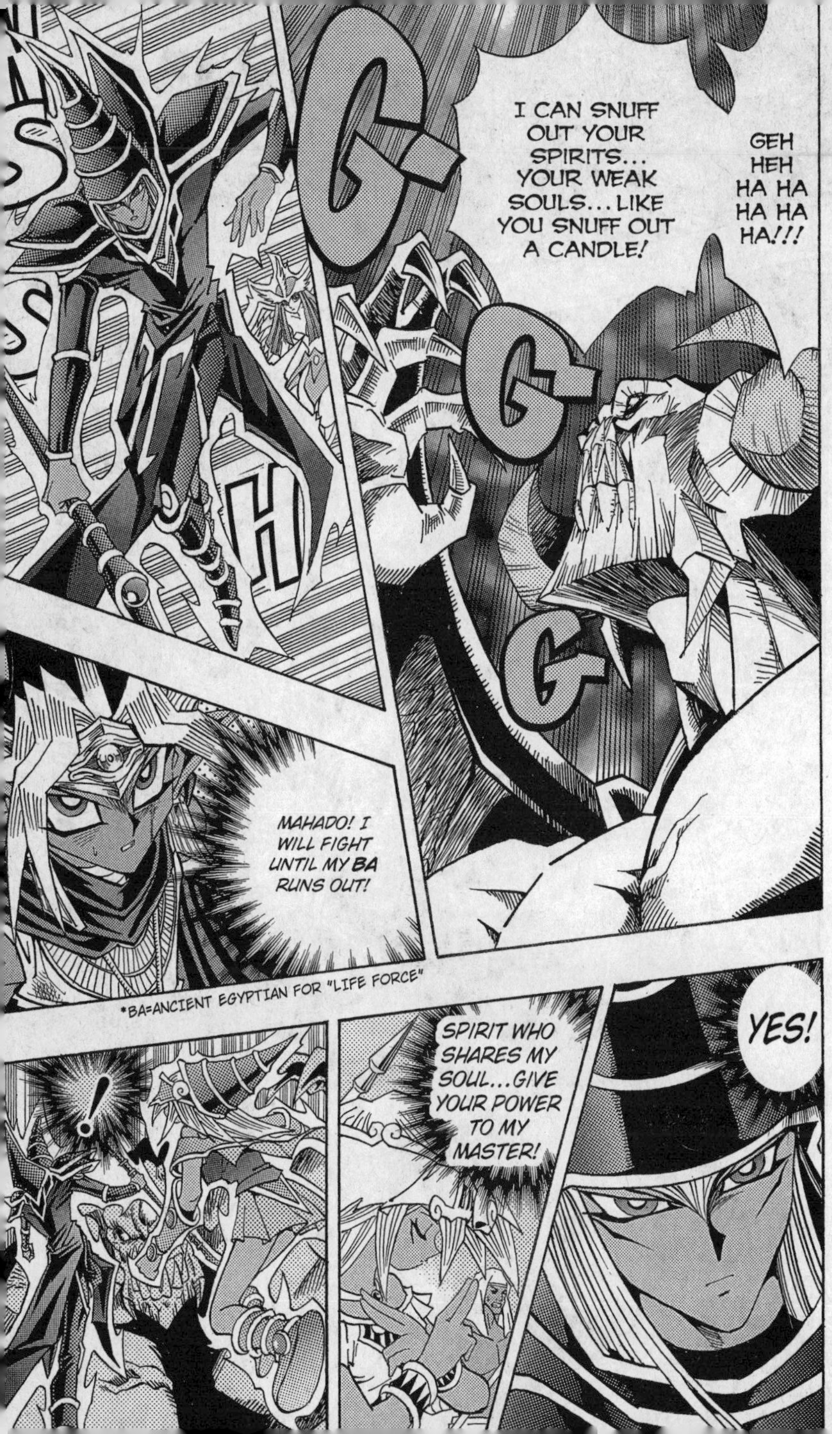
I CAN SNUFF OUT YOUR SPIRITS... YOUR WEAK SOULS... LIKE YOU SNUFF OUT A CANDLE!
GEH HEH HA HA HA HA HA!!!
G
G
G
H
MAHADO! I WILL FIGHT UNTIL MY BA RUNS OUT!
*BA=ANCIENT EGYPTIAN FOR "LIFE FORCE"
YES!
SPIRIT WHO SHARES MY SOUL...GIVE YOUR POWER TO MY MASTER!
!

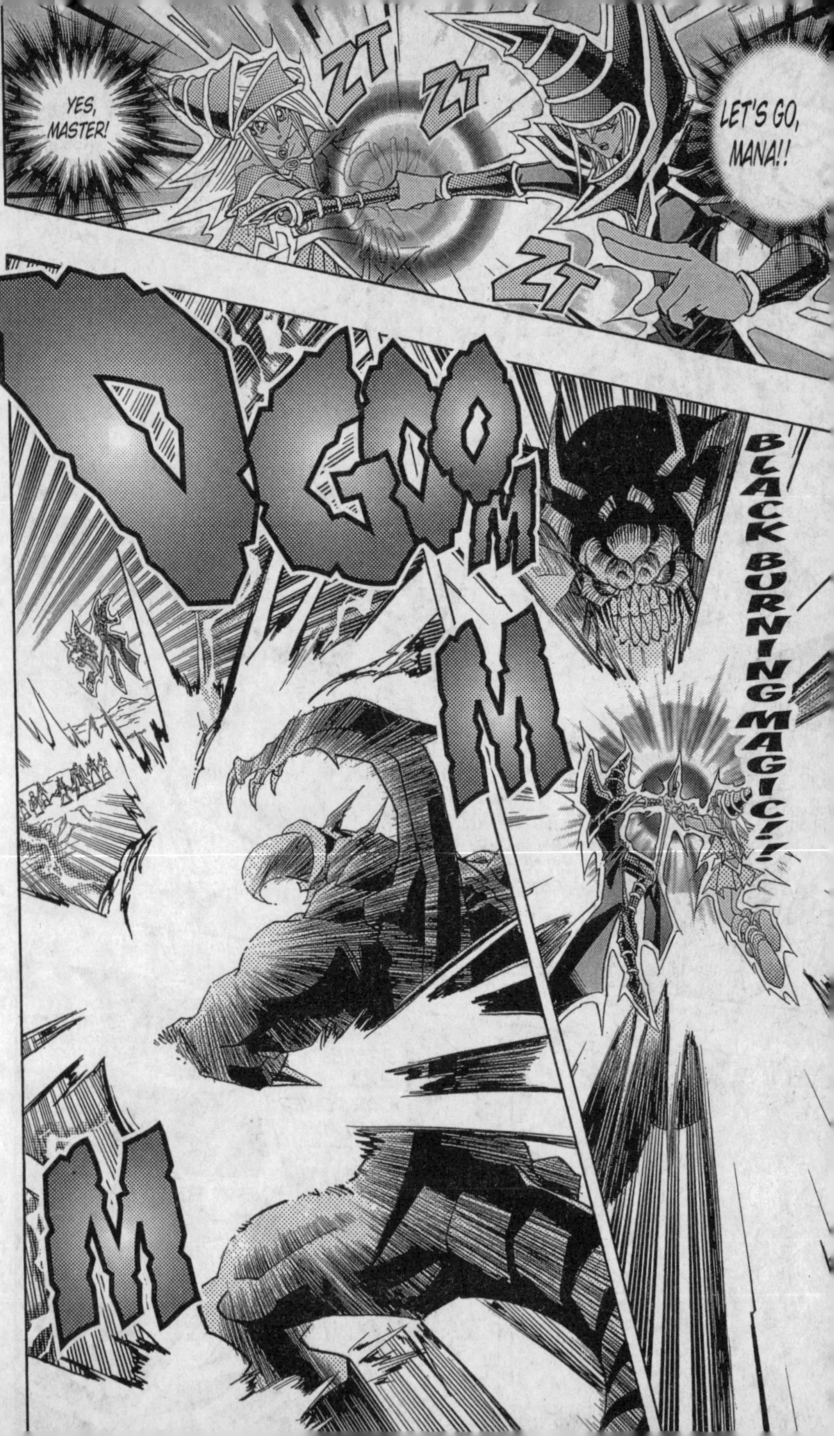
LET'S GO, MANA!!
YES, MASTER!
ZT
ZT
ZT
BLACK BURNING MAGIC!!!
DOOMMM

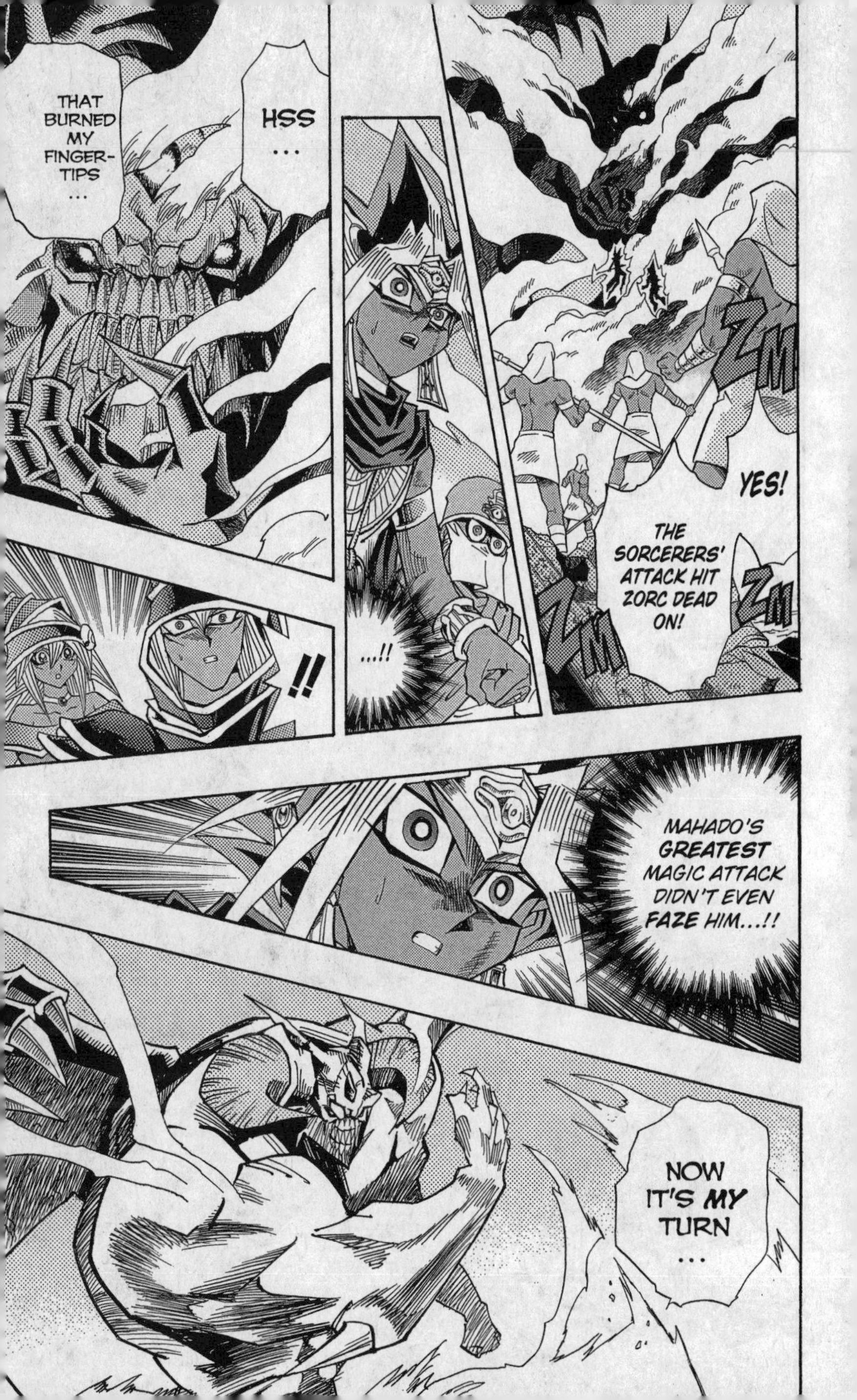
ZM
YES!
THE SORCERERS' ATTACK HIT ZORC DEAD ON!
ZM
ZM
...!!
HSS ...
THAT BURNED MY FINGER-TIPS ...
!!
MAHADO'S **GREATEST** MAGIC ATTACK DIDN'T EVEN **FAZE** HIM...!!
NOW IT'S **MY** TURN ...

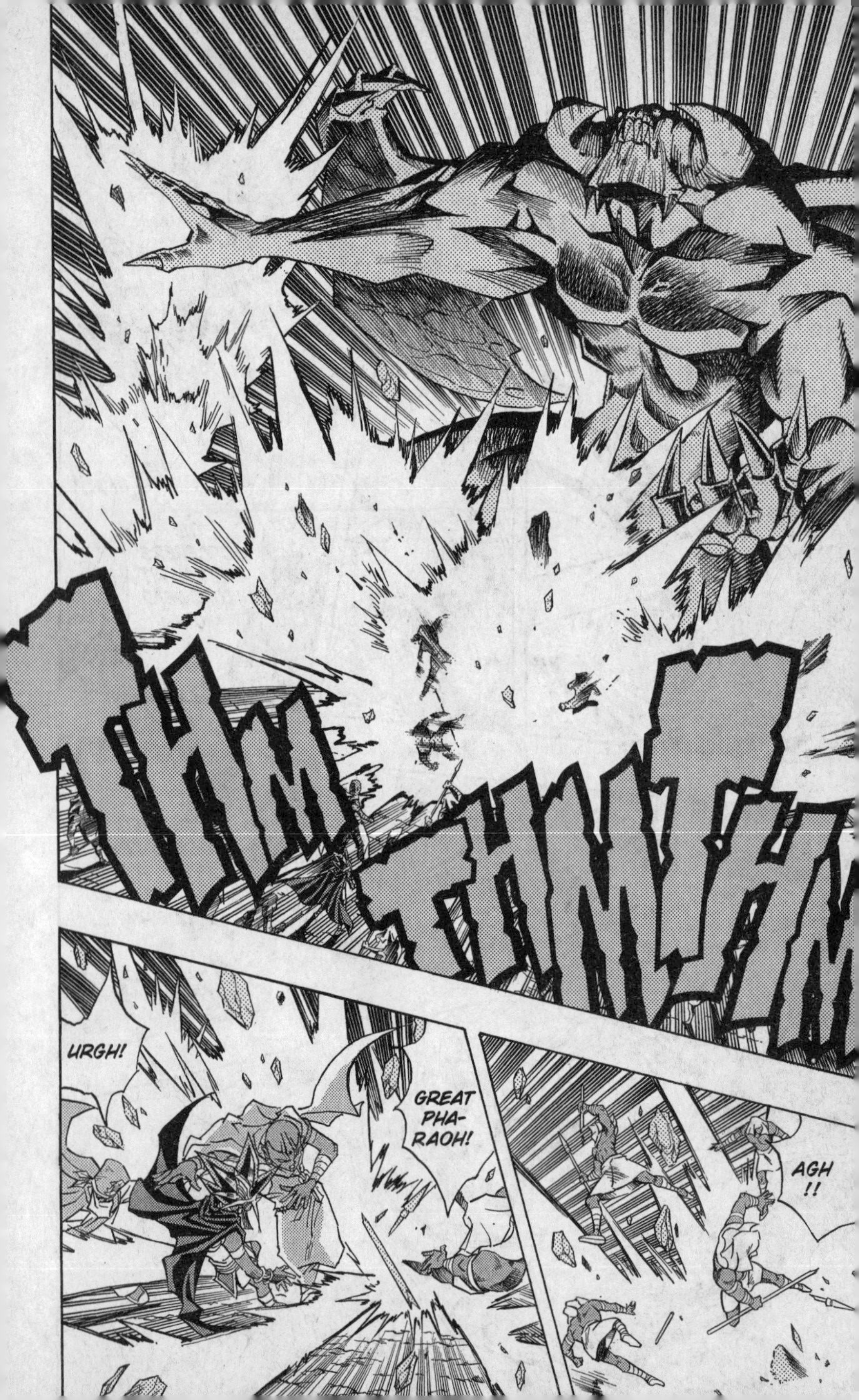
AGH!!
GREAT PHA-RAOH!
URGH!

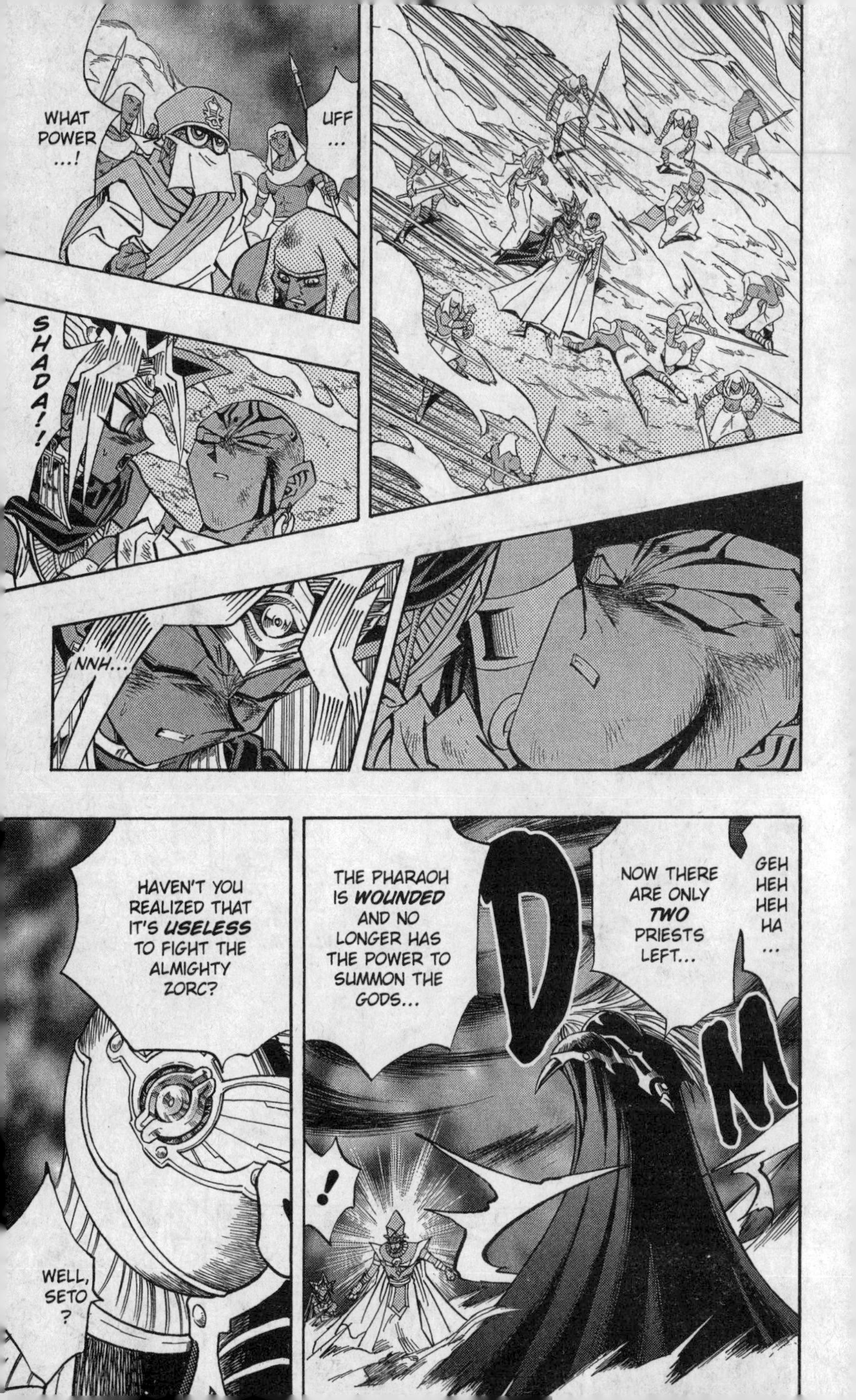
UFF ...
WHAT POWER ...!
SHADA!!
NNH...
GEH HEH HEH HA ...
NOW THERE ARE ONLY **TWO** PRIESTS LEFT...
D M
THE PHARAOH IS **WOUNDED** AND NO LONGER HAS THE POWER TO SUMMON THE GODS...
!
HAVEN'T YOU REALIZED THAT IT'S **USELESS** TO FIGHT THE ALMIGHTY ZORC?
WELL, SETO ?

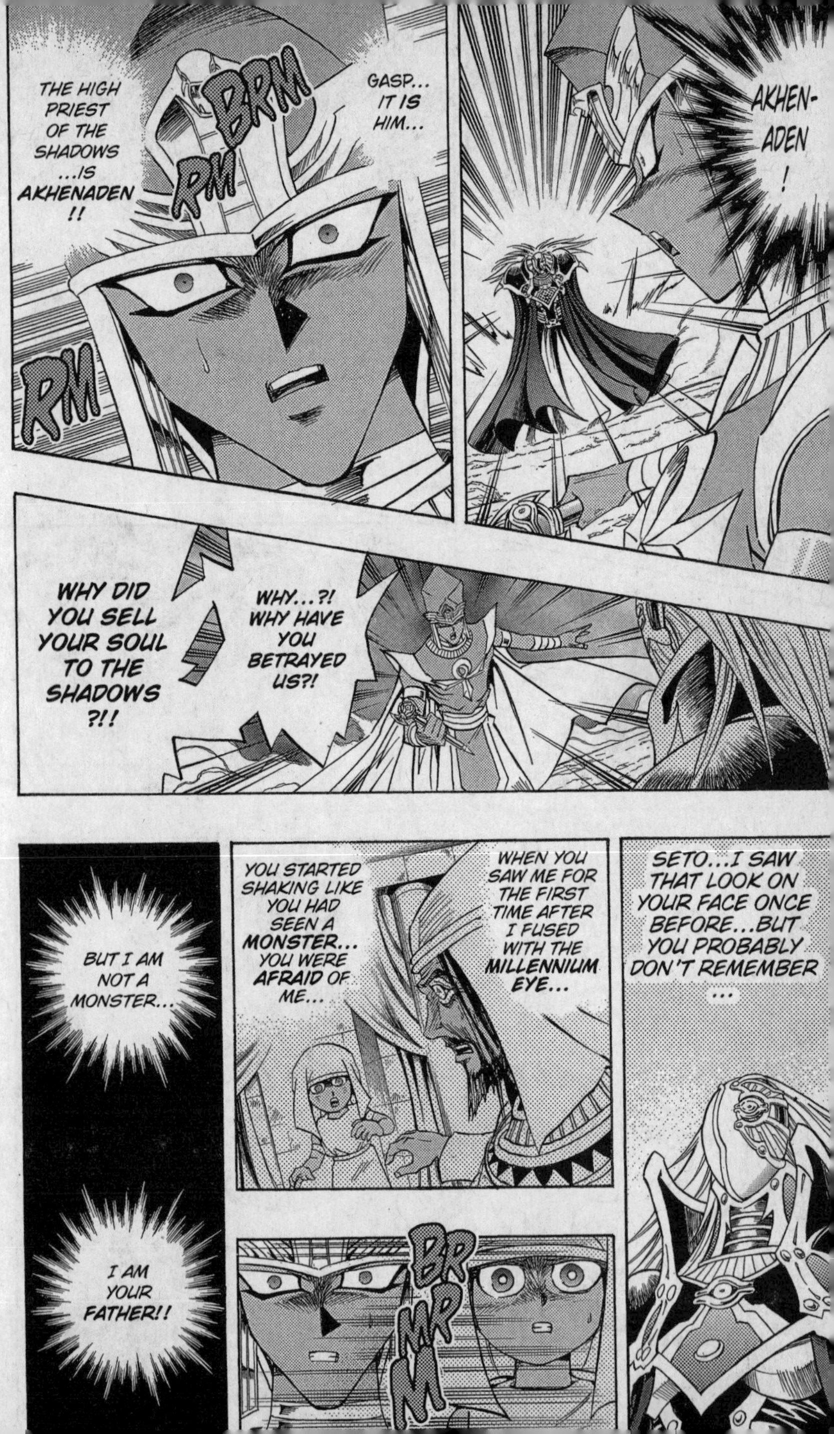
AKHEN-ADEN!
GASP... IT IS HIM...
BRM
RM
THE HIGH PRIEST OF THE SHADOWS ...IS AKHENADEN!!
RM
WHY...?! WHY HAVE YOU BETRAYED US?!
WHY DID YOU SELL YOUR SOUL TO THE SHADOWS?!!
SETO...I SAW THAT LOOK ON YOUR FACE ONCE BEFORE...BUT YOU PROBABLY DON'T REMEMBER...
WHEN YOU SAW ME FOR THE FIRST TIME AFTER I FUSED WITH THE MILLENNIUM EYE...
YOU STARTED SHAKING LIKE YOU HAD SEEN A MONSTER... YOU WERE AFRAID OF ME...
BRMRM
BUT I AM NOT A MONSTER...
I AM YOUR FATHER!!

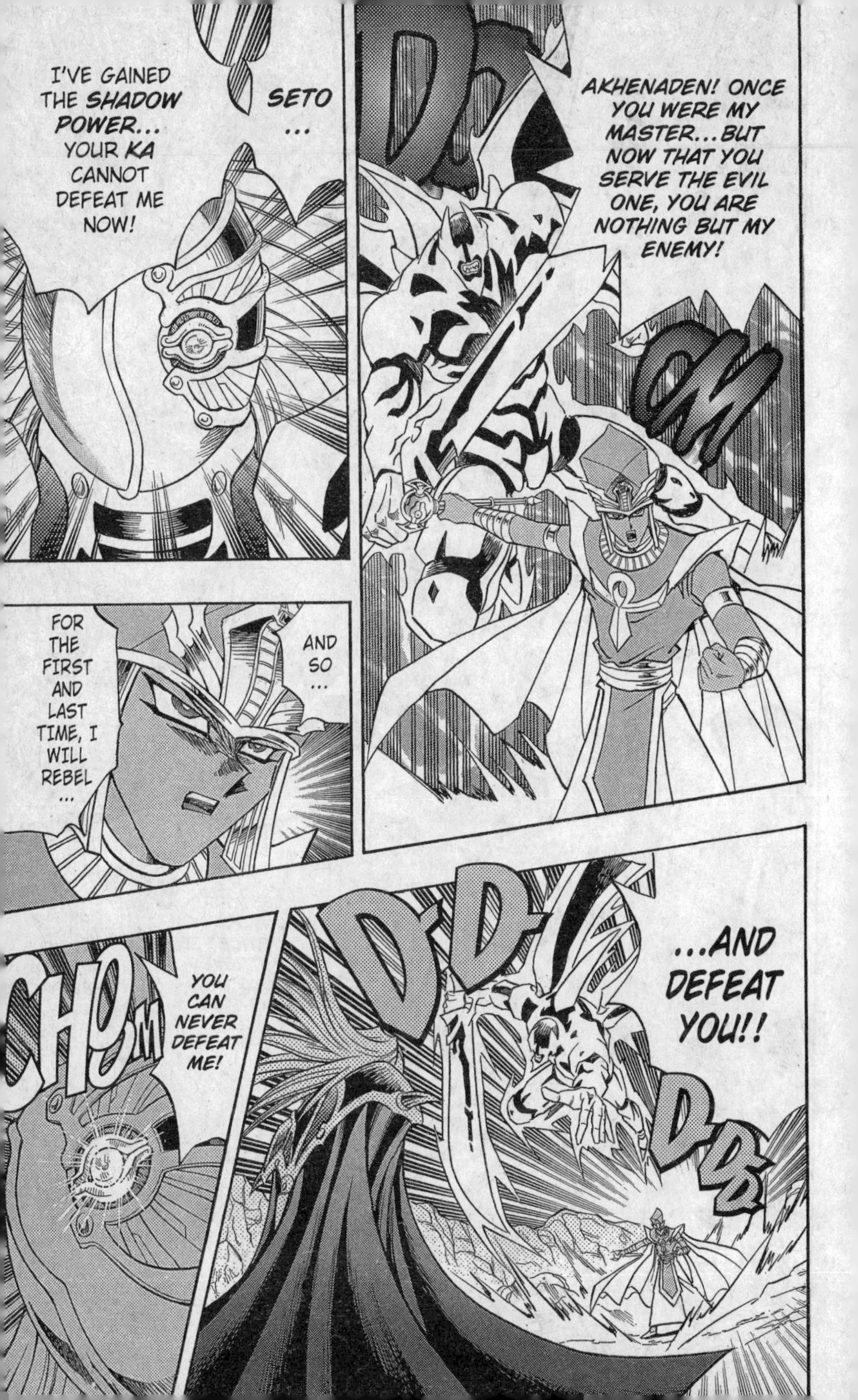
AKHENADEN! ONCE YOU WERE MY MASTER...BUT NOW THAT YOU SERVE THE EVIL ONE, YOU ARE NOTHING BUT MY ENEMY!
SETO ...
I'VE GAINED THE SHADOW POWER... YOUR KA CANNOT DEFEAT ME NOW!
AND SO ...
FOR THE FIRST AND LAST TIME, I WILL REBEL ...
DD
...AND DEFEAT YOU!!
YOU CAN NEVER DEFEAT ME!
CHOOM

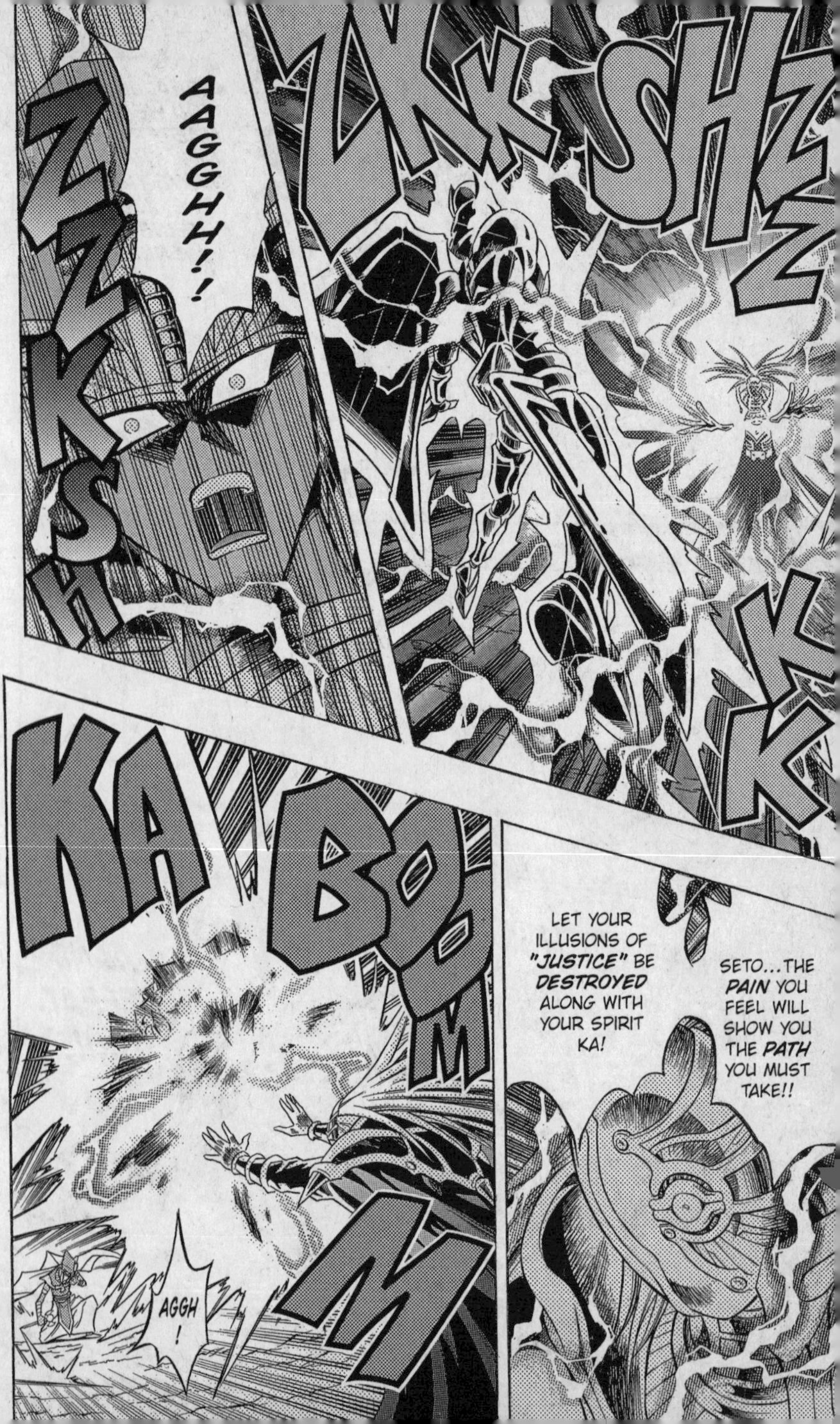
ZKKSHZZ
KKK
AAGGHH!!
ZZKSH
SETO...THE *PAIN* YOU FEEL WILL SHOW YOU THE *PATH* YOU MUST TAKE!!
LET YOUR ILLUSIONS OF *"JUSTICE"* BE *DESTROYED* ALONG WITH YOUR SPIRIT KA!
KABOOM
AGGH!

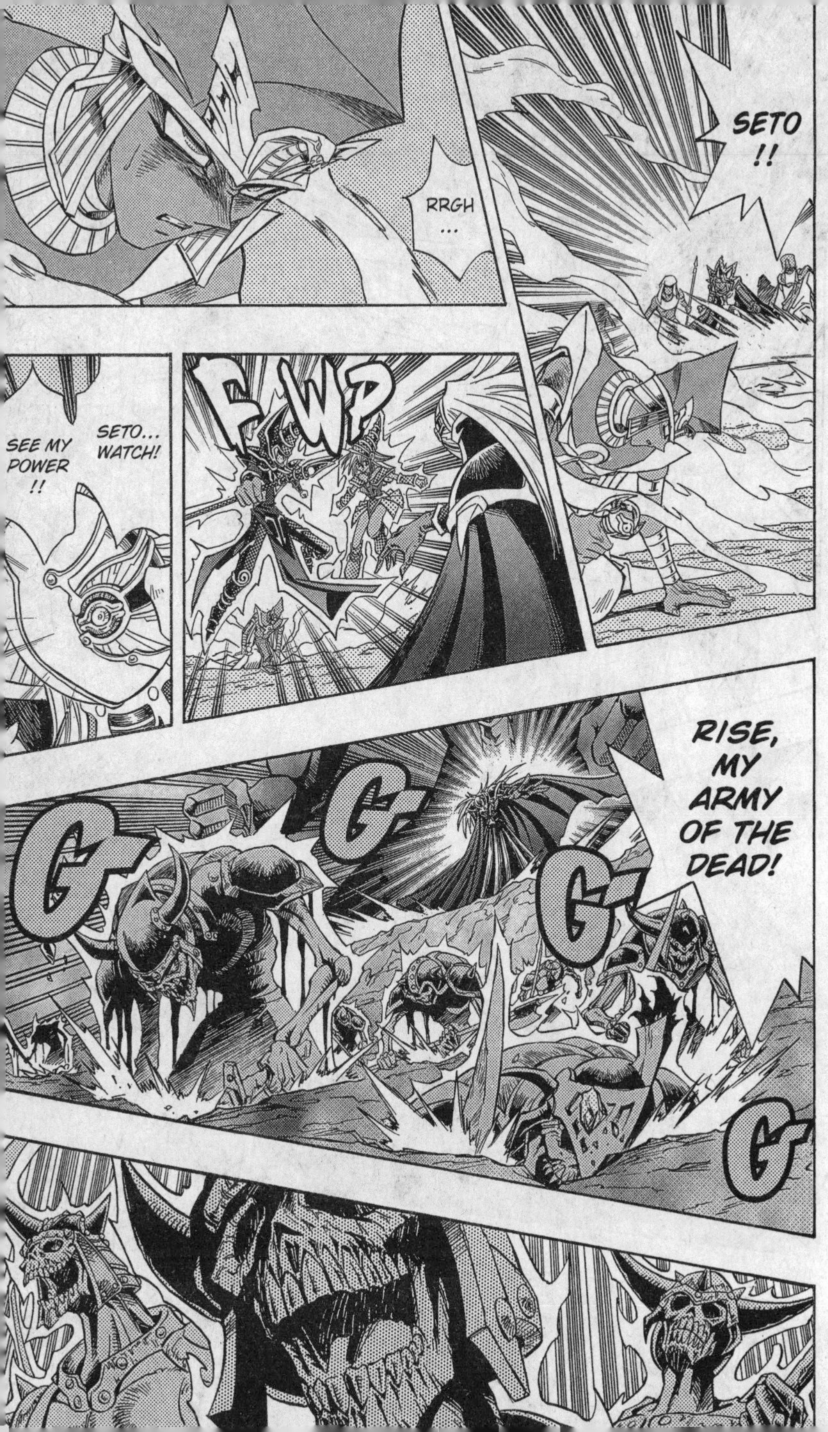
SETO !!
RRGH ...
FWP
SETO... WATCH!
SEE MY POWER !!
RISE, MY ARMY OF THE DEAD!
G
G
G
G
G

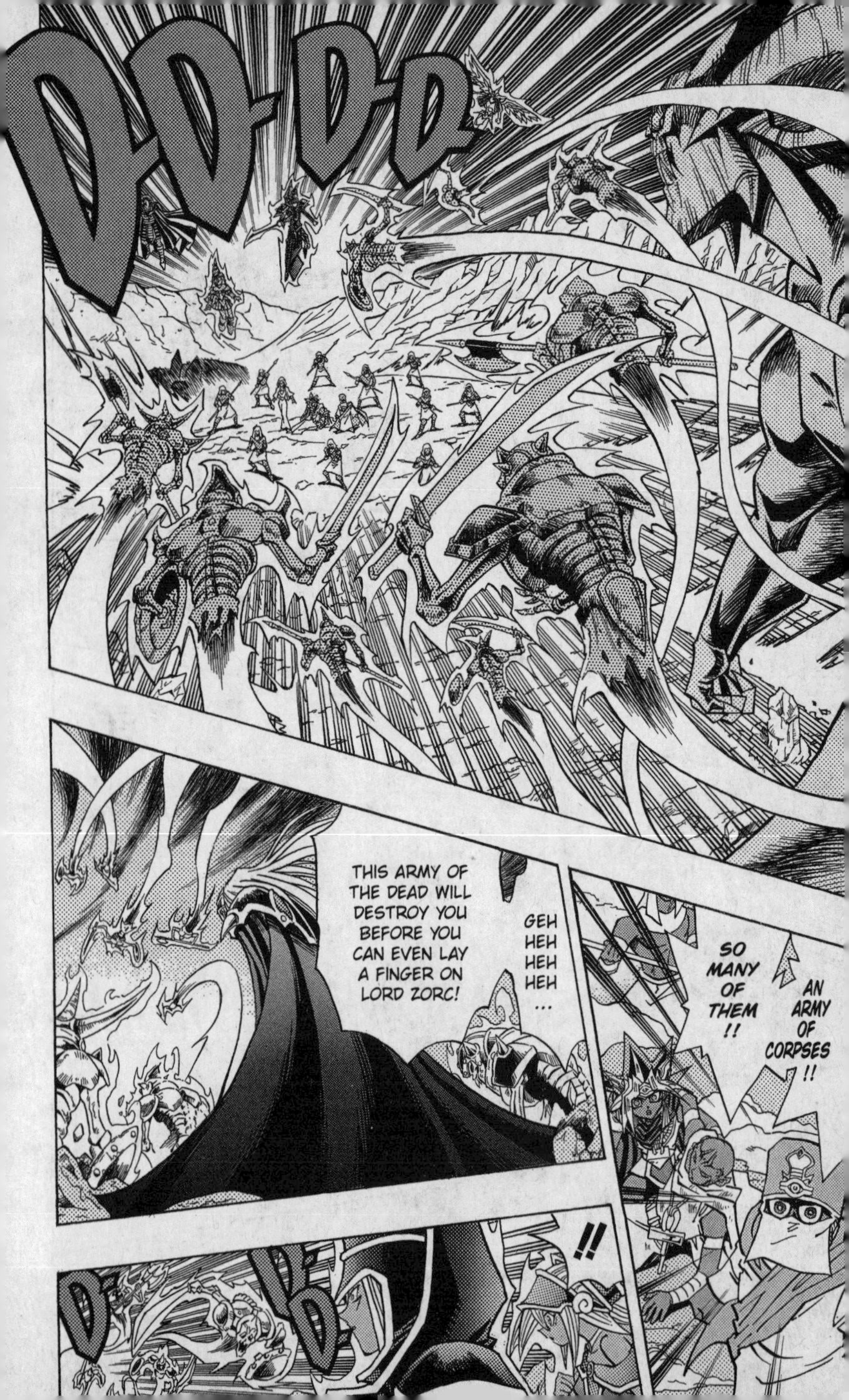
AN ARMY OF CORPSES!!
SO MANY OF THEM!!
GEH HEH HEH HEH...
THIS ARMY OF THE DEAD WILL DESTROY YOU BEFORE YOU CAN EVEN LAY A FINGER ON LORD ZORC!
!!

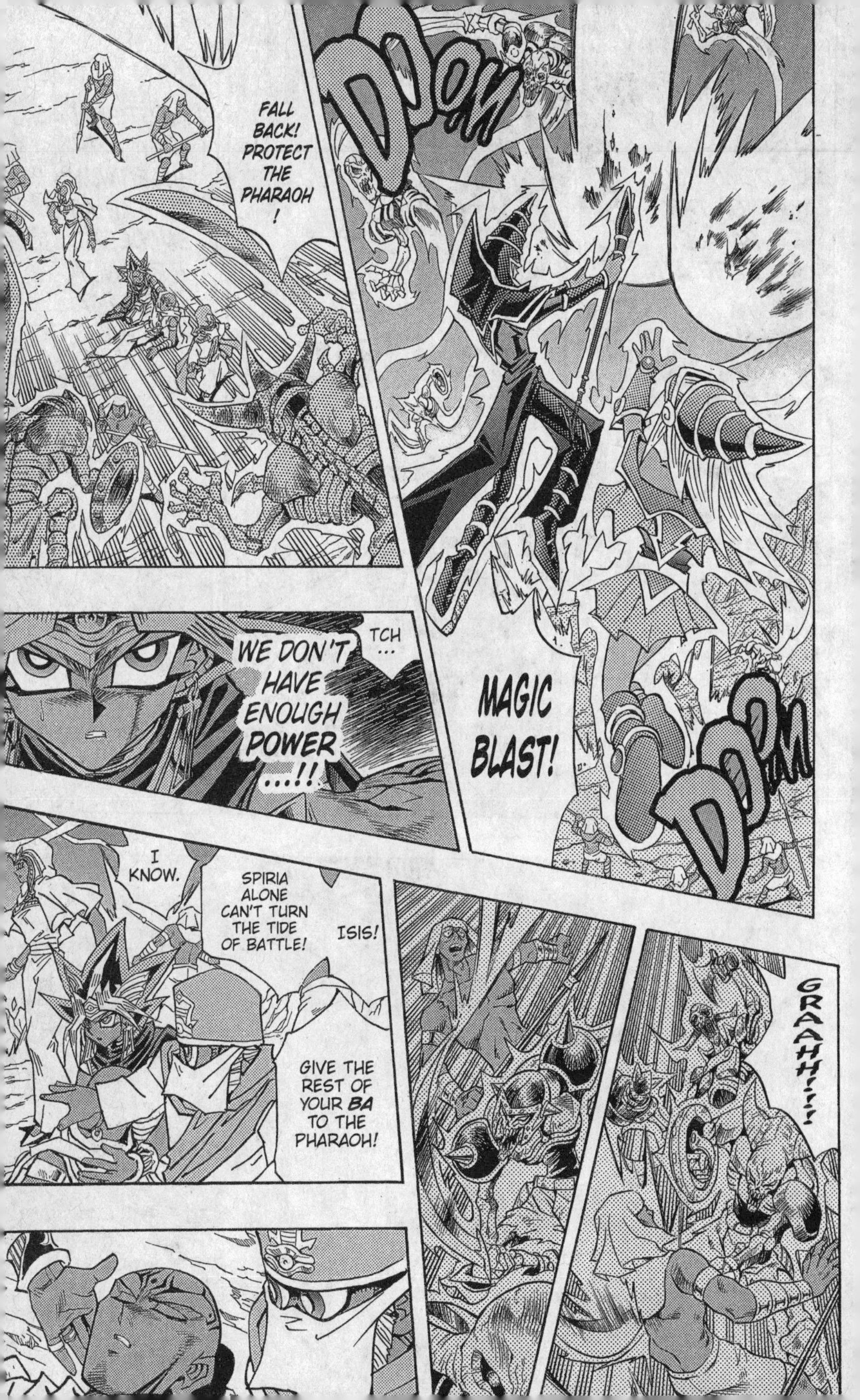

DOOM
MAGIC BLAST!
DOOOM
FALL BACK! PROTECT THE PHARAOH!
TCH...
WE DON'T HAVE ENOUGH POWER ...!!
GRAAHH!!!
I KNOW.
SPIRIA ALONE CAN'T TURN THE TIDE OF BATTLE!
ISIS!
GIVE THE REST OF YOUR *BA* TO THE PHARAOH!

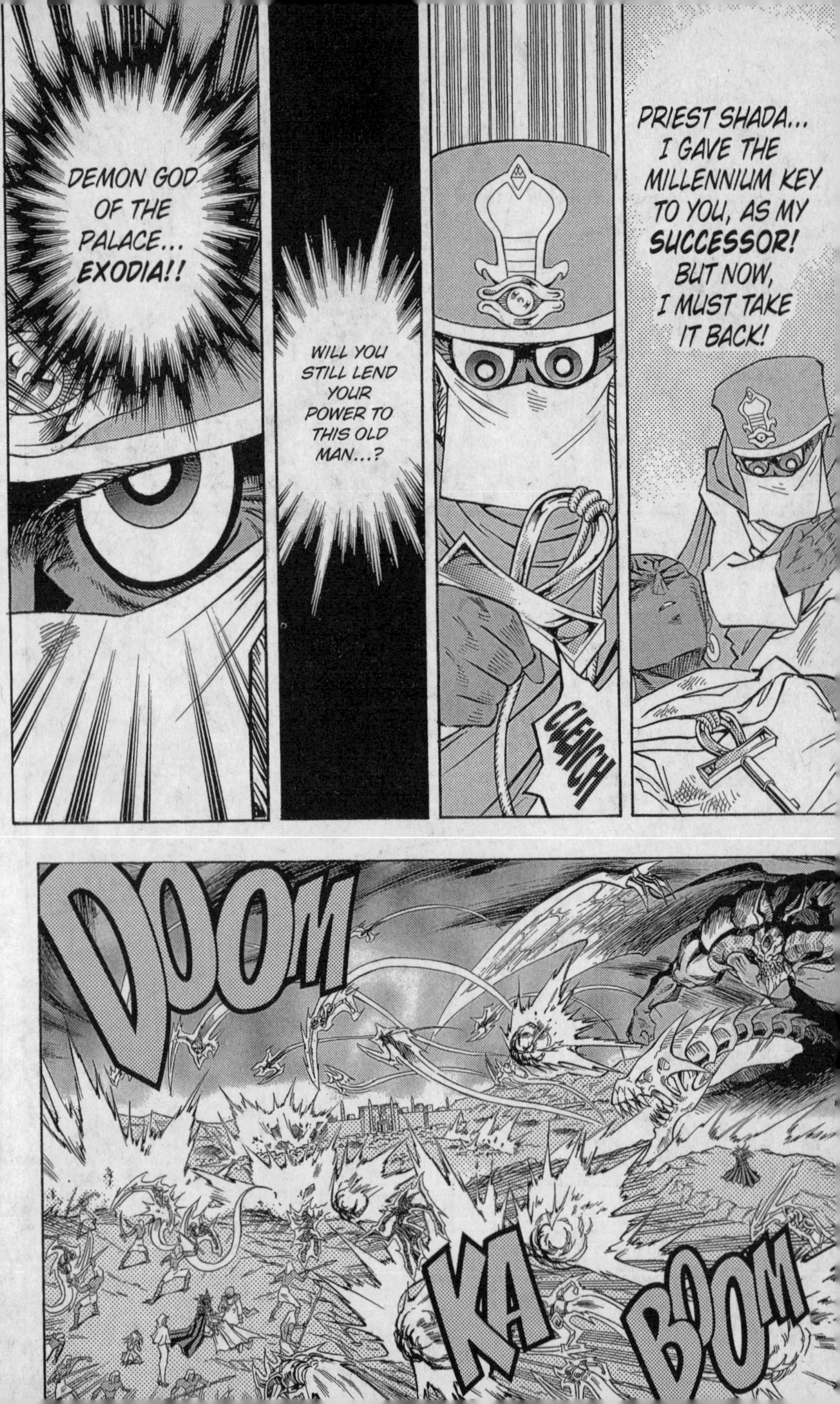
PRIEST SHADA... I GAVE THE MILLENNIUM KEY TO YOU, AS MY SUCCESSOR! BUT NOW, I MUST TAKE IT BACK!
CLENCH
WILL YOU STILL LEND YOUR POWER TO THIS OLD MAN...?
DEMON GOD OF THE PALACE... EXODIA!!
DOOM
KA
BOOM

READ THIS WAY

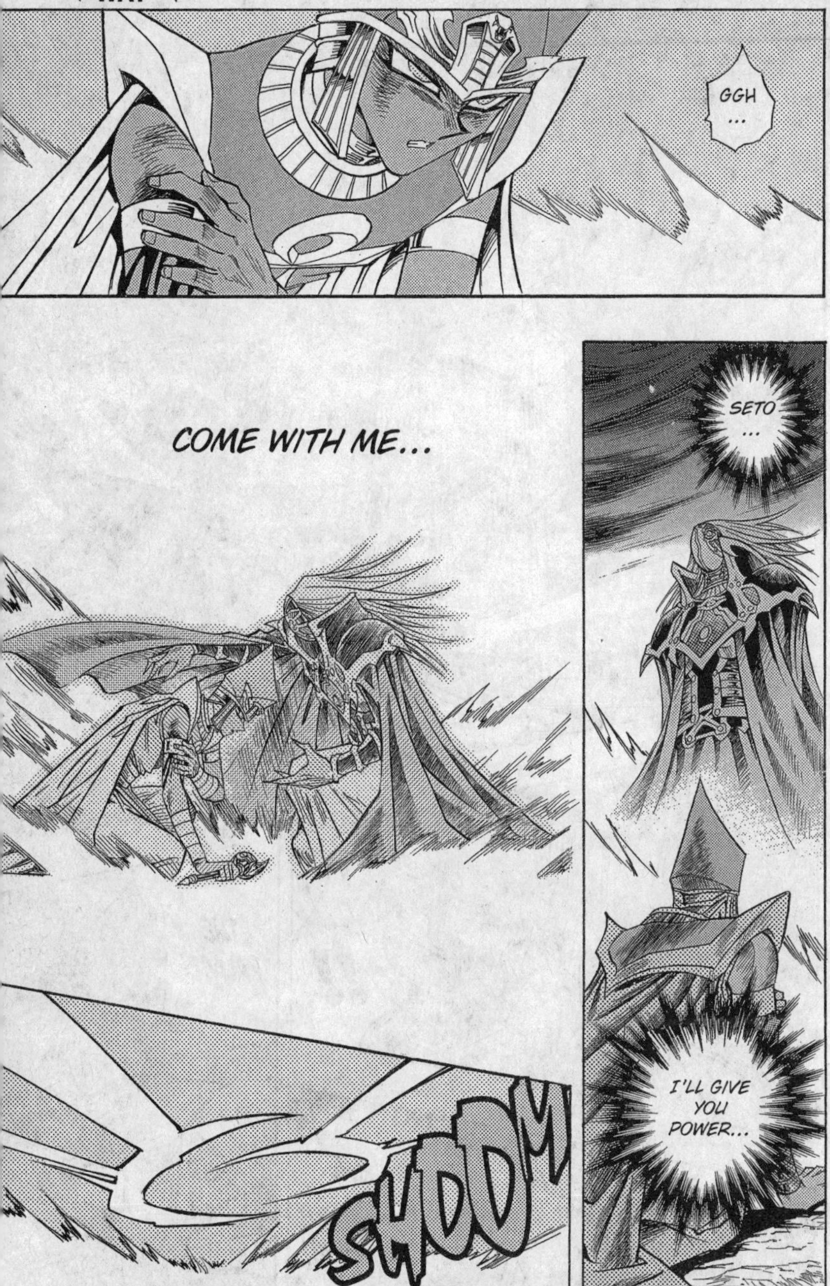
GGH ...
SETO ...
I'LL GIVE YOU POWER...
COME WITH ME...
SHOOM

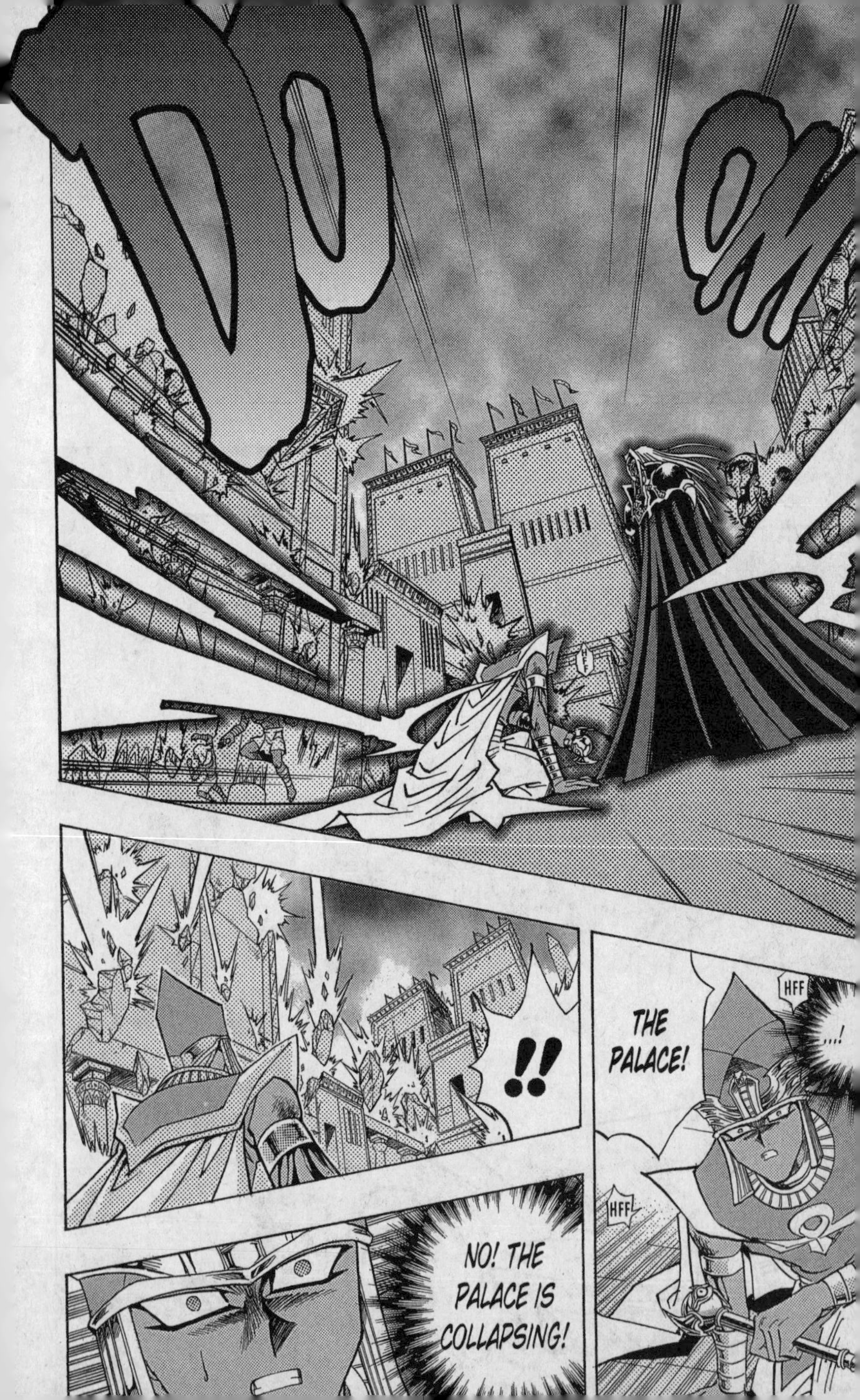
DOOM
HFF
HFF
...!
THE PALACE!
HFF
!!
NO! THE PALACE IS COLLAPSING!

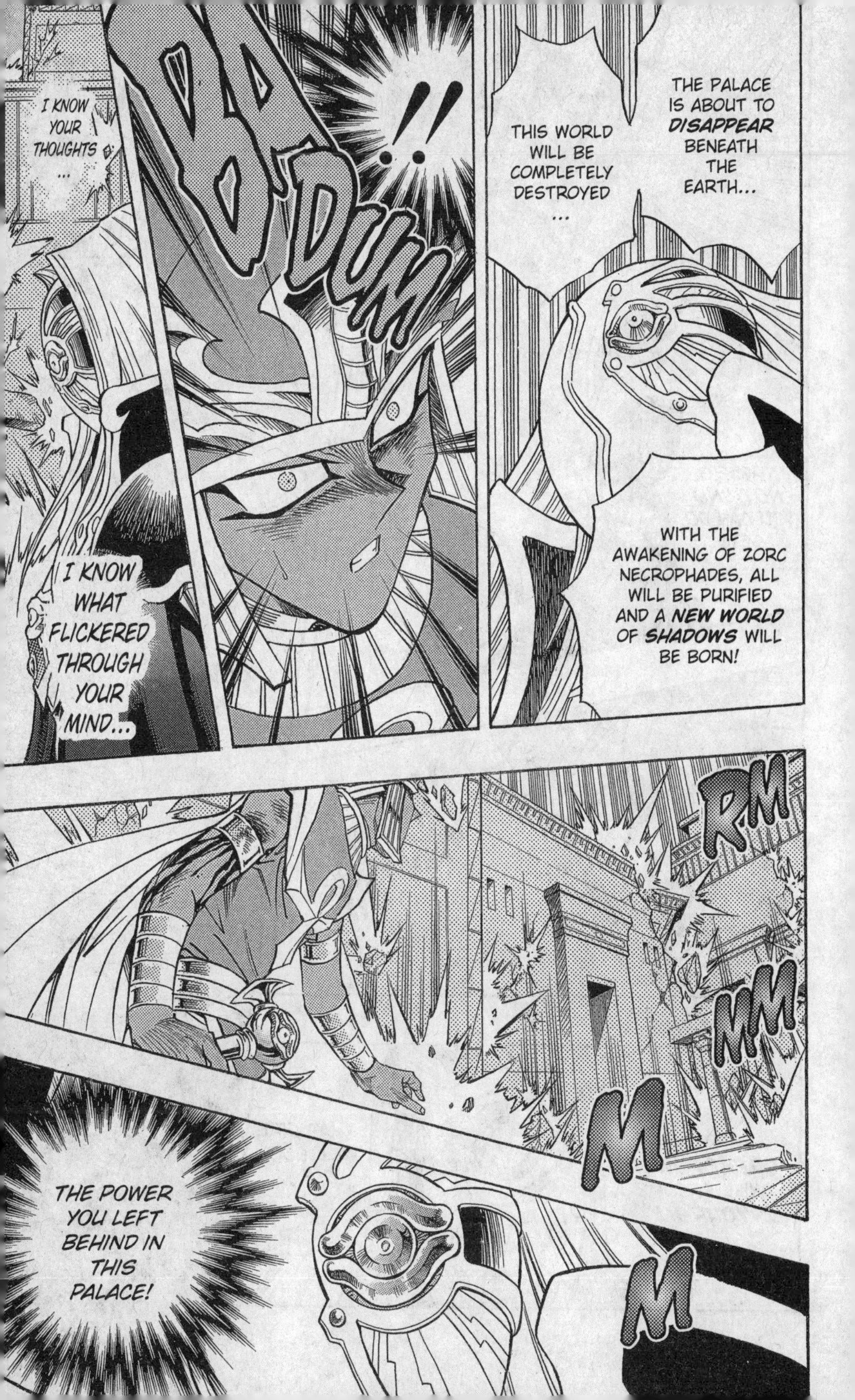
THE PALACE IS ABOUT TO ***DISAPPEAR*** BENEATH THE EARTH...
THIS WORLD WILL BE COMPLETELY DESTROYED ...
WITH THE AWAKENING OF ZORC NECROPHADES, ALL WILL BE PURIFIED AND A ***NEW WORLD*** OF ***SHADOWS*** WILL BE BORN!
BA DUM!!
I KNOW YOUR THOUGHTS ...
I KNOW WHAT FLICKERED THROUGH YOUR MIND...
RM
MM
M
THE POWER YOU LEFT BEHIND IN THIS PALACE!
M

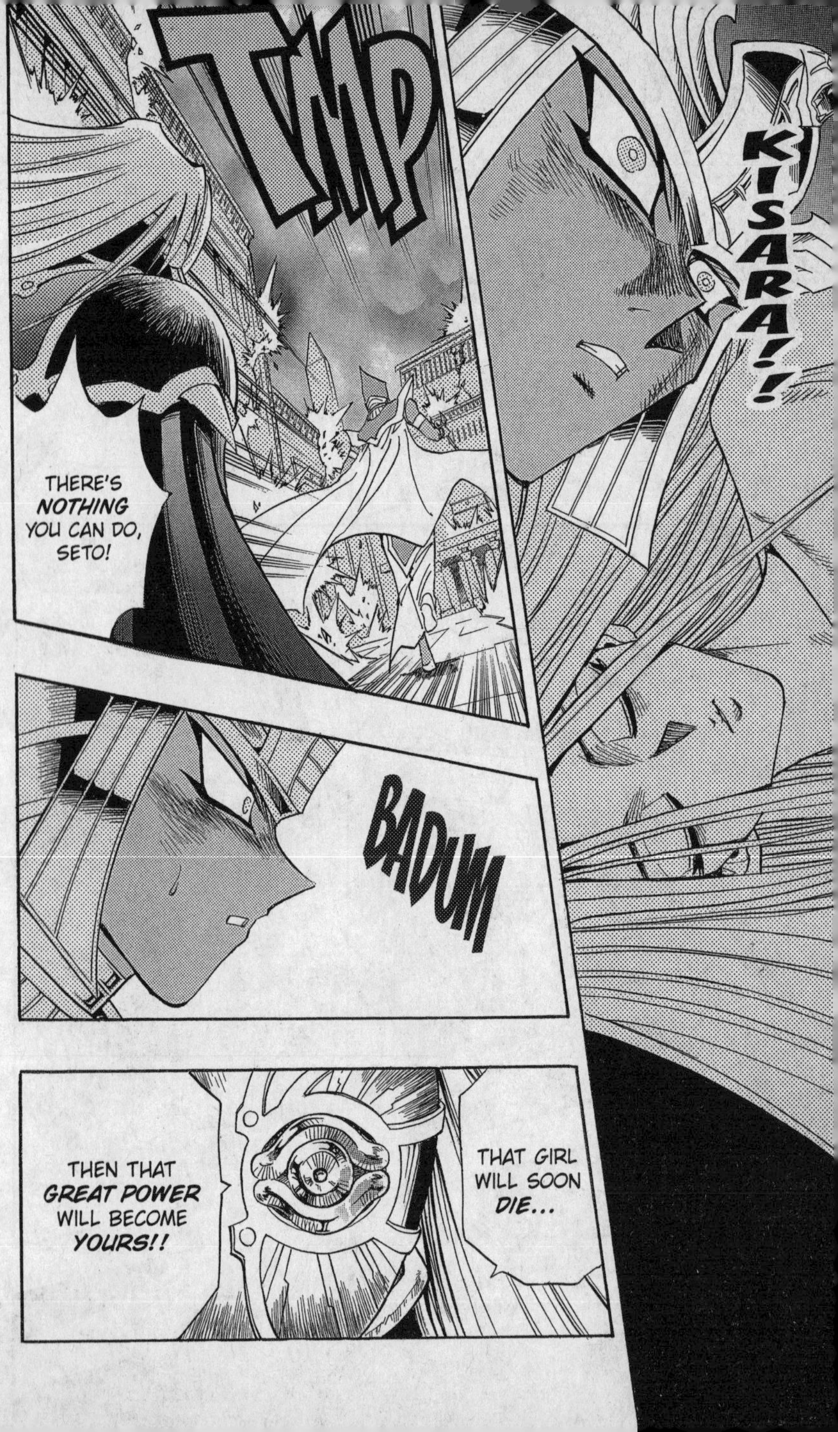
KISARA!!
TMP
THERE'S NOTHING YOU CAN DO, SETO!
BADUM
THAT GIRL WILL SOON DIE...
THEN THAT GREAT POWER WILL BECOME YOURS!!

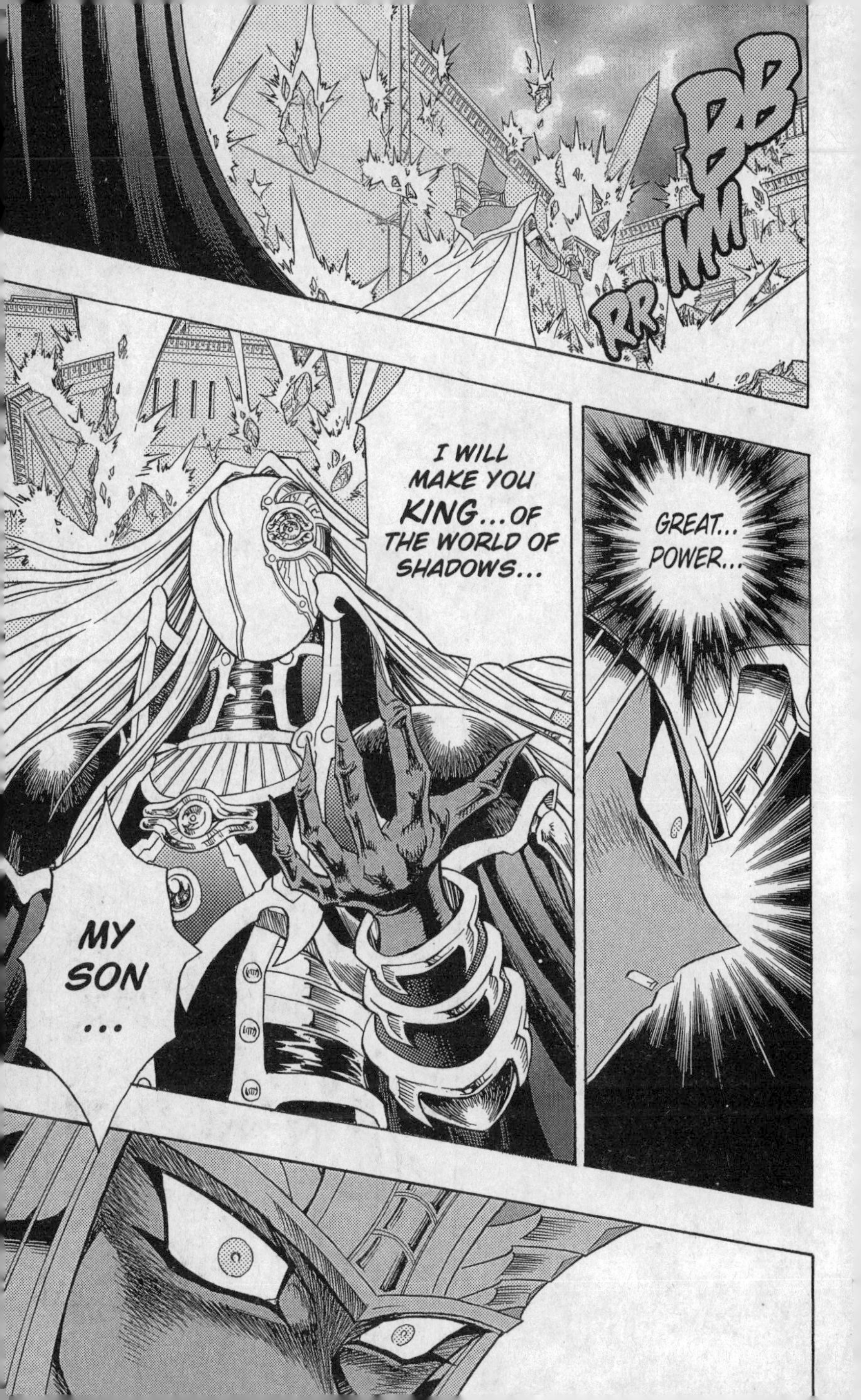
RRMMBB
GREAT... POWER...
I WILL MAKE YOU KING...OF THE WORLD OF SHADOWS...
MY SON ...

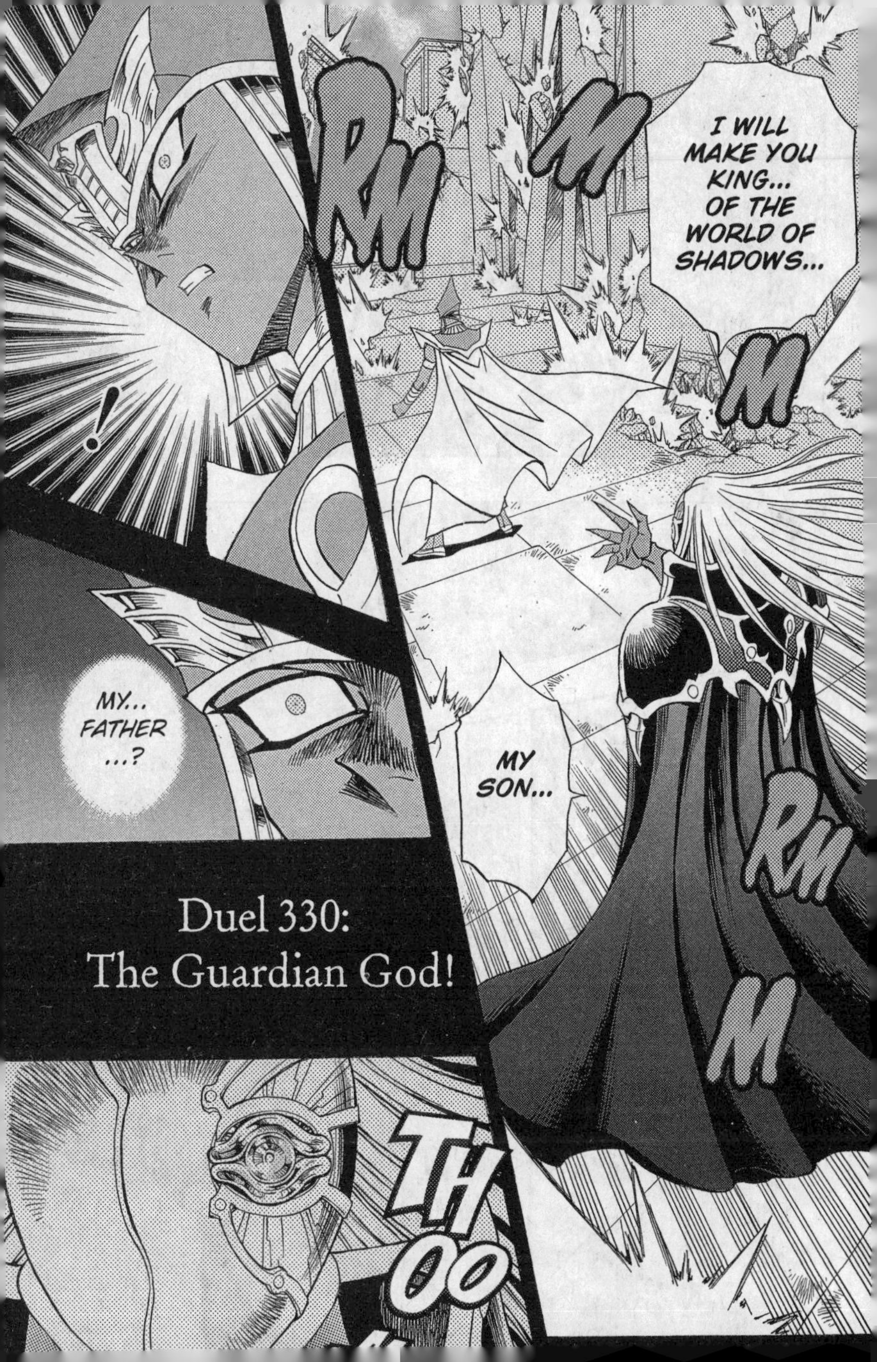

RMMM
I WILL MAKE YOU KING... OF THE WORLD OF SHADOWS...
MY SON...
RMM
THOO
!
MY... FATHER ...?
Duel 330: The Guardian God!

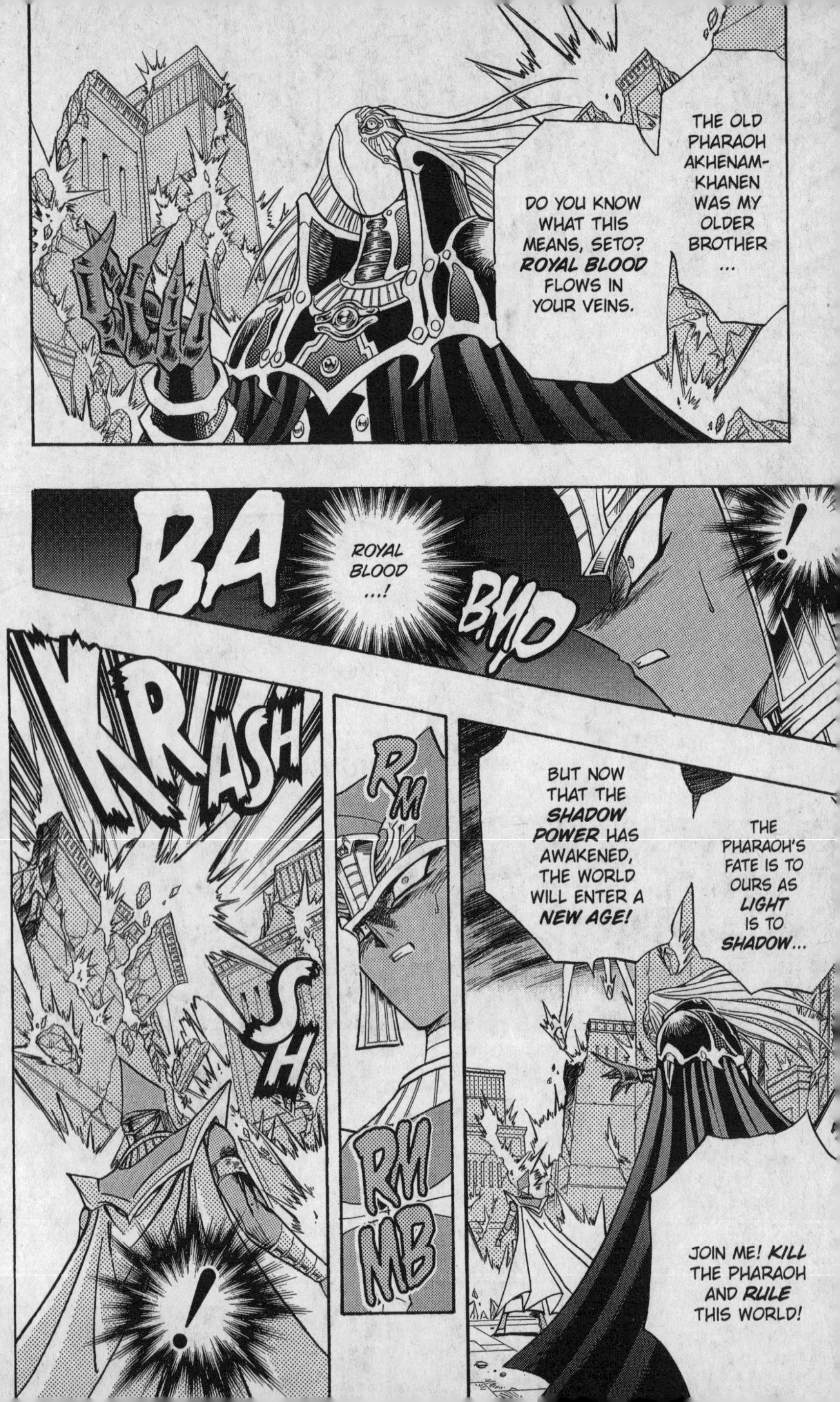
THE OLD PHARAOH AKHENAMKHANEN WAS MY OLDER BROTHER ...
DO YOU KNOW WHAT THIS MEANS, SETO? ROYAL BLOOD FLOWS IN YOUR VEINS.
!
BA
ROYAL BLOOD ...!
THE PHARAOH'S FATE IS TO OURS AS LIGHT IS TO SHADOW...
BUT NOW THAT THE SHADOW POWER HAS AWAKENED, THE WORLD WILL ENTER A NEW AGE!
JOIN ME! KILL THE PHARAOH AND RULE THIS WORLD!
RM
RMMB
KRASH
!

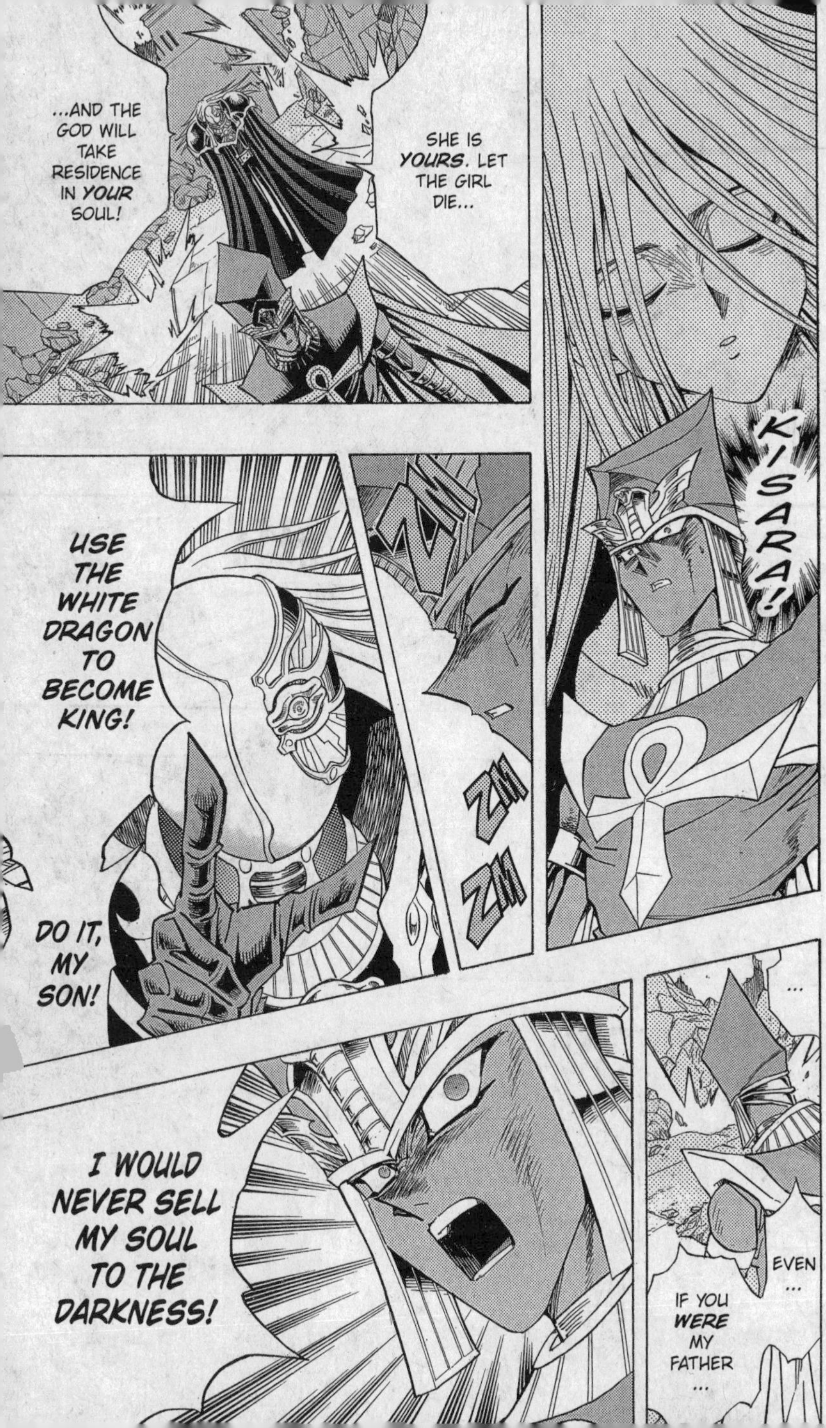
KISARA!
SHE IS YOURS. LET THE GIRL DIE...
...AND THE GOD WILL TAKE RESIDENCE IN YOUR SOUL!
ZM
ZM
ZM
USE THE WHITE DRAGON TO BECOME KING!
DO IT, MY SON!
...
EVEN...
IF YOU WERE MY FATHER...
I WOULD NEVER SELL MY SOUL TO THE DARKNESS!

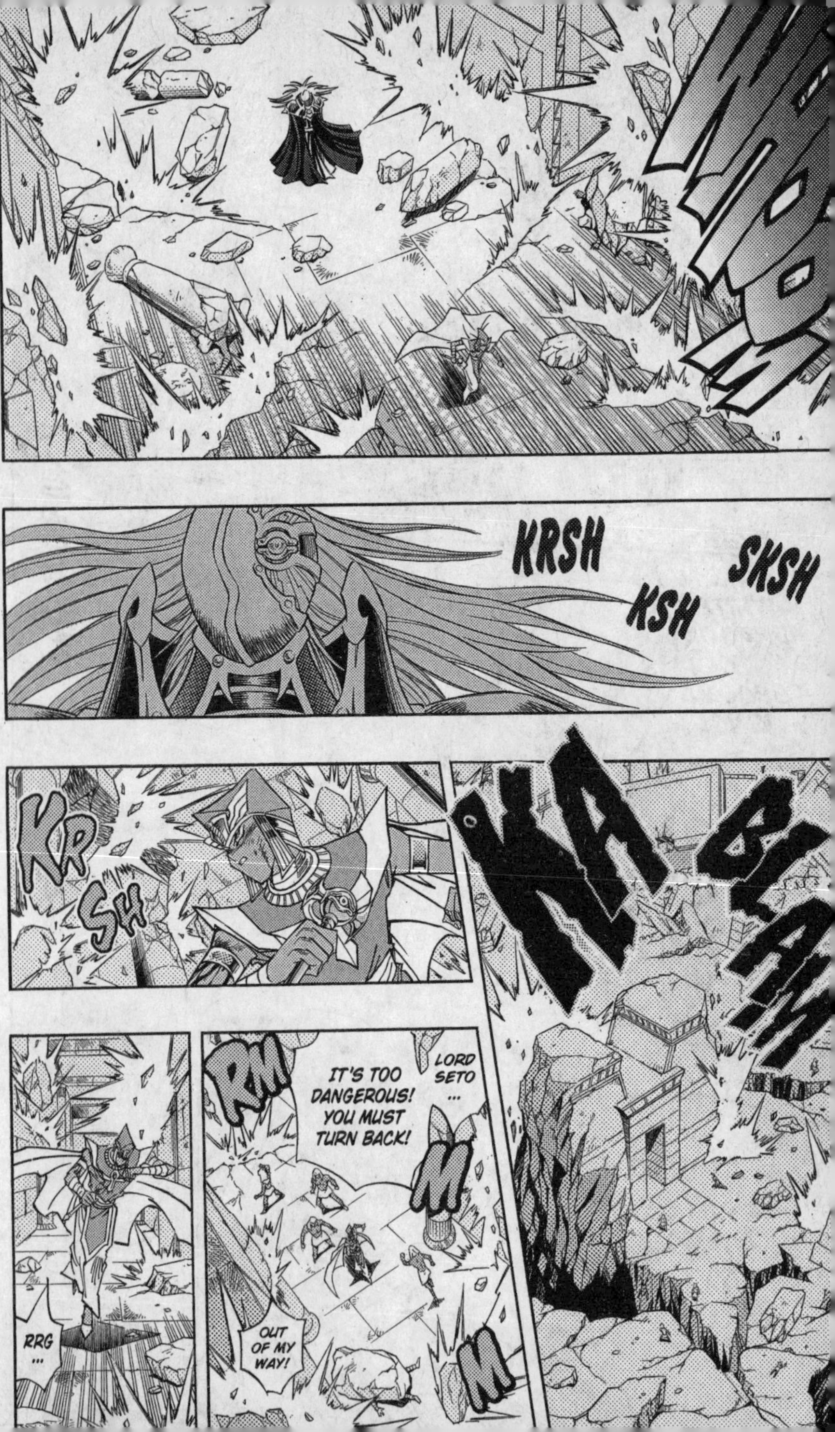
SKSH
KRSH
KSH
KA-BLAM
KRSH
LORD SETO...
IT'S TOO DANGEROUS! YOU MUST TURN BACK!
RM
M
OUT OF MY WAY!
M
RRG...

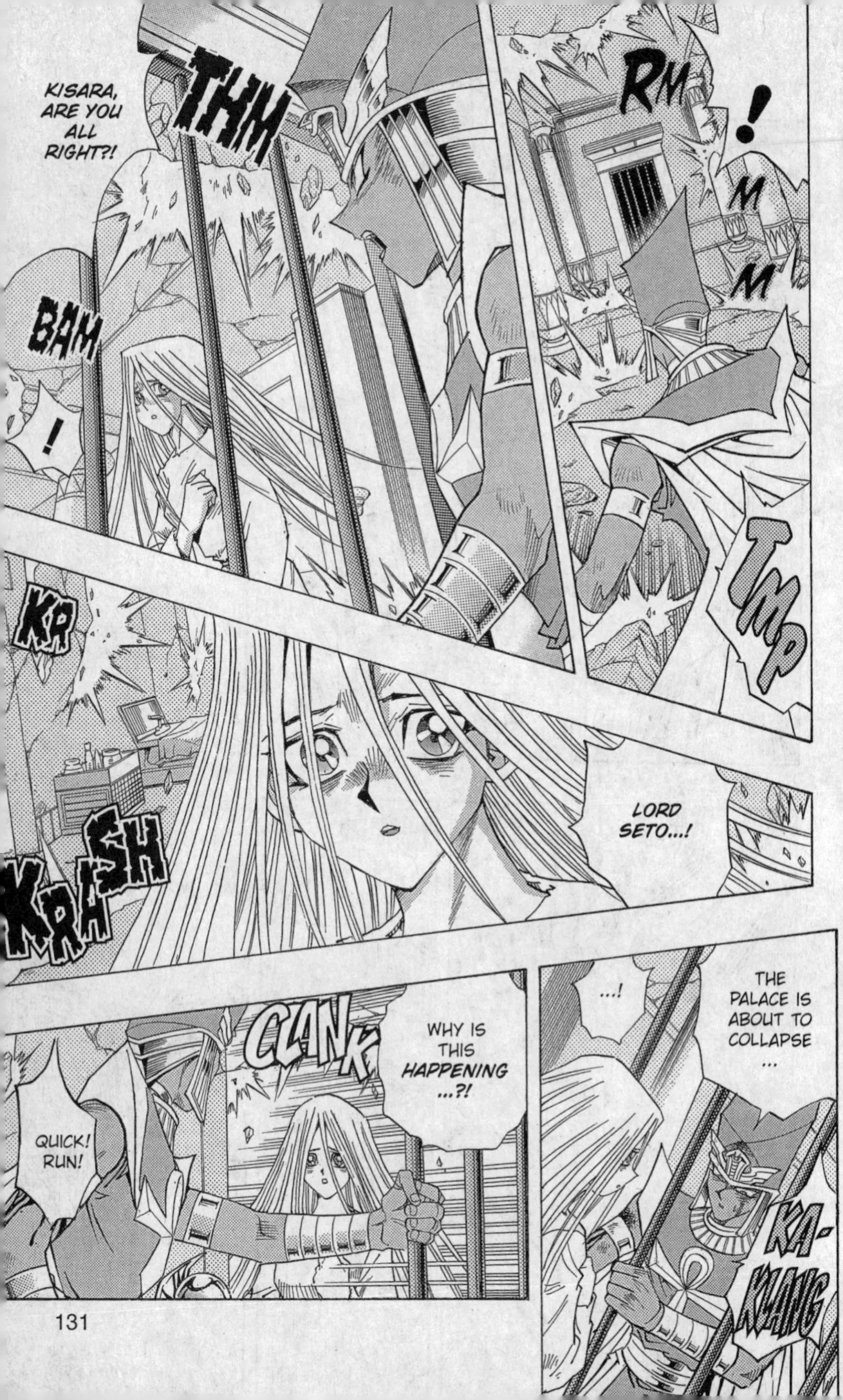

RMMM
!
TMP
KISARA, ARE YOU ALL RIGHT?!
THM
BAM
!
KR
LORD SETO...!
KRASH
...!
THE PALACE IS ABOUT TO COLLAPSE ...
KA-KLANG
WHY IS THIS HAPPENING ...?!
CLANK
QUICK! RUN!

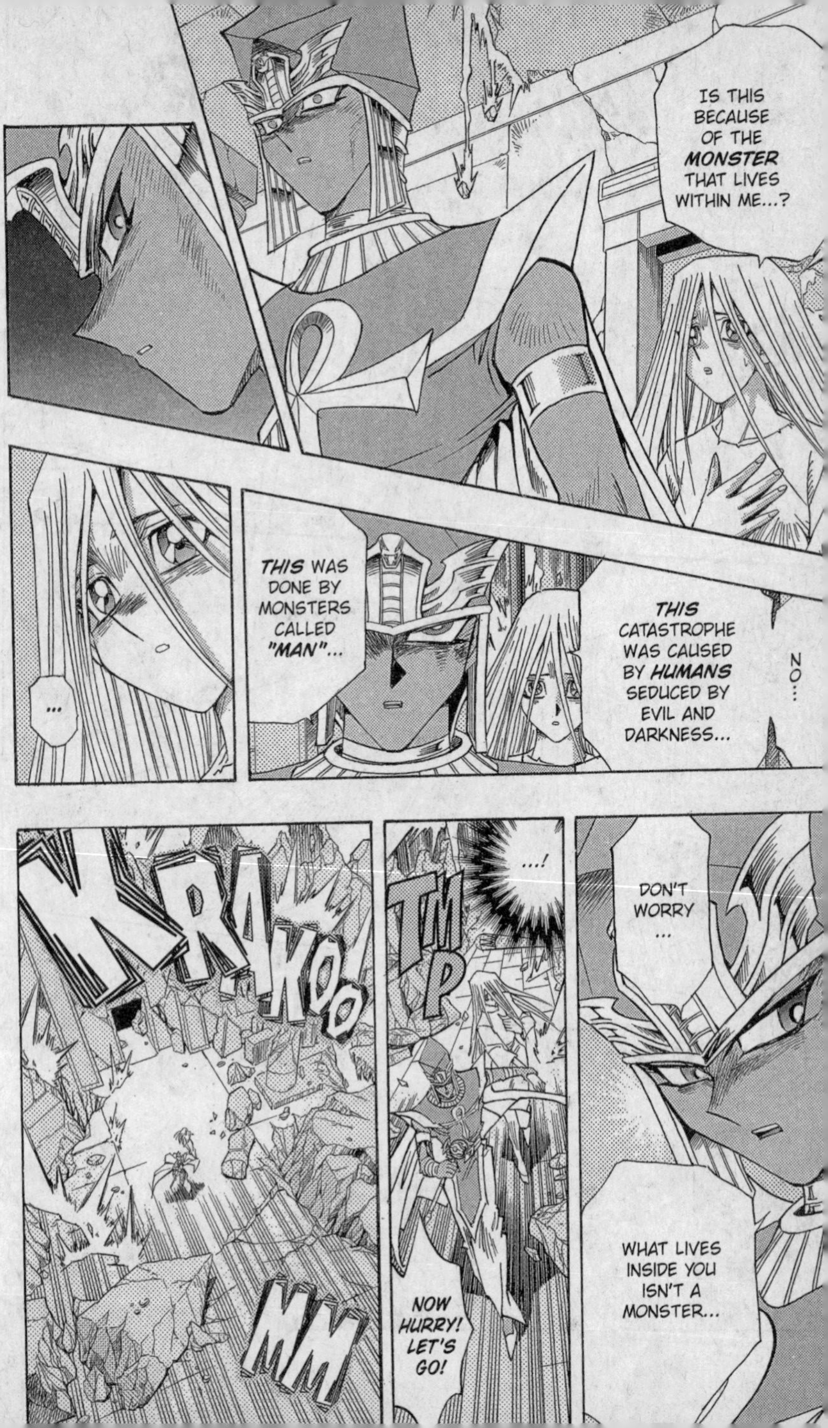

IS THIS BECAUSE OF THE ***MONSTER*** THAT LIVES WITHIN ME...?
NO...
THIS CATASTROPHE WAS CAUSED BY ***HUMANS*** SEDUCED BY EVIL AND DARKNESS...
THIS WAS DONE BY MONSTERS CALLED ***"MAN"***...
...
DON'T WORRY...
WHAT LIVES INSIDE YOU ISN'T A MONSTER...
...!
TMP
NOW HURRY! LET'S GO!
KRAKOOMM

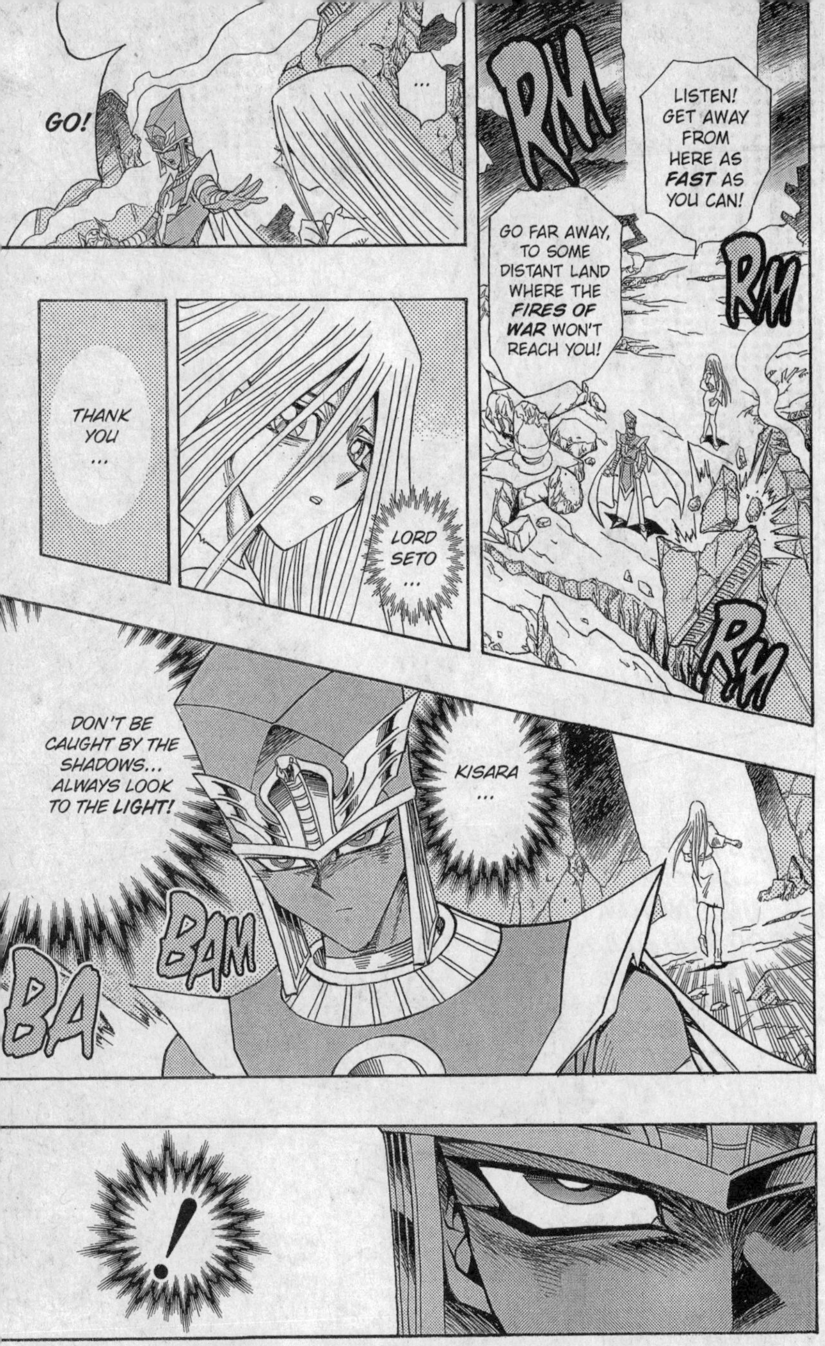

RM
LISTEN! GET AWAY FROM HERE AS FAST AS YOU CAN!
GO FAR AWAY, TO SOME DISTANT LAND WHERE THE FIRES OF WAR WON'T REACH YOU!
RM
RM
...
GO!
LORD SETO ...
THANK YOU ...
KISARA ...
DON'T BE CAUGHT BY THE SHADOWS... ALWAYS LOOK TO THE LIGHT!
BAM
BA
!

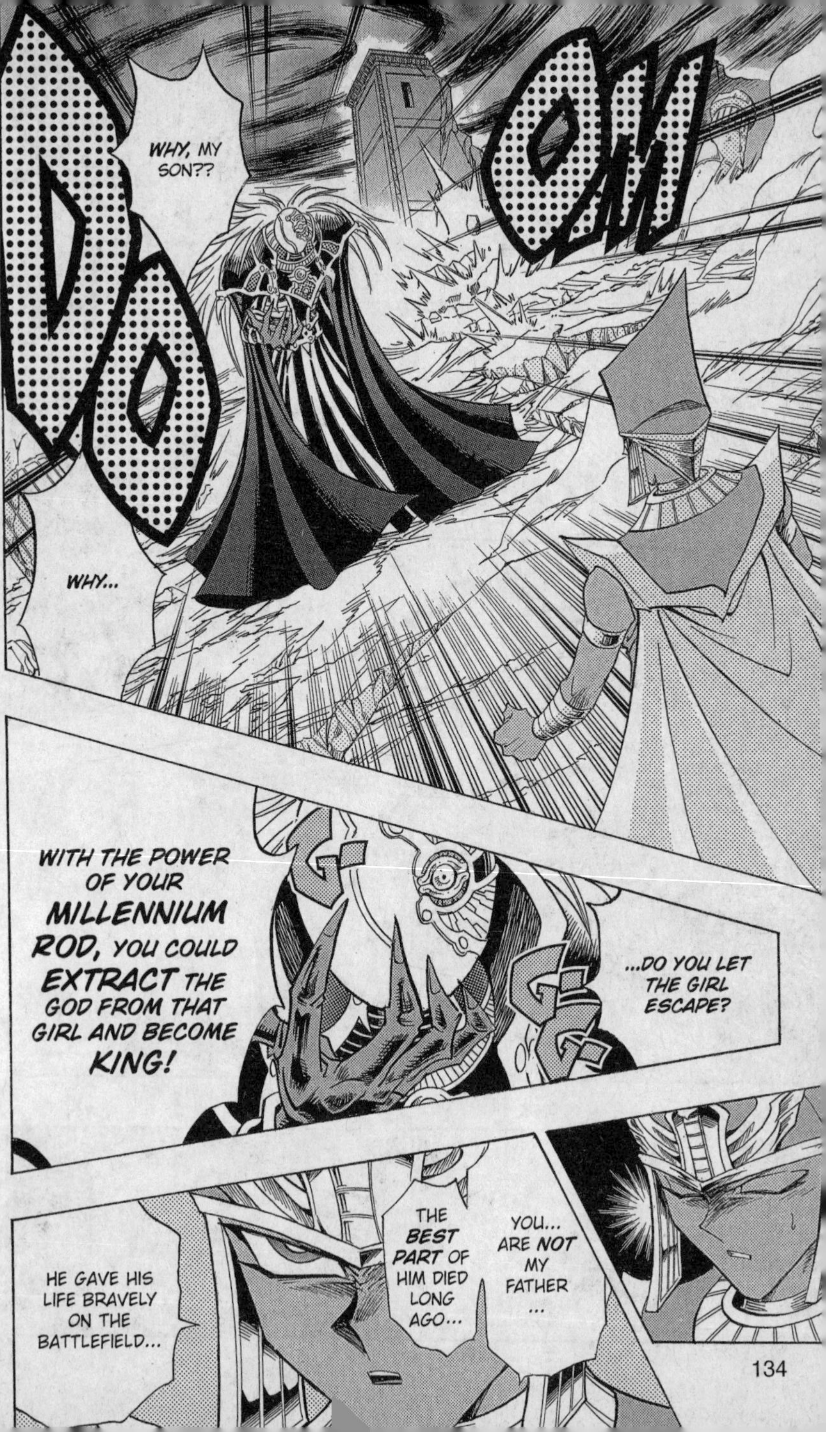
WHY, MY SON??
WHY...
...DO YOU LET THE GIRL ESCAPE?
WITH THE POWER OF YOUR MILLENNIUM ROD, YOU COULD EXTRACT THE GOD FROM THAT GIRL AND BECOME KING!
YOU... ARE NOT MY FATHER ...
THE BEST PART OF HIM DIED LONG AGO...
HE GAVE HIS LIFE BRAVELY ON THE BATTLEFIELD...

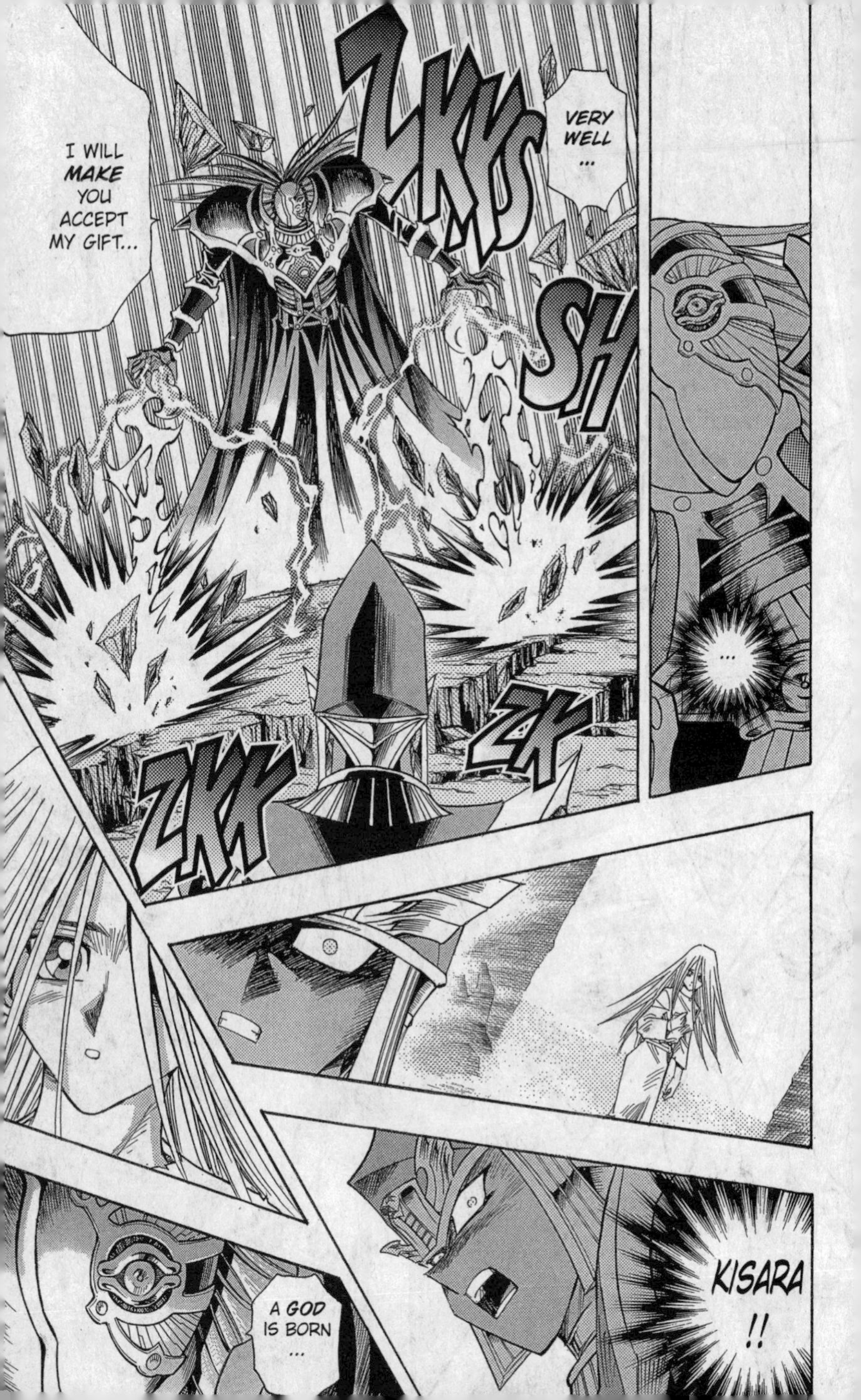
...
VERY WELL ...
ZKYS
SH
I WILL MAKE YOU ACCEPT MY GIFT...
ZK
ZKK
KISARA !!
A GOD IS BORN ...

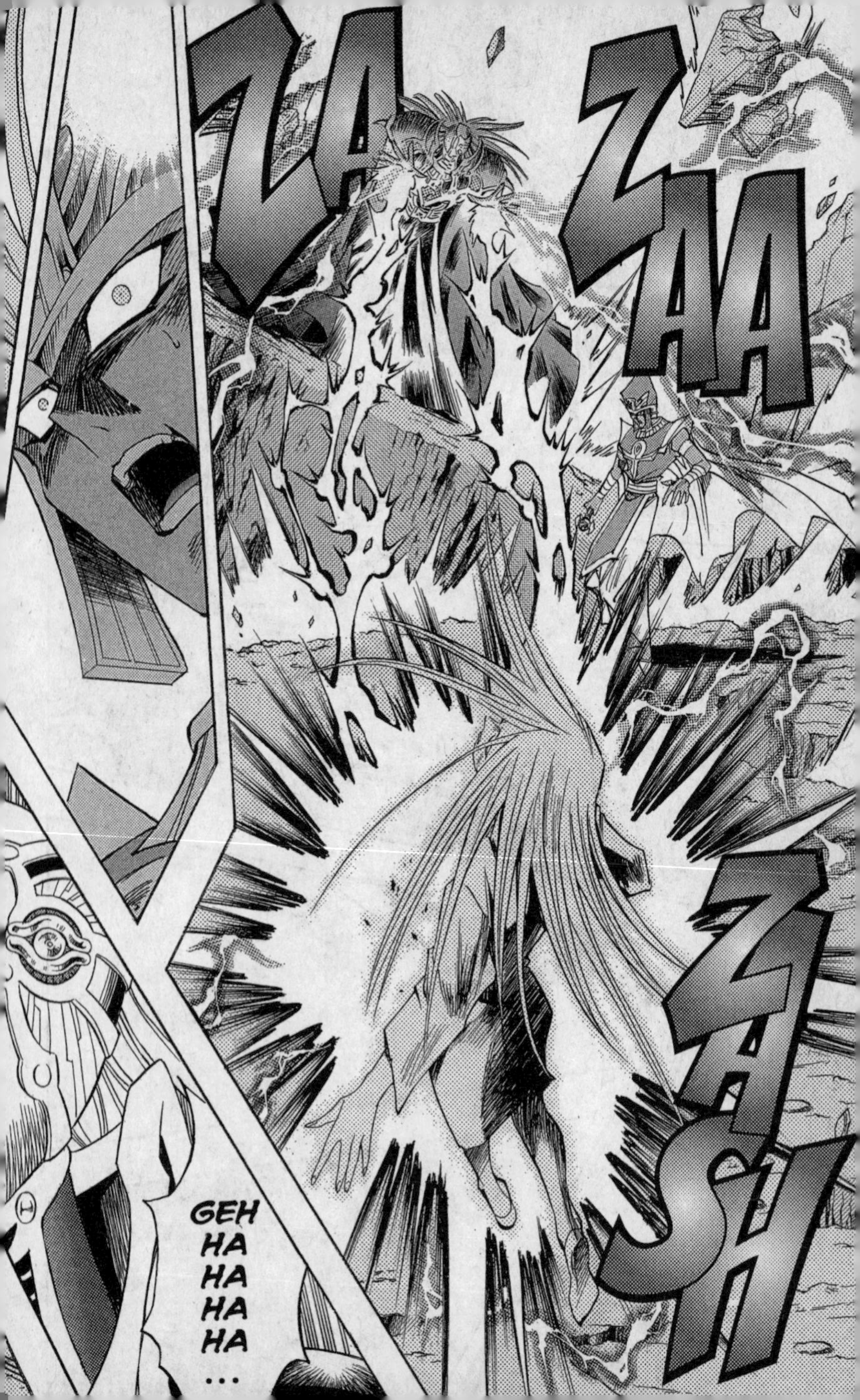
ZAA
ZA
ZASH
GEH HA HA HA HA ...

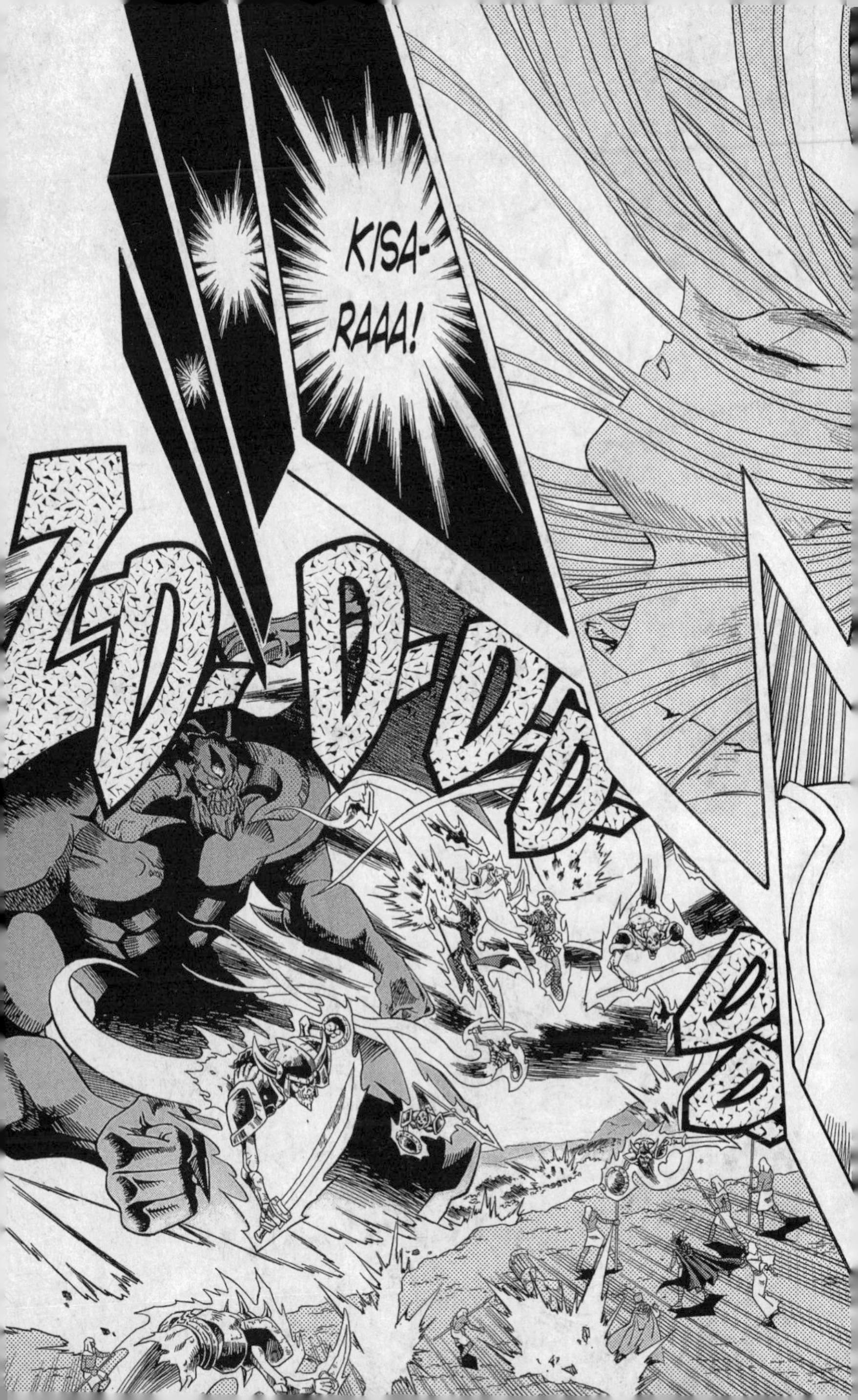
KISA-
RAAA!

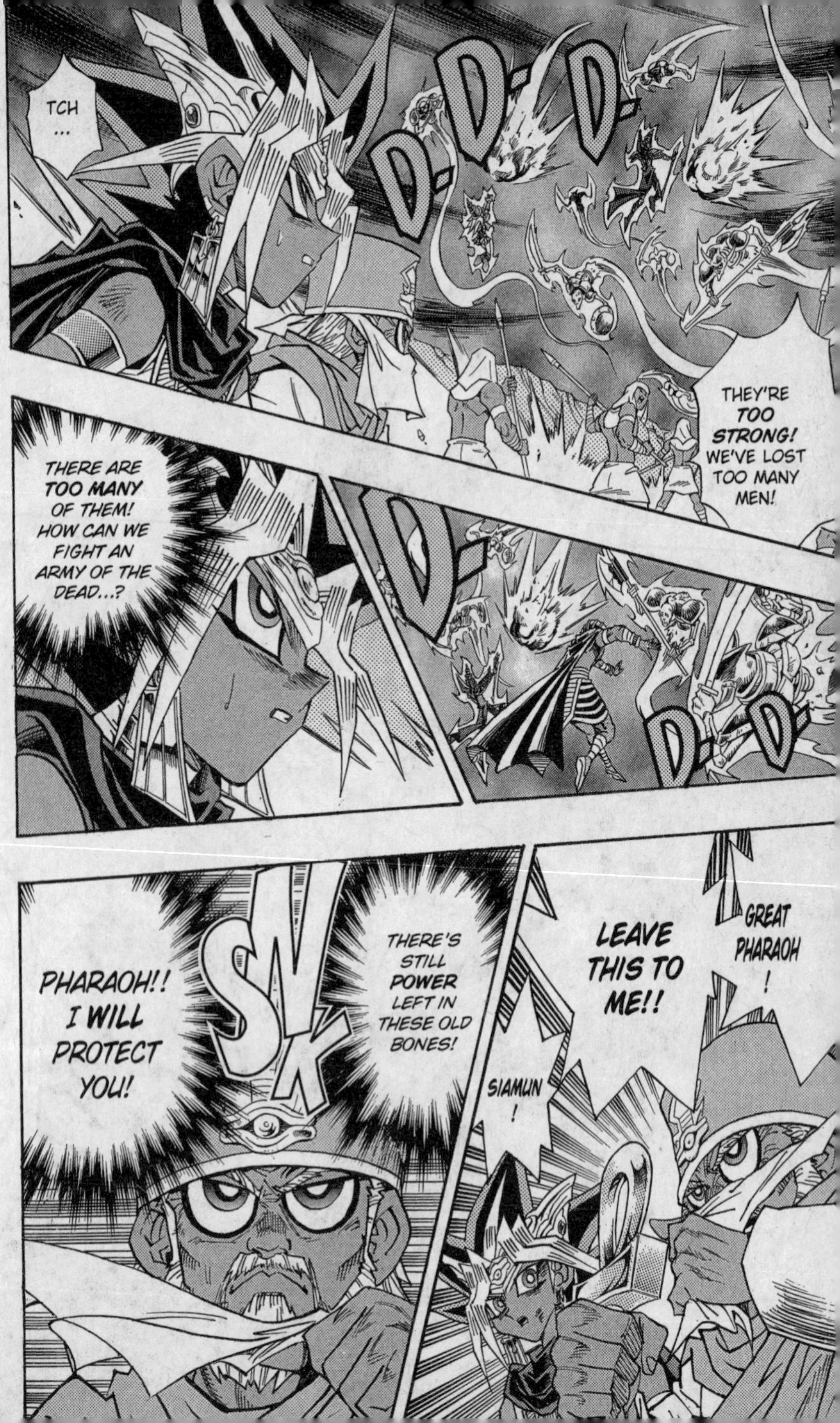
D-D-D-D
TCH ...
THEY'RE TOO STRONG! WE'VE LOST TOO MANY MEN!
D-
D-D-
THERE ARE TOO MANY OF THEM! HOW CAN WE FIGHT AN ARMY OF THE DEAD...?
GREAT PHARAOH!
LEAVE THIS TO ME!!
SIAMUN!
THERE'S STILL POWER LEFT IN THESE OLD BONES!
SK
PHARAOH!! I WILL PROTECT YOU!

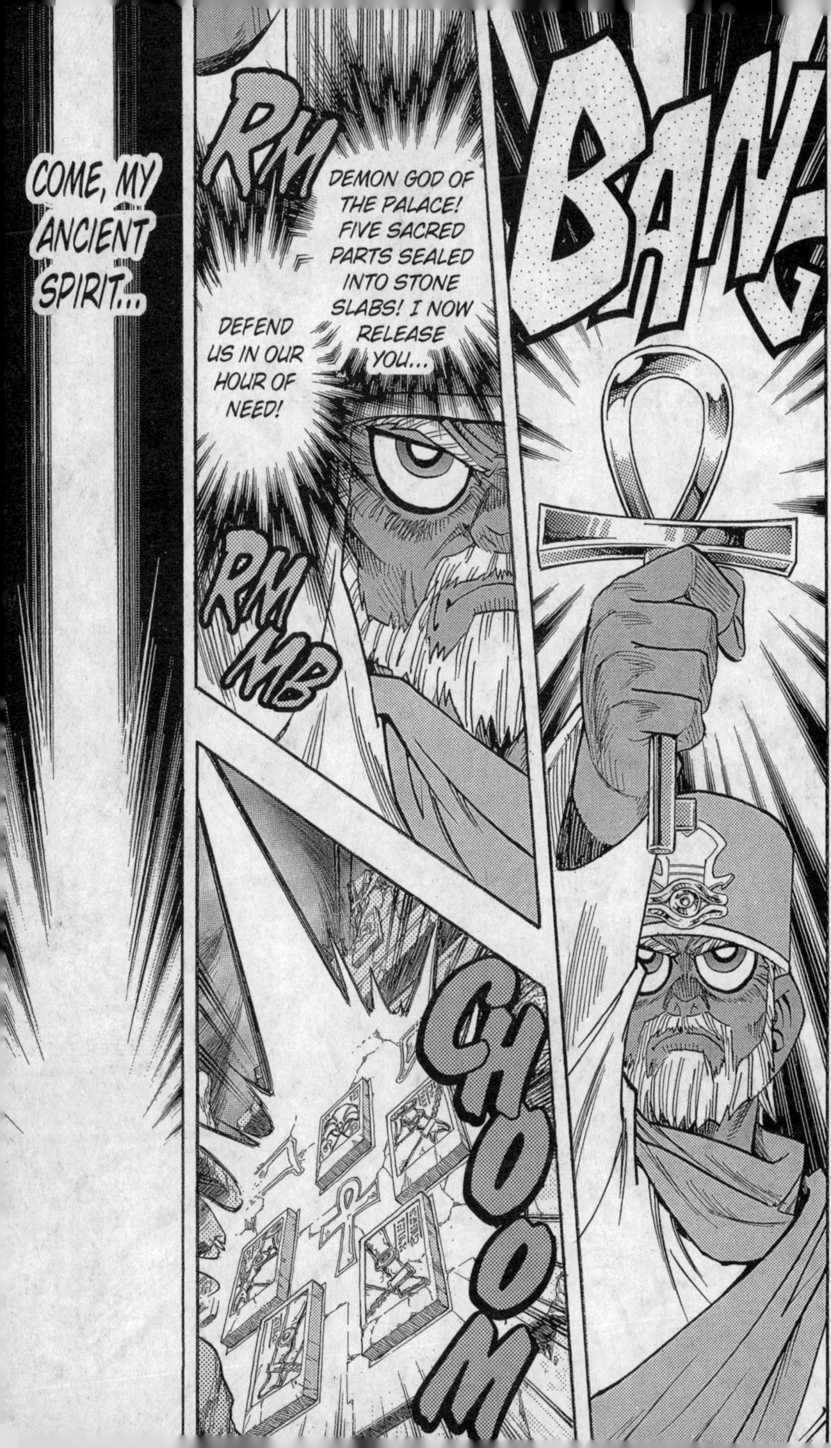
BANG
RM
DEMON GOD OF THE PALACE! FIVE SACRED PARTS SEALED INTO STONE SLABS! I NOW RELEASE YOU...
DEFEND US IN OUR HOUR OF NEED!
RMMB
CHOOM
COME, MY ANCIENT SPIRIT...

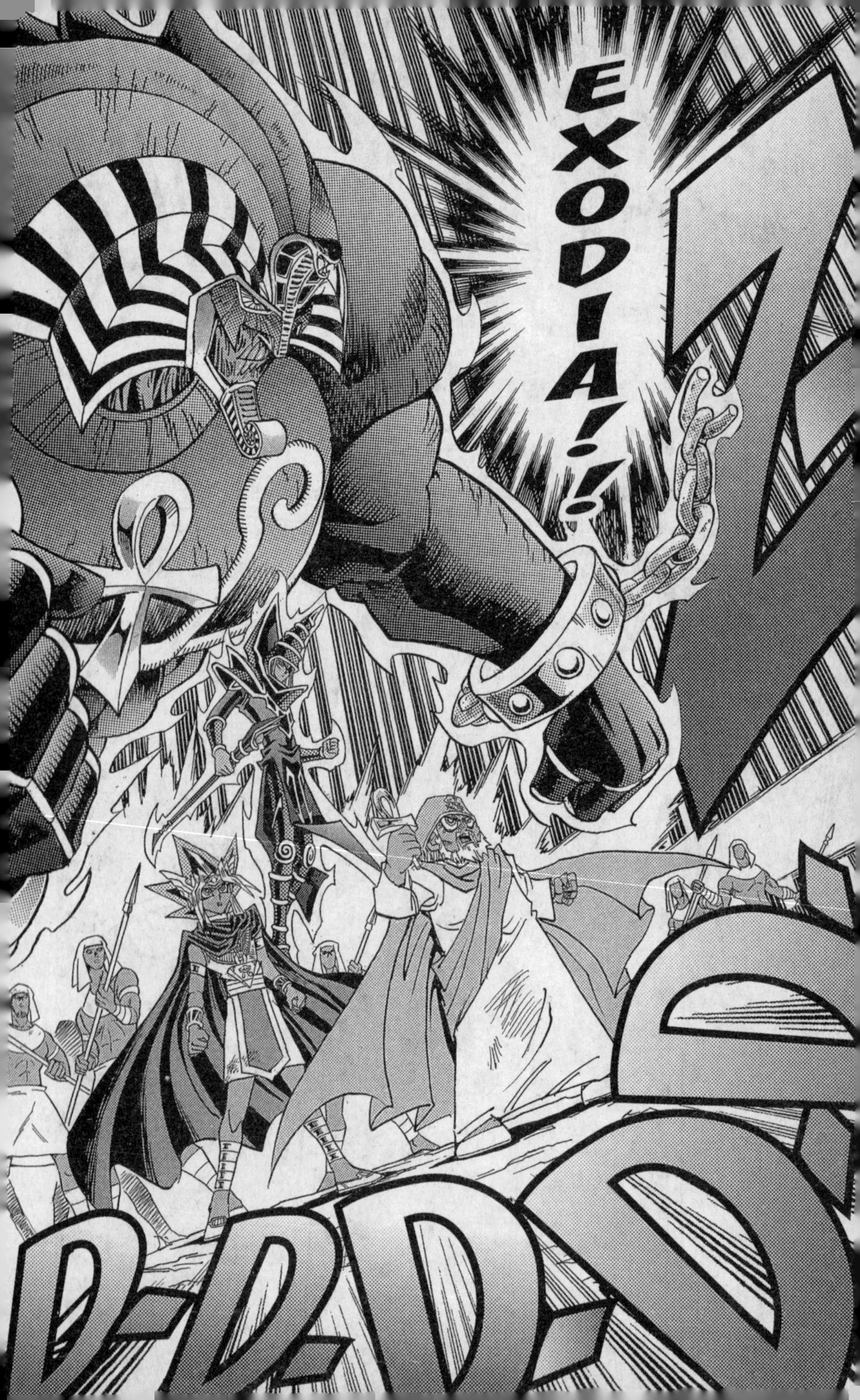
EXODIA!!

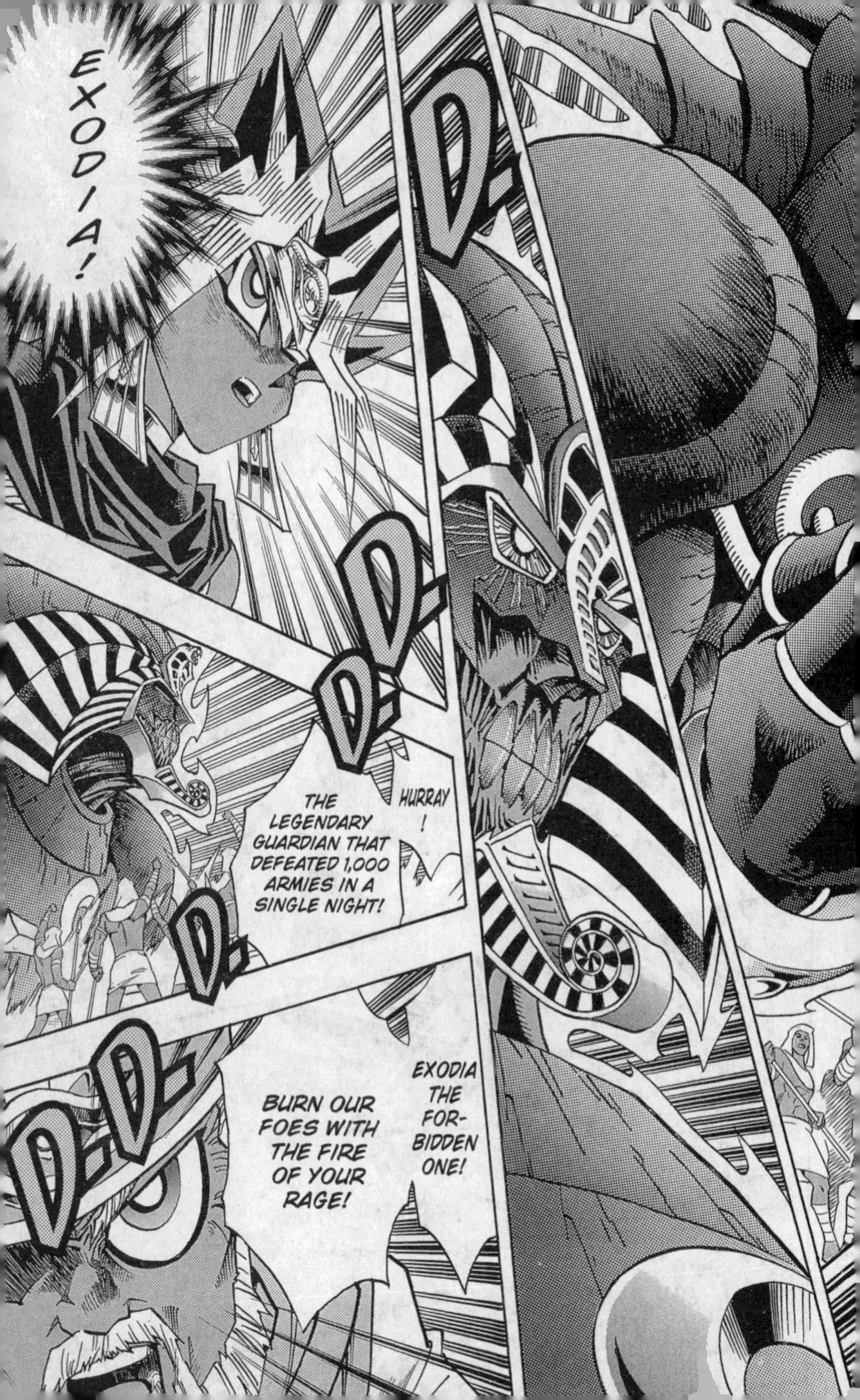
EXODIA!
HURRAY!
THE LEGENDARY GUARDIAN THAT DEFEATED 1,000 ARMIES IN A SINGLE NIGHT!
EXODIA THE FOR-BIDDEN ONE!
BURN OUR FOES WITH THE FIRE OF YOUR RAGE!

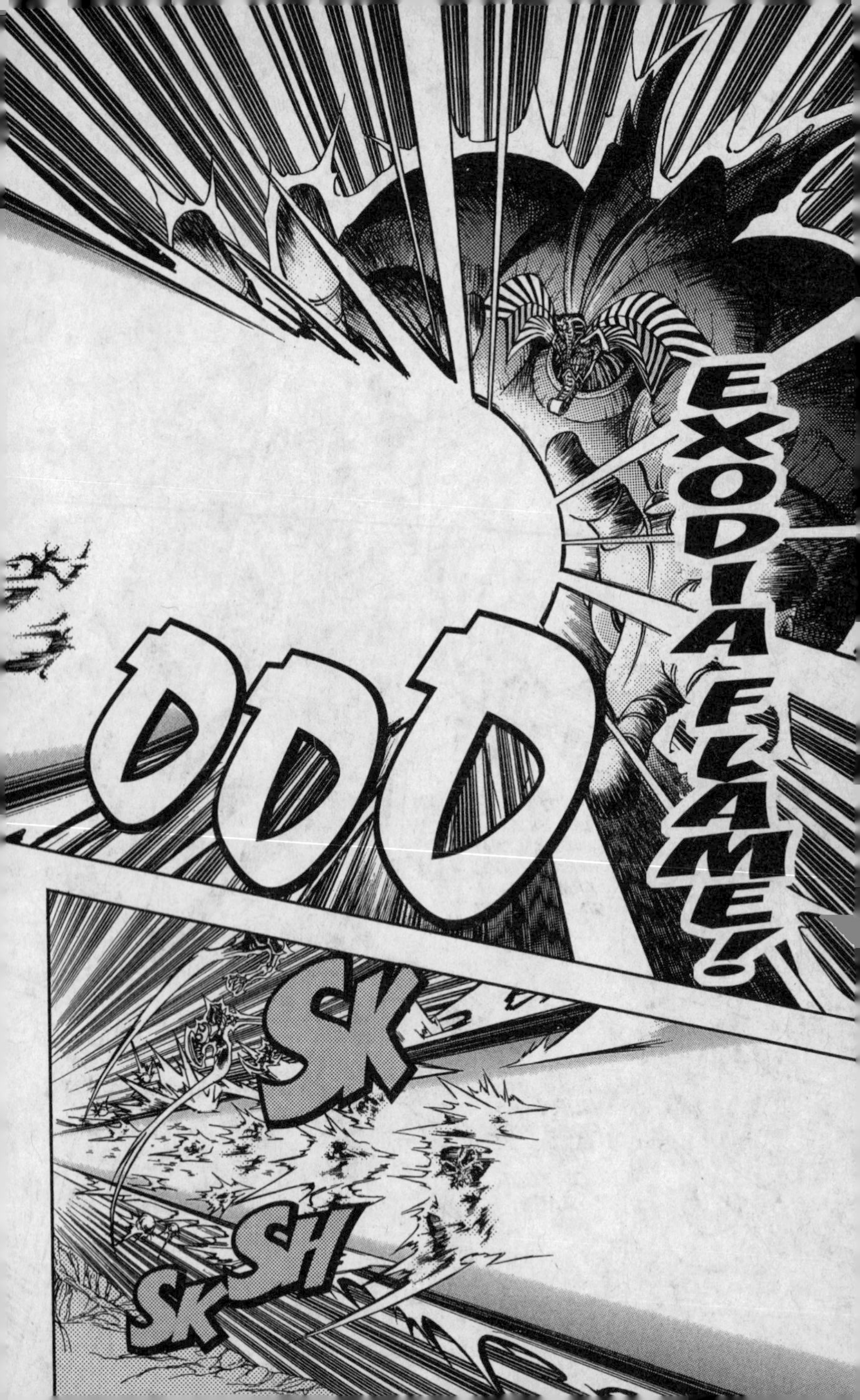

EXODIA AFLAME!
DDD
SK
SKSH

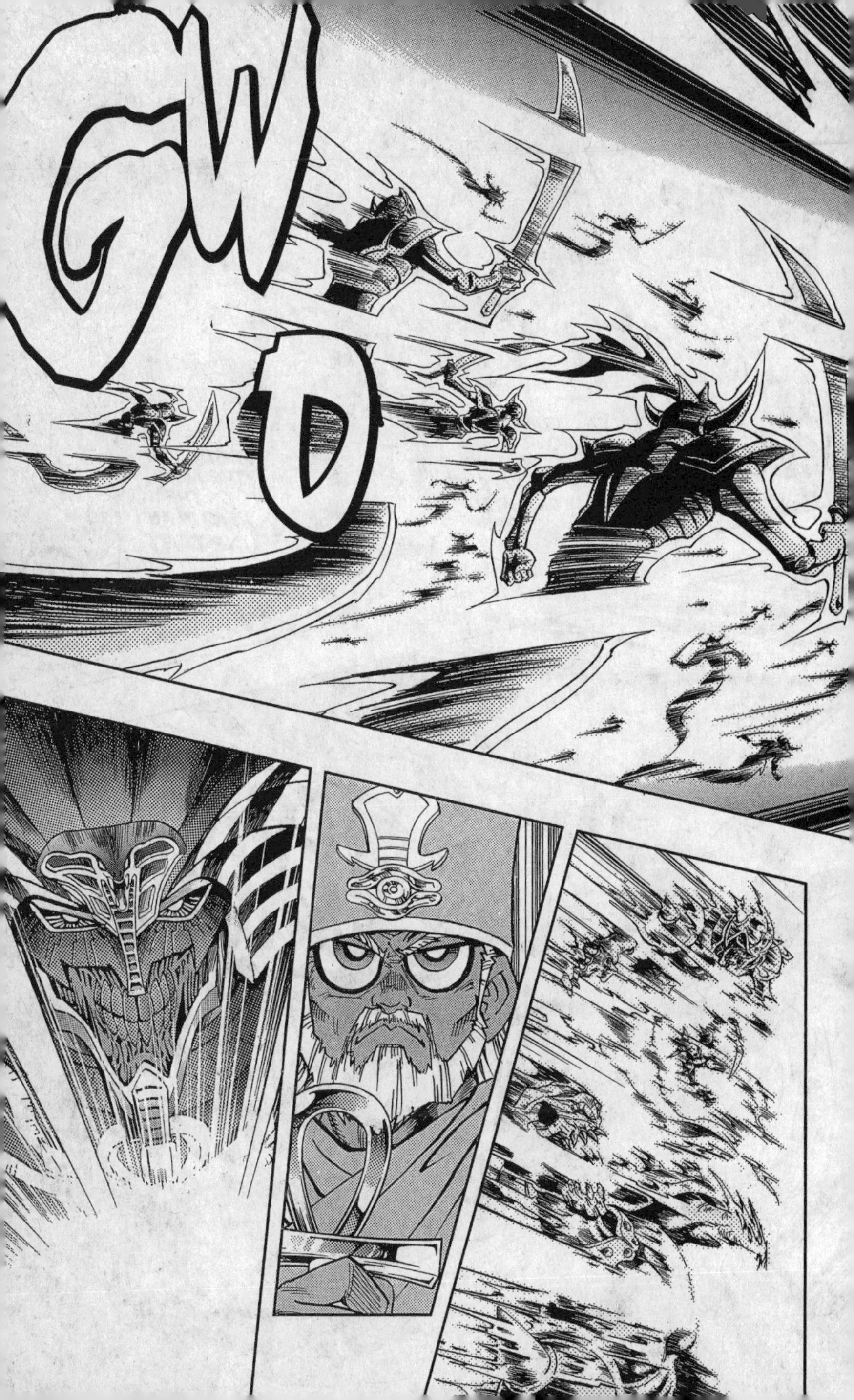
GWD

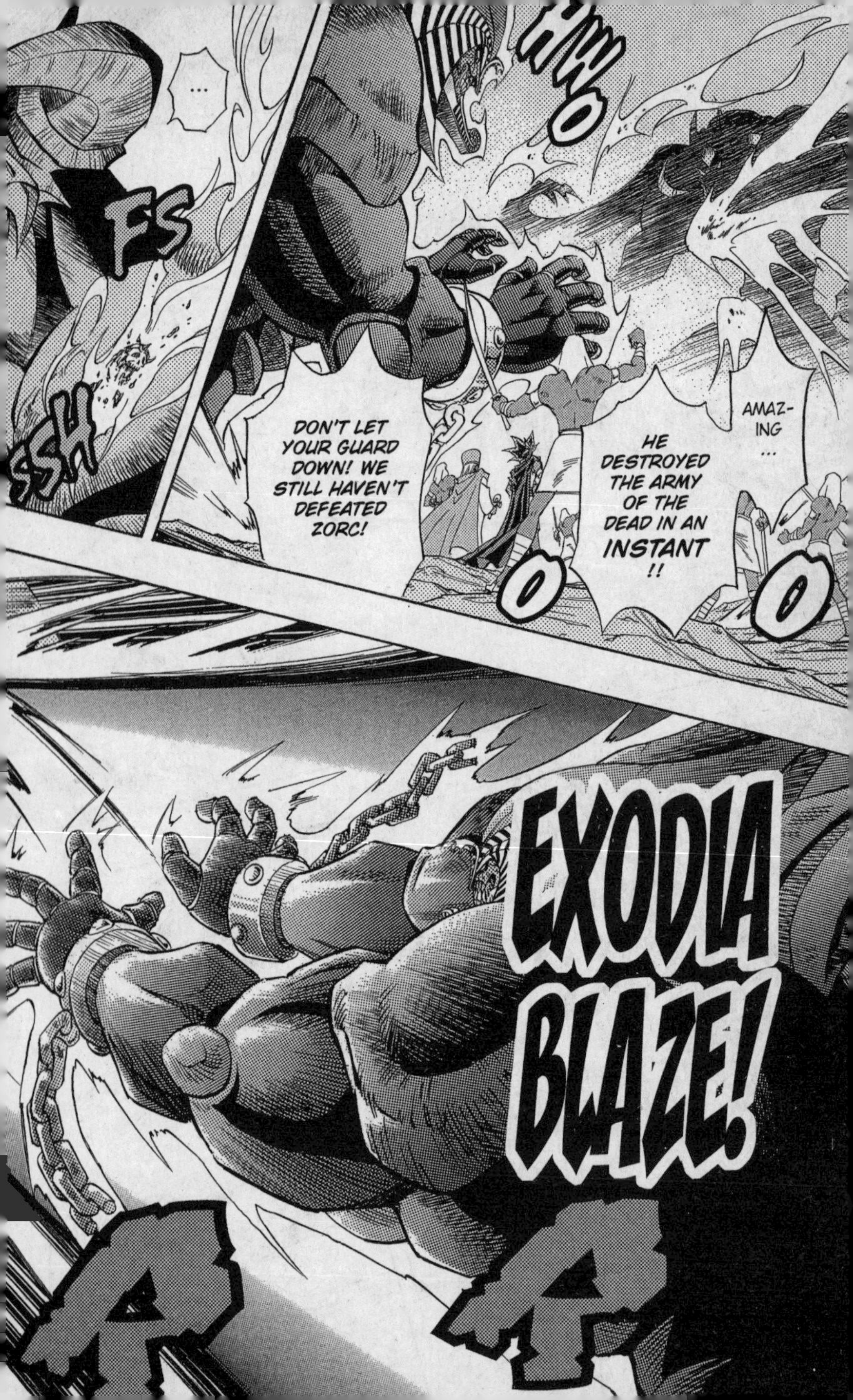
AMAZ-ING ...
HE DESTROYED THE ARMY OF THE DEAD IN AN INSTANT !!
O
DON'T LET YOUR GUARD DOWN! WE STILL HAVEN'T DEFEATED ZORC!
O
...
FS
SSH
EXODIA BLAZE!

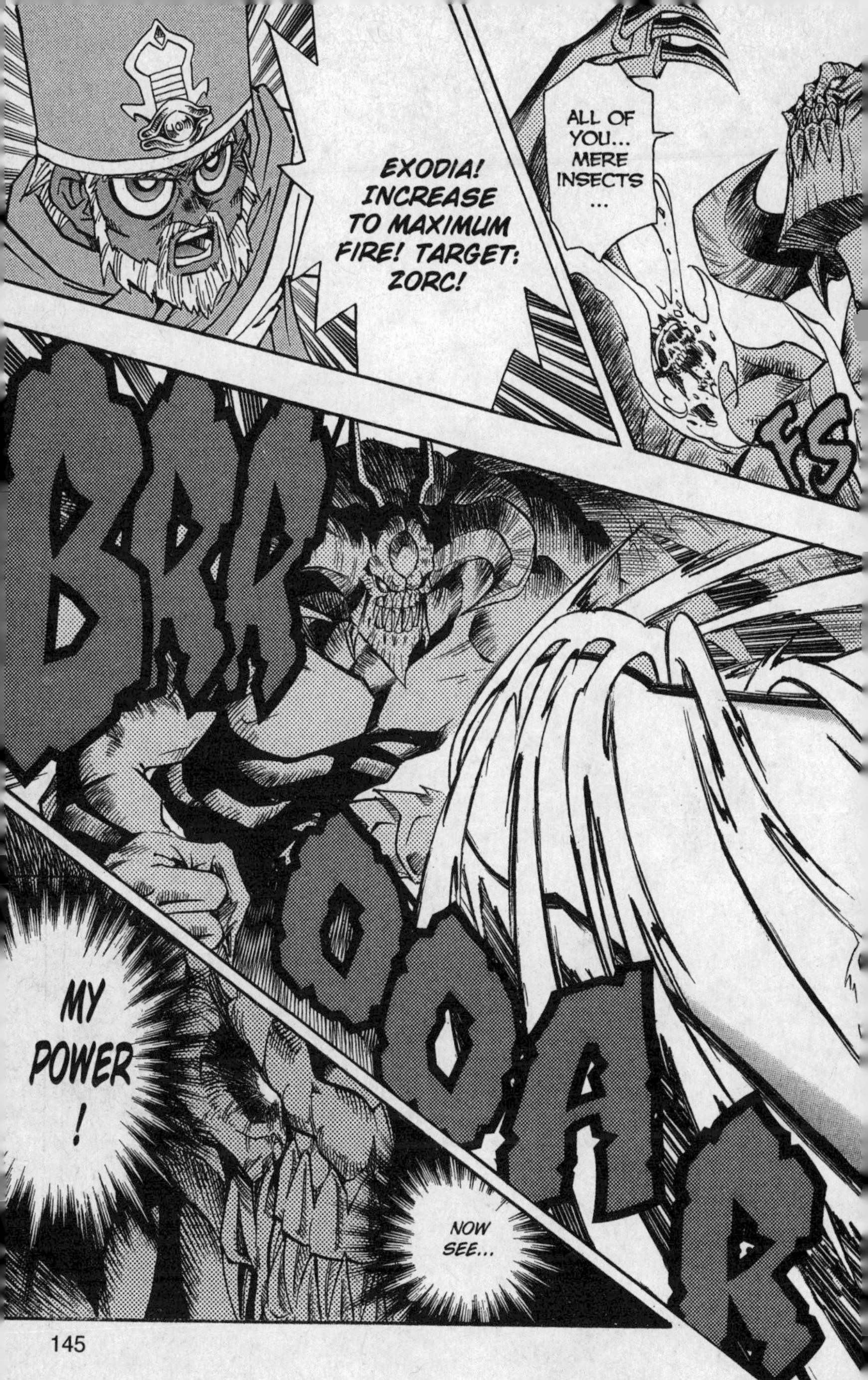
ALL OF YOU... MERE INSECTS ...
FS
EXODIA! INCREASE TO MAXIMUM FIRE! TARGET: ZORC!
BAAOOOAR
NOW SEE...
MY POWER !

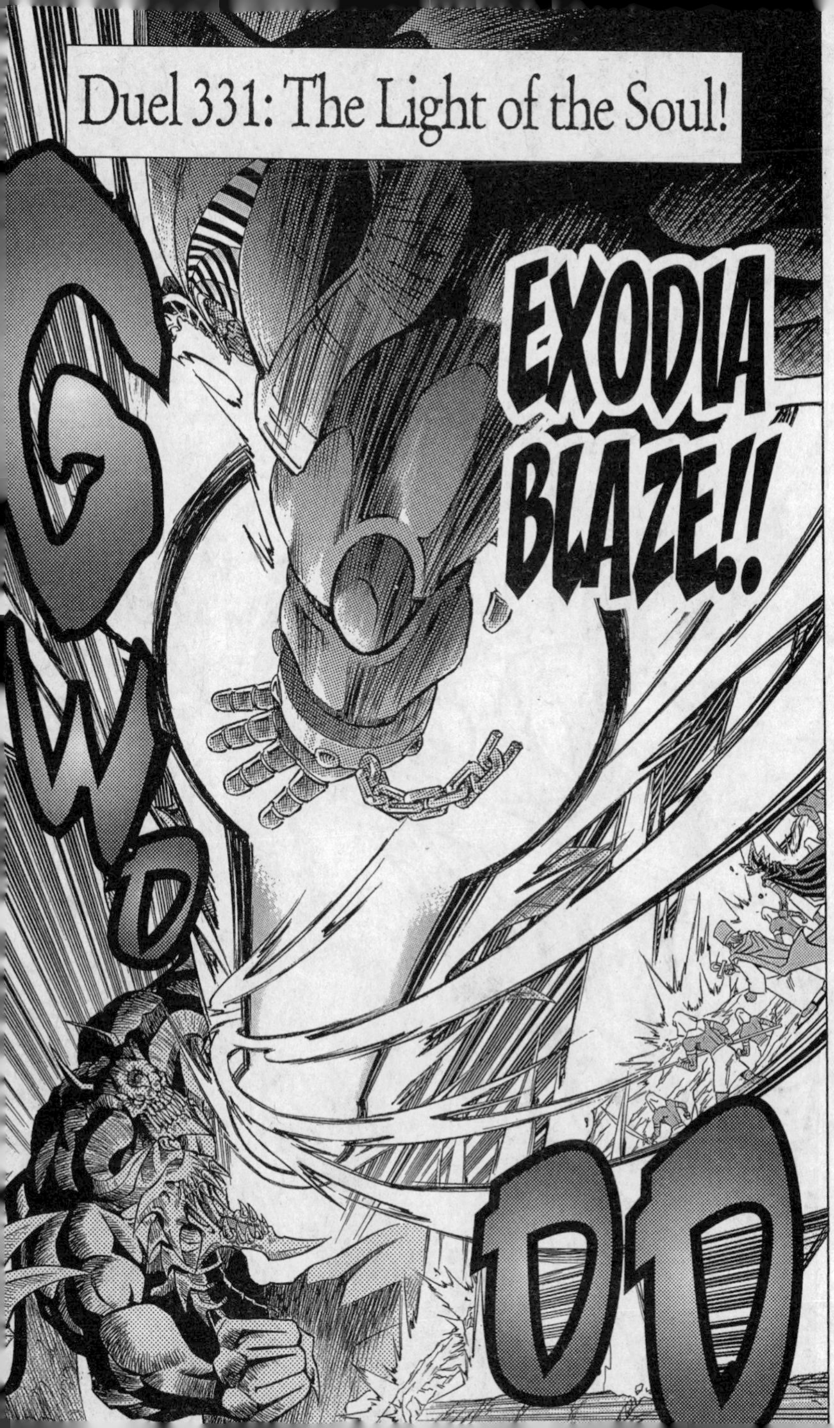
Duel 331: The Light of the Soul!
EXODIA BLAZE!!

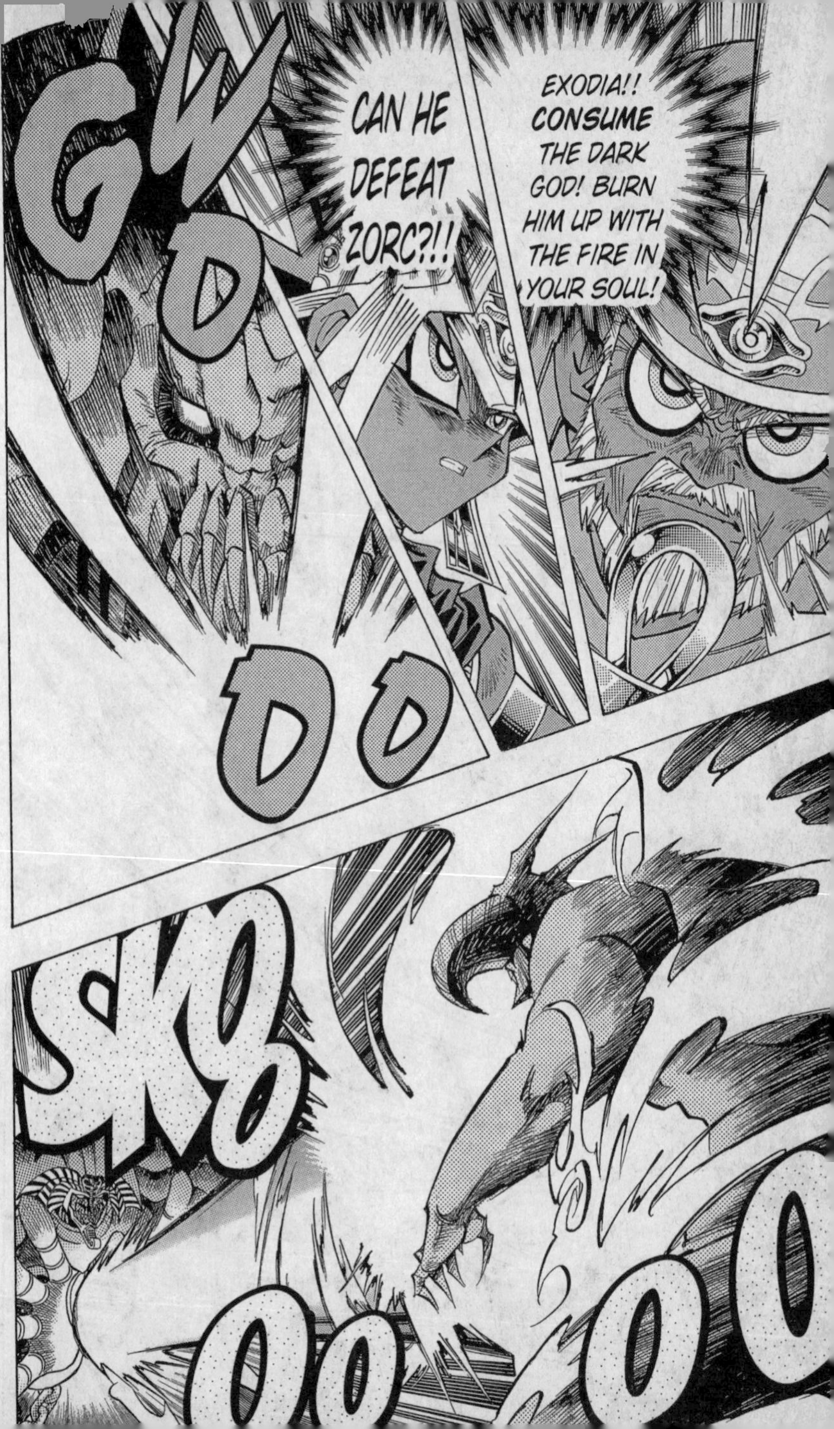
EXODIA!! CONSUME THE DARK GOD! BURN HIM UP WITH THE FIRE IN YOUR SOUL!
CAN HE DEFEAT ZORC?!!

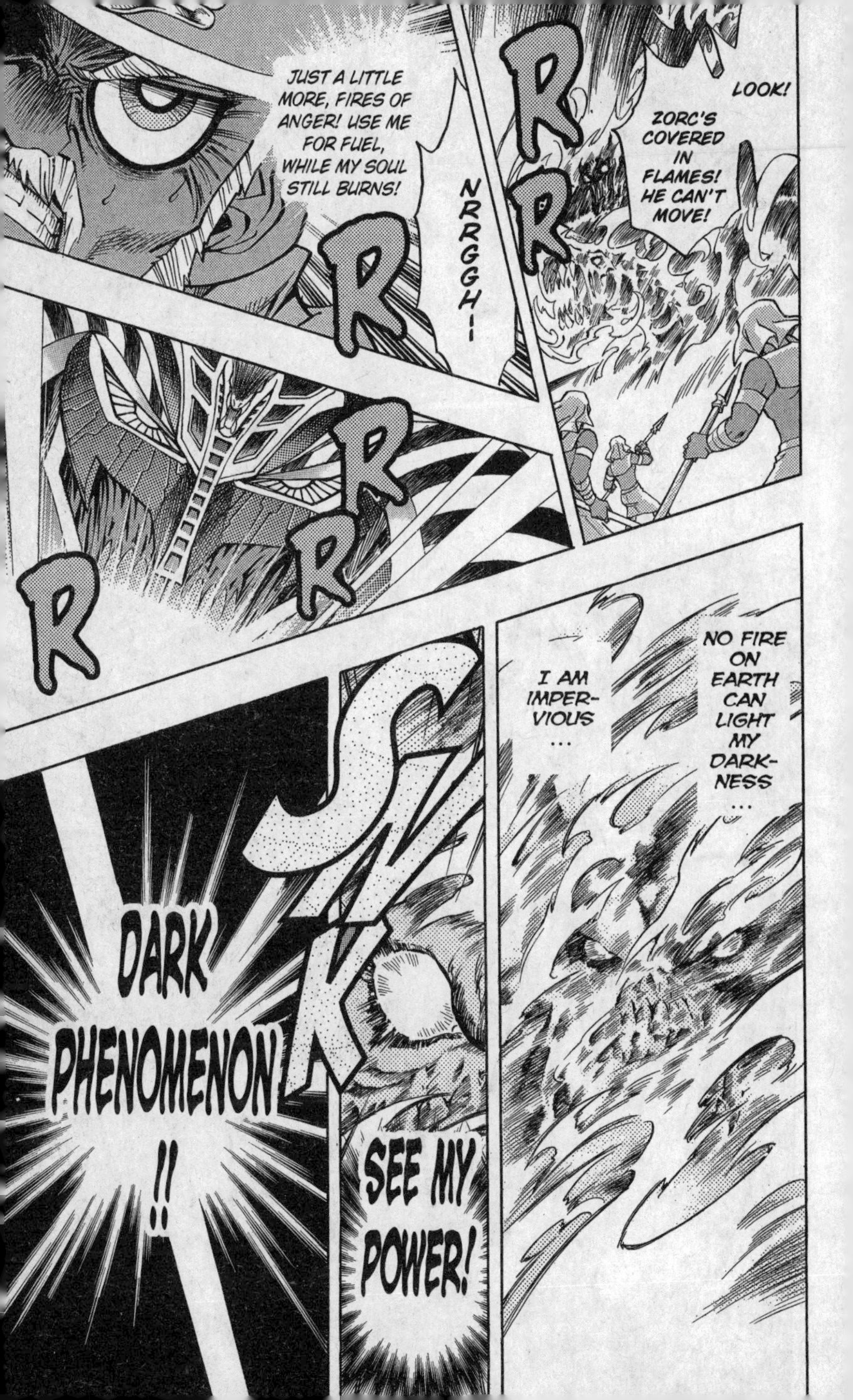
LOOK!
ZORC'S COVERED IN FLAMES! HE CAN'T MOVE!
R R
JUST A LITTLE MORE, FIRES OF ANGER! USE ME FOR FUEL, WHILE MY SOUL STILL BURNS!
NRRGGH!
R
R R R
NO FIRE ON EARTH CAN LIGHT MY DARKNESS ...
I AM IMPERVIOUS ...
SK
SEE MY POWER!
DARK PHENOMENON!!

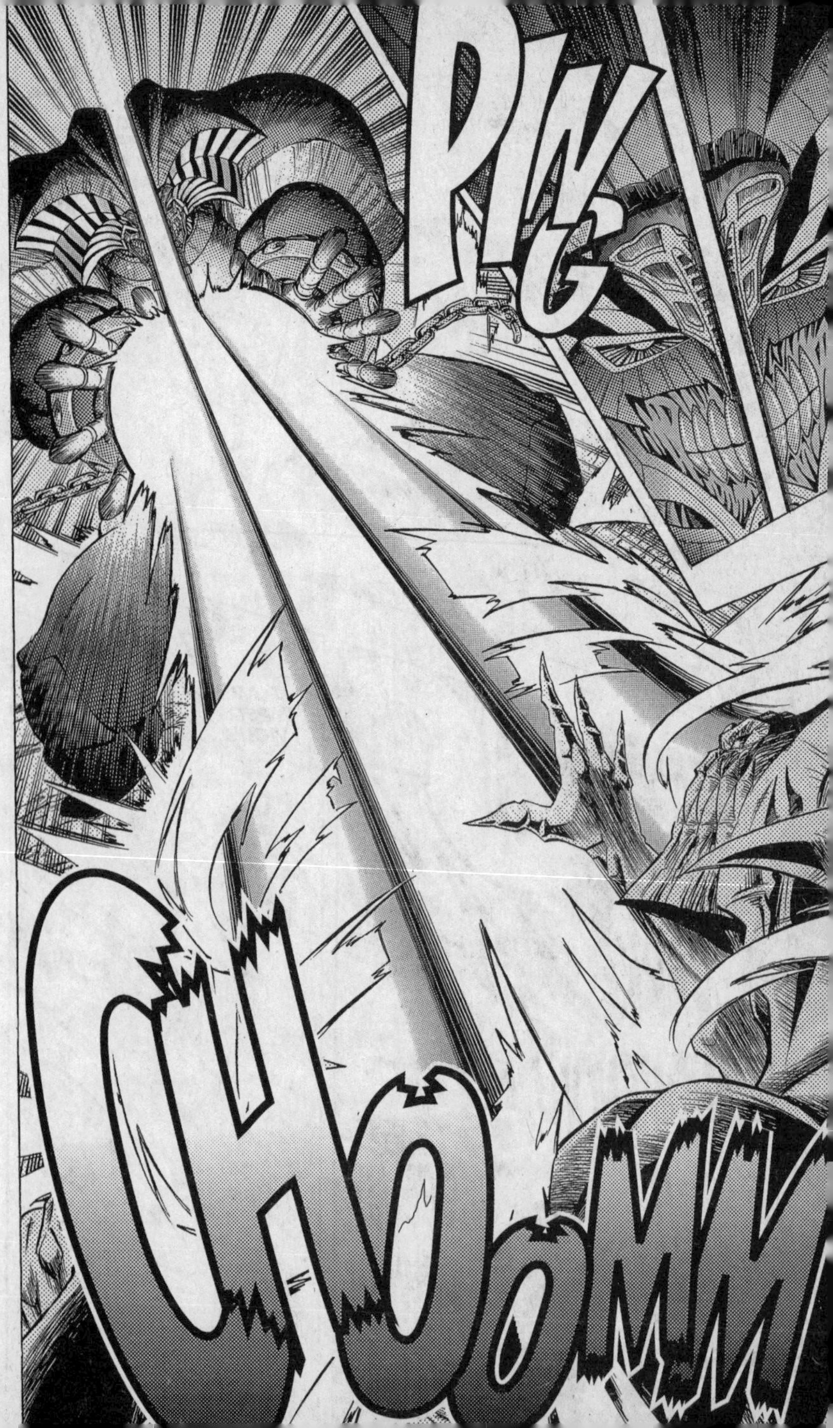
PING
CHOOMM

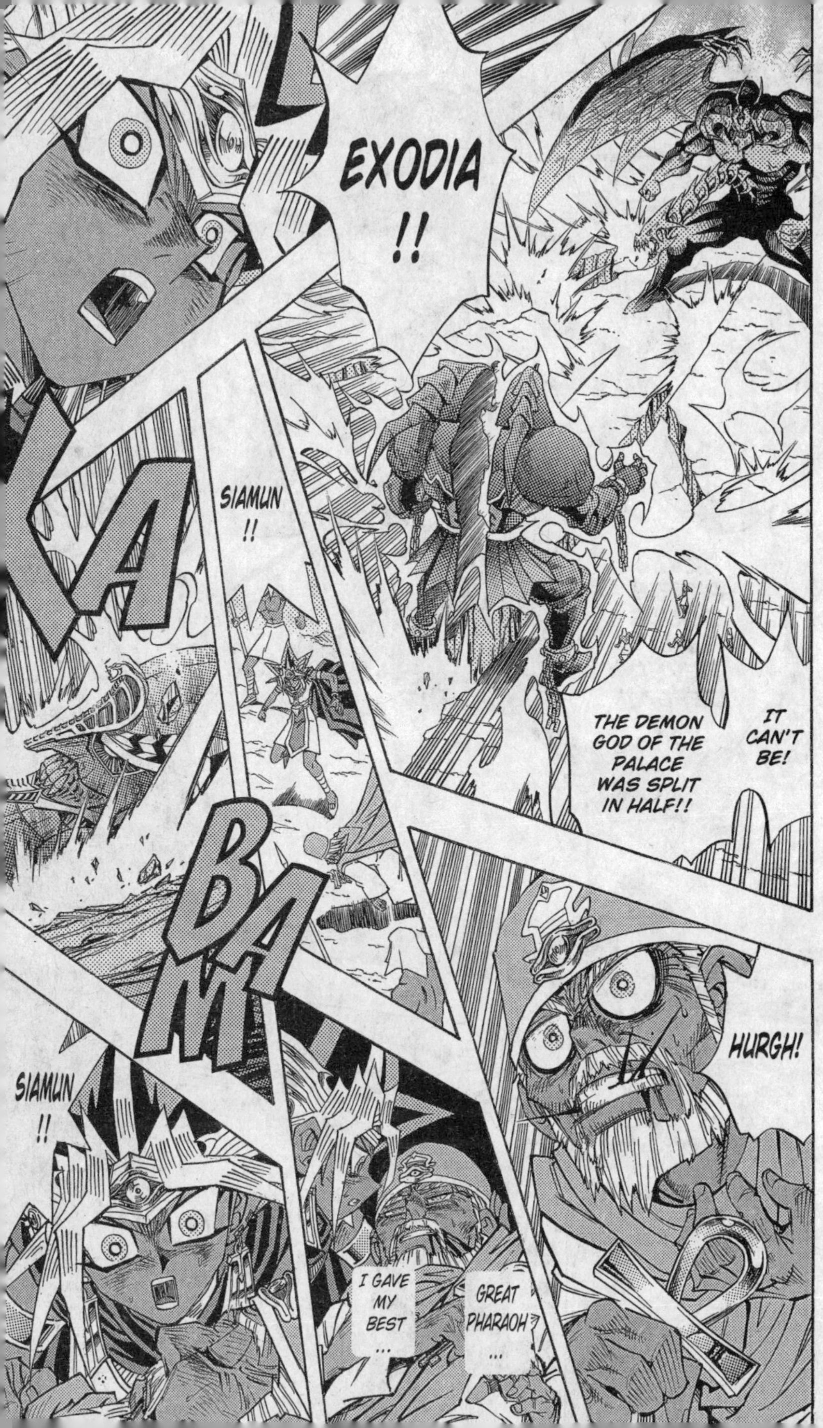

EXODIA !!
IT CAN'T BE!
THE DEMON GOD OF THE PALACE WAS SPLIT IN HALF!!
SIAMUN !!
KA BAM
HURGH!
GREAT PHARAOH ...
I GAVE MY BEST ...
SIAMUN !!

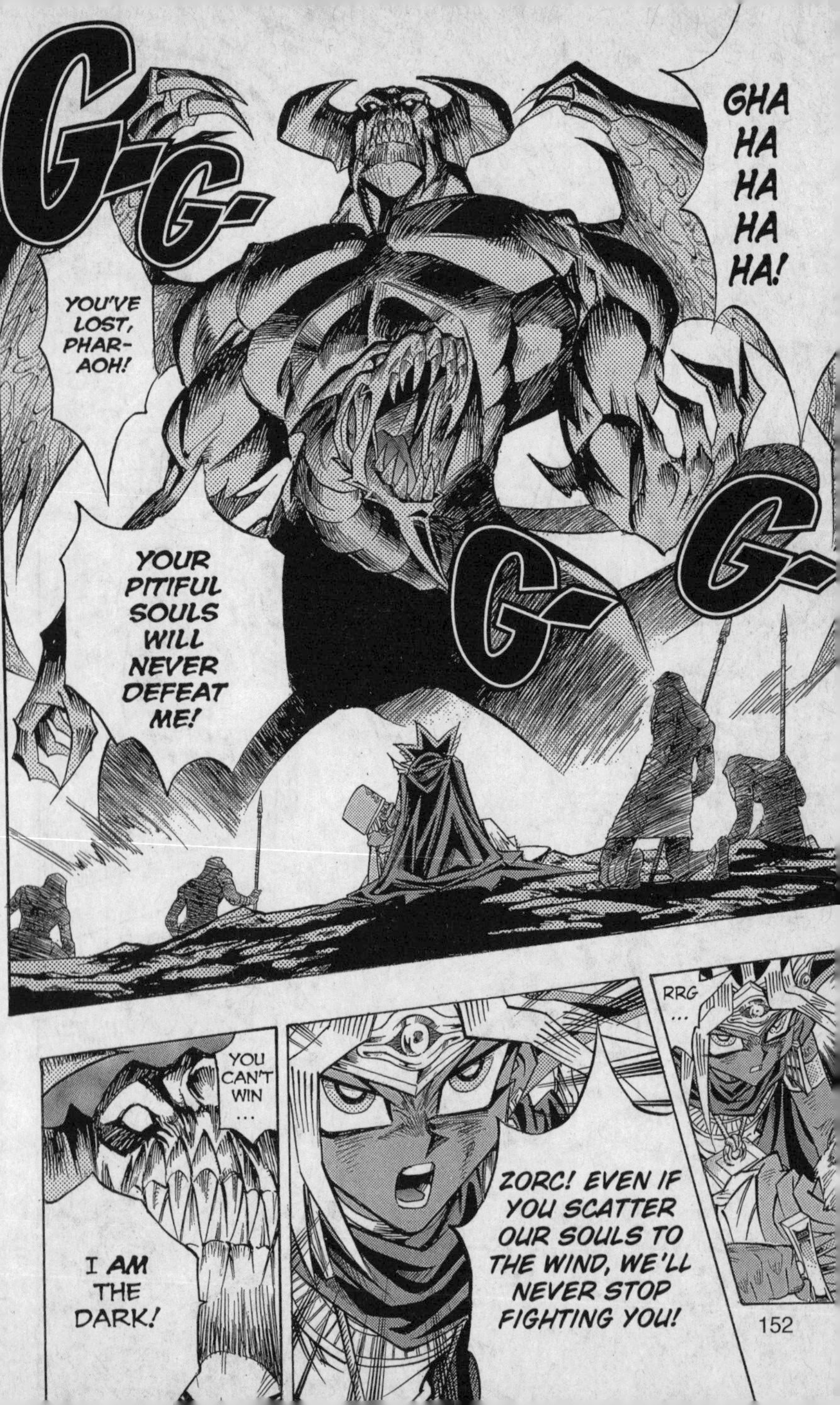
GHA HA HA HA HA!
G-G-
YOU'VE LOST, PHARAOH!
G-G-
YOUR PITIFUL SOULS WILL NEVER DEFEAT ME!
RRG...
ZORC! EVEN IF YOU SCATTER OUR SOULS TO THE WIND, WE'LL NEVER STOP FIGHTING YOU!
YOU CAN'T WIN...
I AM THE DARK!

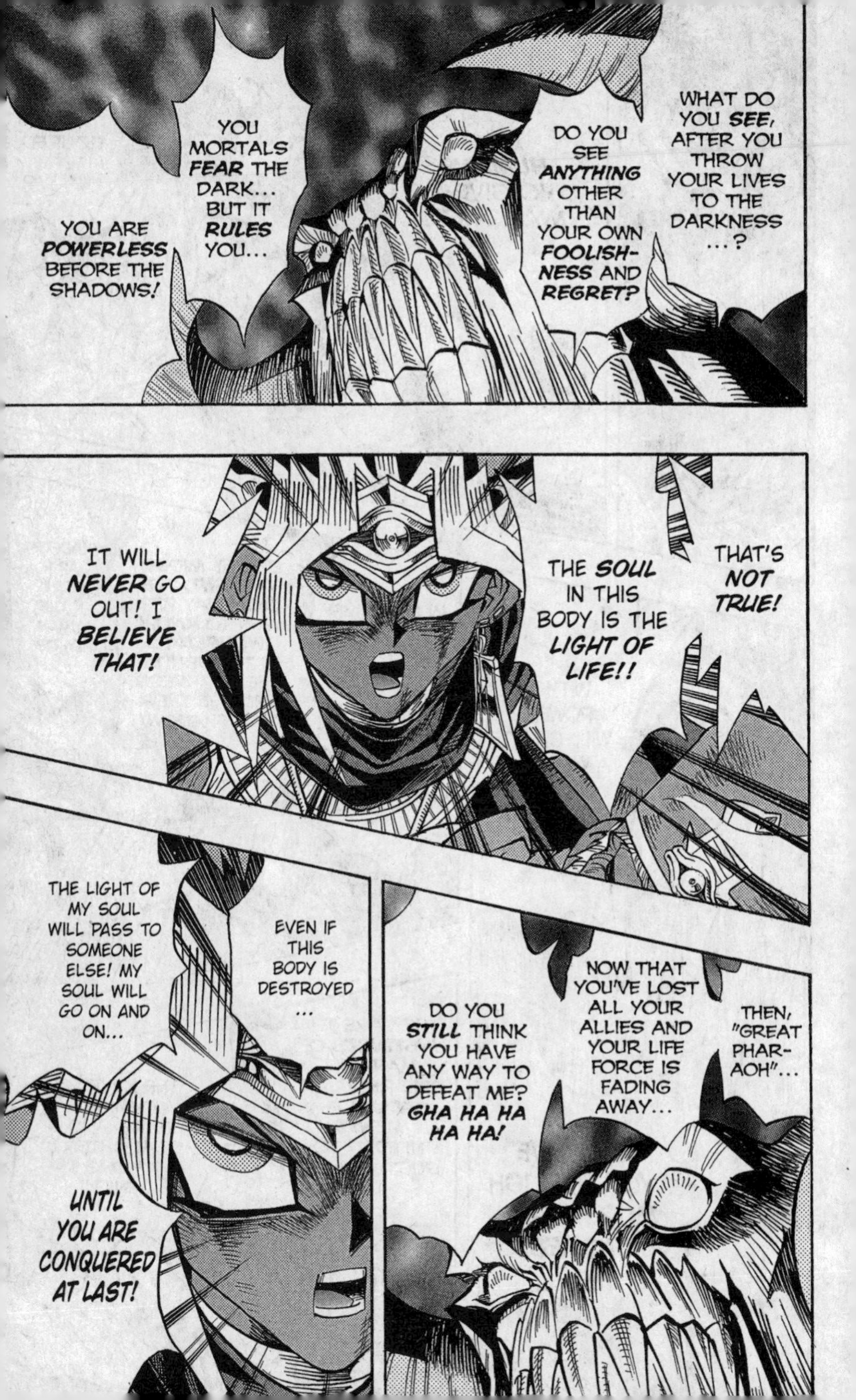
WHAT DO YOU SEE, AFTER YOU THROW YOUR LIVES TO THE DARKNESS ...?
DO YOU SEE ANYTHING OTHER THAN YOUR OWN FOOLISHNESS AND REGRET?
YOU MORTALS FEAR THE DARK... BUT IT RULES YOU...
YOU ARE POWERLESS BEFORE THE SHADOWS!
THAT'S NOT TRUE!
THE SOUL IN THIS BODY IS THE LIGHT OF LIFE!!
IT WILL NEVER GO OUT! I BELIEVE THAT!
THEN, "GREAT PHARAOH"...
NOW THAT YOU'VE LOST ALL YOUR ALLIES AND YOUR LIFE FORCE IS FADING AWAY...
DO YOU STILL THINK YOU HAVE ANY WAY TO DEFEAT ME? GHA HA HA HA HA!
EVEN IF THIS BODY IS DESTROYED ...
THE LIGHT OF MY SOUL WILL PASS TO SOMEONE ELSE! MY SOUL WILL GO ON AND ON...
UNTIL YOU ARE CONQUERED AT LAST!

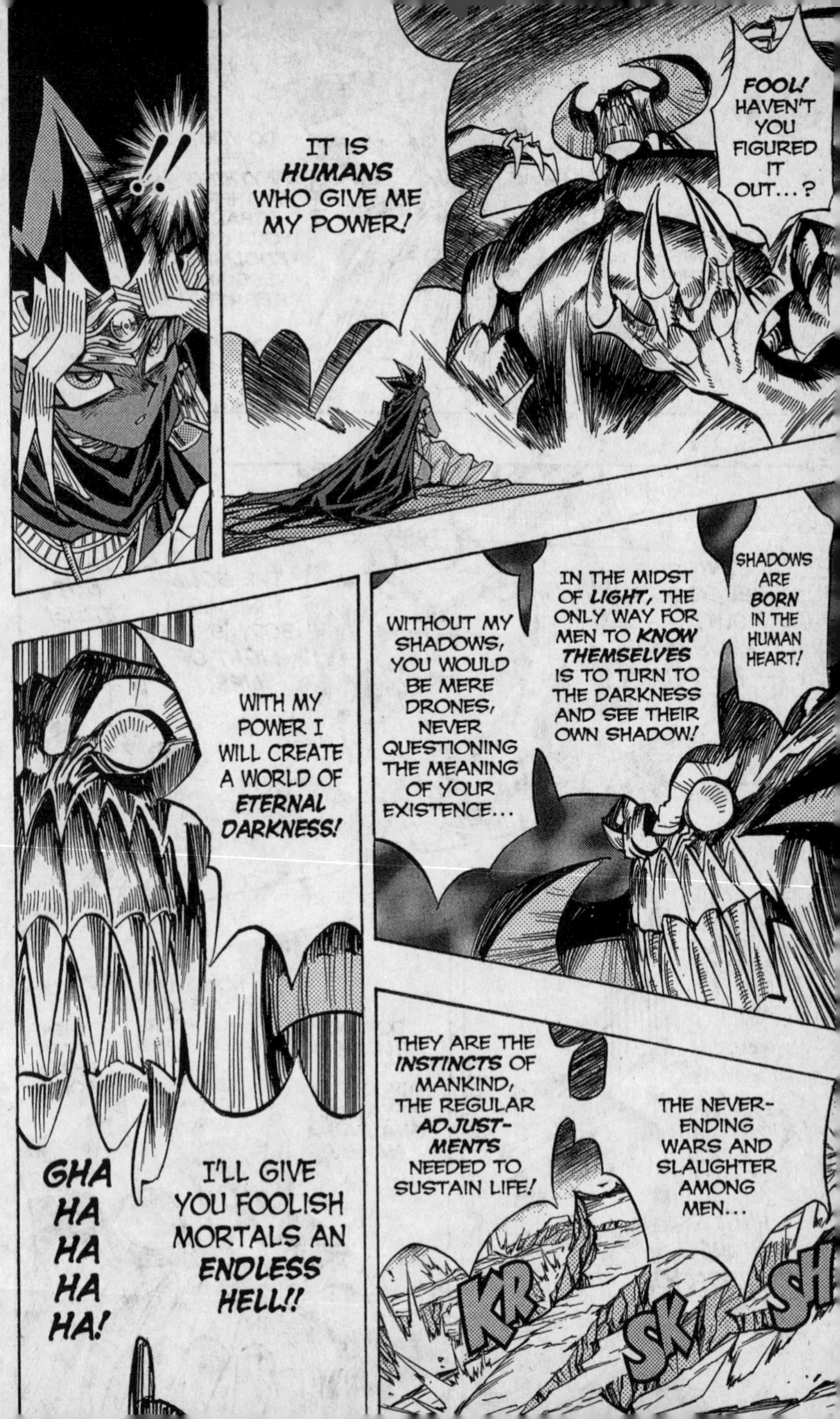
FOOL! HAVEN'T YOU FIGURED IT OUT...?
IT IS HUMANS WHO GIVE ME MY POWER!
!!
SHADOWS ARE BORN IN THE HUMAN HEART!
IN THE MIDST OF LIGHT, THE ONLY WAY FOR MEN TO KNOW THEMSELVES IS TO TURN TO THE DARKNESS AND SEE THEIR OWN SHADOW!
WITHOUT MY SHADOWS, YOU WOULD BE MERE DRONES, NEVER QUESTIONING THE MEANING OF YOUR EXISTENCE...
THE NEVER-ENDING WARS AND SLAUGHTER AMONG MEN...
THEY ARE THE INSTINCTS OF MANKIND, THE REGULAR ADJUST-MENTS NEEDED TO SUSTAIN LIFE!
KR
SKA
SH
WITH MY POWER I WILL CREATE A WORLD OF ETERNAL DARKNESS!
I'LL GIVE YOU FOOLISH MORTALS AN ENDLESS HELL!!
GHA HA HA HA HA!

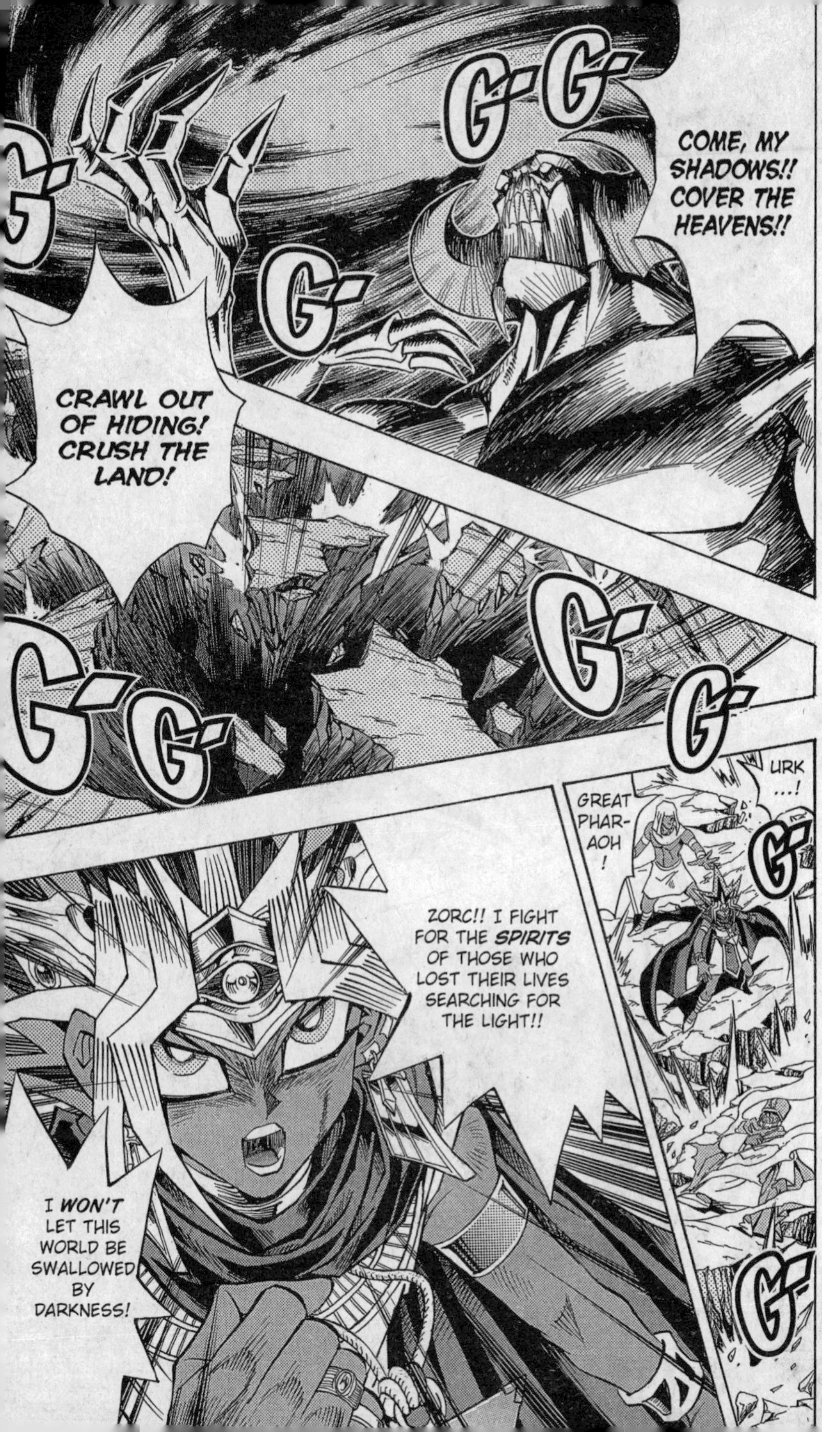
G-G-
COME, MY SHADOWS!! COVER THE HEAVENS!!
G-
G-
CRAWL OUT OF HIDING! CRUSH THE LAND!
G-
G-
G-G-
URK ...!
GREAT PHARAOH!
G-
G-
ZORC!! I FIGHT FOR THE *SPIRITS* OF THOSE WHO LOST THEIR LIVES SEARCHING FOR THE LIGHT!!
I *WON'T* LET THIS WORLD BE SWALLOWED BY DARKNESS!

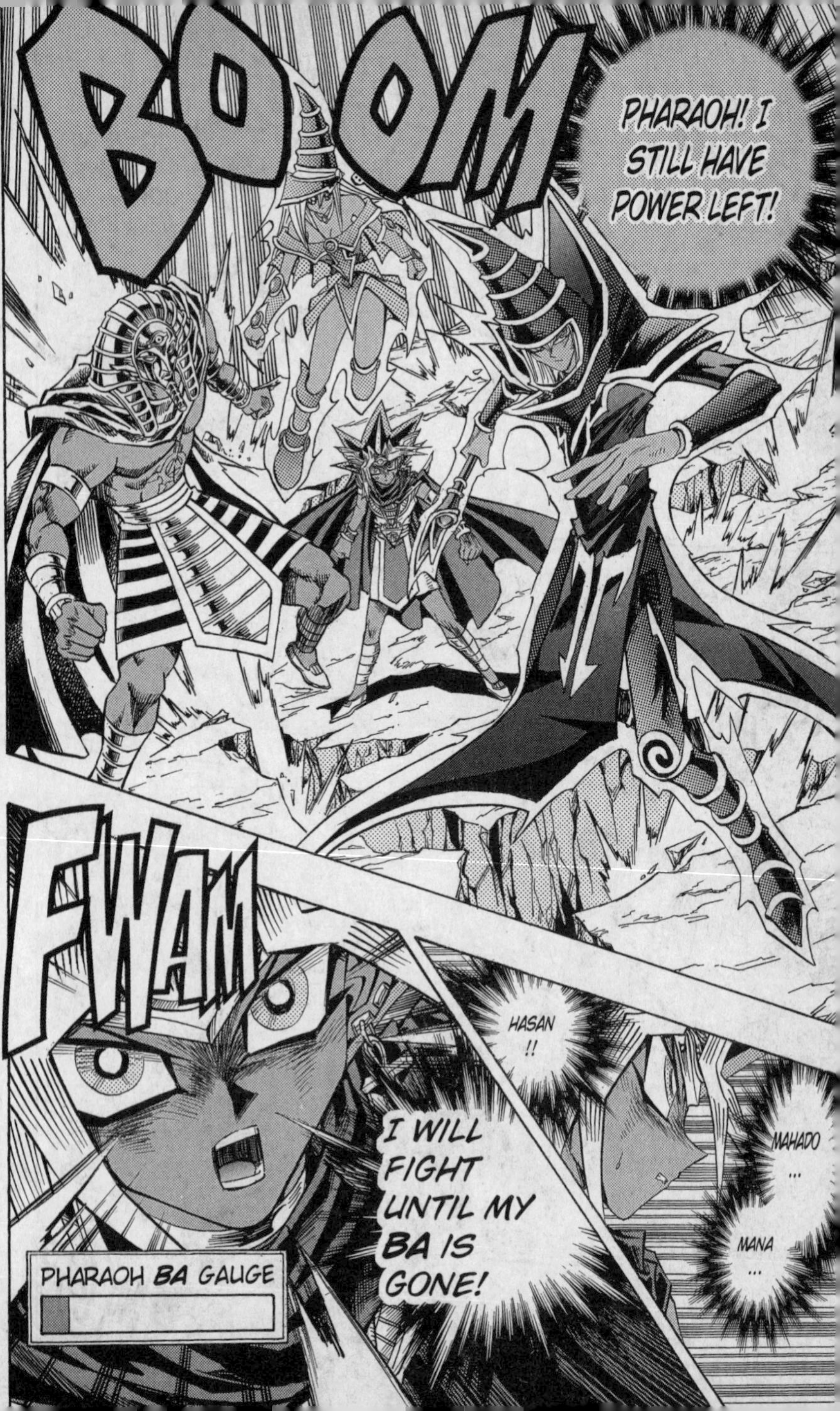
BOOM
PHARAOH! I STILL HAVE POWER LEFT!
HASAN !!
MAHADO ...
MANA ...
FWAM
I WILL FIGHT UNTIL MY BA IS GONE!
PHARAOH BA GAUGE

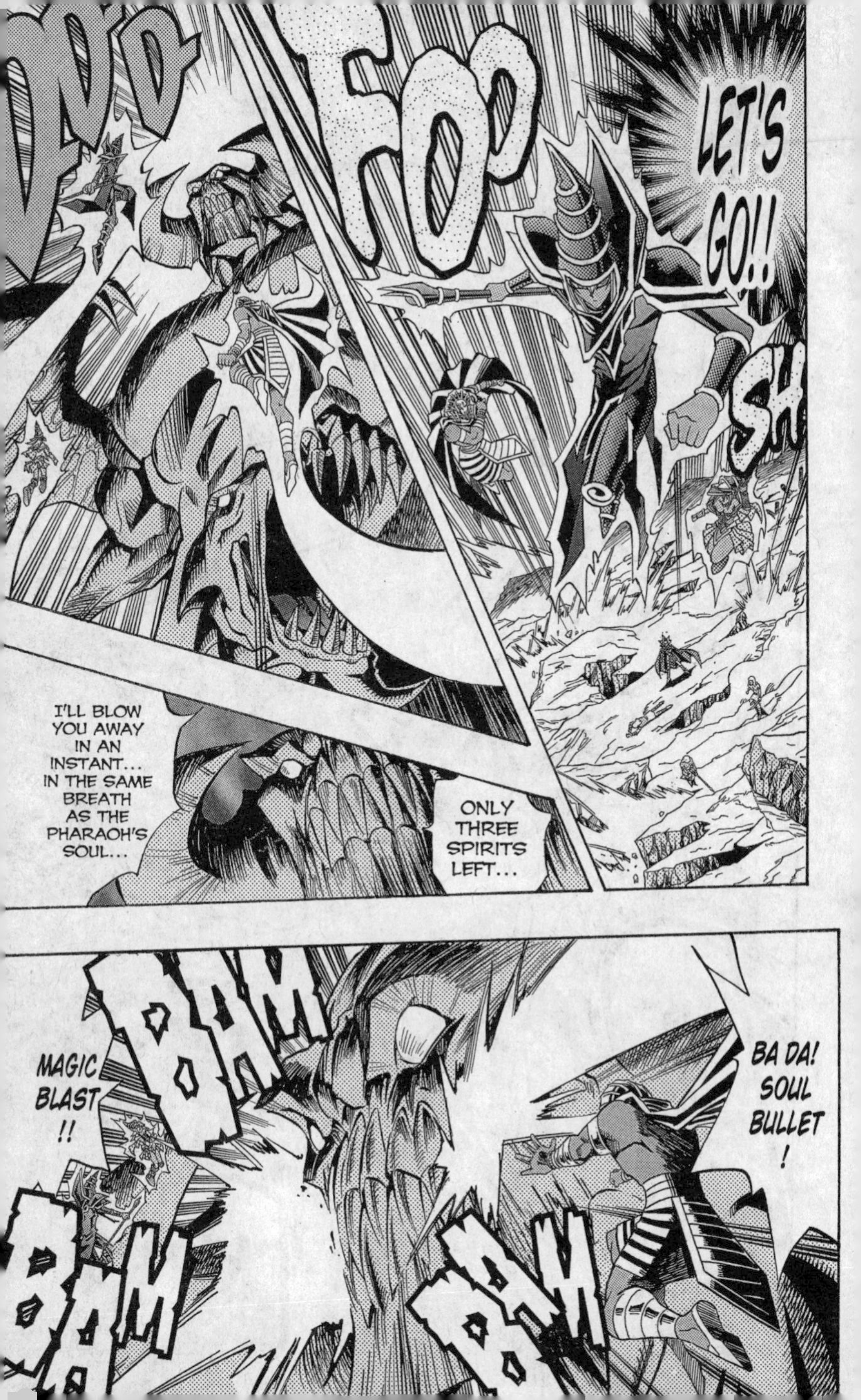
LET'S GO!!
ONLY THREE SPIRITS LEFT...
I'LL BLOW YOU AWAY IN AN INSTANT... IN THE SAME BREATH AS THE PHARAOH'S SOUL...
BA DA! SOUL BULLET!
BAM
MAGIC BLAST!!
BAM
BAM

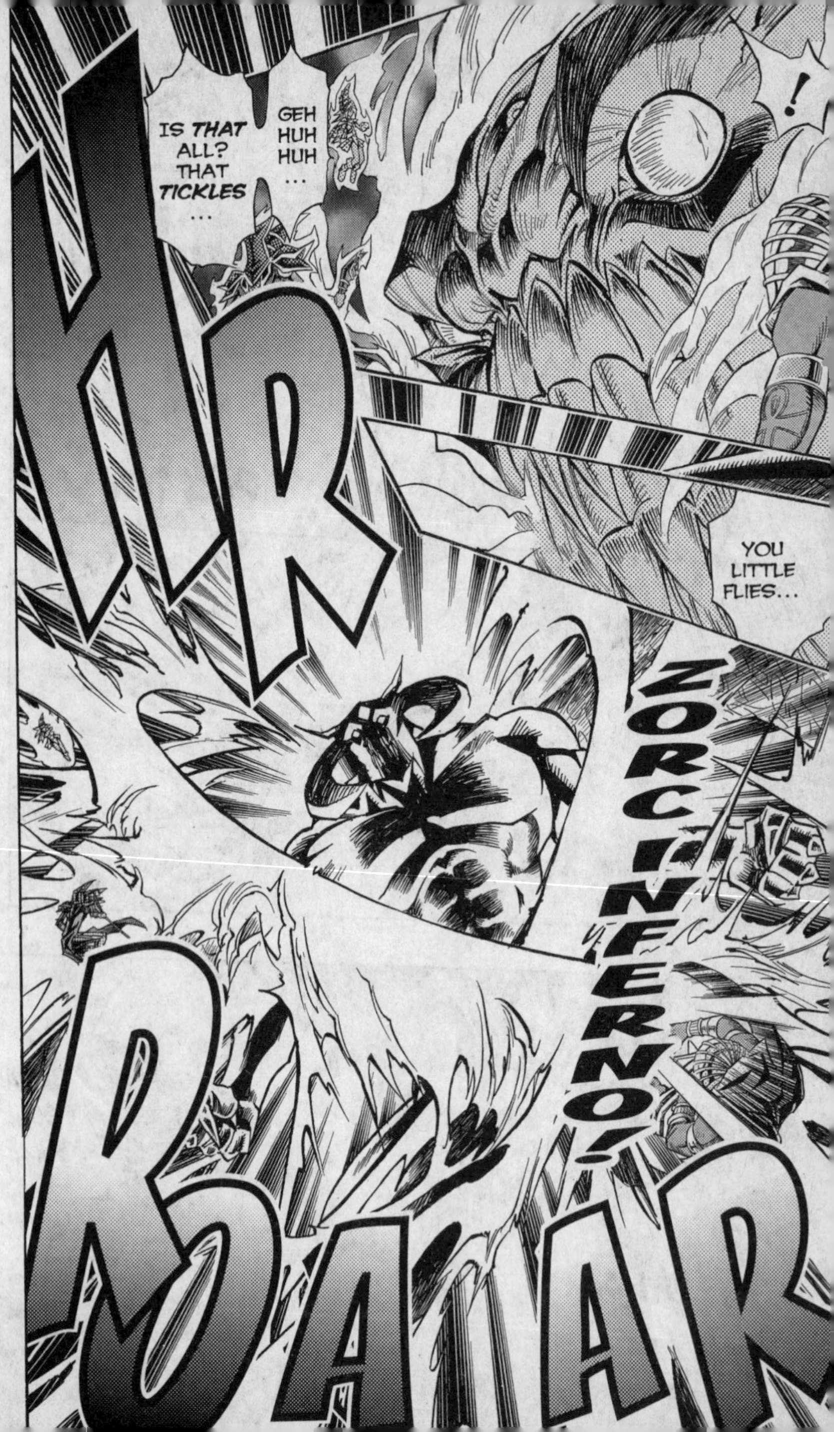

!
GEH HUH HUH ...
IS THAT ALL? THAT TICKLES ...
YOU LITTLE FLIES...
ZORC INFERNO!!

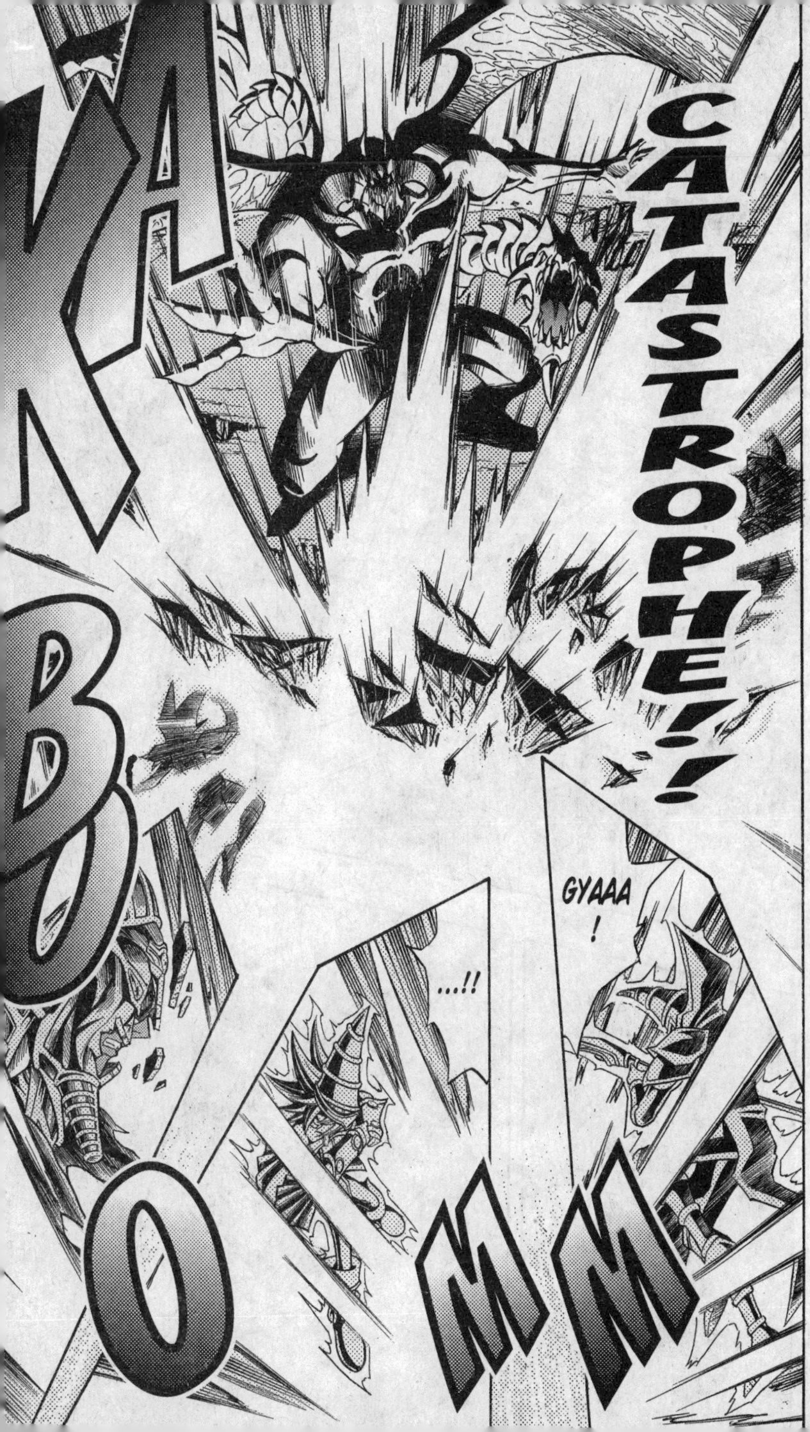
CATASTROPHE!!!
BOOMM
GYAAA!
...!!

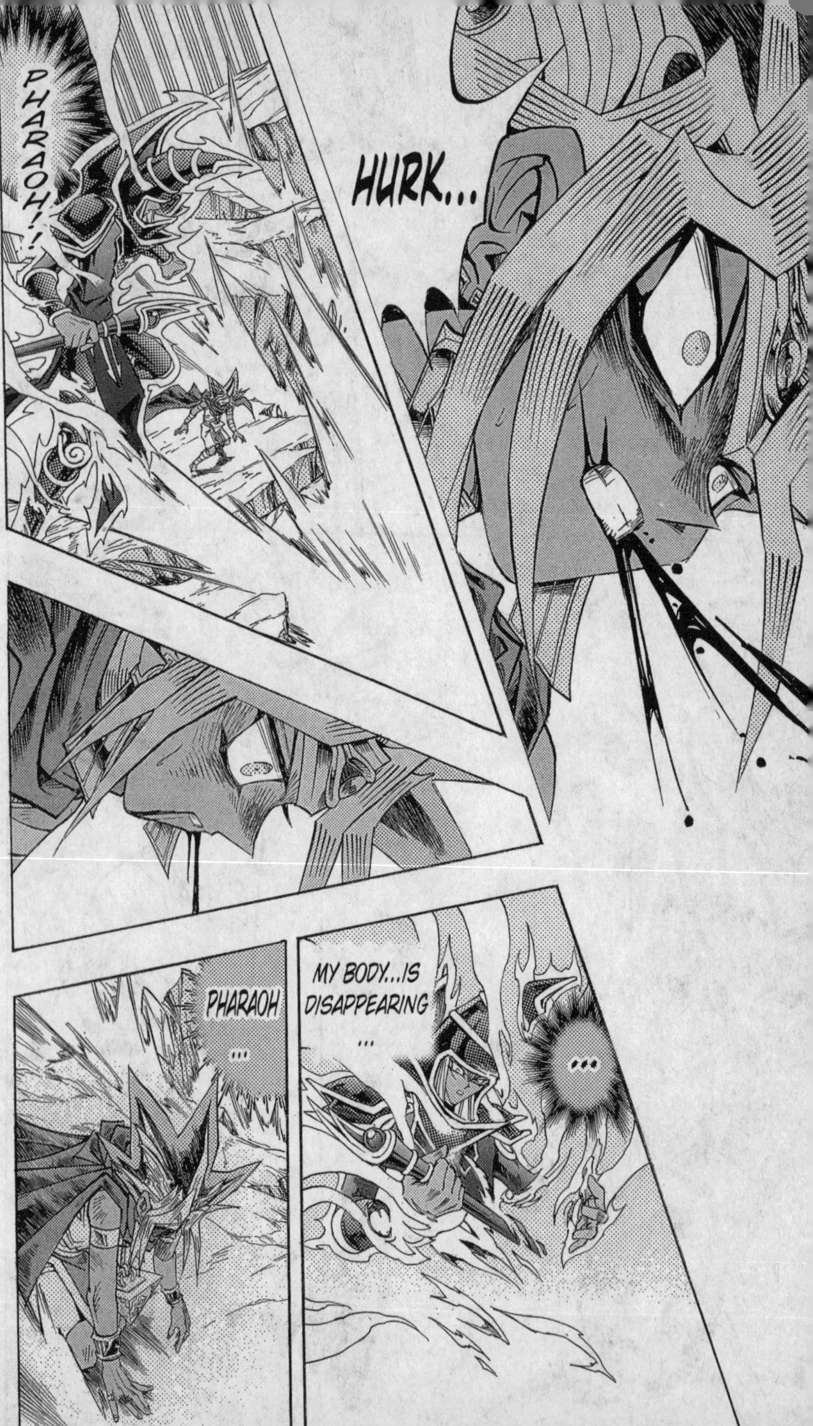
HURK...
PHARAOH!!
MY BODY...IS DISAPPEARING ...
...
PHARAOH ...

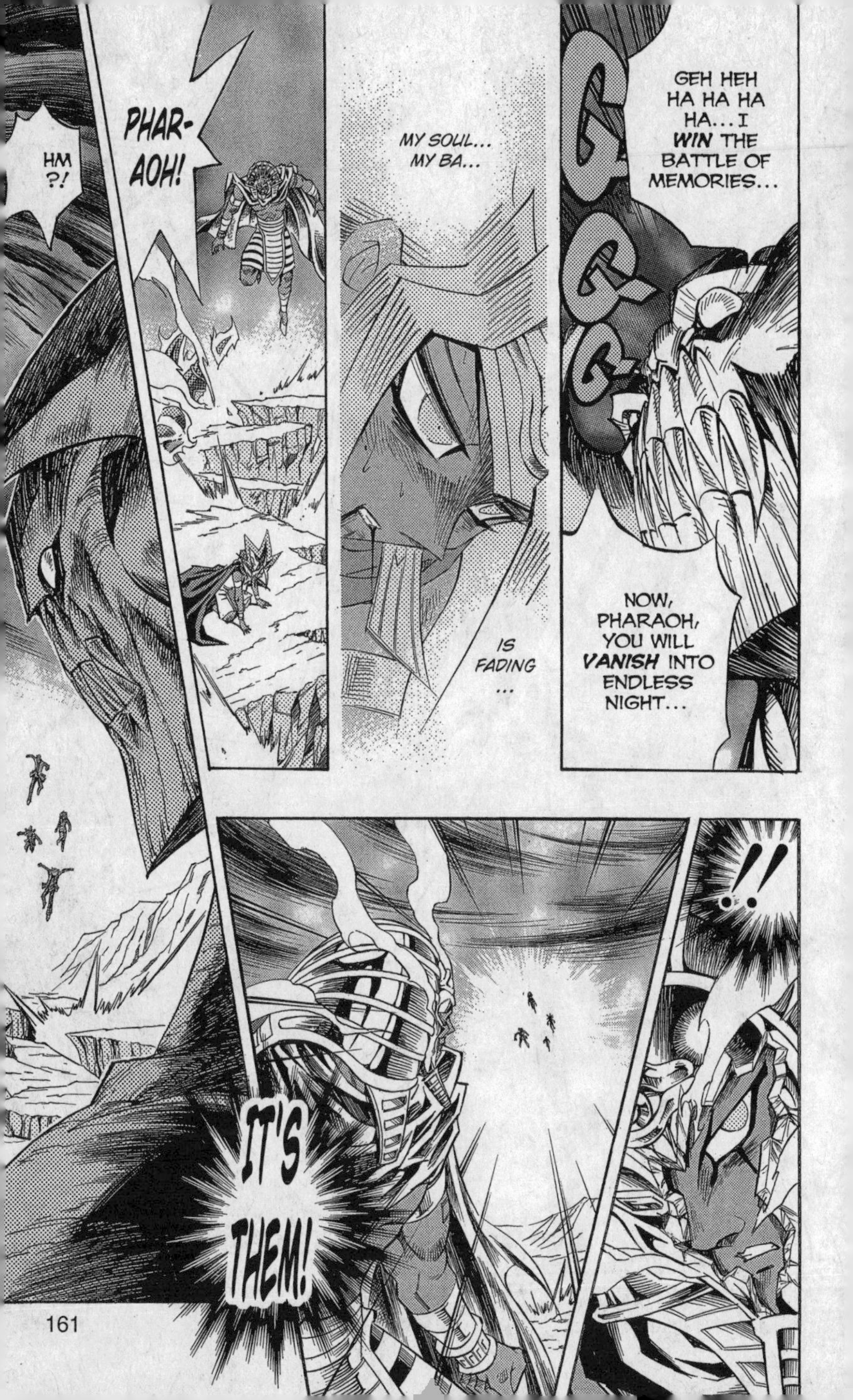
GEH HEH HA HA HA HA... I WIN THE BATTLE OF MEMORIES...
NOW, PHARAOH, YOU WILL VANISH INTO ENDLESS NIGHT...
MY SOUL... MY BA...
IS FADING ...
PHAR-AOH!
HM ?!
!!
IT'S THEM!

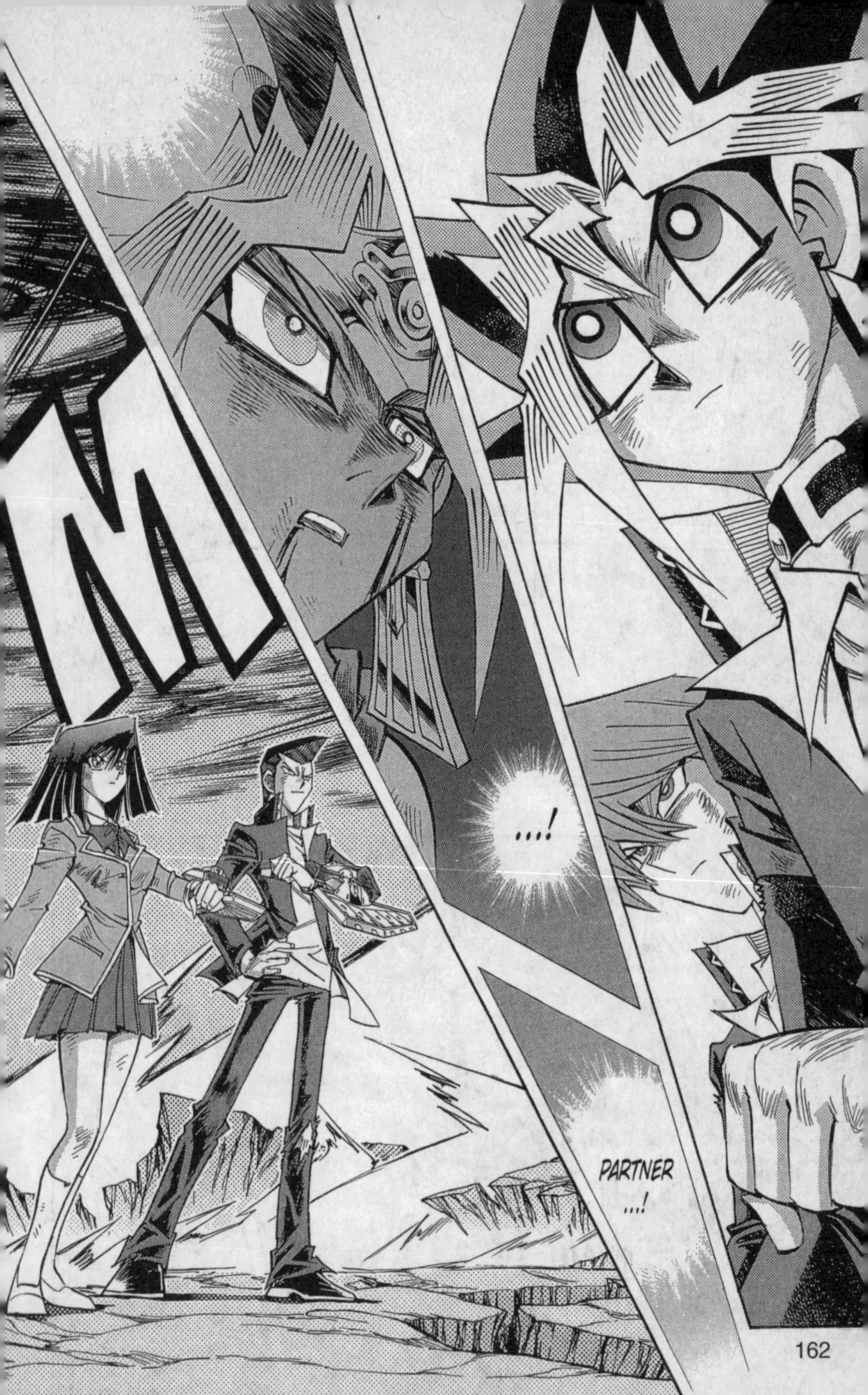
...!
PARTNER ...!

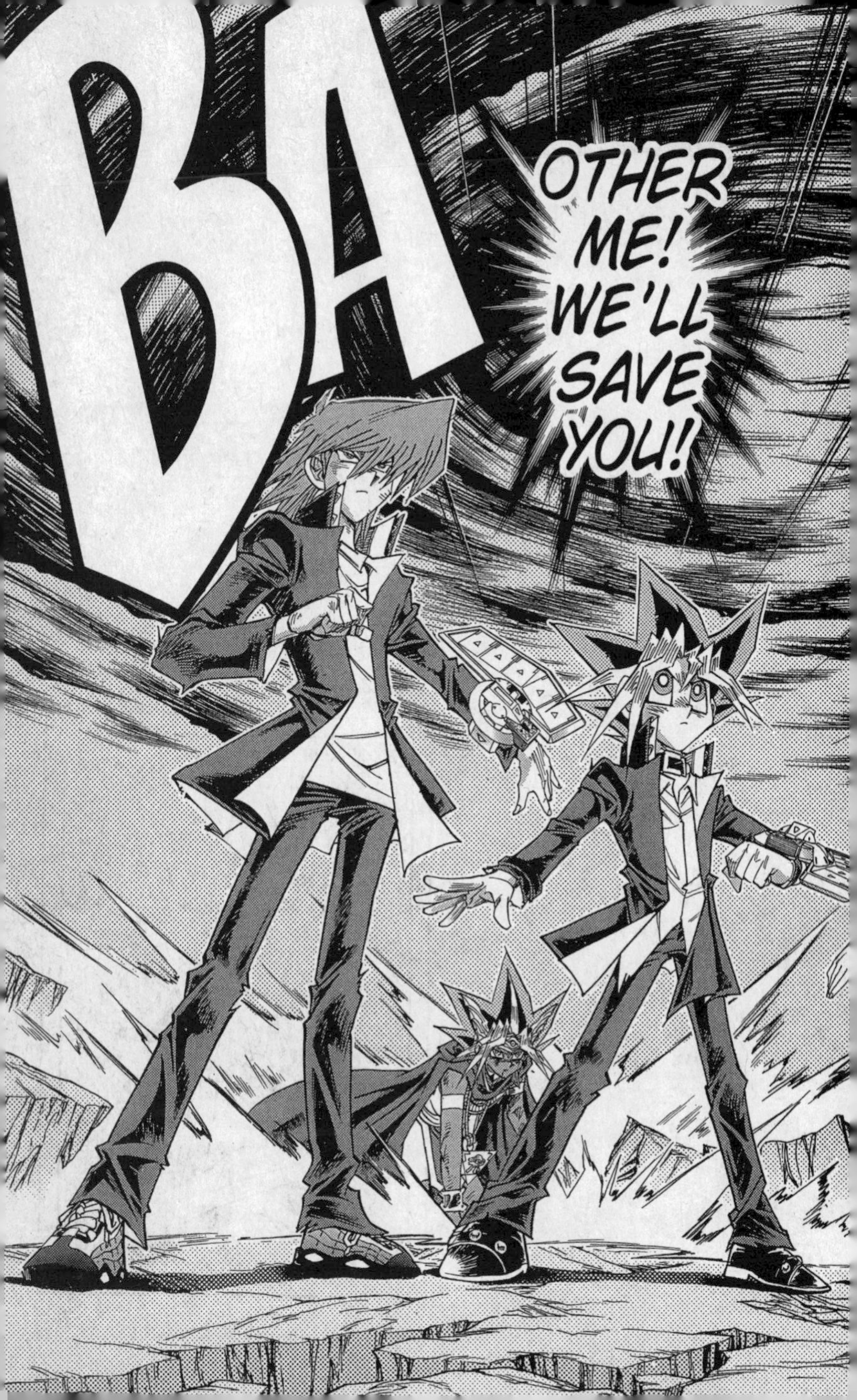
BA
OTHER ME! WE'LL SAVE YOU!

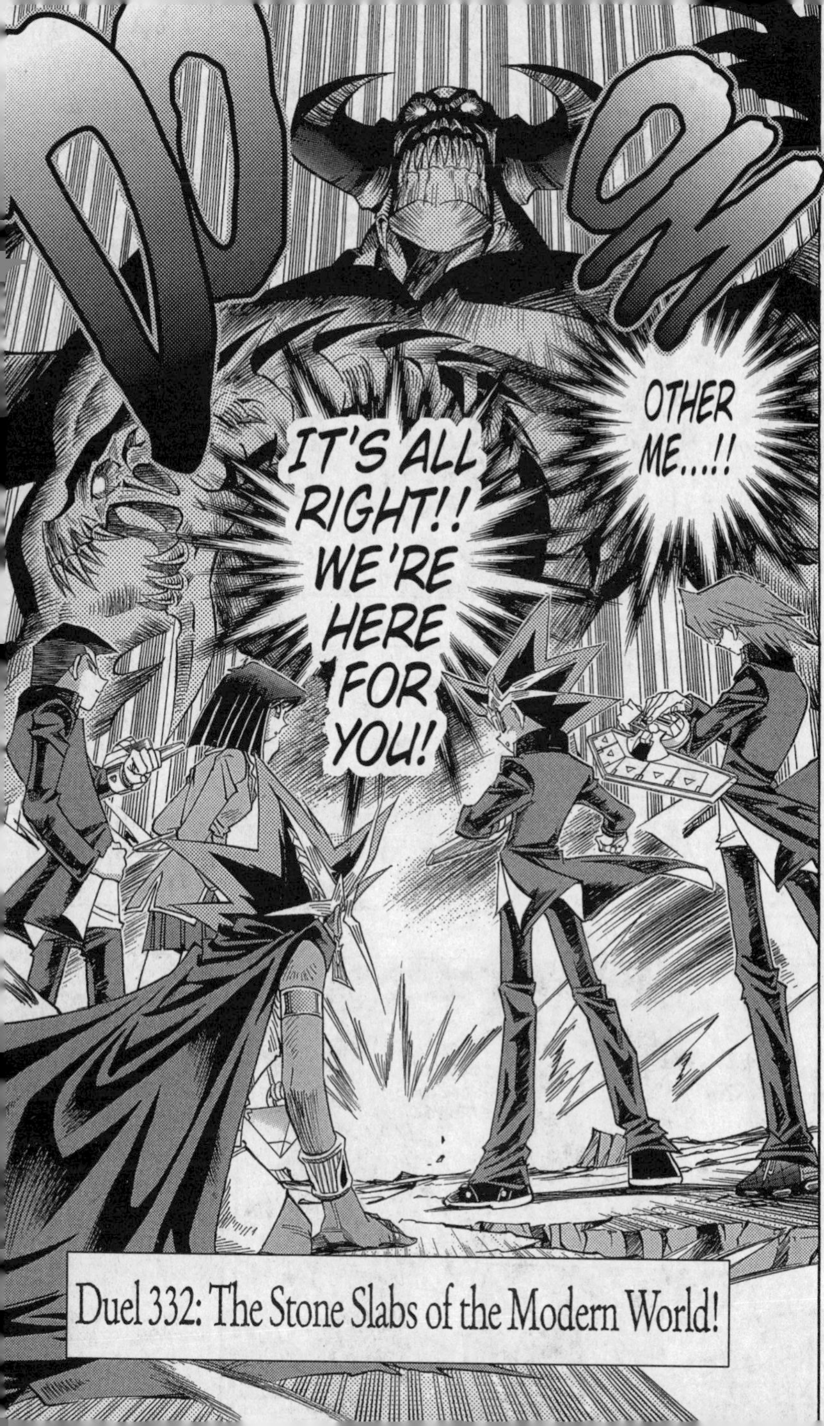
OTHER ME...!!
IT'S ALL RIGHT!! WE'RE HERE FOR YOU!

Duel 332: The Stone Slabs of the Modern World!

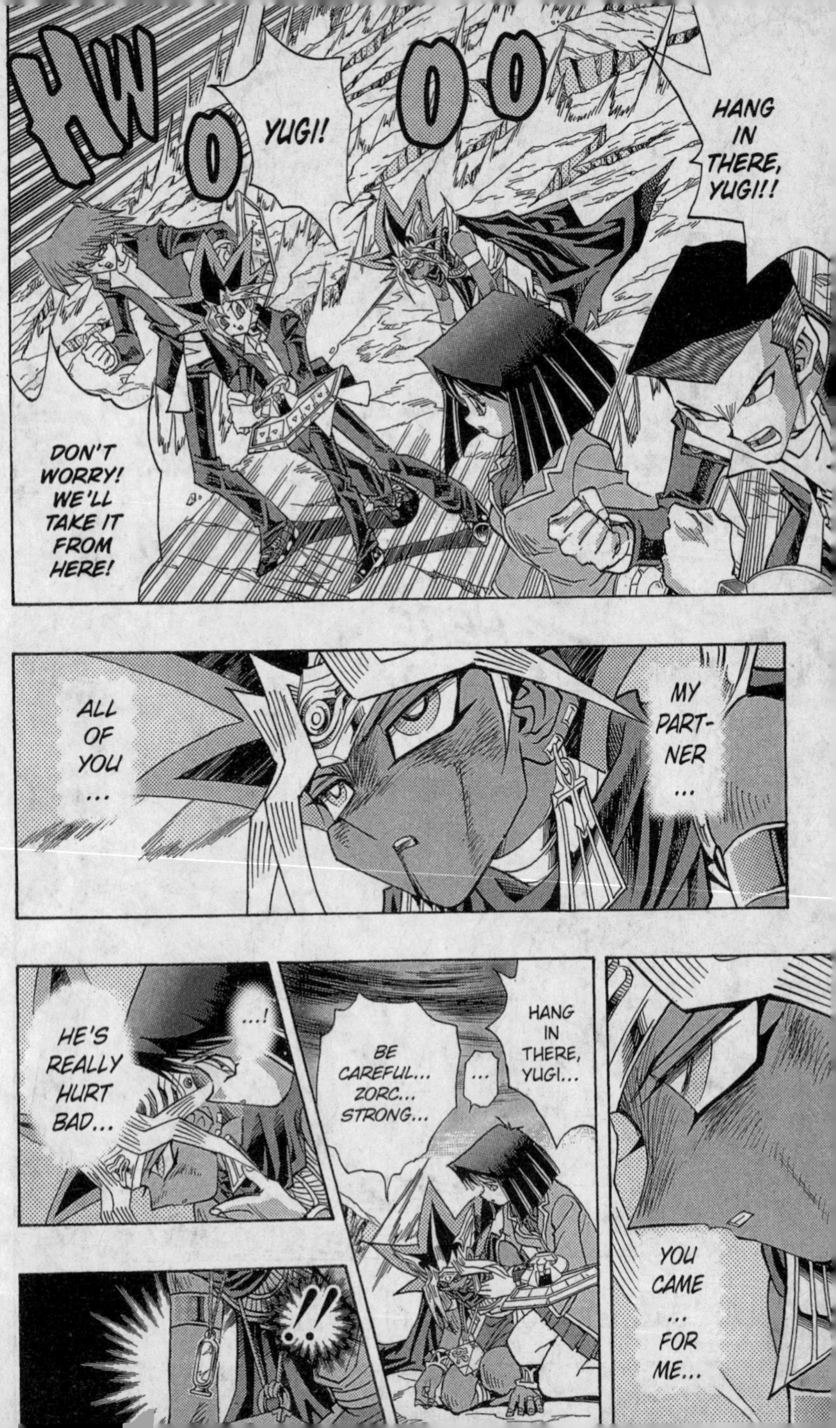
HANG IN THERE, YUGI!!
YUGI!
HWOOOO
DON'T WORRY! WE'LL TAKE IT FROM HERE!
MY PARTNER ...
ALL OF YOU ...
YOU CAME ... FOR ME...
HANG IN THERE, YUGI...
...
BE CAREFUL... ZORC... STRONG...
...!
HE'S REALLY HURT BAD...
!!

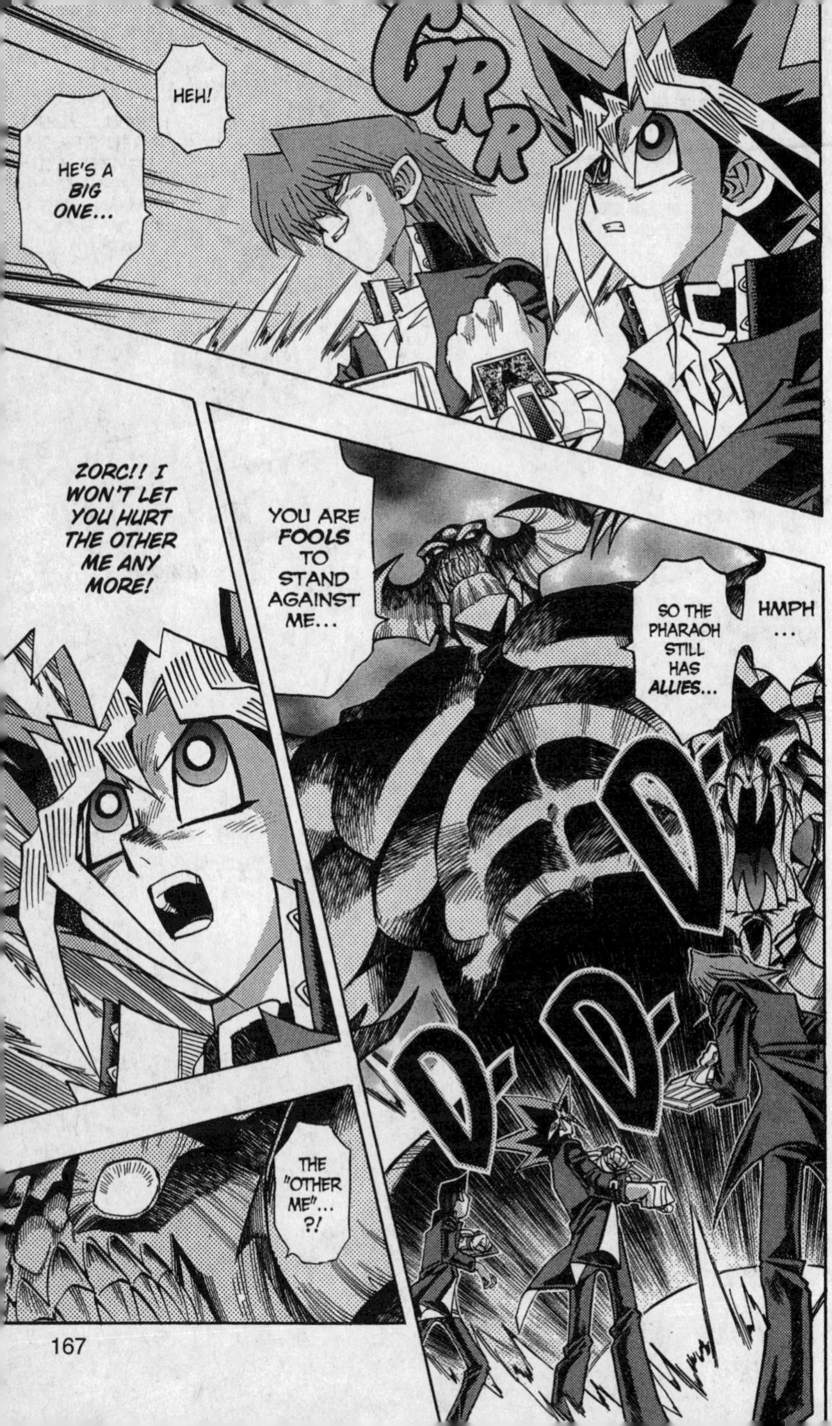
GRR
HEH!
HE'S A BIG ONE...
HMPH ...
SO THE PHARAOH STILL HAS ALLIES...
YOU ARE FOOLS TO STAND AGAINST ME...
ZORC!! I WON'T LET YOU HURT THE OTHER ME ANY MORE!
THE "OTHER ME"... ?!

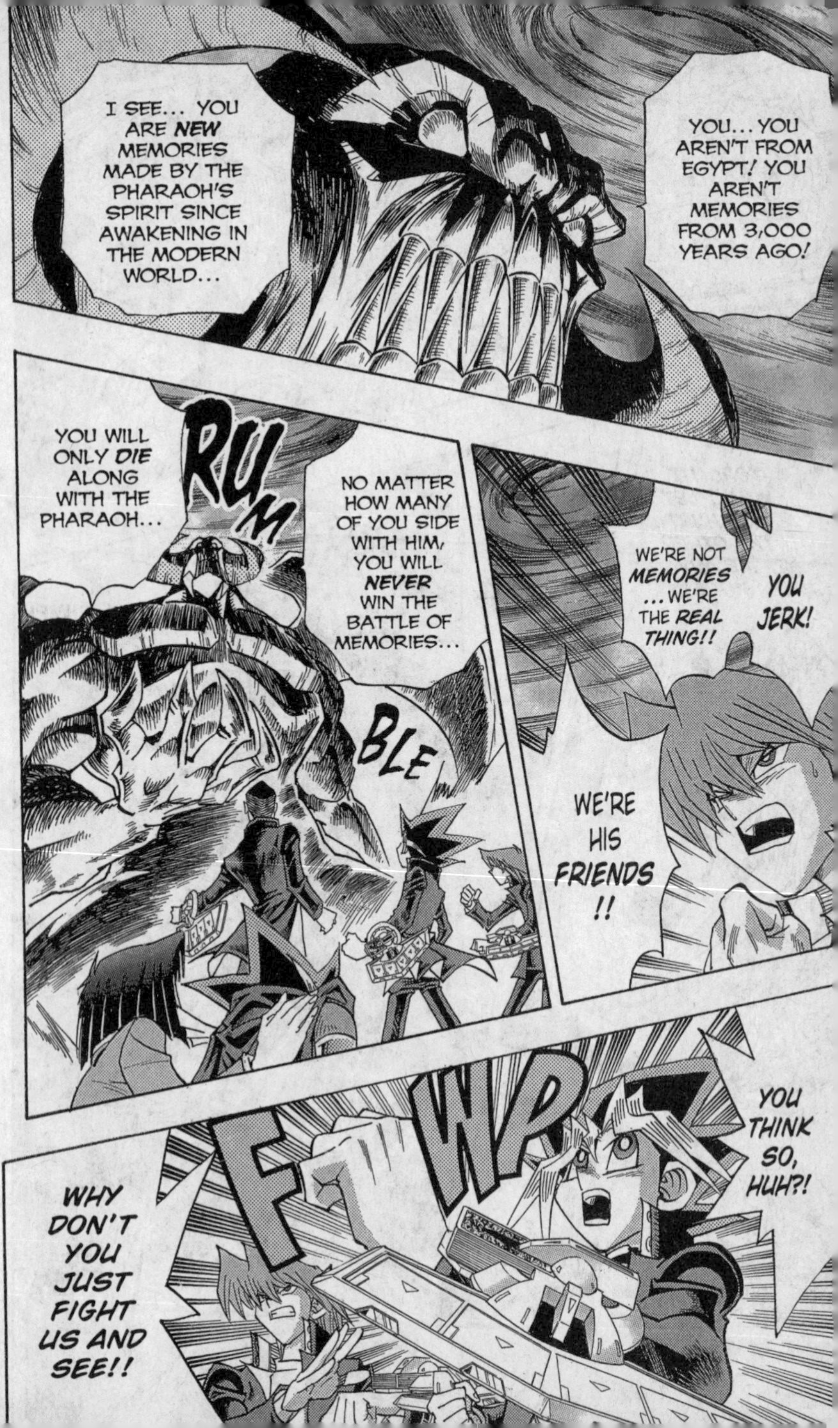
YOU... YOU AREN'T FROM EGYPT! YOU AREN'T MEMORIES FROM 3,000 YEARS AGO!
I SEE... YOU ARE NEW MEMORIES MADE BY THE PHARAOH'S SPIRIT SINCE AWAKENING IN THE MODERN WORLD...
YOU JERK!
WE'RE NOT MEMORIES ...WE'RE THE REAL THING!!
WE'RE HIS FRIENDS!!
NO MATTER HOW MANY OF YOU SIDE WITH HIM, YOU WILL NEVER WIN THE BATTLE OF MEMORIES...
YOU WILL ONLY DIE ALONG WITH THE PHARAOH...
RUMBLE
YOU THINK SO, HUH?!
FWP
WHY DON'T YOU JUST FIGHT US AND SEE!!

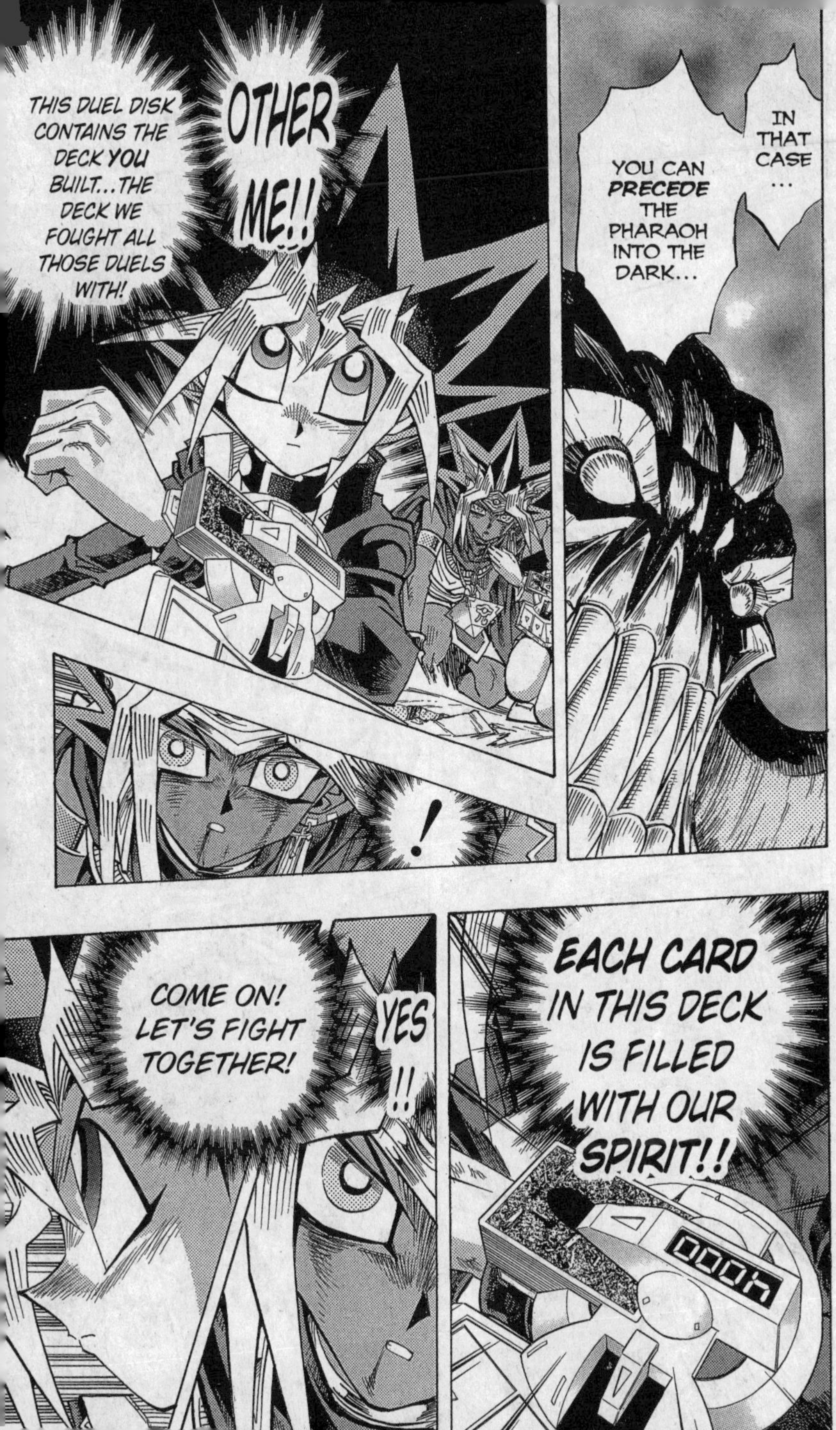
IN THAT CASE...
YOU CAN PRECEDE THE PHARAOH INTO THE DARK...
OTHER ME!!
THIS DUEL DISK CONTAINS THE DECK YOU BUILT...THE DECK WE FOUGHT ALL THOSE DUELS WITH!
!
EACH CARD IN THIS DECK IS FILLED WITH OUR SPIRIT!!
YES!!
COME ON! LET'S FIGHT TOGETHER!
4000

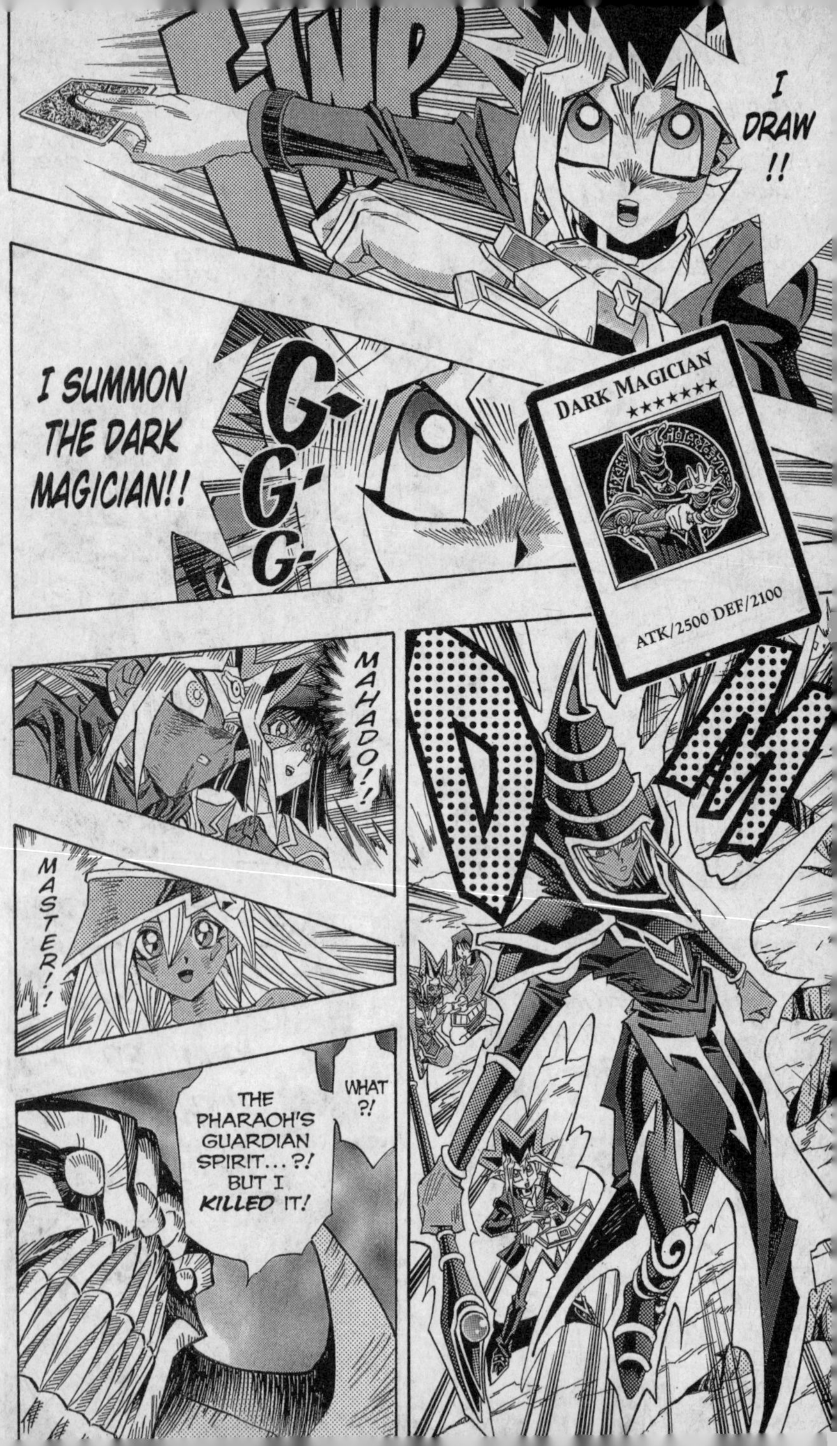

I DRAW !!
G- G- G-
I SUMMON THE DARK MAGICIAN!!
DARK MAGICIAN
ATK/2500 DEF/2100
MAHADO!!
MASTER!!
WHAT ?!
THE PHARAOH'S GUARDIAN SPIRIT...?! BUT I KILLED IT!

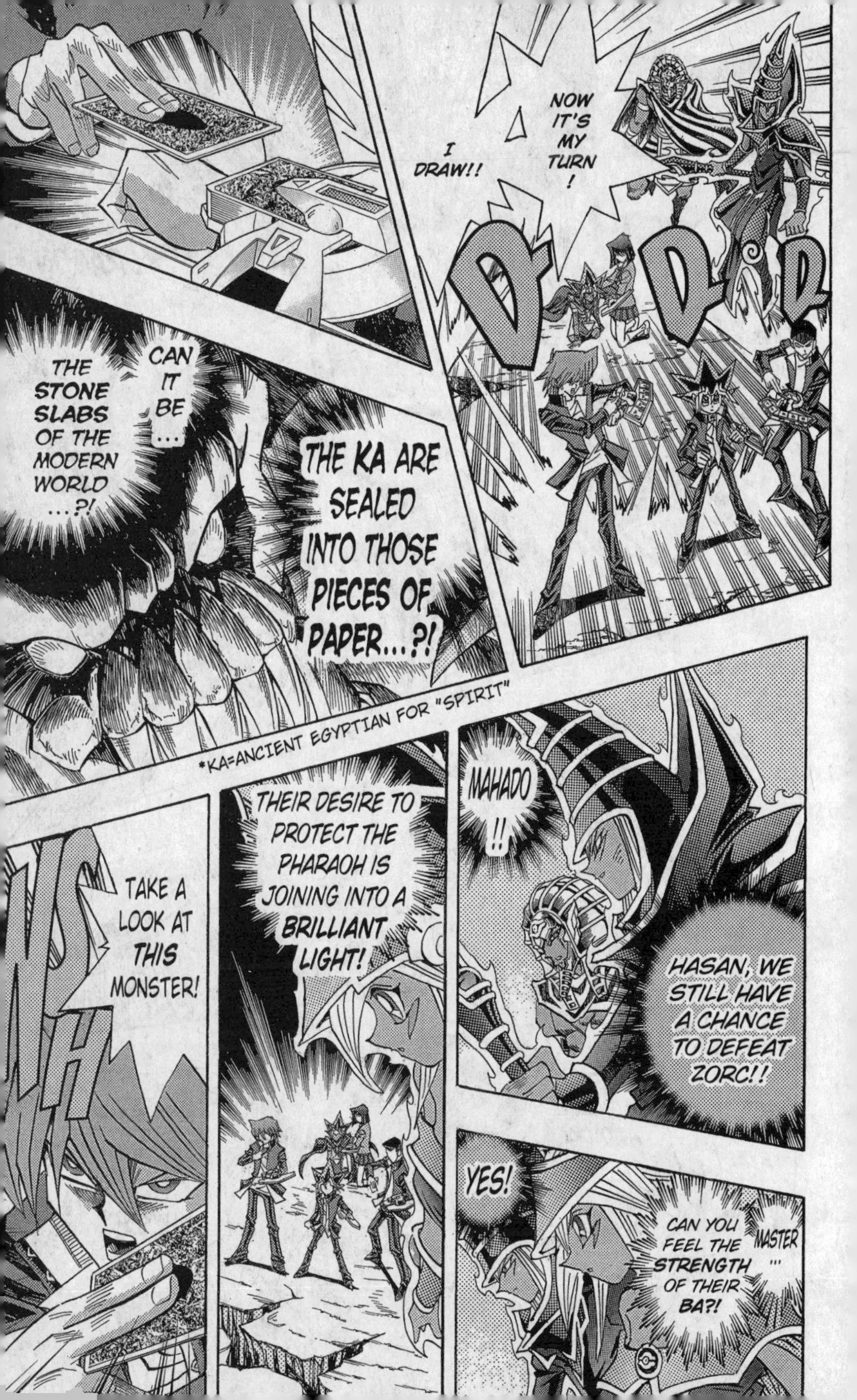
NOW IT'S MY TURN!
I DRAW!!
CAN IT BE...
THE STONE SLABS OF THE MODERN WORLD...?!
THE KA ARE SEALED INTO THOSE PIECES OF PAPER...?!
*KA=ANCIENT EGYPTIAN FOR "SPIRIT"
MAHADO!!
HASAN, WE STILL HAVE A CHANCE TO DEFEAT ZORC!!
YES!
MASTER...
CAN YOU FEEL THE STRENGTH OF THEIR BA?!
THEIR DESIRE TO PROTECT THE PHARAOH IS JOINING INTO A BRILLIANT LIGHT!
TAKE A LOOK AT THIS MONSTER!

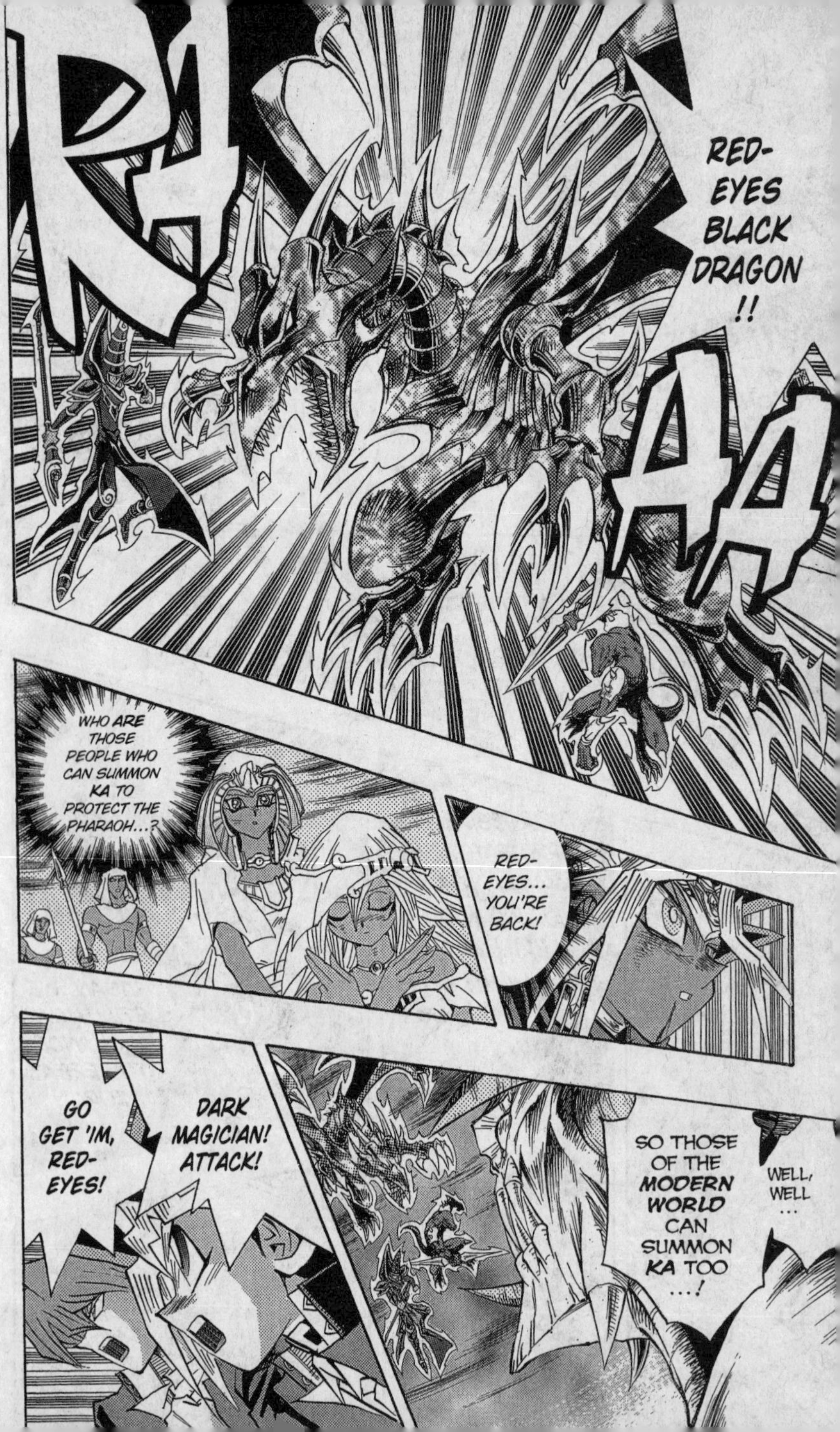
RED-EYES BLACK DRAGON!!
RED-EYES... YOU'RE BACK!
WHO ARE THOSE PEOPLE WHO CAN SUMMON KA TO PROTECT THE PHARAOH...?
WELL, WELL...
SO THOSE OF THE MODERN WORLD CAN SUMMON KA TOO...!
DARK MAGICIAN! ATTACK!
GO GET 'IM, RED-EYES!

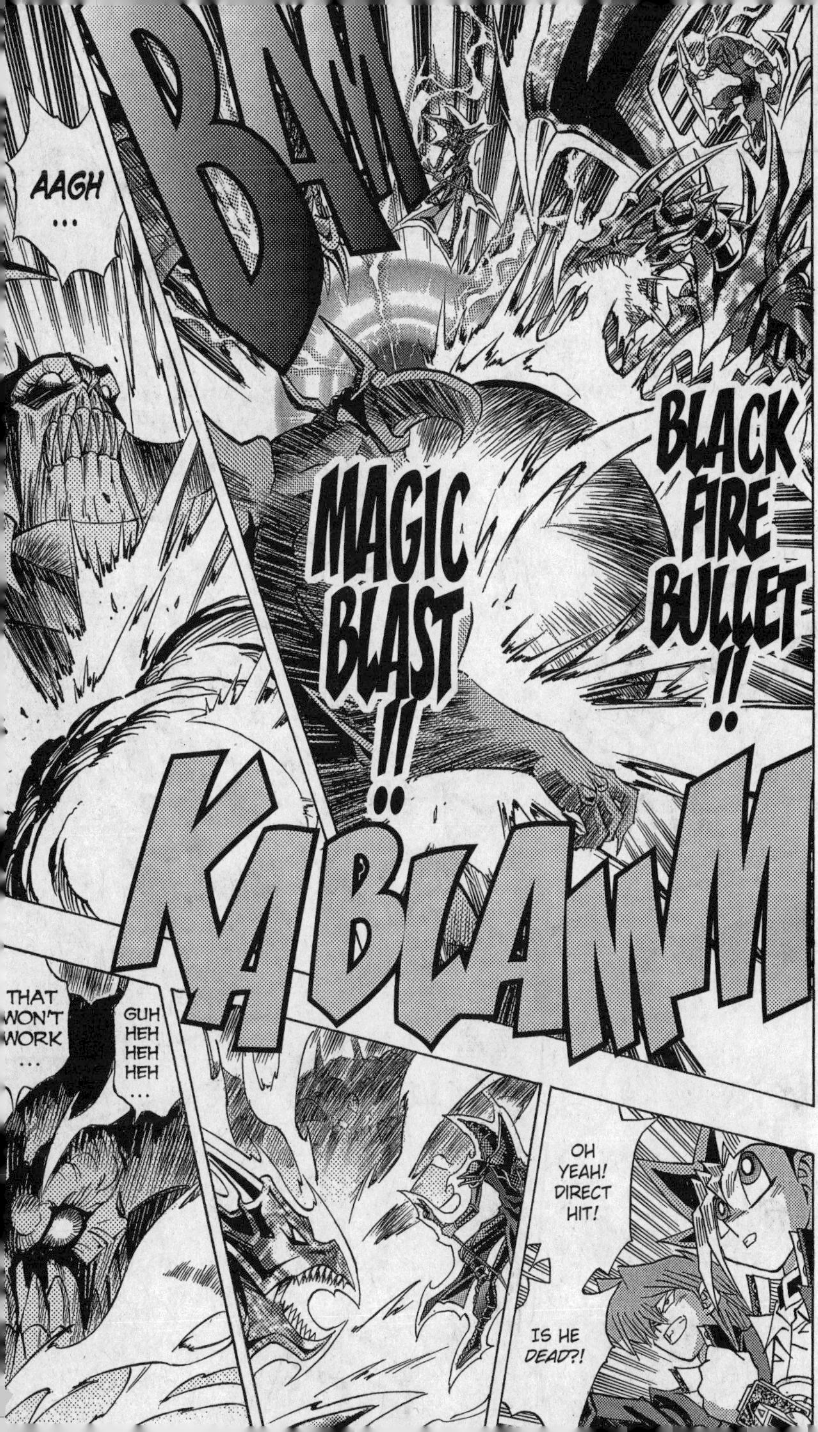
BAM
BLACK FIRE BULLET!!
MAGIC BLAST!!
KABLAMM
AAGH...
OH YEAH! DIRECT HIT!
IS HE DEAD?!
GUH HEH HEH HEH...
THAT WON'T WORK...

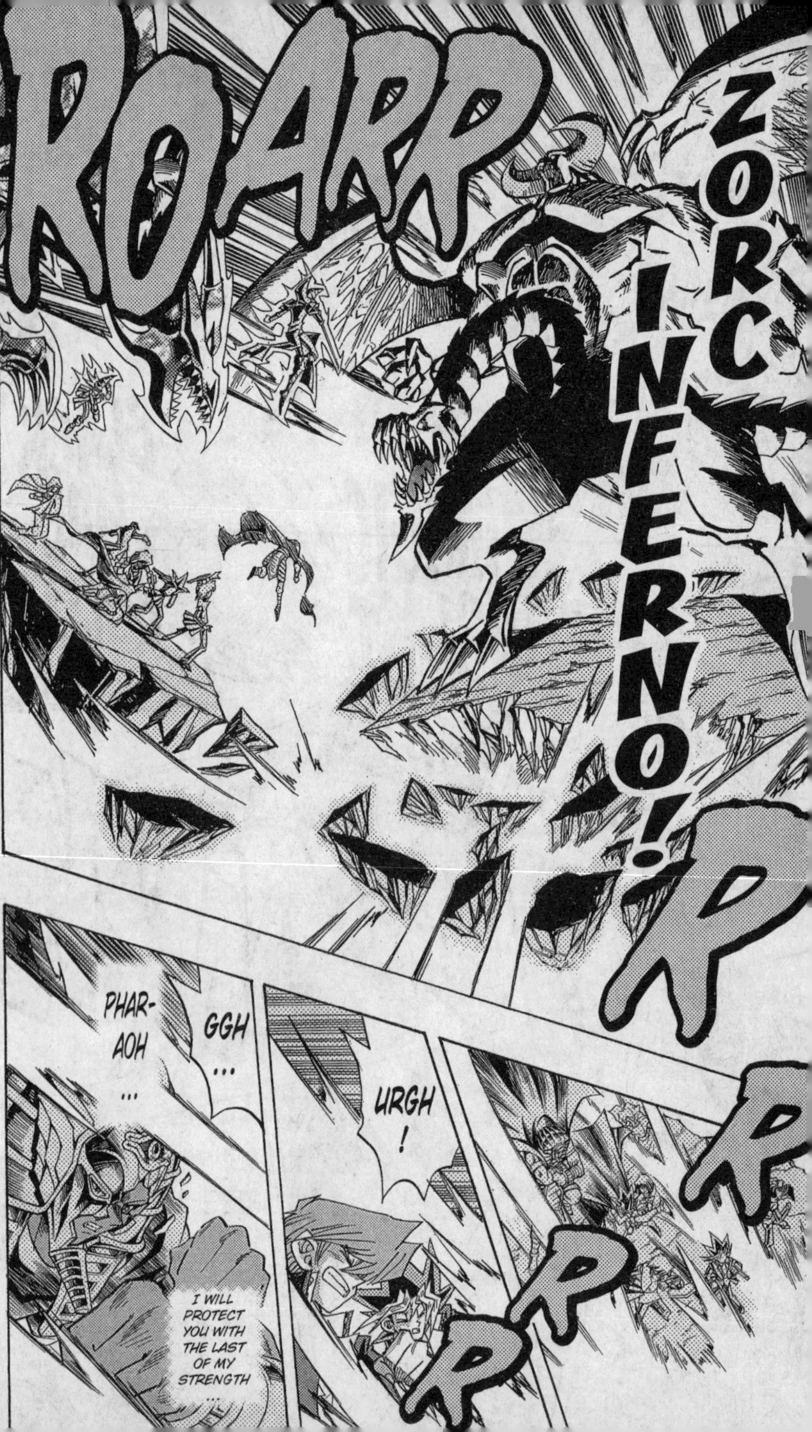
ROARR
ZORC INFERNO!
RRRR
URGH !
GGH ...
PHAR-AOH ...
I WILL PROTECT YOU WITH THE LAST OF MY STRENGTH ...

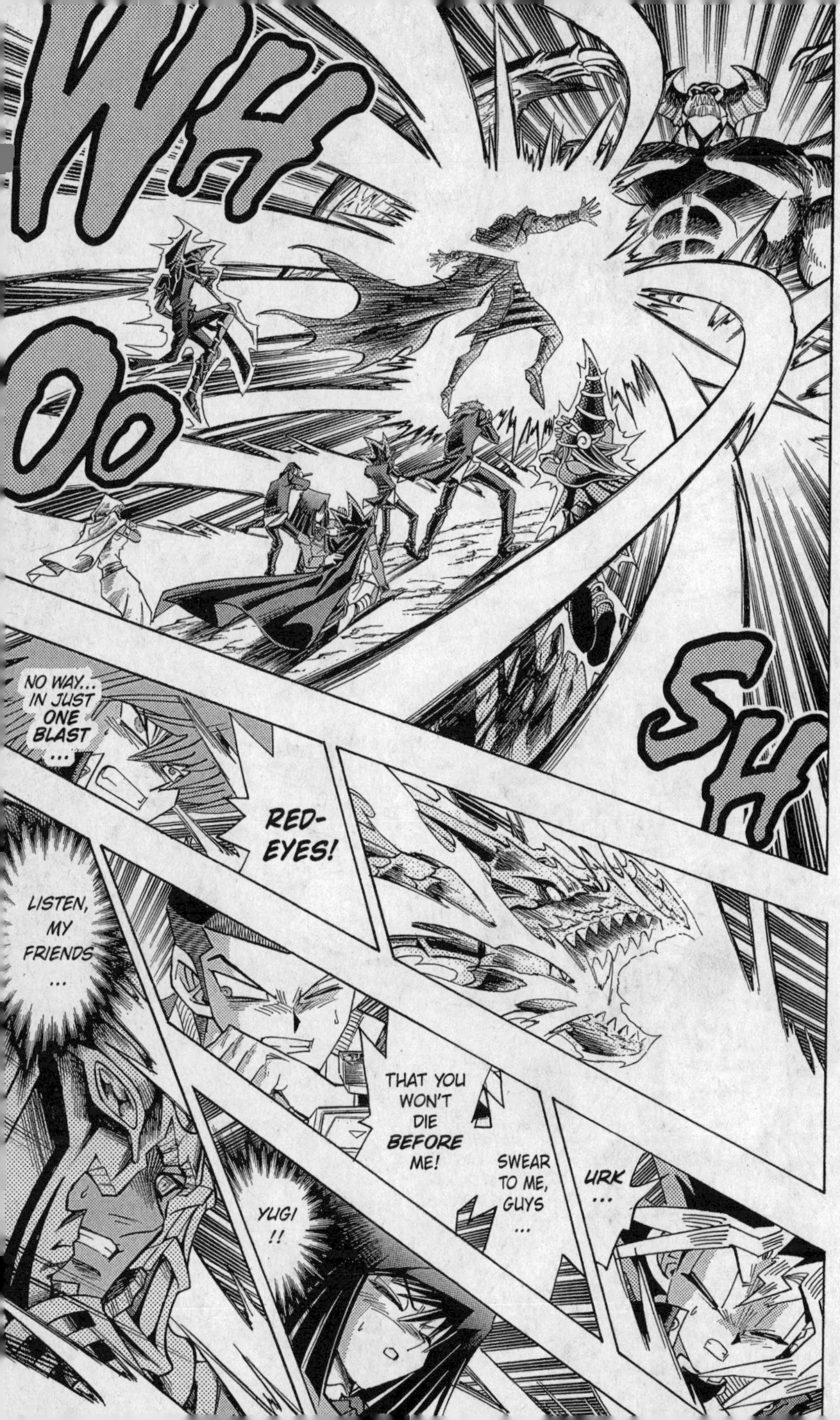
WH
OO
SH
RED-EYES!
NO WAY... IN JUST ONE BLAST...
LISTEN, MY FRIENDS...
SWEAR TO ME, GUYS...
THAT YOU WON'T DIE BEFORE ME!
URK...
YUGI!!

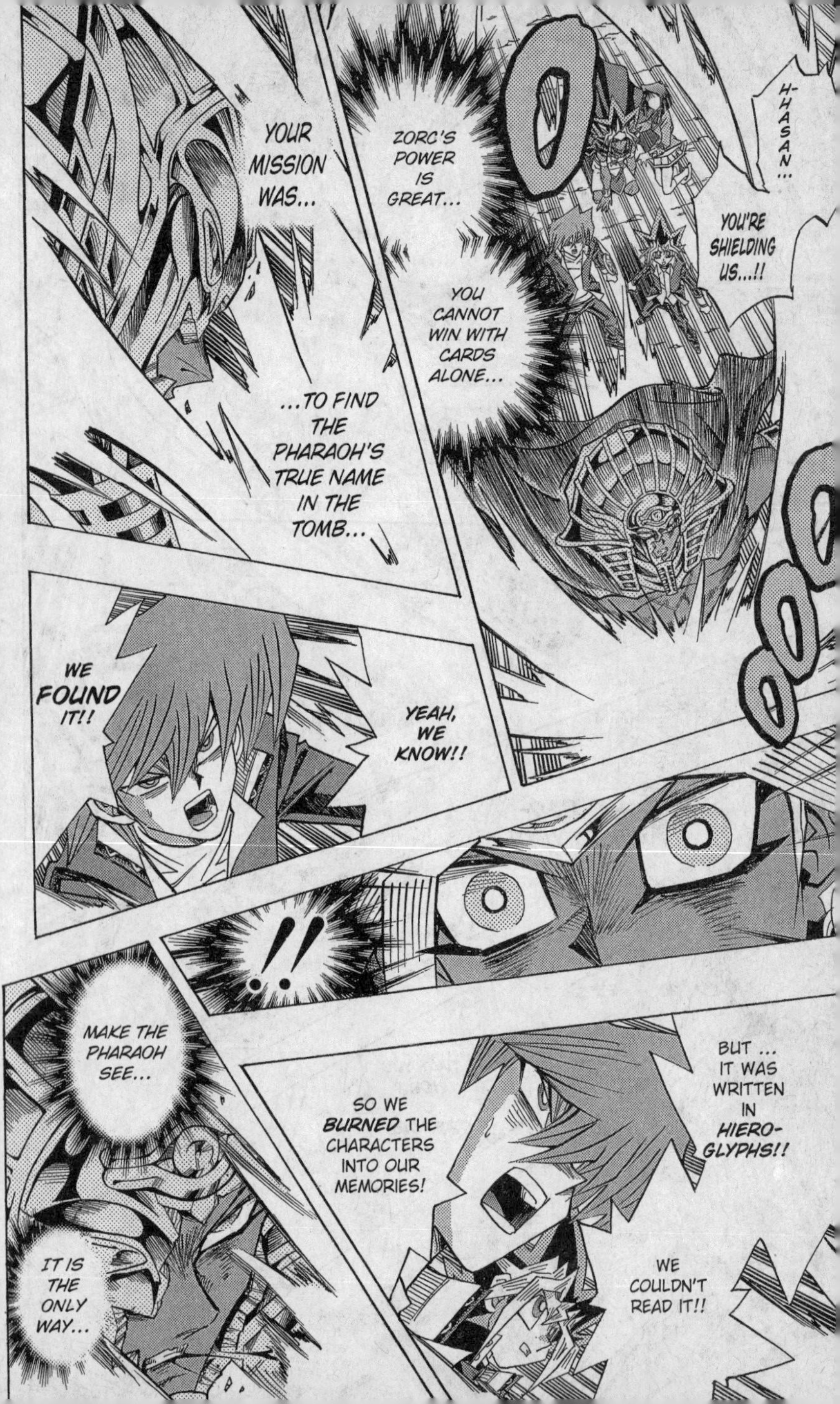
H-HASAN...!!
YOU'RE SHIELDING US...!!
ZORC'S POWER IS GREAT...
YOU CANNOT WIN WITH CARDS ALONE...
YOUR MISSION WAS...
...TO FIND THE PHARAOH'S TRUE NAME IN THE TOMB...
!!
YEAH, WE KNOW!!
WE FOUND IT!!
BUT ... IT WAS WRITTEN IN HIERO-GLYPHS!!
WE COULDN'T READ IT!!
SO WE BURNED THE CHARACTERS INTO OUR MEMORIES!
MAKE THE PHARAOH SEE...
IT IS THE ONLY WAY...

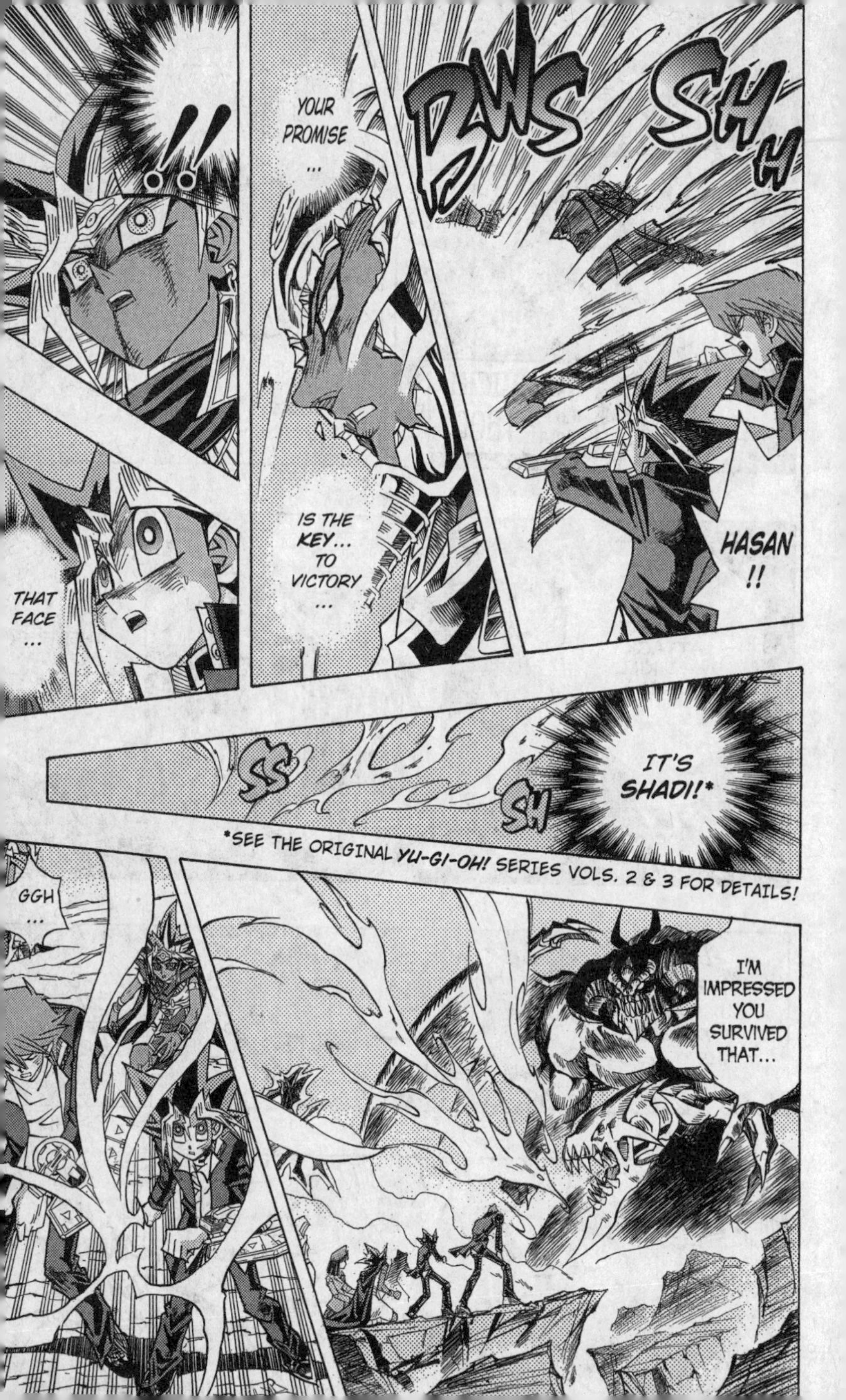
BAWS
SHH
HASAN !!
YOUR PROMISE ...
IS THE KEY... TO VICTORY ...
!!
THAT FACE ...
SS
SH
IT'S SHADI!*
*SEE THE ORIGINAL YU-GI-OH! SERIES VOLS. 2 & 3 FOR DETAILS!
I'M IMPRESSED YOU SURVIVED THAT...
GGH ...

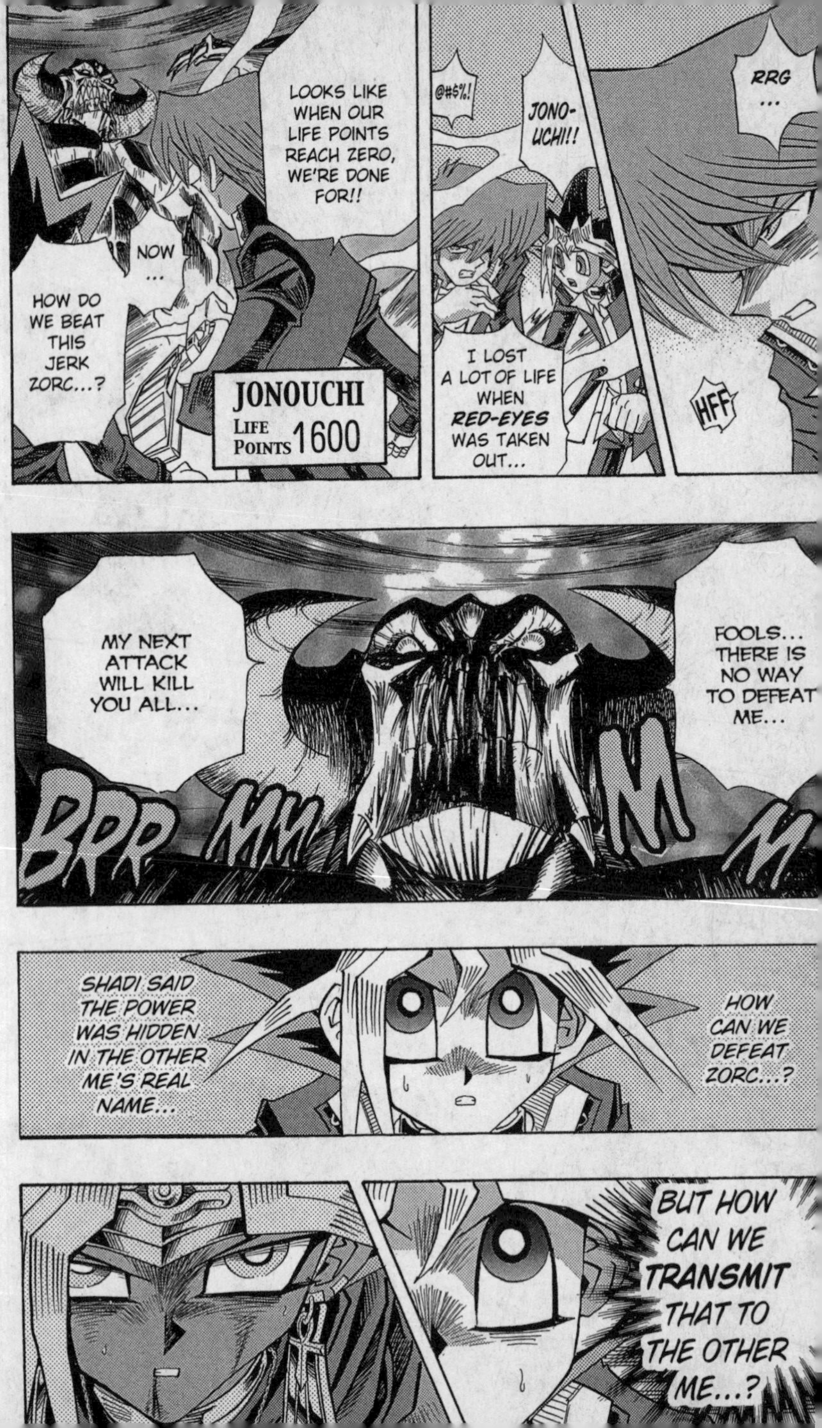
RRG ...
HFF
@#$%!
JONO-UCHI!!
I LOST A LOT OF LIFE WHEN RED-EYES WAS TAKEN OUT...
LOOKS LIKE WHEN OUR LIFE POINTS REACH ZERO, WE'RE DONE FOR!!
NOW ...
HOW DO WE BEAT THIS JERK ZORC...?
JONOUCHI LIFE POINTS 1600
FOOLS... THERE IS NO WAY TO DEFEAT ME...
MY NEXT ATTACK WILL KILL YOU ALL...
BRR MM M M
HOW CAN WE DEFEAT ZORC...?
SHADI SAID THE POWER WAS HIDDEN IN THE OTHER ME'S REAL NAME...
BUT HOW CAN WE TRANSMIT THAT TO THE OTHER ME...?

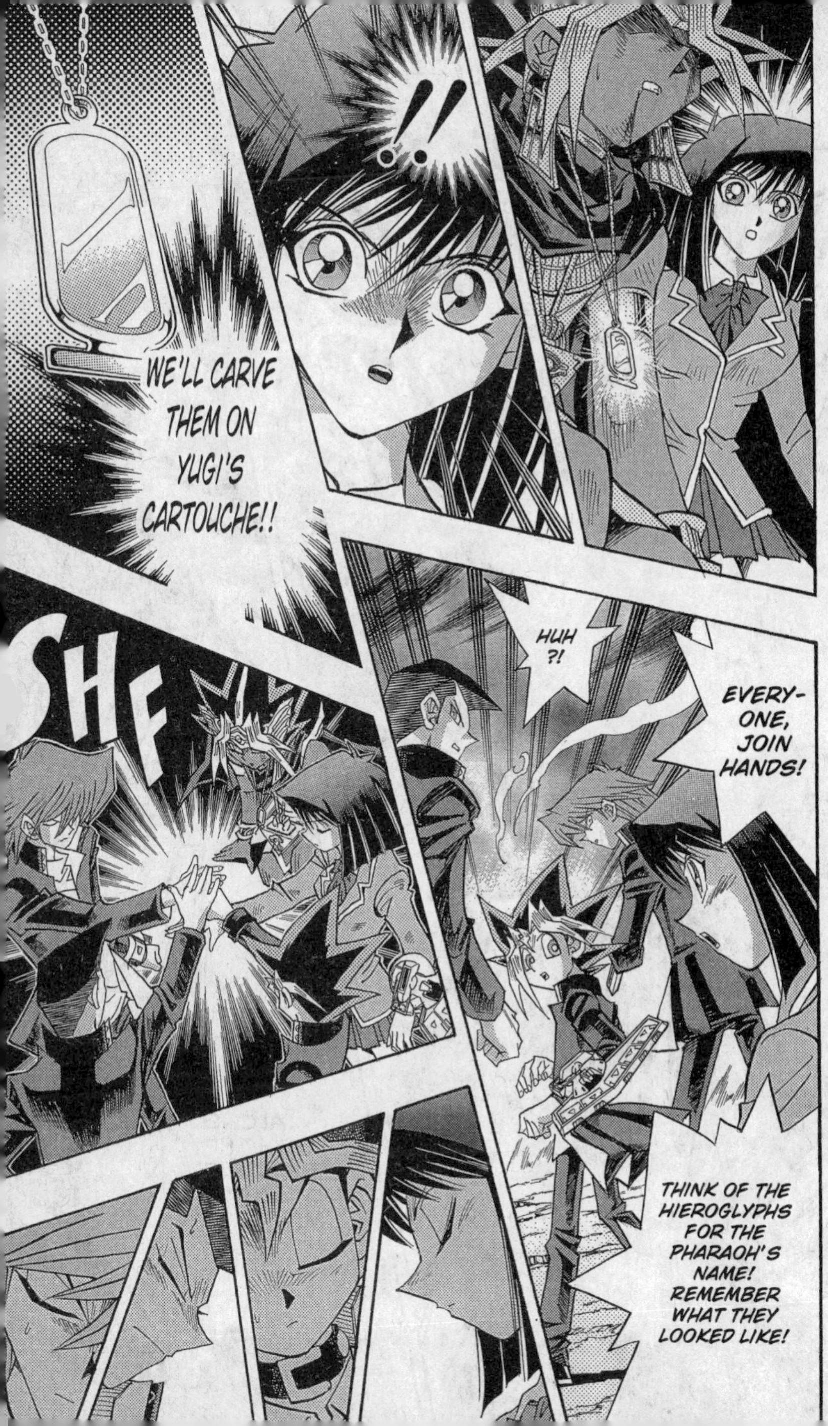
!!
WE'LL CARVE THEM ON YUGI'S CARTOUCHE!!
HUH ?!
EVERY-ONE, JOIN HANDS!
THINK OF THE HIEROGLYPHS FOR THE PHARAOH'S NAME! REMEMBER WHAT THEY LOOKED LIKE!
SHF

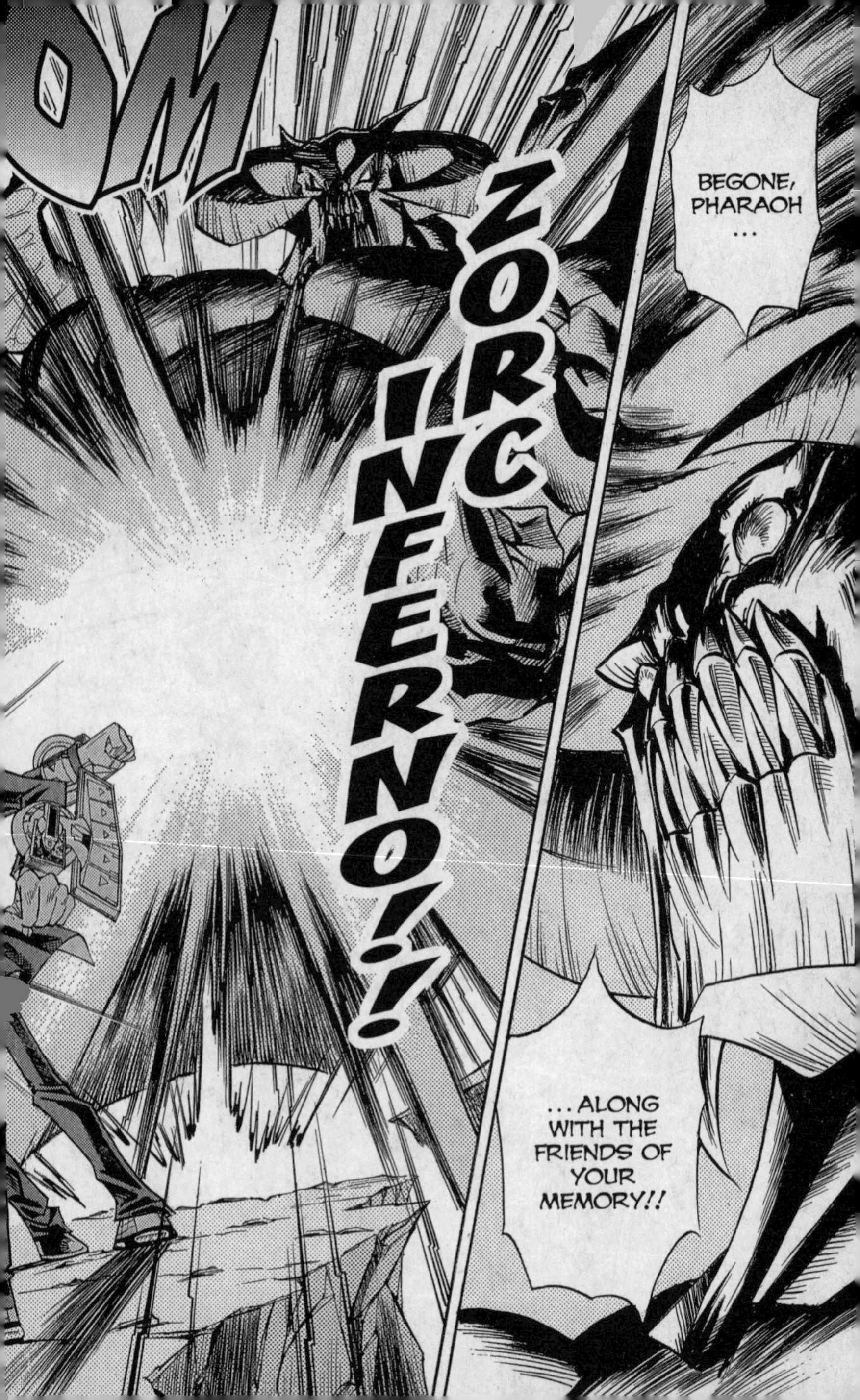
BEGONE, PHARAOH ...
...ALONG WITH THE FRIENDS OF YOUR MEMORY!!
OM
ZORC INFERNO!!

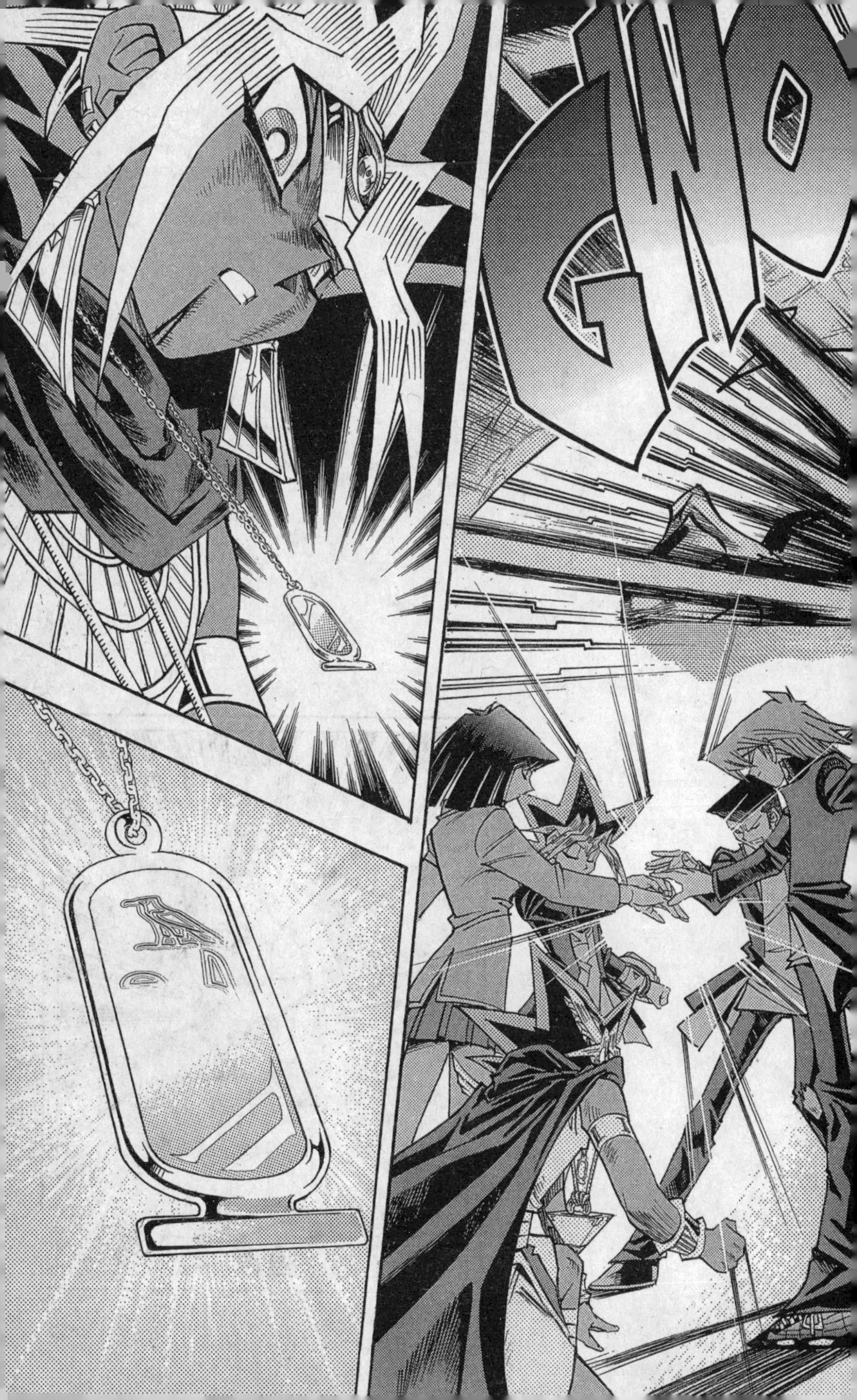
GWO

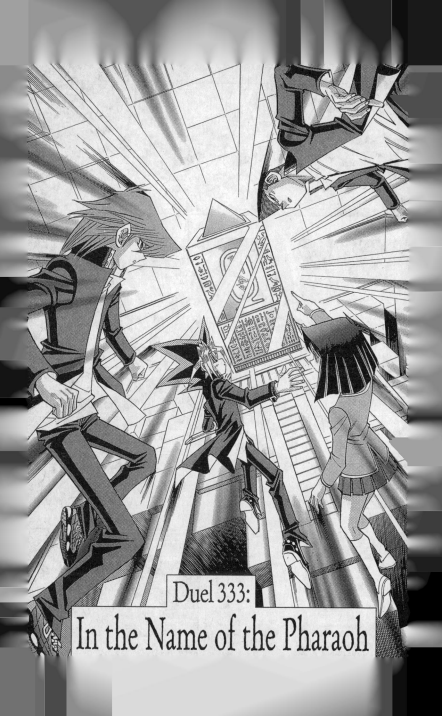

Duel 333:
In the Name of the Pharaoh

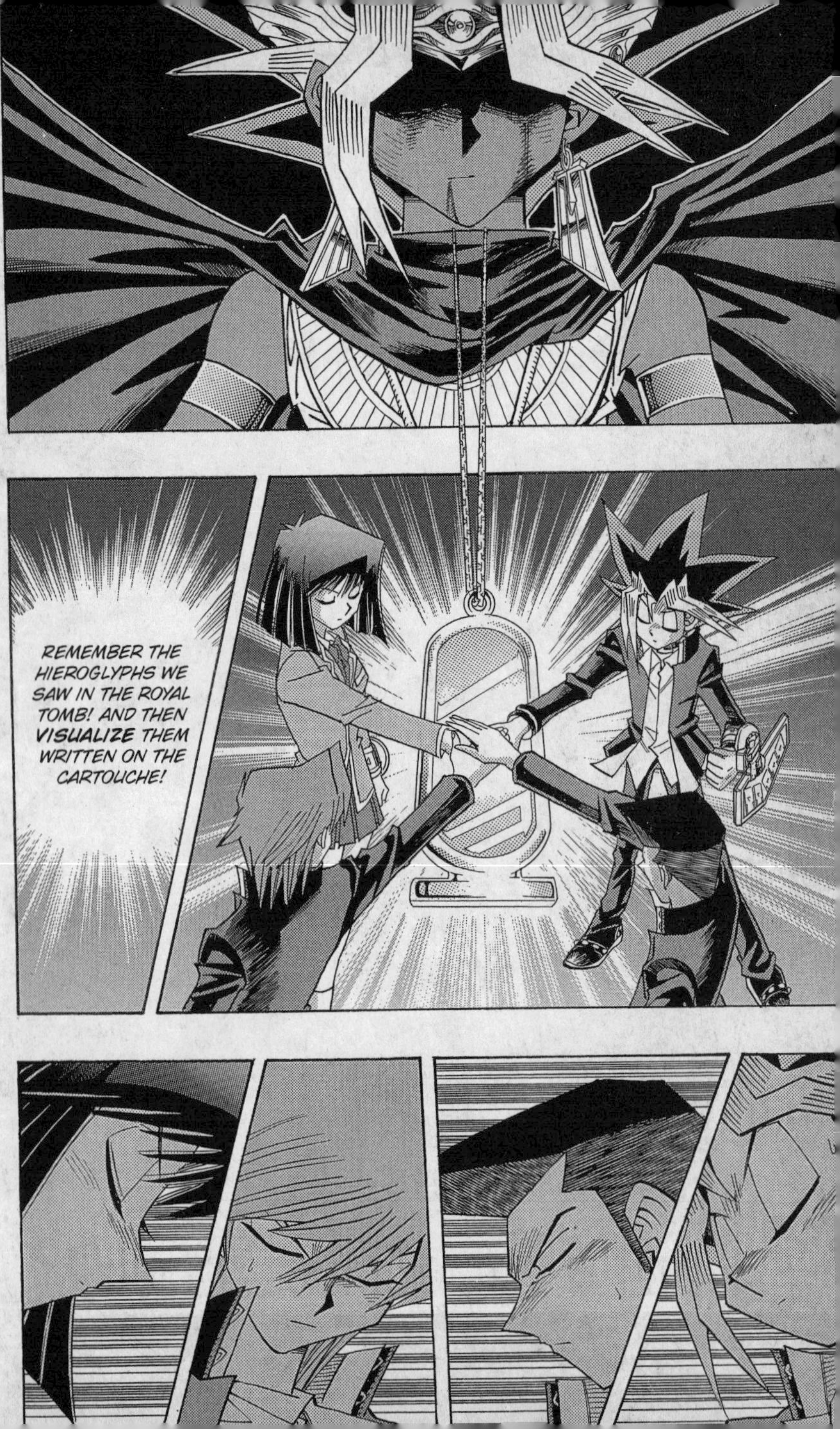
REMEMBER THE HIEROGLYPHS WE SAW IN THE ROYAL TOMB! AND THEN **VISUALIZE** THEM WRITTEN ON THE CARTOUCHE!

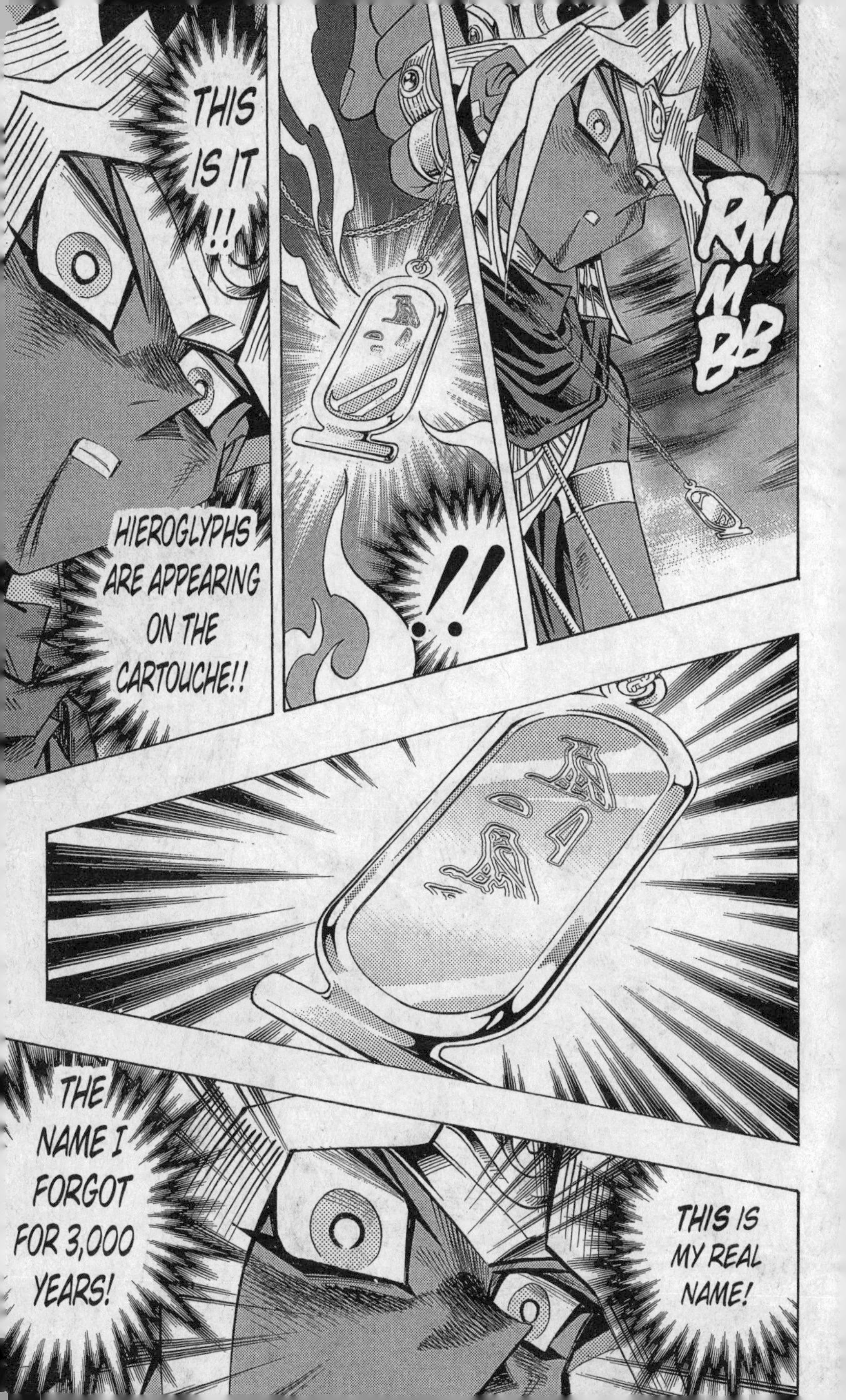
RMMBB
!!
THIS IS IT!!
HIEROGLYPHS ARE APPEARING ON THE CARTOUCHE!!
THIS IS MY REAL NAME!
THE NAME I FORGOT FOR 3,000 YEARS!

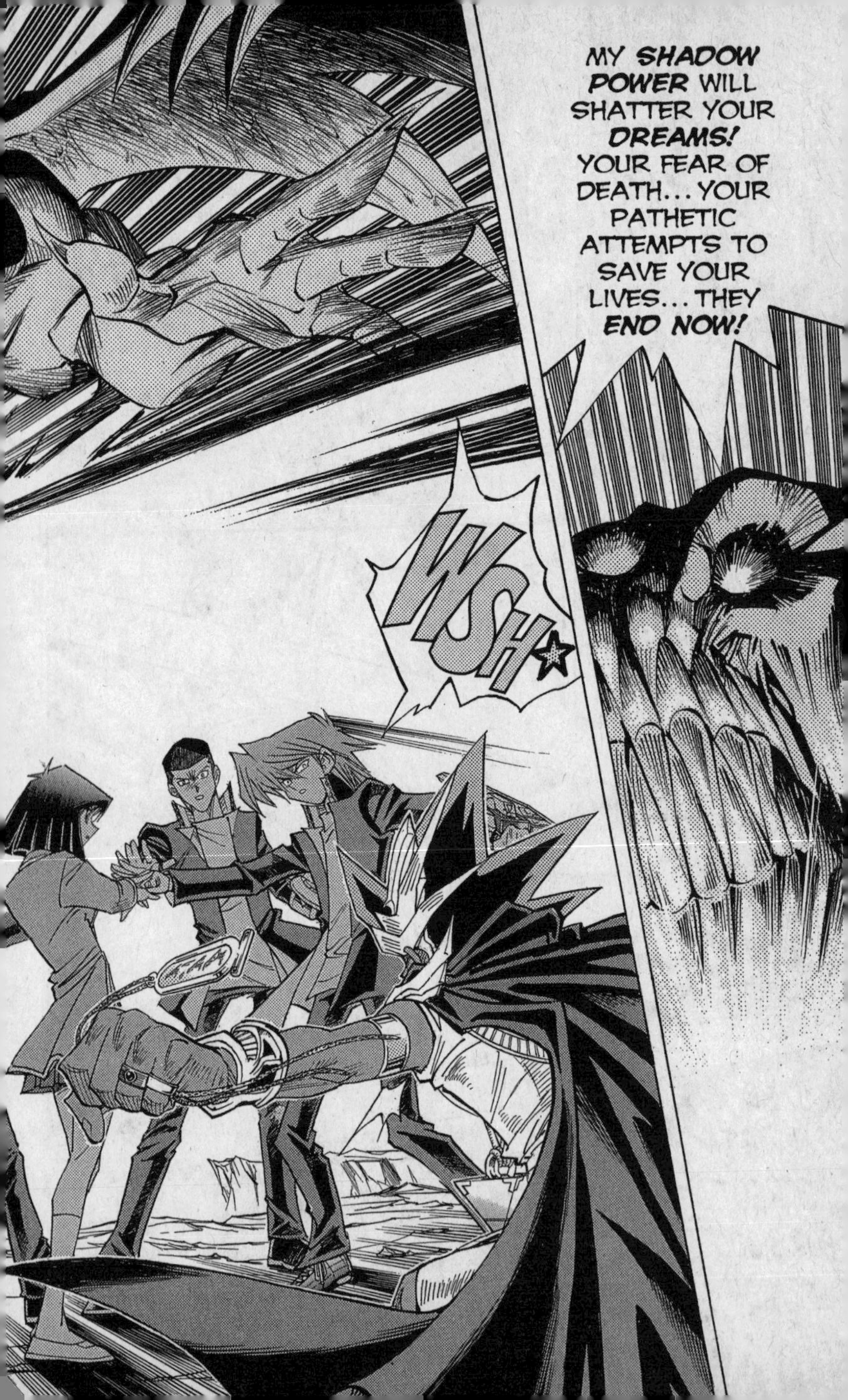
MY SHADOW POWER WILL SHATTER YOUR DREAMS! YOUR FEAR OF DEATH... YOUR PATHETIC ATTEMPTS TO SAVE YOUR LIVES... THEY END NOW!
WSH☆

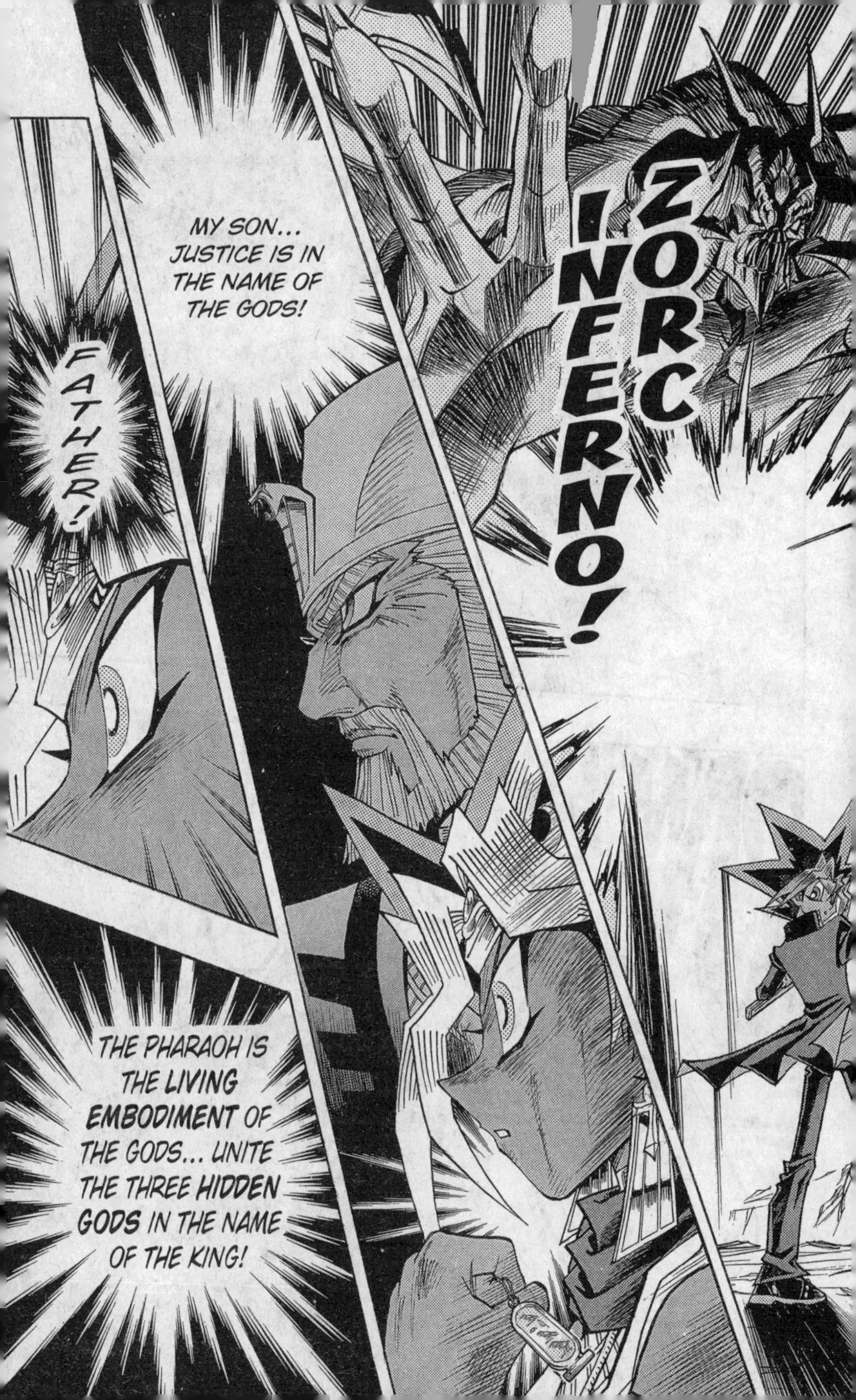
ZORC INFERNO!
MY SON... JUSTICE IS IN THE NAME OF THE GODS!
FATHER!
THE PHARAOH IS THE LIVING EMBODIMENT OF THE GODS... UNITE THE THREE HIDDEN GODS IN THE NAME OF THE KING!

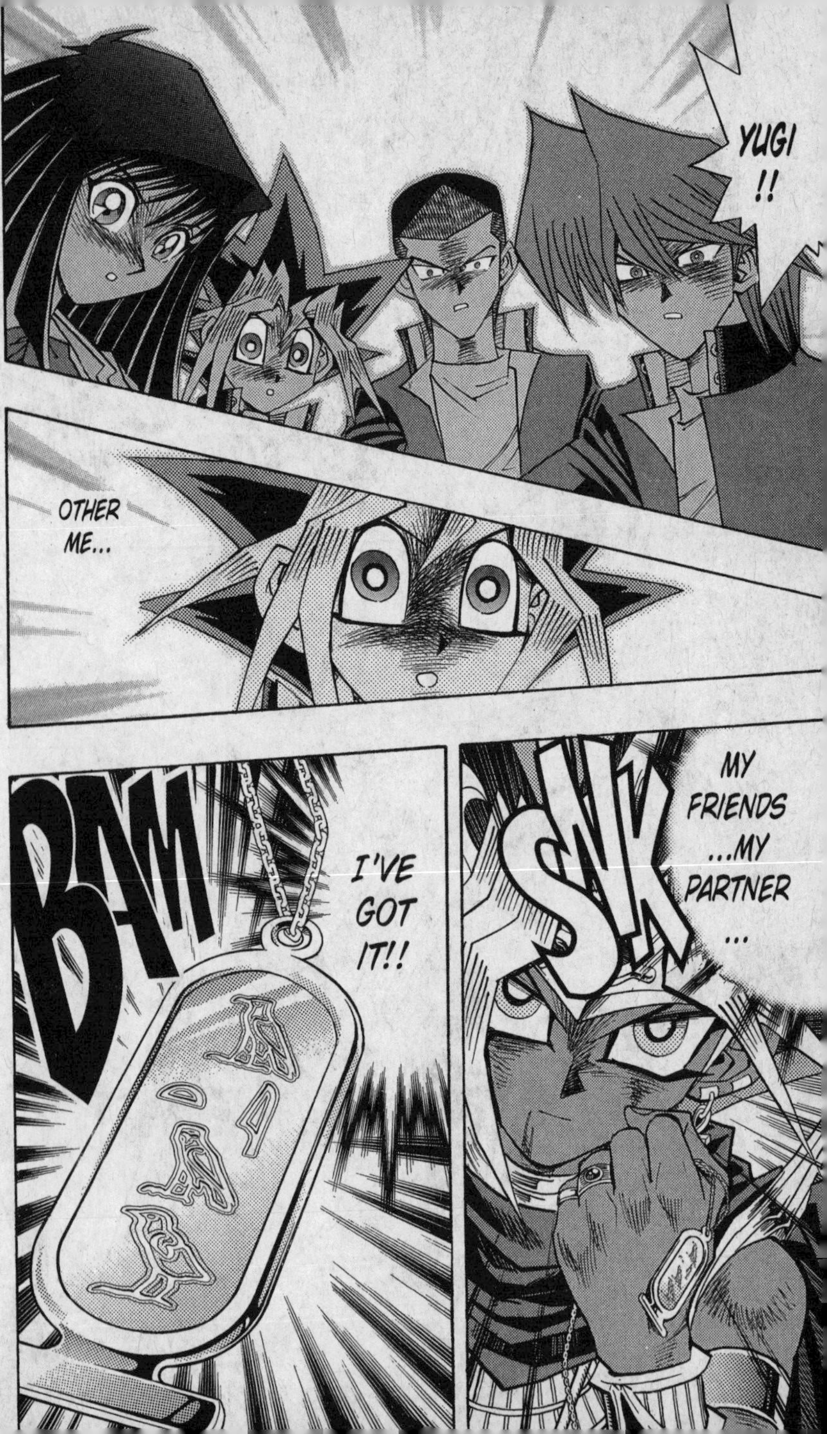
YUGI !!
OTHER ME...
MY FRIENDS ...MY PARTNER ...
SNK
I'VE GOT IT!!
BAM

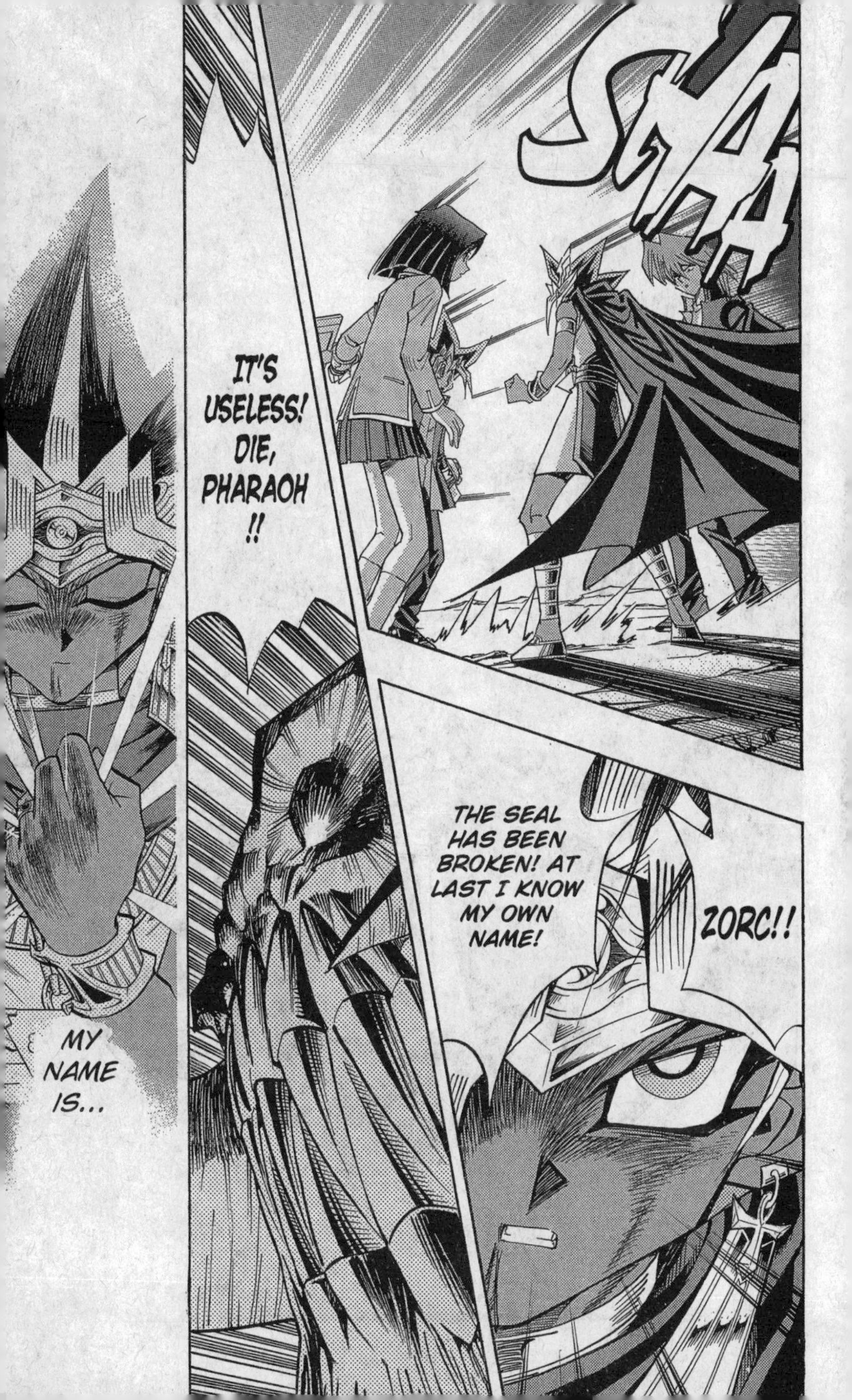

IT'S USELESS! DIE, PHARAOH!!
THE SEAL HAS BEEN BROKEN! AT LAST I KNOW MY OWN NAME!
ZORC!!
MY NAME IS...

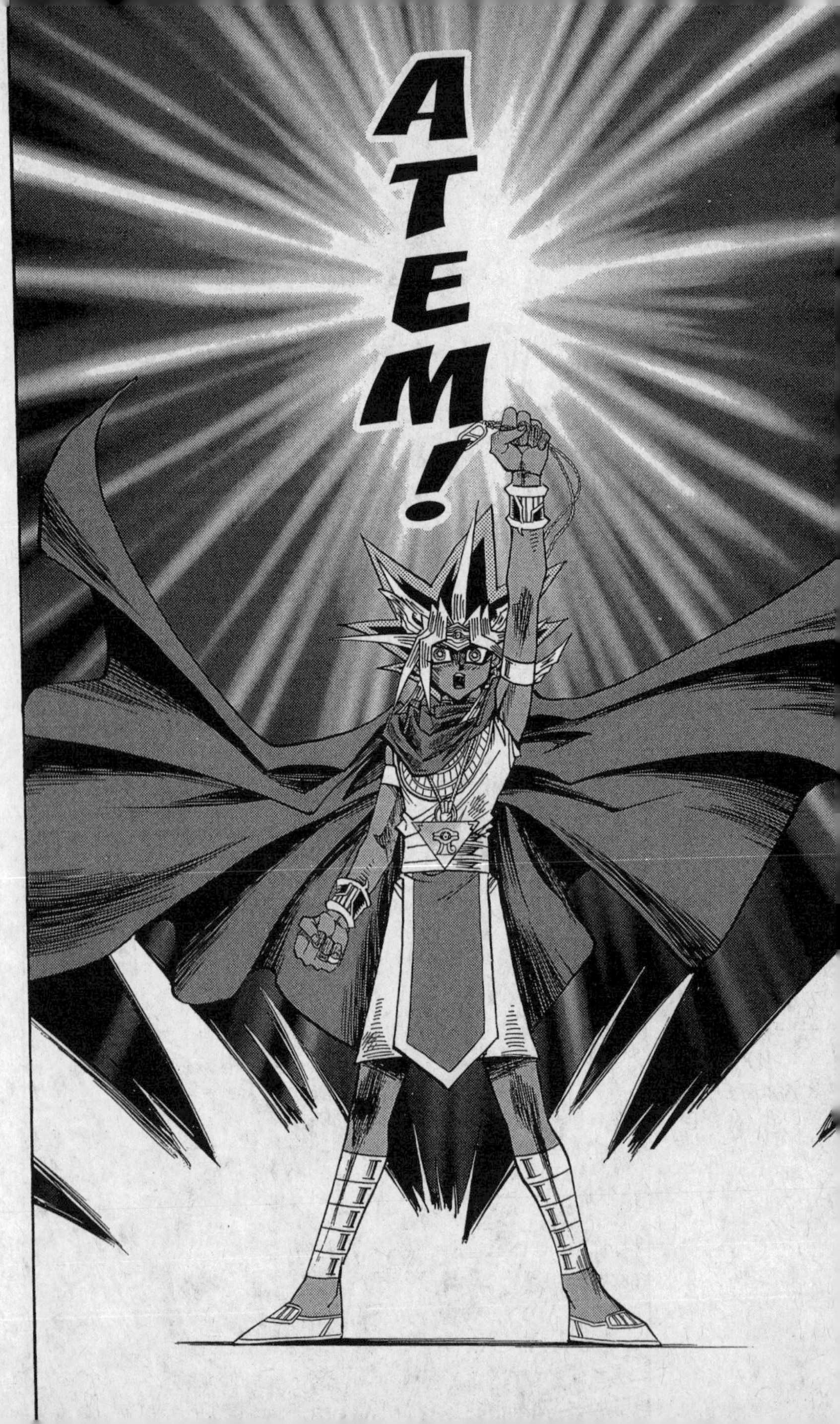
ATEM!

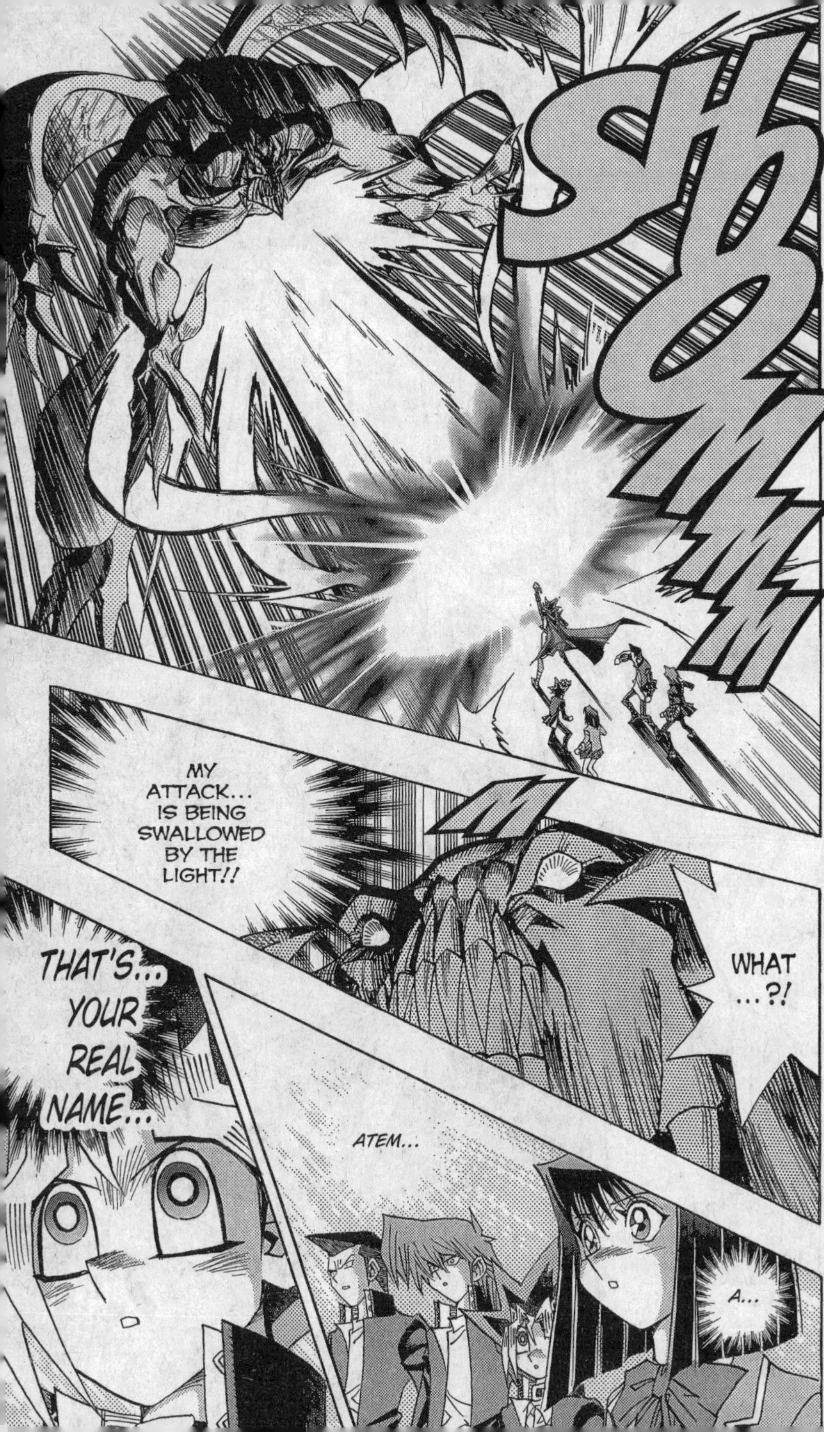
SHOOMMM
MY ATTACK... IS BEING SWALLOWED BY THE LIGHT!!
WHAT ...?!
A...
ATEM...
THAT'S... YOUR REAL NAME...

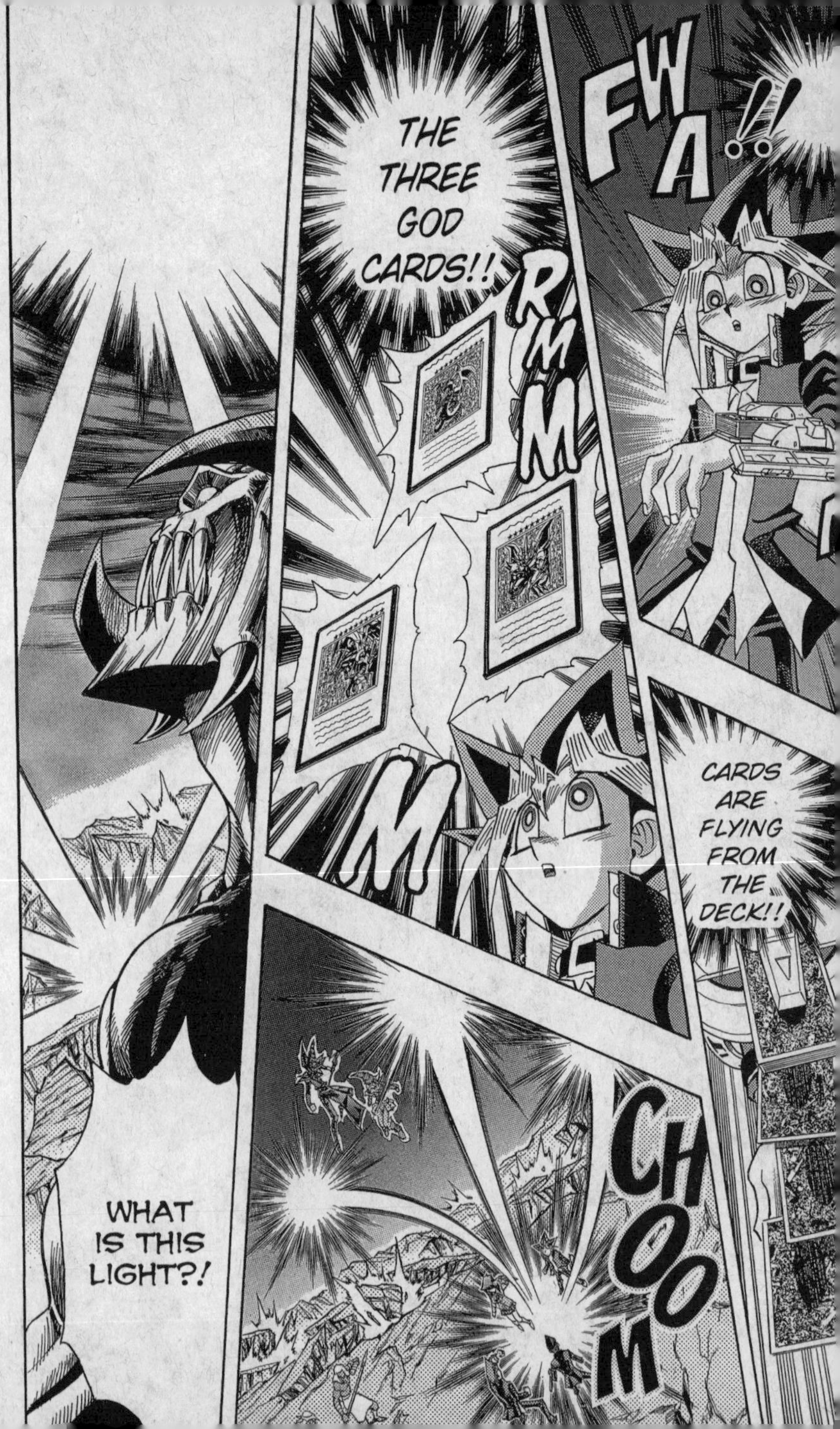
FWA!!
THE THREE GOD CARDS!!
RMMMM
CARDS ARE FLYING FROM THE DECK!!
CHOOOM
WHAT IS THIS LIGHT?!

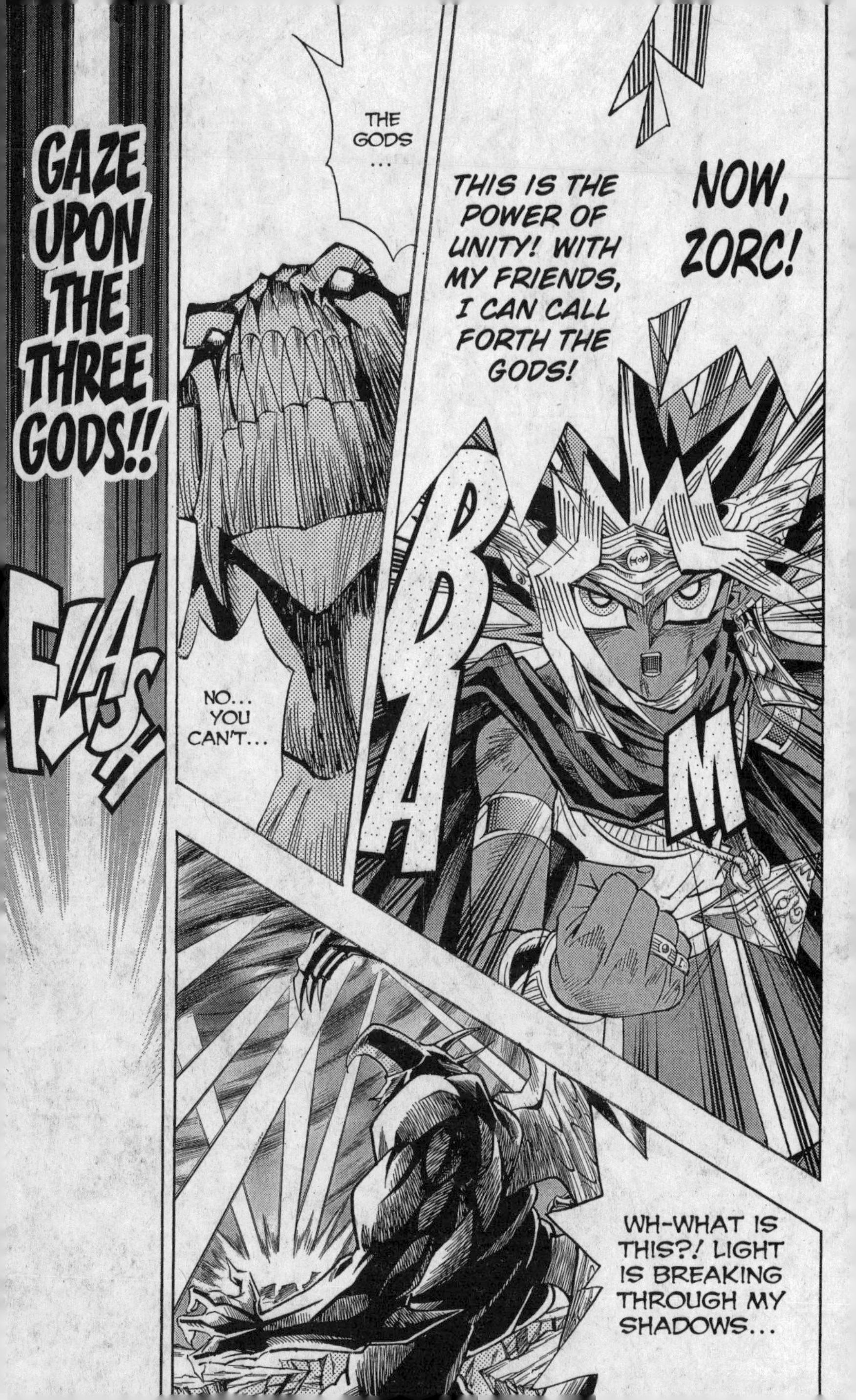
NOW, ZORC!
THIS IS THE POWER OF UNITY! WITH MY FRIENDS, I CAN CALL FORTH THE GODS!
BAM
THE GODS ...
NO... YOU CAN'T...
WH-WHAT IS THIS?! LIGHT IS BREAKING THROUGH MY SHADOWS...
GAZE UPON THE THREE GODS!!
FLASH!!

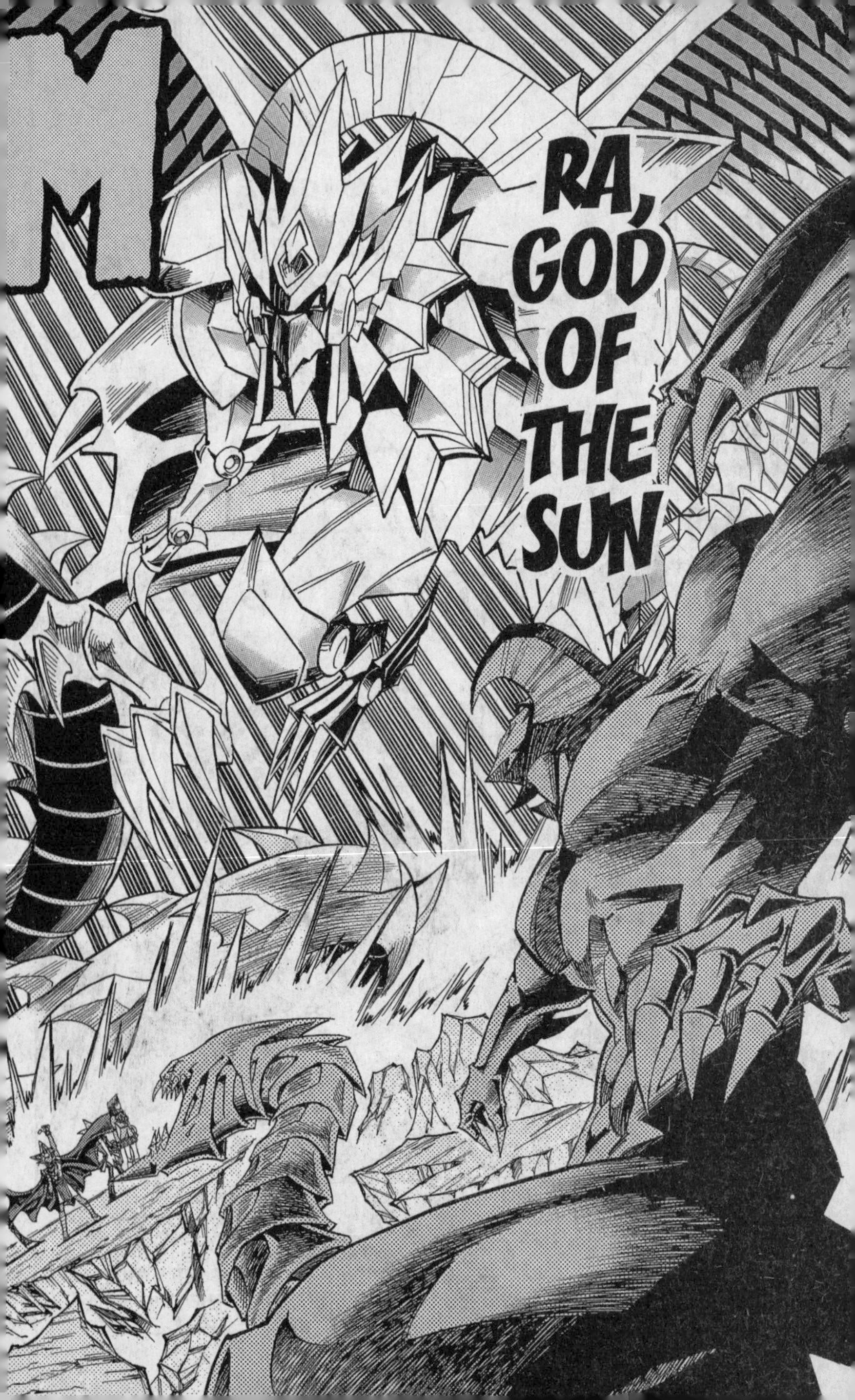
RA, GOD OF THE SUN

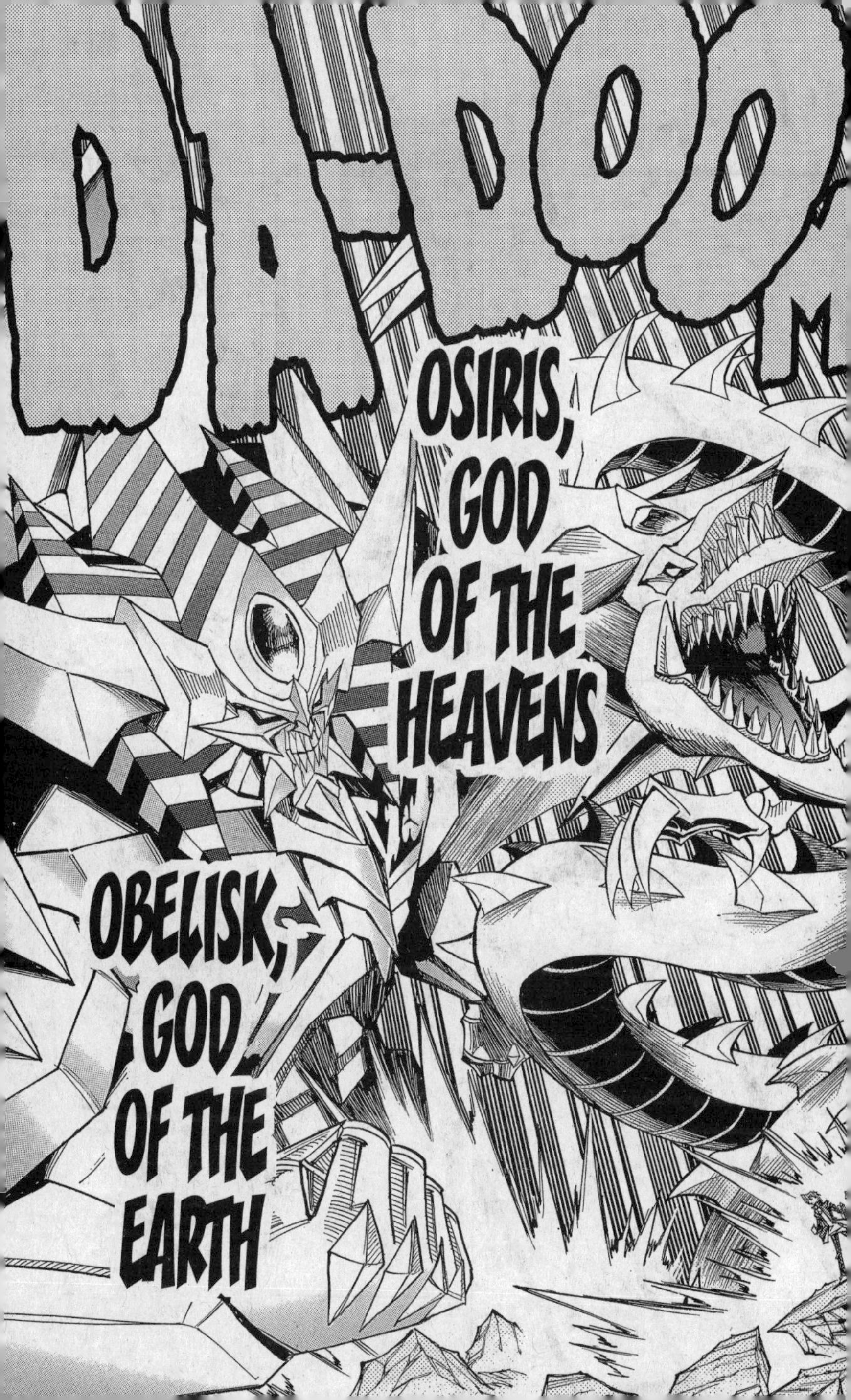
DA-DOO
OSIRIS, GOD OF THE HEAVENS
OBELISK, GOD OF THE EARTH

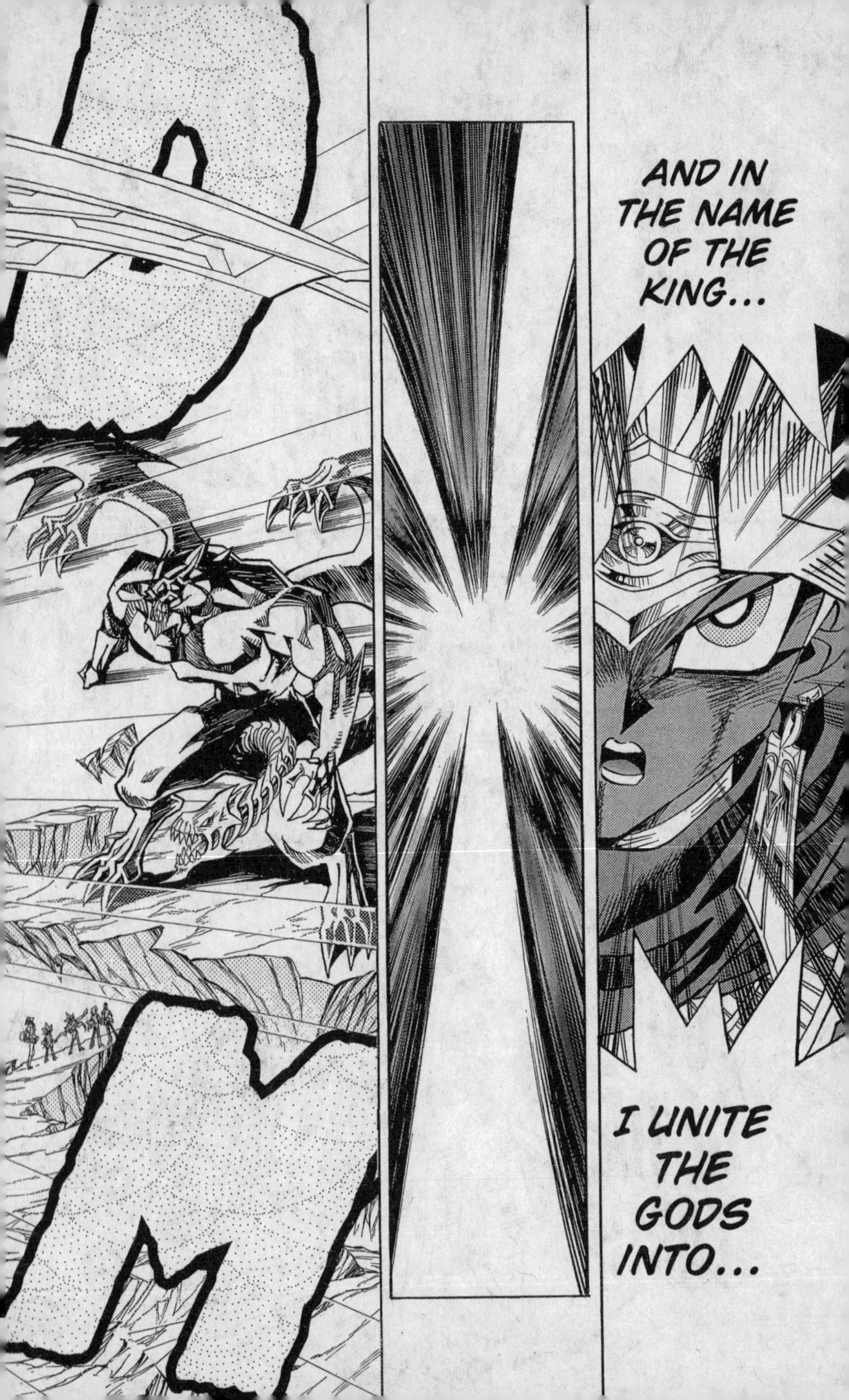
AND IN THE NAME OF THE KING...
I UNITE THE GODS INTO...

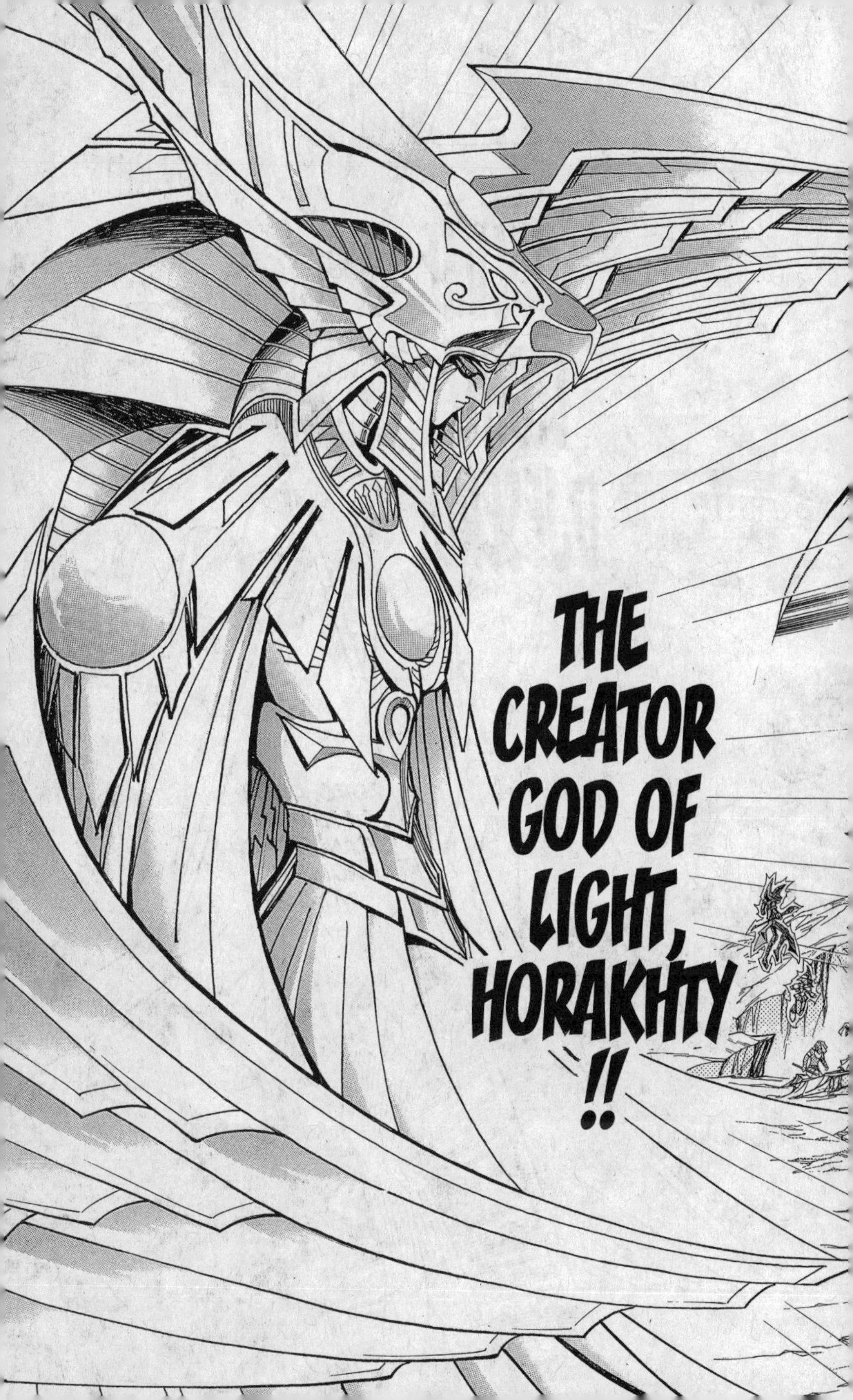
THE CREATOR GOD OF LIGHT, HORAKHTY!!

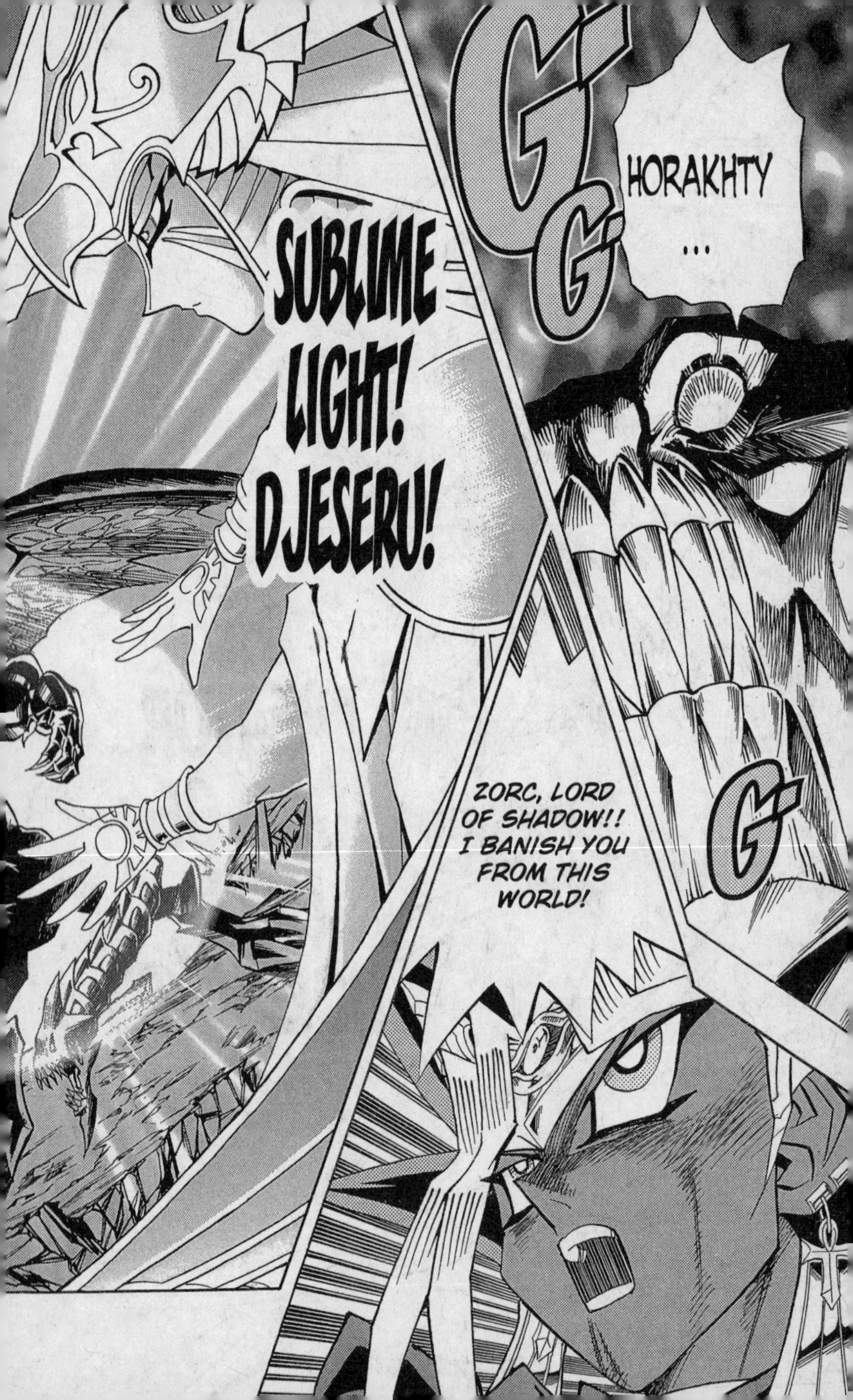
G G
HORAKHTY ...
G
ZORC, LORD OF SHADOW!! I BANISH YOU FROM THIS WORLD!
SUBLIME LIGHT! DJESERU!

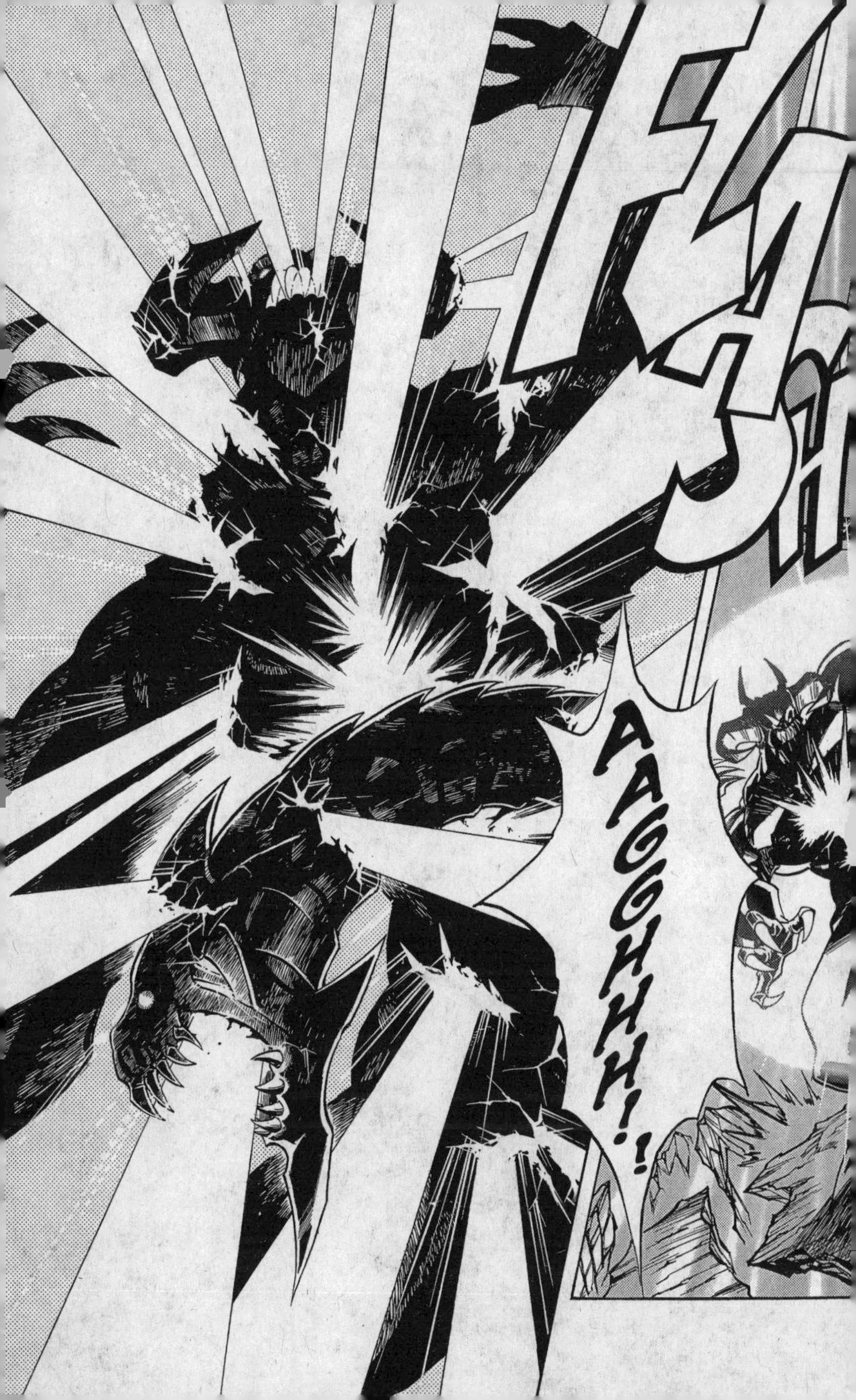
AAGGHHH!!

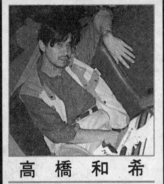

高橋和希

TO ALL OF YOU WHO'VE SUPPORTED
ME...YOU HAVE MY DEEPEST THANKS.

—KAZUKI TAKAHASHI, 2004

SHONEN JUMP MANGA

Yu-Gi-Oh!
Millennium World

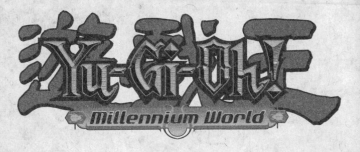

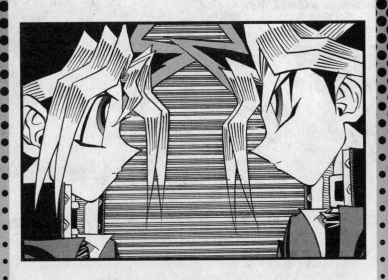

Vol. 38

THROUGH THE LAST DOOR

STORY AND ART BY

KAZUKI TAKAHASHI

THE MAIN CHARACTERS

YUGI MUTOU

むとうゆうぎ
武藤遊戯

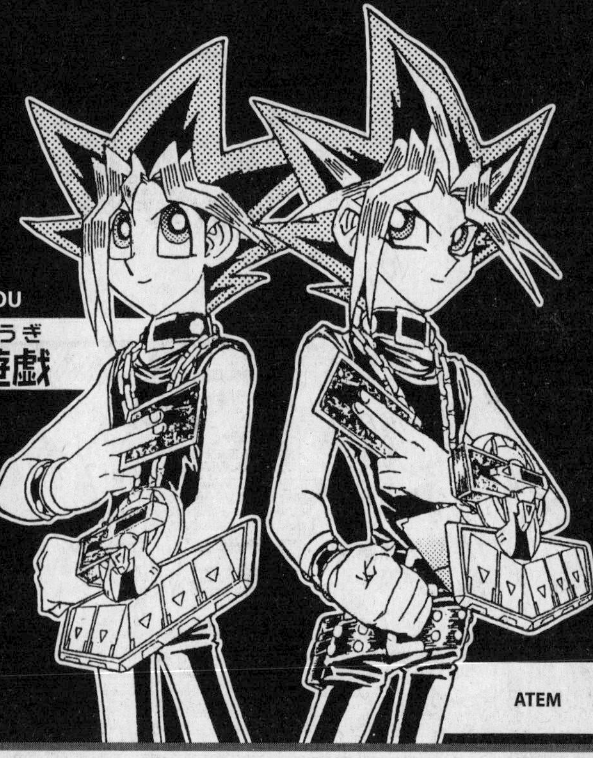

ATEM

Soon Akhenaden surrendered to the dark side and summoned Zorc Necrophades, who attacked Egypt with an army of the dead. Then Bakura revealed the truth: the "world of memories" is a simulation, a shadow role-playing game based on Yu-Gi-Oh's memories of the past! Yu-Gi-Oh and the priests (including Akhenaden's son Seto) fought bravely against Zorc and Bakura, knowing that only the winner could escape the role-playing game alive. All hope seemed lost, until Yugi's friends followed Yu-Gi-Oh into the game. There, they found the key to victory: the pharaoh's true name, which had been forgotten for 3,000 years.

The ancient Egyptians believed that magic dwelled in a person's name. When Yu-Gi-Oh spoke his true name, "Atem," the three Great Gods of Egypt appeared. Merging into one, the creator god Horakhty, they blasted Zorc with a beam of light...!

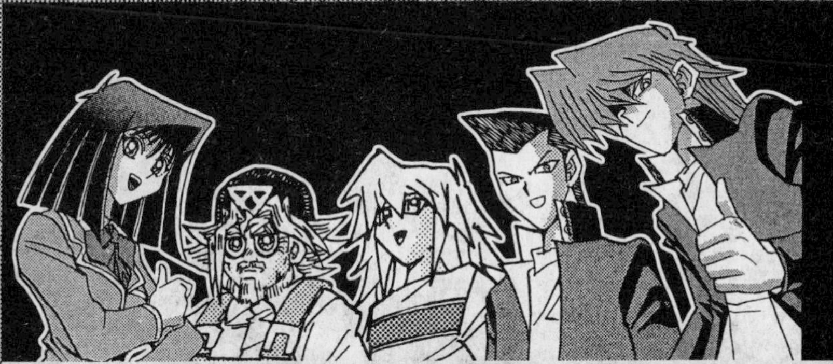

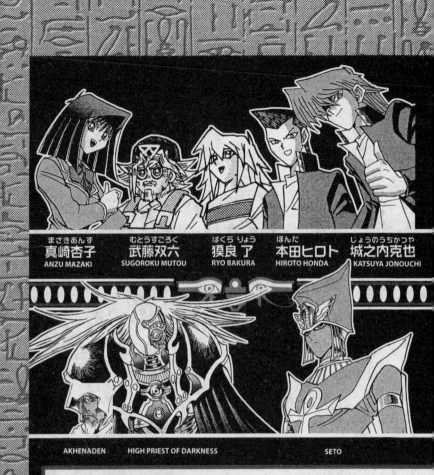

まざきあんず
真崎杏子
ANZU MAZAKI

むとうすごろく
武藤双六
SUGOROKU MUTOU

ばくら りょう
獏良 了
RYO BAKURA

ほんだ
本田ヒロト
HIROTO HONDA

じょうのうちかつや
城之内克也
KATSUYA JONOUCHI

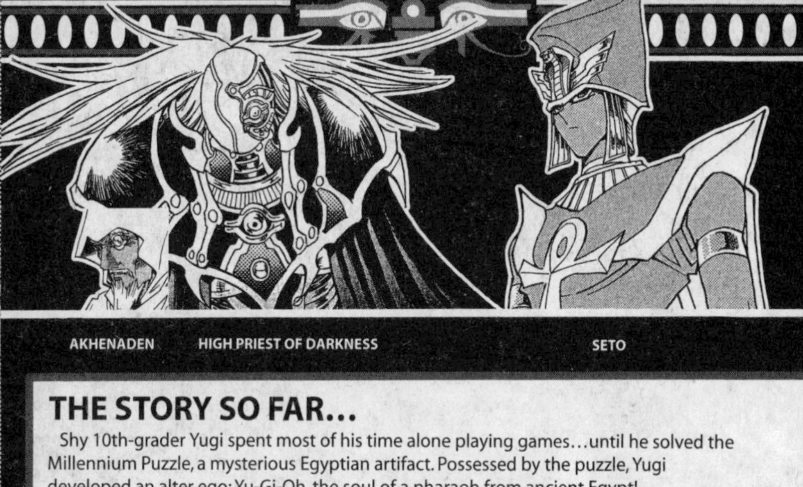

AKHENADEN

HIGH PRIEST OF DARKNESS

SETO

THE STORY SO FAR...

Shy 10th-grader Yugi spent most of his time alone playing games...until he solved the Millennium Puzzle, a mysterious Egyptian artifact. Possessed by the puzzle, Yugi developed an alter ego: Yu-Gi-Oh, the soul of a pharaoh from ancient Egypt!

Discovering that the card game "Duel Monsters" was of Ancient Egyptian origin, Yu-Gi-Oh collected the three Egyptian God Cards and used them to travel into the "world of memories" of his own life 3,000 years ago. There, he found that he was the pharaoh, served by priests who used the seven magic Millennium Items.

But unbeknownst even to the pharaoh, the Millennium Items were stained with blood. Created by the high priest Akhenaden, the Millennium Items owed their power to a mass human sacrifice! Their bloody origin had infused the Millennium Items with an evil spirit: the dark god Zorc Necrophades, who tempted Akhenaden with untold power. In the modern world, Zorc's servant was Bakura, a piece of Zorc's consciousness who dwelled in the Millennium Ring.

Vol. 38

CONTENTS

Duel 334	The Survivors	207
Duel 335	White Dragon, Black Magician	227
Duel 336	He Who Inherits the Light	247
Duel 337	Over the Nile!!	267
Duel 338	The Rite of the Duel!!	287
Duel 339	Yugi vs. Atem!!	307
Duel 340	The Ties That Bind	327
Duel 341	The Master of Servants	347
Duel 342	The Last Gamble!!	367
Last Duel	The Journey of the King	387
Afterword		420

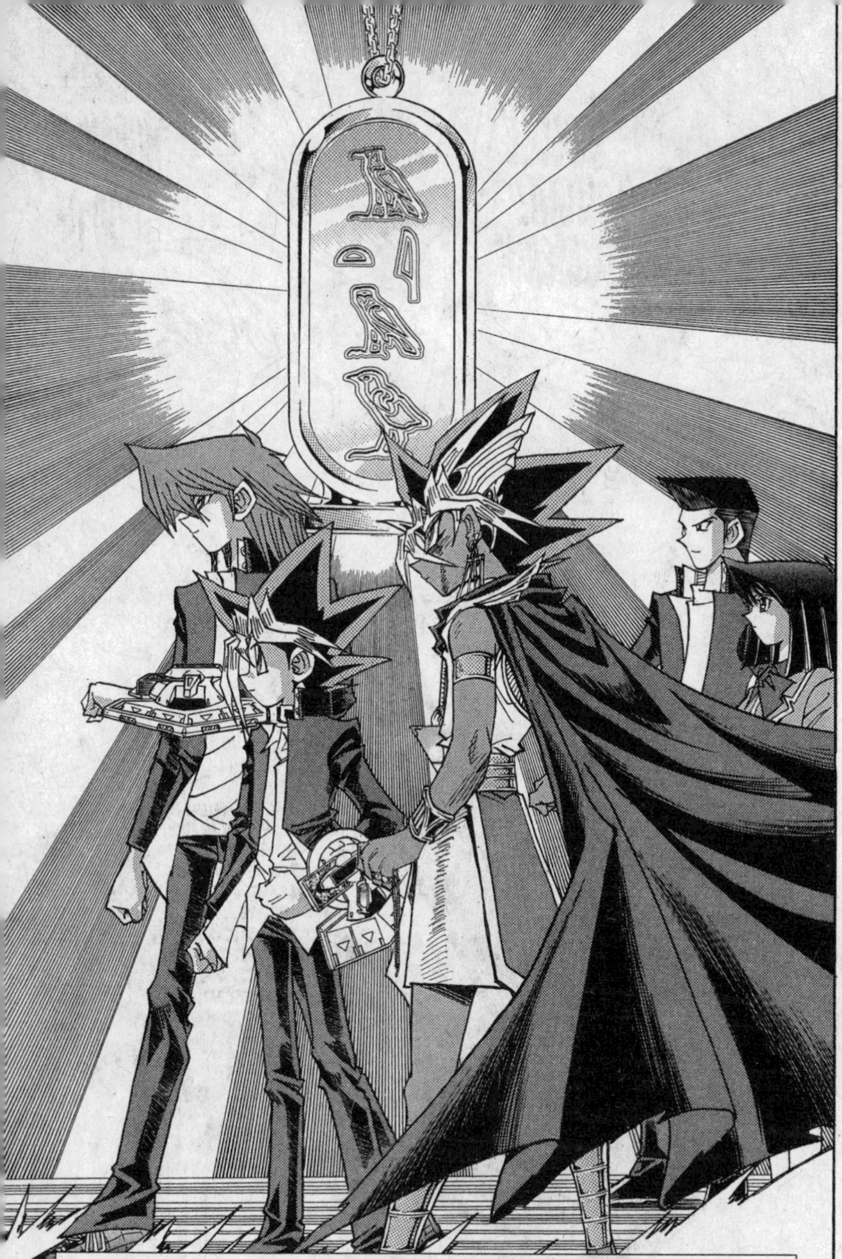

Duel 334: The Survivors

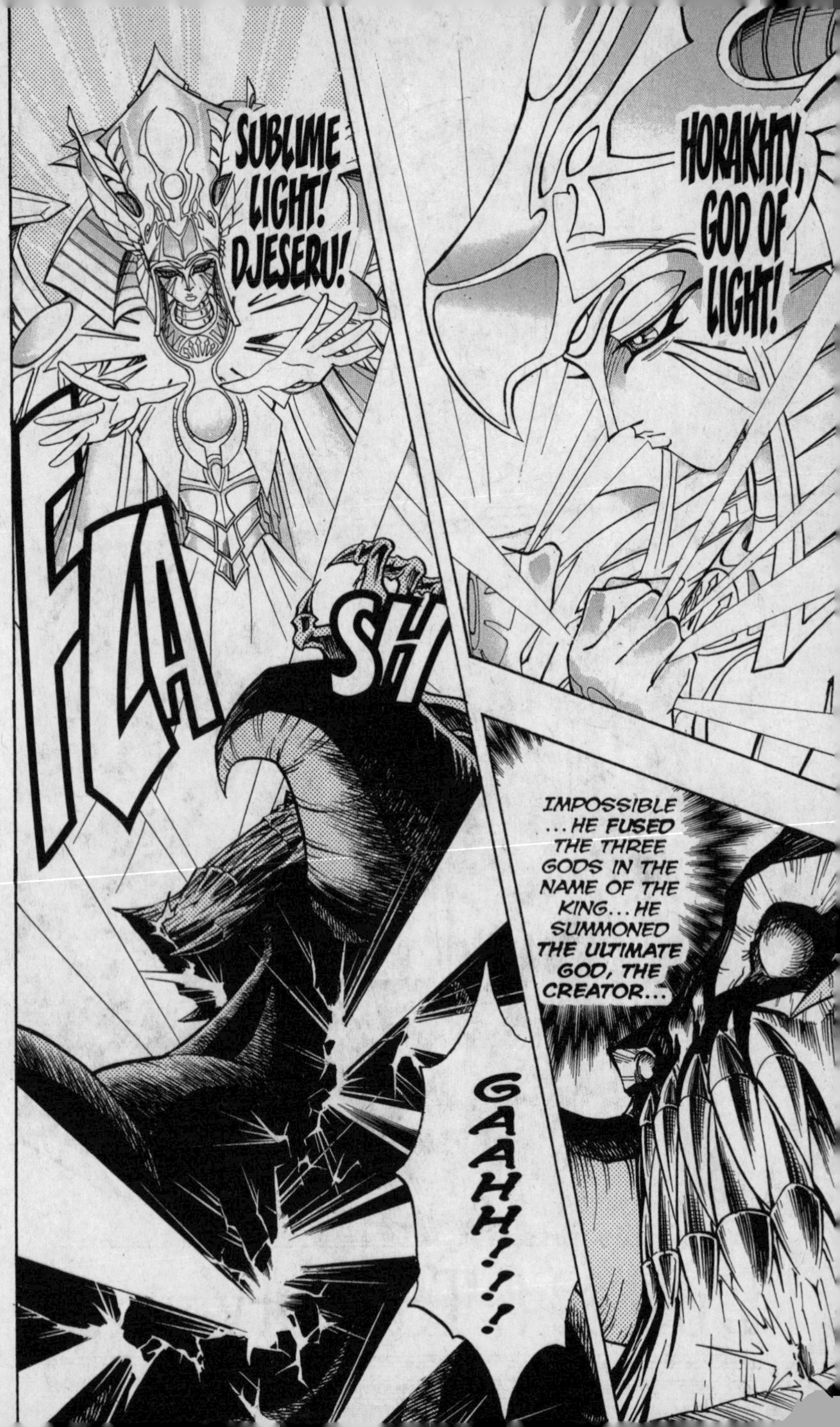
HORAKHTY, GOD OF LIGHT!
SUBLIME LIGHT! DJESERU!
FLASH
IMPOSSIBLE ...HE FUSED THE THREE GODS IN THE NAME OF THE KING...HE SUMMONED THE ULTIMATE GOD, THE CREATOR...
GAAHH!!!

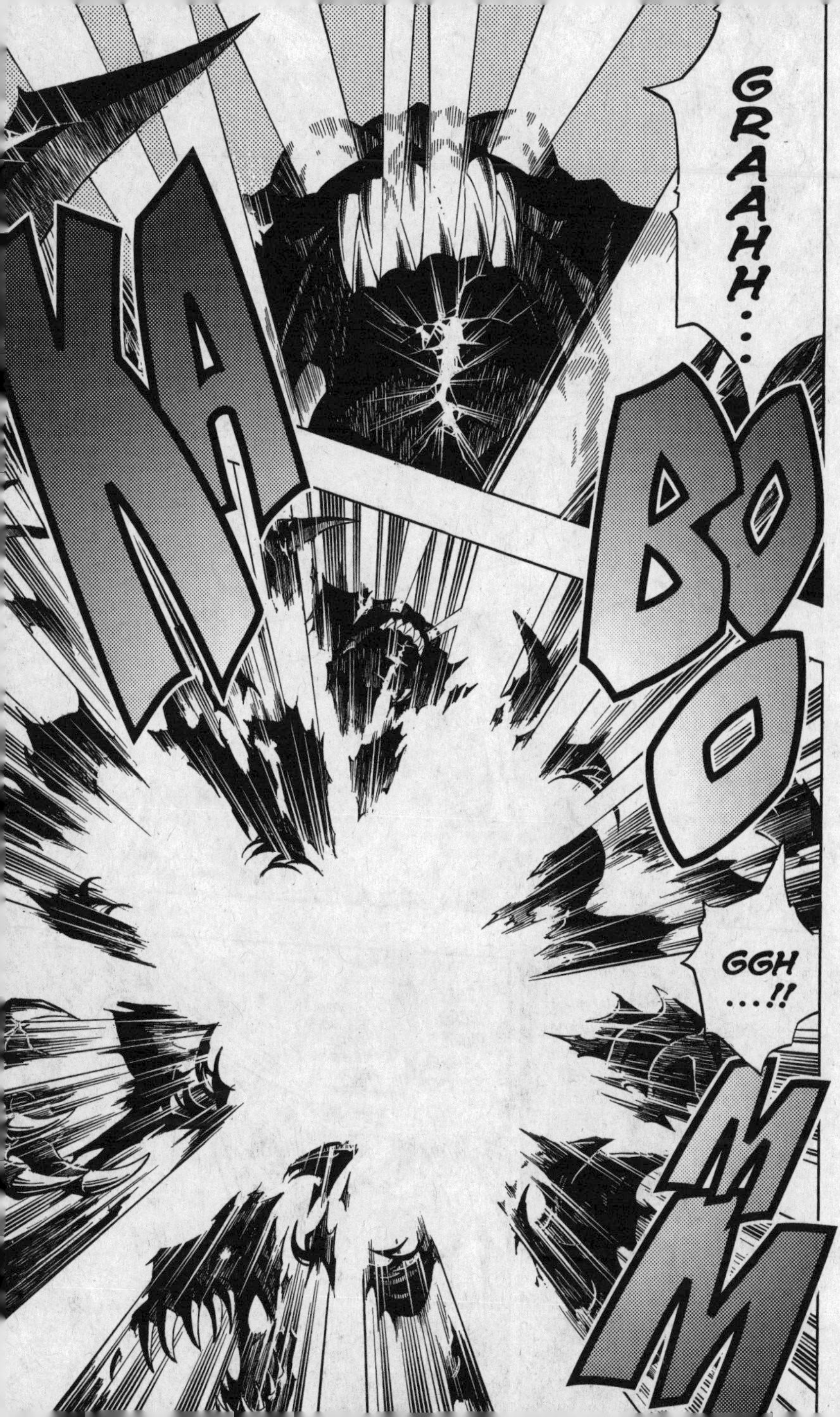
GRAAHH...
KA
BOOMM
GGH ...!!

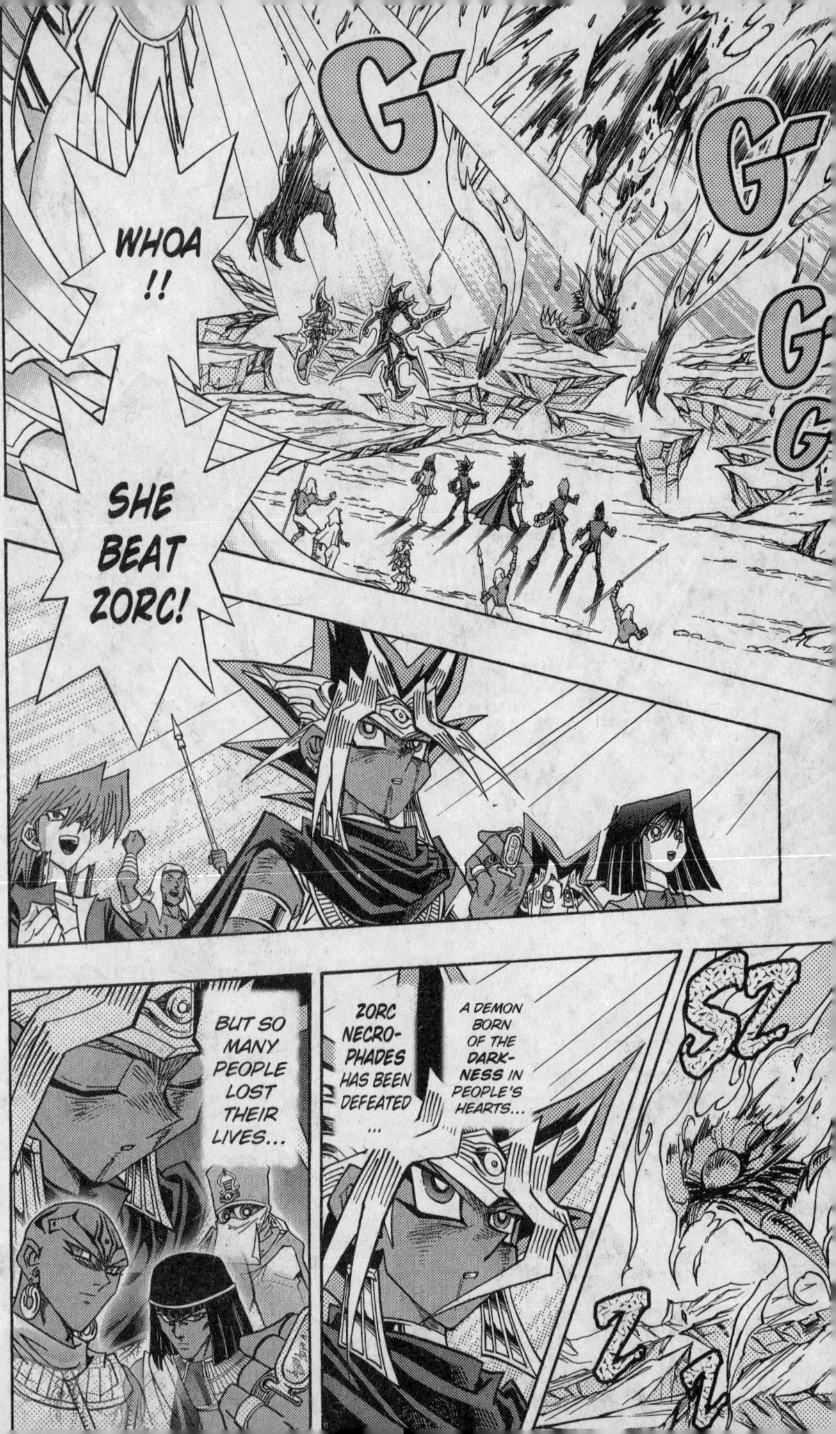
G
G
G
G
WHOA !!
SHE BEAT ZORC!
SZ
Z
A DEMON BORN OF THE DARKNESS IN PEOPLE'S HEARTS...
ZORC NECROPHADES HAS BEEN DEFEATED...
BUT SO MANY PEOPLE LOST THEIR LIVES...

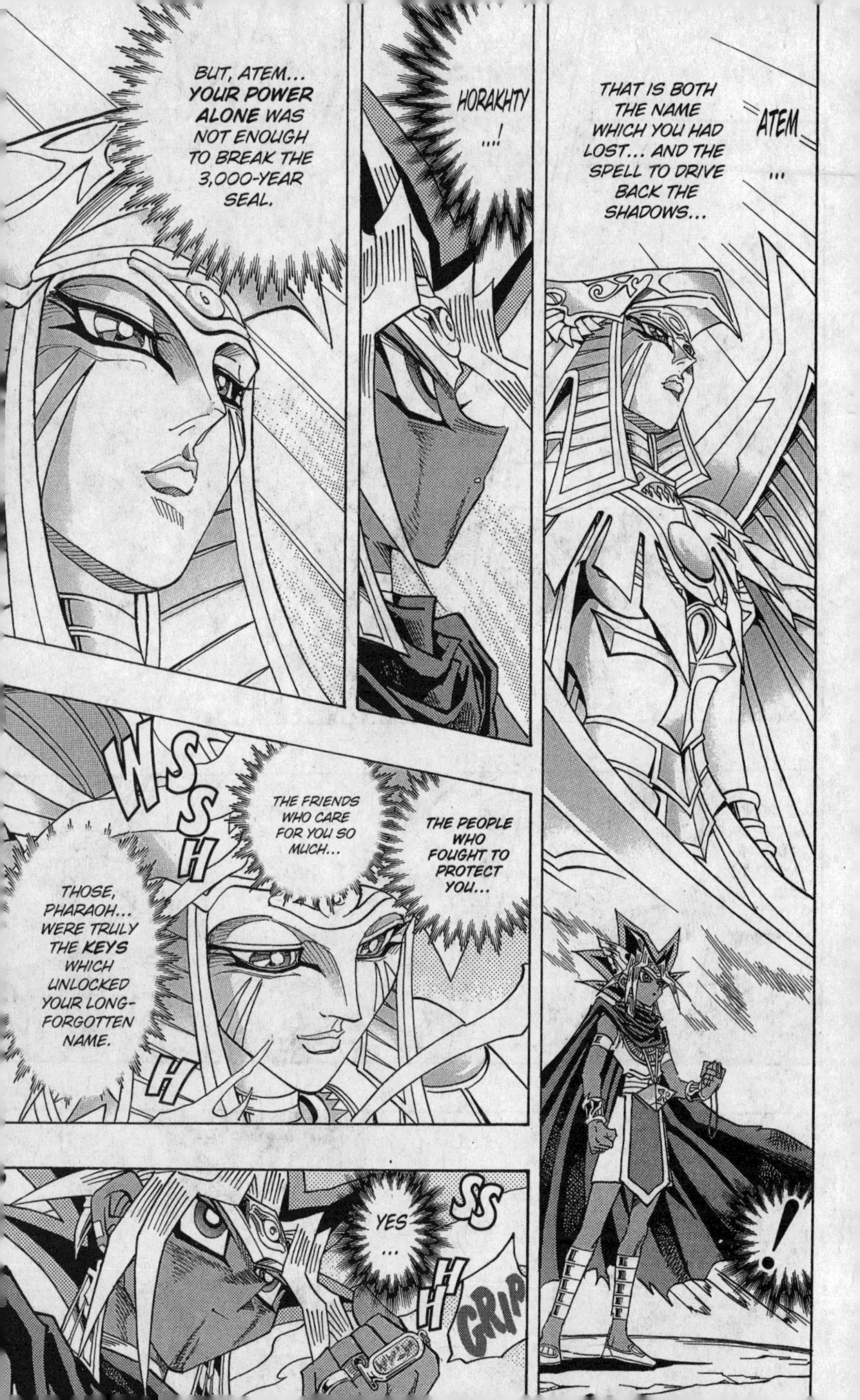

ATEM ...
THAT IS BOTH THE NAME WHICH YOU HAD LOST... AND THE SPELL TO DRIVE BACK THE SHADOWS...
!
HORAKHTY ...!
BUT, ATEM... YOUR POWER ALONE WAS NOT ENOUGH TO BREAK THE 3,000-YEAR SEAL.
WSSH
THE PEOPLE WHO FOUGHT TO PROTECT YOU...
THE FRIENDS WHO CARE FOR YOU SO MUCH...
THOSE, PHARAOH... WERE TRULY THE KEYS WHICH UNLOCKED YOUR LONG-FORGOTTEN NAME.
H
SSHHHH
YES ...
GRIP

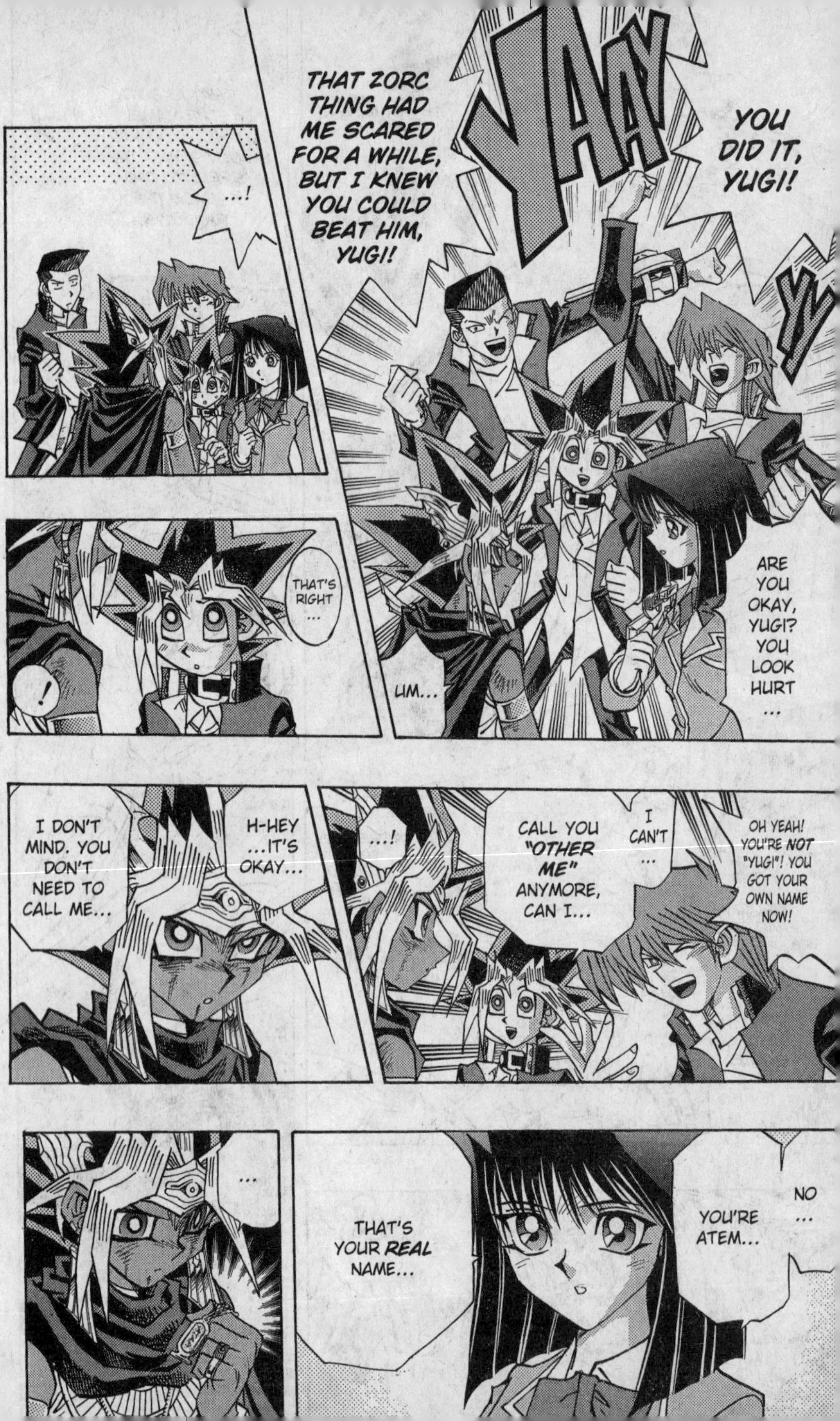
YAAY
YOU DID IT, YUGI!
YY
THAT ZORC THING HAD ME SCARED FOR A WHILE, BUT I KNEW YOU COULD BEAT HIM, YUGI!
ARE YOU OKAY, YUGI? YOU LOOK HURT...
UM...
...!
THAT'S RIGHT...
!
OH YEAH! YOU'RE *NOT* "YUGI"! YOU GOT YOUR OWN NAME NOW!
I CAN'T...
CALL YOU *"OTHER ME"* ANYMORE, CAN I...
...!
H-HEY ...IT'S OKAY...
I DON'T MIND. YOU DON'T NEED TO CALL ME...
NO...
YOU'RE ATEM...
THAT'S YOUR *REAL* NAME...
...

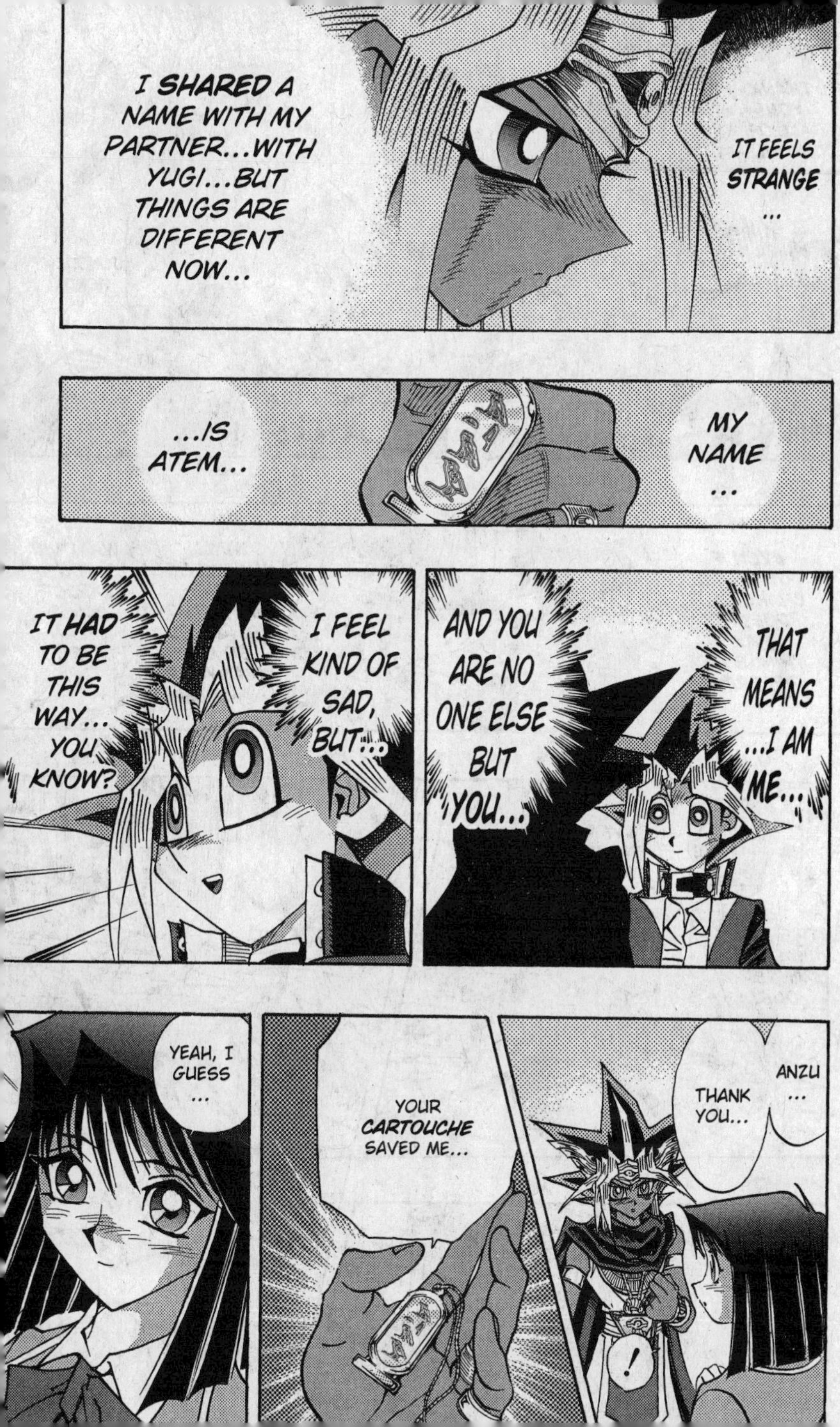
IT FEELS STRANGE...
I SHARED A NAME WITH MY PARTNER...WITH YUGI...BUT THINGS ARE DIFFERENT NOW...
MY NAME...
...IS ATEM...
THAT MEANS ...I AM ME...
AND YOU ARE NO ONE ELSE BUT YOU...
I FEEL KIND OF SAD, BUT...
IT HAD TO BE THIS WAY... YOU KNOW?
ANZU...
THANK YOU...
!
YOUR CARTOUCHE SAVED ME...
YEAH, I GUESS...

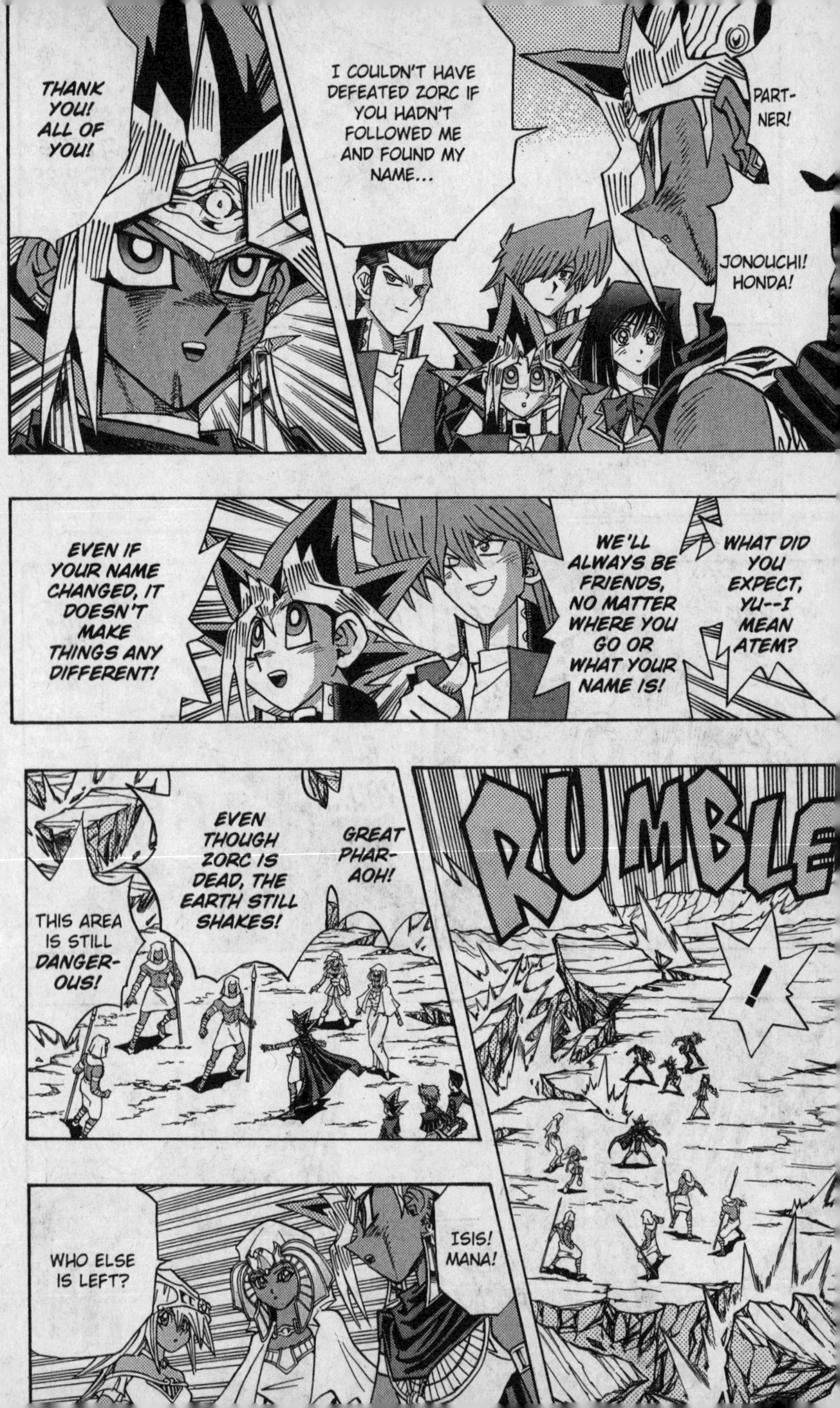
PART-NER!
JONOUCHI! HONDA!
I COULDN'T HAVE DEFEATED ZORC IF YOU HADN'T FOLLOWED ME AND FOUND MY NAME...
THANK YOU! ALL OF YOU!
WHAT DID YOU EXPECT, YU--I MEAN ATEM?
WE'LL ALWAYS BE FRIENDS, NO MATTER WHERE YOU GO OR WHAT YOUR NAME IS!
EVEN IF YOUR NAME CHANGED, IT DOESN'T MAKE THINGS ANY DIFFERENT!
RUMBLE
!
GREAT PHAR-AOH!
EVEN THOUGH ZORC IS DEAD, THE EARTH STILL SHAKES!
THIS AREA IS STILL DANGER-OUS!
ISIS! MANA!
WHO ELSE IS LEFT?

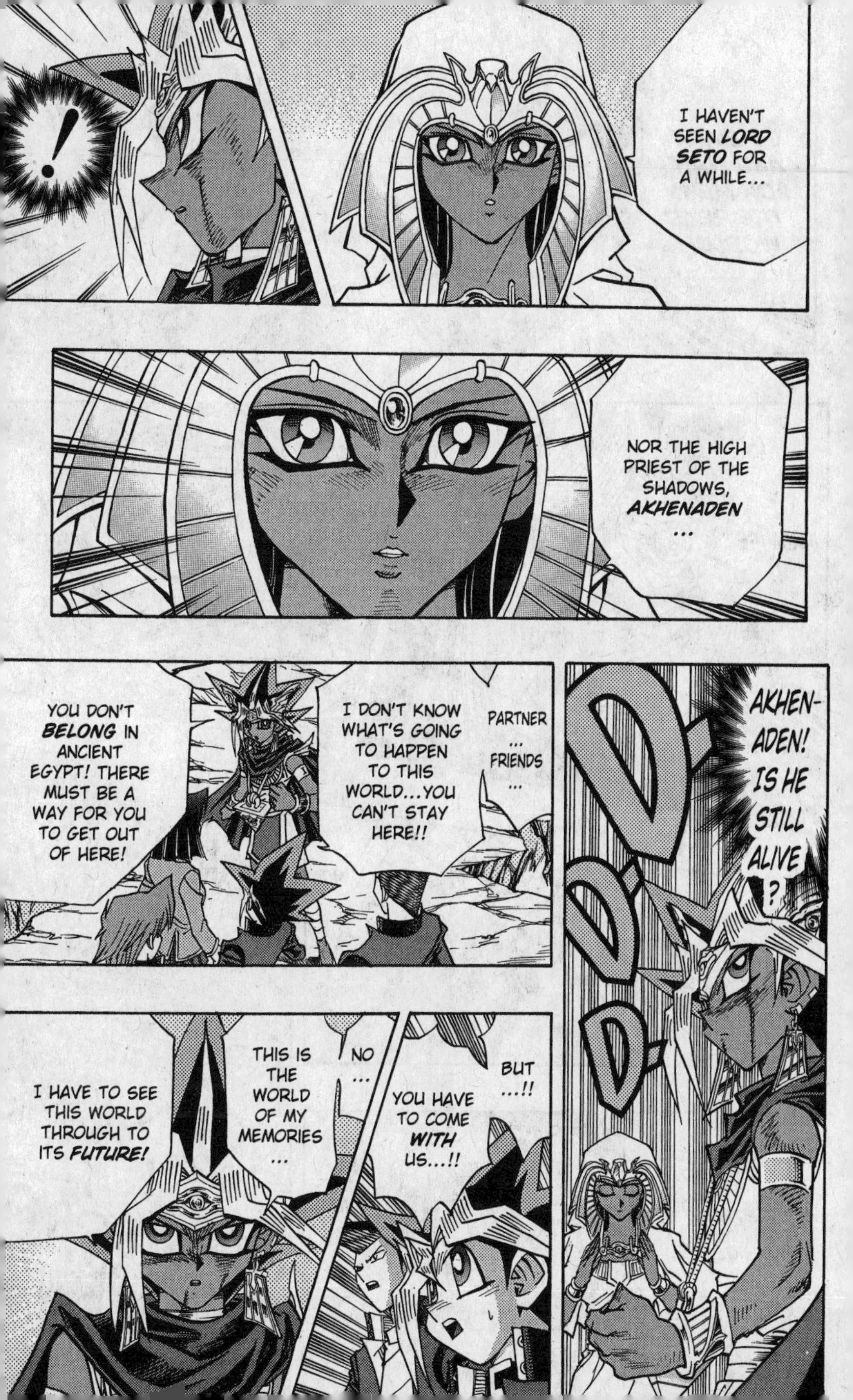
I HAVEN'T SEEN LORD SETO FOR A WHILE...
!
NOR THE HIGH PRIEST OF THE SHADOWS, AKHENADEN...
AKHEN-ADEN! IS HE STILL ALIVE?
PARTNER... FRIENDS...
I DON'T KNOW WHAT'S GOING TO HAPPEN TO THIS WORLD...YOU CAN'T STAY HERE!!
YOU DON'T BELONG IN ANCIENT EGYPT! THERE MUST BE A WAY FOR YOU TO GET OUT OF HERE!
BUT...!!
YOU HAVE TO COME WITH US...!!
NO...
THIS IS THE WORLD OF MY MEMORIES...
I HAVE TO SEE THIS WORLD THROUGH TO ITS FUTURE!

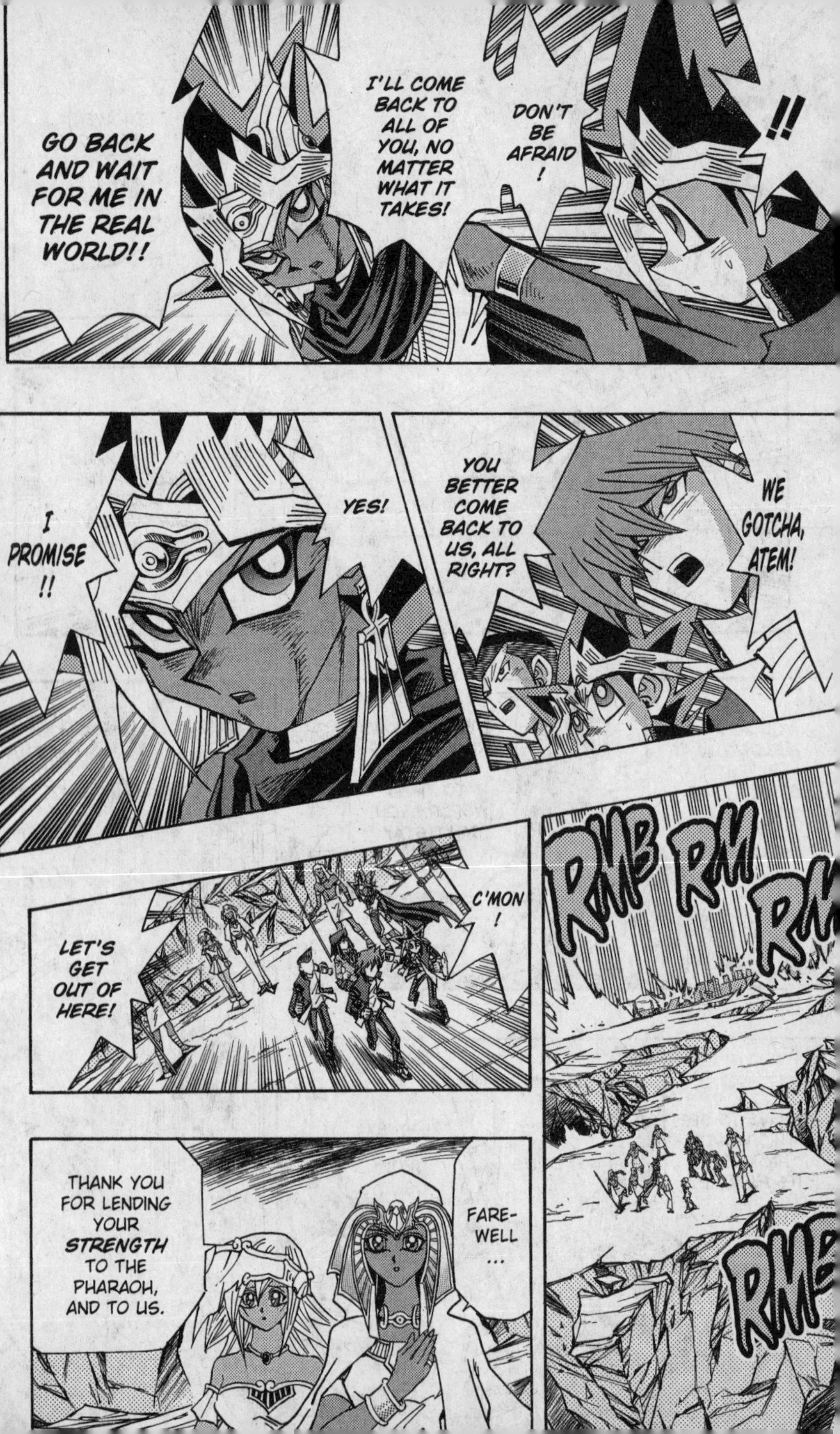
!!
DON'T BE AFRAID!
I'LL COME BACK TO ALL OF YOU, NO MATTER WHAT IT TAKES!
GO BACK AND WAIT FOR ME IN THE REAL WORLD!!
WE GOTCHA, ATEM!
YOU BETTER COME BACK TO US, ALL RIGHT?
YES!
I PROMISE!!
RMB RM
RM
RMB
C'MON!
LET'S GET OUT OF HERE!
FAREWELL...
THANK YOU FOR LENDING YOUR STRENGTH TO THE PHARAOH, AND TO US.

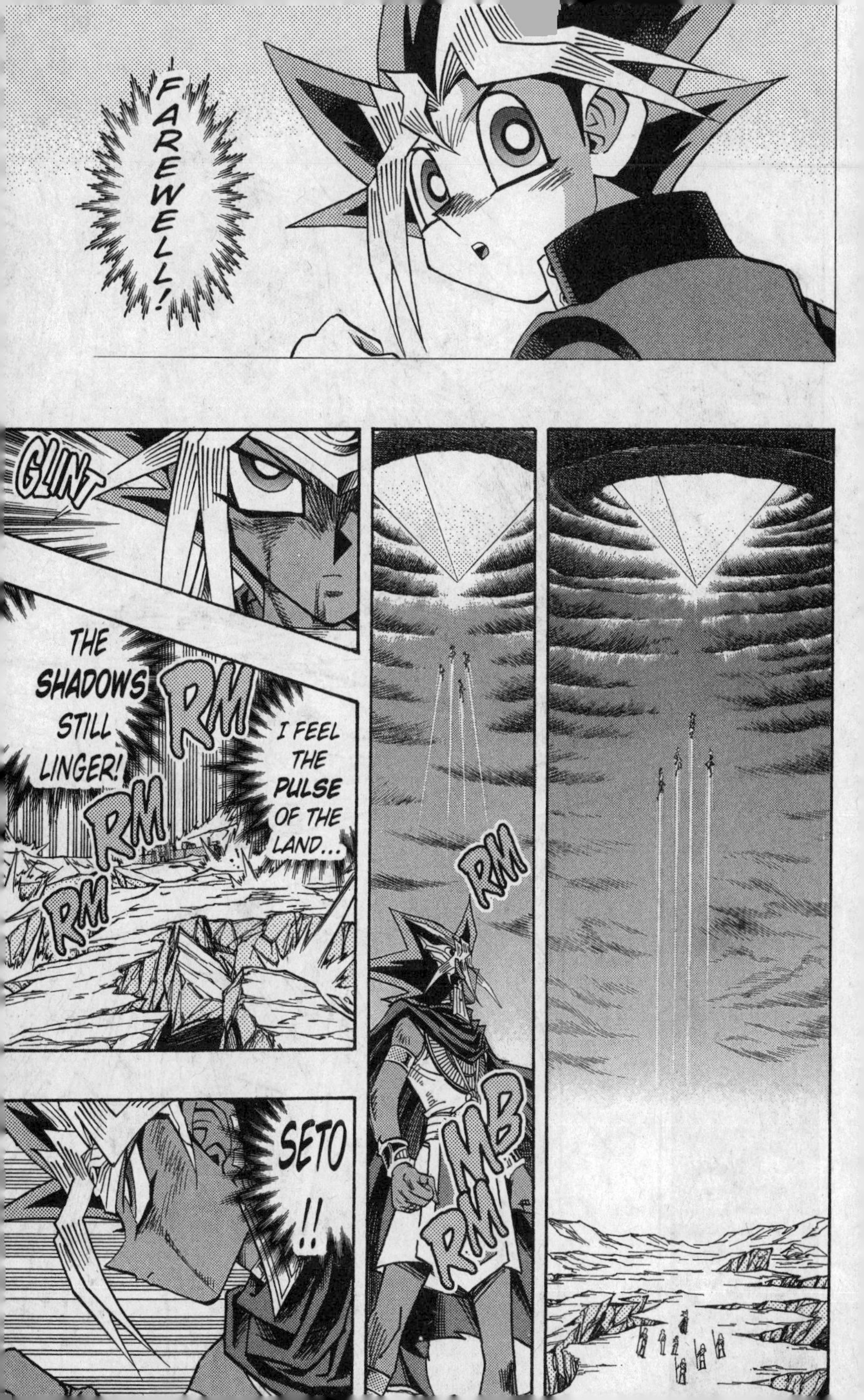
FAREWELL!
RM
RMB
RM
GLINT
I FEEL THE PULSE OF THE LAND...
THE SHADOWS STILL LINGER!
RM
RM
RM
SETO!!

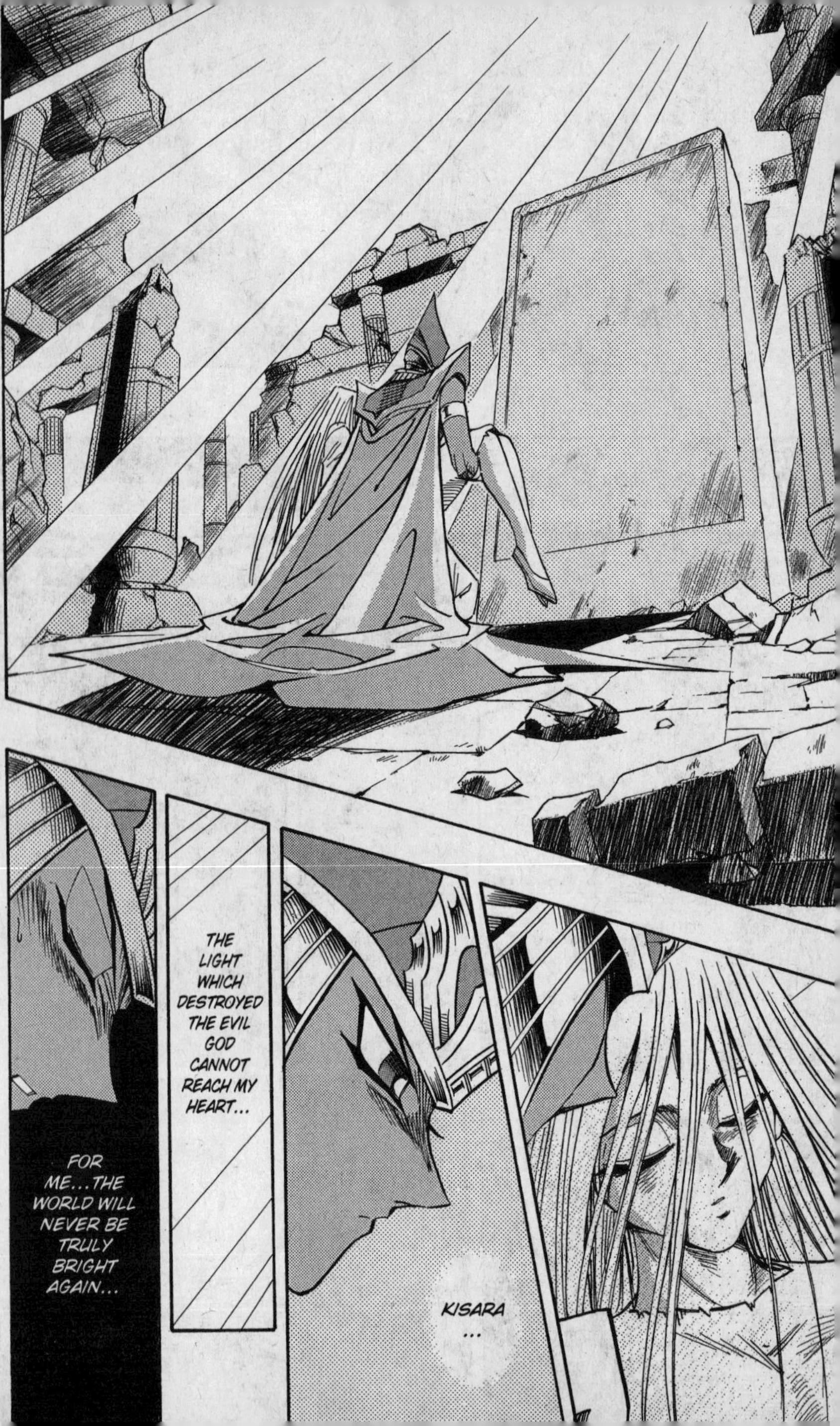
KISARA ...
THE LIGHT WHICH DESTROYED THE EVIL GOD CANNOT REACH MY HEART...
FOR ME...THE WORLD WILL NEVER BE TRULY BRIGHT AGAIN...

READ THIS WAY

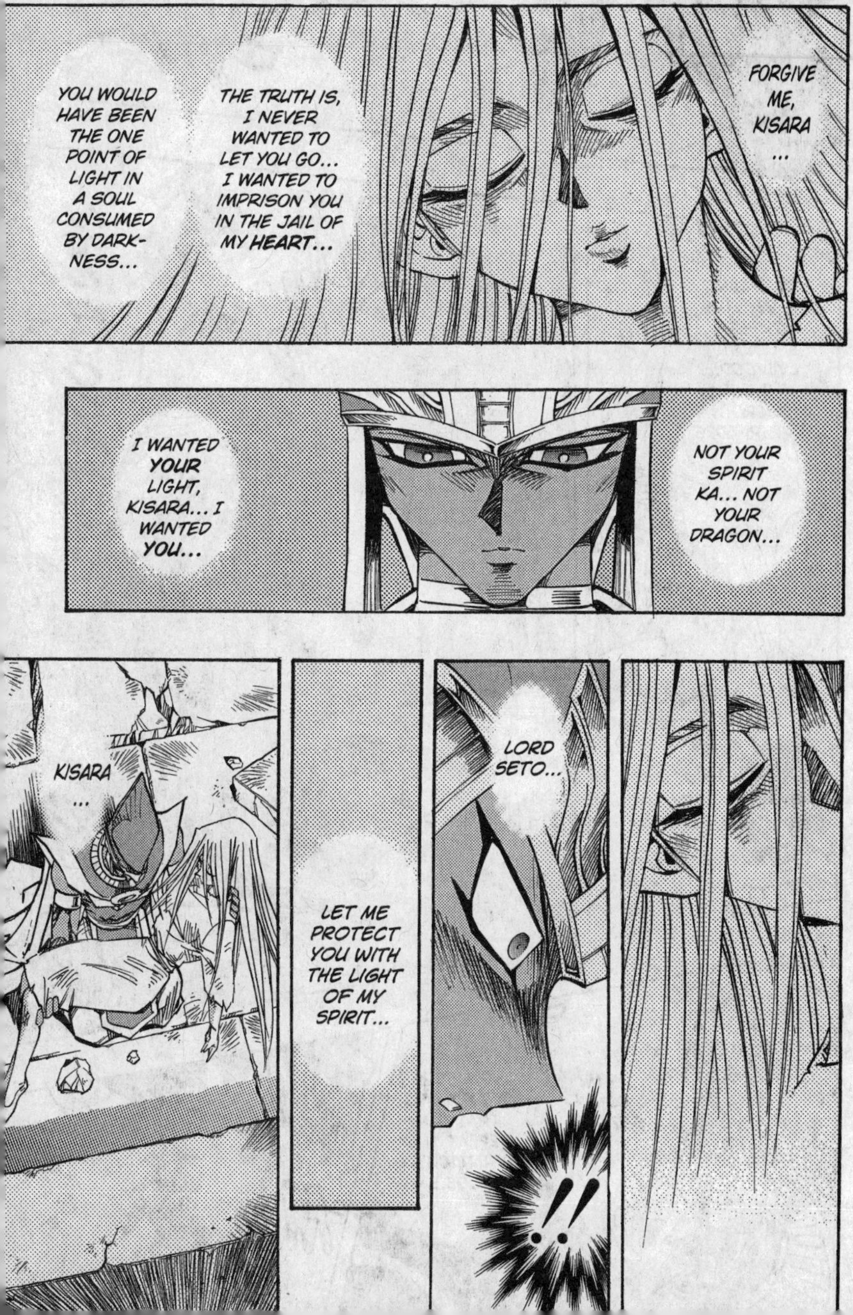
FORGIVE ME, KISARA ...
THE TRUTH IS, I NEVER WANTED TO LET YOU GO... I WANTED TO IMPRISON YOU IN THE JAIL OF MY HEART...
YOU WOULD HAVE BEEN THE ONE POINT OF LIGHT IN A SOUL CONSUMED BY DARKNESS...
NOT YOUR SPIRIT KA... NOT YOUR DRAGON...
I WANTED YOUR LIGHT, KISARA... I WANTED YOU...
LORD SETO...
!!
LET ME PROTECT YOU WITH THE LIGHT OF MY SPIRIT...
KISARA ...

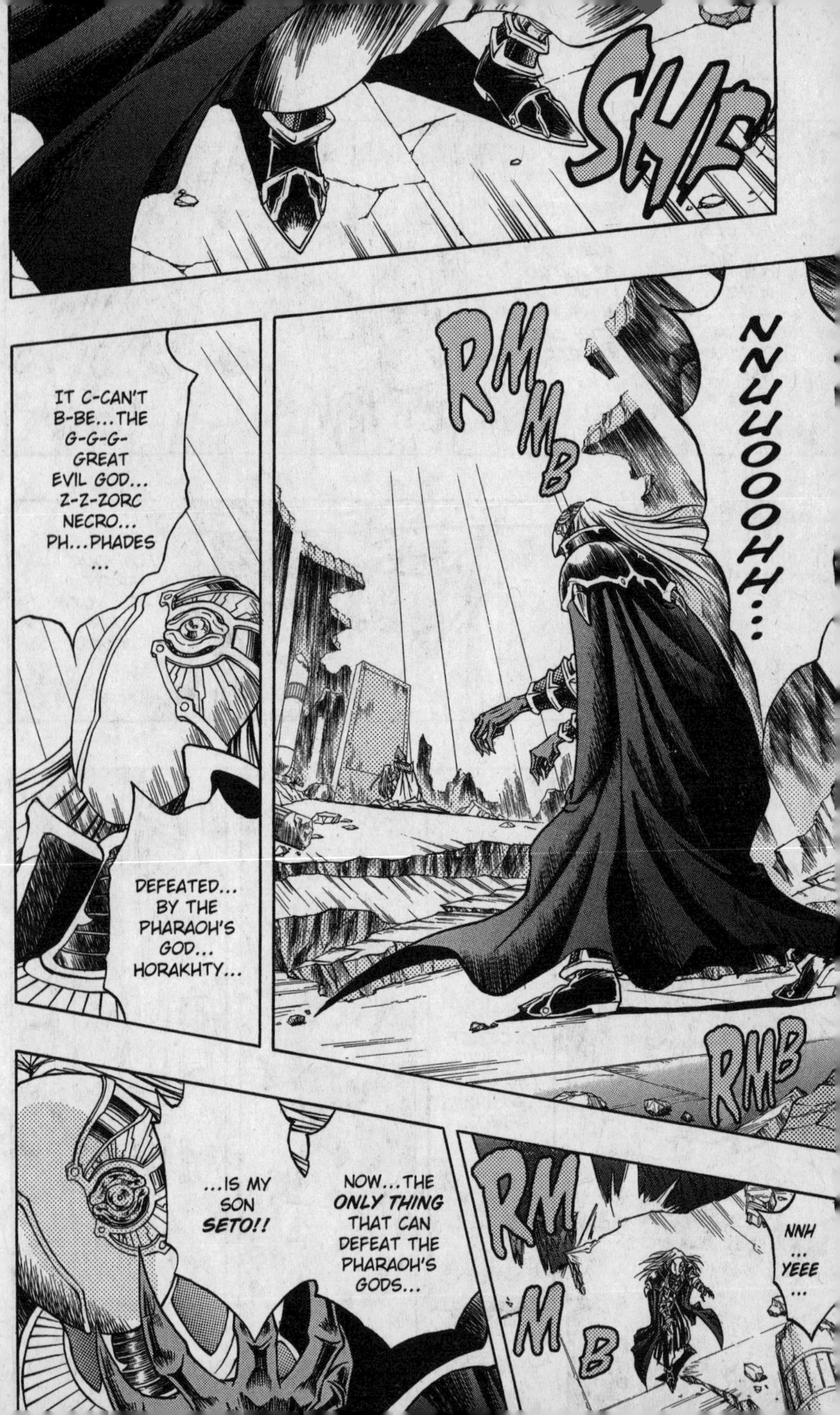
SHF
NNUOOOOHH...
RMMB
IT C-CAN'T B-BE...THE G-G-G-GREAT EVIL GOD... Z-Z-ZORC NECRO... PH...PHADES ...
DEFEATED... BY THE PHARAOH'S GOD... HORAKHTY...
RMB
NNH ... YEEE ...
RM M B
NOW...THE *ONLY THING* THAT CAN DEFEAT THE PHARAOH'S GODS...
...IS MY SON ***SETO!!***

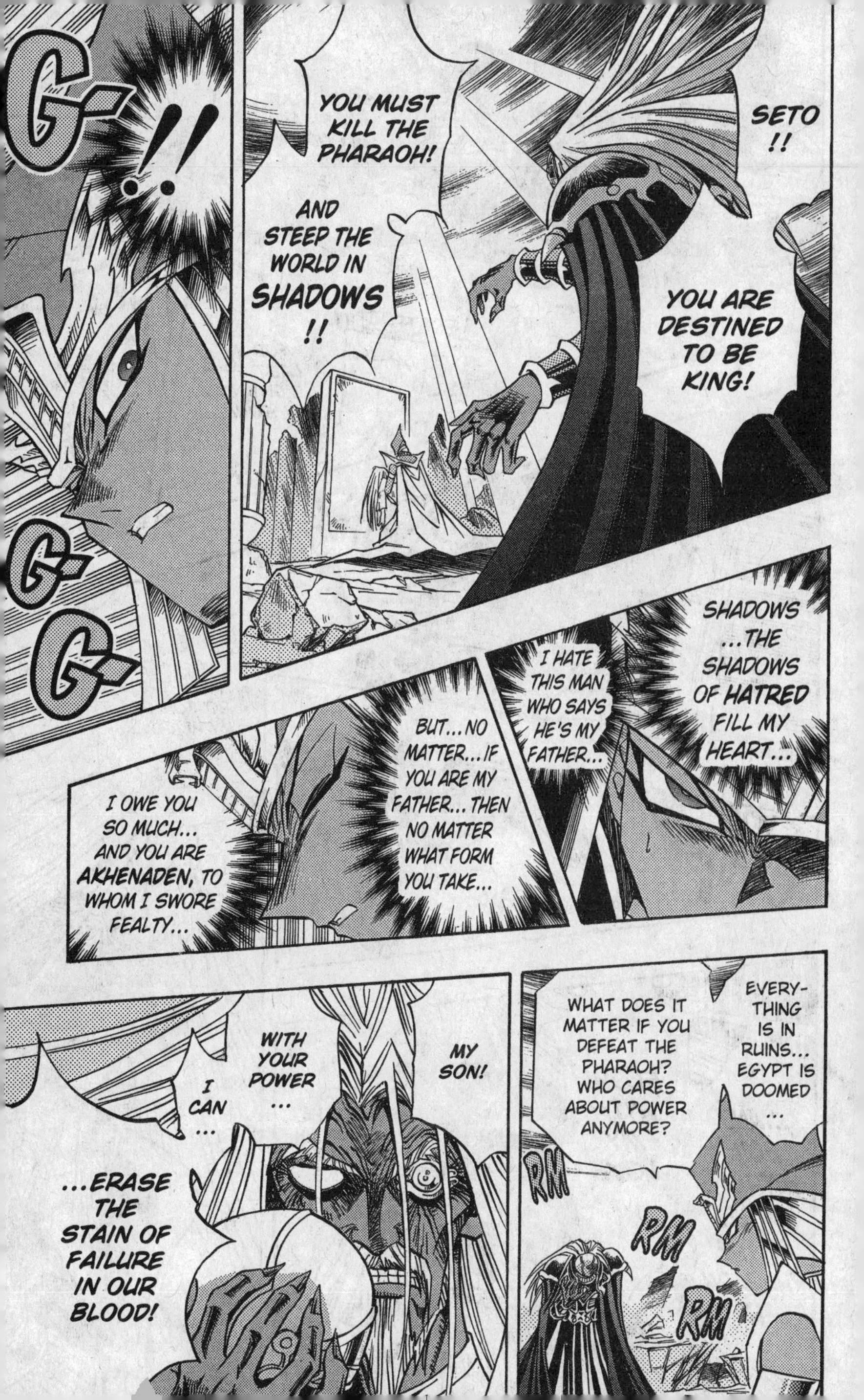
SETO!!
YOU ARE DESTINED TO BE KING!
YOU MUST KILL THE PHARAOH!
AND STEEP THE WORLD IN SHADOWS!!
G-!!
GG
SHADOWS ...THE SHADOWS OF HATRED FILL MY HEART...
I HATE THIS MAN WHO SAYS HE'S MY FATHER...
BUT... NO MATTER... IF YOU ARE MY FATHER... THEN NO MATTER WHAT FORM YOU TAKE...
I OWE YOU SO MUCH... AND YOU ARE AKHENADEN, TO WHOM I SWORE FEALTY...
EVERY-THING IS IN RUINS... EGYPT IS DOOMED...
WHAT DOES IT MATTER IF YOU DEFEAT THE PHARAOH? WHO CARES ABOUT POWER ANYMORE?
RM
RM
RM
MY SON!
WITH YOUR POWER...
I CAN...
...ERASE THE STAIN OF FAILURE IN OUR BLOOD!

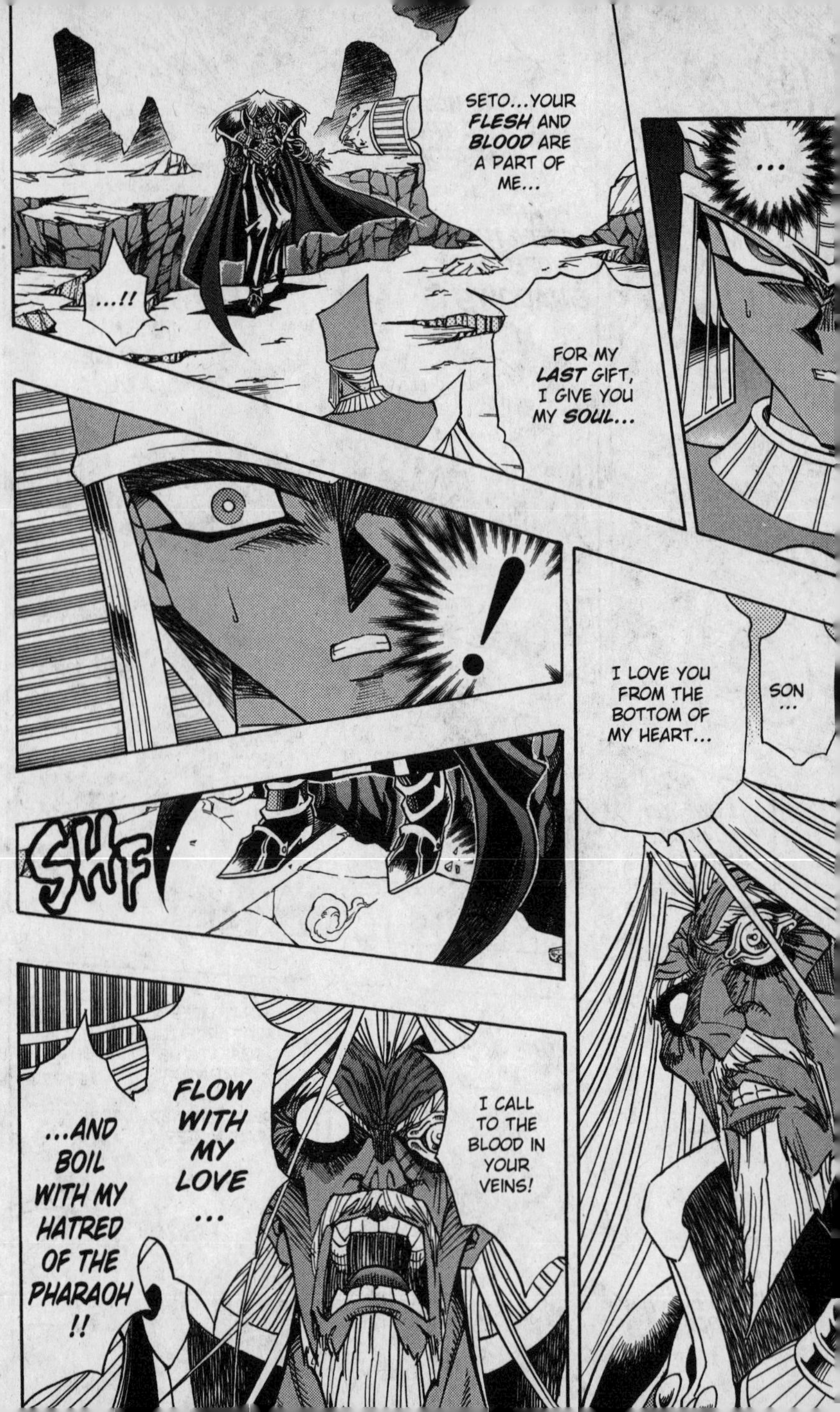
...
SETO...YOUR FLESH AND BLOOD ARE A PART OF ME...
...!!
FOR MY LAST GIFT, I GIVE YOU MY SOUL...
I LOVE YOU FROM THE BOTTOM OF MY HEART...
SON...
!
SHF
I CALL TO THE BLOOD IN YOUR VEINS!
FLOW WITH MY LOVE...
...AND BOIL WITH MY HATRED OF THE PHARAOH!!

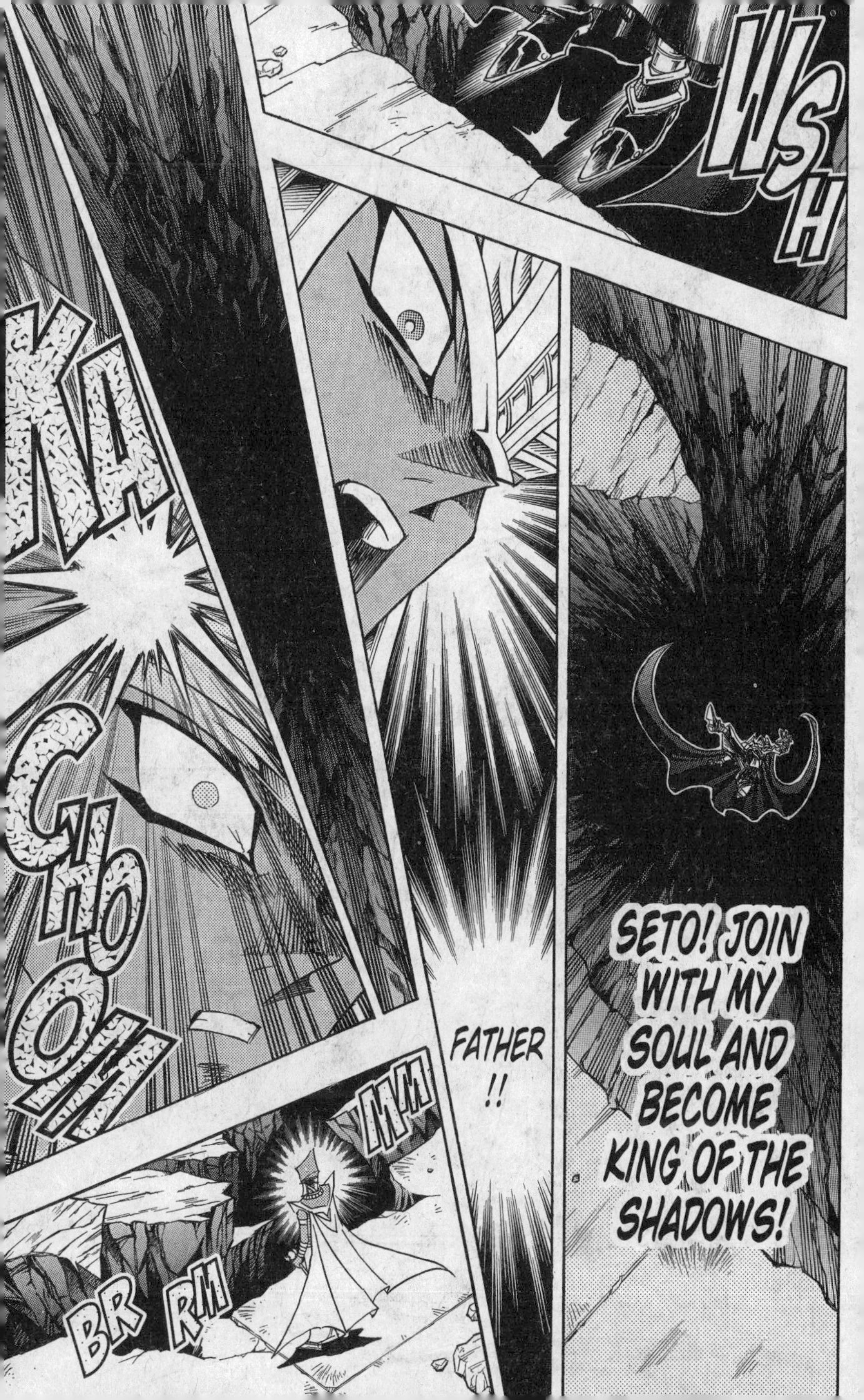
WSH
SETO! JOIN WITH MY SOUL AND BECOME KING OF THE SHADOWS!
FATHER !!
KA
CHOOM
MM
BR RM

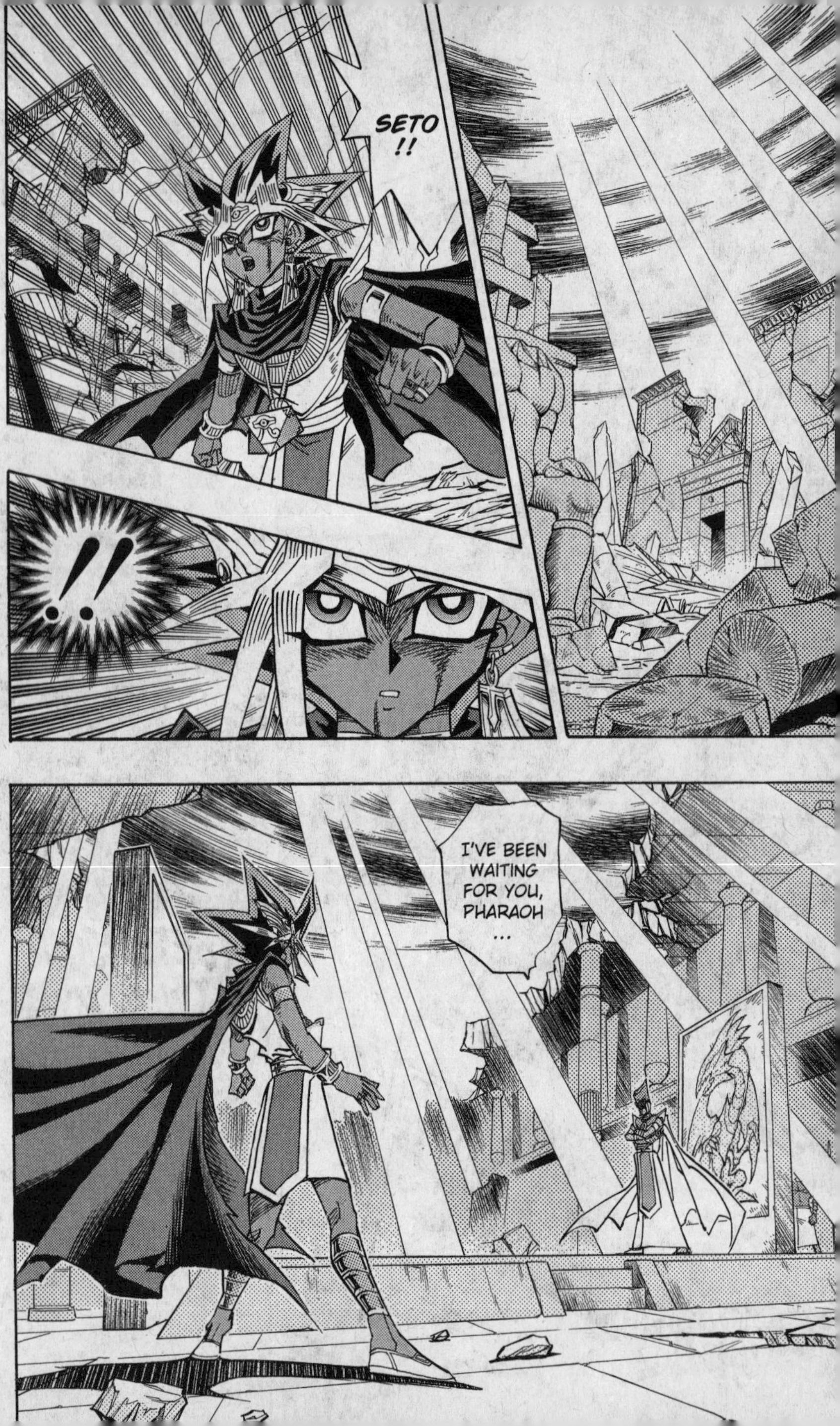
SETO !!
!!
I'VE BEEN WAITING FOR YOU, PHARAOH ...

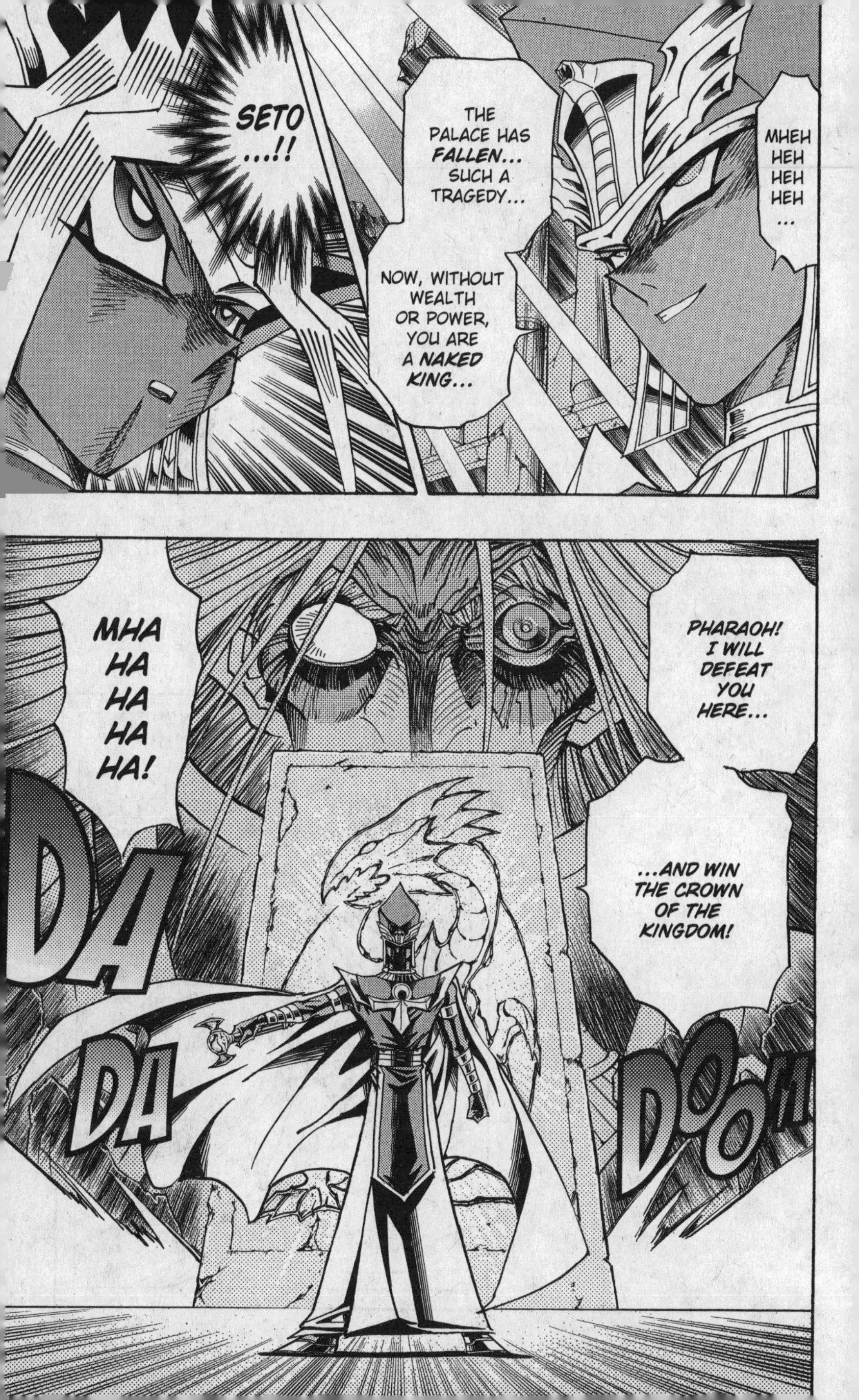
MHEH HEH HEH HEH...
THE PALACE HAS FALLEN... SUCH A TRAGEDY...
NOW, WITHOUT WEALTH OR POWER, YOU ARE A NAKED KING...
SETO...!!
PHARAOH! I WILL DEFEAT YOU HERE...
...AND WIN THE CROWN OF THE KINGDOM!
DOOO
MHA HA HA HA HA!
DA
DA

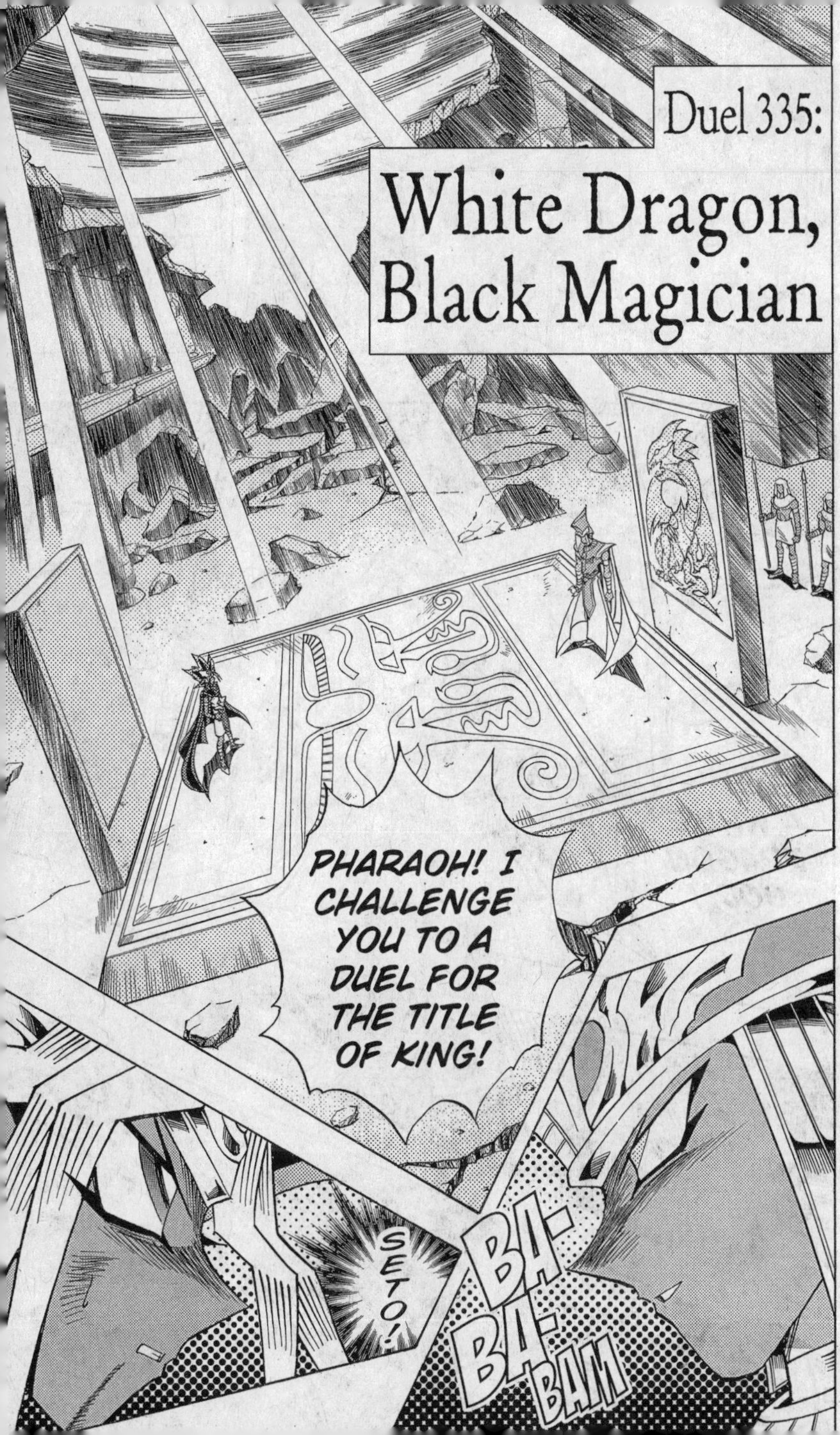
Duel 335:
White Dragon, Black Magician
PHARAOH! I CHALLENGE YOU TO A DUEL FOR THE TITLE OF KING!
BA-BA-BAM
SETO!

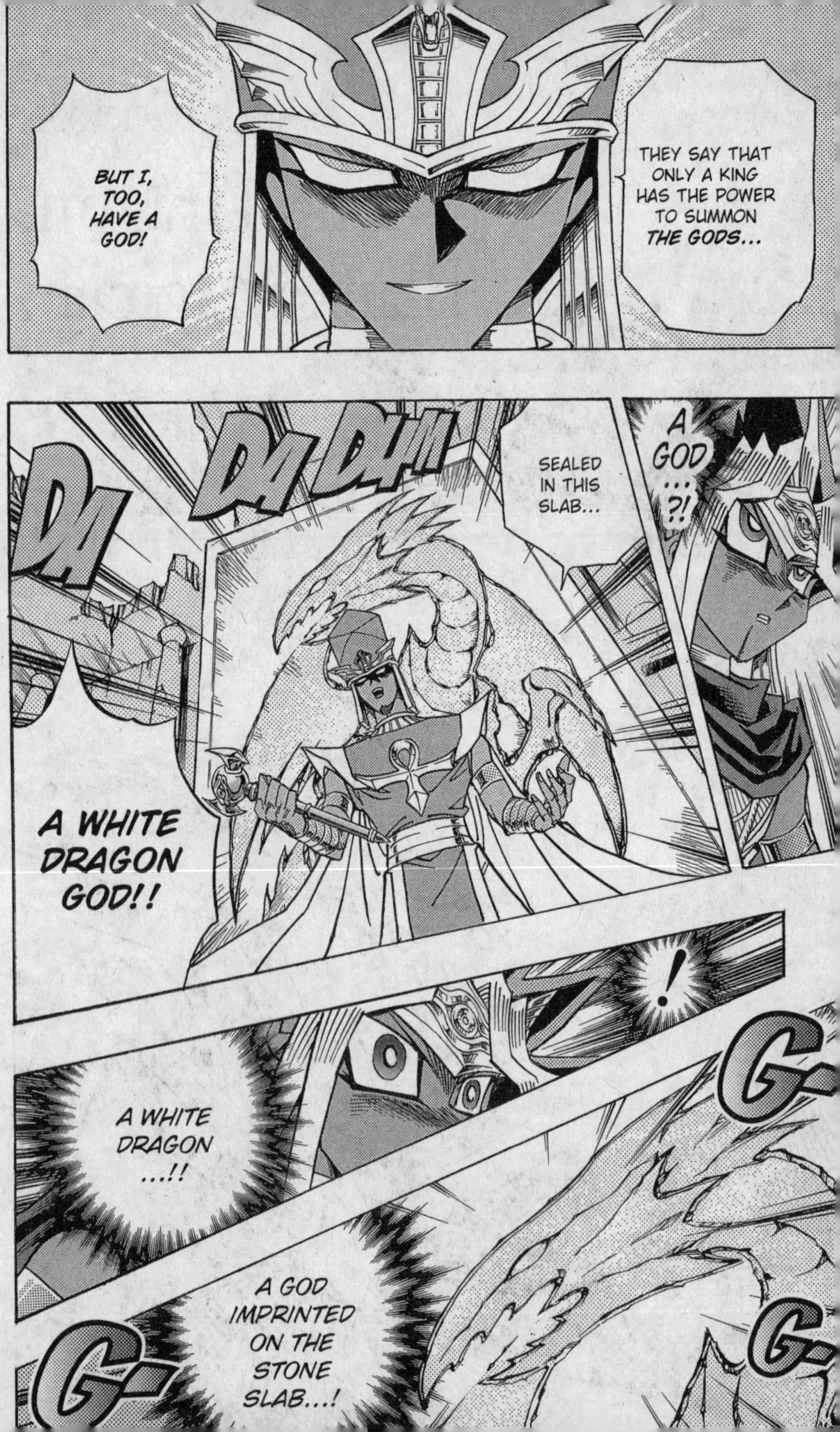
THEY SAY THAT ONLY A KING HAS THE POWER TO SUMMON *THE GODS...*
BUT I, TOO, HAVE A GOD!
A GOD...?!
SEALED IN THIS SLAB...
DA DA DUM
A WHITE DRAGON GOD!!
!
G-
A WHITE DRAGON...!!
A GOD IMPRINTED ON THE STONE SLAB...!
G-
G-

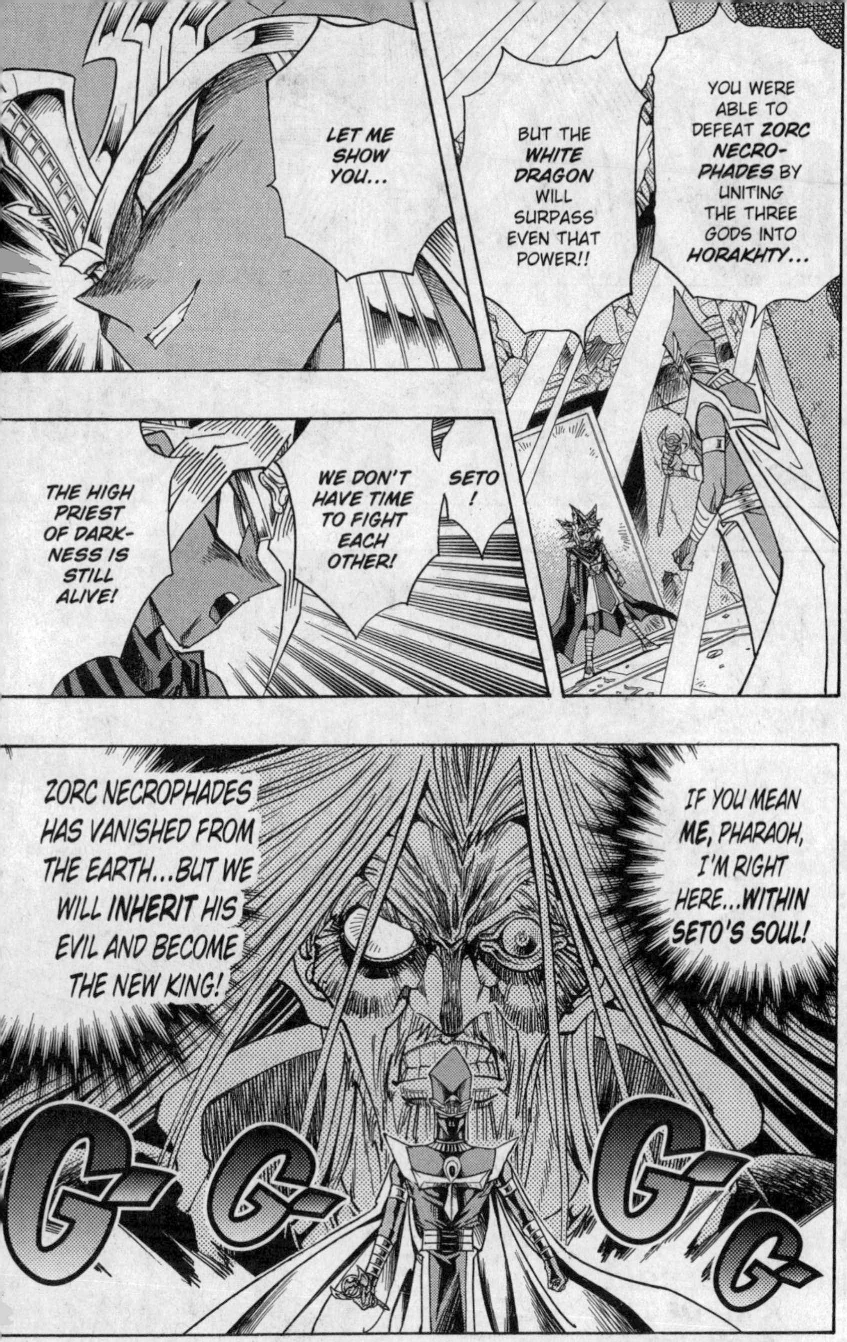
YOU WERE ABLE TO DEFEAT ZORC NECROPHADES BY UNITING THE THREE GODS INTO HORAKHTY...
BUT THE WHITE DRAGON WILL SURPASS EVEN THAT POWER!!
LET ME SHOW YOU...
SETO!
WE DON'T HAVE TIME TO FIGHT EACH OTHER!
THE HIGH PRIEST OF DARKNESS IS STILL ALIVE!
IF YOU MEAN ME, PHARAOH, I'M RIGHT HERE...WITHIN SETO'S SOUL!
ZORC NECROPHADES HAS VANISHED FROM THE EARTH...BUT WE WILL INHERIT HIS EVIL AND BECOME THE NEW KING!
G-G-G-G

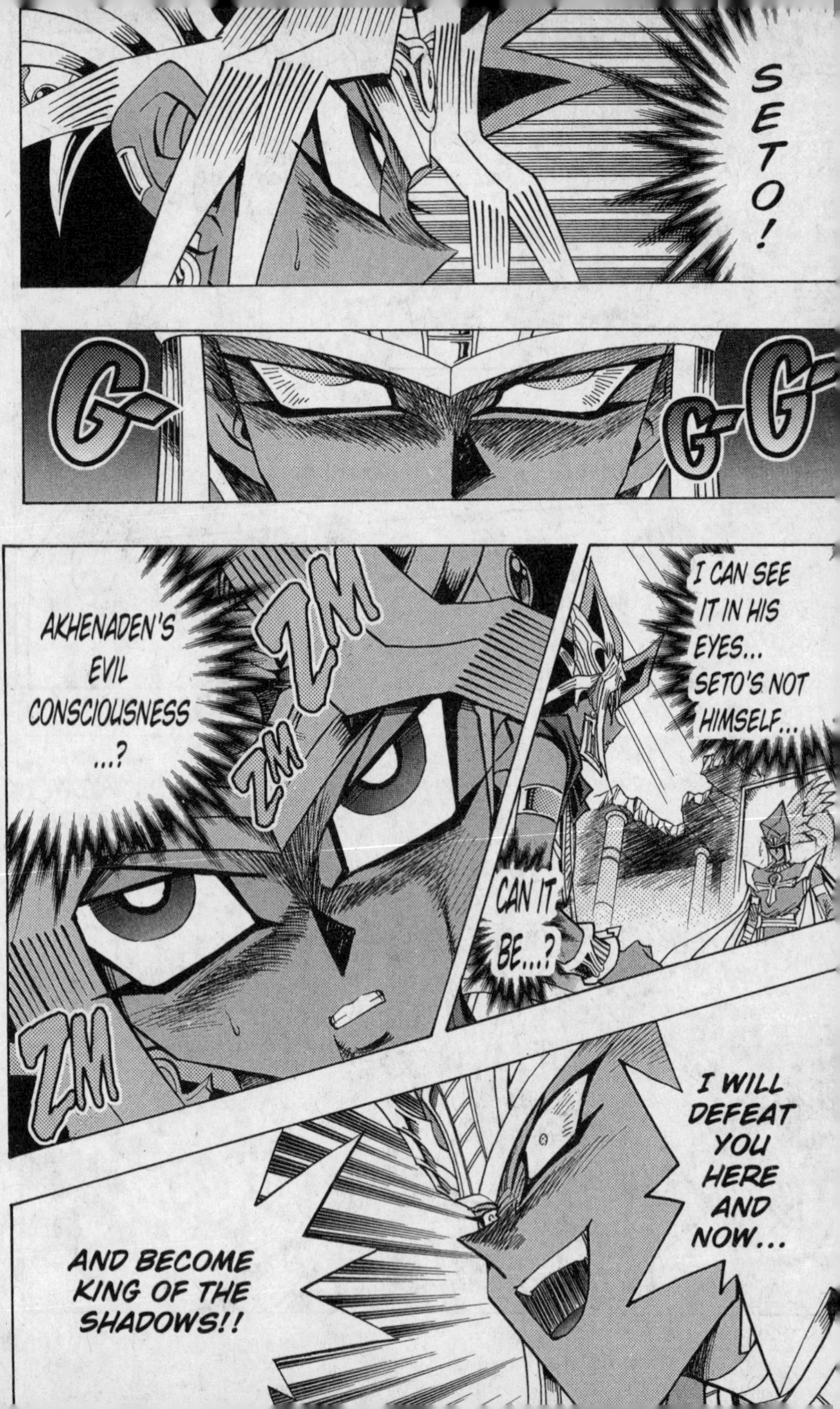
SETO!
G-G-
G-
I CAN SEE IT IN HIS EYES... SETO'S NOT HIMSELF...
CAN IT BE...?
AKHENADEN'S EVIL CONSCIOUSNESS ...?
ZM ZM
ZM
ZM
I WILL DEFEAT YOU HERE AND NOW...
AND BECOME KING OF THE SHADOWS!!

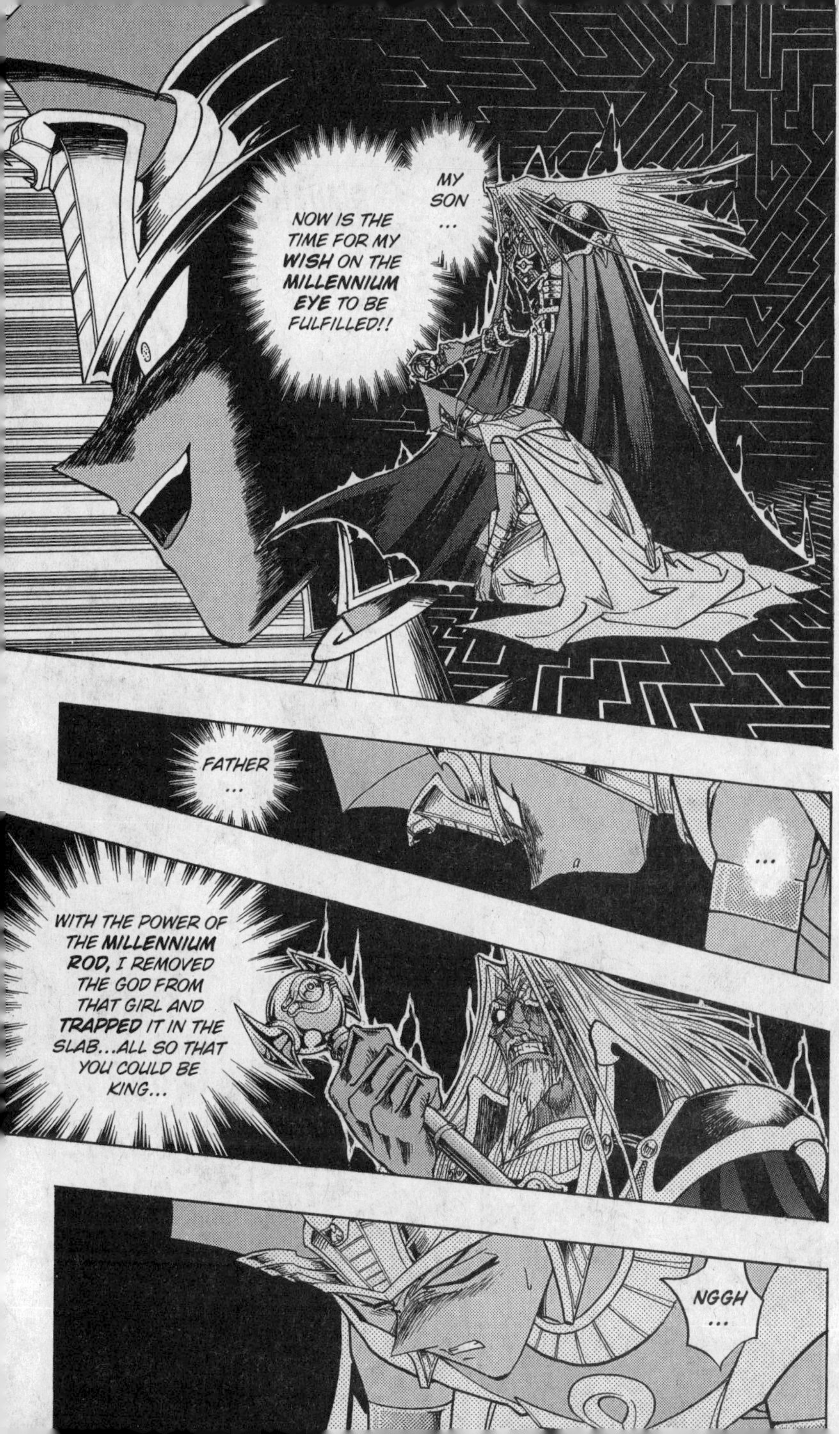
MY SON ...
NOW IS THE TIME FOR MY WISH ON THE MILLENNIUM EYE TO BE FULFILLED!!
FATHER ...
...
WITH THE POWER OF THE MILLENNIUM ROD, I REMOVED THE GOD FROM THAT GIRL AND TRAPPED IT IN THE SLAB...ALL SO THAT YOU COULD BE KING...
NGGH ...

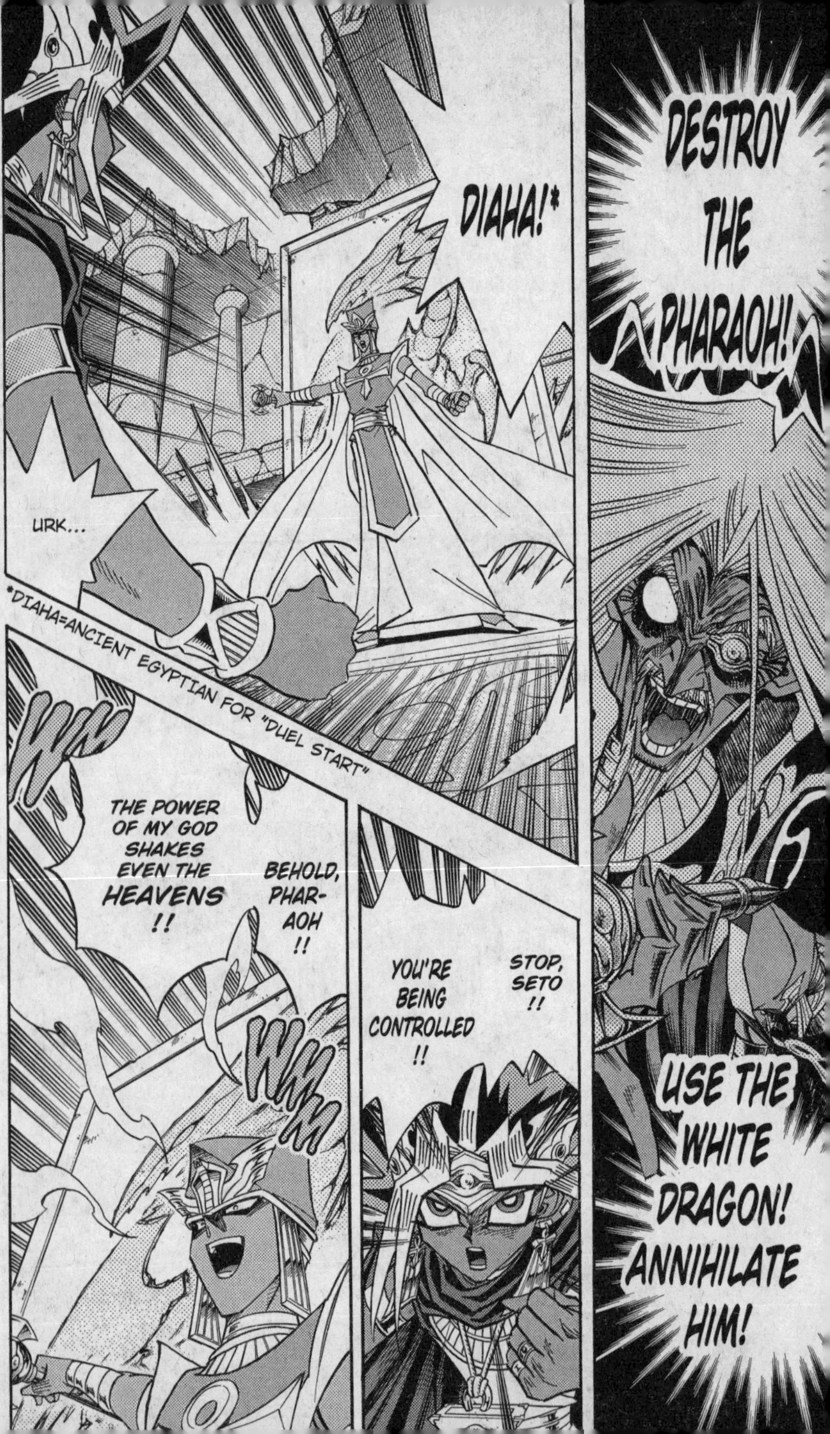
DESTROY THE PHARAOH!
USE THE WHITE DRAGON! ANNIHILATE HIM!
DIAHA!*
URK...
*DIAHA=ANCIENT EGYPTIAN FOR "DUEL START"
STOP, SETO!!
YOU'RE BEING CONTROLLED!!
BEHOLD, PHARAOH!!
THE POWER OF MY GOD SHAKES EVEN THE HEAVENS!!

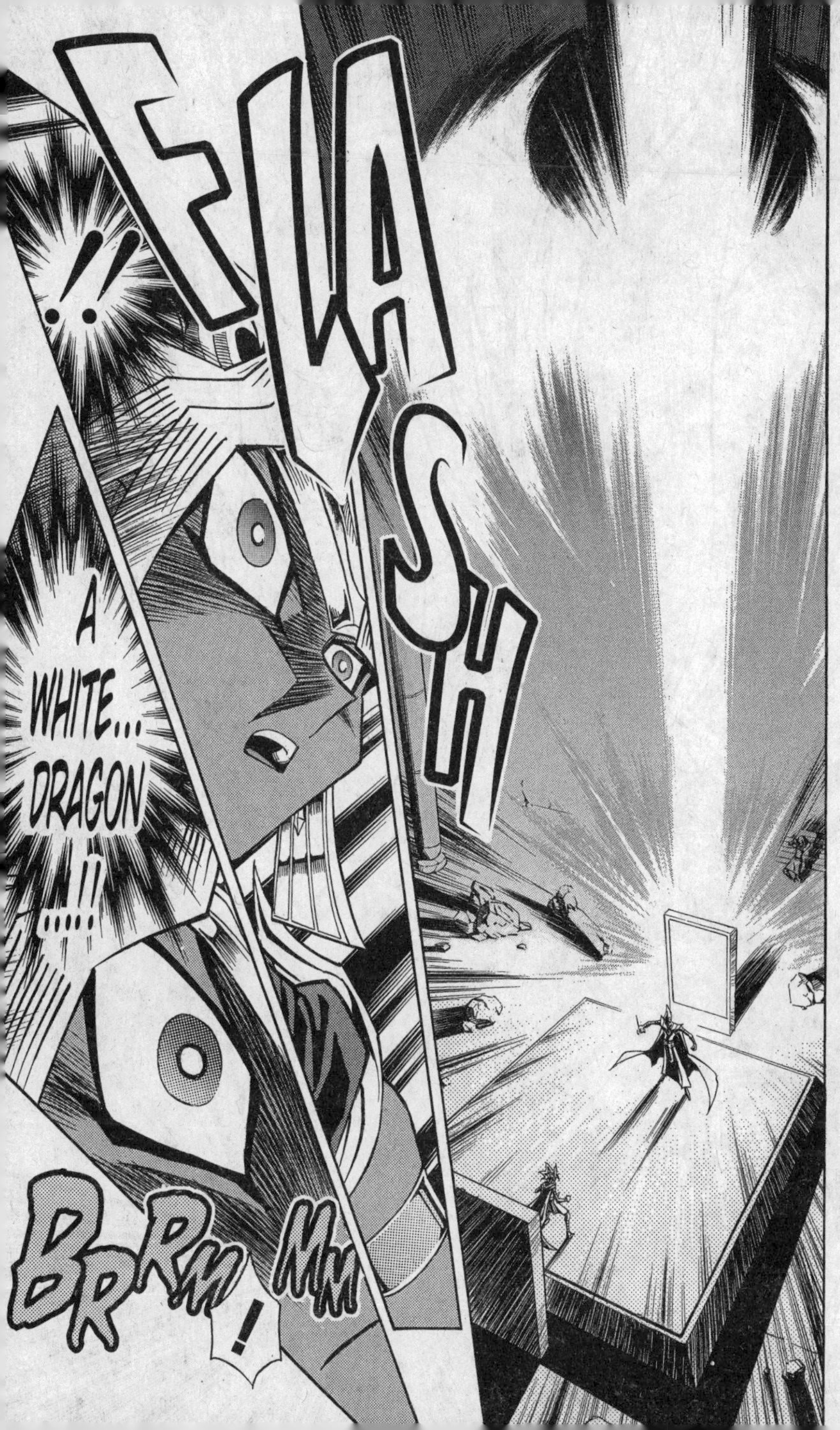
FLASH
!!
A WHITE... DRAGON ...!!
BRRMMM!

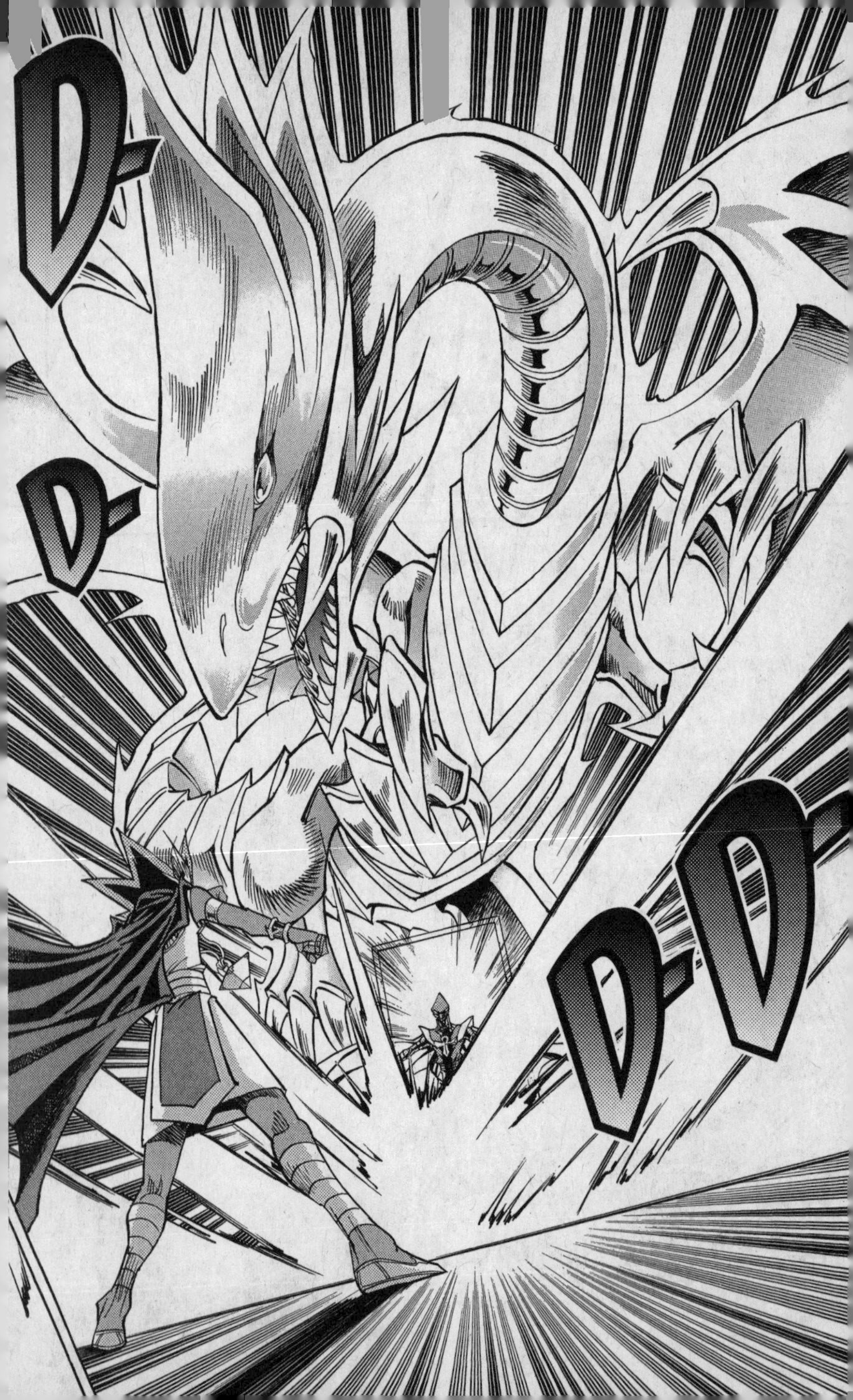
D-
D-
D-D-

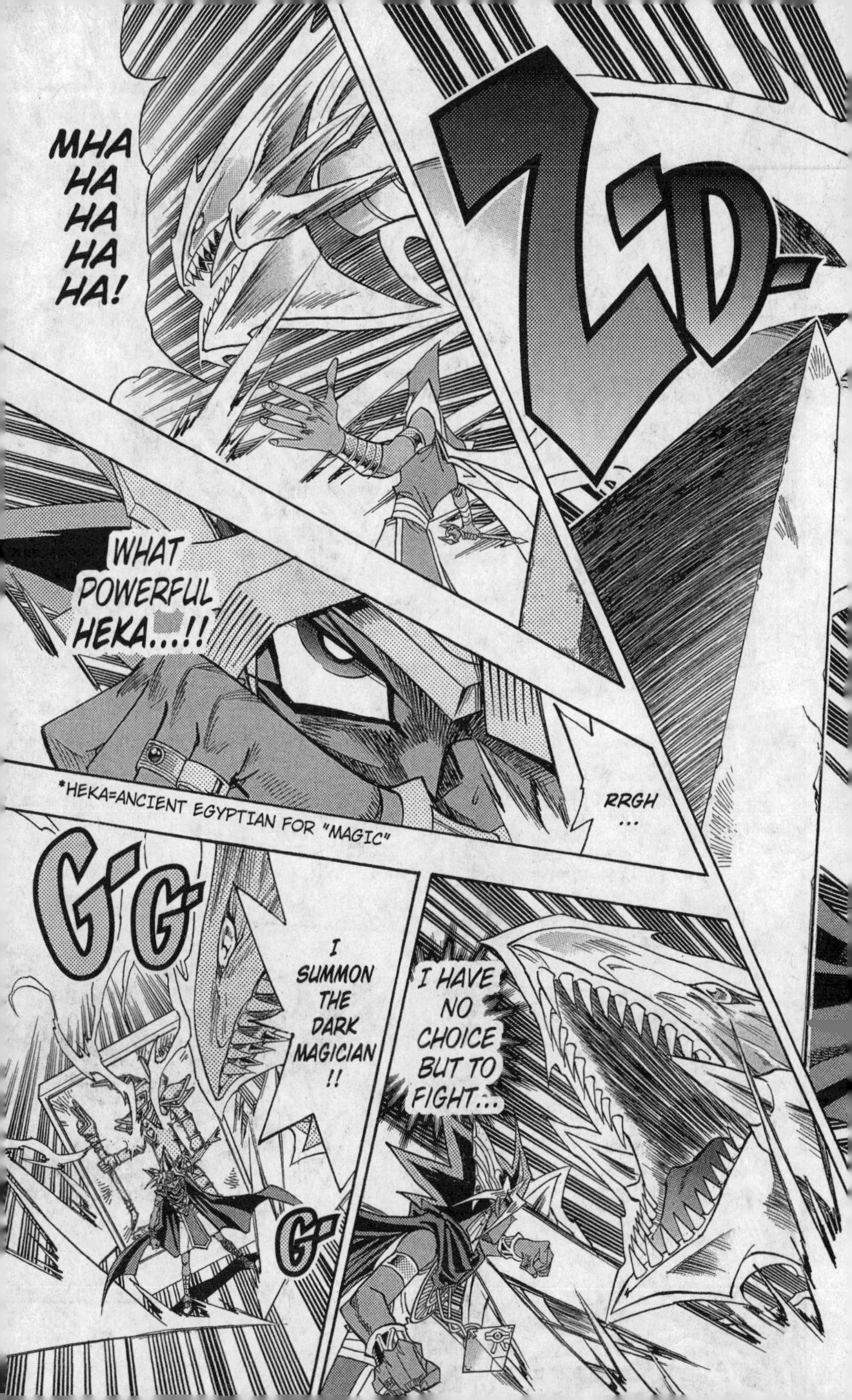
ZD
MHA HA HA HA HA!
RRGH...
WHAT POWERFUL HEKA...!!
*HEKA=ANCIENT EGYPTIAN FOR "MAGIC"
I HAVE NO CHOICE BUT TO FIGHT...
G
I SUMMON THE DARK MAGICIAN!!
GG

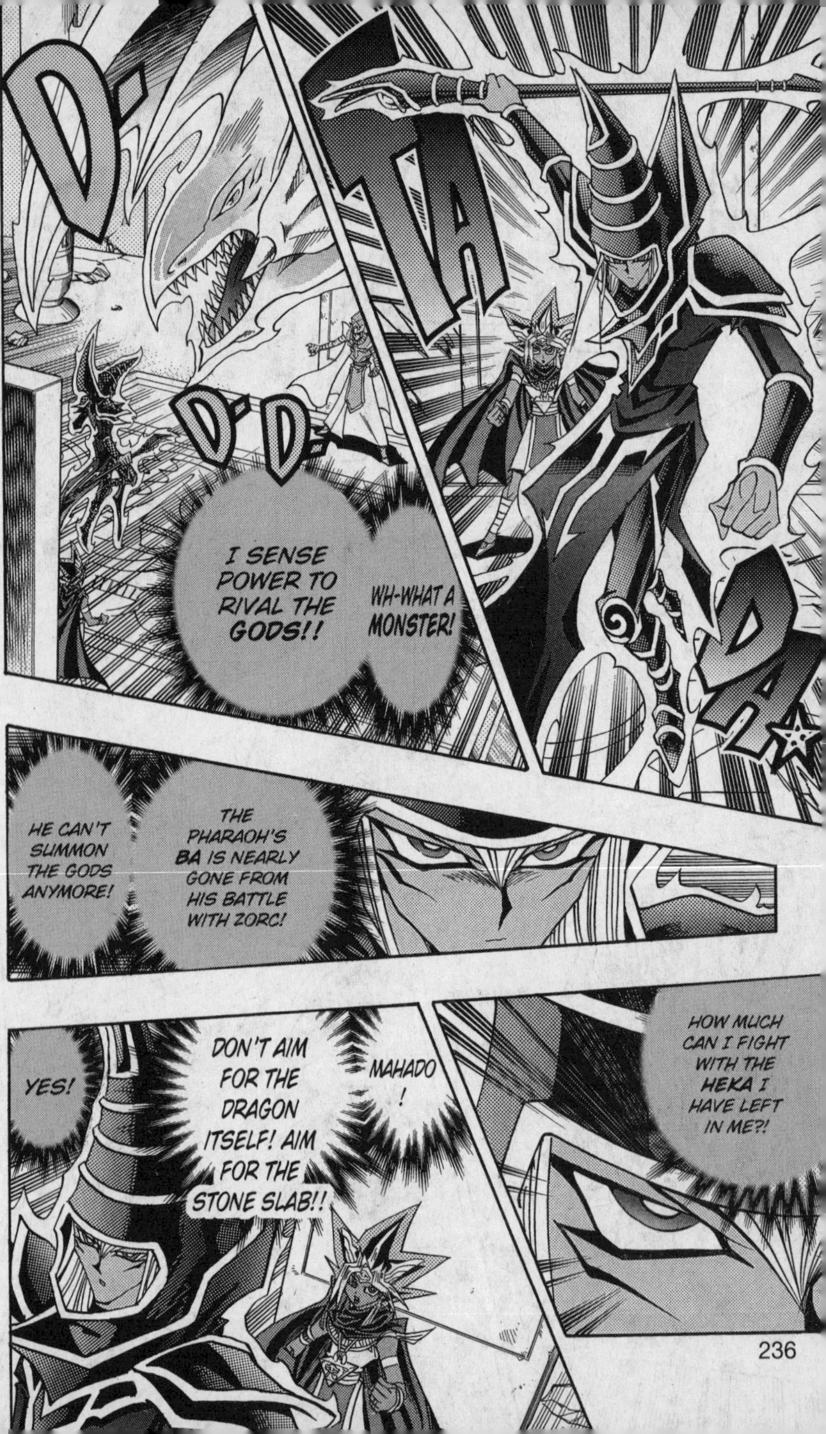
TA
DA
D-
D-D-
WH-WHAT A MONSTER!
I SENSE POWER TO RIVAL THE GODS!!
THE PHARAOH'S BA IS NEARLY GONE FROM HIS BATTLE WITH ZORC!
HE CAN'T SUMMON THE GODS ANYMORE!
HOW MUCH CAN I FIGHT WITH THE HEKA I HAVE LEFT IN ME?!
MAHADO!
DON'T AIM FOR THE DRAGON ITSELF! AIM FOR THE STONE SLAB!!
YES!

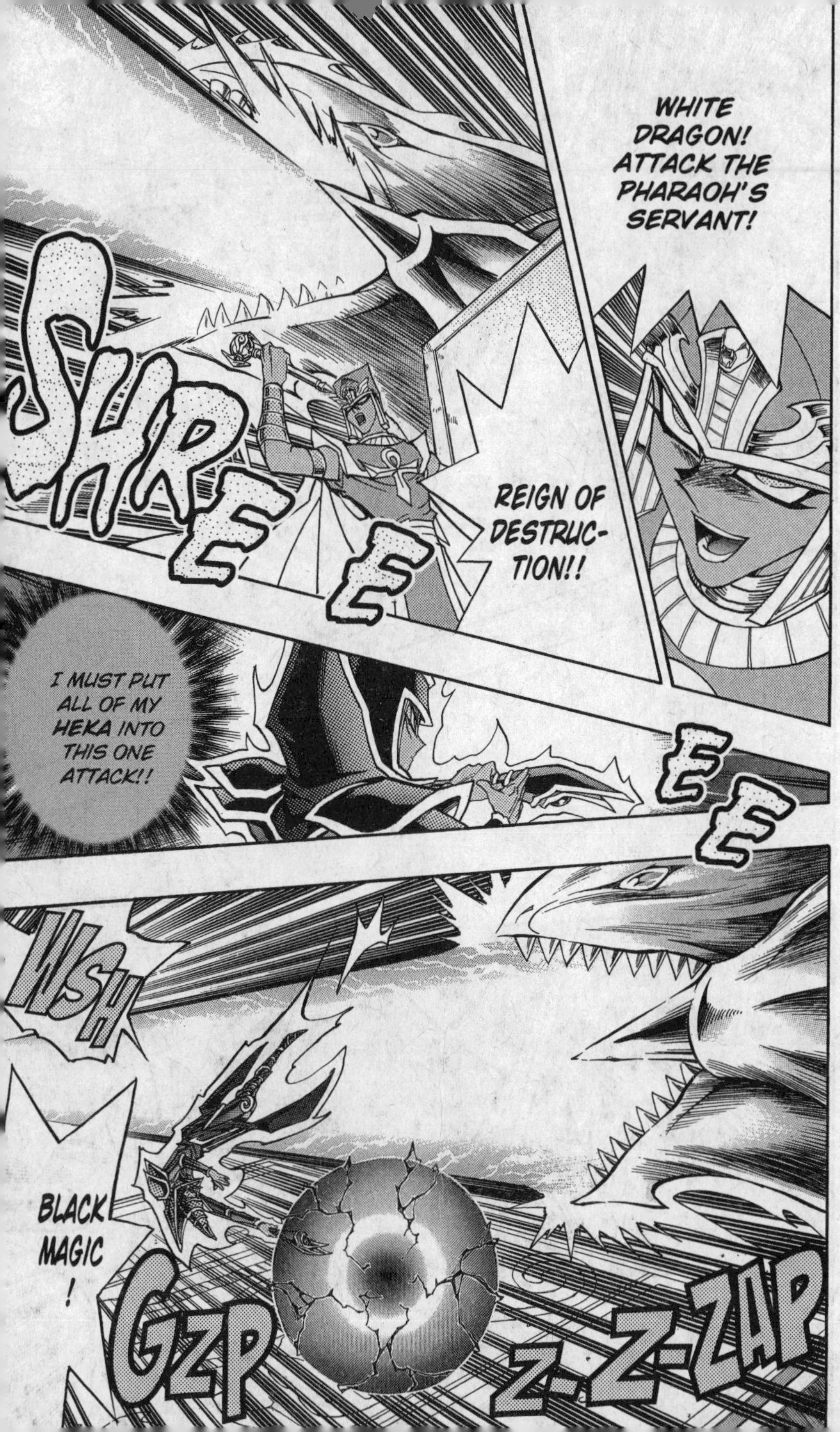
WHITE DRAGON! ATTACK THE PHARAOH'S SERVANT!
REIGN OF DESTRUCTION!!
SHREEE
I MUST PUT ALL OF MY HEKA INTO THIS ONE ATTACK!!
EE
WISH
BLACK MAGIC!
GZP
Z-Z-ZAP

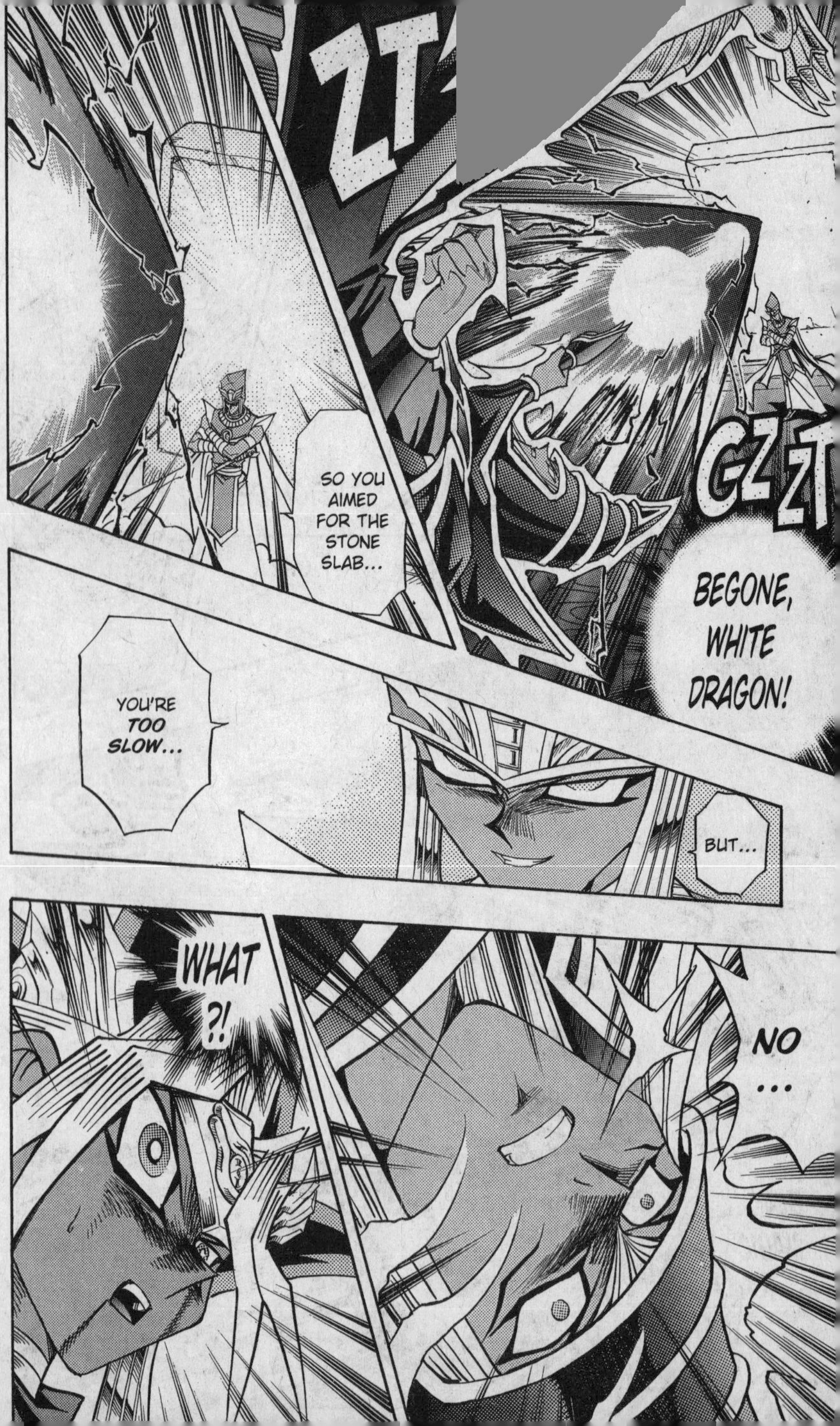
GZ ZT
BEGONE, WHITE DRAGON!
ZT
SO YOU AIMED FOR THE STONE SLAB...
BUT...
YOU'RE *TOO SLOW*...
NO ...
WHAT ?!

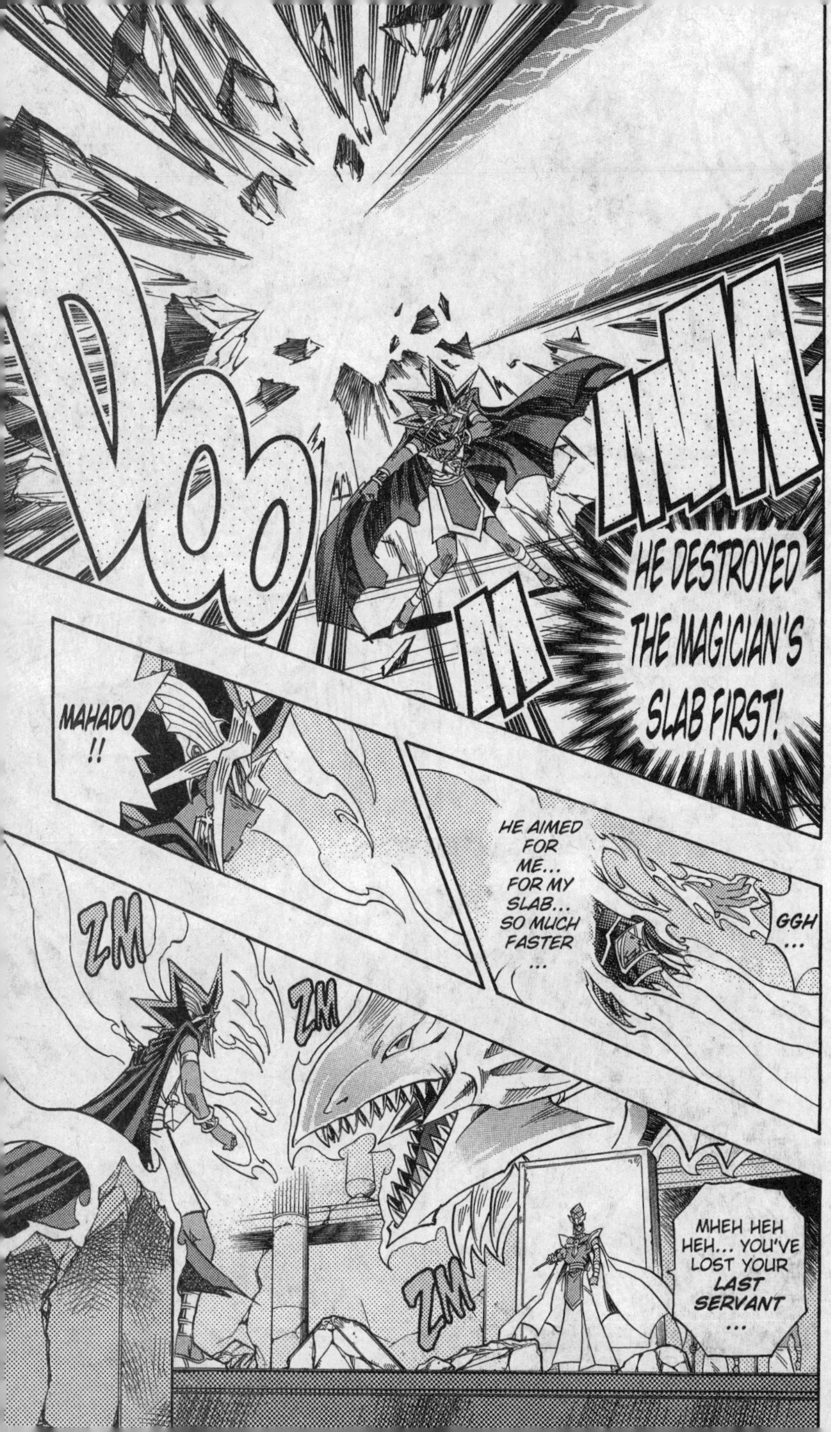
DOOOMMMM
HE DESTROYED THE MAGICIAN'S SLAB FIRST!
GGH...
HE AIMED FOR ME... FOR MY SLAB... SO MUCH FASTER...
MAHADO !!
MHEH HEH HEH... YOU'VE LOST YOUR LAST SERVANT...
ZM
ZM
ZM

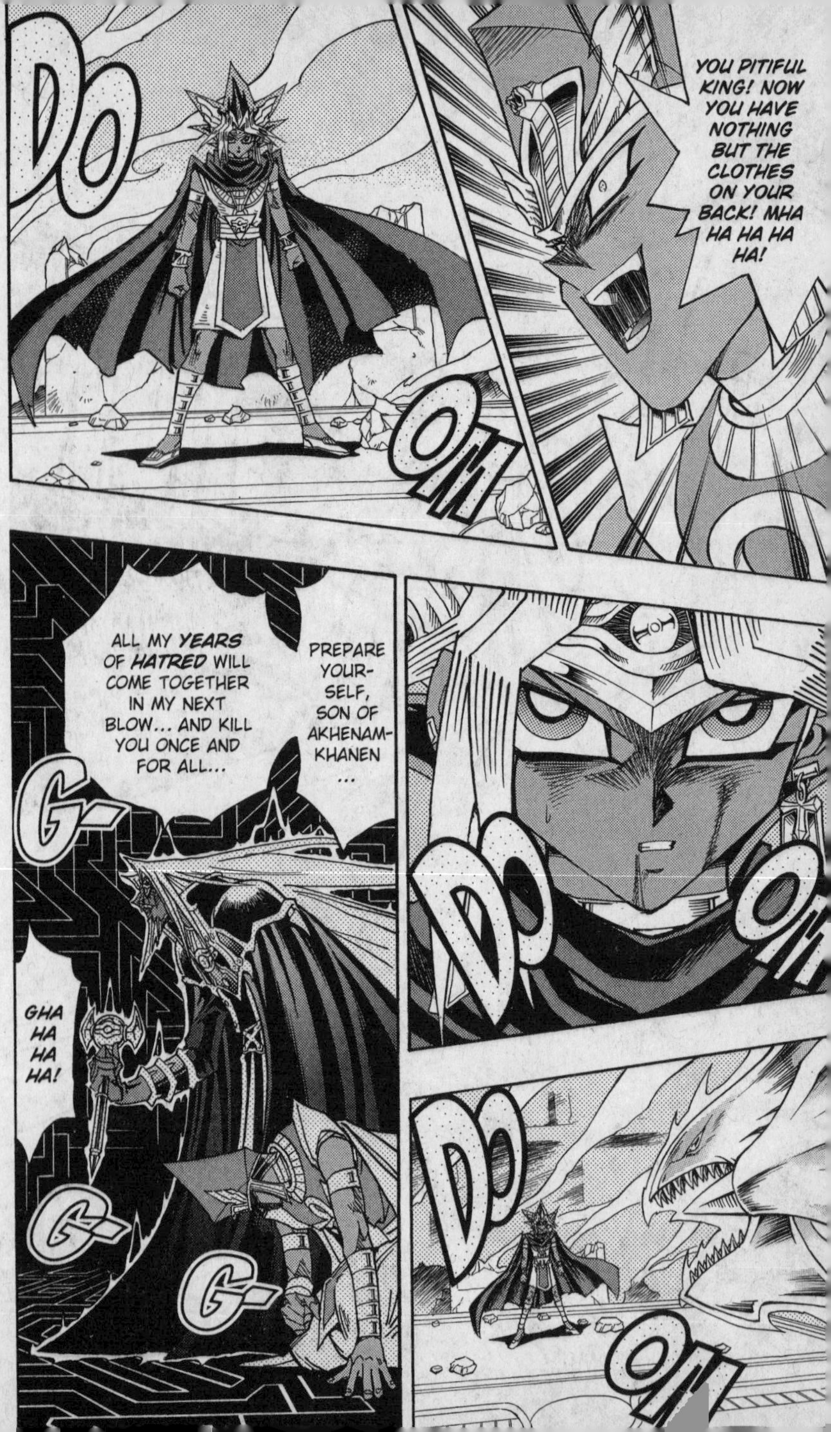
YOU PITIFUL KING! NOW YOU HAVE NOTHING BUT THE CLOTHES ON YOUR BACK! MHA HA HA HA HA!
DO
OM
DO
DO
PREPARE YOURSELF, SON OF AKHENAMKHANEN ...
ALL MY *YEARS* OF *HATRED* WILL COME TOGETHER IN MY NEXT BLOW... AND KILL YOU ONCE AND FOR ALL...
G-
GHA HA HA HA HA!
G-
G-

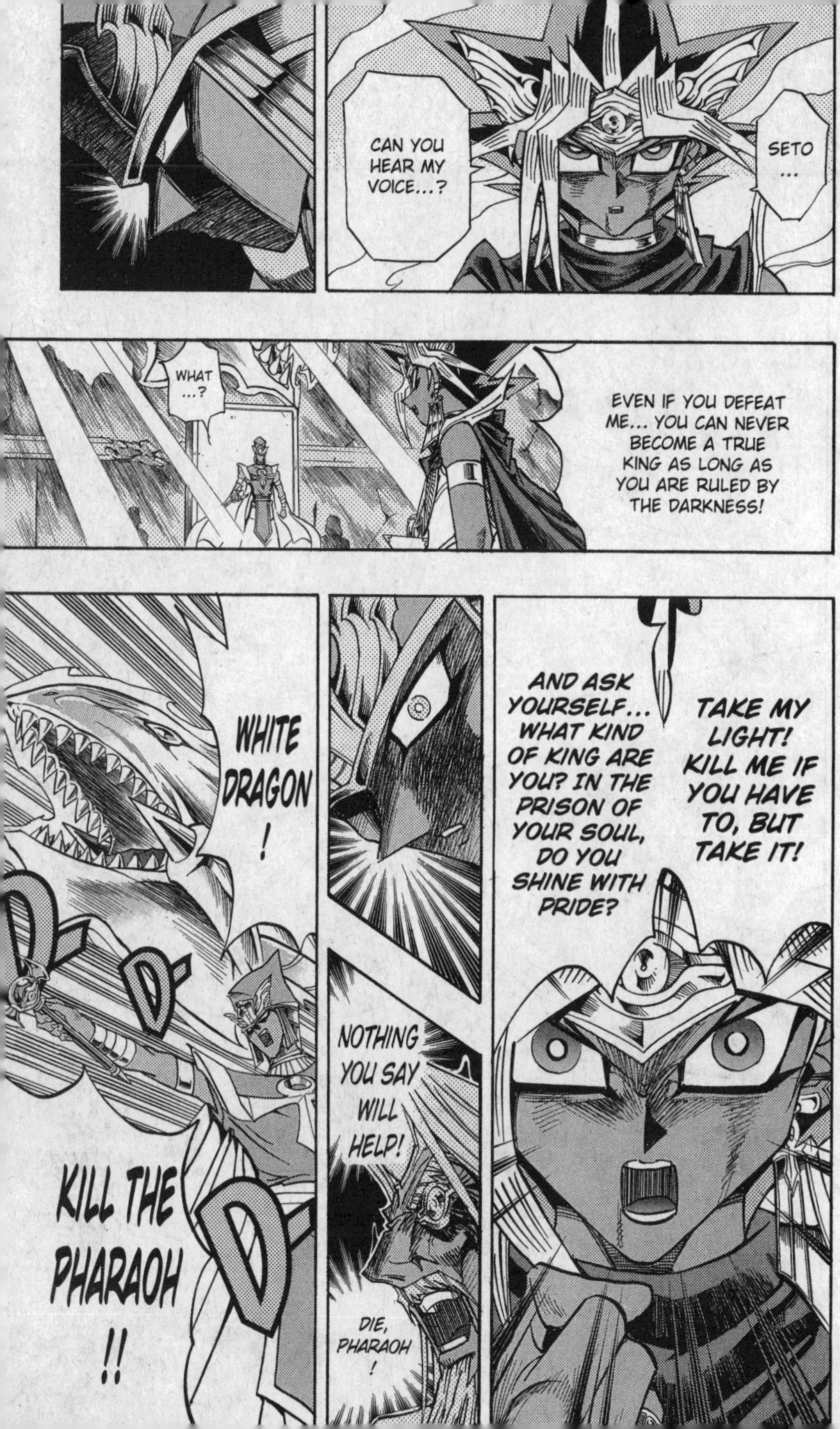

SETO ...
CAN YOU HEAR MY VOICE...?
EVEN IF YOU DEFEAT ME... YOU CAN NEVER BECOME A TRUE KING AS LONG AS YOU ARE RULED BY THE DARKNESS!
WHAT ...?
TAKE MY LIGHT! KILL ME IF YOU HAVE TO, BUT TAKE IT!
AND ASK YOURSELF... WHAT KIND OF KING ARE YOU? IN THE PRISON OF YOUR SOUL, DO YOU SHINE WITH PRIDE?
NOTHING YOU SAY WILL HELP!
DIE, PHARAOH!
WHITE DRAGON!
KILL THE PHARAOH!!

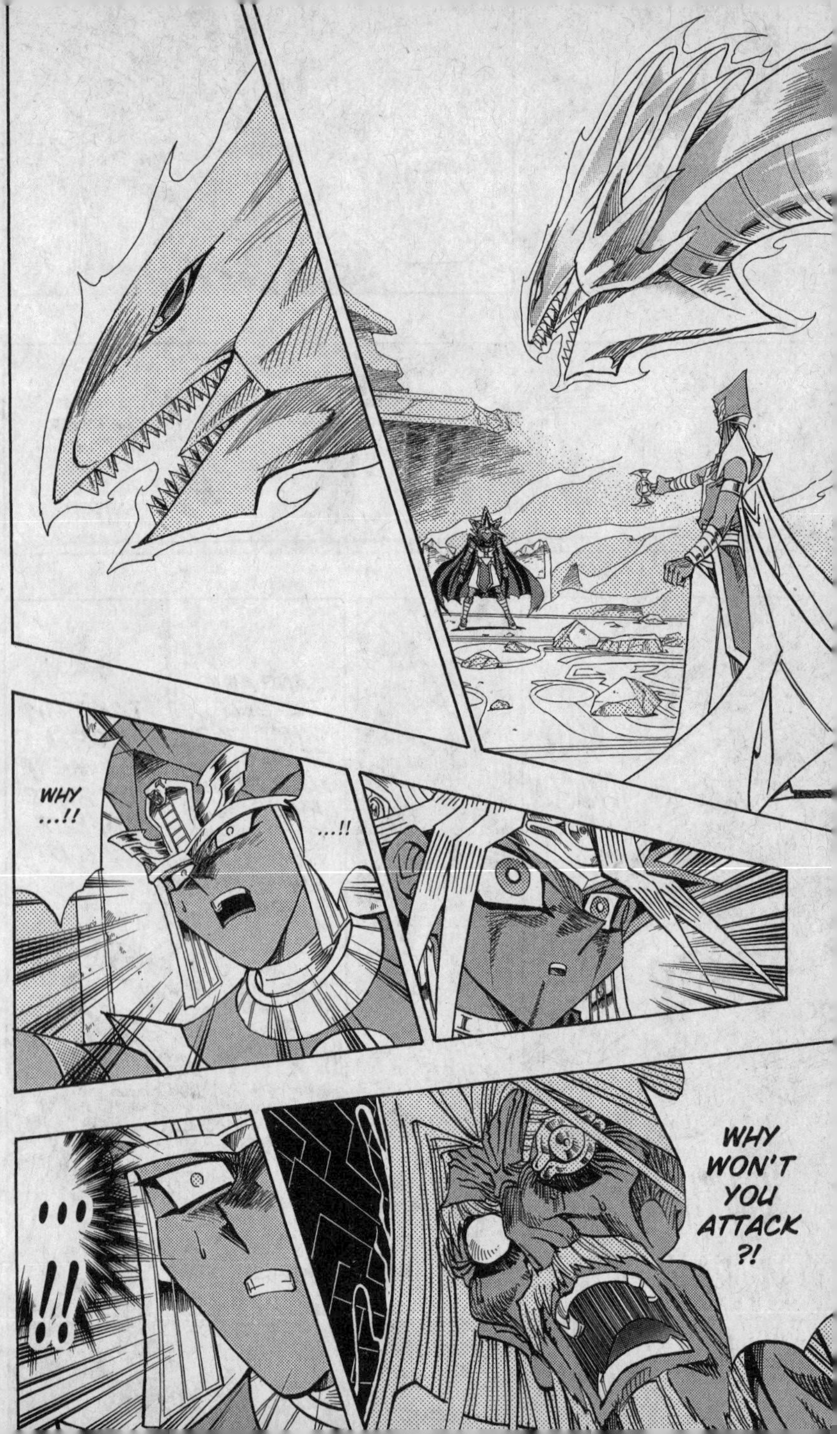
...!!
WHY ...!!
WHY WON'T YOU ATTACK ?!
...!!

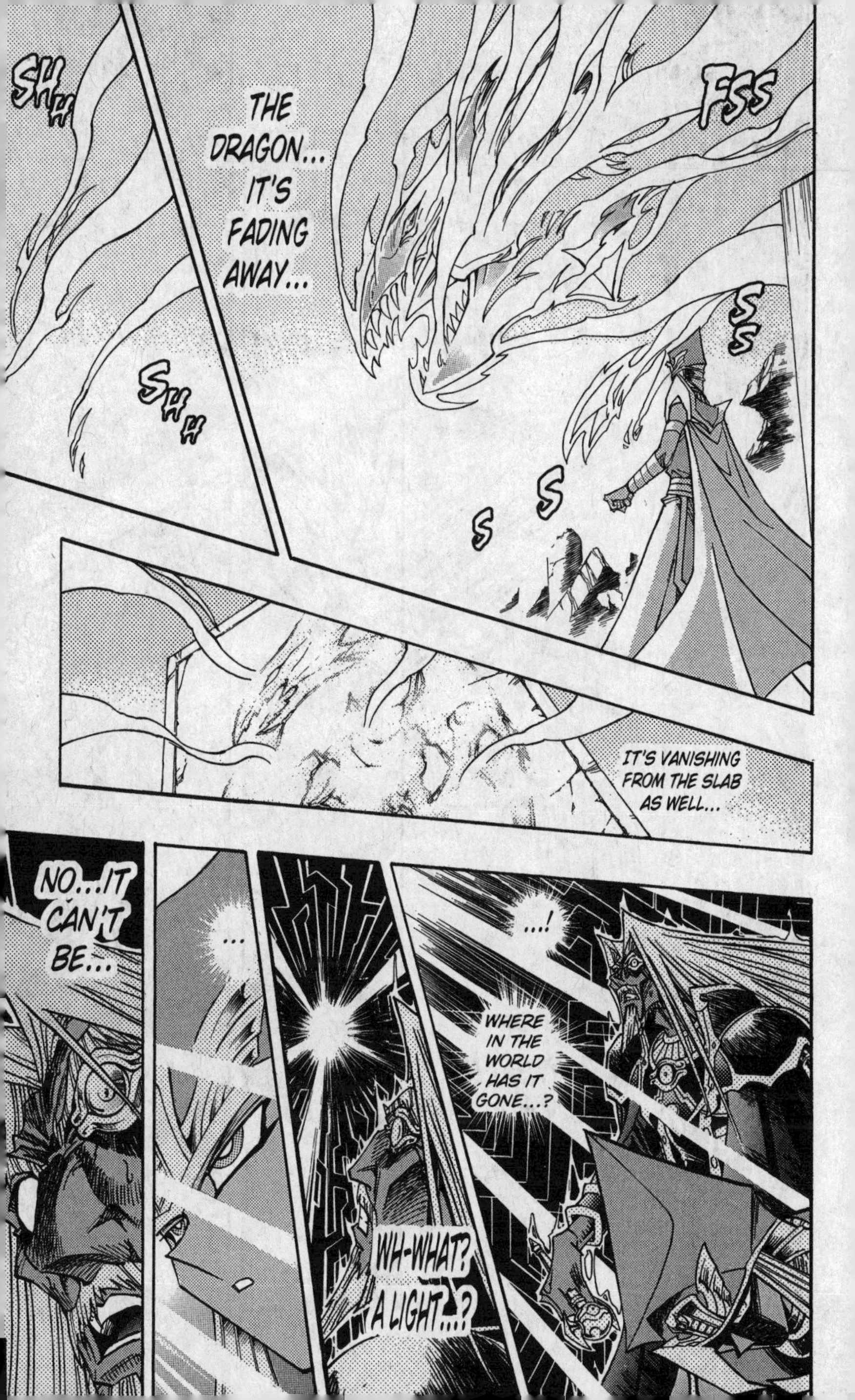
FSS
THE DRAGON... IT'S FADING AWAY...
SHH
SS
SHH
S
S
IT'S VANISHING FROM THE SLAB AS WELL...
...!
WHERE IN THE WORLD HAS IT GONE...?
WH-WHAT? A LIGHT...?
...
NO...IT CAN'T BE...

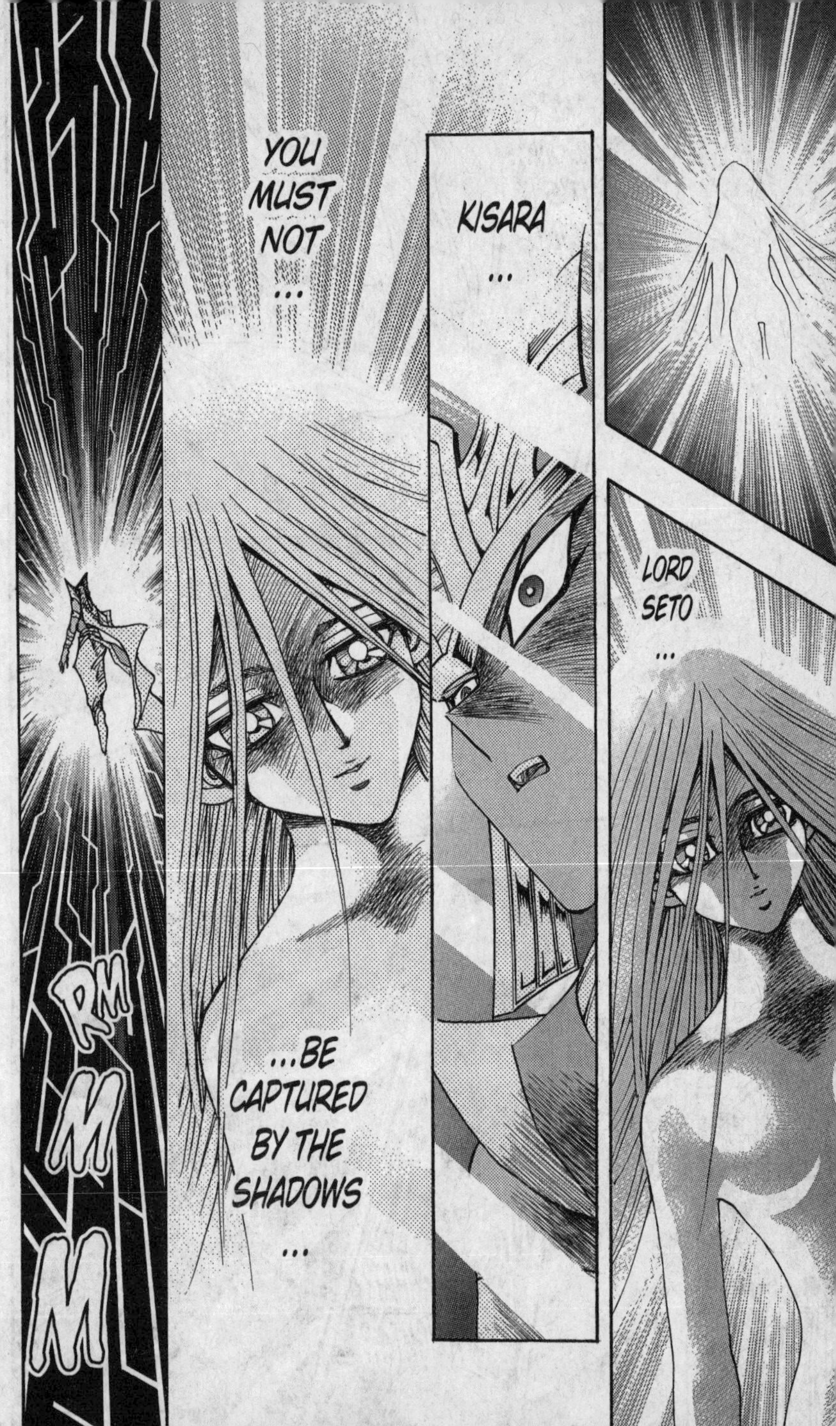
LORD SETO ...
KISARA ...
YOU MUST NOT ...
...BE CAPTURED BY THE SHADOWS ...
RMMM

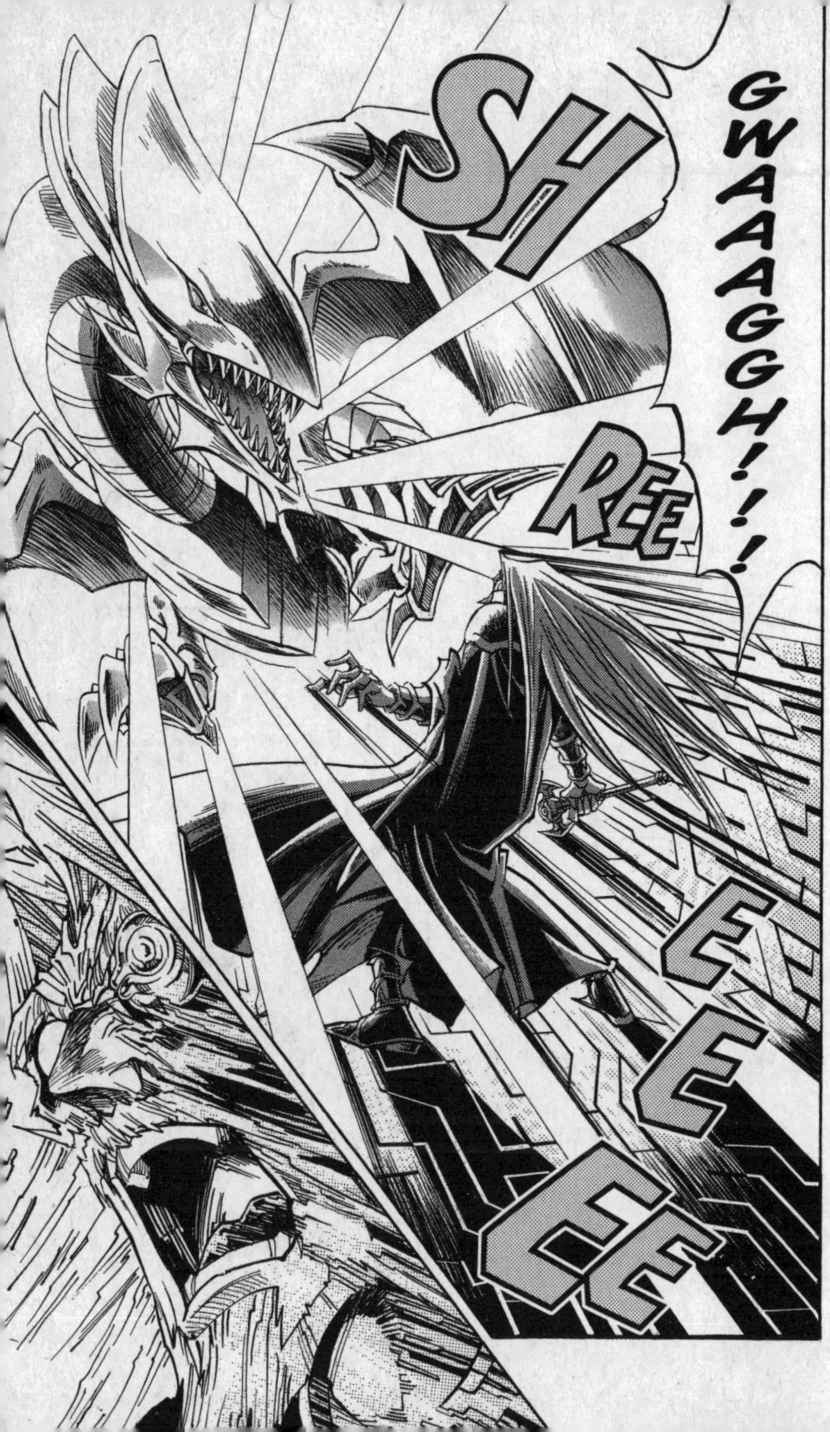
GWAAAGGH!!!
SHREEEEEEE

Duel 336: He Who Inherits the Light

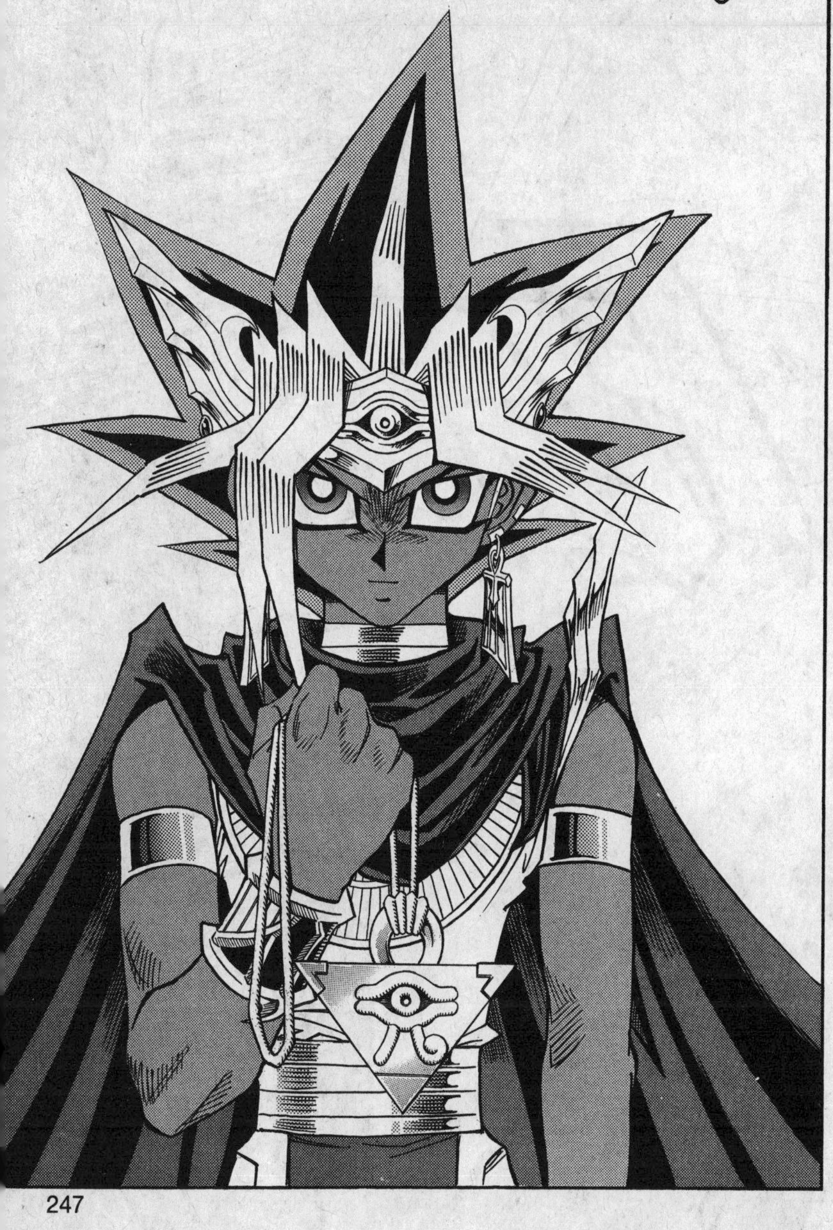

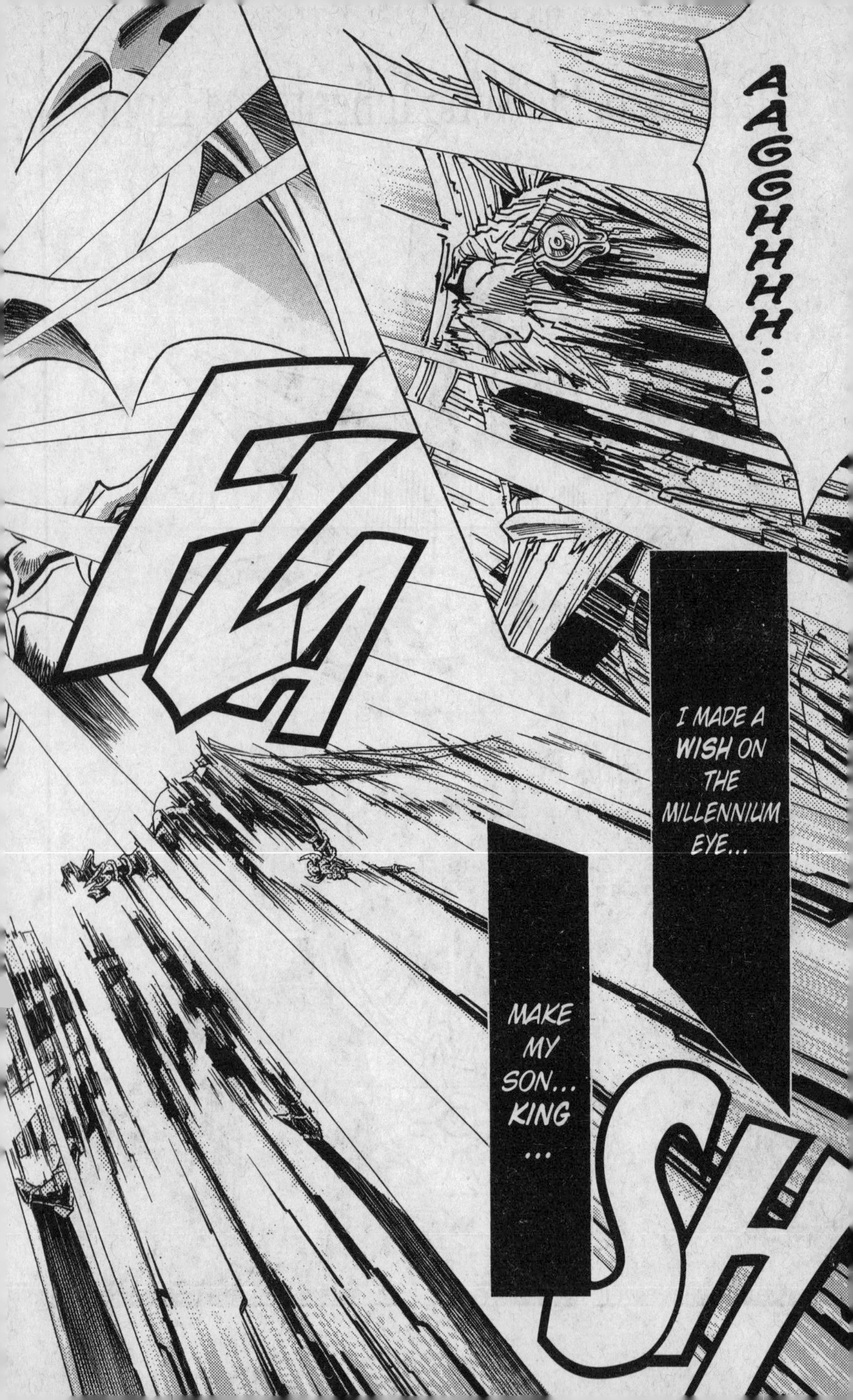
AAGGHHHH...
I MADE A WISH ON THE MILLENNIUM EYE...
MAKE MY SON... KING ...

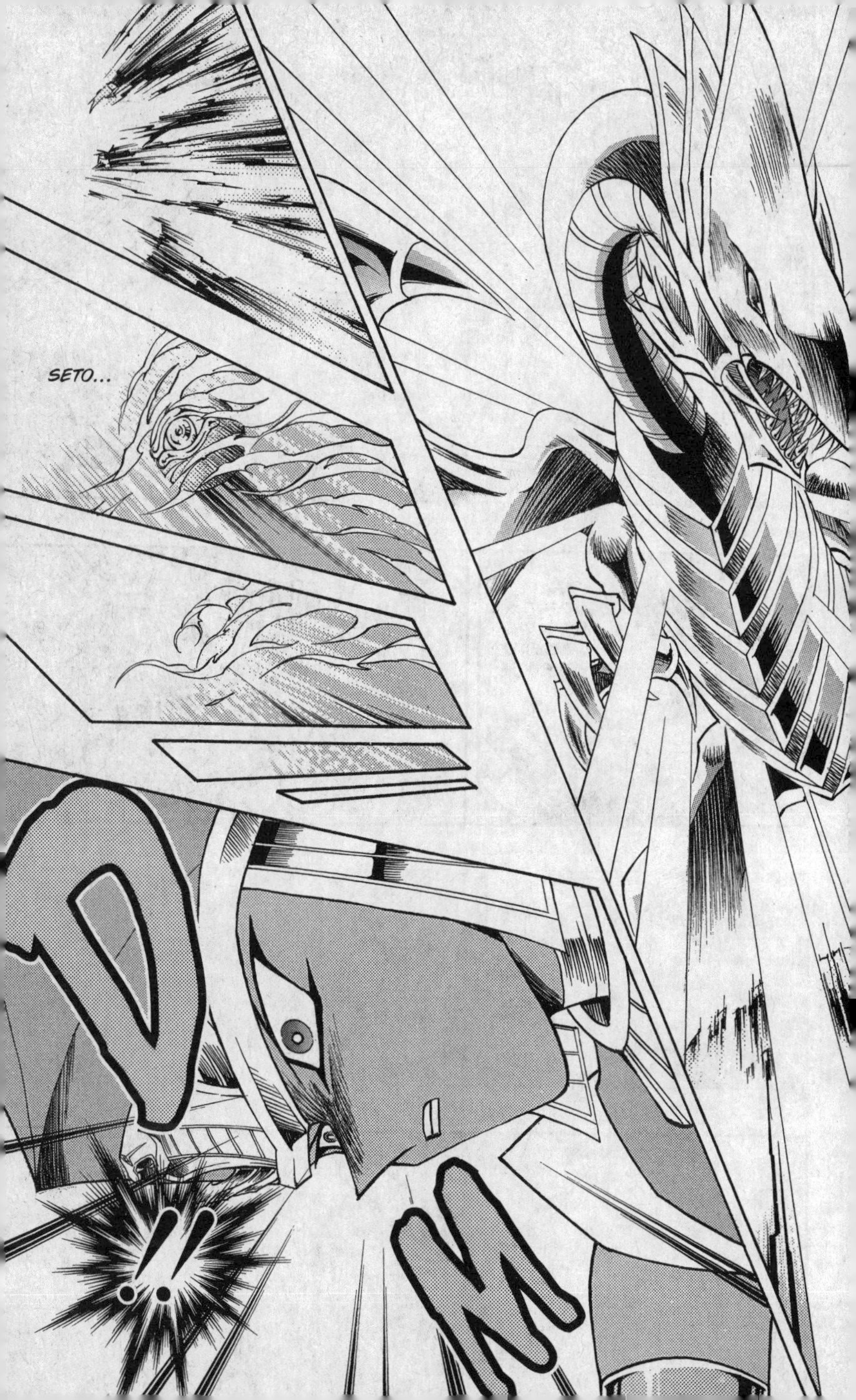
SETO...
!!

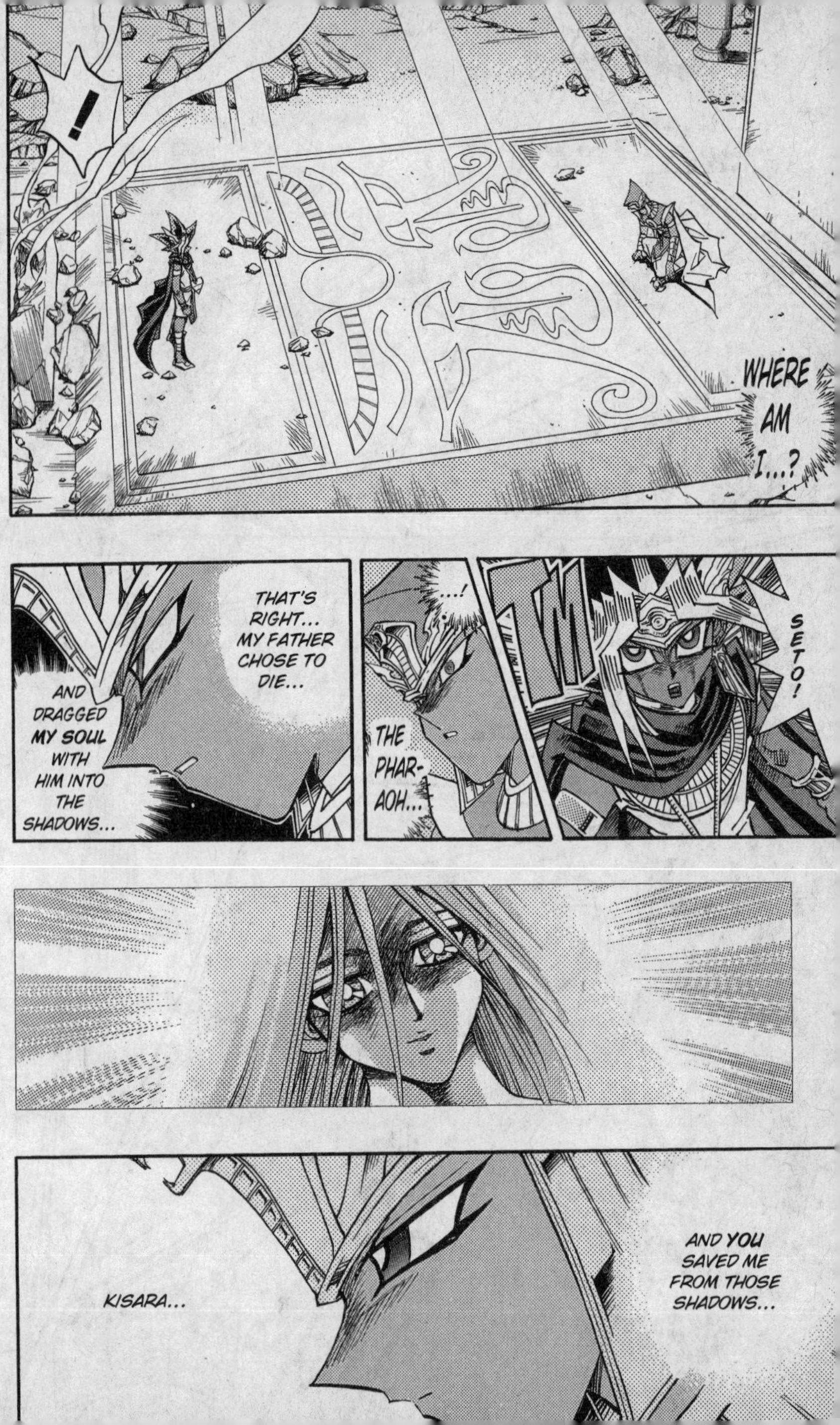

!
WHERE AM I...?
SETO!
...!
THE PHAR-AOH...
THAT'S RIGHT... MY FATHER CHOSE TO DIE...
AND DRAGGED **MY SOUL** WITH HIM INTO THE SHADOWS...
AND **YOU** SAVED ME FROM THOSE SHADOWS...
KISARA...

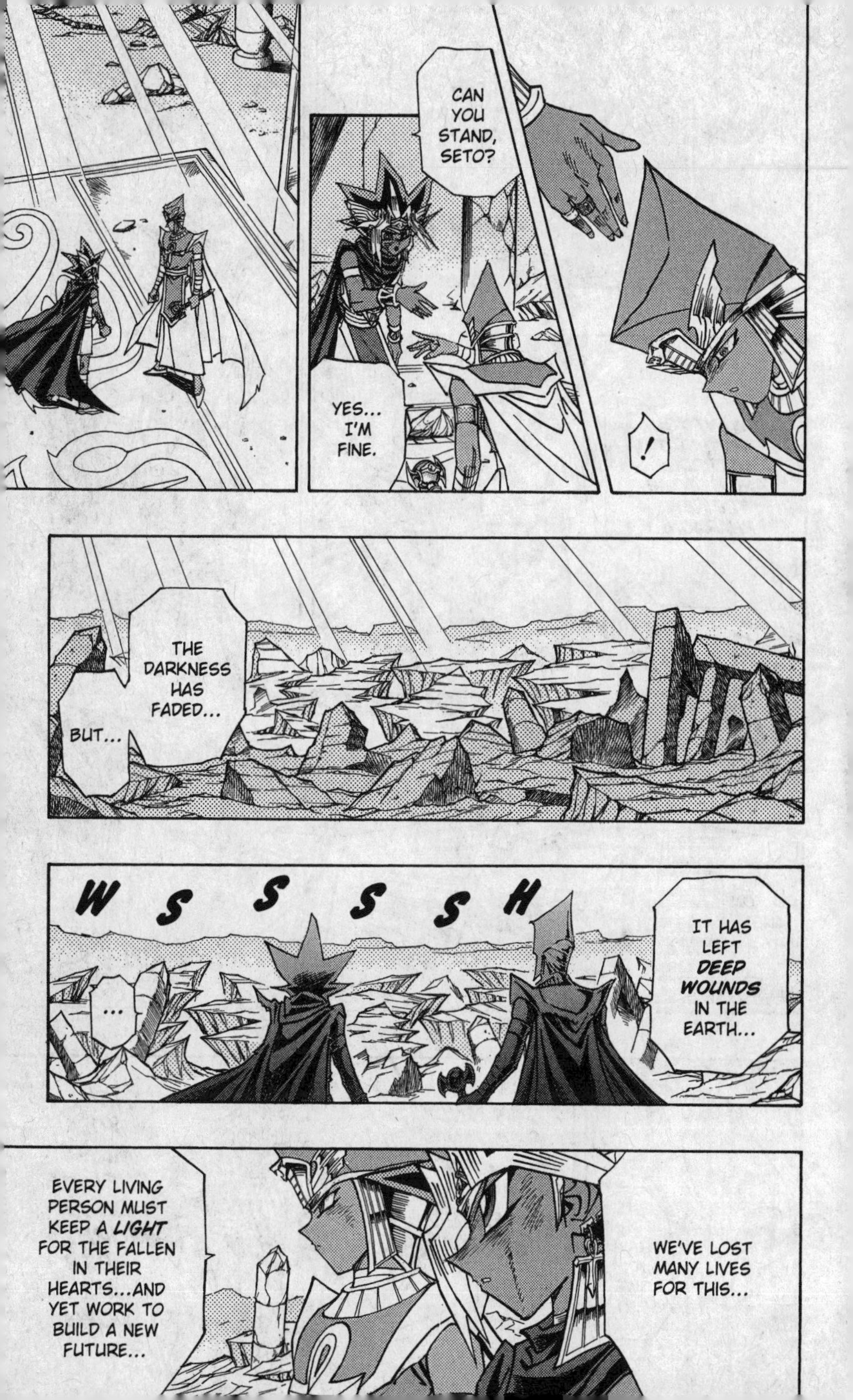
!
CAN YOU STAND, SETO?
YES... I'M FINE.
THE DARKNESS HAS FADED...
BUT...
IT HAS LEFT DEEP WOUNDS IN THE EARTH...
WSSSSH
...
WE'VE LOST MANY LIVES FOR THIS...
EVERY LIVING PERSON MUST KEEP A LIGHT FOR THE FALLEN IN THEIR HEARTS...AND YET WORK TO BUILD A NEW FUTURE...

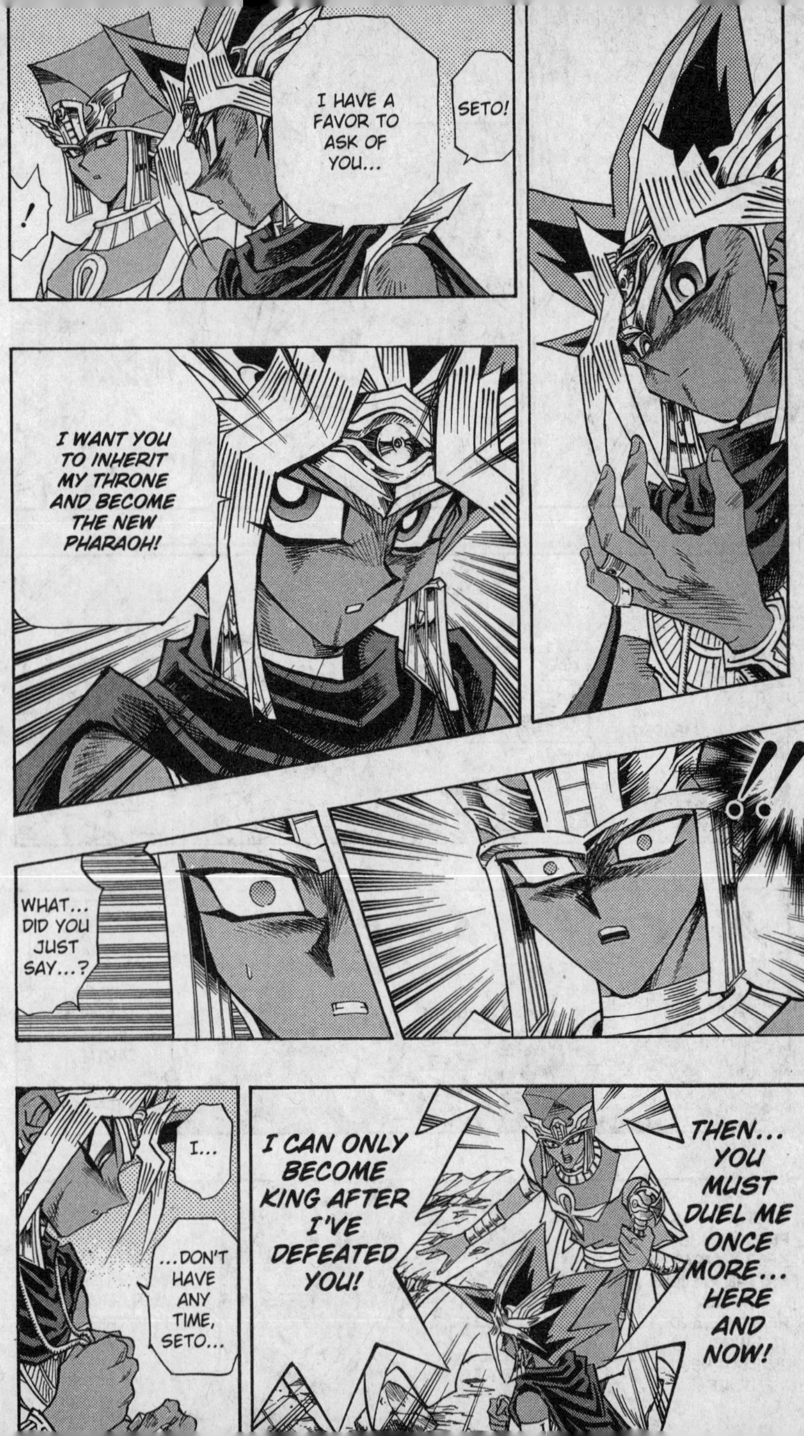
SETO!
I HAVE A FAVOR TO ASK OF YOU...
!
I WANT YOU TO INHERIT MY THRONE AND BECOME THE NEW PHARAOH!
!!
WHAT... DID YOU JUST SAY...?
THEN... YOU MUST DUEL ME ONCE MORE... HERE AND NOW!
I CAN ONLY BECOME KING AFTER I'VE DEFEATED YOU!
I...
...DON'T HAVE ANY TIME, SETO...

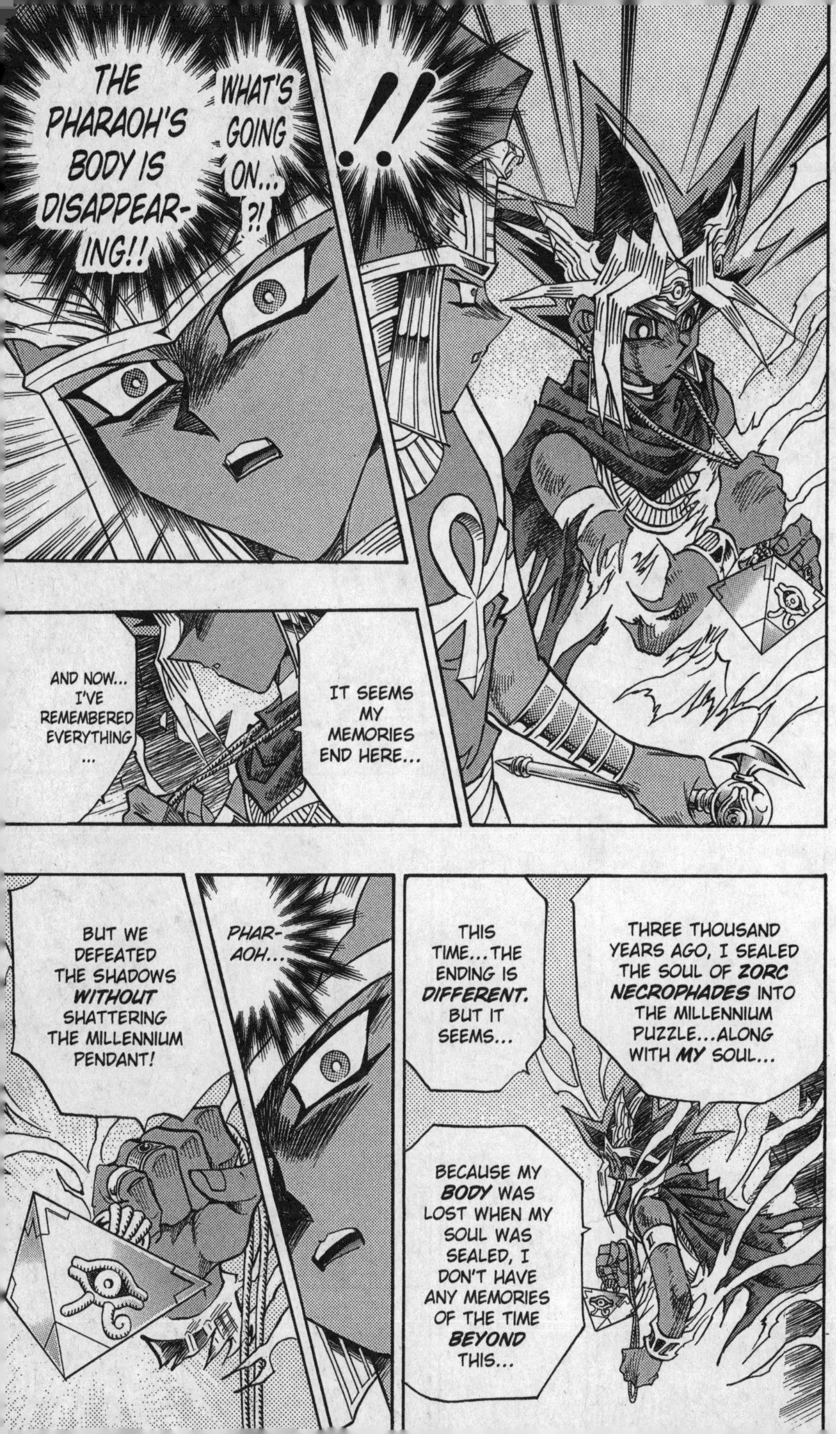
!!
WHAT'S GOING ON... ?!
THE PHARAOH'S BODY IS DISAPPEAR-ING!!
IT SEEMS MY MEMORIES END HERE...
AND NOW... I'VE REMEMBERED EVERYTHING ...
THREE THOUSAND YEARS AGO, I SEALED THE SOUL OF ZORC NECROPHADES INTO THE MILLENNIUM PUZZLE...ALONG WITH MY SOUL...
THIS TIME...THE ENDING IS DIFFERENT. BUT IT SEEMS...
BECAUSE MY BODY WAS LOST WHEN MY SOUL WAS SEALED, I DON'T HAVE ANY MEMORIES OF THE TIME BEYOND THIS...
PHAR-AOH...
BUT WE DEFEATED THE SHADOWS WITHOUT SHATTERING THE MILLENNIUM PENDANT!

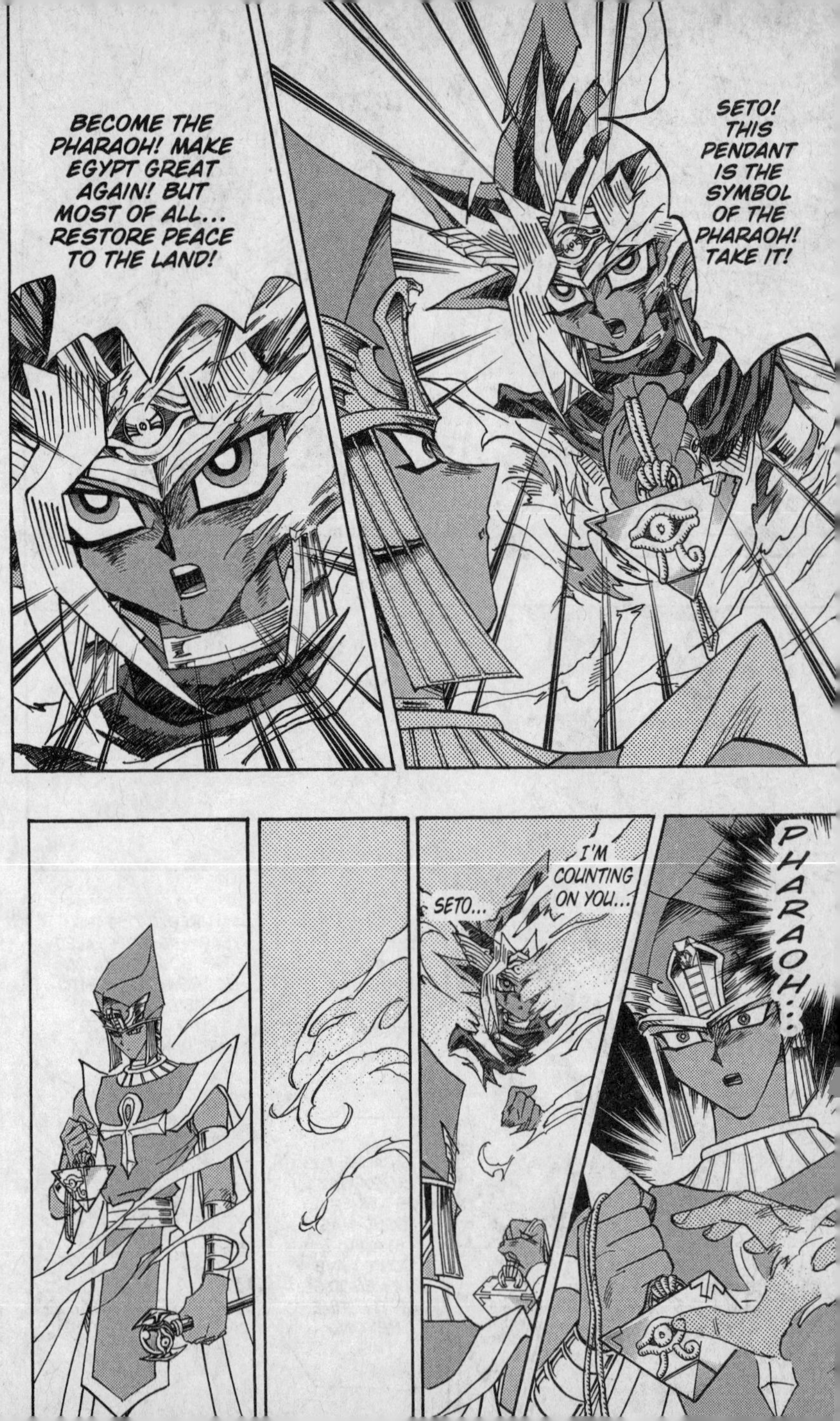
SETO! THIS PENDANT IS THE SYMBOL OF THE PHARAOH! TAKE IT!
BECOME THE PHARAOH! MAKE EGYPT GREAT AGAIN! BUT MOST OF ALL... RESTORE PEACE TO THE LAND!
PHARAOH...
I'M COUNTING ON YOU...
SETO...

READ THIS WAY

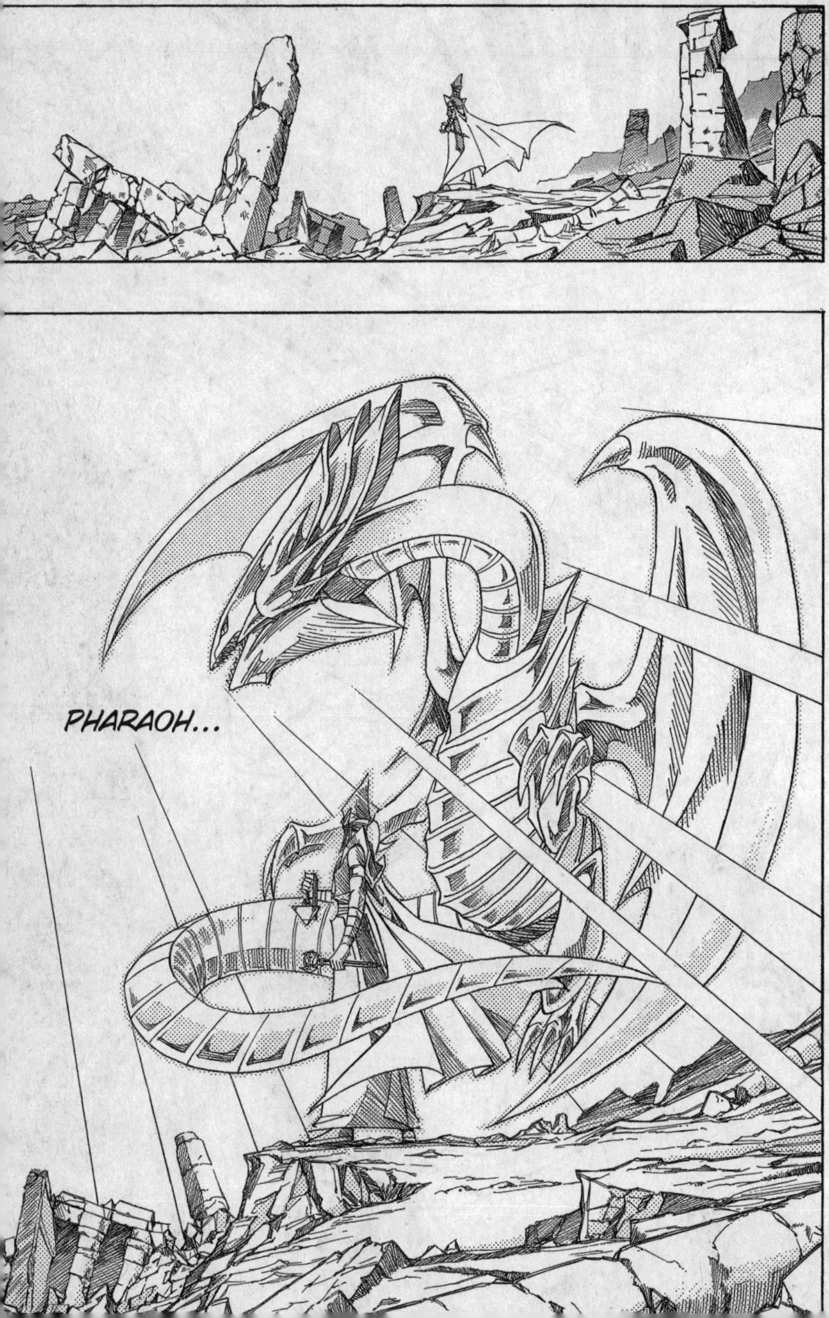
PHARAOH...

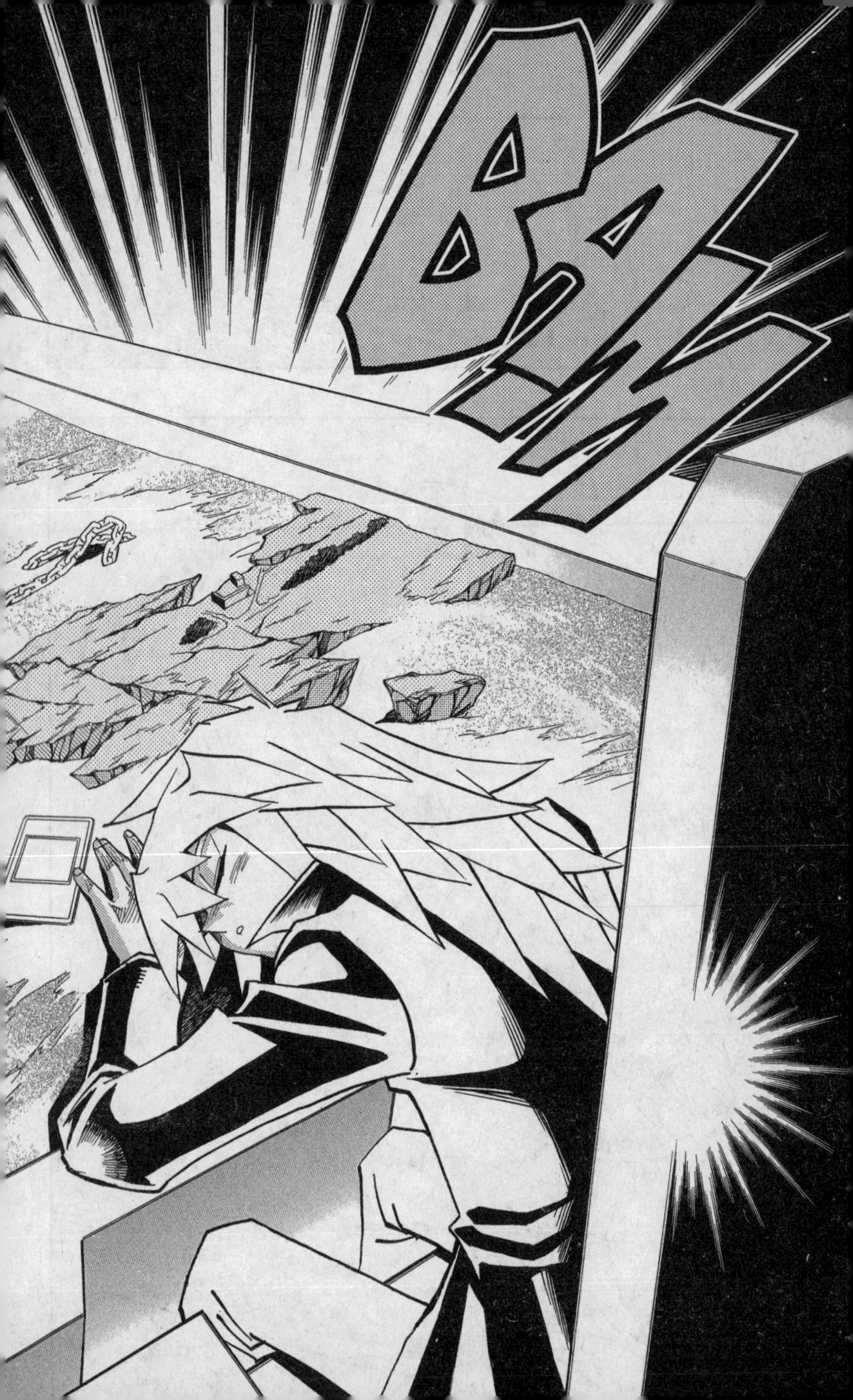
BASH

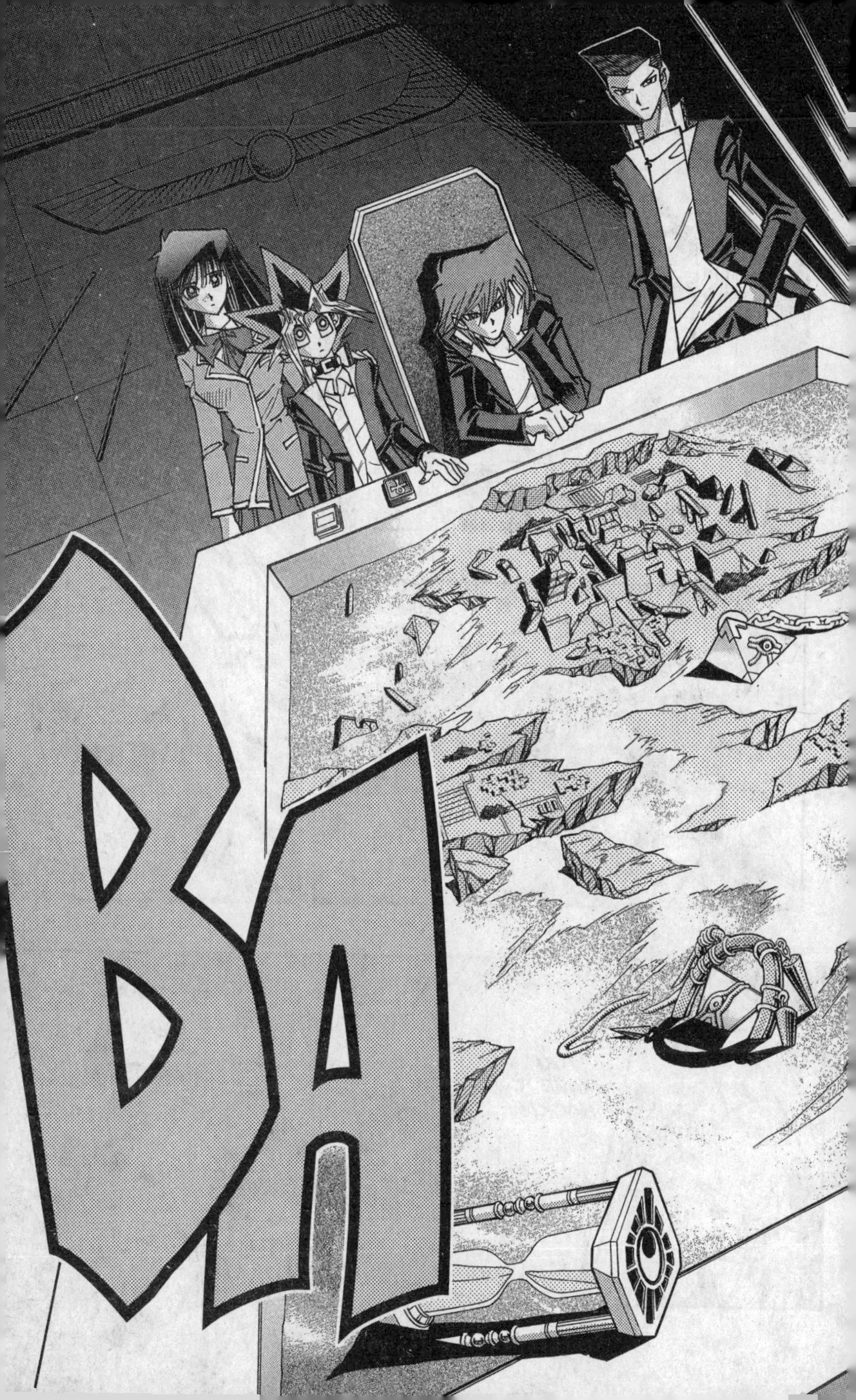
BA

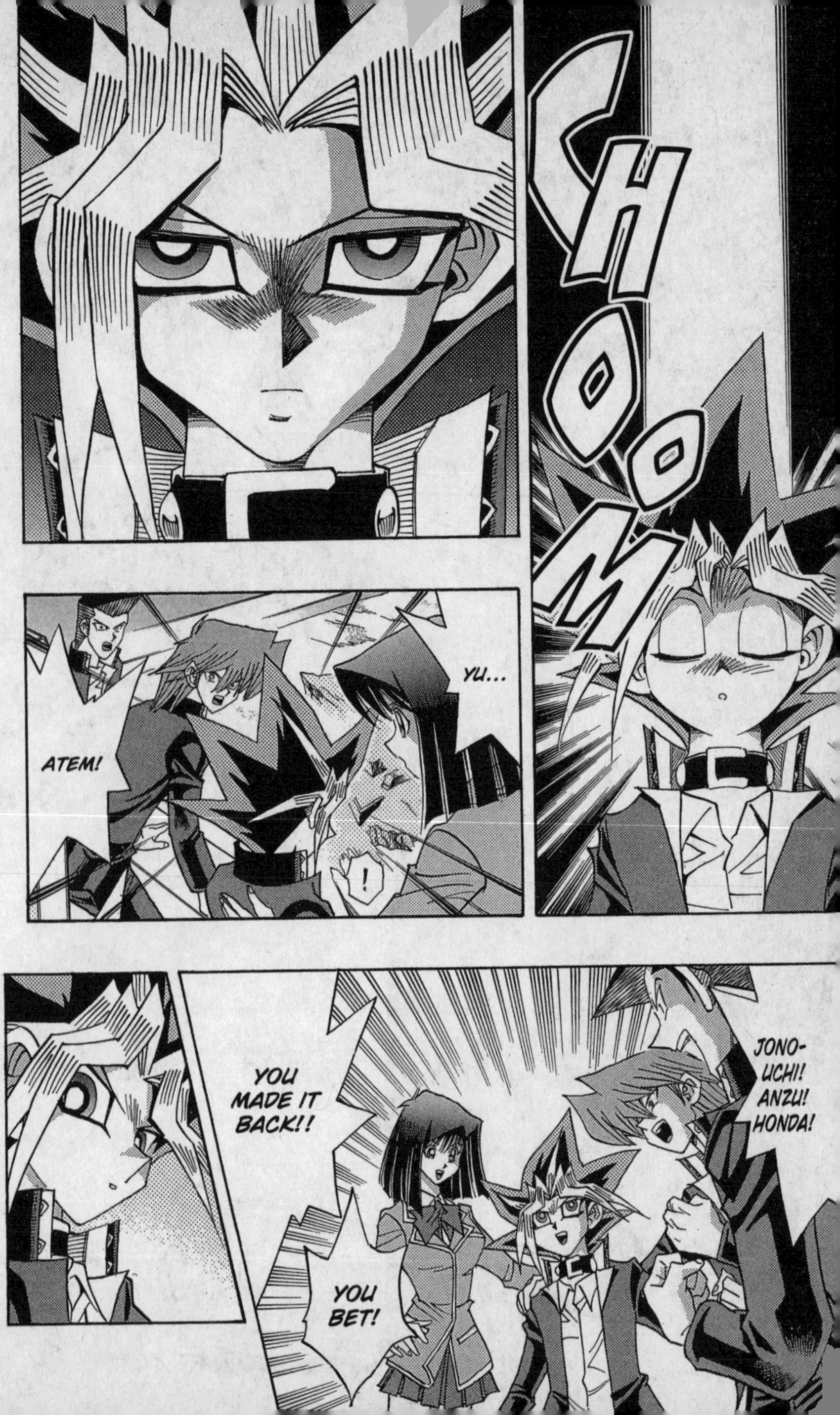
CHOOOM
YU...
ATEM!
!
JONO-UCHI! ANZU! HONDA!
YOU MADE IT BACK!!
YOU BET!

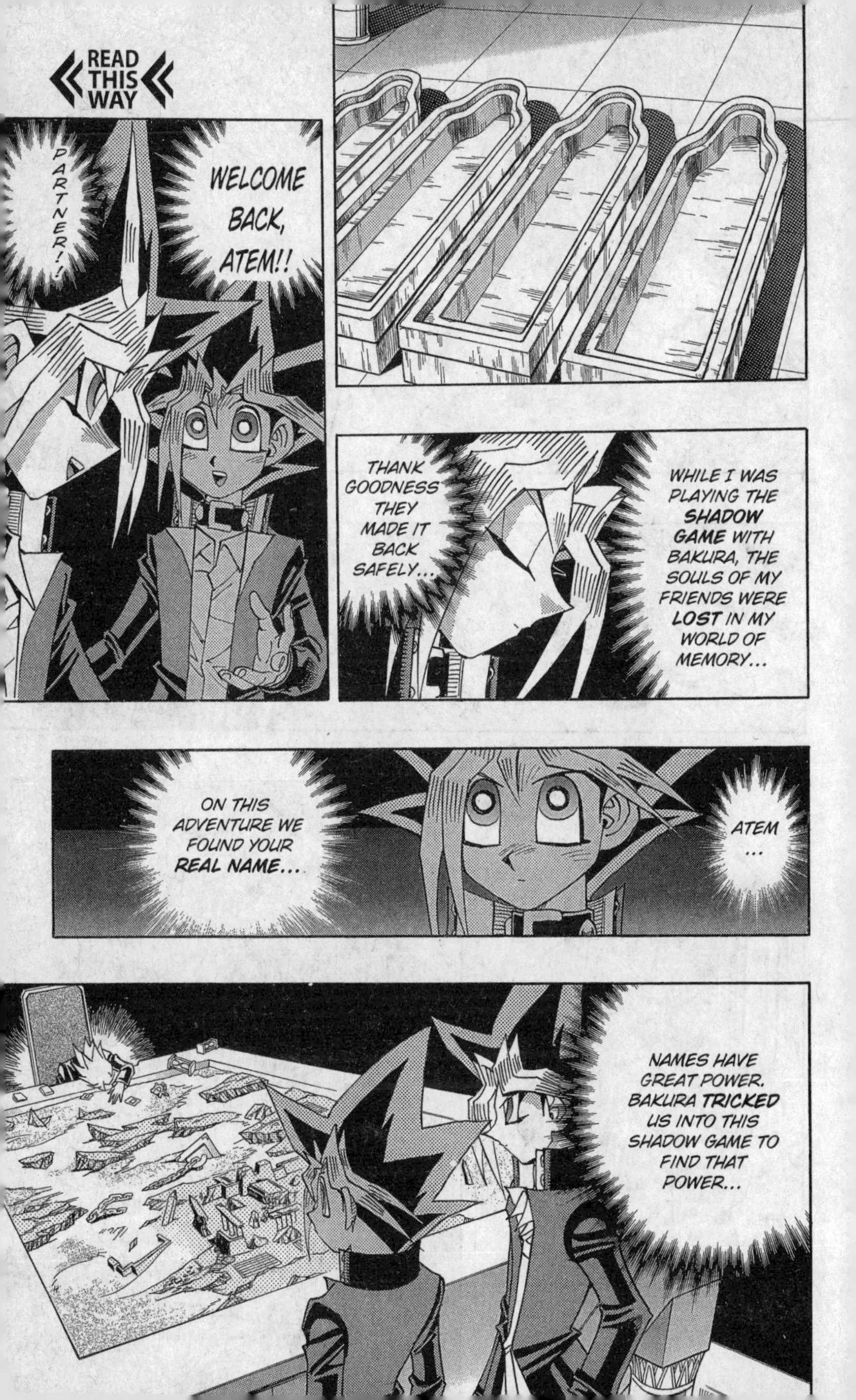
READ THIS WAY
WHILE I WAS PLAYING THE SHADOW GAME WITH BAKURA, THE SOULS OF MY FRIENDS WERE LOST IN MY WORLD OF MEMORY...
THANK GOODNESS THEY MADE IT BACK SAFELY...
WELCOME BACK, ATEM!!
PARTNER!!
ATEM...
ON THIS ADVENTURE WE FOUND YOUR REAL NAME...
NAMES HAVE GREAT POWER. BAKURA TRICKED US INTO THIS SHADOW GAME TO FIND THAT POWER...

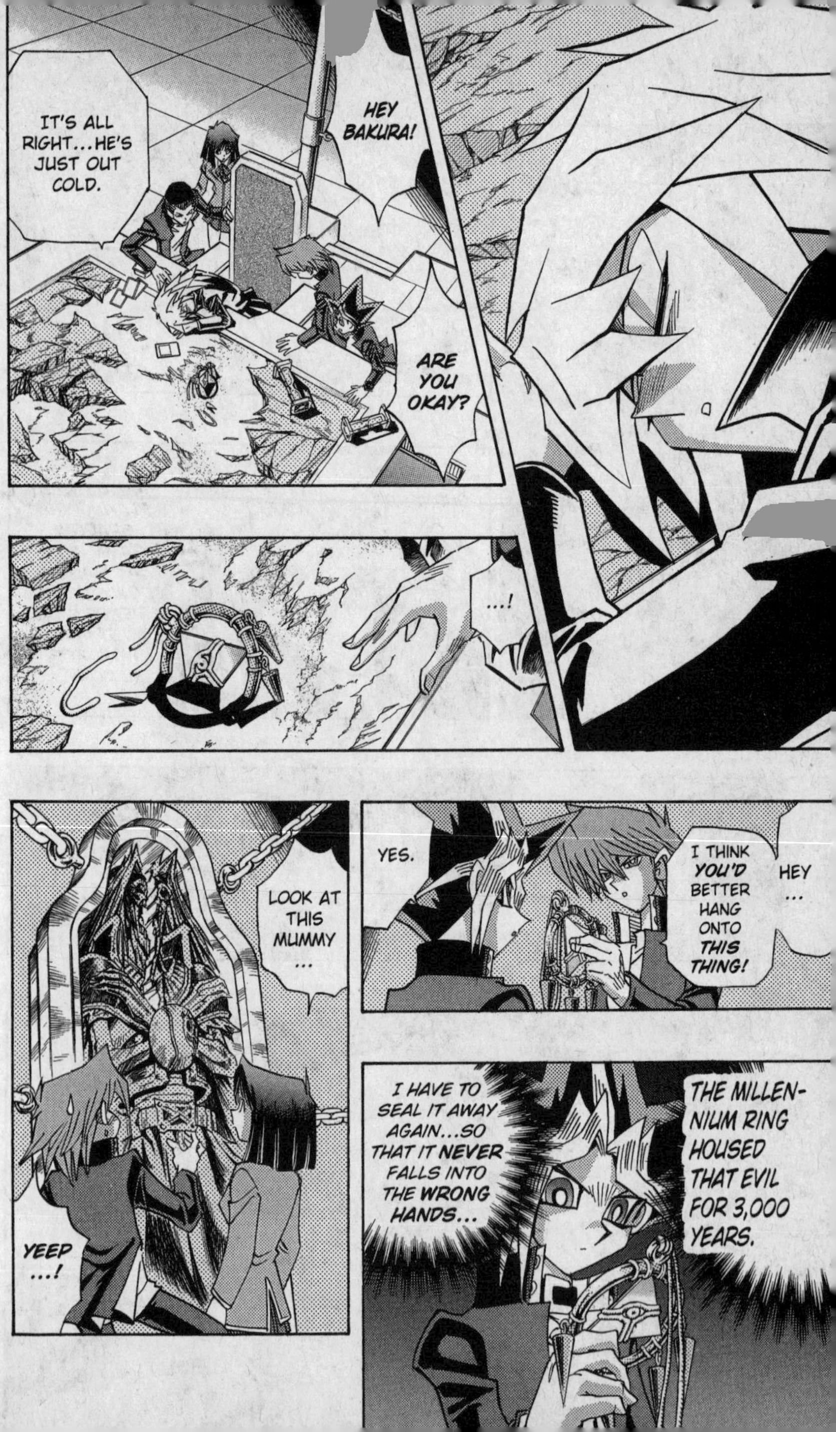

HEY BAKURA!
ARE YOU OKAY?
IT'S ALL RIGHT...HE'S JUST OUT COLD.
...!
HEY...
I THINK YOU'D BETTER HANG ONTO THIS THING!
YES.
THE MILLEN-NIUM RING HOUSED THAT EVIL FOR 3,000 YEARS.
I HAVE TO SEAL IT AWAY AGAIN...SO THAT IT NEVER FALLS INTO THE WRONG HANDS...
LOOK AT THIS MUMMY...
YEEP...!

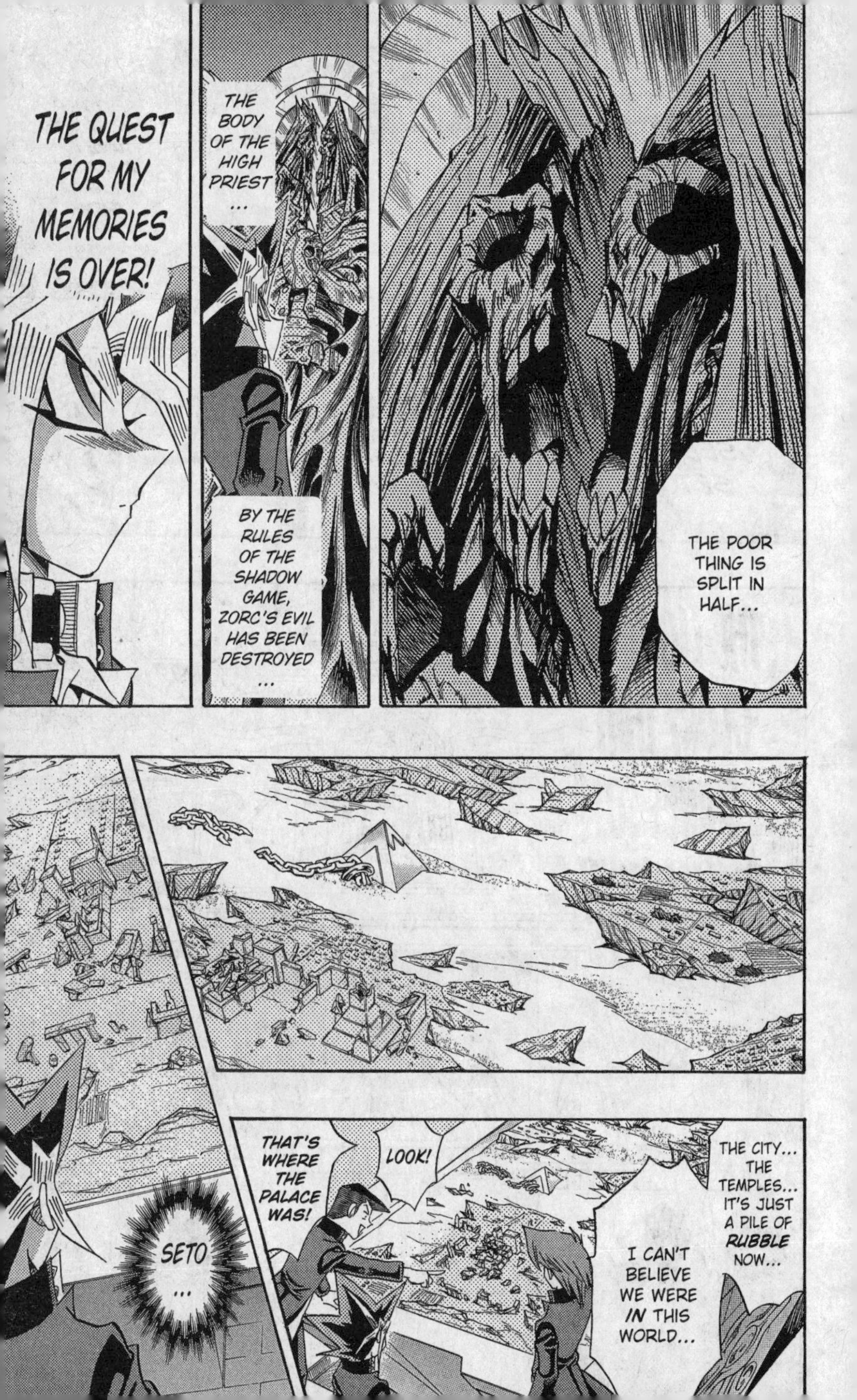
THE POOR THING IS SPLIT IN HALF...
THE BODY OF THE HIGH PRIEST ...
BY THE RULES OF THE SHADOW GAME, ZORC'S EVIL HAS BEEN DESTROYED ...
THE QUEST FOR MY MEMORIES IS OVER!
THE CITY... THE TEMPLES... IT'S JUST A PILE OF RUBBLE NOW...
I CAN'T BELIEVE WE WERE IN THIS WORLD...
LOOK!
THAT'S WHERE THE PALACE WAS!
SETO ...

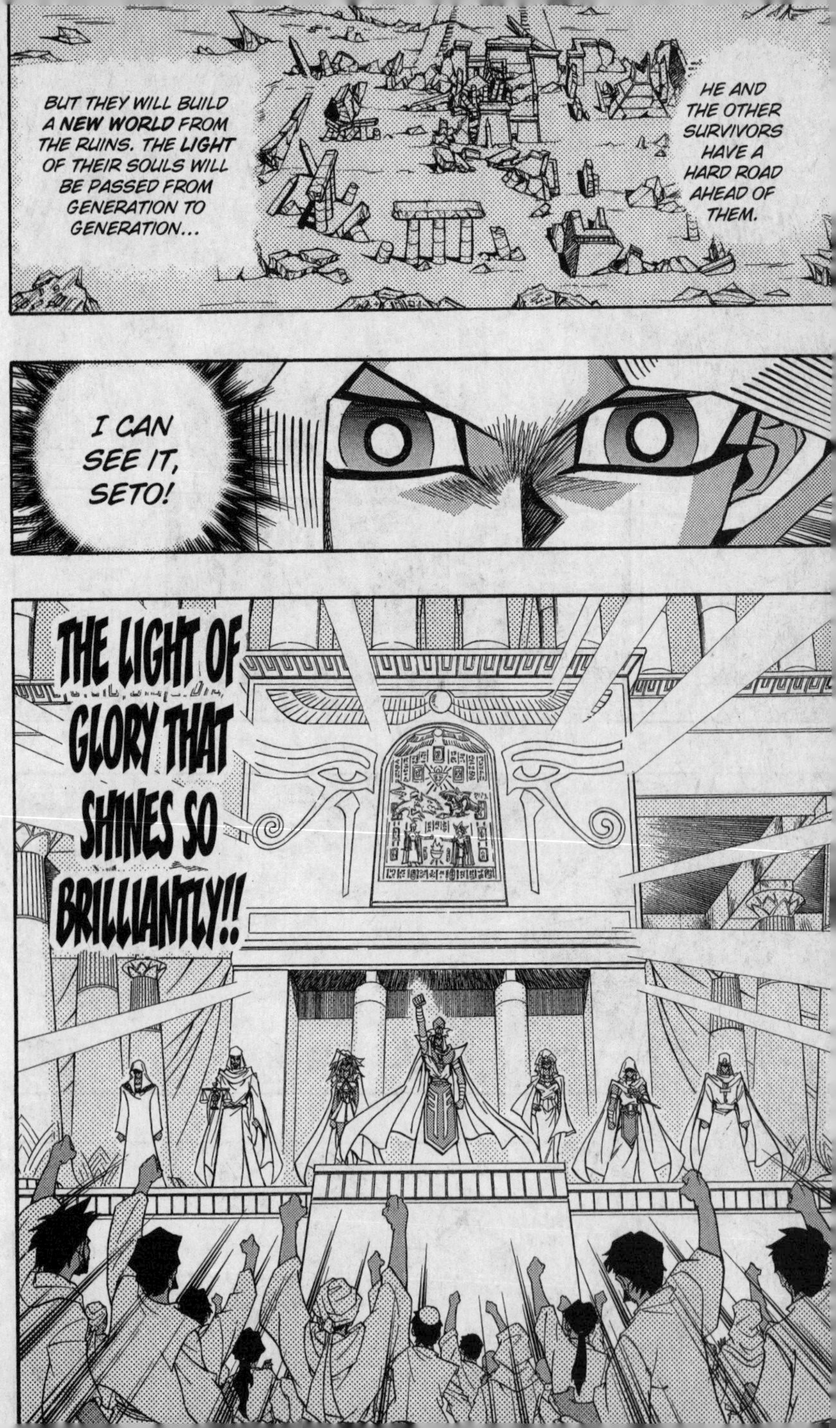
HE AND THE OTHER SURVIVORS HAVE A HARD ROAD AHEAD OF THEM.
BUT THEY WILL BUILD A NEW WORLD FROM THE RUINS. THE LIGHT OF THEIR SOULS WILL BE PASSED FROM GENERATION TO GENERATION...
I CAN SEE IT, SETO!
THE LIGHT OF GLORY THAT SHINES SO BRILLIANTLY!!

FWP

YES!

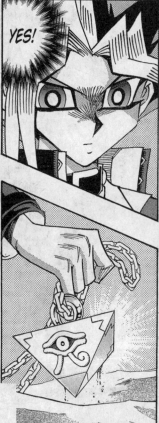

IT'S ALMOST TIME...

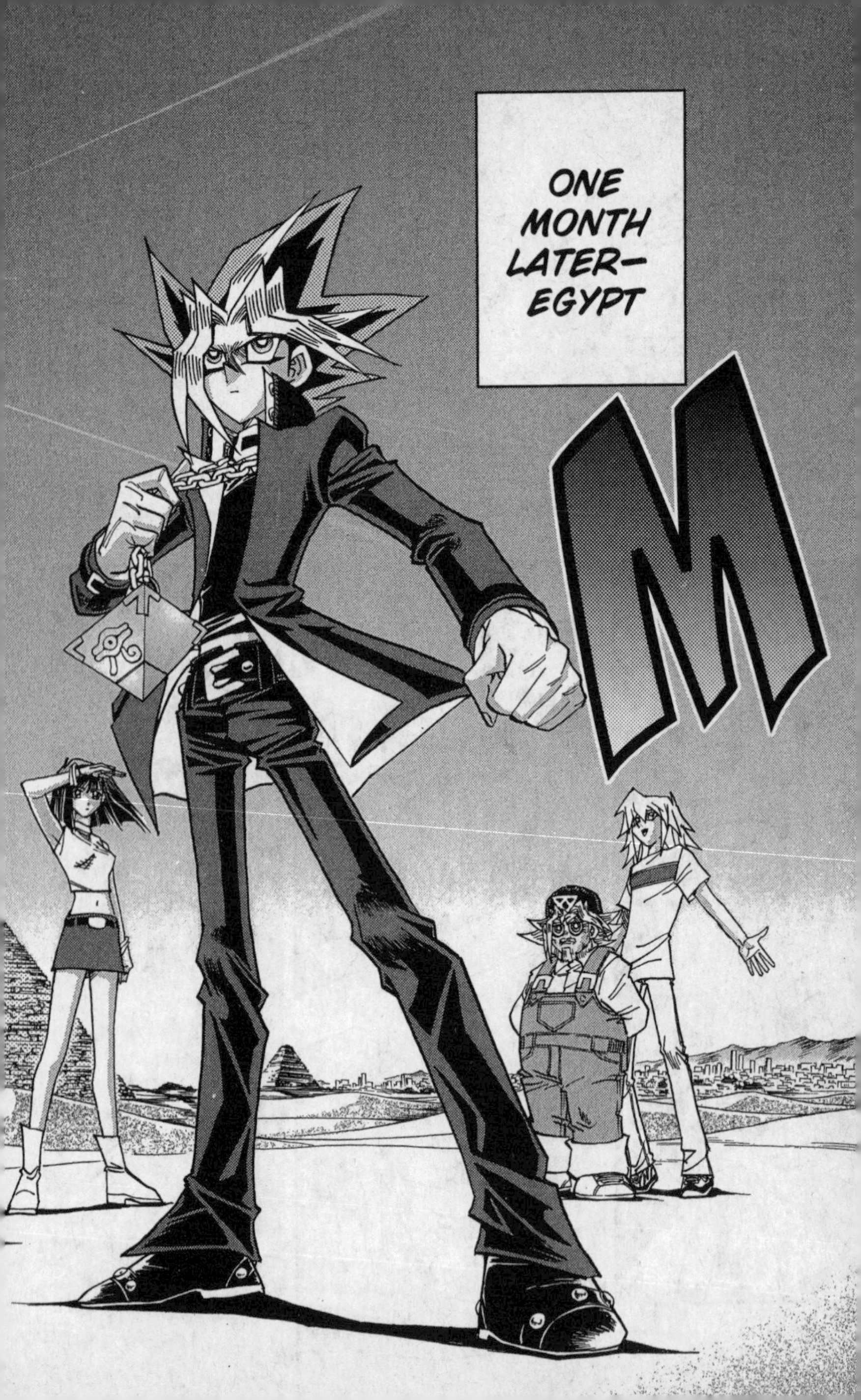
ONE MONTH LATER– EGYPT
M

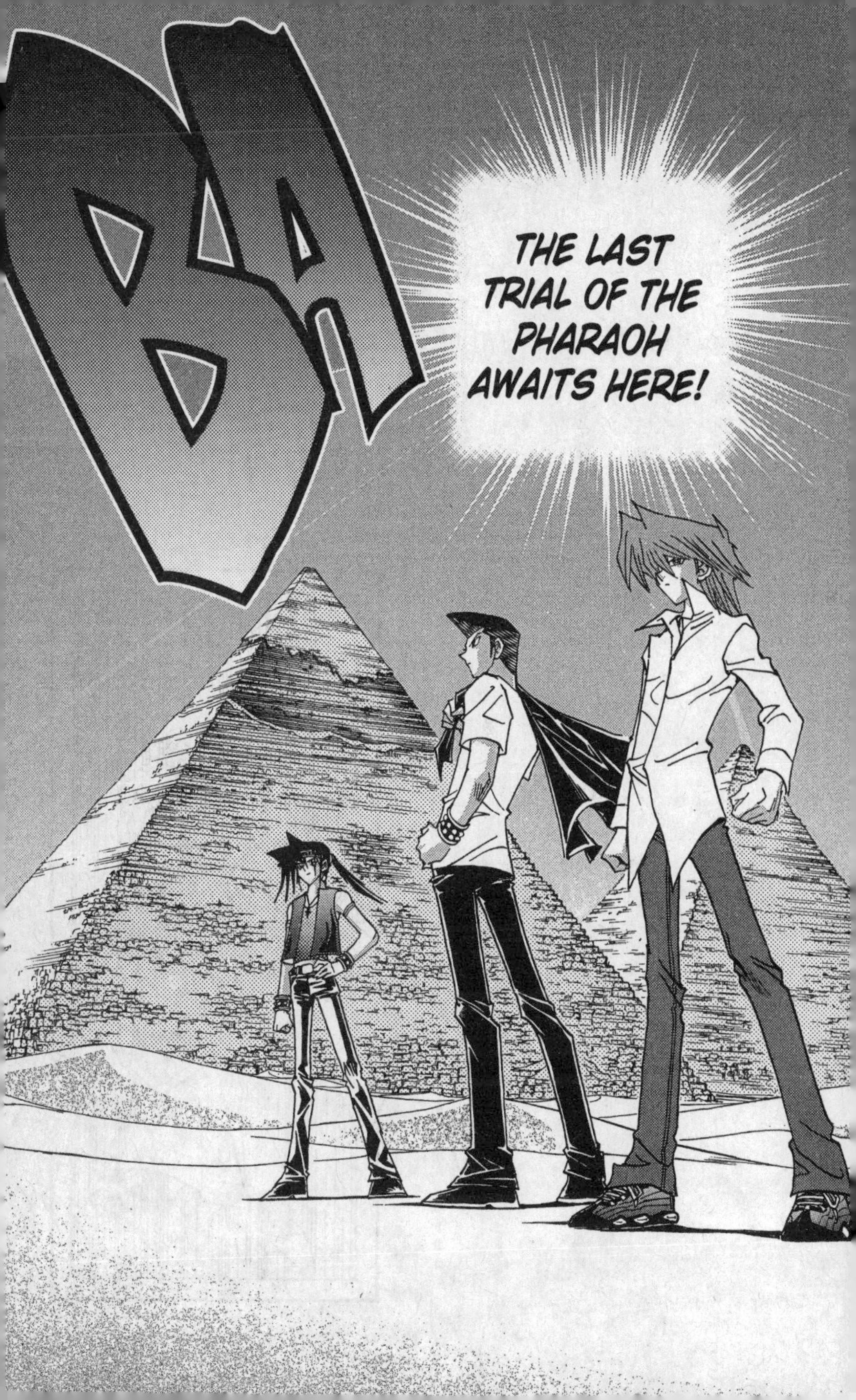
BA
THE LAST TRIAL OF THE PHARAOH AWAITS HERE!

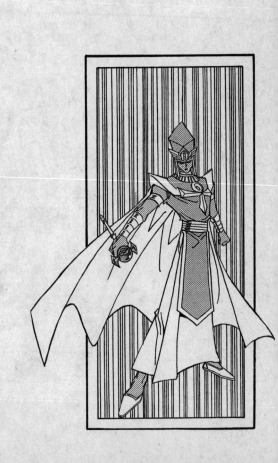

Duel 337: Over the Nile!!

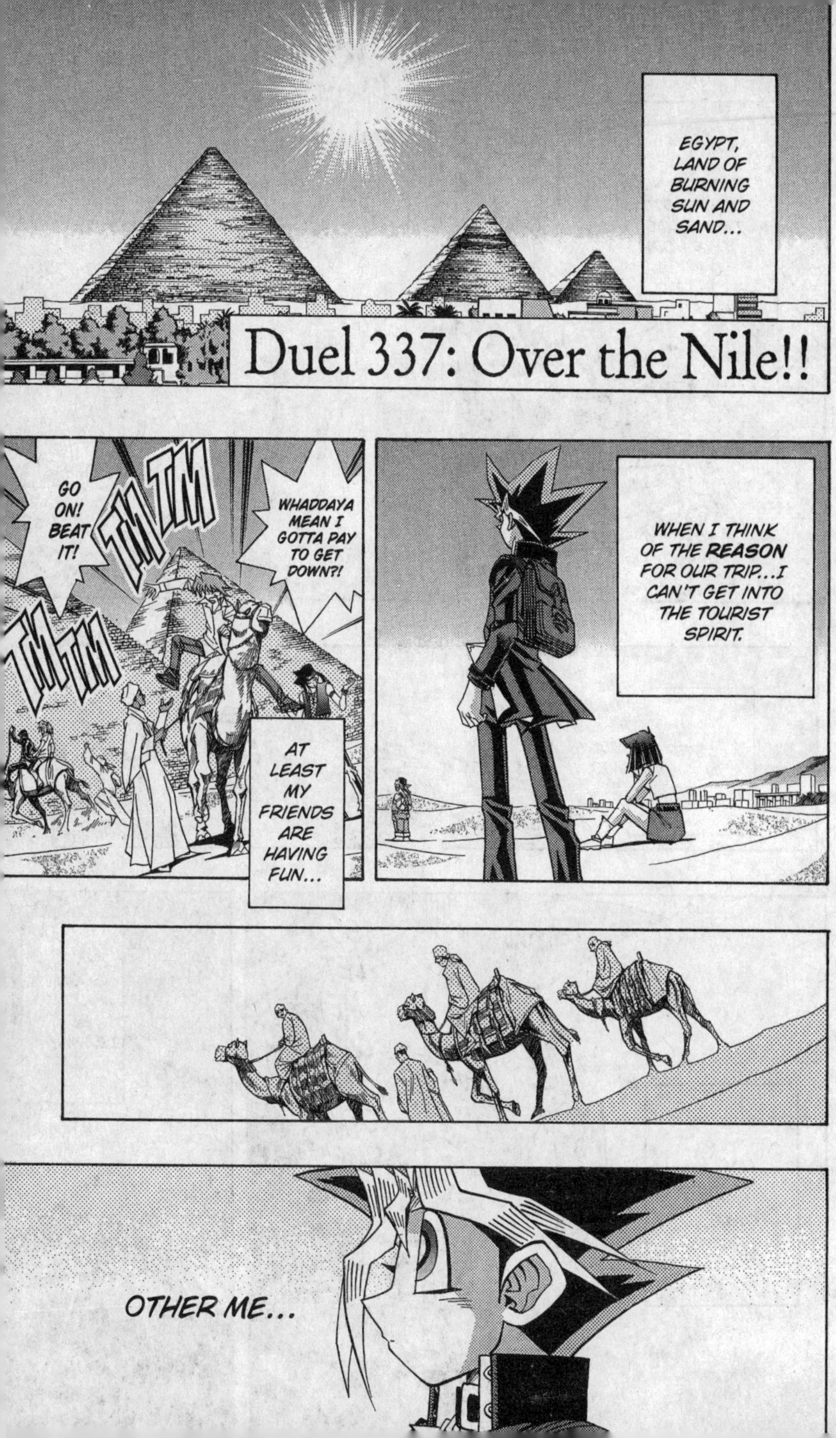
EGYPT, LAND OF BURNING SUN AND SAND...
WHEN I THINK OF THE **REASON** FOR OUR TRIP...I CAN'T GET INTO THE TOURIST SPIRIT.
WHADDAYA MEAN I GOTTA PAY TO GET DOWN?!
TM TM
GO ON! BEAT IT!
TM TM
AT LEAST MY FRIENDS ARE HAVING FUN...
OTHER ME...

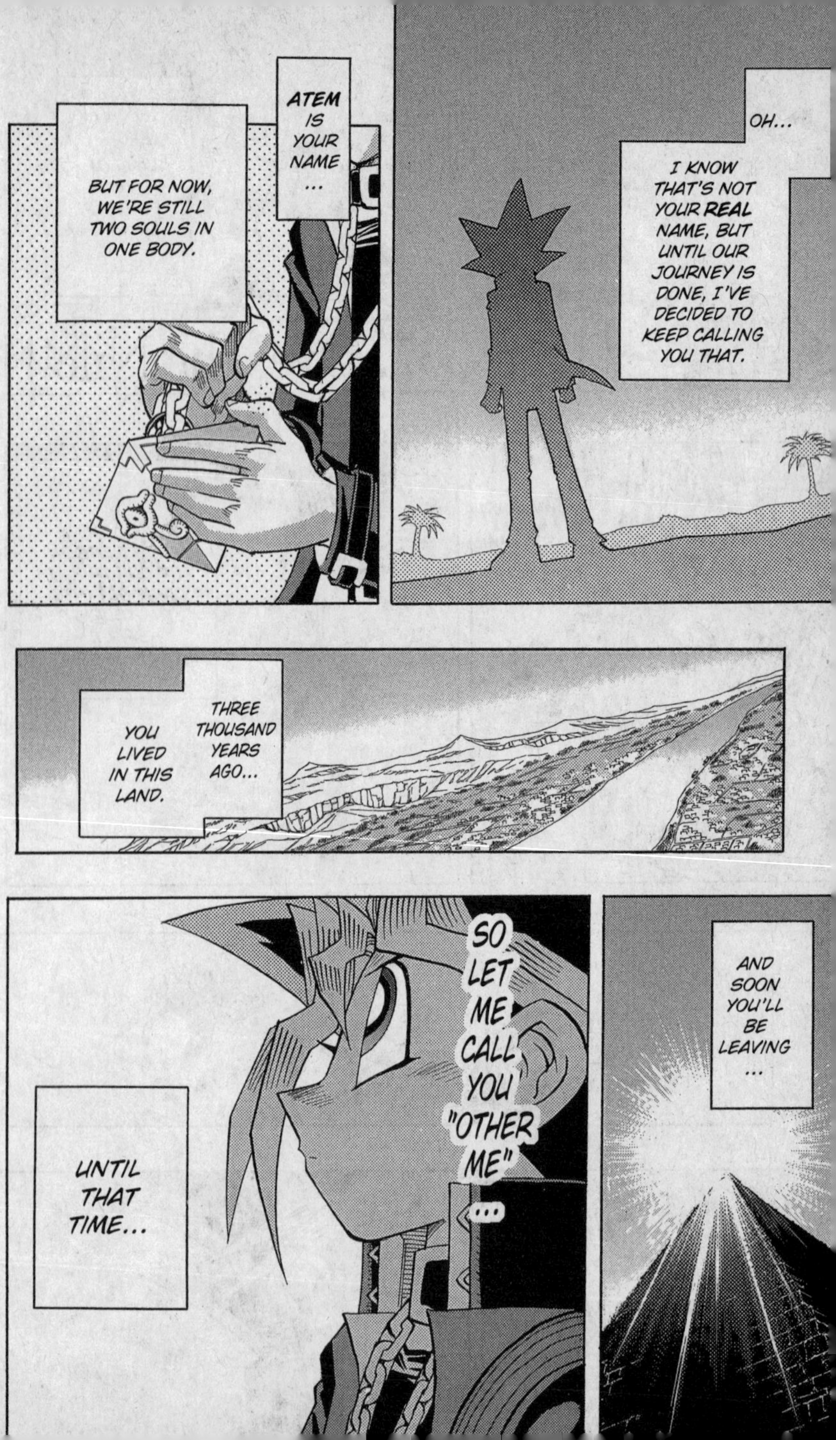
OH...
I KNOW THAT'S NOT YOUR **REAL** NAME, BUT UNTIL OUR JOURNEY IS DONE, I'VE DECIDED TO KEEP CALLING YOU THAT.
ATEM IS YOUR NAME ...
BUT FOR NOW, WE'RE STILL TWO SOULS IN ONE BODY.
THREE THOUSAND YEARS AGO...
YOU LIVED IN THIS LAND.
AND SOON YOU'LL BE LEAVING ...
SO LET ME CALL YOU "OTHER ME" ...
UNTIL THAT TIME...

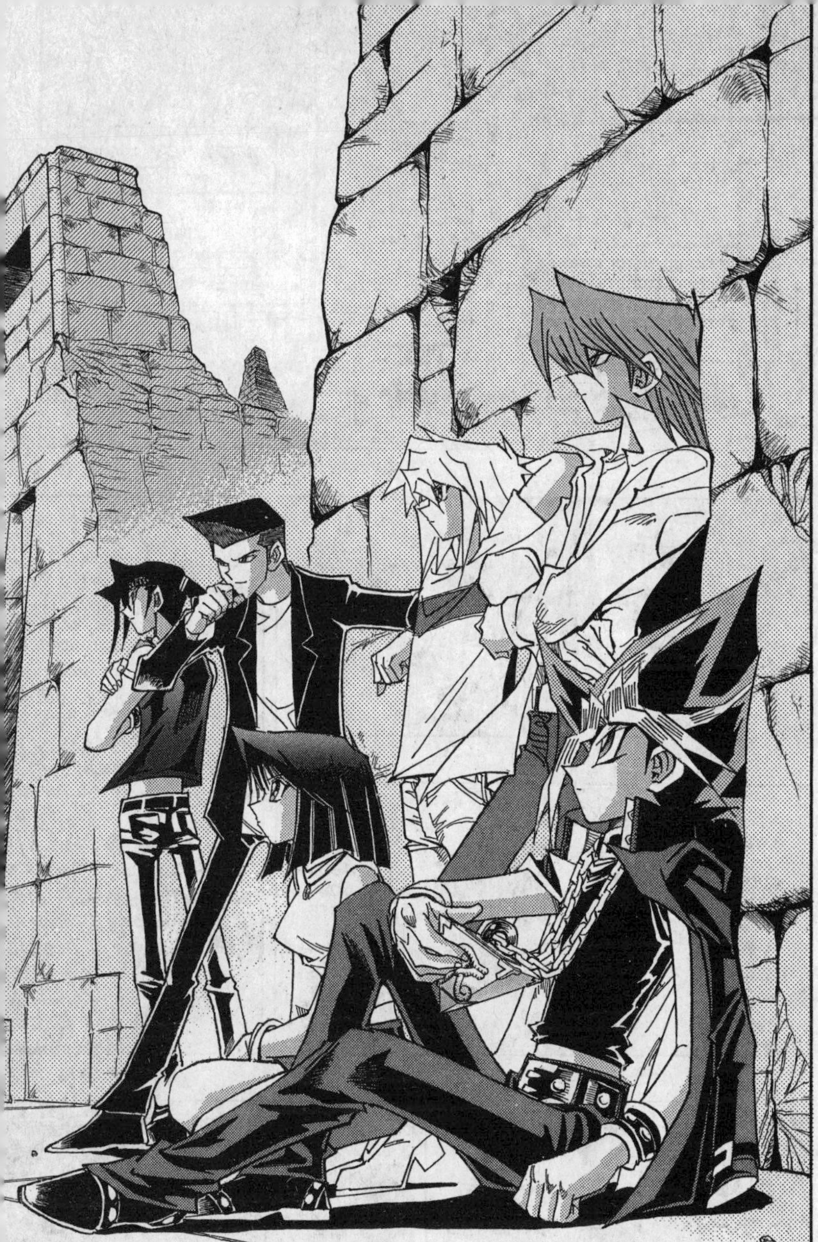

Duel 337: Over the Nile!!

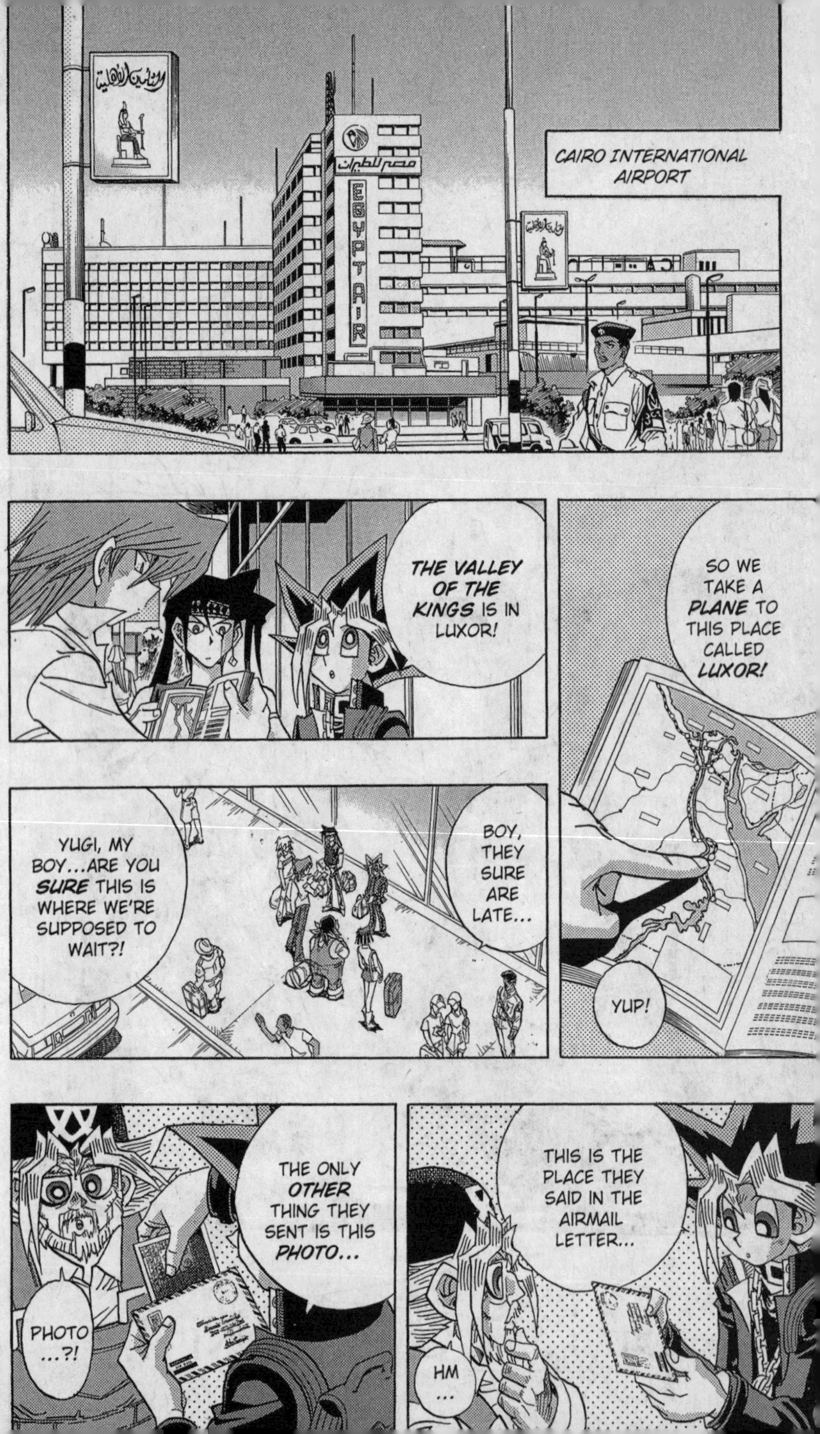
CAIRO INTERNATIONAL AIRPORT
EGYPTAIR
SO WE TAKE A ***PLANE*** TO THIS PLACE CALLED ***LUXOR!***
YUP!
THE VALLEY OF THE KINGS IS IN LUXOR!
BOY, THEY SURE ARE LATE...
YUGI, MY BOY...ARE YOU ***SURE*** THIS IS WHERE WE'RE SUPPOSED TO WAIT?!
THIS IS THE PLACE THEY SAID IN THE AIRMAIL LETTER...
HM...
THE ONLY ***OTHER*** THING THEY SENT IS THIS ***PHOTO...***
PHOTO...?!

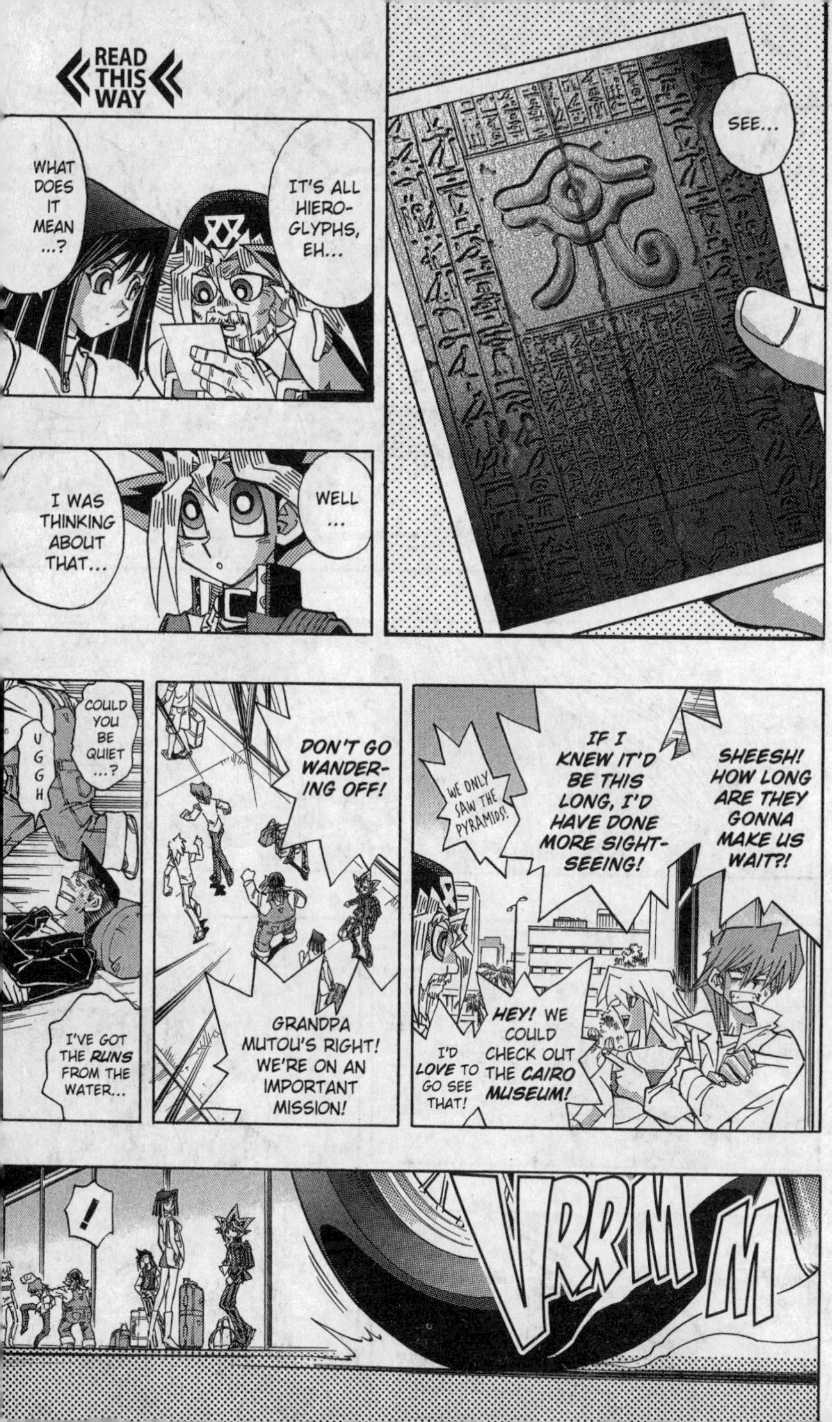
READ THIS WAY
SEE...
IT'S ALL HIERO-GLYPHS, EH...
WHAT DOES IT MEAN ...?
WELL ...
I WAS THINKING ABOUT THAT...
SHEESH! HOW LONG ARE THEY GONNA MAKE US WAIT?!
IF I KNEW IT'D BE THIS LONG, I'D HAVE DONE MORE SIGHT-SEEING!
WE ONLY SAW THE PYRAMIDS!
HEY! WE COULD CHECK OUT THE CAIRO MUSEUM!
I'D LOVE TO GO SEE THAT!
DON'T GO WANDER-ING OFF!
GRANDPA MUTOU'S RIGHT! WE'RE ON AN IMPORTANT MISSION!
COULD YOU BE QUIET ...?
UGGH
I'VE GOT THE RUNS FROM THE WATER...
VRRMM
!

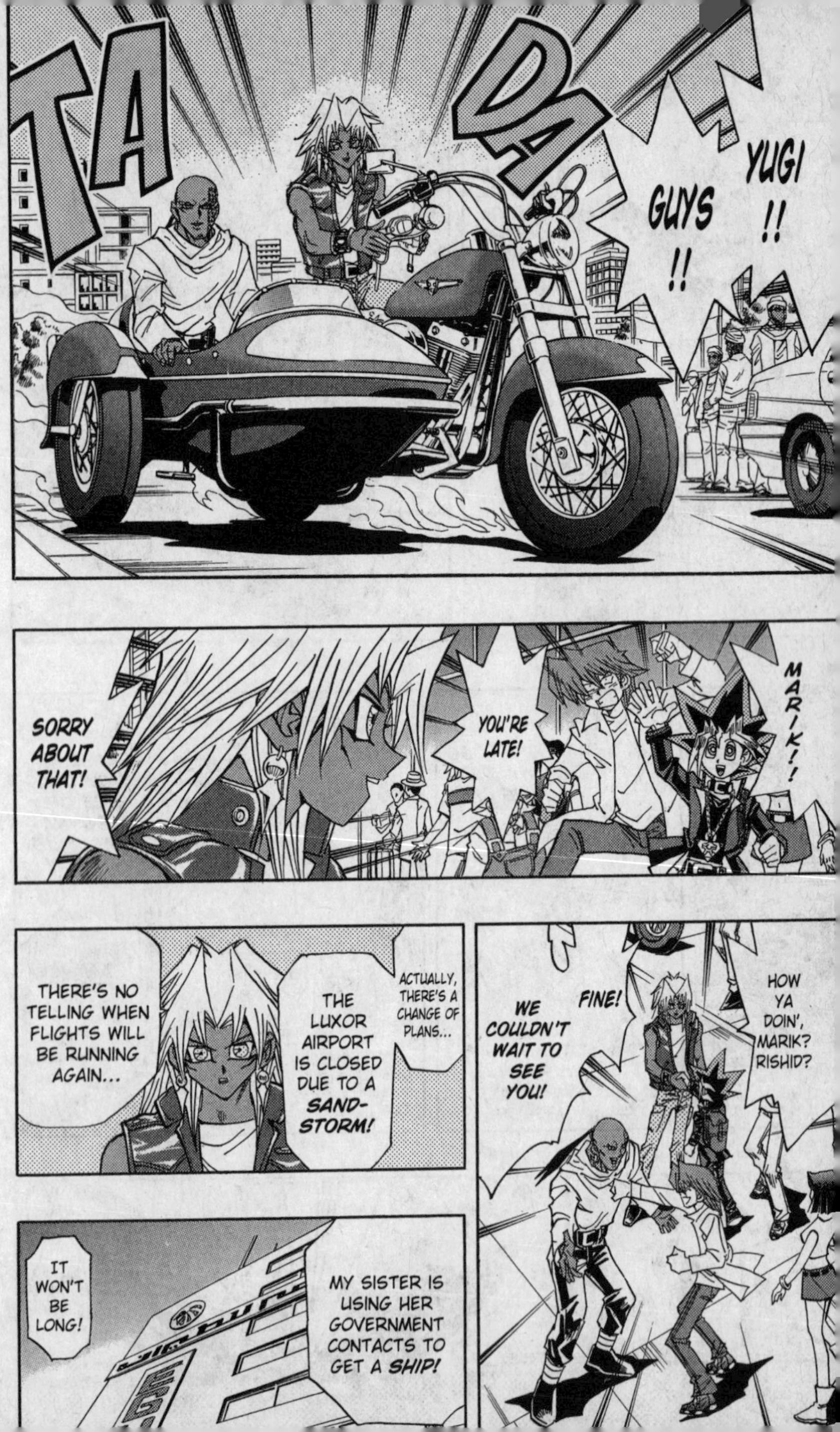
YUGI !!
GUYS !!
TA DA
MARIK!!
YOU'RE LATE!
SORRY ABOUT THAT!
HOW YA DOIN', MARIK? RISHID?
FINE!
WE COULDN'T WAIT TO SEE YOU!
ACTUALLY, THERE'S A CHANGE OF PLANS...
THE LUXOR AIRPORT IS CLOSED DUE TO A SANDSTORM!
THERE'S NO TELLING WHEN FLIGHTS WILL BE RUNNING AGAIN...
MY SISTER IS USING HER GOVERNMENT CONTACTS TO GET A SHIP!
IT WON'T BE LONG!

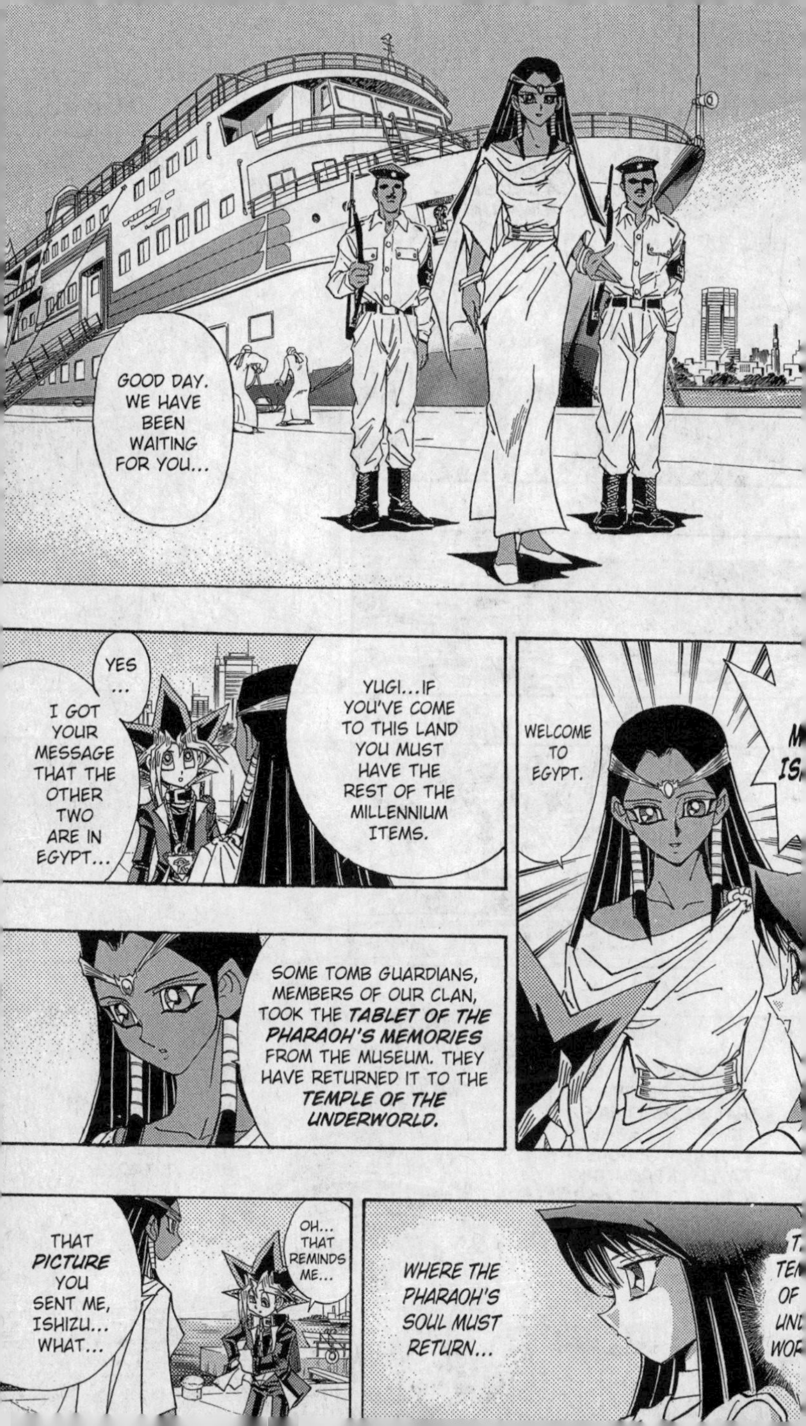
GOOD DAY. WE HAVE BEEN WAITING FOR YOU...
WELCOME TO EGYPT.
YUGI...IF YOU'VE COME TO THIS LAND YOU MUST HAVE THE REST OF THE MILLENNIUM ITEMS.
YES...
I GOT YOUR MESSAGE THAT THE OTHER TWO ARE IN EGYPT...
SOME TOMB GUARDIANS, MEMBERS OF OUR CLAN, TOOK THE *TABLET OF THE PHARAOH'S MEMORIES* FROM THE MUSEUM. THEY HAVE RETURNED IT TO THE *TEMPLE OF THE UNDERWORLD.*
WHERE THE PHARAOH'S SOUL MUST RETURN...
OH... THAT REMINDS ME...
THAT *PICTURE* YOU SENT ME, ISHIZU... WHAT...

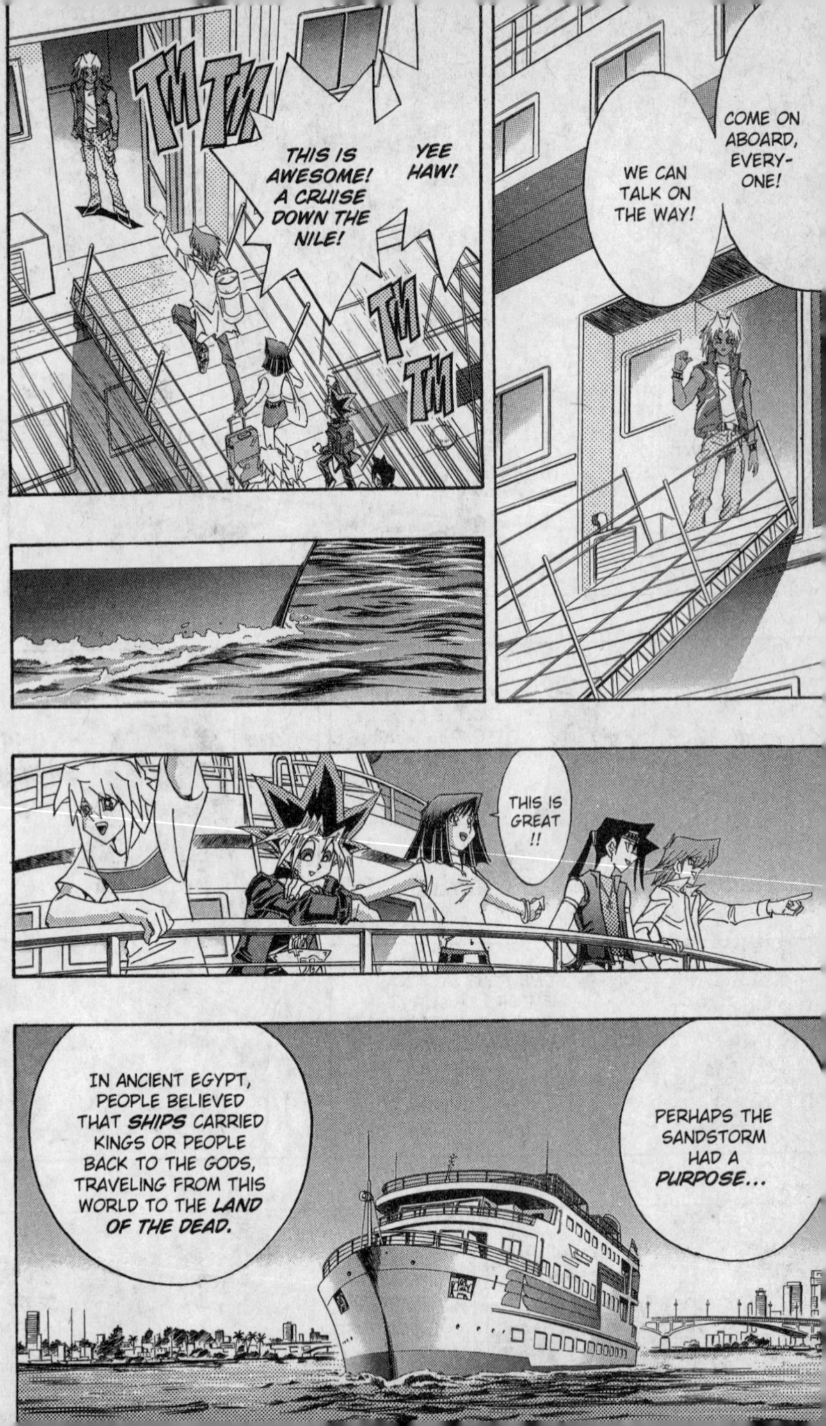
COME ON ABOARD, EVERY-ONE!
WE CAN TALK ON THE WAY!
TM TM
YEE HAW!
THIS IS AWESOME! A CRUISE DOWN THE NILE!
TM TM
THIS IS GREAT !!
PERHAPS THE SANDSTORM HAD A PURPOSE...
IN ANCIENT EGYPT, PEOPLE BELIEVED THAT SHIPS CARRIED KINGS OR PEOPLE BACK TO THE GODS, TRAVELING FROM THIS WORLD TO THE LAND OF THE DEAD.

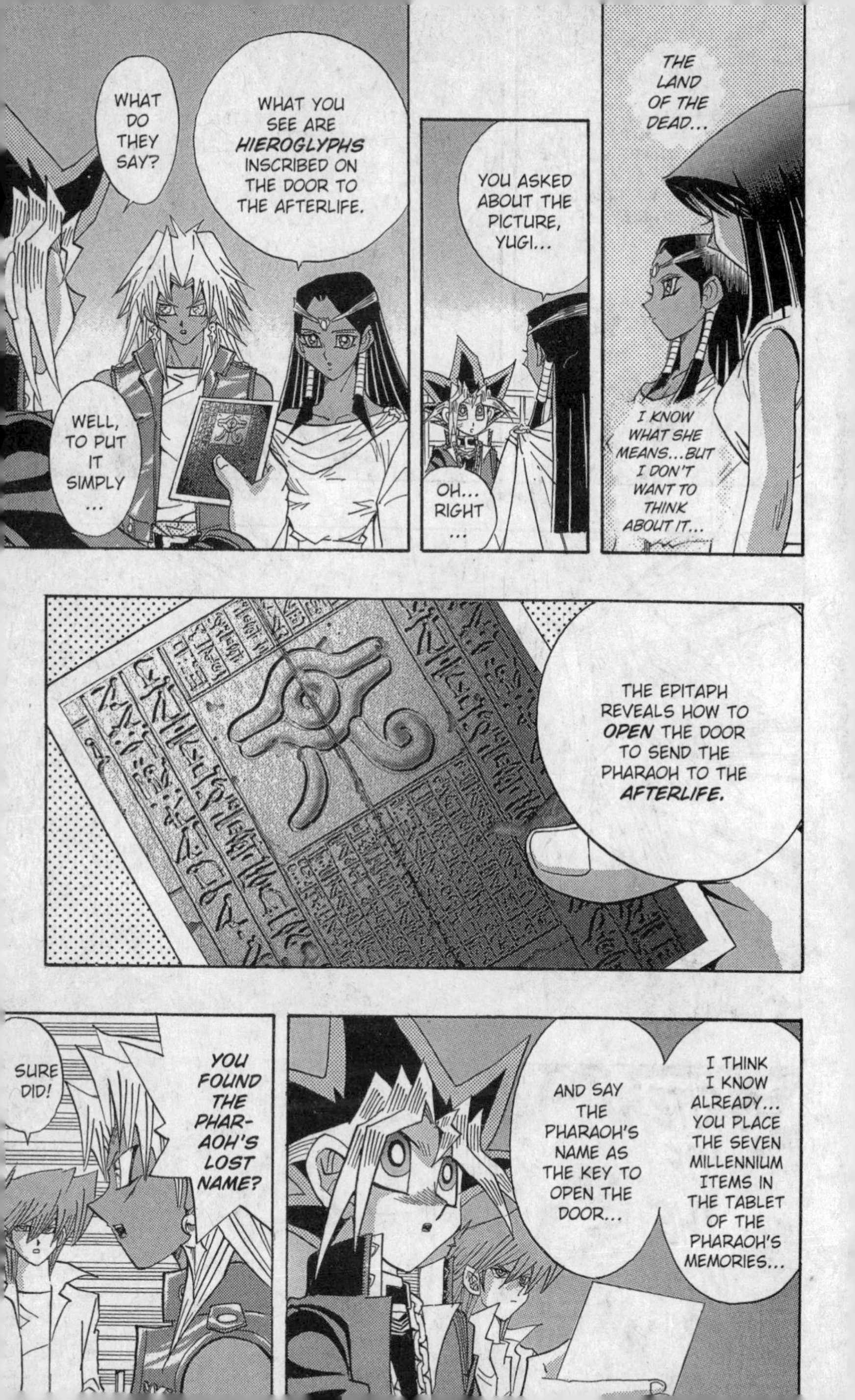

THE LAND OF THE DEAD...
I KNOW WHAT SHE MEANS...BUT I DON'T WANT TO THINK ABOUT IT...
YOU ASKED ABOUT THE PICTURE, YUGI...
OH... RIGHT ...
WHAT YOU SEE ARE **HIEROGLYPHS** INSCRIBED ON THE DOOR TO THE AFTERLIFE.
WHAT DO THEY SAY?
WELL, TO PUT IT SIMPLY ...
THE EPITAPH REVEALS HOW TO **OPEN** THE DOOR TO SEND THE PHARAOH TO THE **AFTERLIFE.**
I THINK I KNOW ALREADY... YOU PLACE THE SEVEN MILLENNIUM ITEMS IN THE TABLET OF THE PHARAOH'S MEMORIES...
AND SAY THE PHARAOH'S NAME AS THE KEY TO OPEN THE DOOR...
YOU FOUND THE PHAR-AOH'S LOST NAME?
SURE DID!

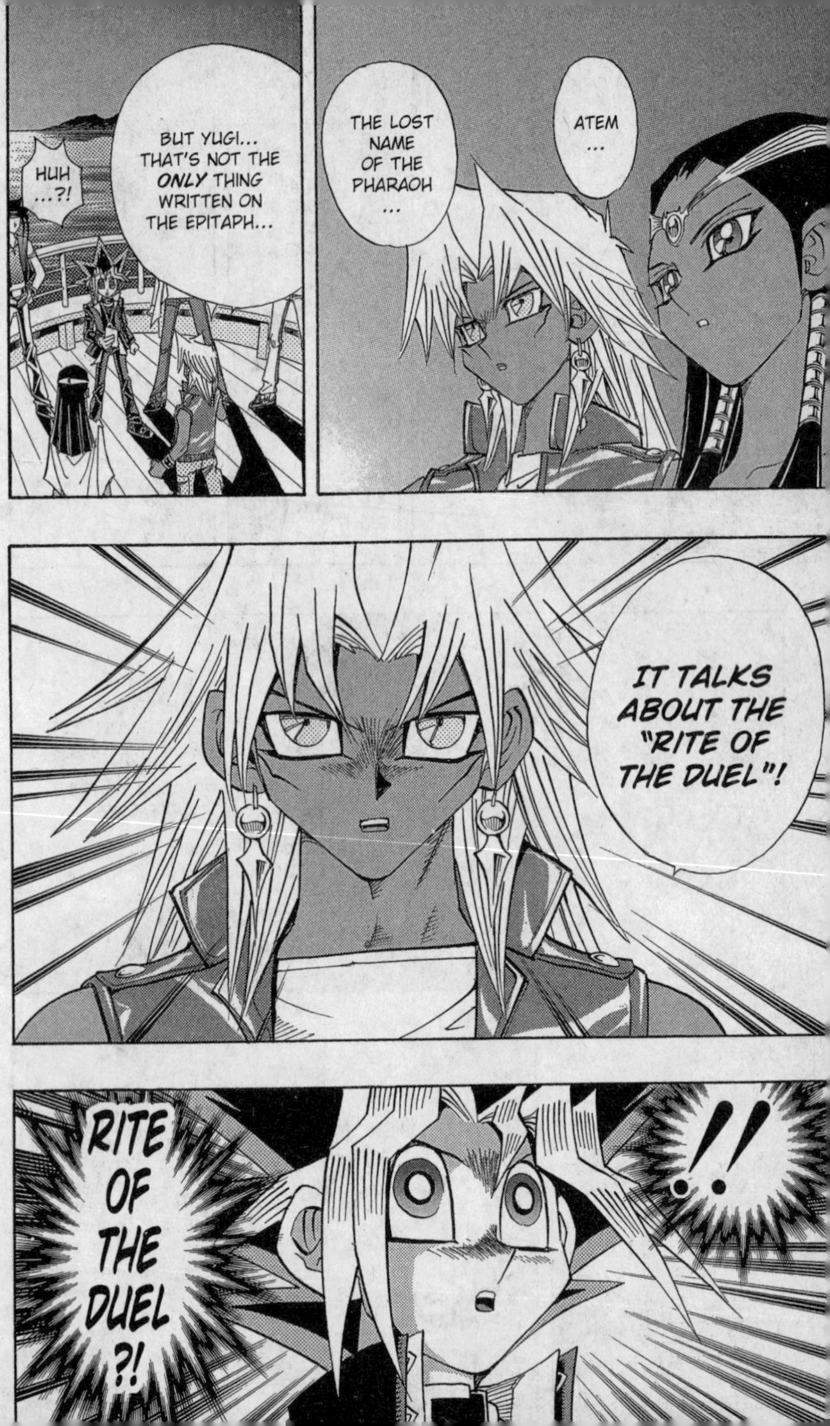
ATEM...
THE LOST NAME OF THE PHARAOH...
BUT YUGI... THAT'S NOT THE *ONLY* THING WRITTEN ON THE EPITAPH...
HUH...?!
IT TALKS ABOUT THE "RITE OF THE DUEL"!
!!
RITE OF THE DUEL?!

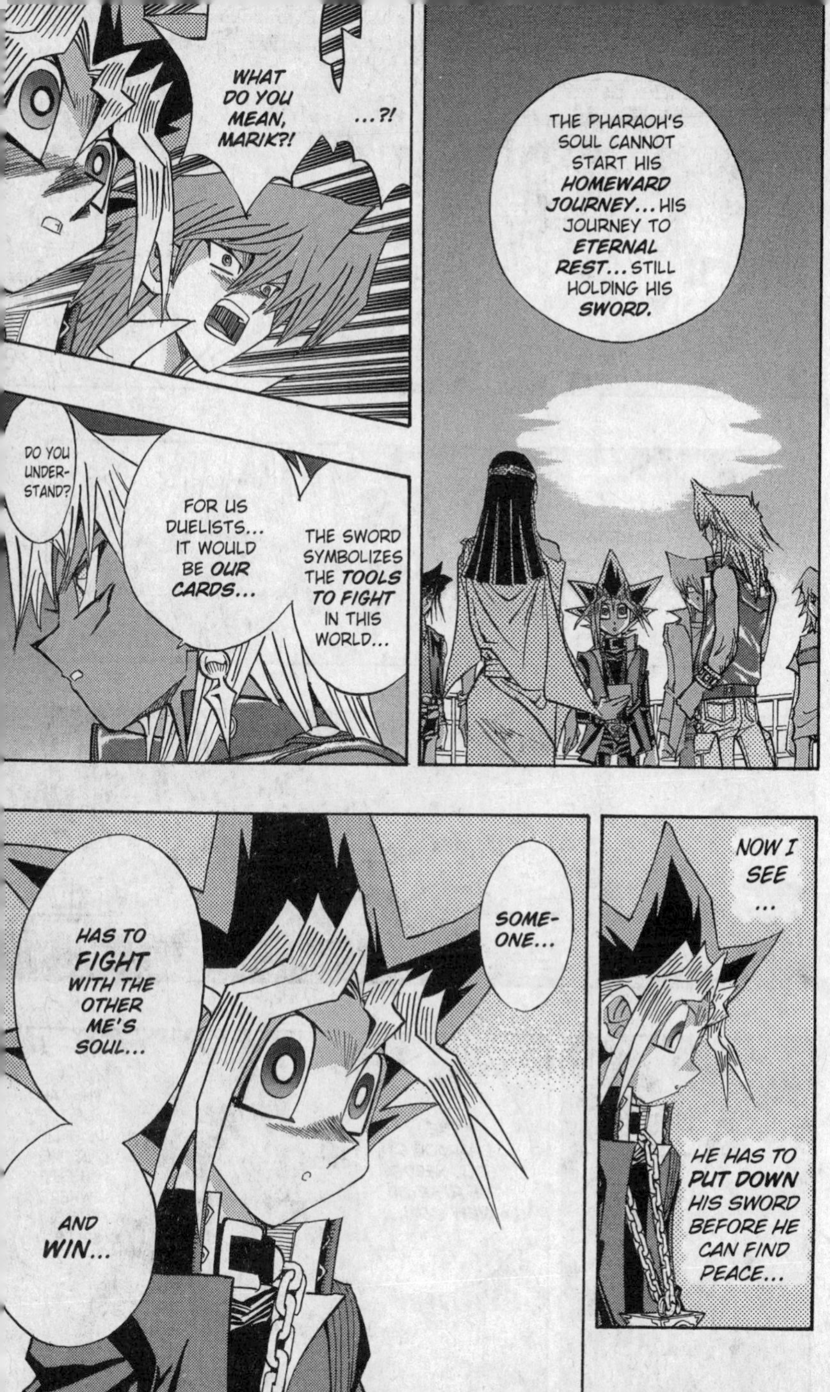
THE PHARAOH'S SOUL CANNOT START HIS HOMEWARD JOURNEY... HIS JOURNEY TO ETERNAL REST... STILL HOLDING HIS SWORD.
...?!
WHAT DO YOU MEAN, MARIK?!
THE SWORD SYMBOLIZES THE TOOLS TO FIGHT IN THIS WORLD...
FOR US DUELISTS... IT WOULD BE OUR CARDS...
DO YOU UNDER-STAND?
NOW I SEE ...
HE HAS TO PUT DOWN HIS SWORD BEFORE HE CAN FIND PEACE...
SOME-ONE...
HAS TO FIGHT WITH THE OTHER ME'S SOUL...
AND WIN...

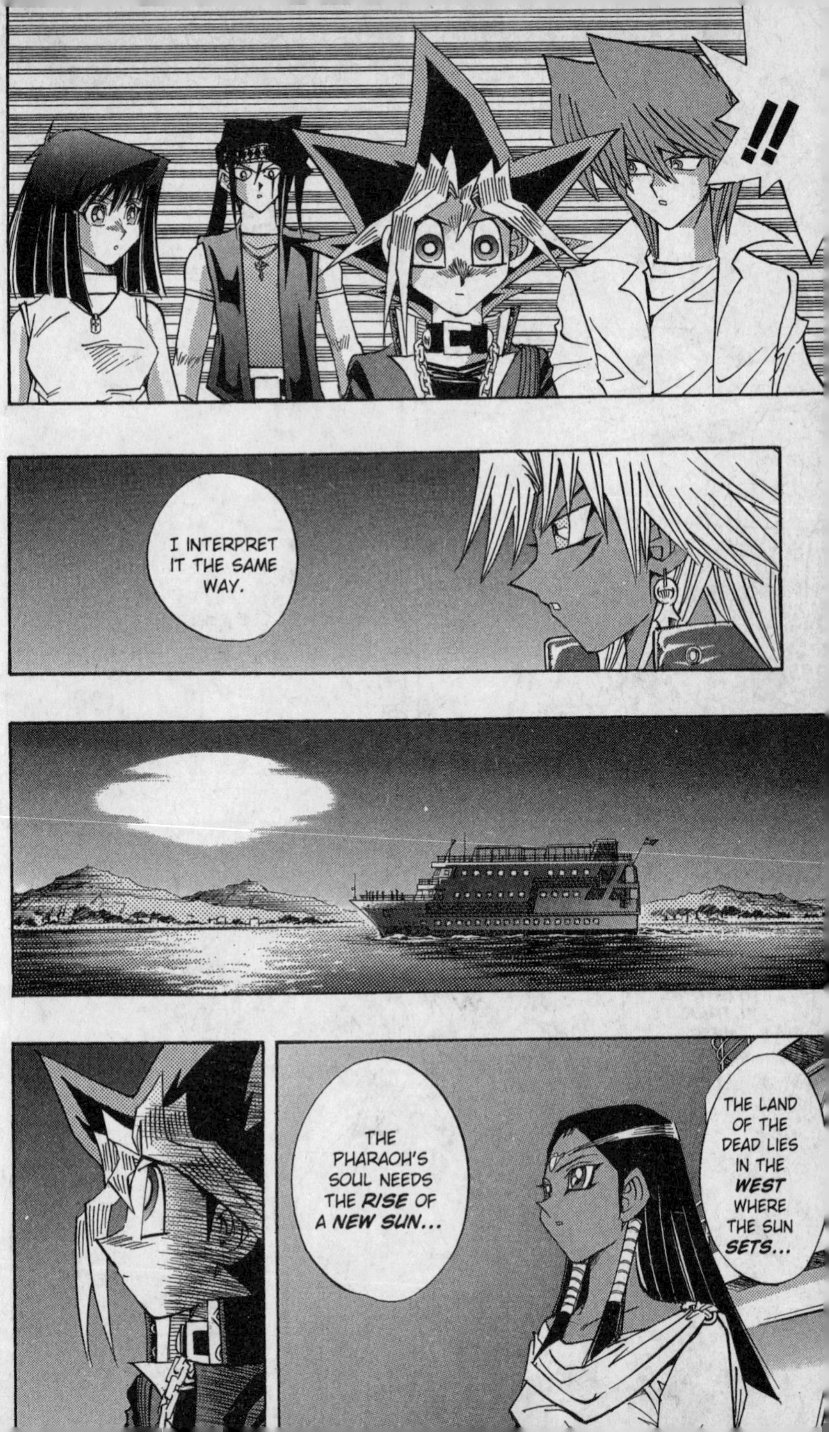
!!
I INTERPRET IT THE SAME WAY.
THE LAND OF THE DEAD LIES IN THE WEST WHERE THE SUN SETS...
THE PHARAOH'S SOUL NEEDS THE RISE OF A NEW SUN...

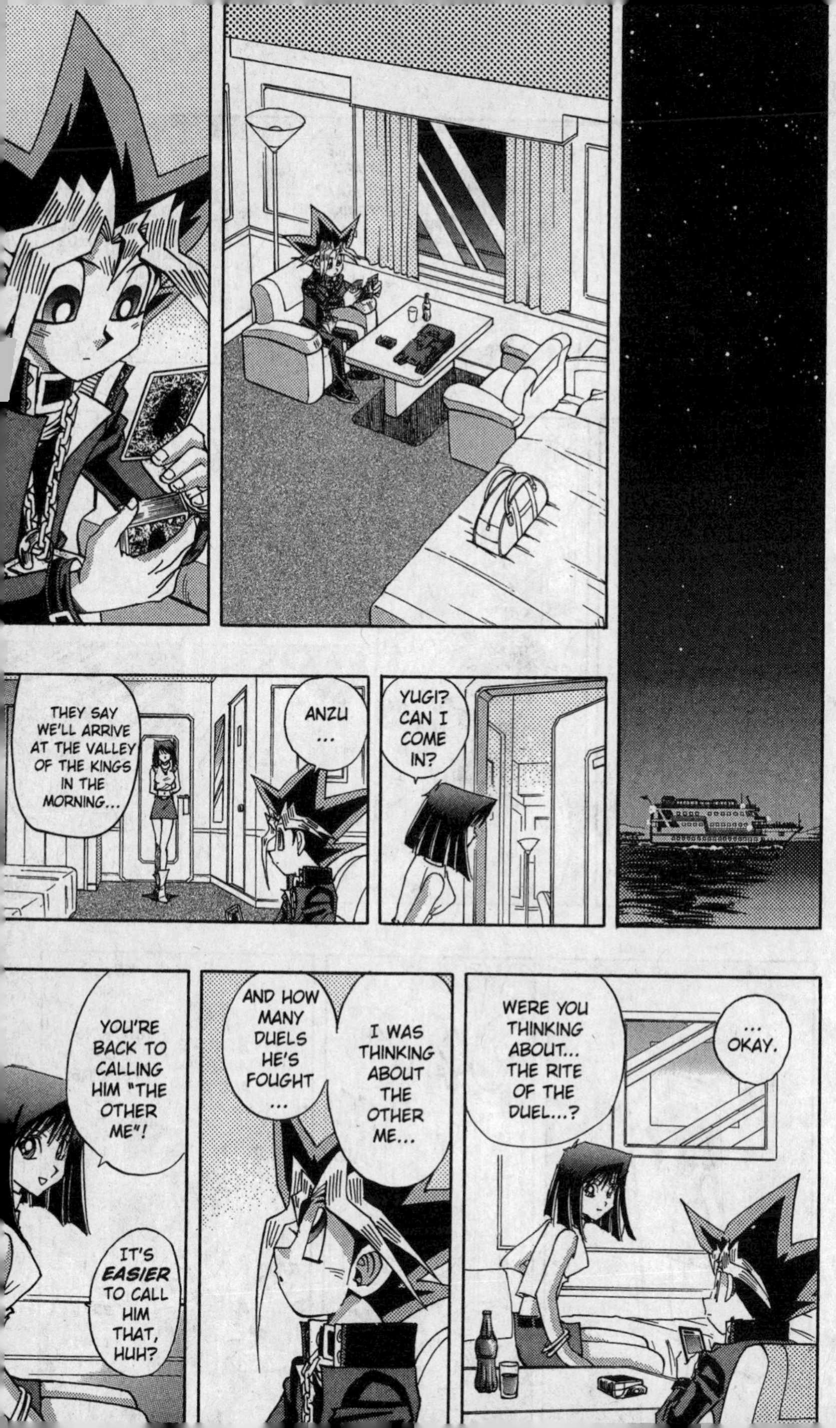
YUGI? CAN I COME IN?
ANZU...
THEY SAY WE'LL ARRIVE AT THE VALLEY OF THE KINGS IN THE MORNING...
...OKAY.
WERE YOU THINKING ABOUT... THE RITE OF THE DUEL...?
I WAS THINKING ABOUT THE OTHER ME...
AND HOW MANY DUELS HE'S FOUGHT...
YOU'RE BACK TO CALLING HIM "THE OTHER ME"!
IT'S *EASIER* TO CALL HIM THAT, HUH?

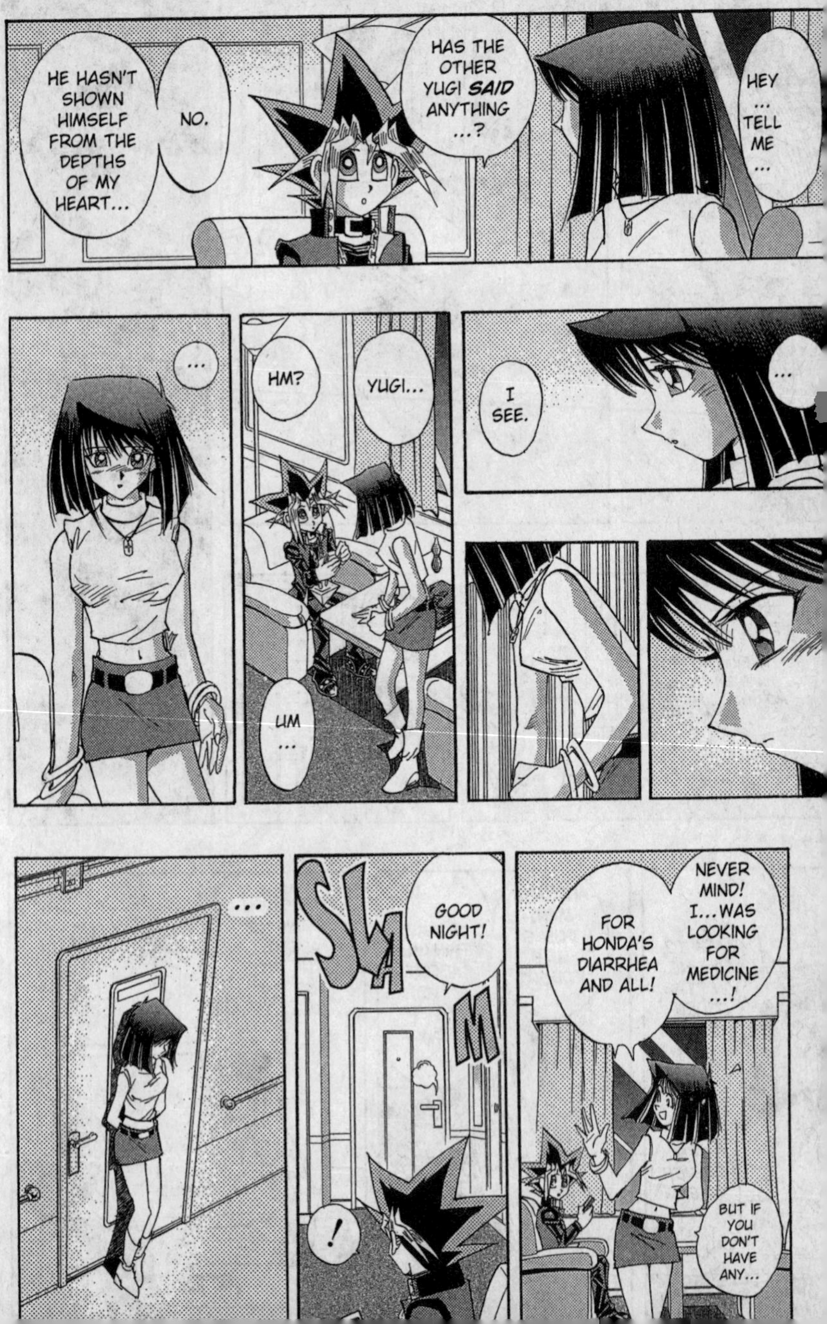
HEY... TELL ME...
HAS THE OTHER YUGI SAID ANYTHING...?
NO.
HE HASN'T SHOWN HIMSELF FROM THE DEPTHS OF MY HEART...
...
I SEE.
YUGI...
HM?
UM...
...
NEVER MIND! I...WAS LOOKING FOR MEDICINE...!
FOR HONDA'S DIARRHEA AND ALL!
BUT IF YOU DON'T HAVE ANY...
GOOD NIGHT!
SLAM
!
...

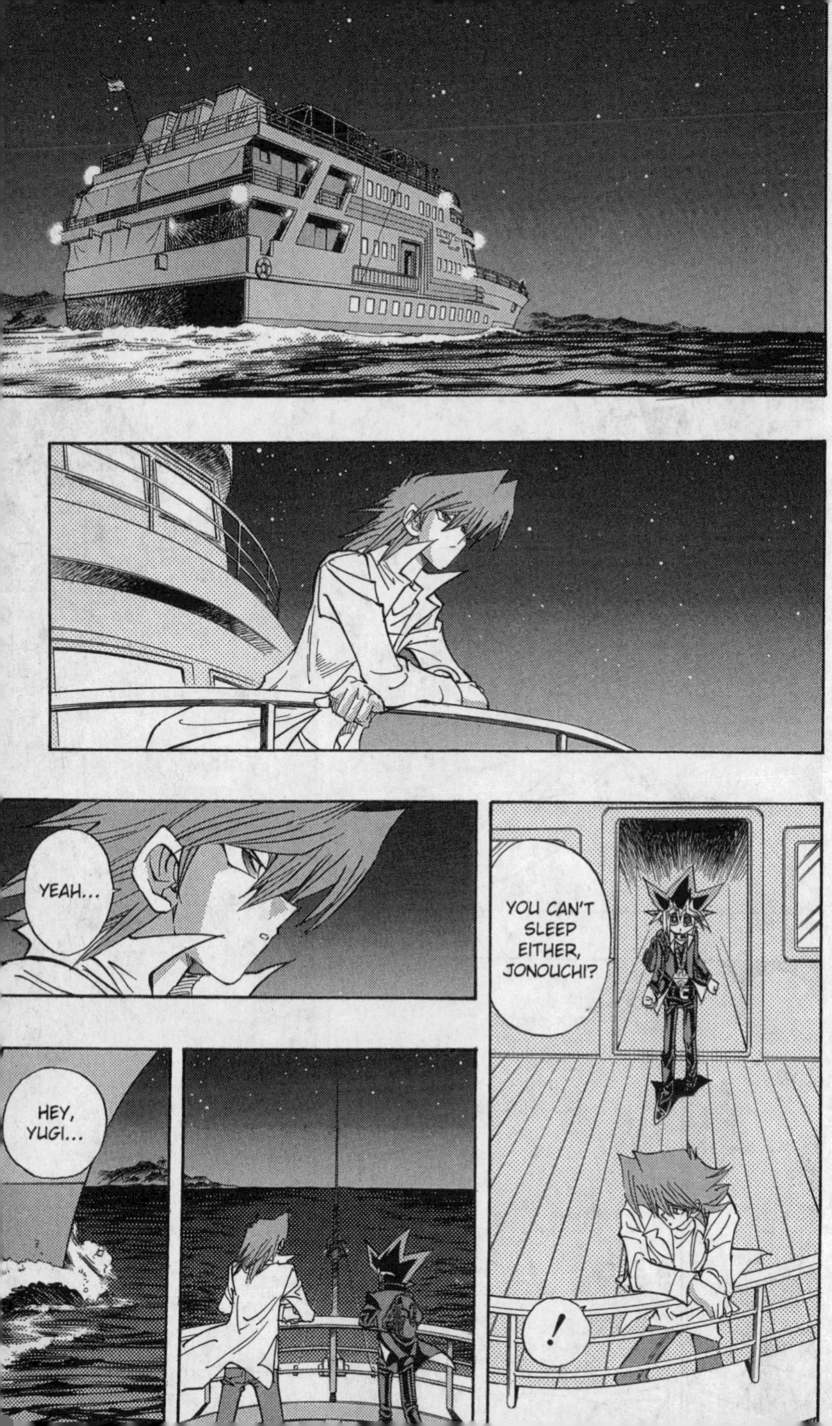

YOU CAN'T SLEEP EITHER, JONOUCHI?
!
YEAH...
HEY, YUGI...

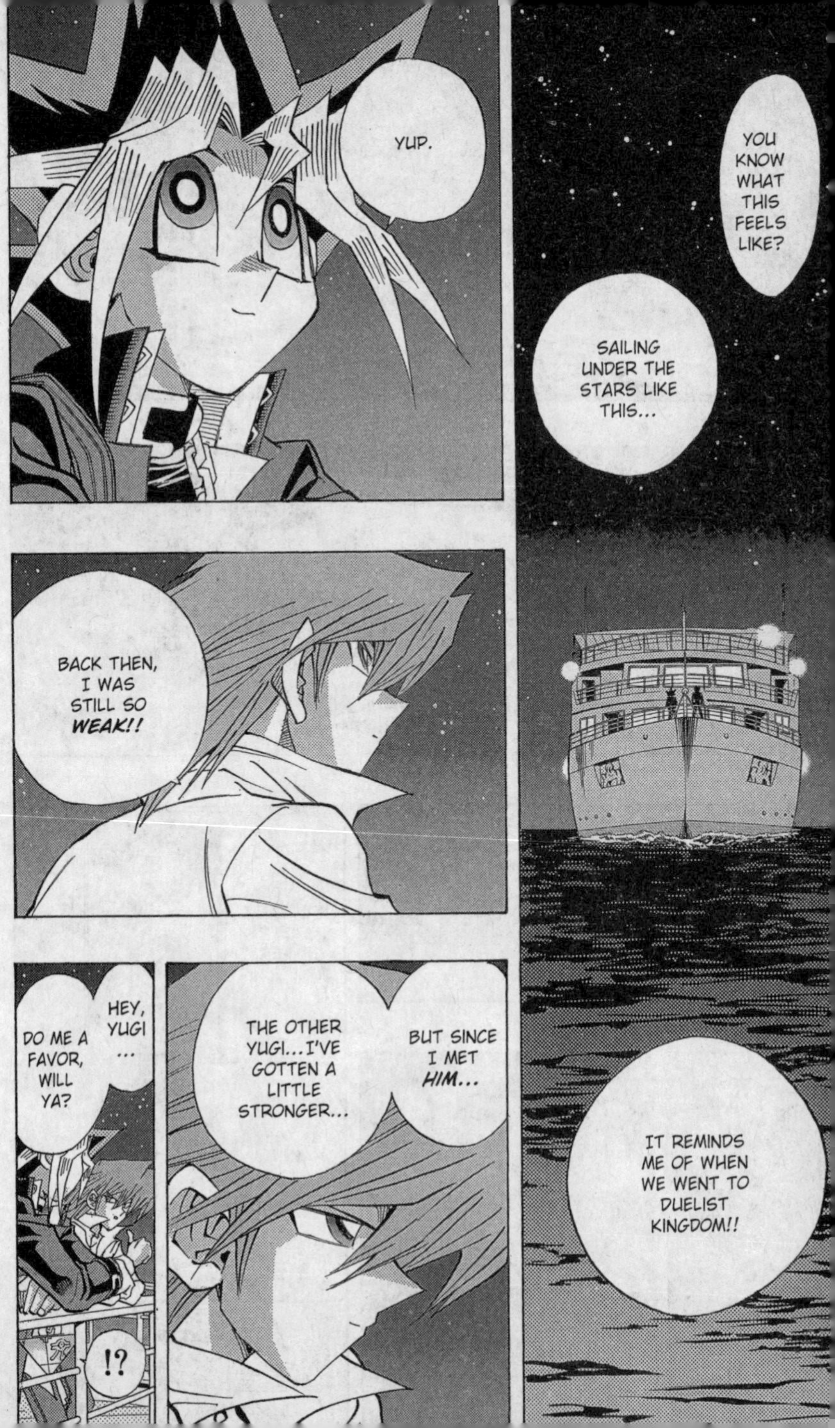
YOU KNOW WHAT THIS FEELS LIKE?
SAILING UNDER THE STARS LIKE THIS...
IT REMINDS ME OF WHEN WE WENT TO DUELIST KINGDOM!!
YUP.
BACK THEN, I WAS STILL SO *WEAK!!*
BUT SINCE I MET *HIM...*
THE OTHER YUGI...I'VE GOTTEN A LITTLE STRONGER...
HEY, YUGI ...
DO ME A FAVOR, WILL YA?
!?

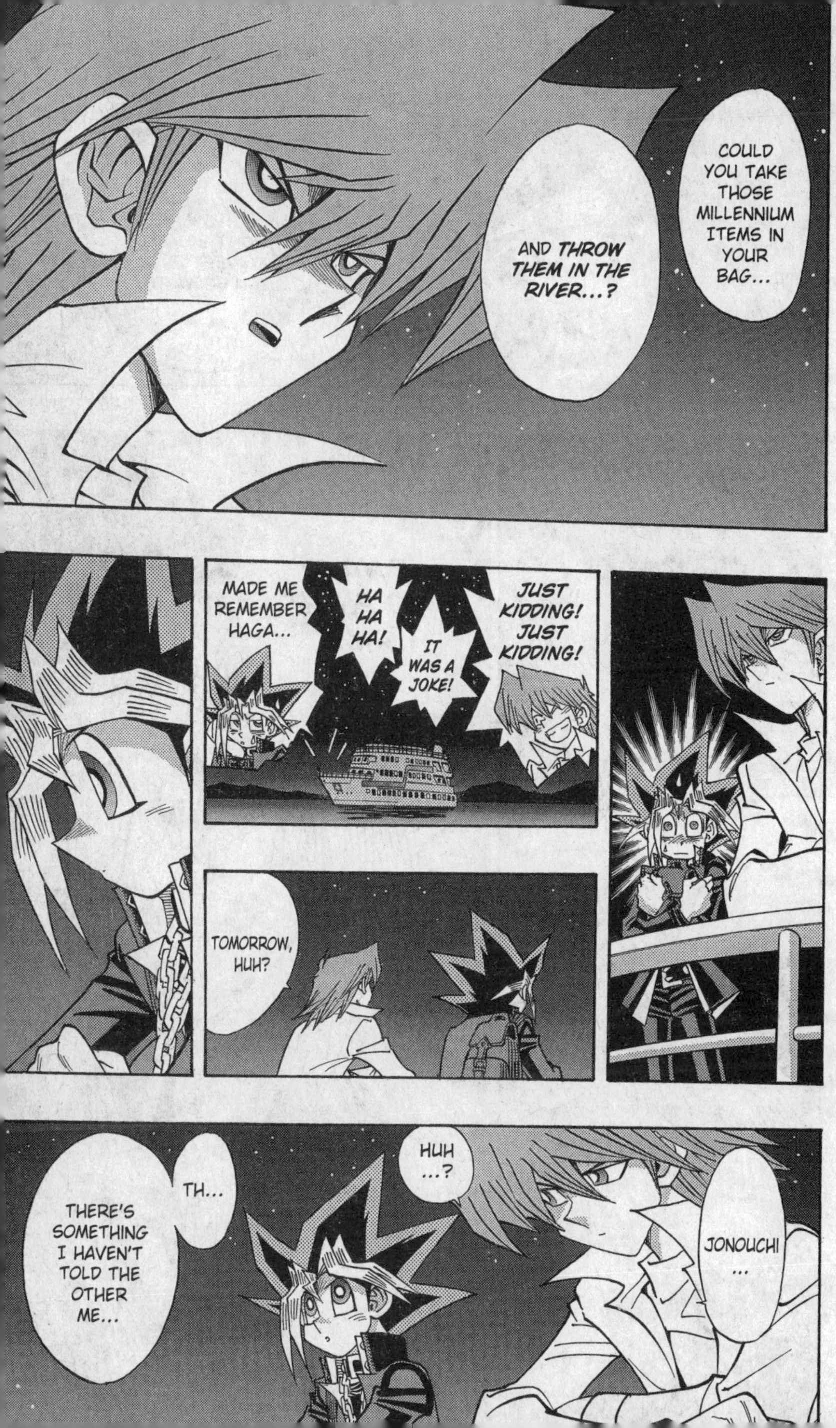
COULD YOU TAKE THOSE MILLENNIUM ITEMS IN YOUR BAG...
AND THROW THEM IN THE RIVER...?
JUST KIDDING! JUST KIDDING!
IT WAS A JOKE!
HA HA HA!
MADE ME REMEMBER HAGA...
TOMORROW, HUH?
JONOUCHI ...
HUH ...?
TH...
THERE'S SOMETHING I HAVEN'T TOLD THE OTHER ME...

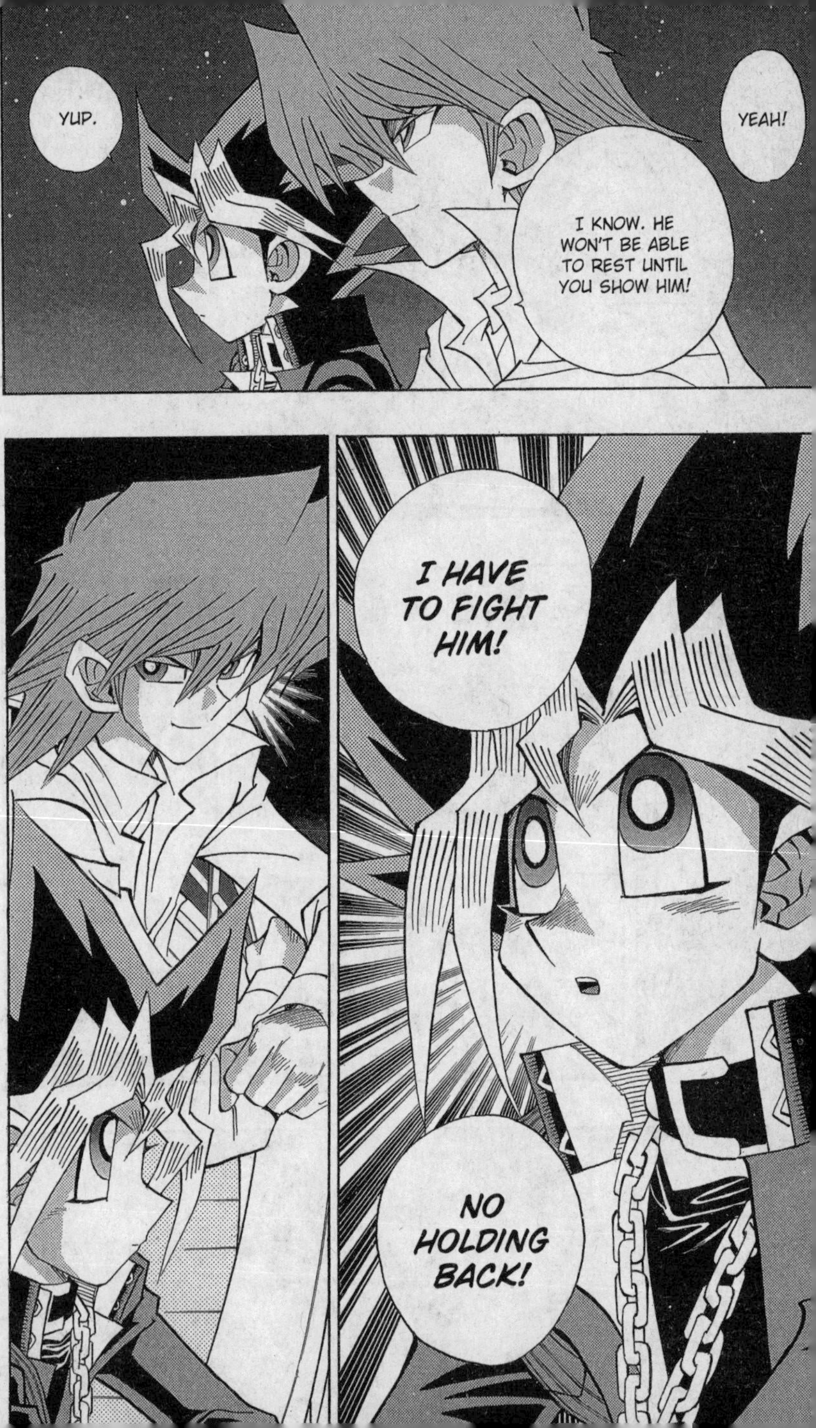
YEAH!
I KNOW. HE WON'T BE ABLE TO REST UNTIL YOU SHOW HIM!
YUP.
I HAVE TO FIGHT HIM!
NO HOLDING BACK!

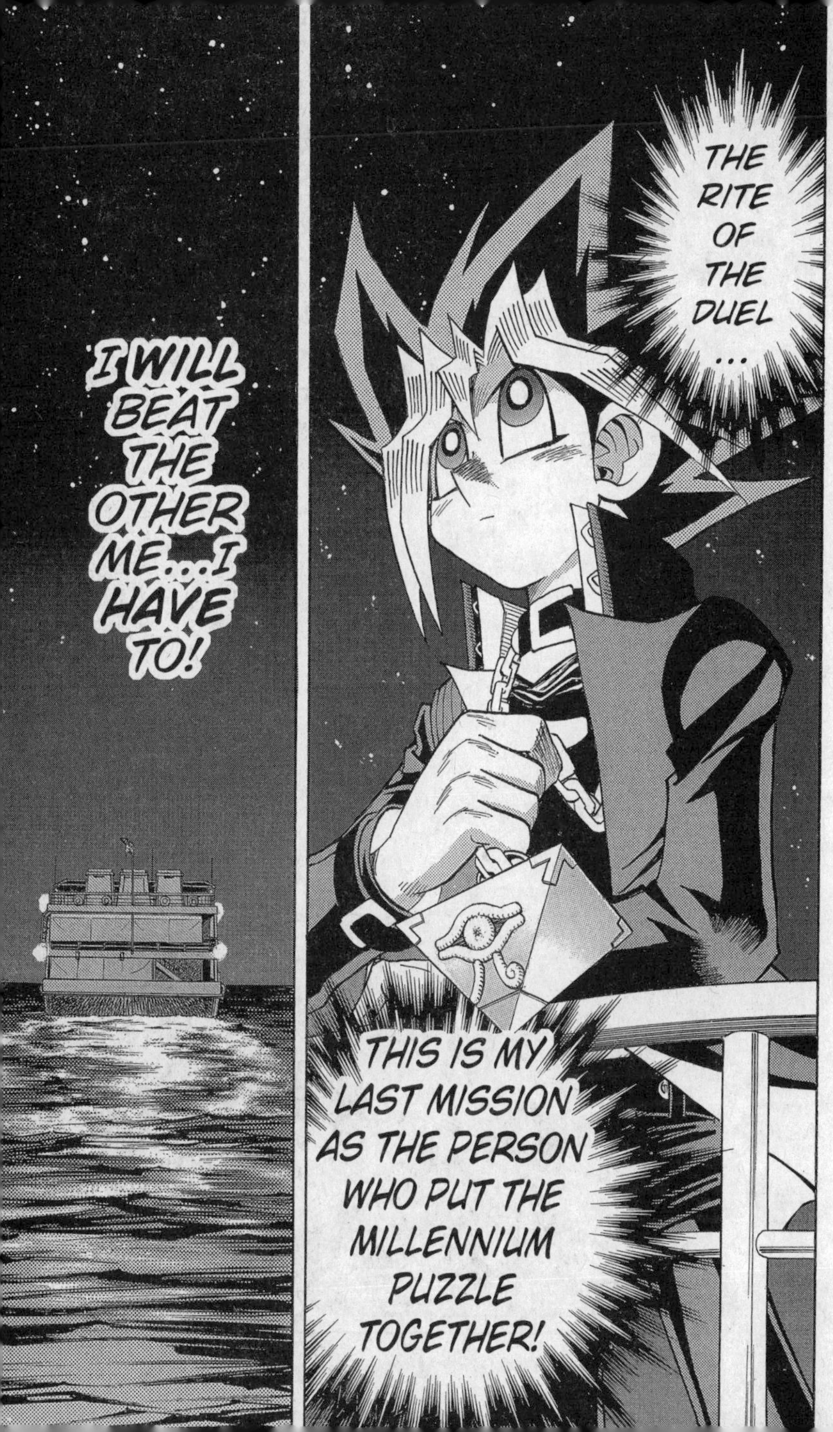
THE RITE OF THE DUEL...
THIS IS MY LAST MISSION AS THE PERSON WHO PUT THE MILLENNIUM PUZZLE TOGETHER!
I WILL BEAT THE OTHER ME...I HAVE TO!

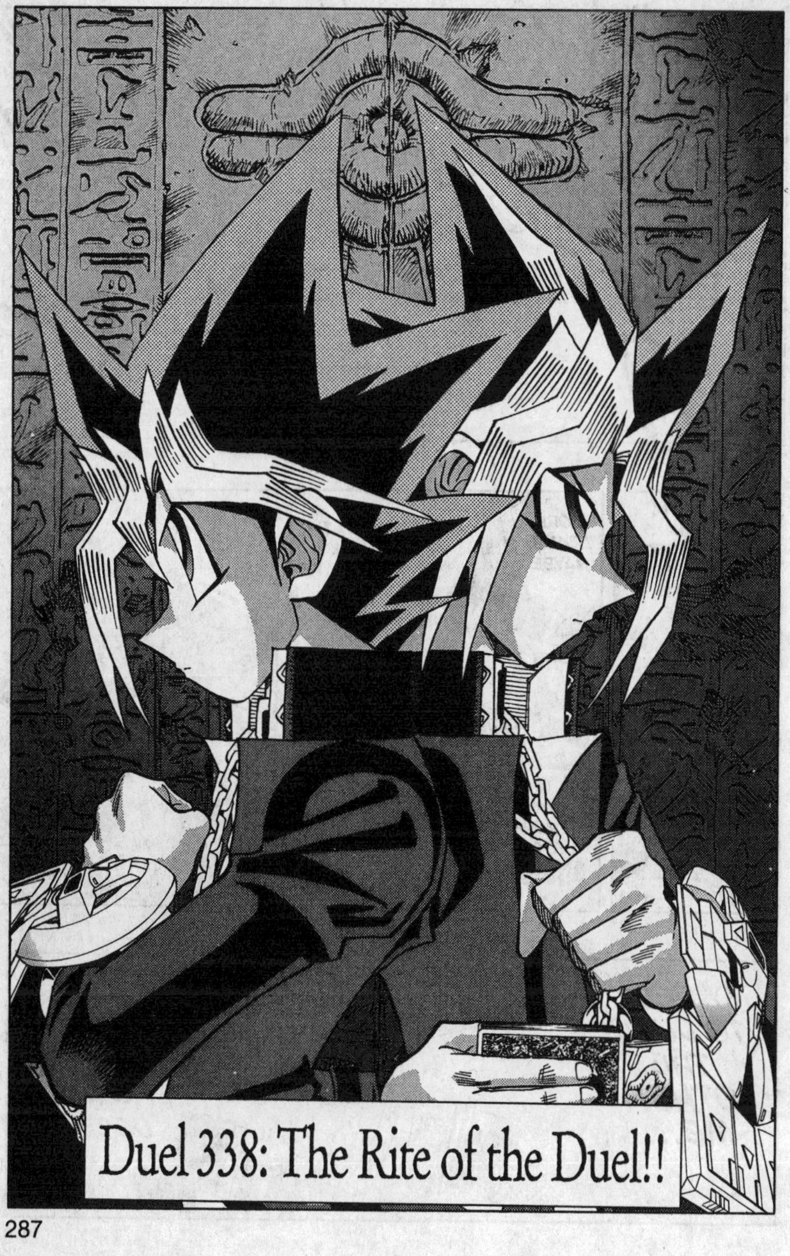
Duel 338: The Rite of the Duel!!

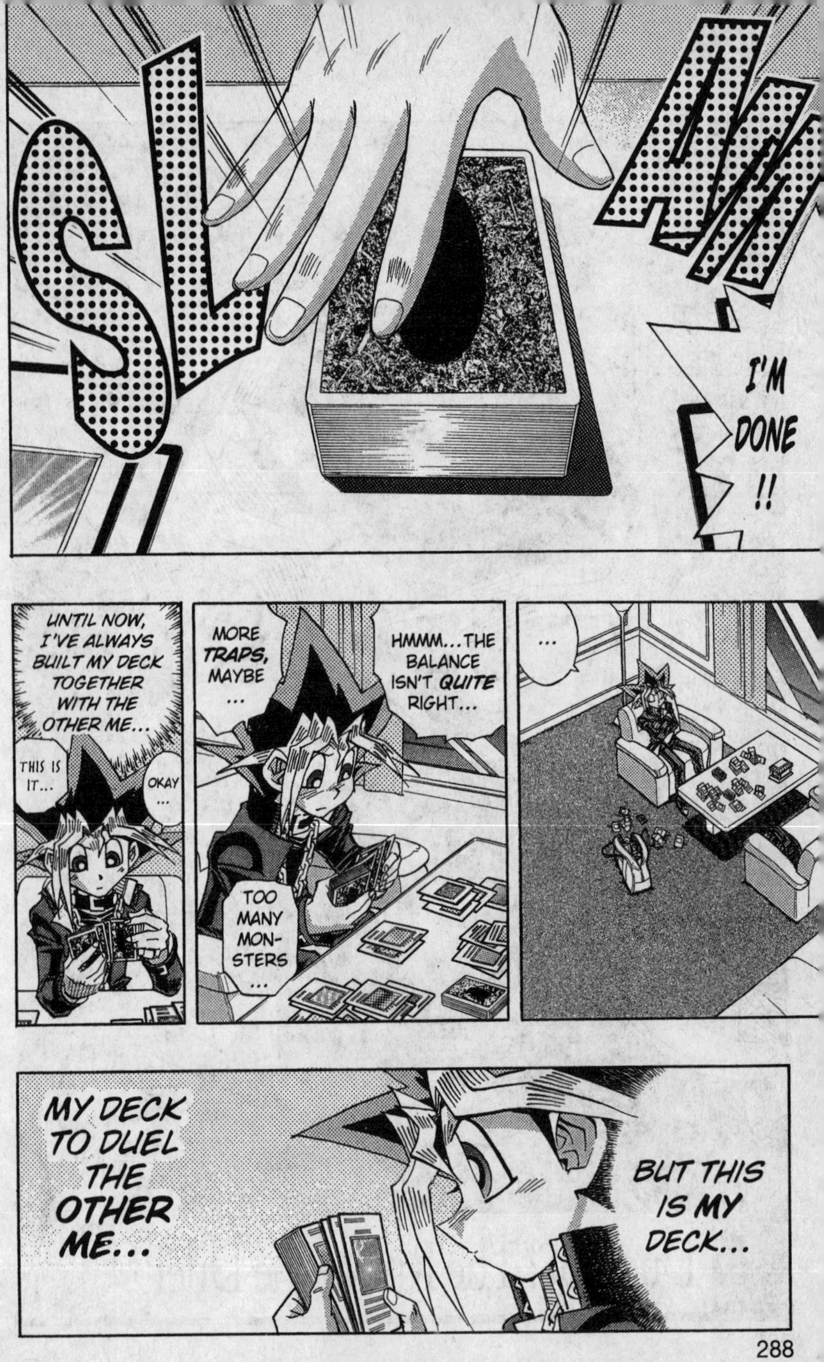
I'M DONE !!
...
HMMM...THE BALANCE ISN'T QUITE RIGHT...
MORE TRAPS, MAYBE ...
TOO MANY MON-STERS ...
UNTIL NOW, I'VE ALWAYS BUILT MY DECK TOGETHER WITH THE OTHER ME...
OKAY ...
THIS IS IT...
BUT THIS IS MY DECK...
MY DECK TO DUEL THE OTHER ME...

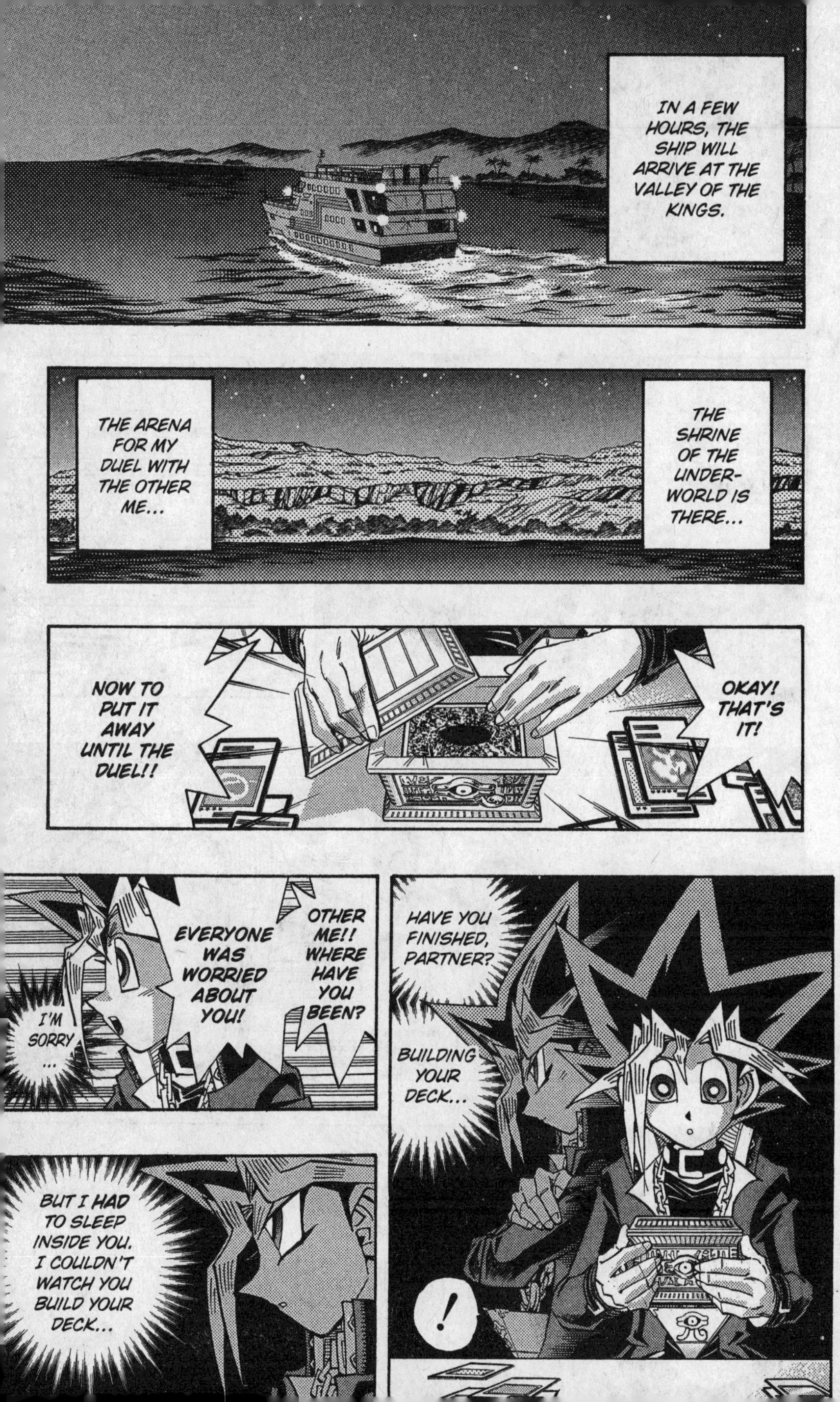

IN A FEW HOURS, THE SHIP WILL ARRIVE AT THE VALLEY OF THE KINGS.
THE SHRINE OF THE UNDER-WORLD IS THERE...
THE ARENA FOR MY DUEL WITH THE OTHER ME...
OKAY! THAT'S IT!
NOW TO PUT IT AWAY UNTIL THE DUEL!!
HAVE YOU FINISHED, PARTNER?
BUILDING YOUR DECK...
!
OTHER ME!! WHERE HAVE YOU BEEN?
EVERYONE WAS WORRIED ABOUT YOU!
I'M SORRY...
BUT I HAD TO SLEEP INSIDE YOU. I COULDN'T WATCH YOU BUILD YOUR DECK...

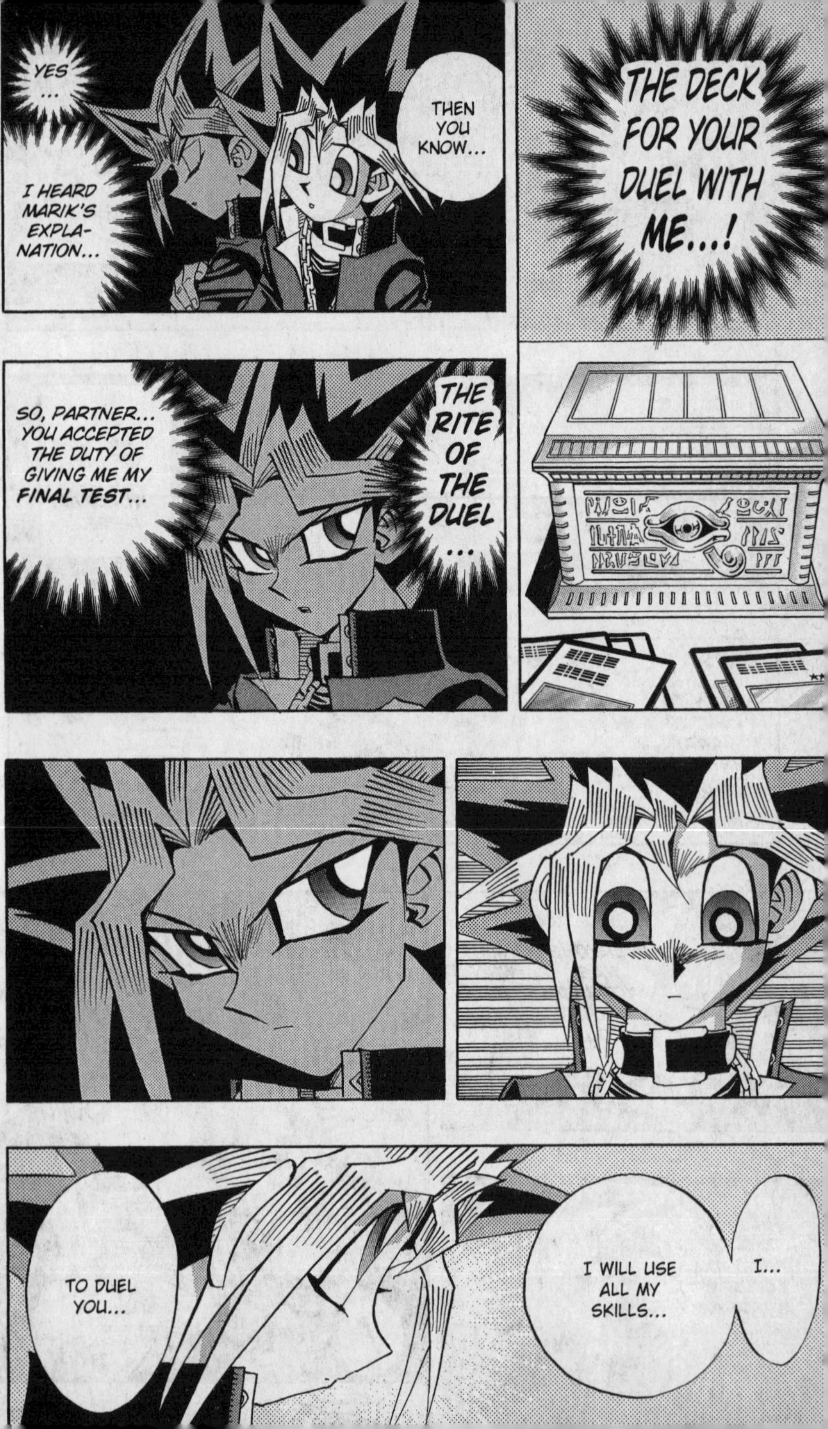
THE DECK FOR YOUR DUEL WITH ME...!
THEN YOU KNOW...
YES...
I HEARD MARIK'S EXPLANATION...
THE RITE OF THE DUEL...
SO, PARTNER... YOU ACCEPTED THE DUTY OF GIVING ME MY FINAL TEST...
I...
I WILL USE ALL MY SKILLS...
TO DUEL YOU...

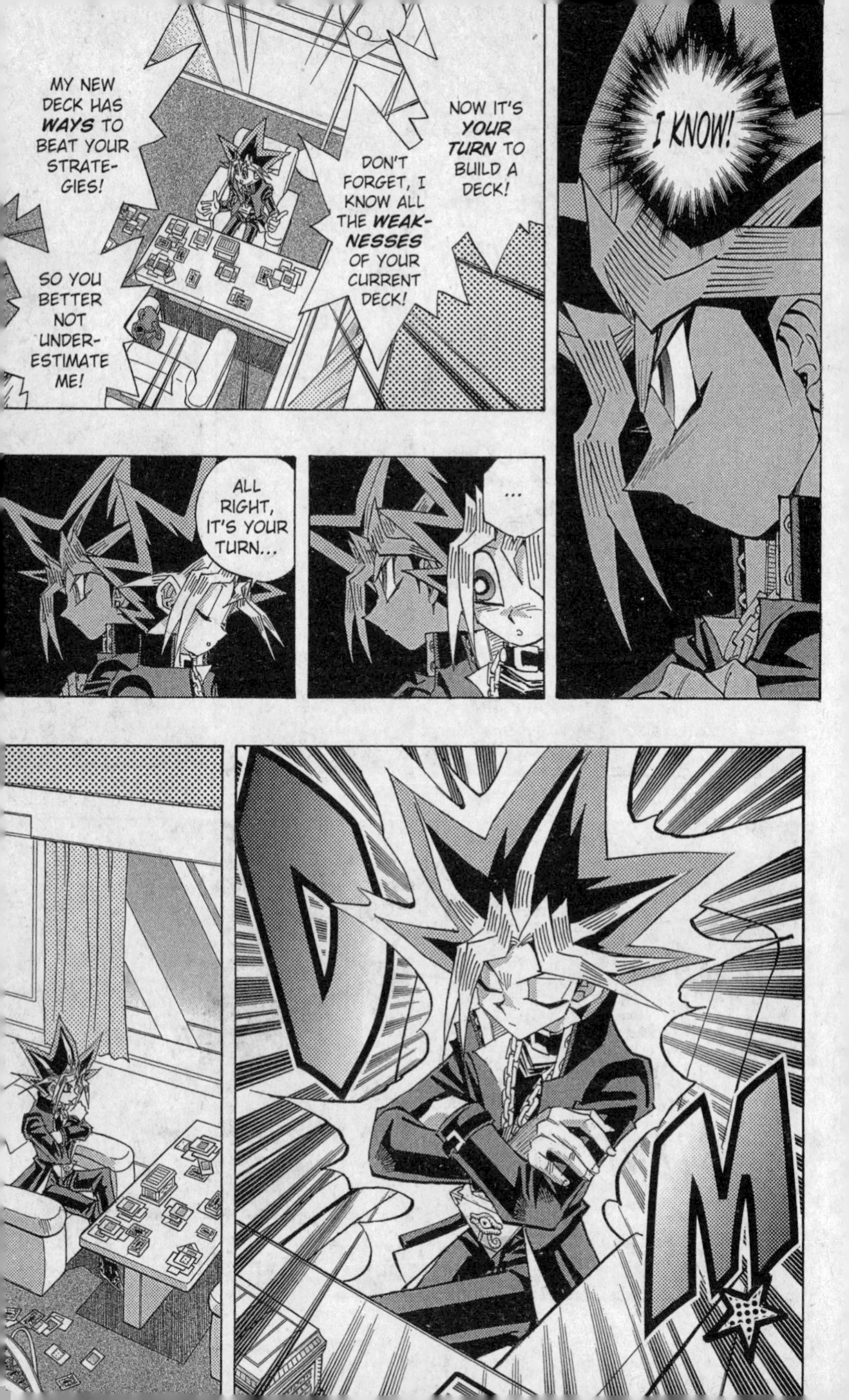

I KNOW!
NOW IT'S YOUR TURN TO BUILD A DECK!
DON'T FORGET, I KNOW ALL THE WEAKNESSES OF YOUR CURRENT DECK!
MY NEW DECK HAS WAYS TO BEAT YOUR STRATEGIES!
SO YOU BETTER NOT UNDERESTIMATE ME!
...
ALL RIGHT, IT'S YOUR TURN...
M

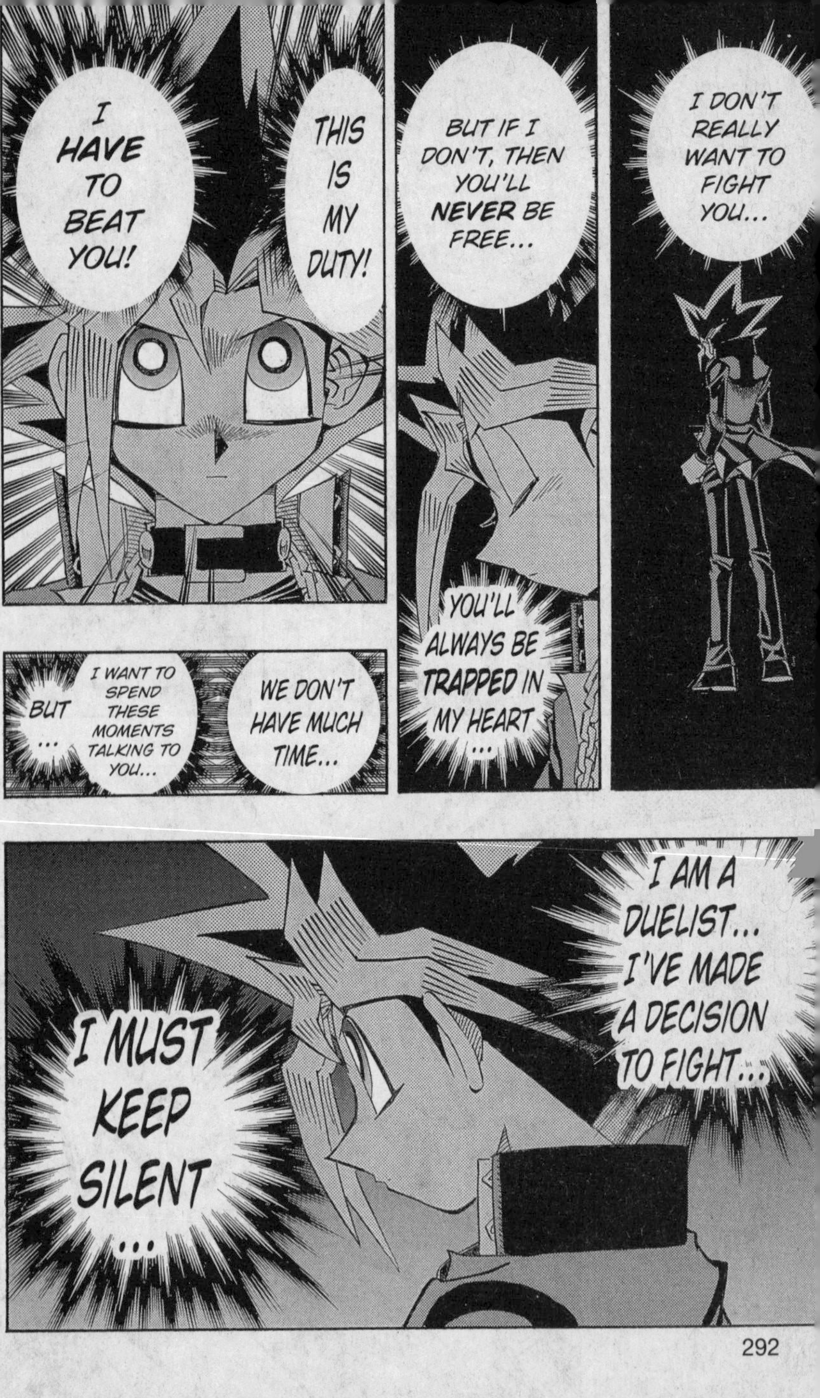
I DON'T REALLY WANT TO FIGHT YOU...
BUT IF I DON'T, THEN YOU'LL NEVER BE FREE...
YOU'LL ALWAYS BE TRAPPED IN MY HEART...
THIS IS MY DUTY!
I HAVE TO BEAT YOU!
WE DON'T HAVE MUCH TIME...
I WANT TO SPEND THESE MOMENTS TALKING TO YOU...
BUT...
I AM A DUELIST... I'VE MADE A DECISION TO FIGHT...
I MUST KEEP SILENT...

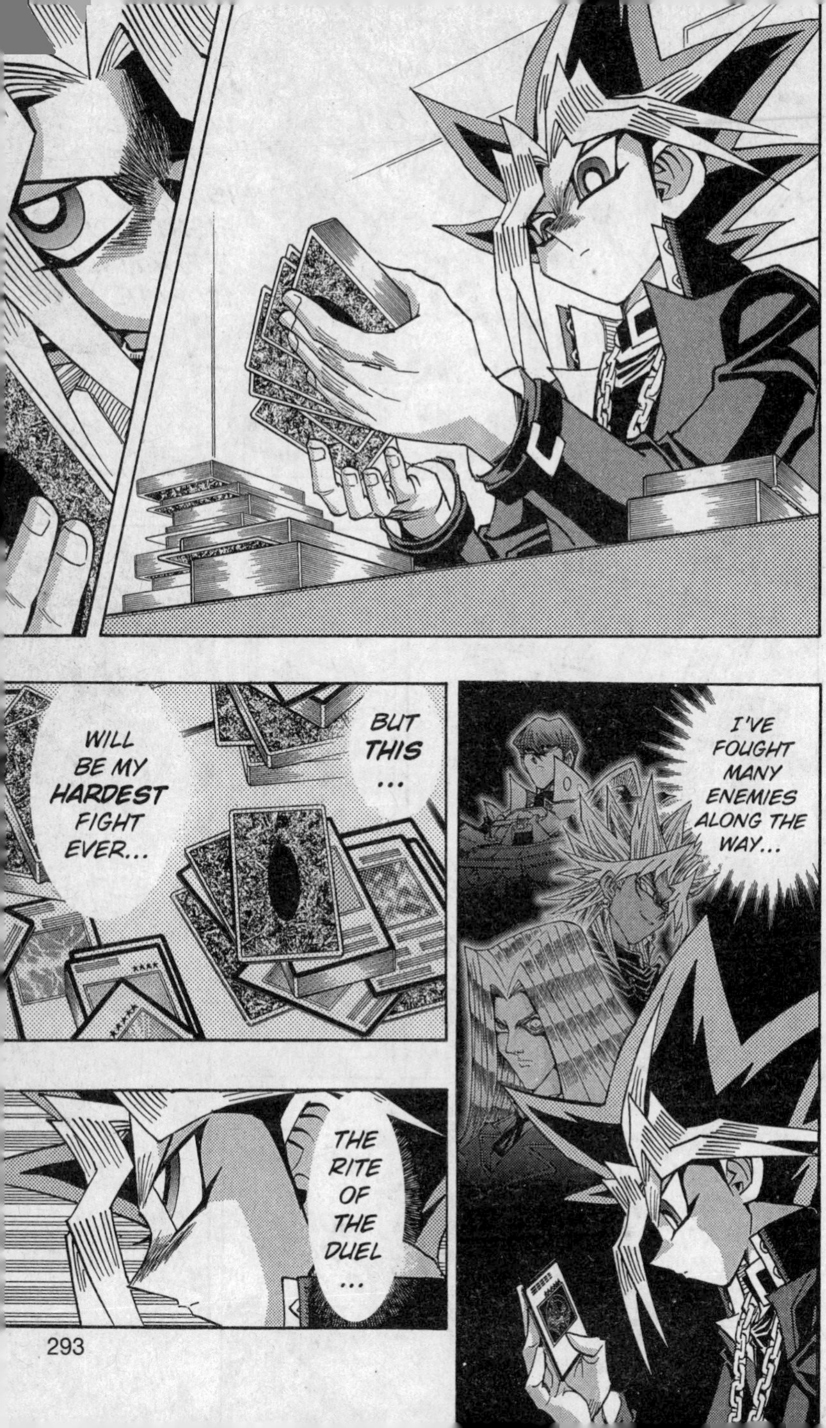
I'VE FOUGHT MANY ENEMIES ALONG THE WAY...
BUT THIS...
WILL BE MY **HARDEST** FIGHT EVER...
THE RITE OF THE DUEL...

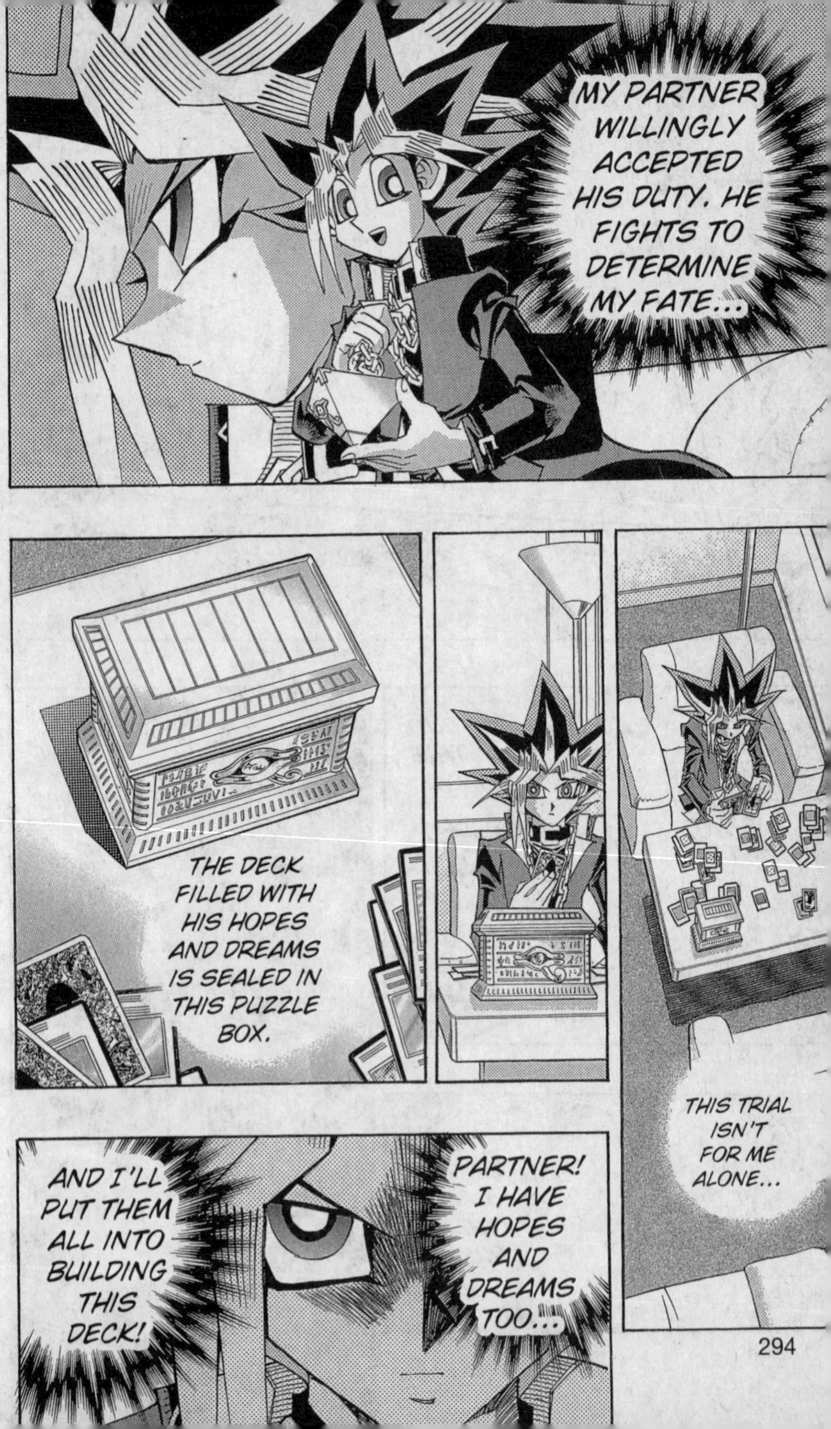
MY PARTNER WILLINGLY ACCEPTED HIS DUTY. HE FIGHTS TO DETERMINE MY FATE...
THIS TRIAL ISN'T FOR ME ALONE...
THE DECK FILLED WITH HIS HOPES AND DREAMS IS SEALED IN THIS PUZZLE BOX.
PARTNER! I HAVE HOPES AND DREAMS TOO...
AND I'LL PUT THEM ALL INTO BUILDING THIS DECK!

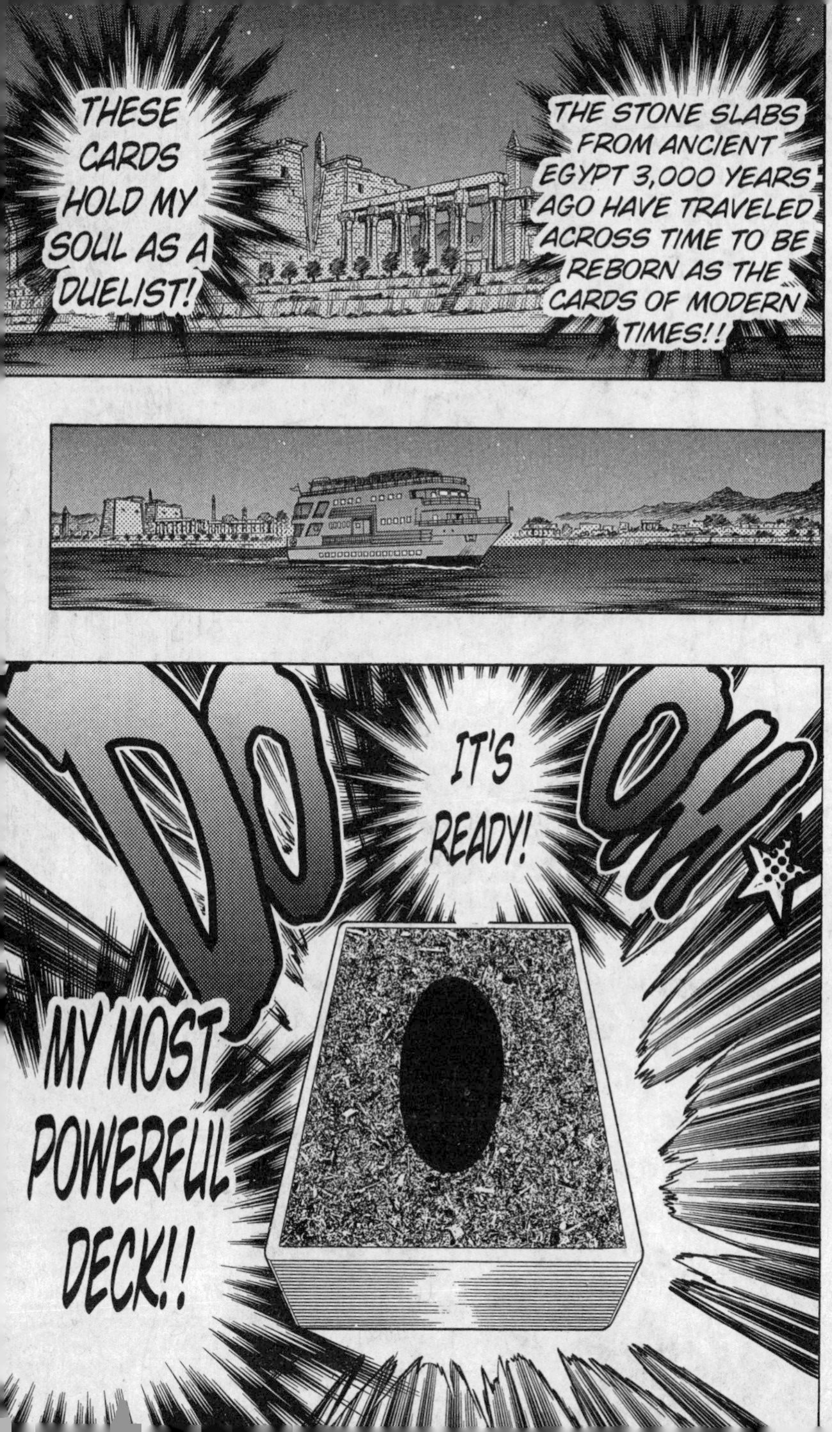
THE STONE SLABS FROM ANCIENT EGYPT 3,000 YEARS AGO HAVE TRAVELED ACROSS TIME TO BE REBORN AS THE CARDS OF MODERN TIMES!!
THESE CARDS HOLD MY SOUL AS A DUELIST!
IT'S READY!
MY MOST POWERFUL DECK!!

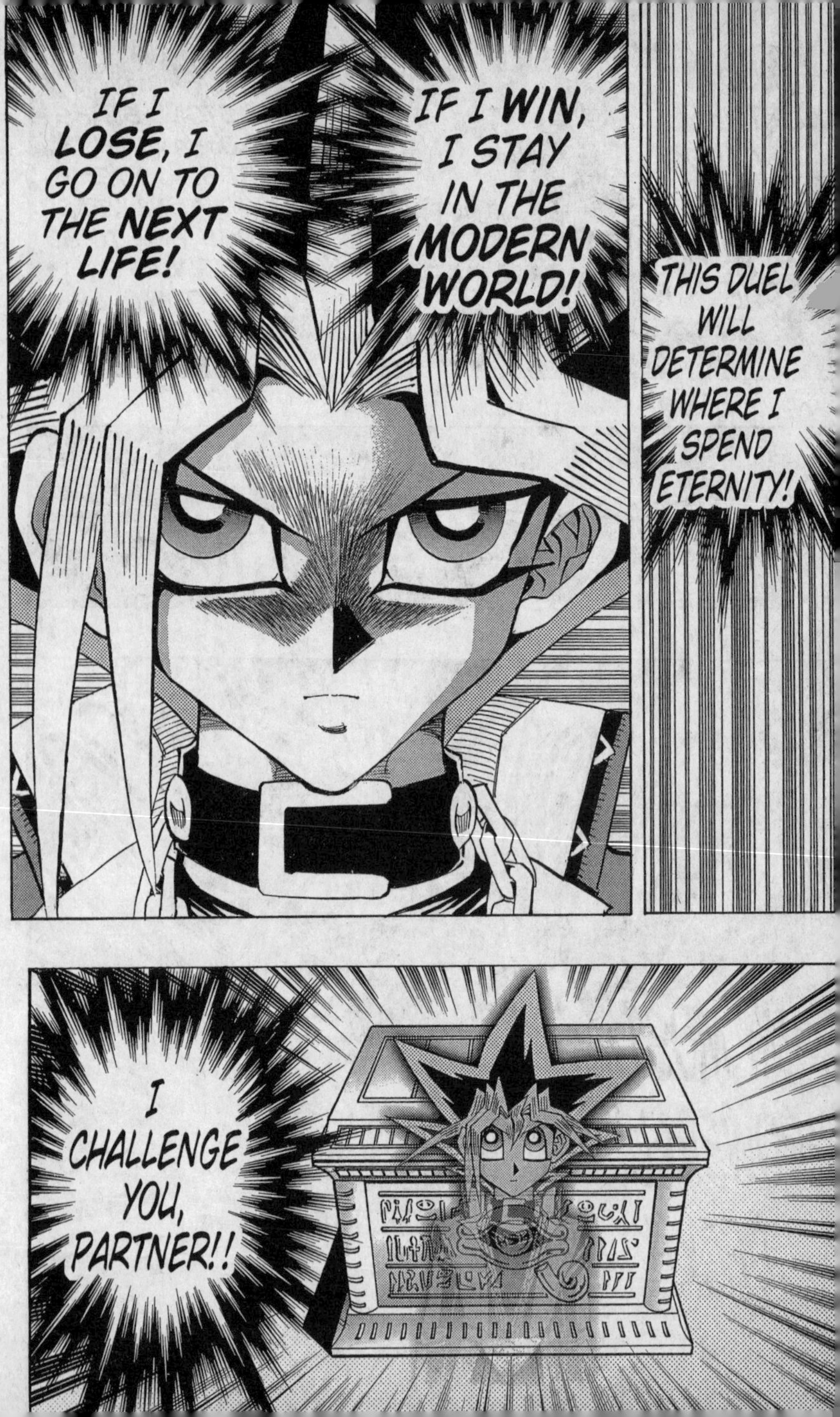
THIS DUEL WILL DETERMINE WHERE I SPEND ETERNITY!
IF I WIN, I STAY IN THE MODERN WORLD!
IF I LOSE, I GO ON TO THE NEXT LIFE!
I CHALLENGE YOU, PARTNER!!

READ THIS WAY

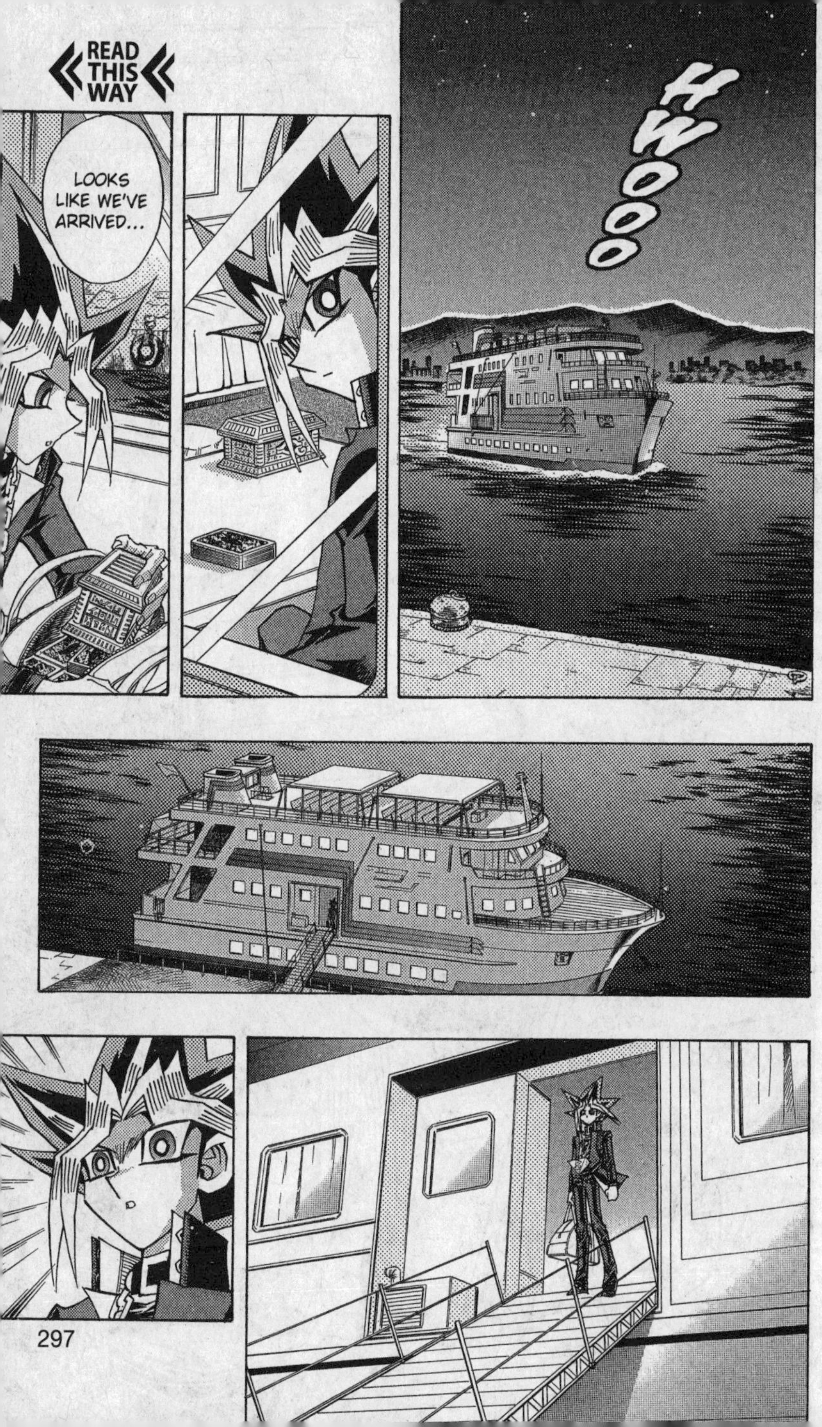
HWOOOO
LOOKS LIKE WE'VE ARRIVED...

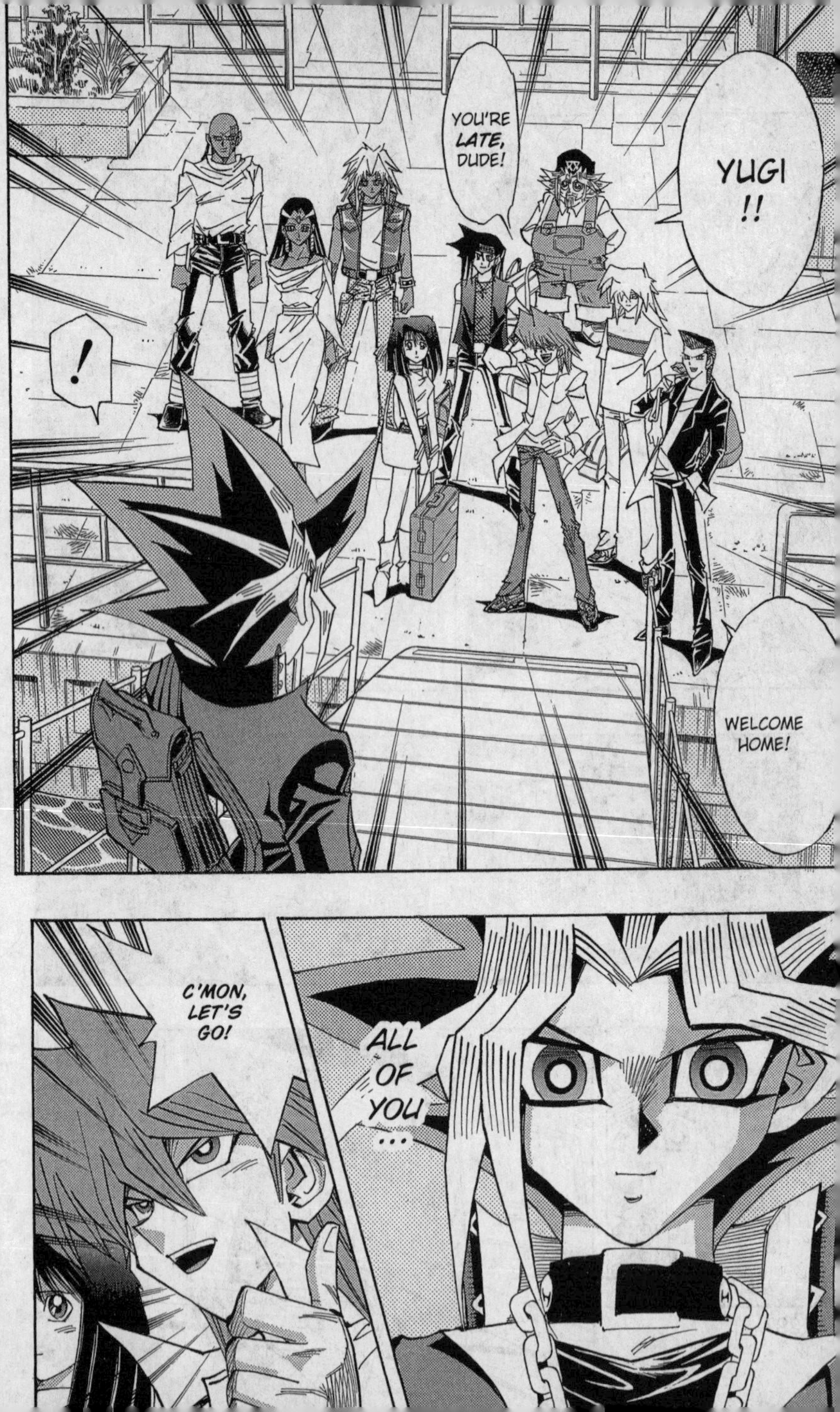
YUGI !!
YOU'RE LATE, DUDE!
WELCOME HOME!
!
ALL OF YOU ...
C'MON, LET'S GO!

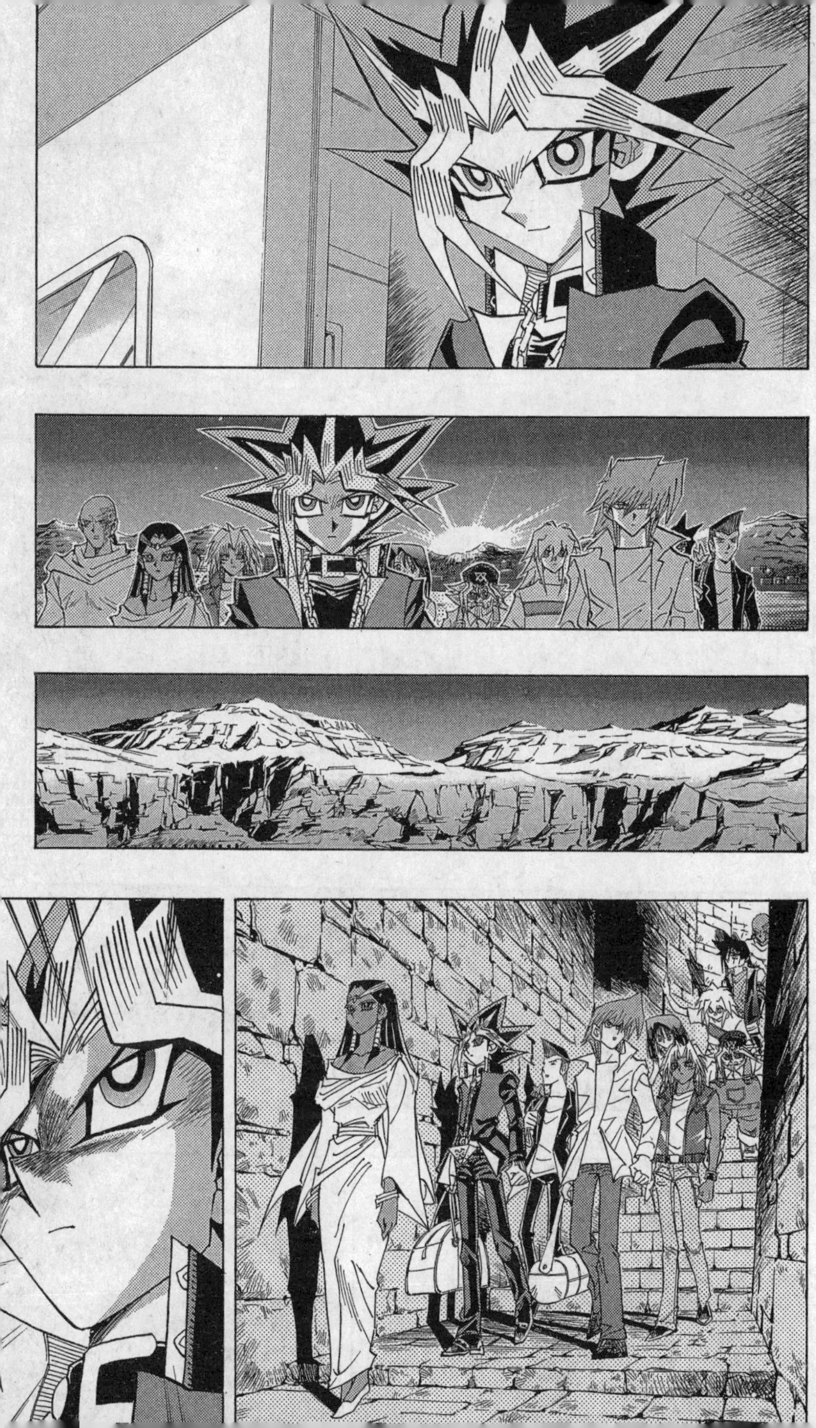

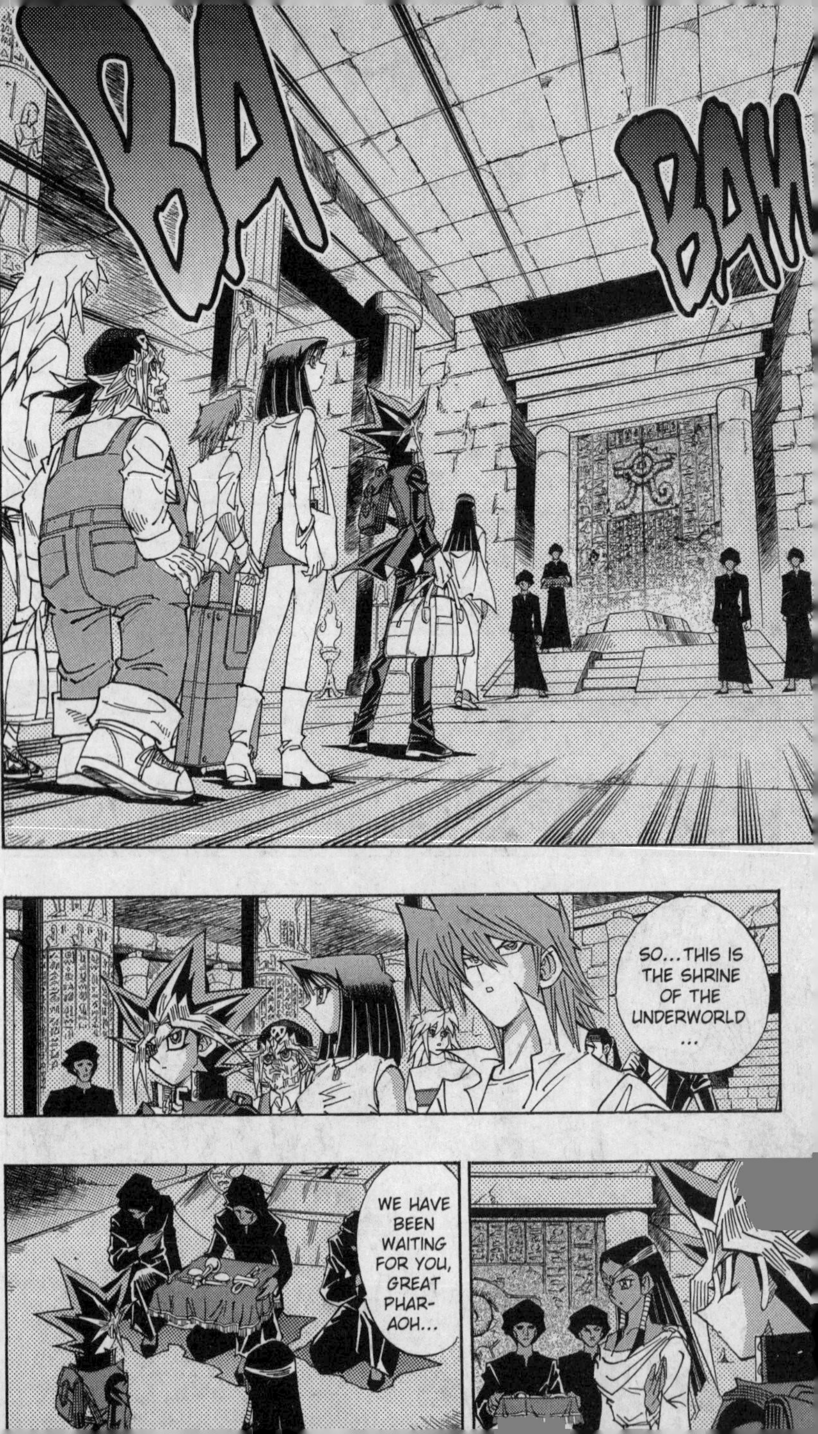
BAM
BA
SO...THIS IS THE SHRINE OF THE UNDERWORLD ...
WE HAVE BEEN WAITING FOR YOU, GREAT PHARAOH...

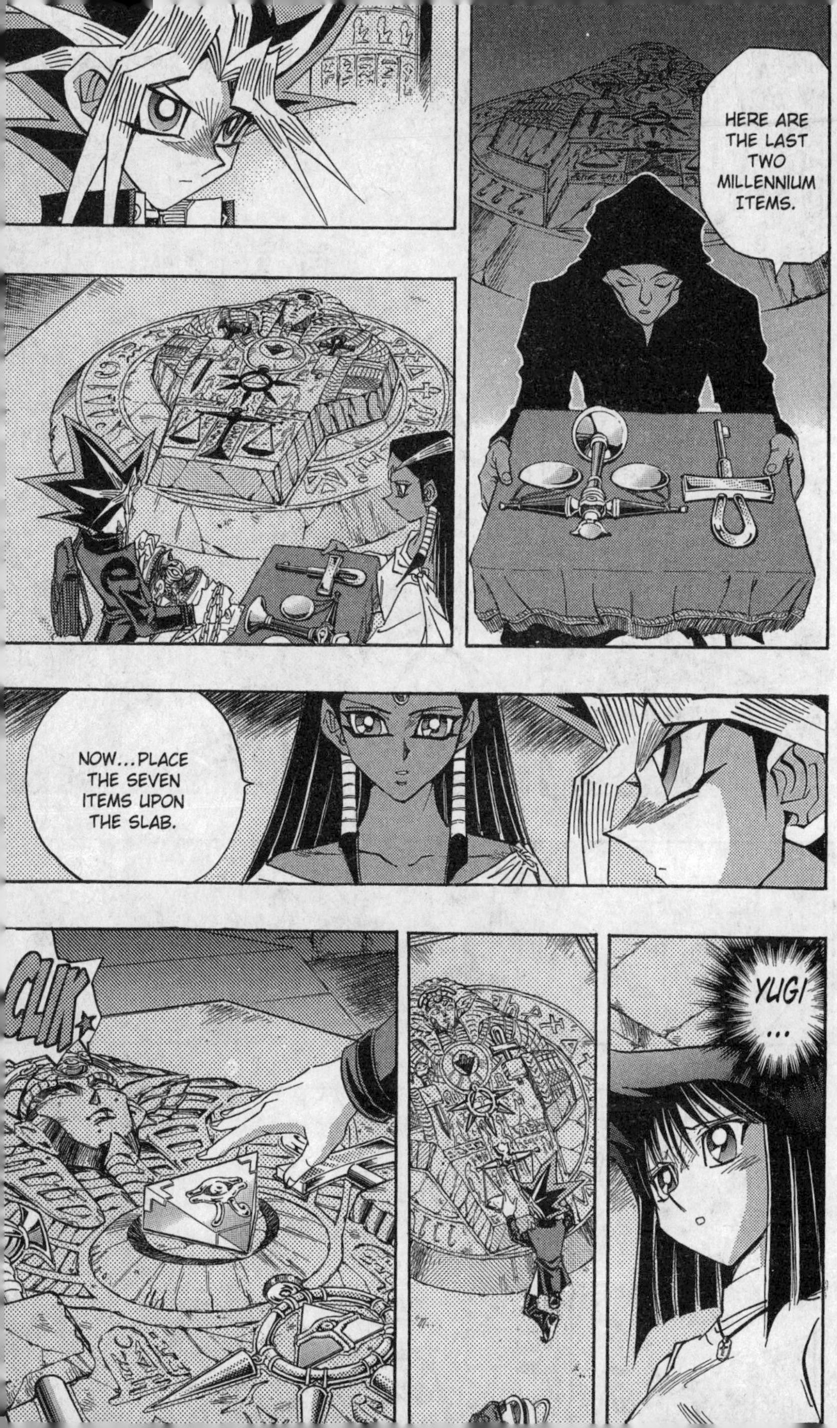
HERE ARE THE LAST TWO MILLENNIUM ITEMS.
NOW...PLACE THE SEVEN ITEMS UPON THE SLAB.
YUGI ...
CLIK

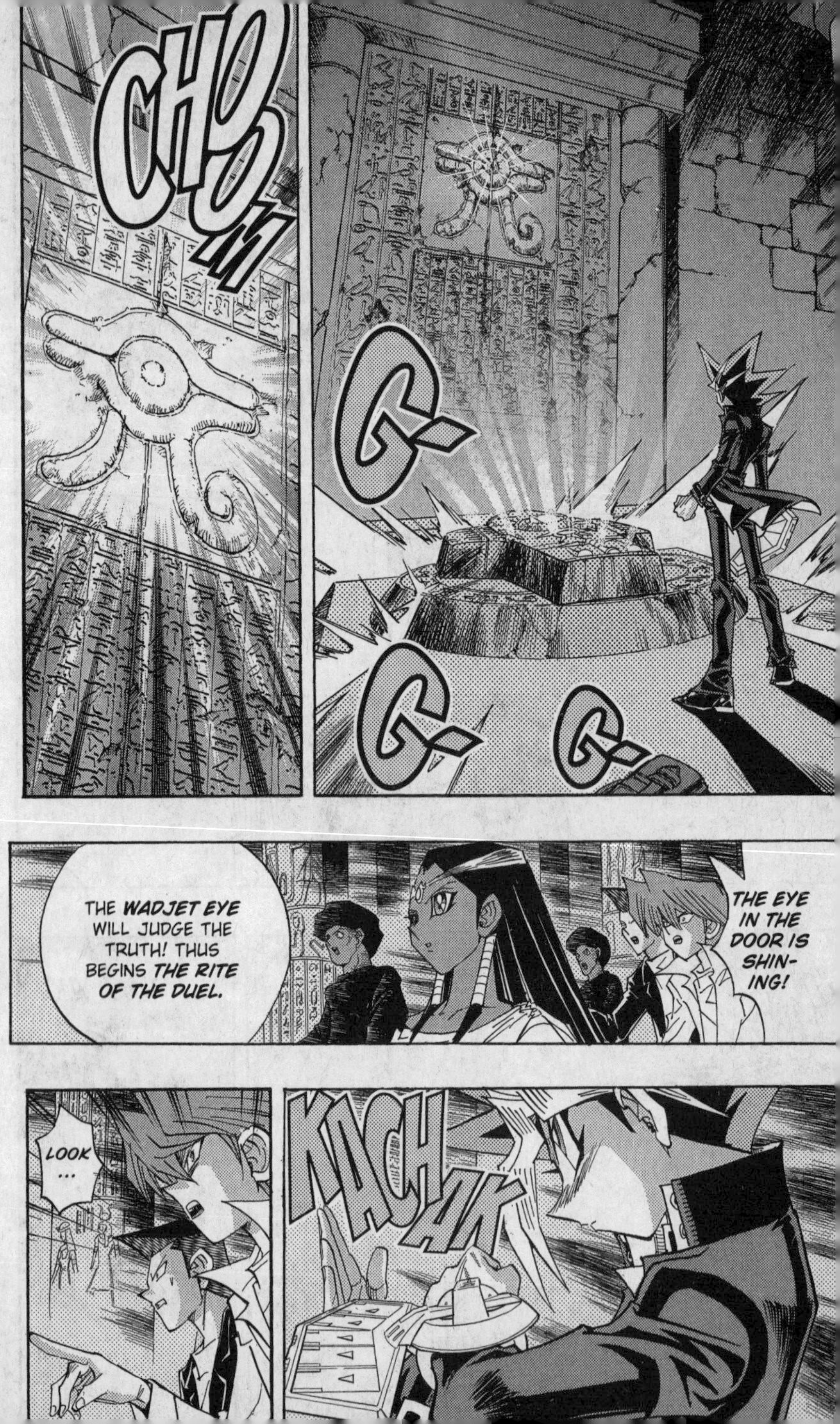
G-
G-
G-
CHOOM
THE EYE IN THE DOOR IS SHINING!
THE WADJET EYE WILL JUDGE THE TRUTH! THUS BEGINS THE RITE OF THE DUEL.
KACHAK
LOOK...

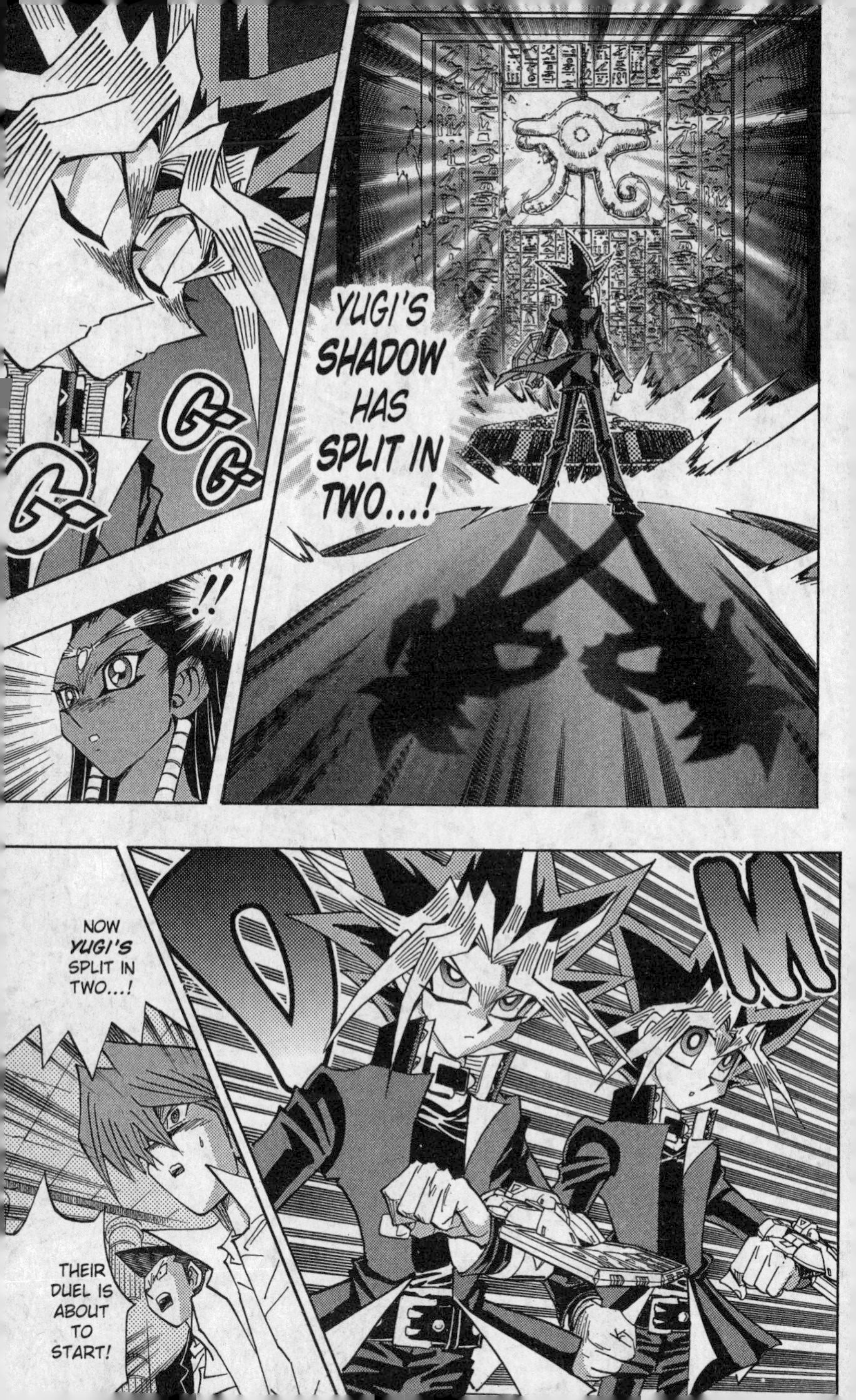

YUGI'S SHADOW HAS SPLIT IN TWO...!
G G
G
!!
M
NOW YUGI'S SPLIT IN TWO...!
THEIR DUEL IS ABOUT TO START!

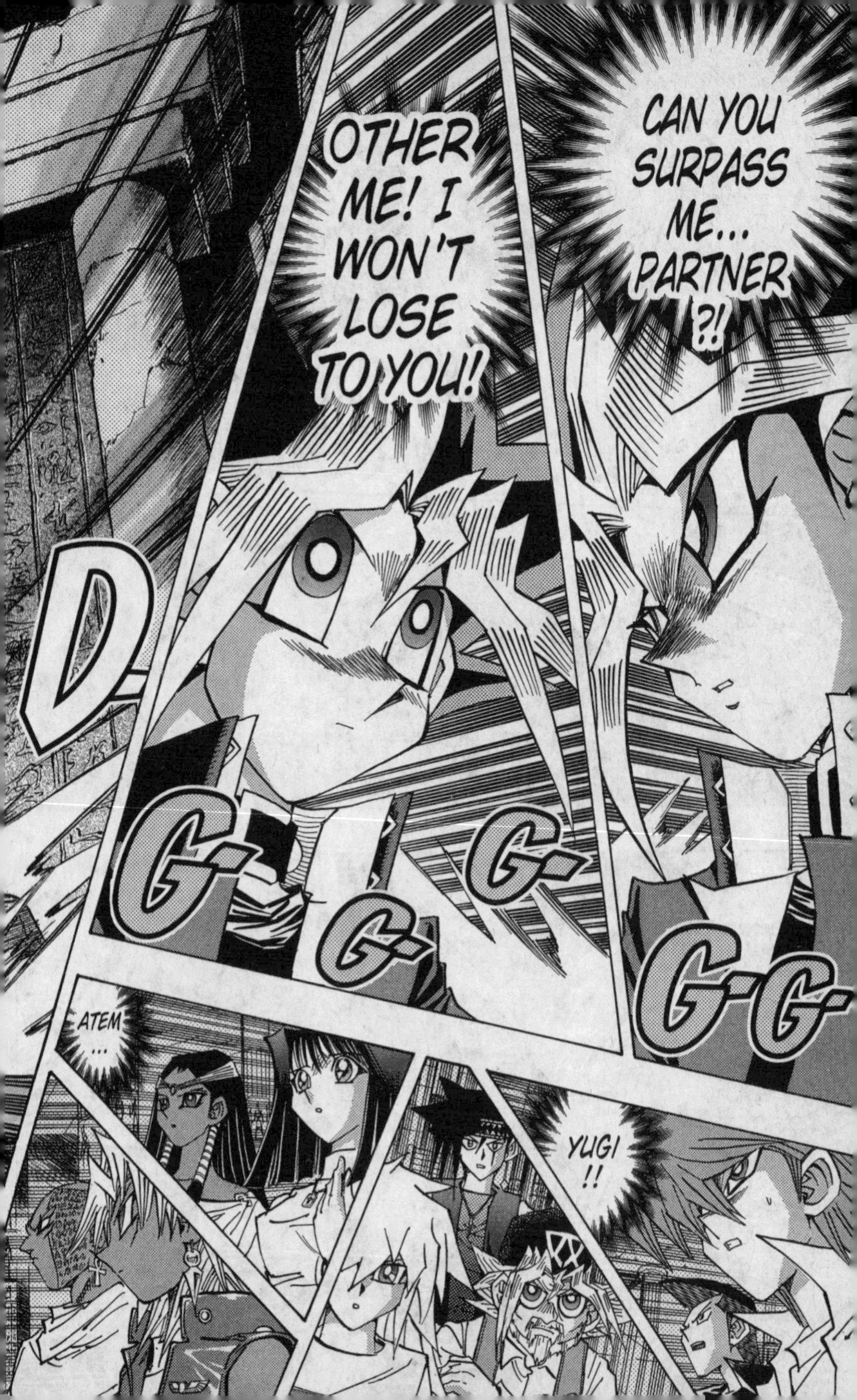
CAN YOU SURPASS ME... PARTNER ?!
G-G-
OTHER ME! I WON'T LOSE TO YOU!
G-G-G-
D
YUGI !!
ATEM ...

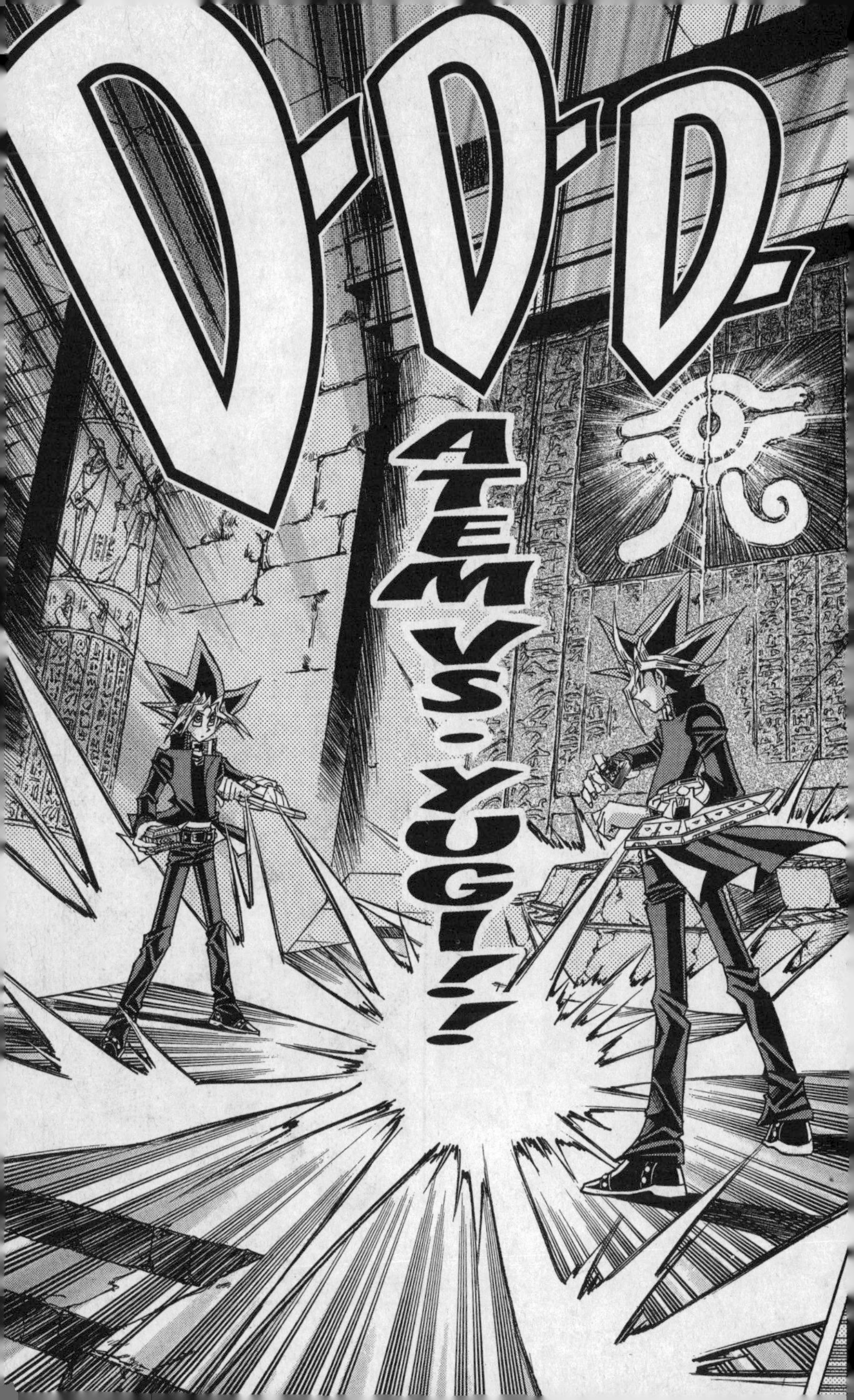
D·D·D·
ATEM VS. YUGI!!

Duel 339: Yugi vs. Atem!!

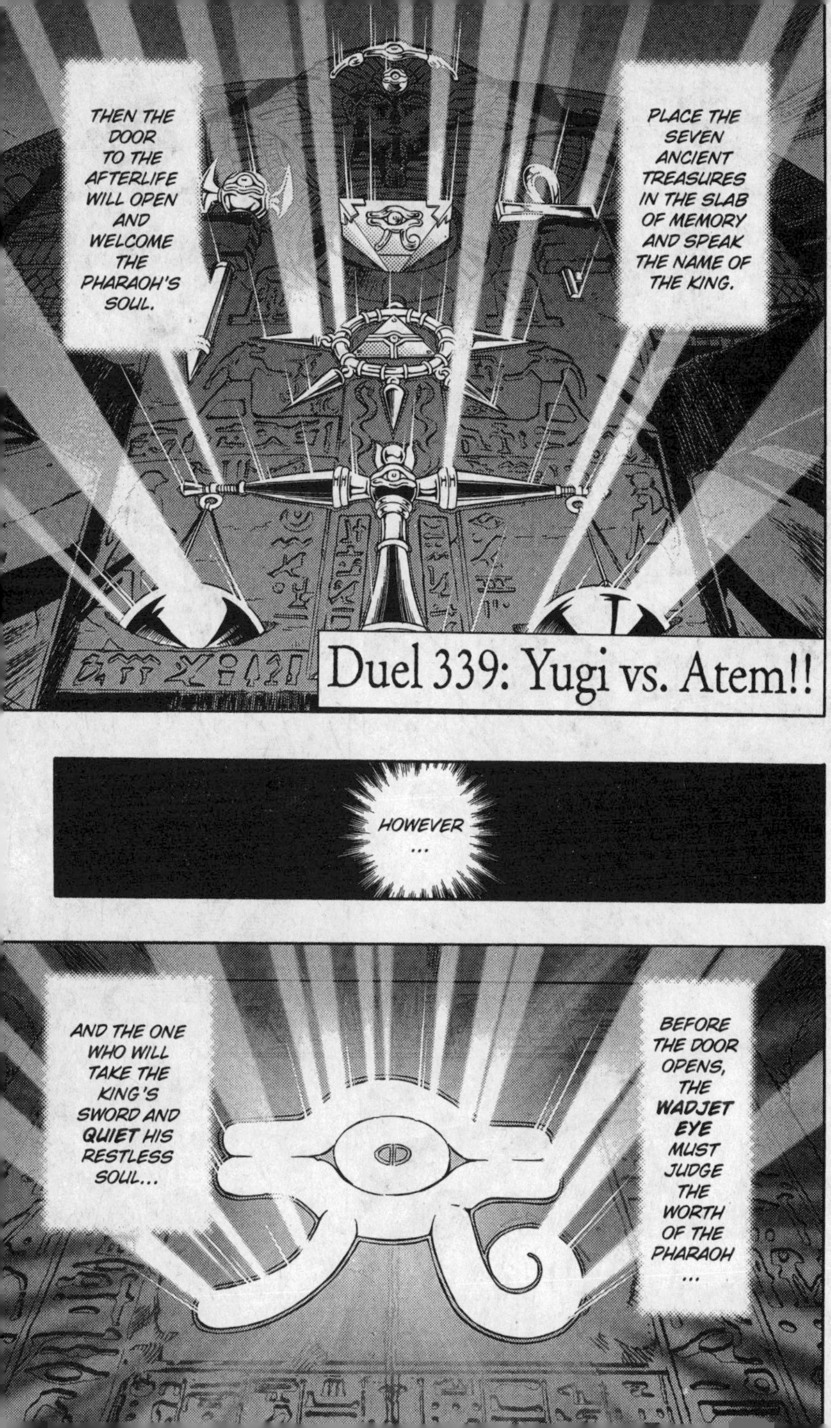

PLACE THE SEVEN ANCIENT TREASURES IN THE SLAB OF MEMORY AND SPEAK THE NAME OF THE KING.
THEN THE DOOR TO THE AFTERLIFE WILL OPEN AND WELCOME THE PHARAOH'S SOUL.
HOWEVER ...
BEFORE THE DOOR OPENS, THE **WADJET EYE** MUST JUDGE THE WORTH OF THE PHARAOH ...
AND THE ONE WHO WILL TAKE THE KING'S SWORD AND **QUIET** HIS RESTLESS SOUL...

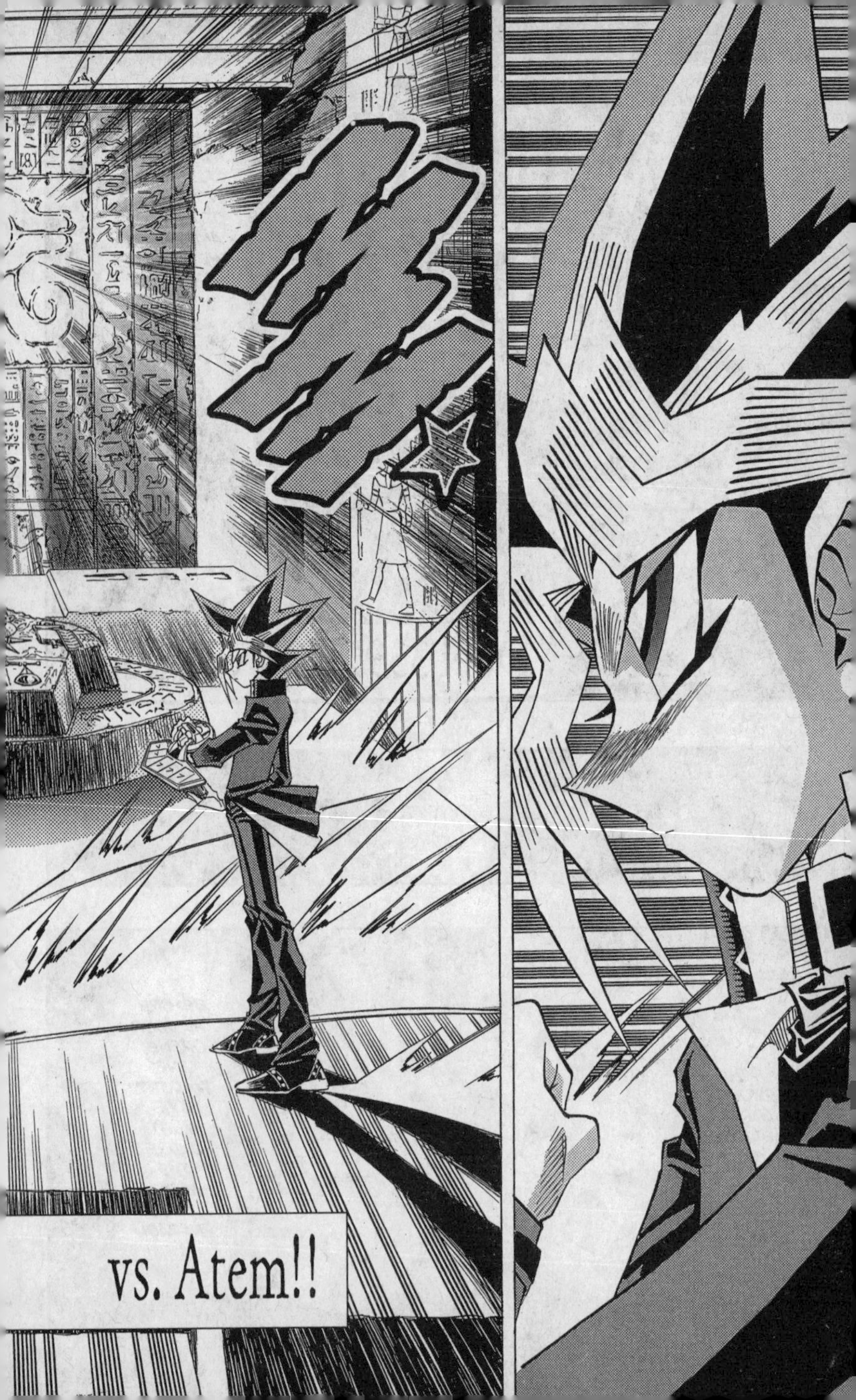
vs. Atem!!

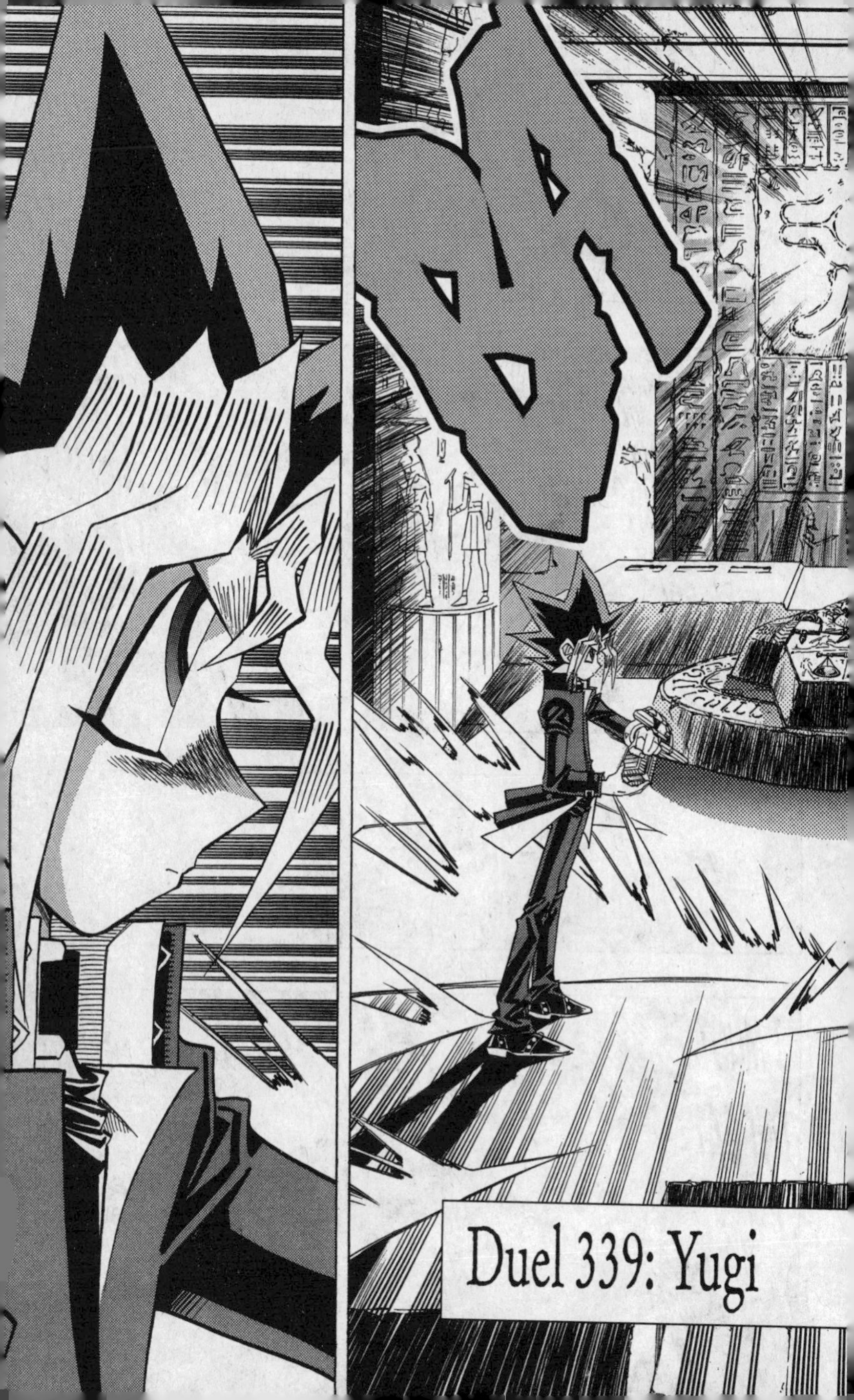
Duel 339: Yugi

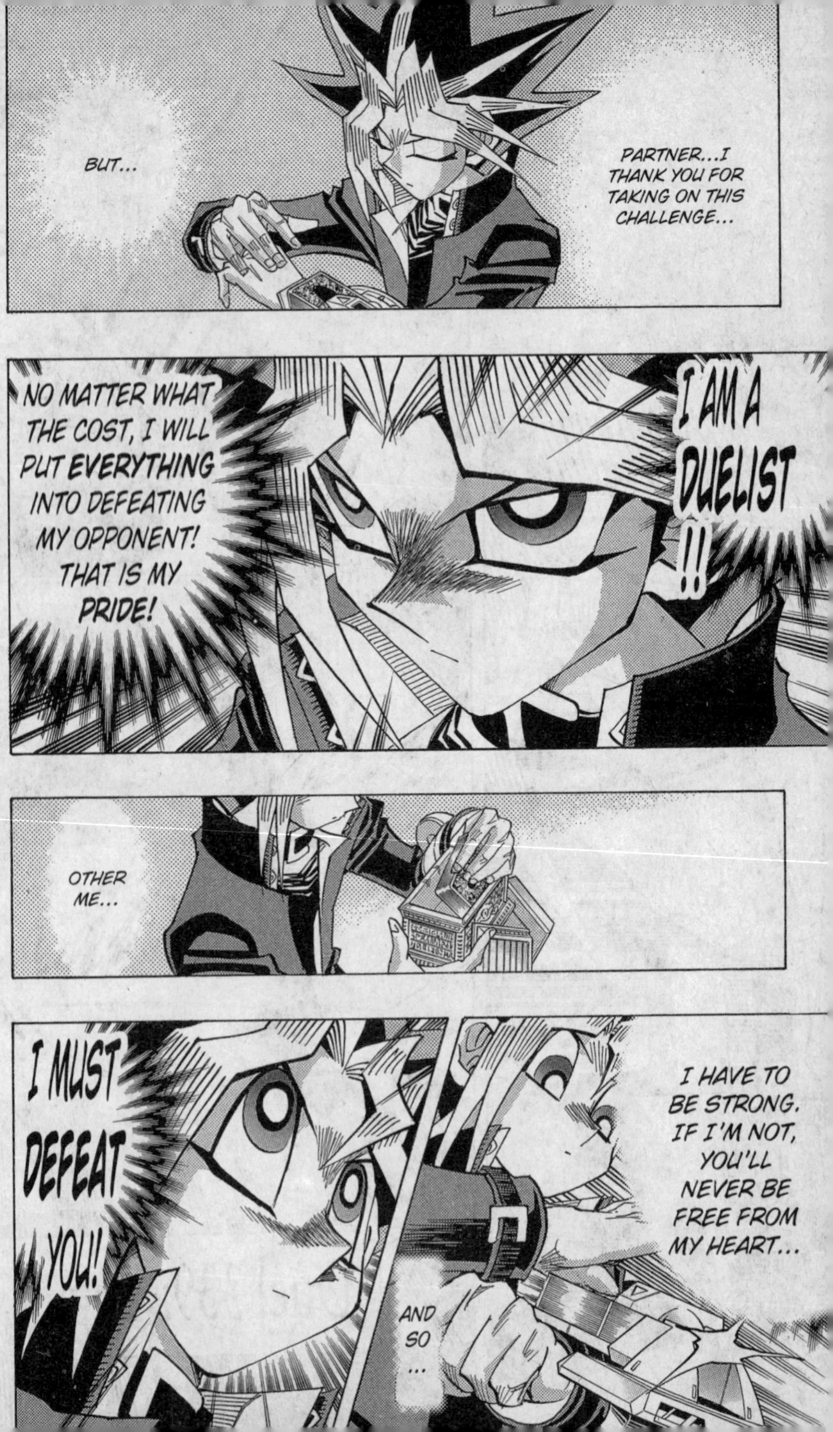
PARTNER...I THANK YOU FOR TAKING ON THIS CHALLENGE...
BUT...
I AM A DUELIST!!
NO MATTER WHAT THE COST, I WILL PUT **EVERYTHING** INTO DEFEATING MY OPPONENT! THAT IS MY **PRIDE!**
OTHER ME...
I HAVE TO BE STRONG. IF I'M NOT, YOU'LL NEVER BE FREE FROM MY HEART...
AND SO...
I MUST DEFEAT YOU!

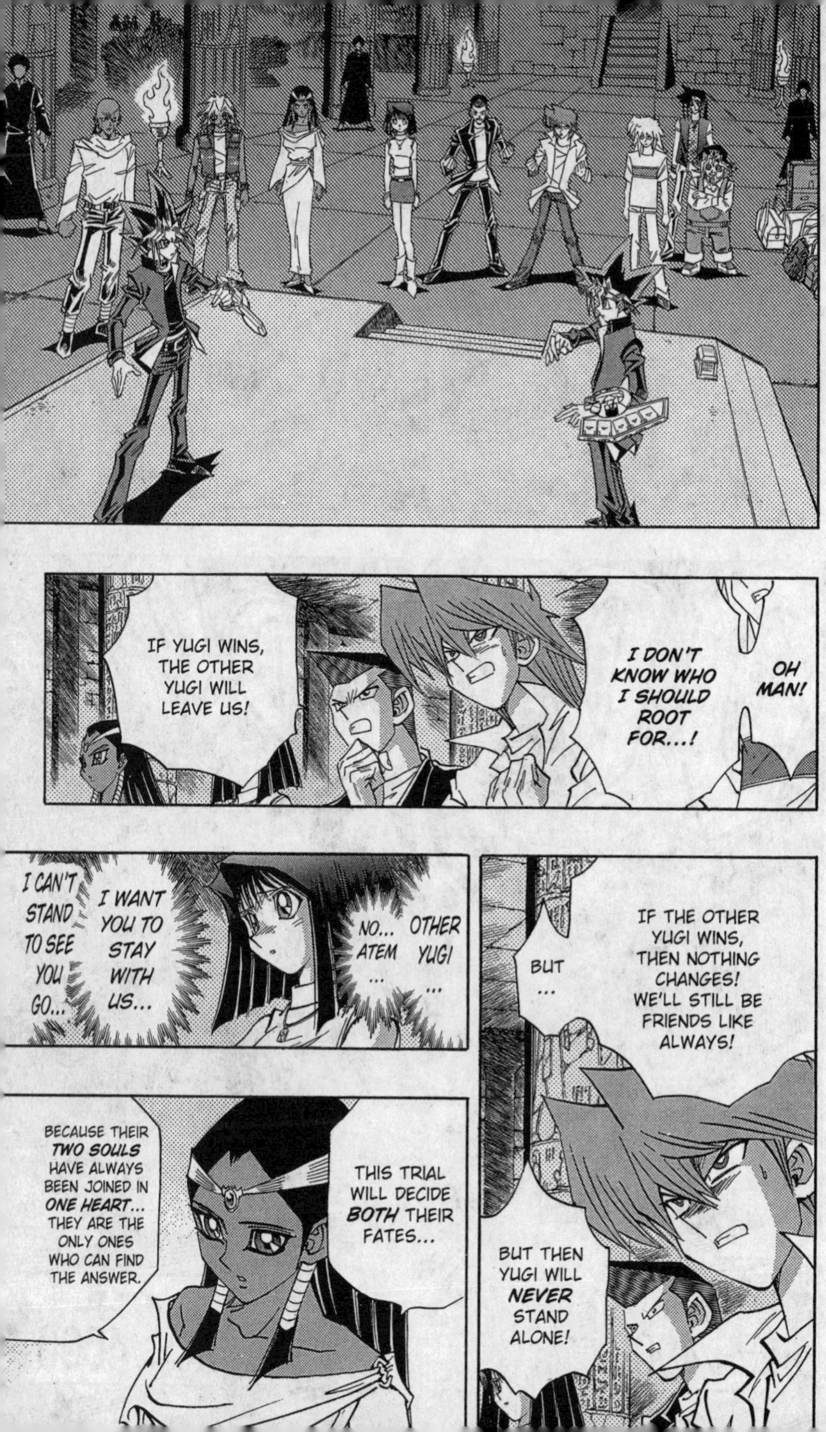
OH MAN!
I DON'T KNOW WHO I SHOULD ROOT FOR...!
IF YUGI WINS, THE OTHER YUGI WILL LEAVE US!
IF THE OTHER YUGI WINS, THEN NOTHING CHANGES! WE'LL STILL BE FRIENDS LIKE ALWAYS!
BUT...
BUT THEN YUGI WILL NEVER STAND ALONE!
OTHER YUGI...
NO... ATEM...
I WANT YOU TO STAY WITH US...
I CAN'T STAND TO SEE YOU GO...
THIS TRIAL WILL DECIDE BOTH THEIR FATES...
BECAUSE THEIR TWO SOULS HAVE ALWAYS BEEN JOINED IN ONE HEART... THEY ARE THE ONLY ONES WHO CAN FIND THE ANSWER.

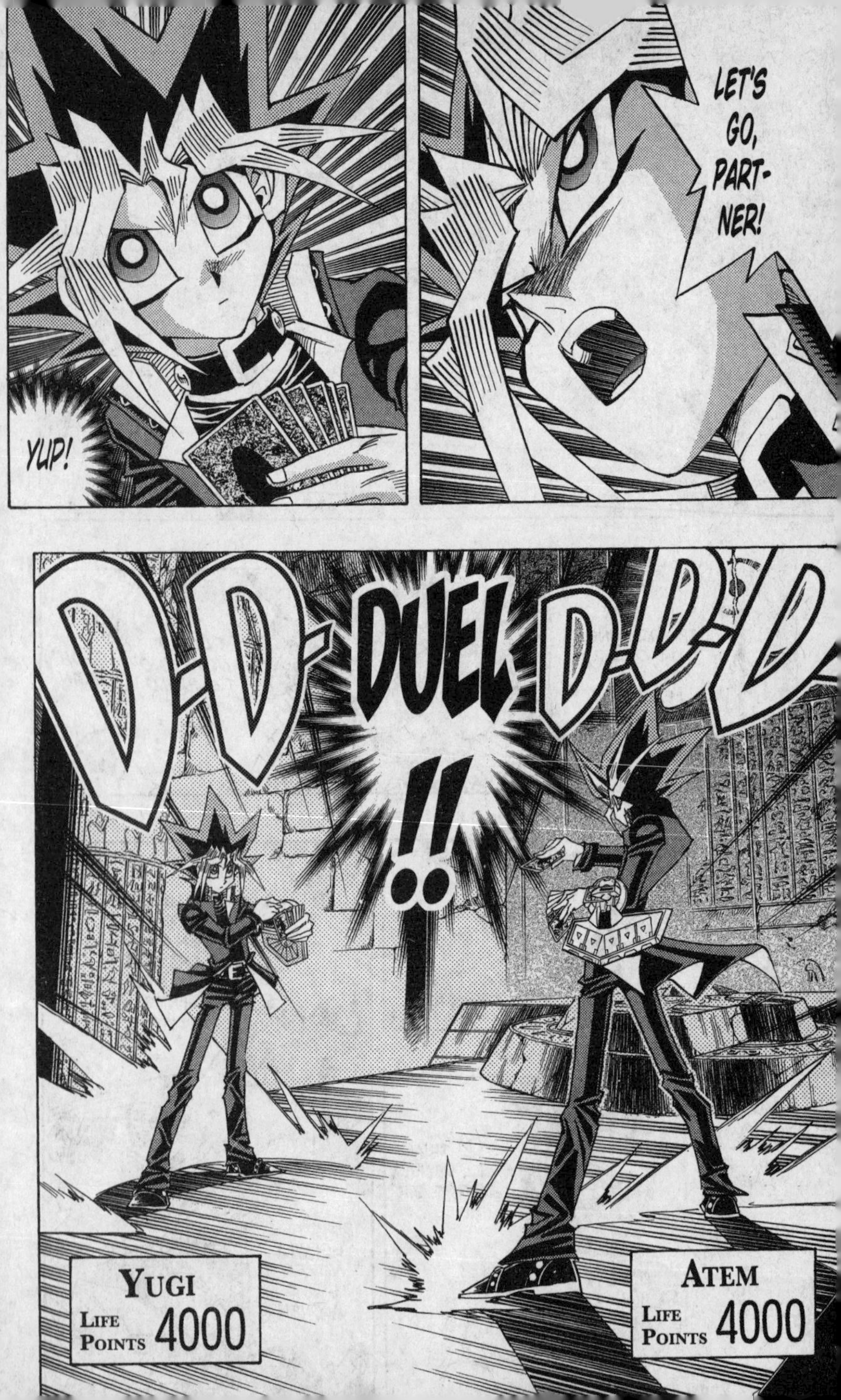
LET'S GO, PART-NER!
YUP!
D-D-DUEL D-D-D
!!
ATEM
LIFE POINTS 4000
YUGI
LIFE POINTS 4000

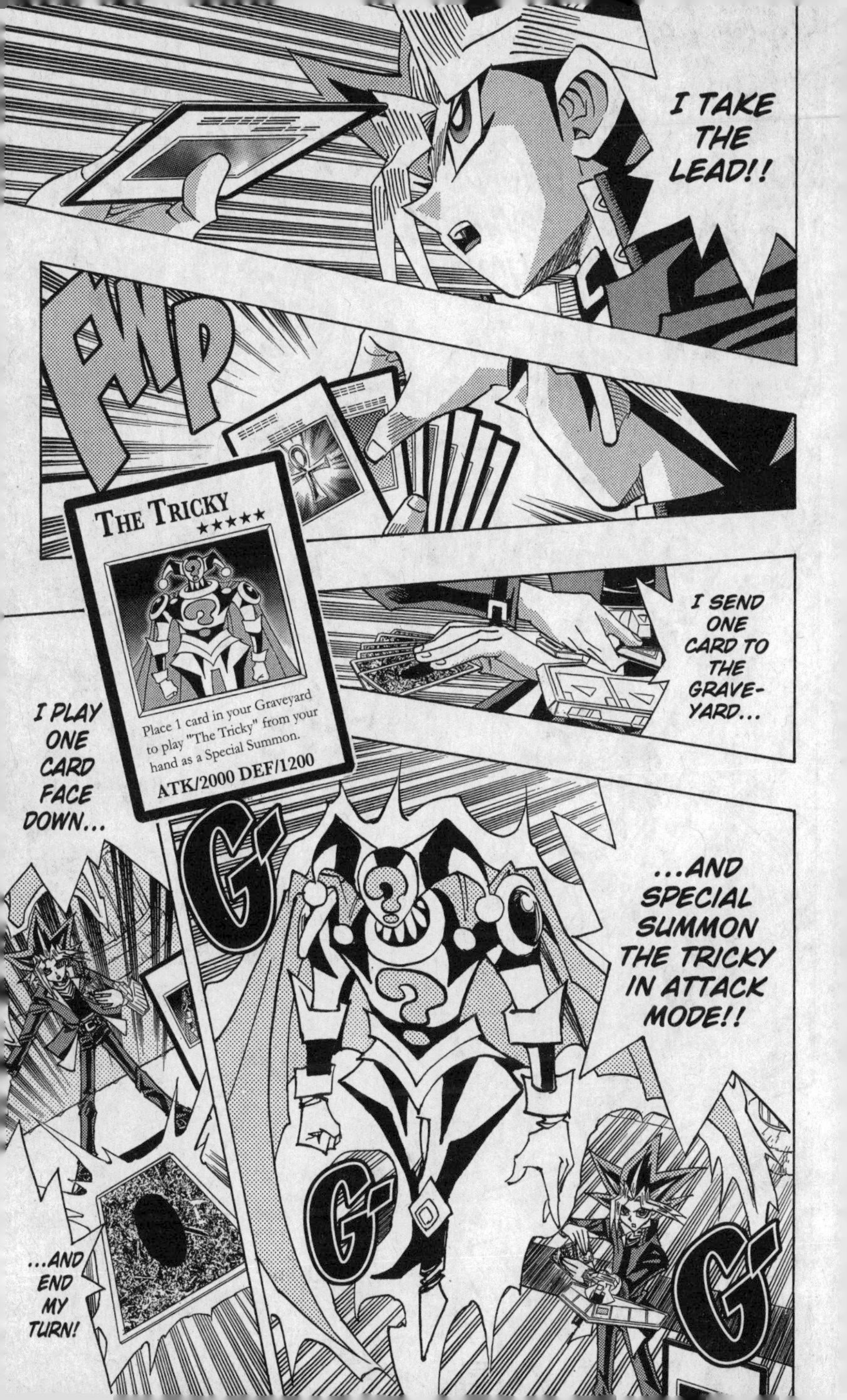
I TAKE THE LEAD!!
PAP
I SEND ONE CARD TO THE GRAVEYARD...
THE TRICKY
★★★★★
Place 1 card in your Graveyard to play "The Tricky" from your hand as a Special Summon.
ATK/2000 DEF/1200
I PLAY ONE CARD FACE DOWN...
...AND SPECIAL SUMMON THE TRICKY IN ATTACK MODE!!
G
G
G
...AND END MY TURN!

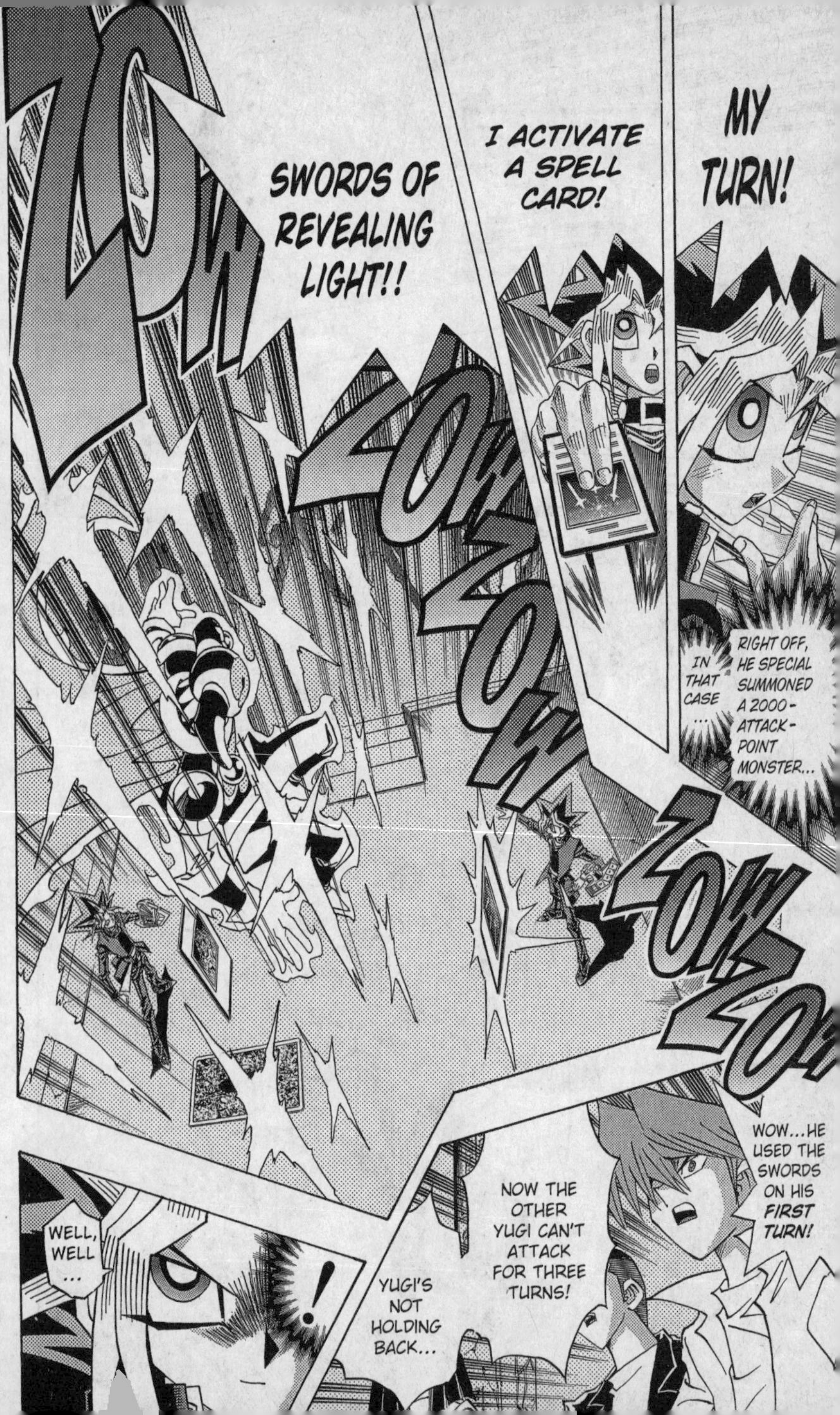
MY TURN!
RIGHT OFF, HE SPECIAL SUMMONED A 2000-ATTACK-POINT MONSTER...
IN THAT CASE...
I ACTIVATE A SPELL CARD!
SWORDS OF REVEALING LIGHT!!
ZOWN
ZOWN ZOWN
ZOWN ZOWN
WOW...HE USED THE SWORDS ON HIS FIRST TURN!
NOW THE OTHER YUGI CAN'T ATTACK FOR THREE TURNS!
YUGI'S NOT HOLDING BACK...
WELL, WELL...
!

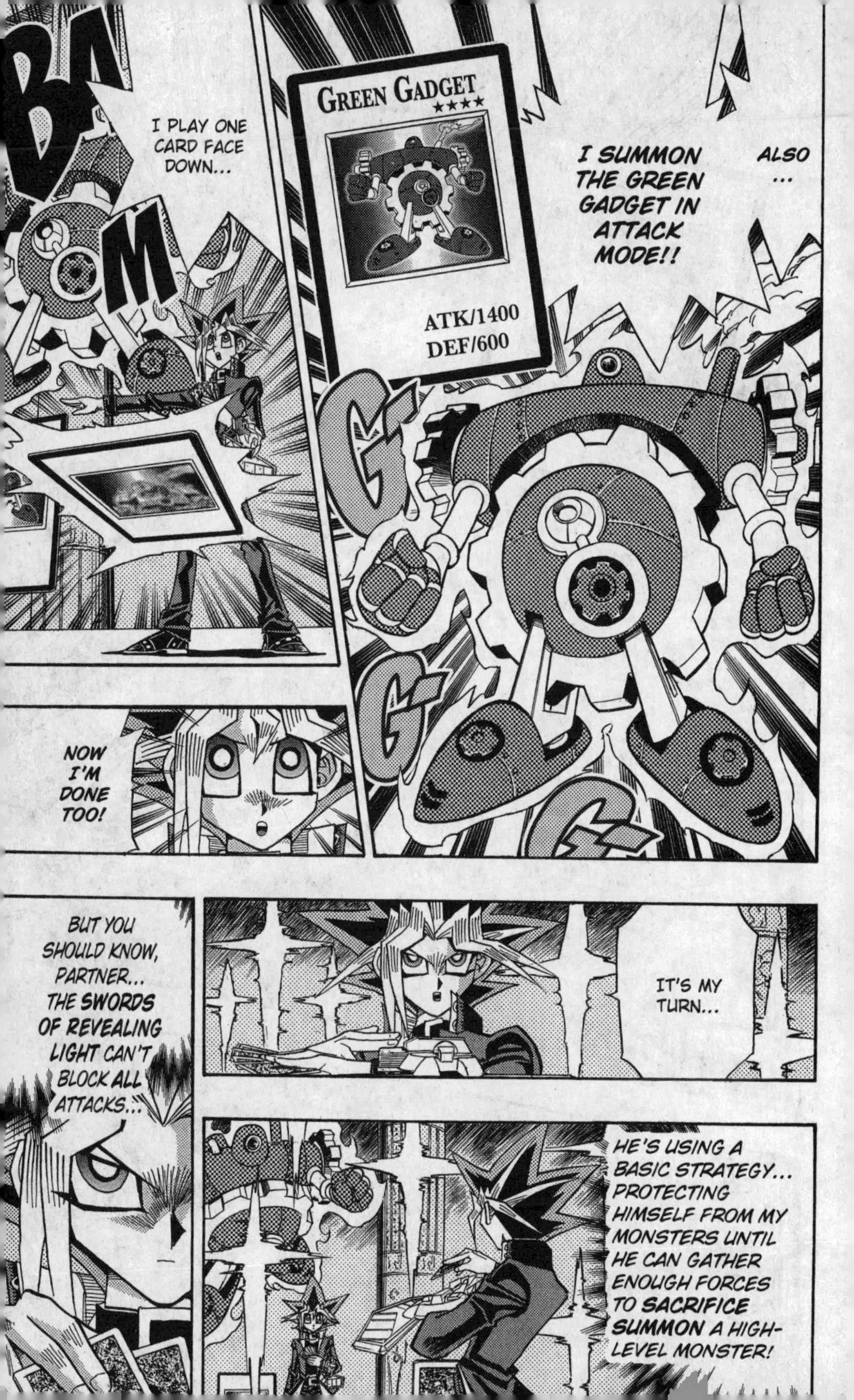
ALSO ...
I SUMMON THE GREEN GADGET IN ATTACK MODE!!
GREEN GADGET
ATK/1400
DEF/600
G
G
G
BAM
BOOM
I PLAY ONE CARD FACE DOWN...
NOW I'M DONE TOO!
IT'S MY TURN...
HE'S USING A BASIC STRATEGY... PROTECTING HIMSELF FROM MY MONSTERS UNTIL HE CAN GATHER ENOUGH FORCES TO SACRIFICE SUMMON A HIGH-LEVEL MONSTER!
BUT YOU SHOULD KNOW, PARTNER... THE SWORDS OF REVEALING LIGHT CAN'T BLOCK ALL ATTACKS...

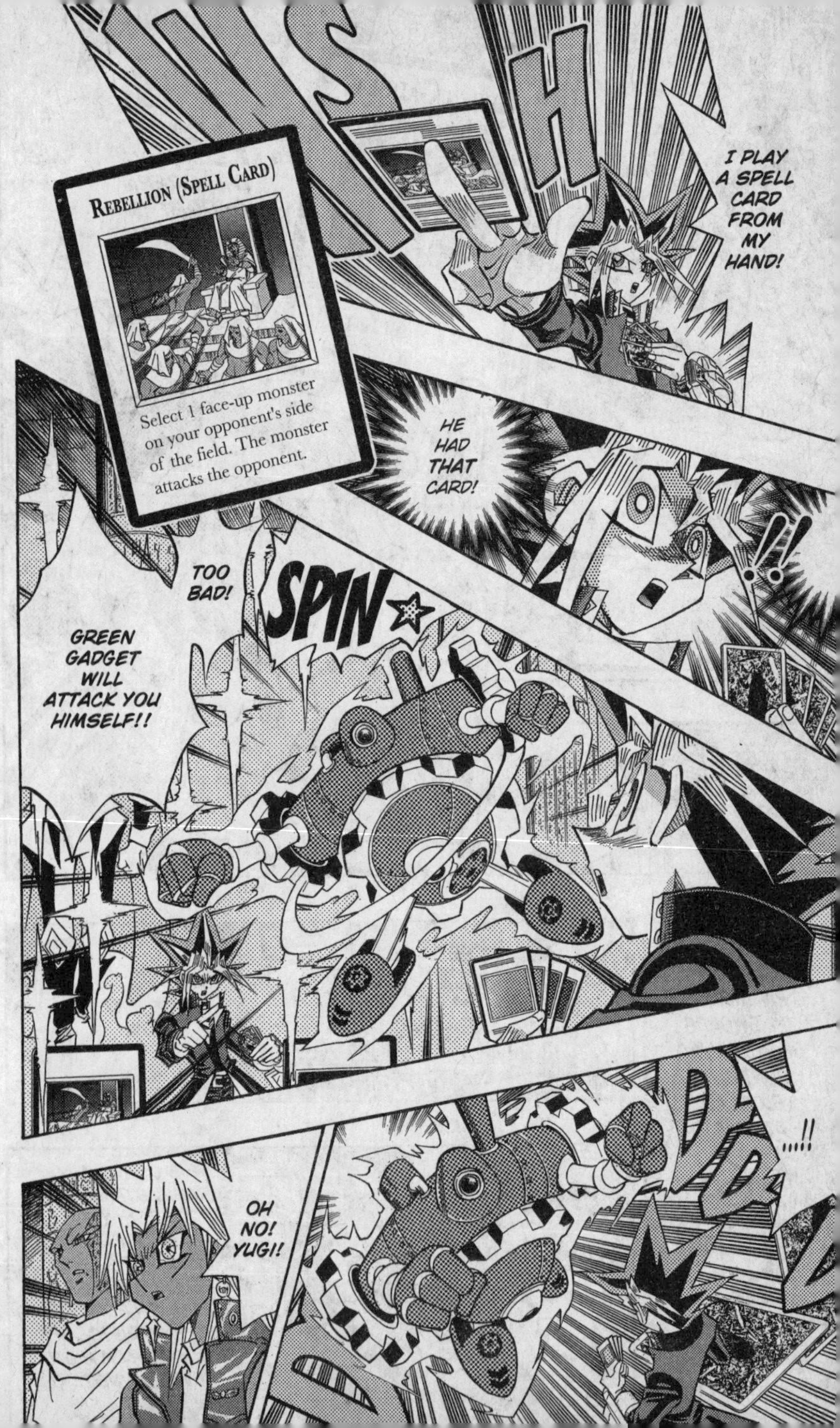
I PLAY A SPELL CARD FROM MY HAND!
REBELLION (SPELL CARD)
Select 1 face-up monster on your opponent's side of the field. The monster attacks the opponent.
HE HAD THAT CARD!
!!
TOO BAD!
GREEN GADGET WILL ATTACK YOU HIMSELF!!
SPIN
...!!
OH NO! YUGI!

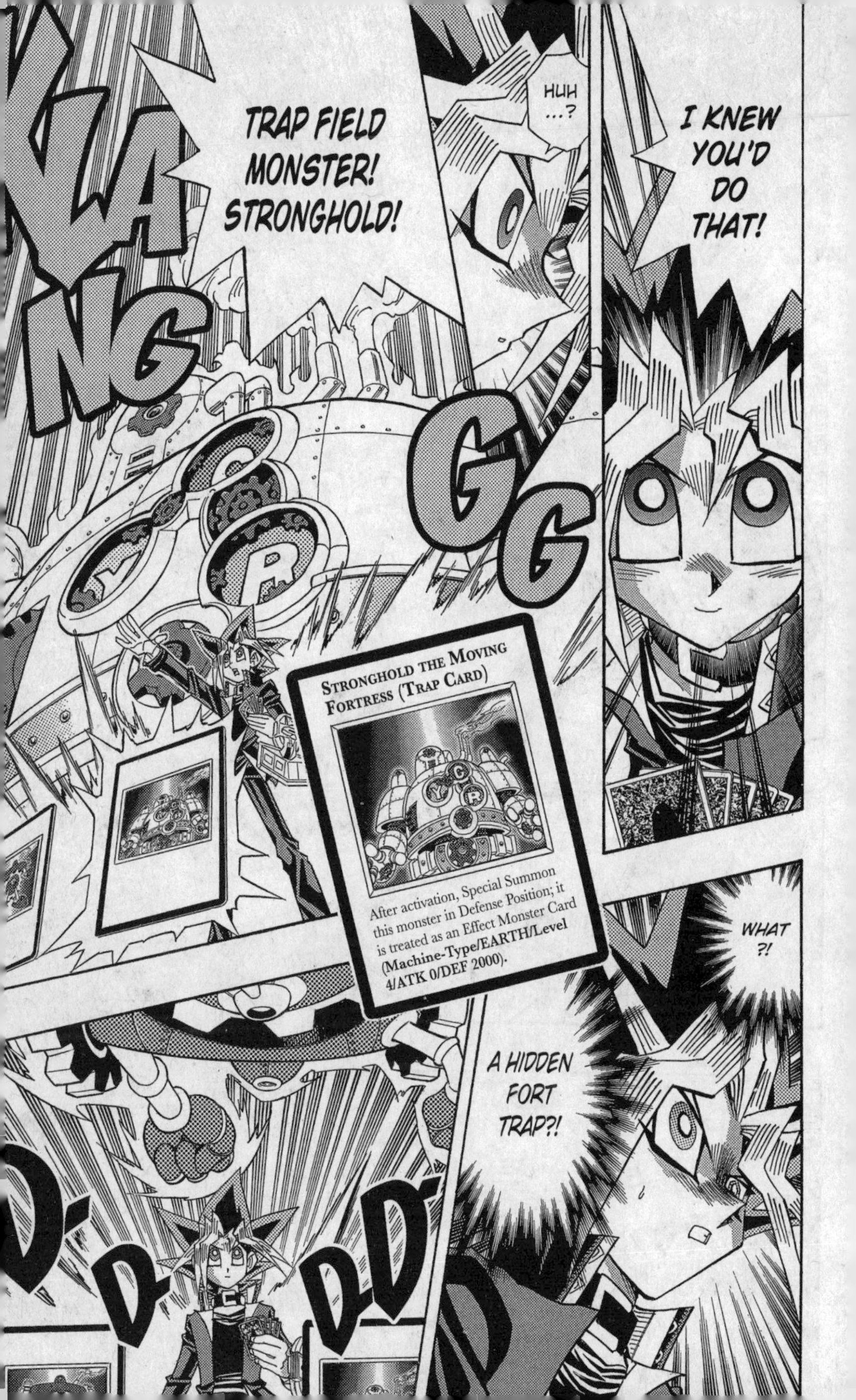
I KNEW YOU'D DO THAT!
HUH ...?
TRAP FIELD MONSTER! STRONGHOLD!
NG
GG
STRONGHOLD THE MOVING FORTRESS (TRAP CARD)
After activation, Special Summon this monster in Defense Position; it is treated as an Effect Monster Card (Machine-Type/EARTH/Level 4/ATK 0/DEF 2000).
WHAT ?!
A HIDDEN FORT TRAP?!

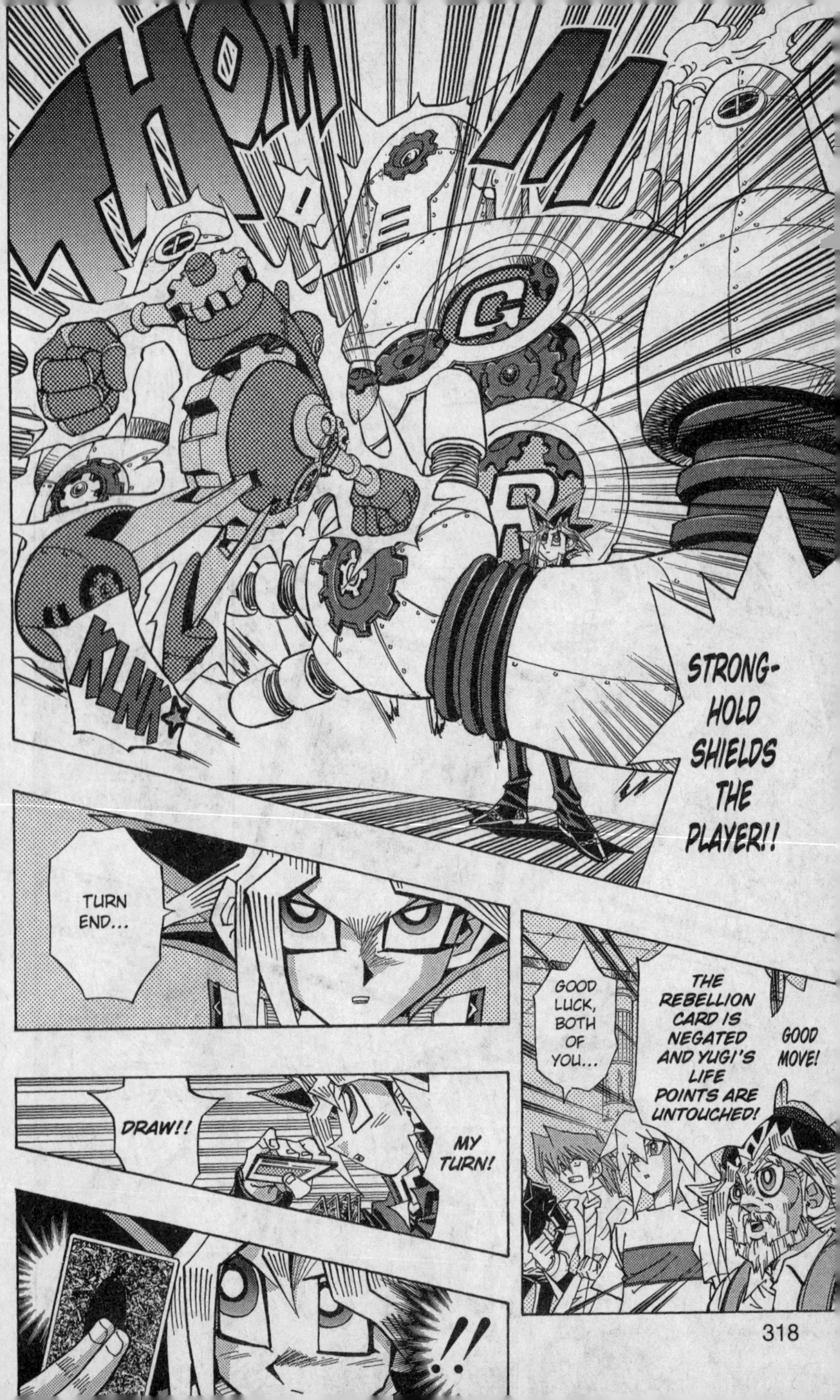
WHOMM
!
KLNK
STRONG-HOLD SHIELDS THE PLAYER!!
TURN END...
GOOD MOVE!
THE REBELLION CARD IS NEGATED AND YUGI'S LIFE POINTS ARE UNTOUCHED!
GOOD LUCK, BOTH OF YOU...
MY TURN!
DRAW!!
!!

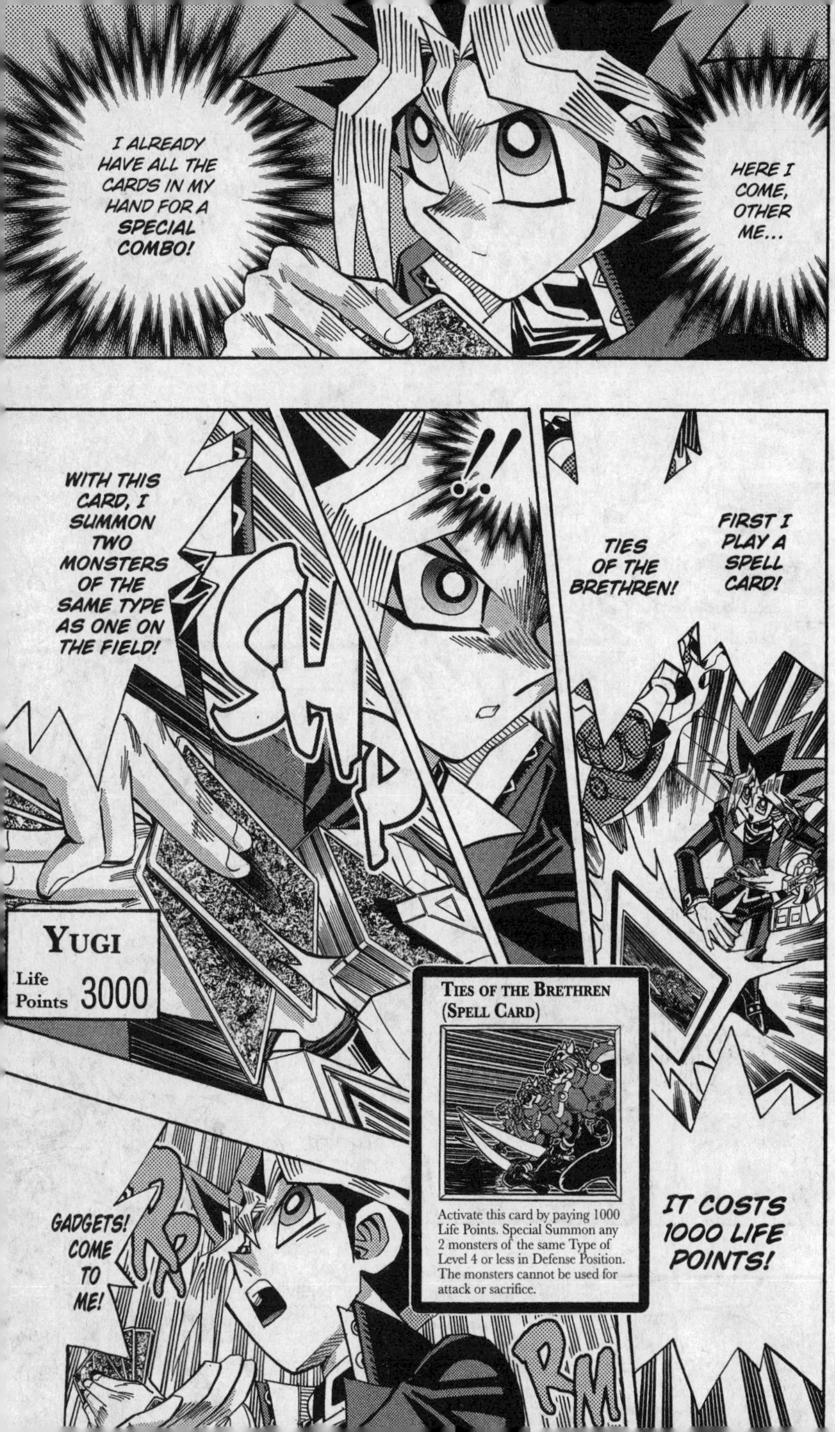
HERE I COME, OTHER ME...
I ALREADY HAVE ALL THE CARDS IN MY HAND FOR A SPECIAL COMBO!
FIRST I PLAY A SPELL CARD!
TIES OF THE BRETHREN!
!!
WITH THIS CARD, I SUMMON TWO MONSTERS OF THE SAME TYPE AS ONE ON THE FIELD!
SHP
YUGI
Life Points 3000
TIES OF THE BRETHREN (SPELL CARD)
Activate this card by paying 1000 Life Points. Special Summon any 2 monsters of the same Type of Level 4 or less in Defense Position. The monsters cannot be used for attack or sacrifice.
IT COSTS 1000 LIFE POINTS!
GADGETS! COME TO ME!
RM

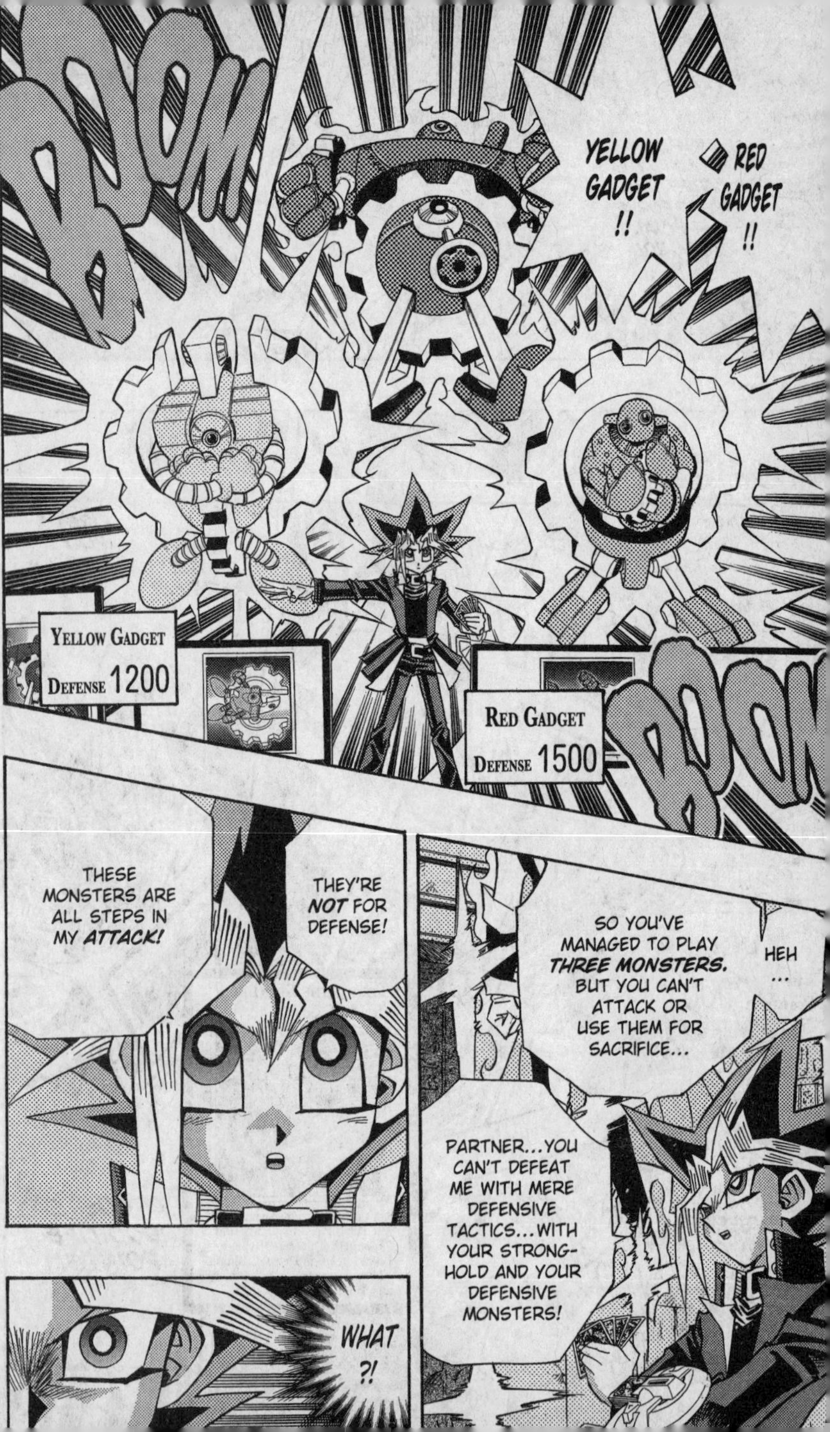
RED GADGET !!
YELLOW GADGET !!
BOOM
YELLOW GADGET DEFENSE 1200
BOOM
RED GADGET DEFENSE 1500
HEH ...
SO YOU'VE MANAGED TO PLAY *THREE MONSTERS.* BUT YOU CAN'T ATTACK OR USE THEM FOR SACRIFICE...
PARTNER...YOU CAN'T DEFEAT ME WITH MERE DEFENSIVE TACTICS...WITH YOUR STRONG-HOLD AND YOUR DEFENSIVE MONSTERS!
THEY'RE *NOT* FOR DEFENSE!
THESE MONSTERS ARE ALL STEPS IN MY *ATTACK!*
WHAT ?!

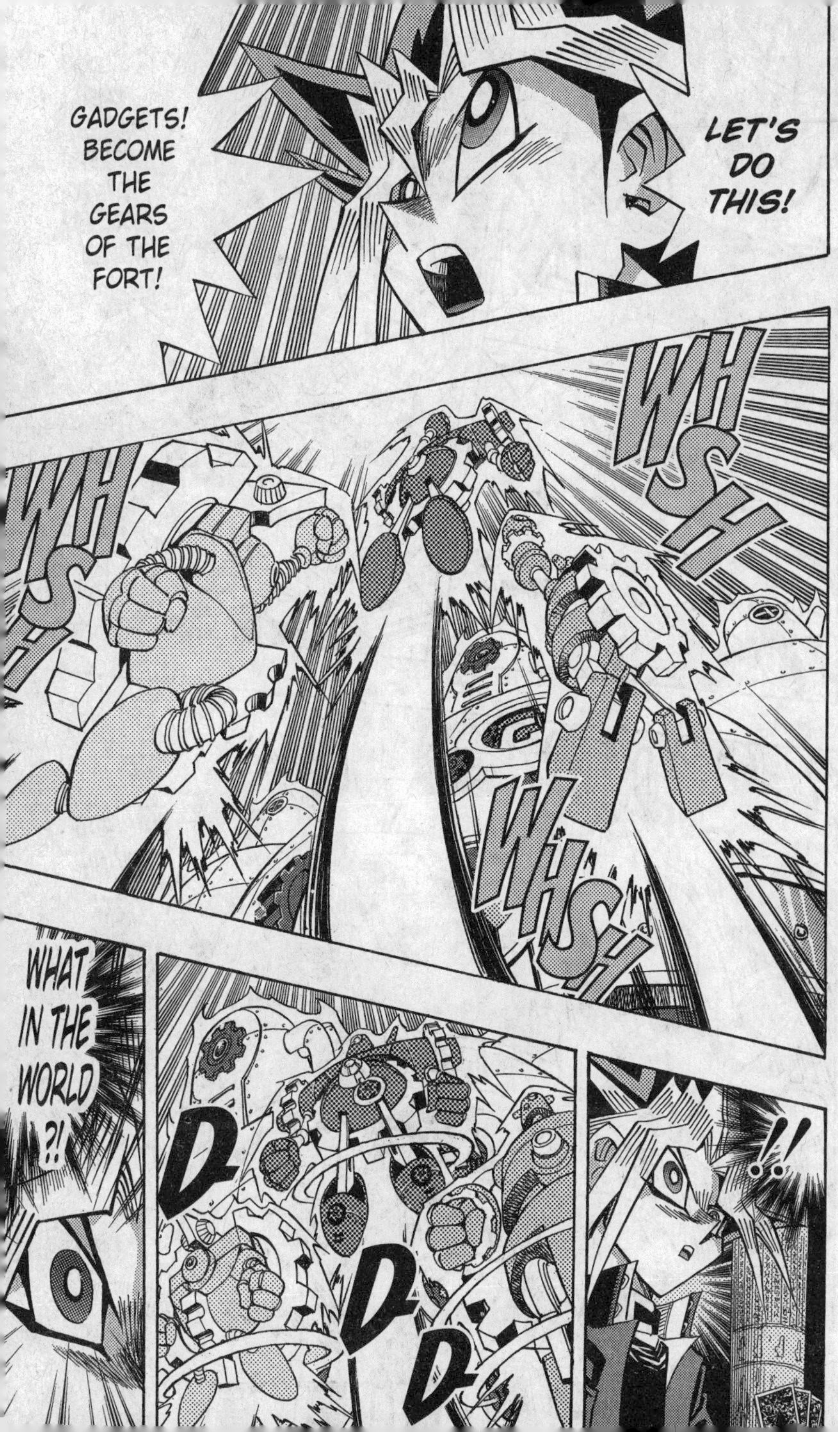

LET'S DO THIS!
GADGETS! BECOME THE GEARS OF THE FORT!
WHSH
WHSH
WHSH
!!
D
D
D
D
WHAT IN THE WORLD ?!

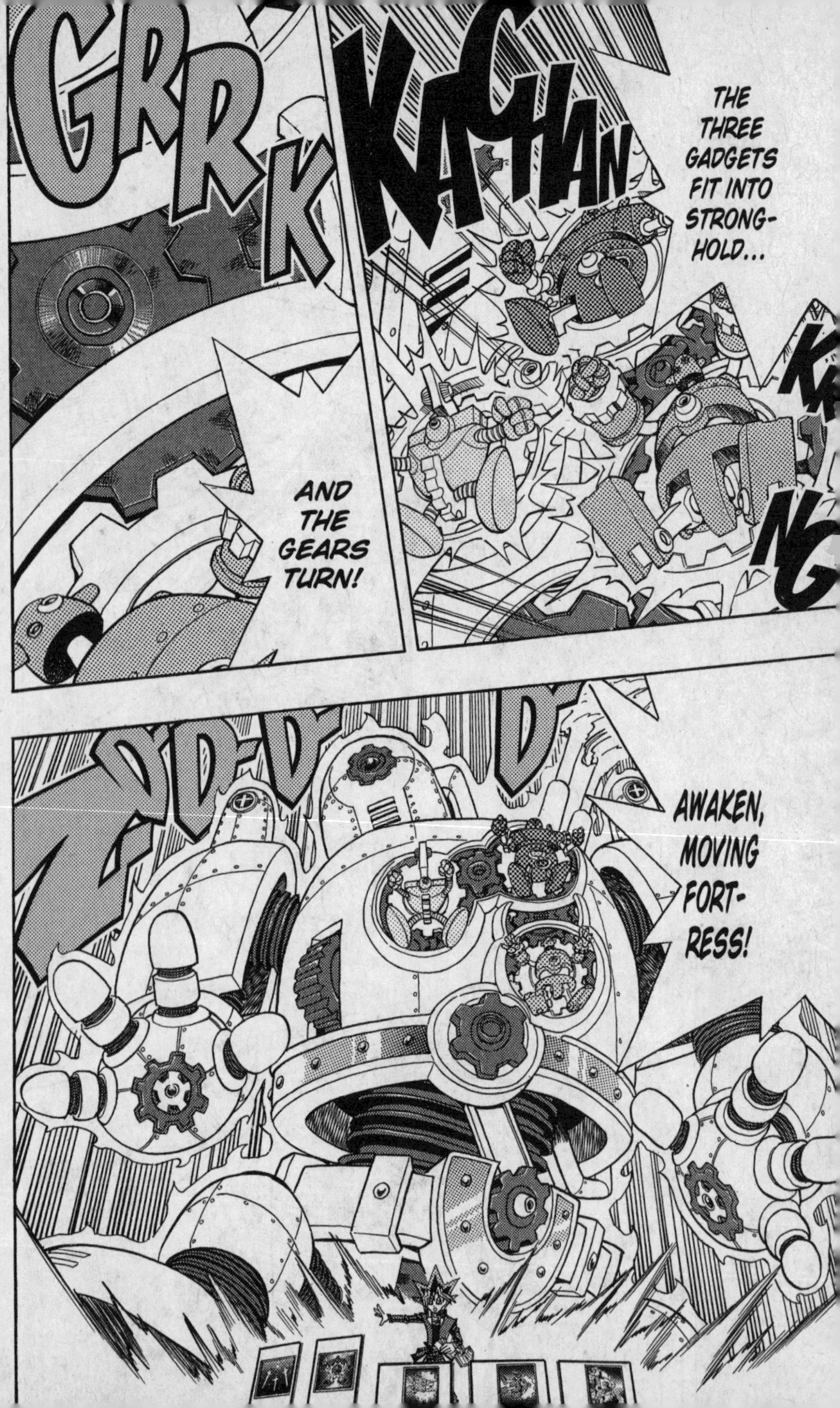
KACHAN
THE THREE GADGETS FIT INTO STRONG-HOLD...
GRRK
AND THE GEARS TURN!
AWAKEN, MOVING FORT-RESS!

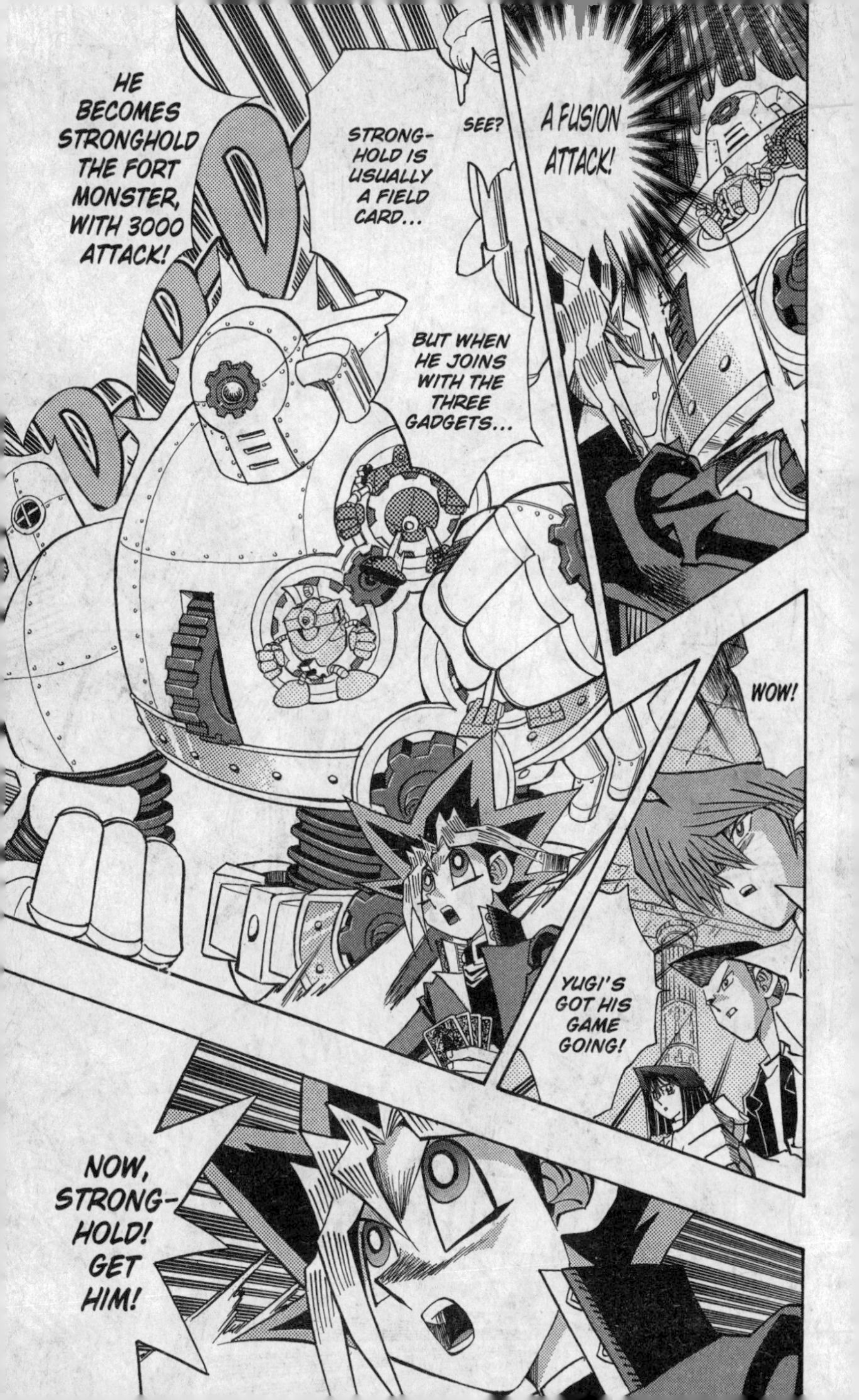
A FUSION ATTACK!
SEE?
STRONG-HOLD IS USUALLY A FIELD CARD...
BUT WHEN HE JOINS WITH THE THREE GADGETS...
HE BECOMES STRONGHOLD THE FORT MONSTER, WITH 3000 ATTACK!
WOW!
YUGI'S GOT HIS GAME GOING!
NOW, STRONG-HOLD! GET HIM!

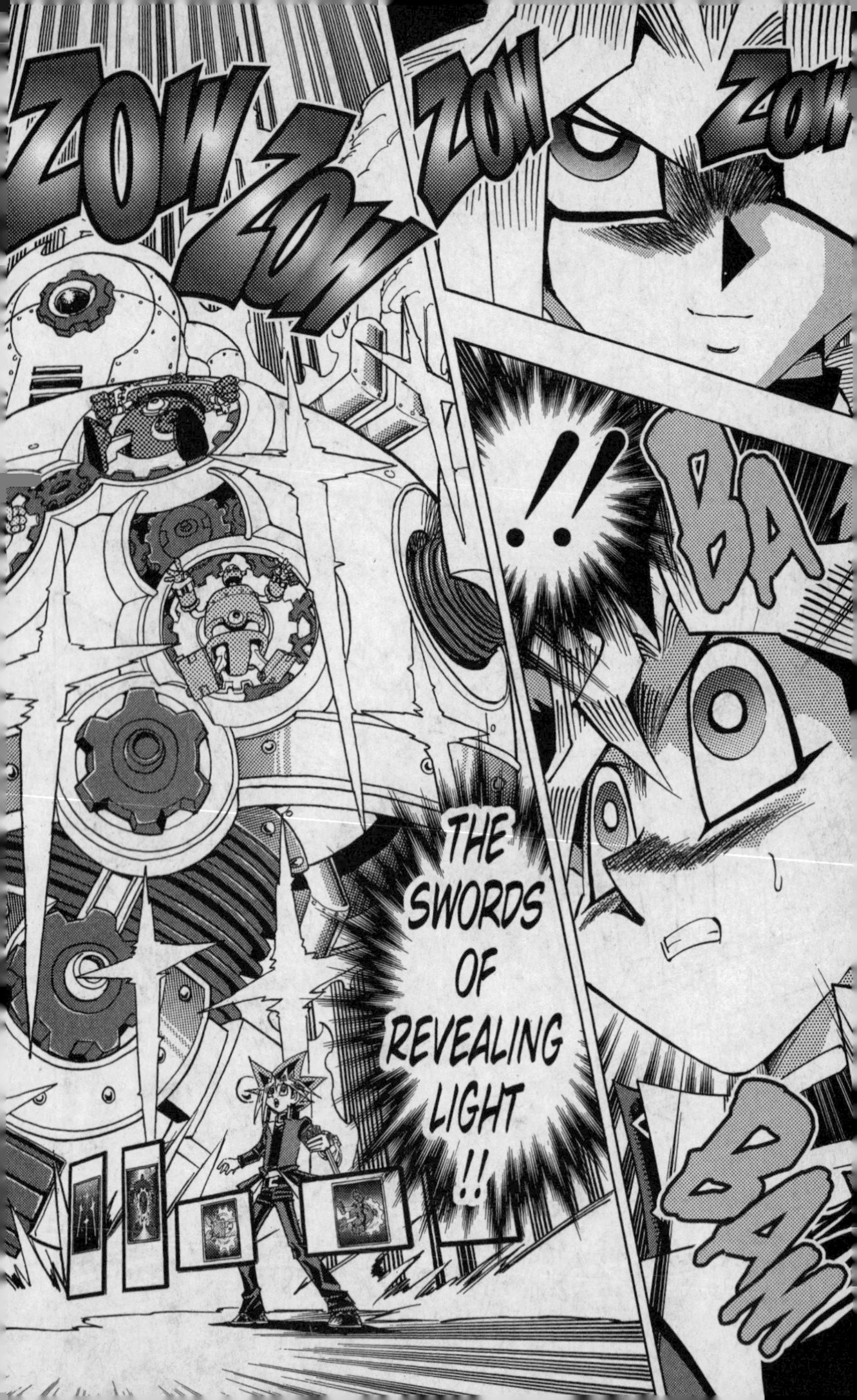
ZOW
!!
ZOW
ZOW
ZOW
THE SWORDS OF REVEALING LIGHT!!

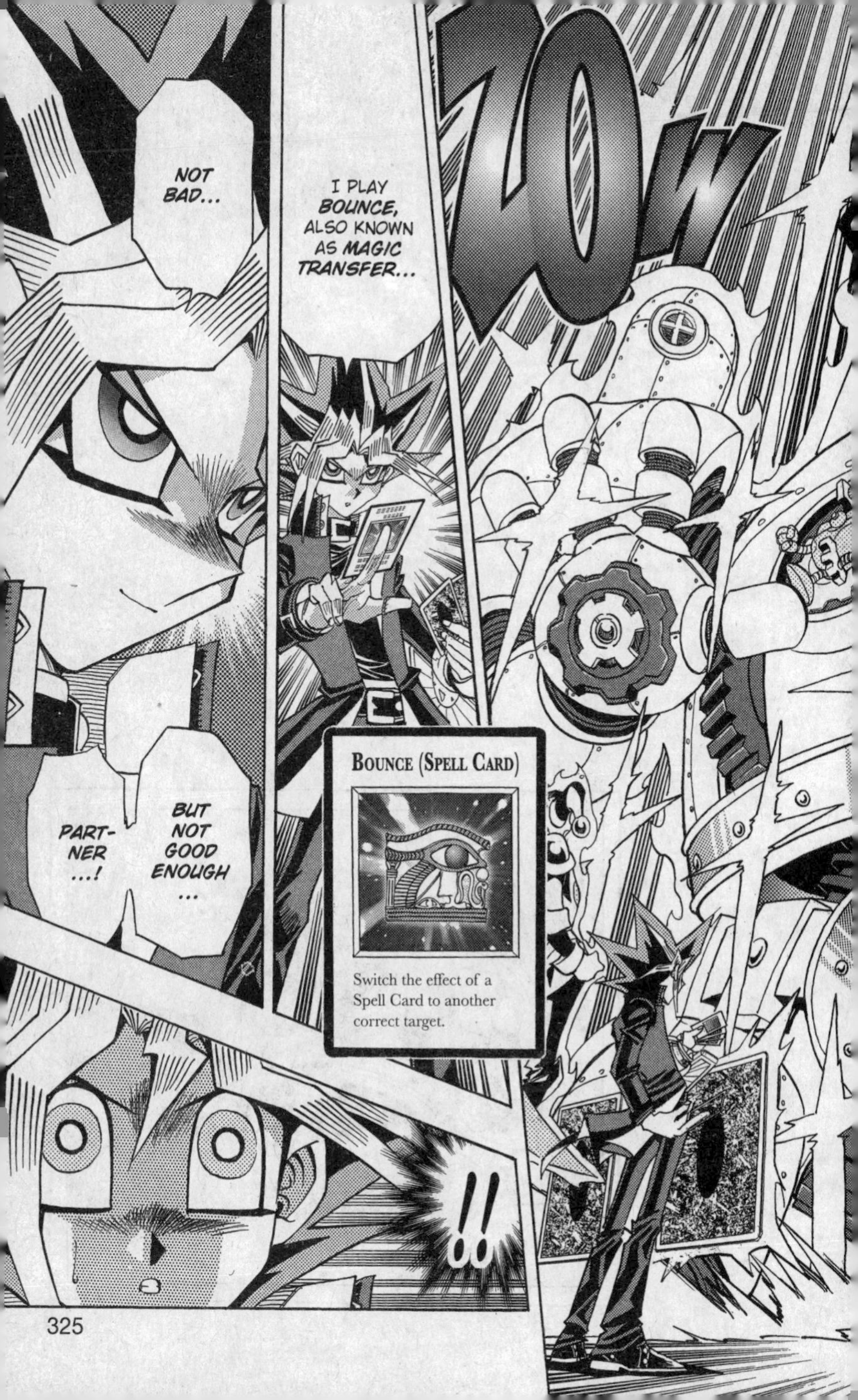
ZOW
I PLAY BOUNCE, ALSO KNOWN AS MAGIC TRANSFER...
BOUNCE (SPELL CARD)
Switch the effect of a Spell Card to another correct target.
NOT BAD...
BUT NOT GOOD ENOUGH...
PARTNER...!
!!

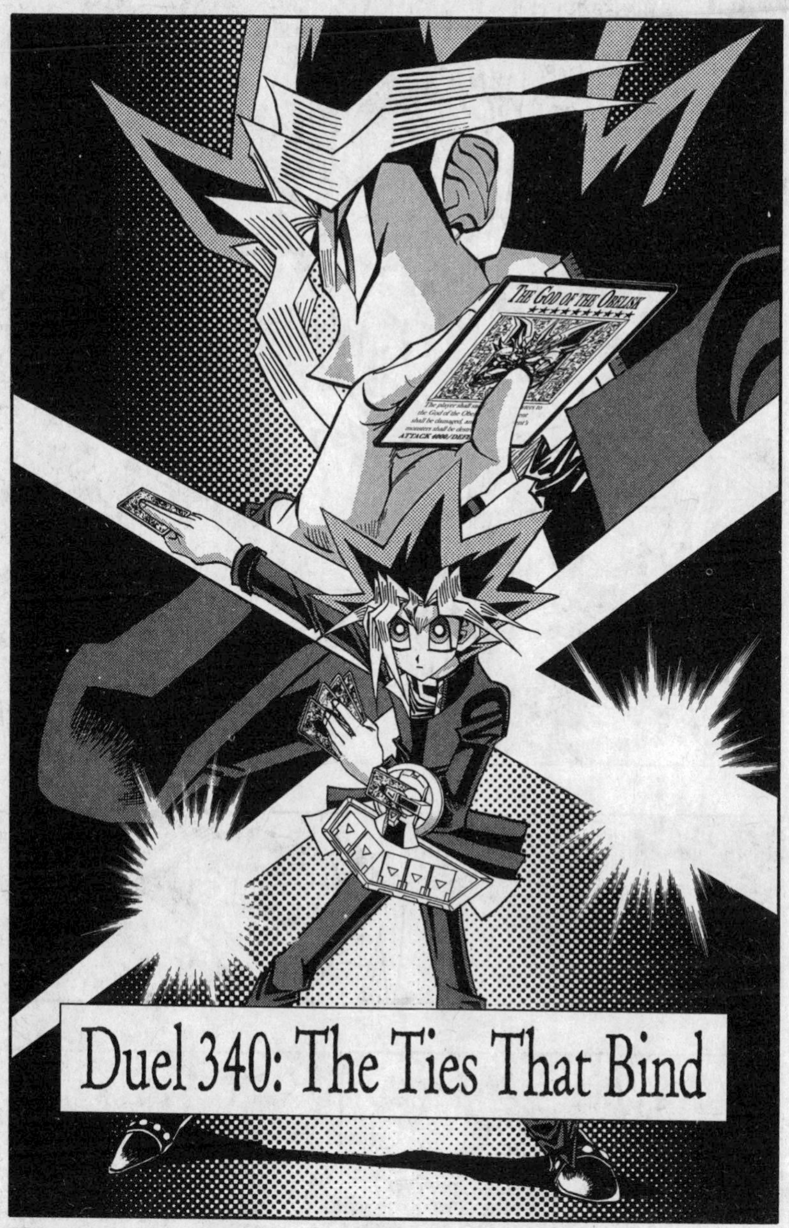
THE GOD OF THE OBELISK
Duel 340: The Ties That Bind

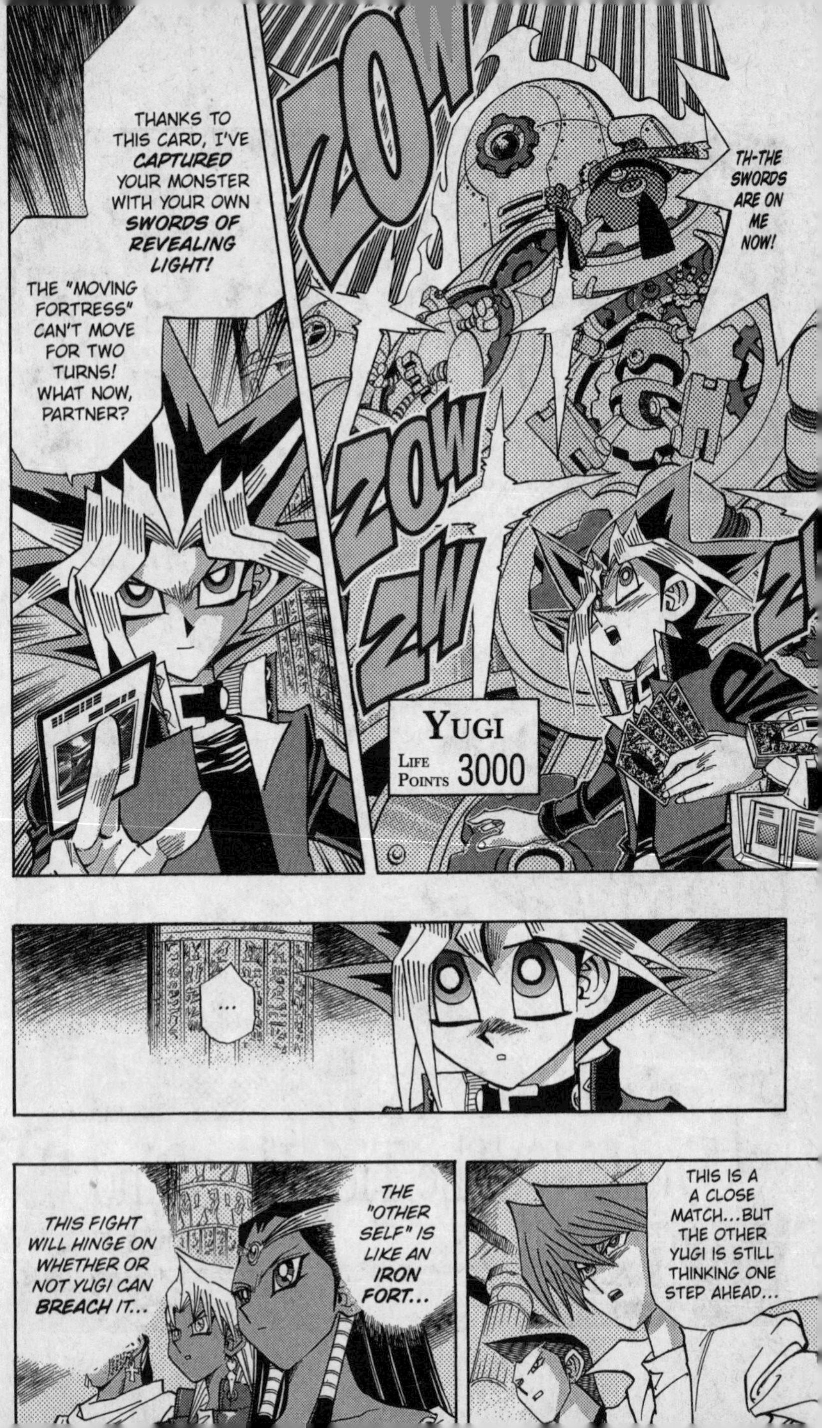

TH-THE SWORDS ARE ON ME NOW!
ZOW
ZW
YUGI
LIFE POINTS 3000
THANKS TO THIS CARD, I'VE **CAPTURED** YOUR MONSTER WITH YOUR OWN **SWORDS OF REVEALING LIGHT!**
THE "MOVING FORTRESS" CAN'T MOVE FOR TWO TURNS! WHAT NOW, PARTNER?
...
THIS IS A A CLOSE MATCH...BUT THE OTHER YUGI IS STILL THINKING ONE STEP AHEAD...
THE "OTHER SELF" IS LIKE AN **IRON FORT...**
THIS FIGHT WILL HINGE ON WHETHER OR NOT YUGI CAN **BREACH** IT...

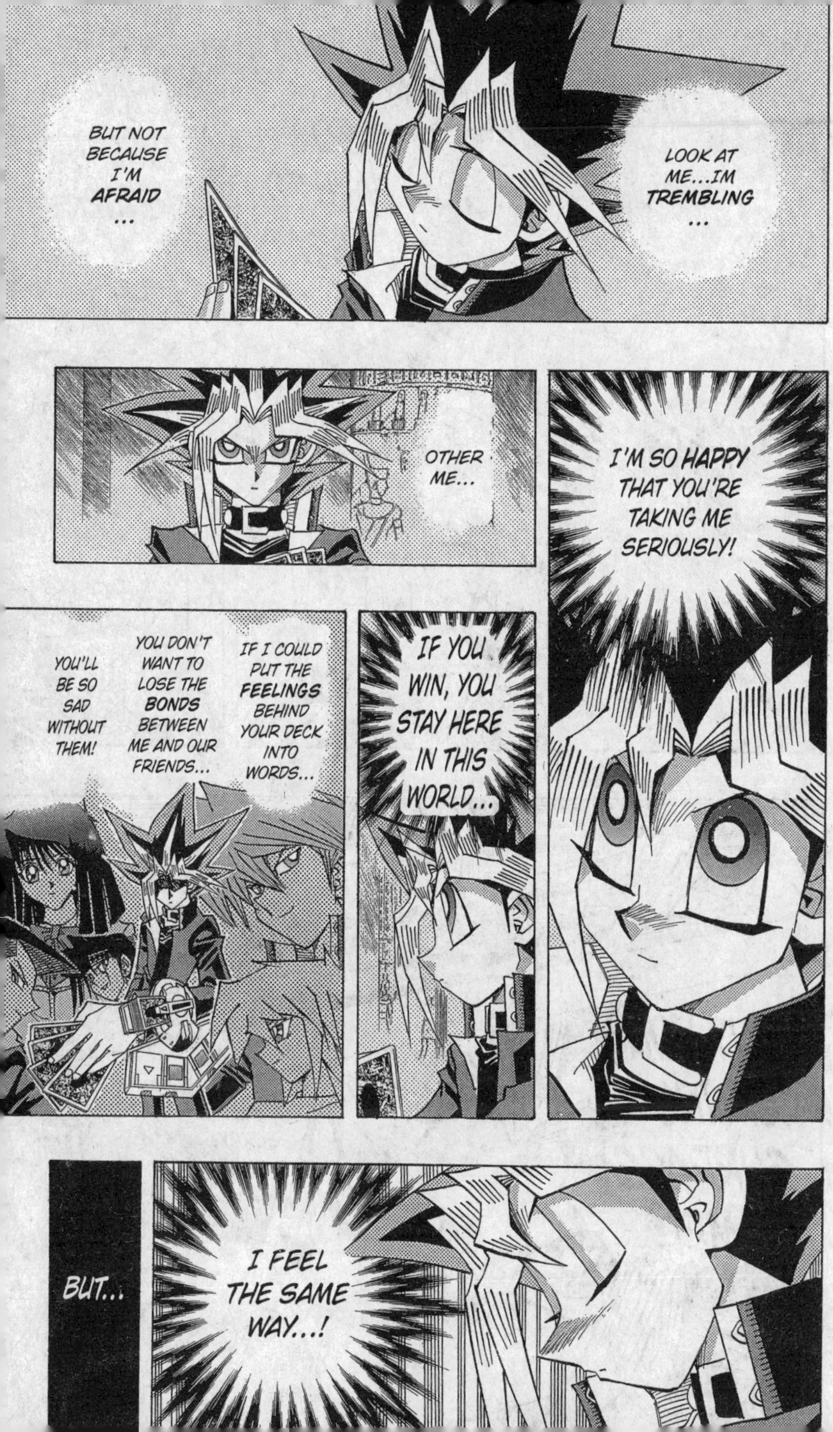
LOOK AT ME...IM TREMBLING...
BUT NOT BECAUSE I'M AFRAID...
I'M SO HAPPY THAT YOU'RE TAKING ME SERIOUSLY!
OTHER ME...
IF YOU WIN, YOU STAY HERE IN THIS WORLD...
IF I COULD PUT THE FEELINGS BEHIND YOUR DECK INTO WORDS...
YOU DON'T WANT TO LOSE THE BONDS BETWEEN ME AND OUR FRIENDS...
YOU'LL BE SO SAD WITHOUT THEM!
I FEEL THE SAME WAY...!
BUT...

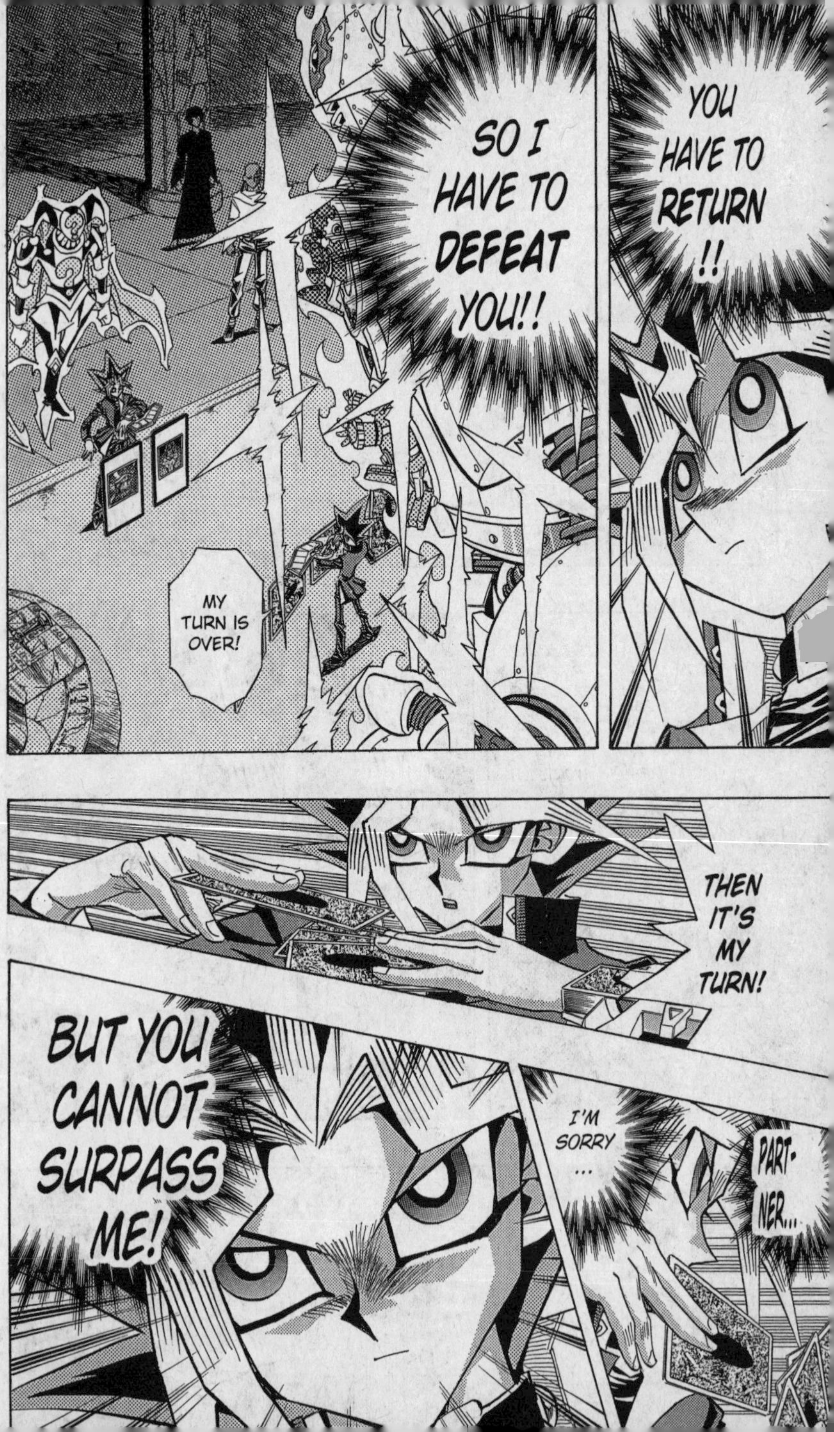
YOU HAVE TO RETURN!!
SO I HAVE TO DEFEAT YOU!!
MY TURN IS OVER!
THEN IT'S MY TURN!
I'M SORRY...
PART-NER...
BUT YOU CANNOT SURPASS ME!

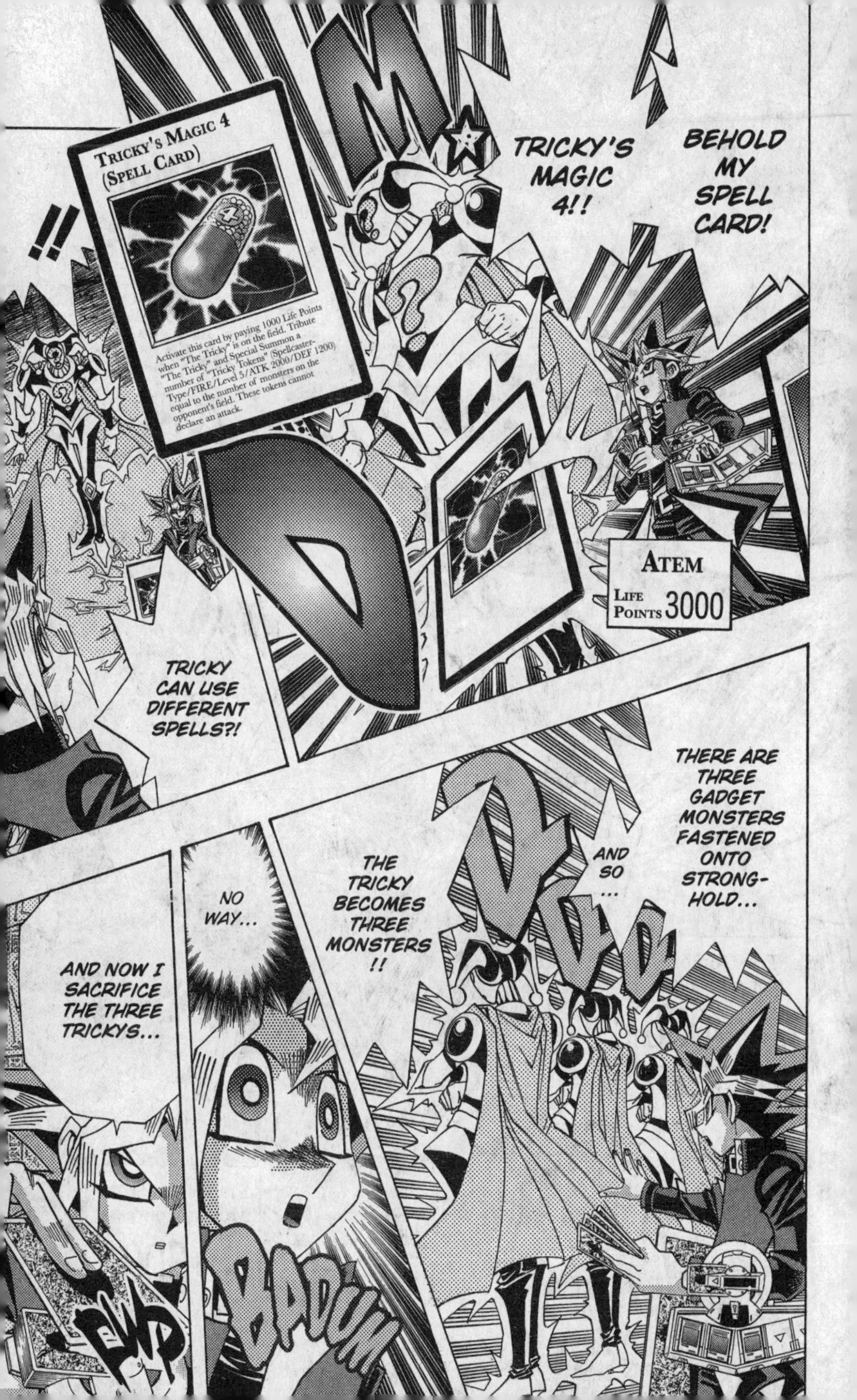
BEHOLD MY SPELL CARD!
TRICKY'S MAGIC 4!!
Tricky's Magic 4
(Spell Card)
Activate this card by paying 1000 Life Points when "The Tricky" is on the field. Tribute "The Tricky" and Special Summon a number of "Tricky Tokens" (Spellcaster-Type/FIRE/Level 5/ATK 2000/DEF 1200) equal to the number of monsters on the opponent's field. These tokens cannot declare an attack.
!!
Atem
Life Points 3000
TRICKY CAN USE DIFFERENT SPELLS?!
THERE ARE THREE GADGET MONSTERS FASTENED ONTO STRONG-HOLD...
AND SO...
THE TRICKY BECOMES THREE MONSTERS!!
NO WAY...
AND NOW I SACRIFICE THE THREE TRICKYS...

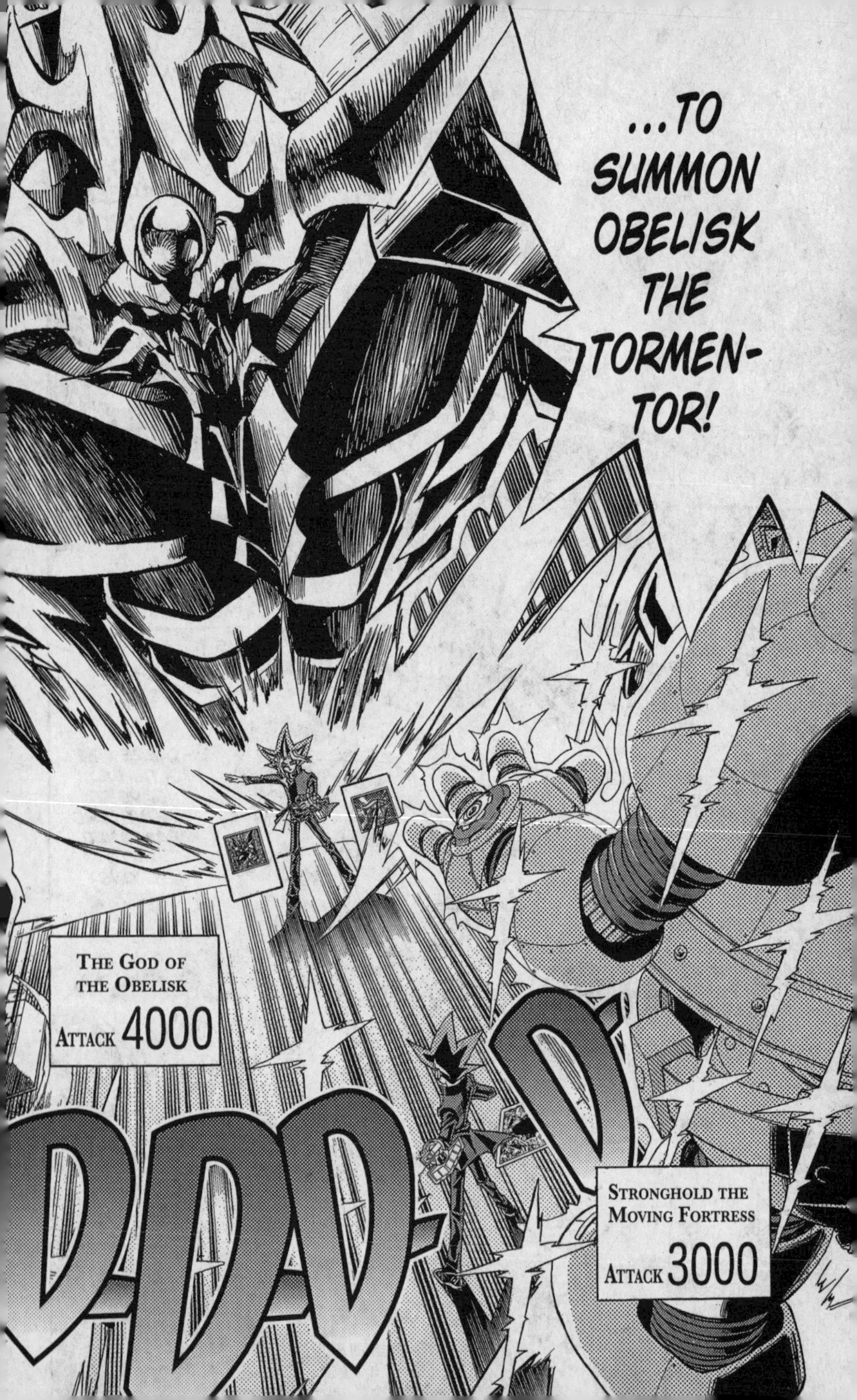
...TO SUMMON OBELISK THE TORMEN-TOR!
THE GOD OF THE OBELISK ATTACK 4000
STRONGHOLD THE MOVING FORTRESS ATTACK 3000

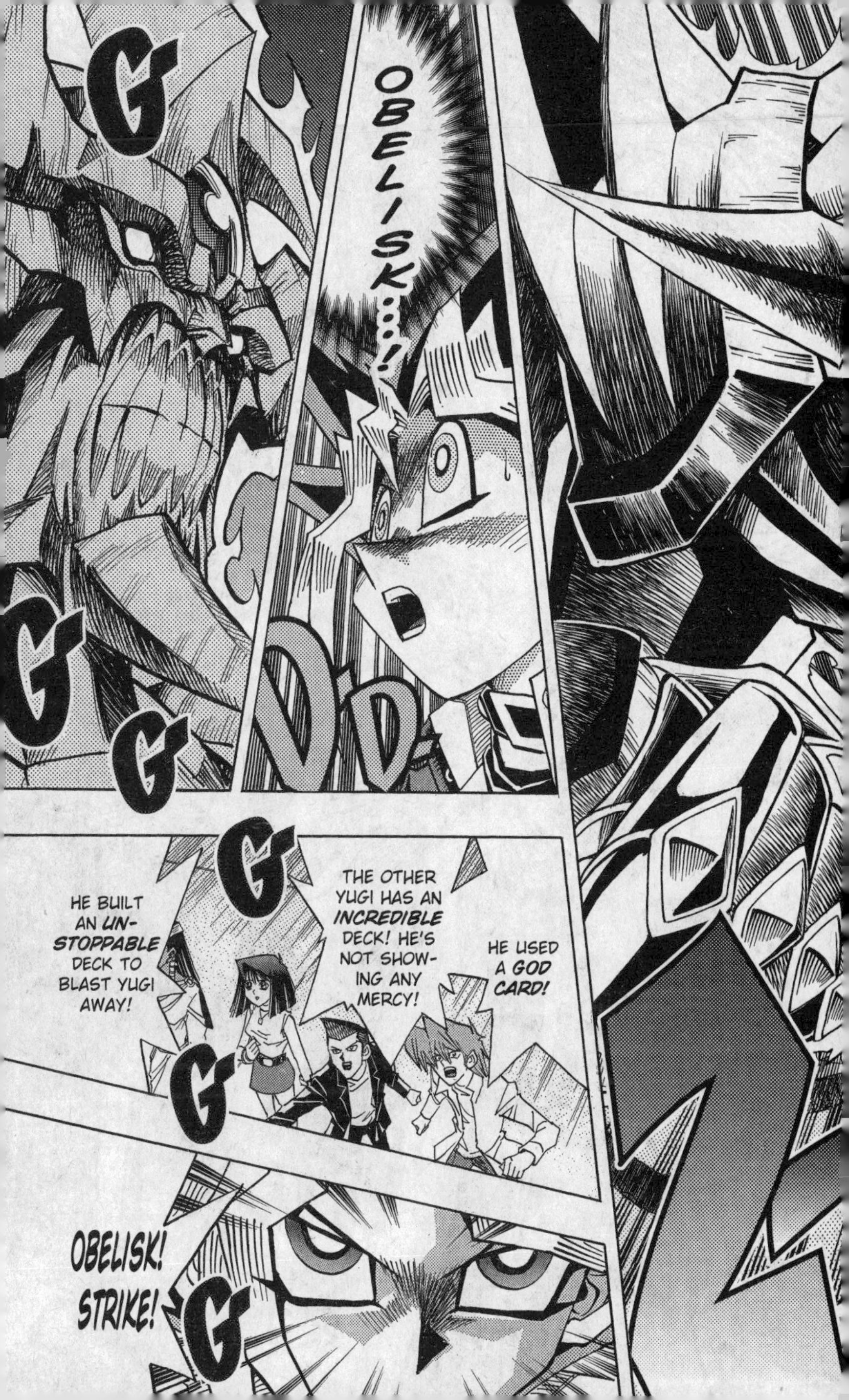
OBELISK...!
DD
GGG
G
HE USED A GOD CARD!
THE OTHER YUGI HAS AN INCREDIBLE DECK! HE'S NOT SHOWING ANY MERCY!
HE BUILT AN UN-STOPPABLE DECK TO BLAST YUGI AWAY!
G
OBELISK! STRIKE!
G

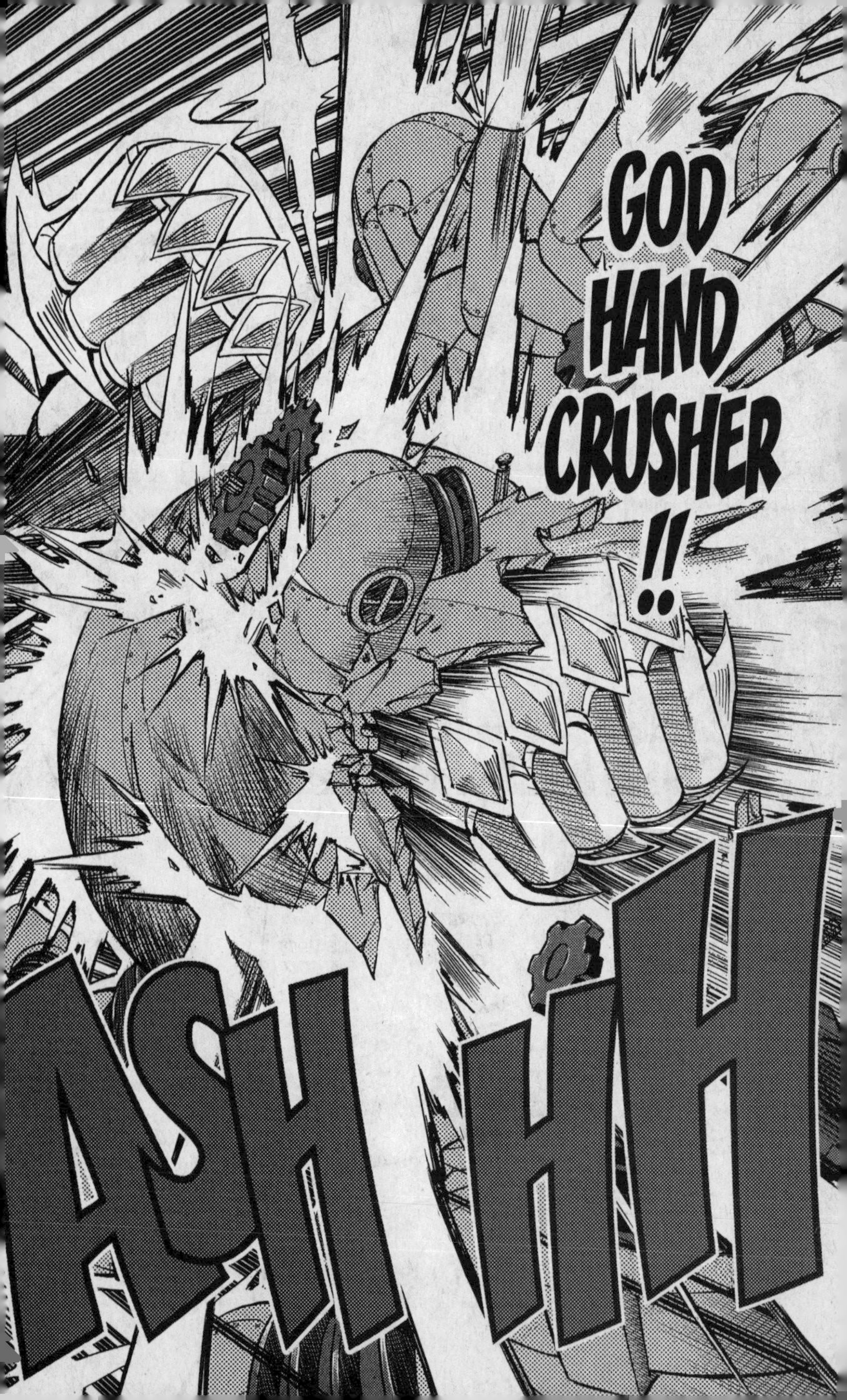
GOD HAND CRUSHER !!
ASHHH

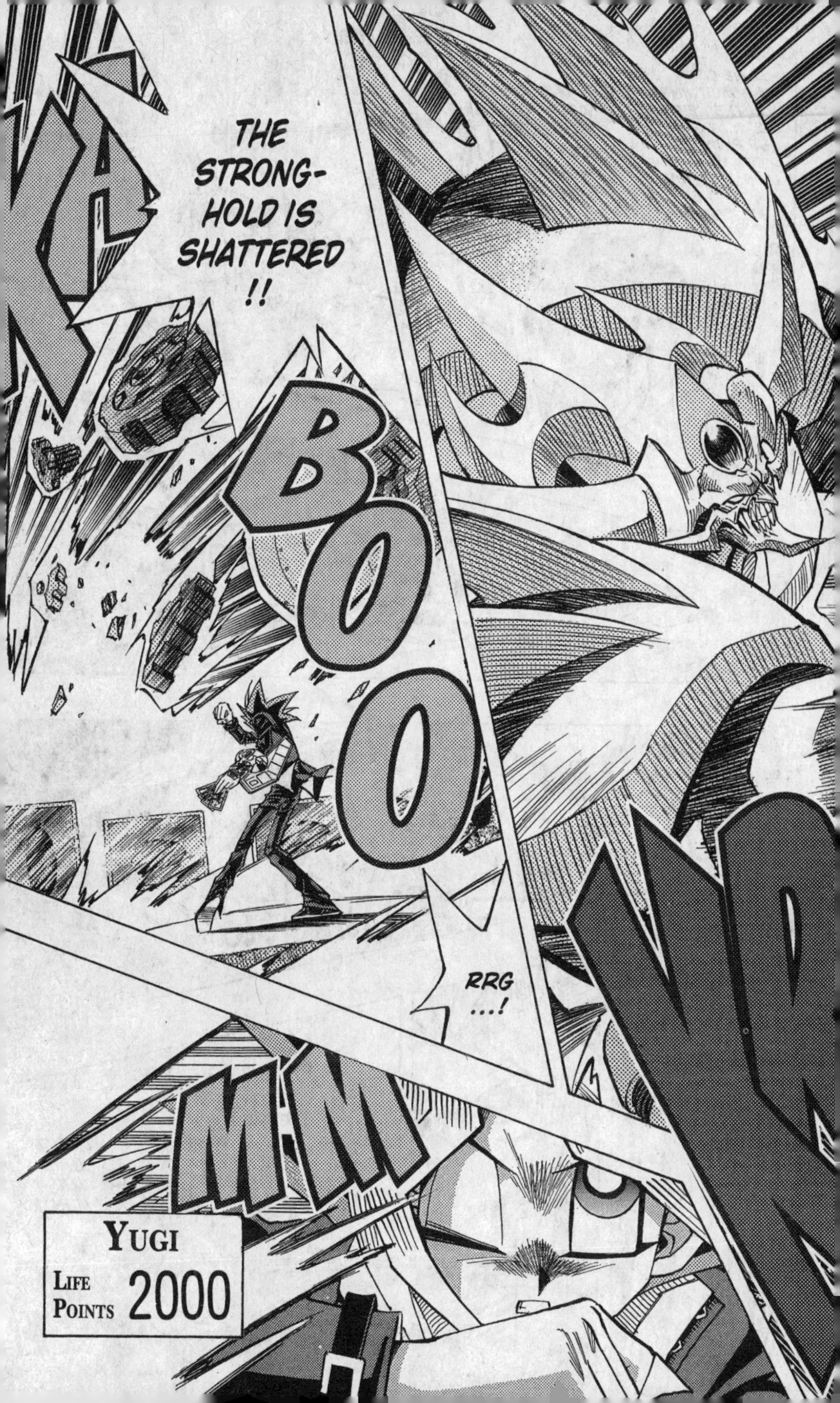
THE STRONG-HOLD IS SHATTERED !!
BOOO
RRG ...!
YUGI
LIFE POINTS 2000

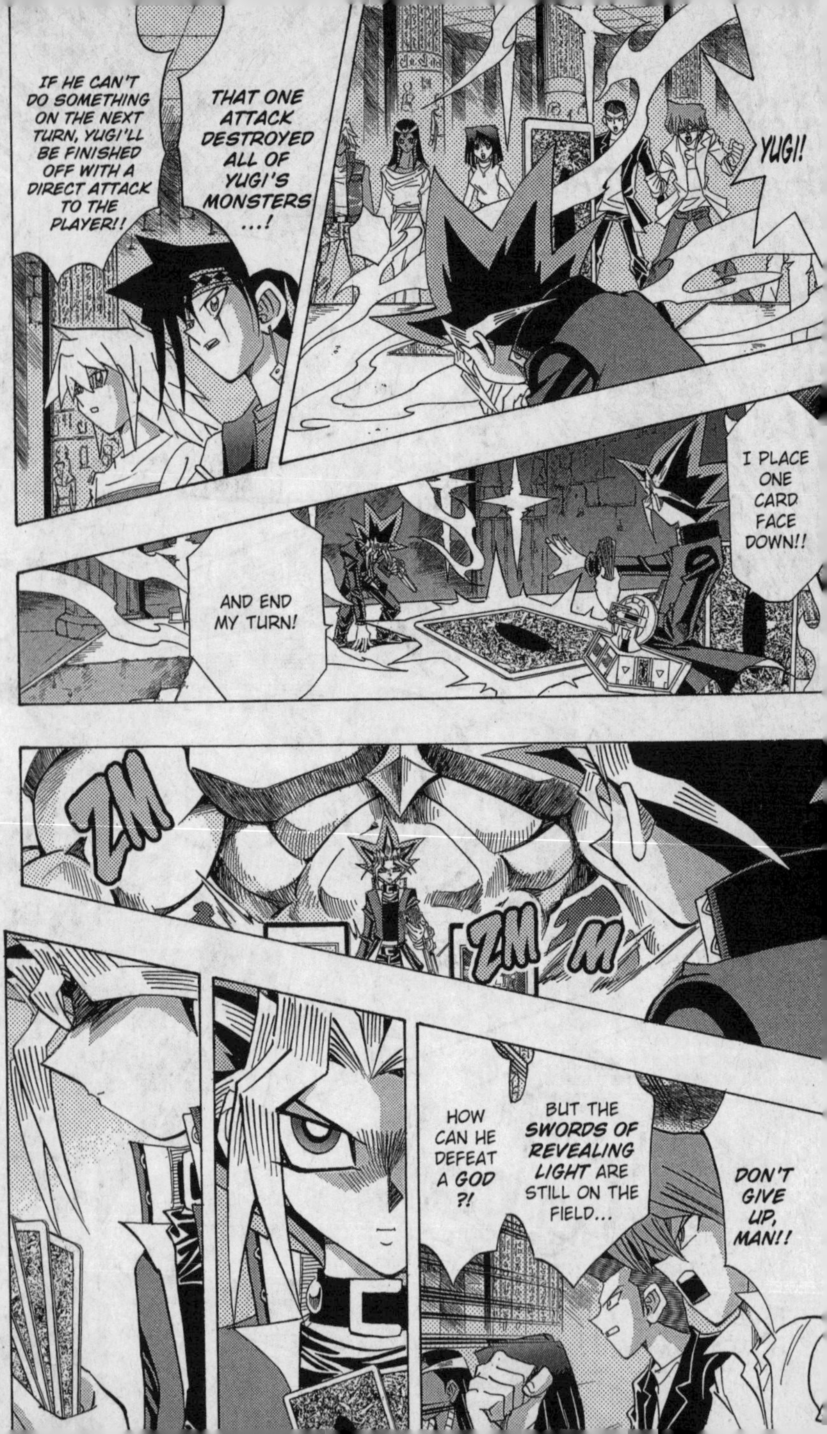
YUGI!!
THAT ONE ATTACK DESTROYED ALL OF YUGI'S MONSTERS ...!
IF HE CAN'T DO SOMETHING ON THE NEXT TURN, YUGI'LL BE FINISHED OFF WITH A DIRECT ATTACK TO THE PLAYER!!
I PLACE ONE CARD FACE DOWN!!
AND END MY TURN!
ZM
ZM M
DON'T GIVE UP, MAN!!
BUT THE SWORDS OF REVEALING LIGHT ARE STILL ON THE FIELD...
HOW CAN HE DEFEAT A GOD ?!

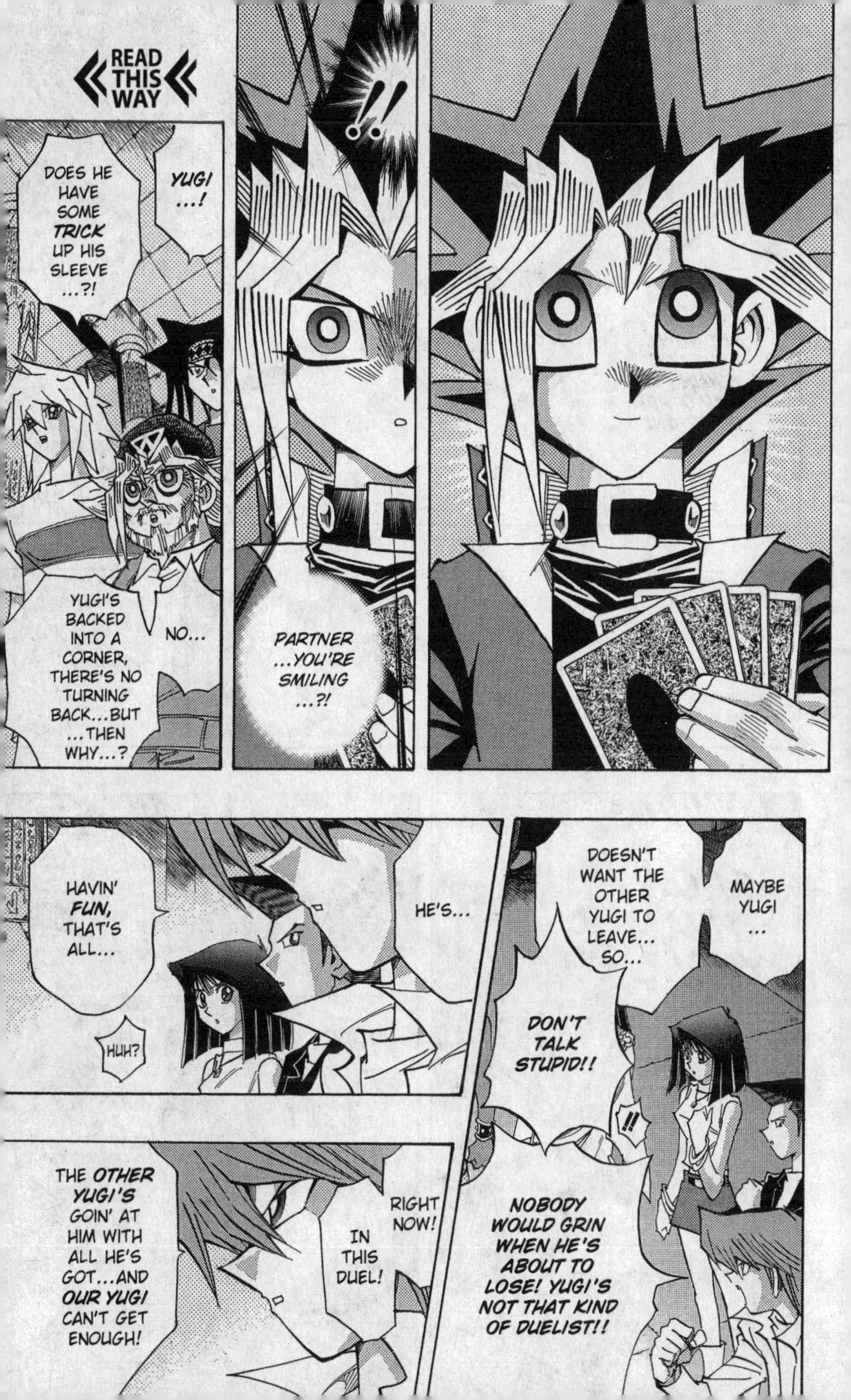
READ THIS WAY
!!
PARTNER ...YOU'RE SMILING ...?!
YUGI ...!
DOES HE HAVE SOME TRICK UP HIS SLEEVE ...?!
NO...
YUGI'S BACKED INTO A CORNER, THERE'S NO TURNING BACK...BUT ...THEN WHY...?
MAYBE YUGI ...
DOESN'T WANT THE OTHER YUGI TO LEAVE... SO...
DON'T TALK STUPID!!
!!
NOBODY WOULD GRIN WHEN HE'S ABOUT TO LOSE! YUGI'S NOT THAT KIND OF DUELIST!!
HE'S...
HAVIN' FUN, THAT'S ALL...
HUH?
RIGHT NOW!
IN THIS DUEL!
THE OTHER YUGI'S GOIN' AT HIM WITH ALL HE'S GOT...AND OUR YUGI CAN'T GET ENOUGH!

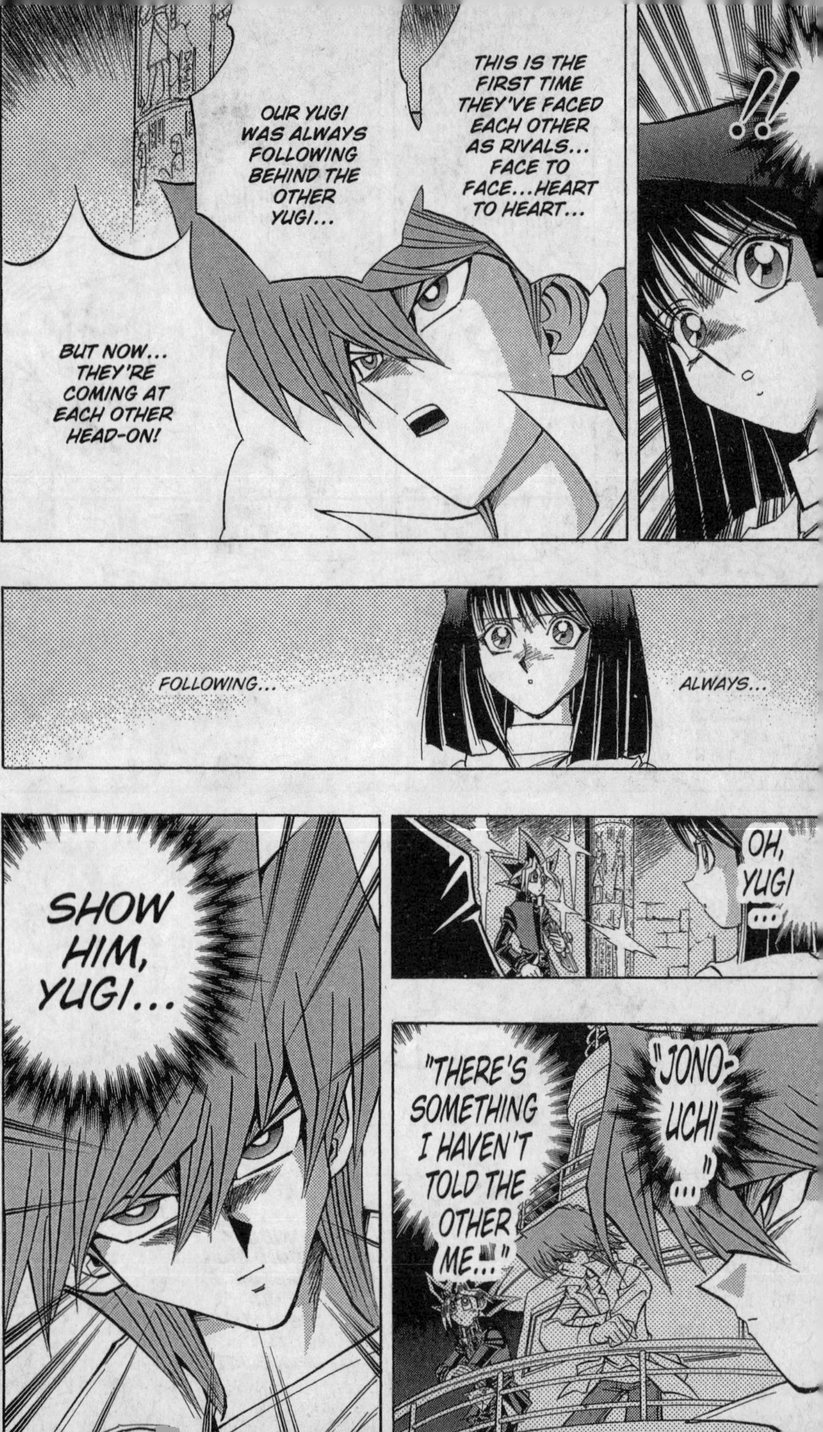
!!
THIS IS THE FIRST TIME THEY'VE FACED EACH OTHER AS RIVALS... FACE TO FACE...HEART TO HEART...
OUR YUGI WAS ALWAYS FOLLOWING BEHIND THE OTHER YUGI...
BUT NOW... THEY'RE COMING AT EACH OTHER HEAD-ON!
ALWAYS...
FOLLOWING...
OH, YUGI...
"JONO-UCHI..."
"THERE'S SOMETHING I HAVEN'T TOLD THE OTHER ME...!"
SHOW HIM, YUGI...

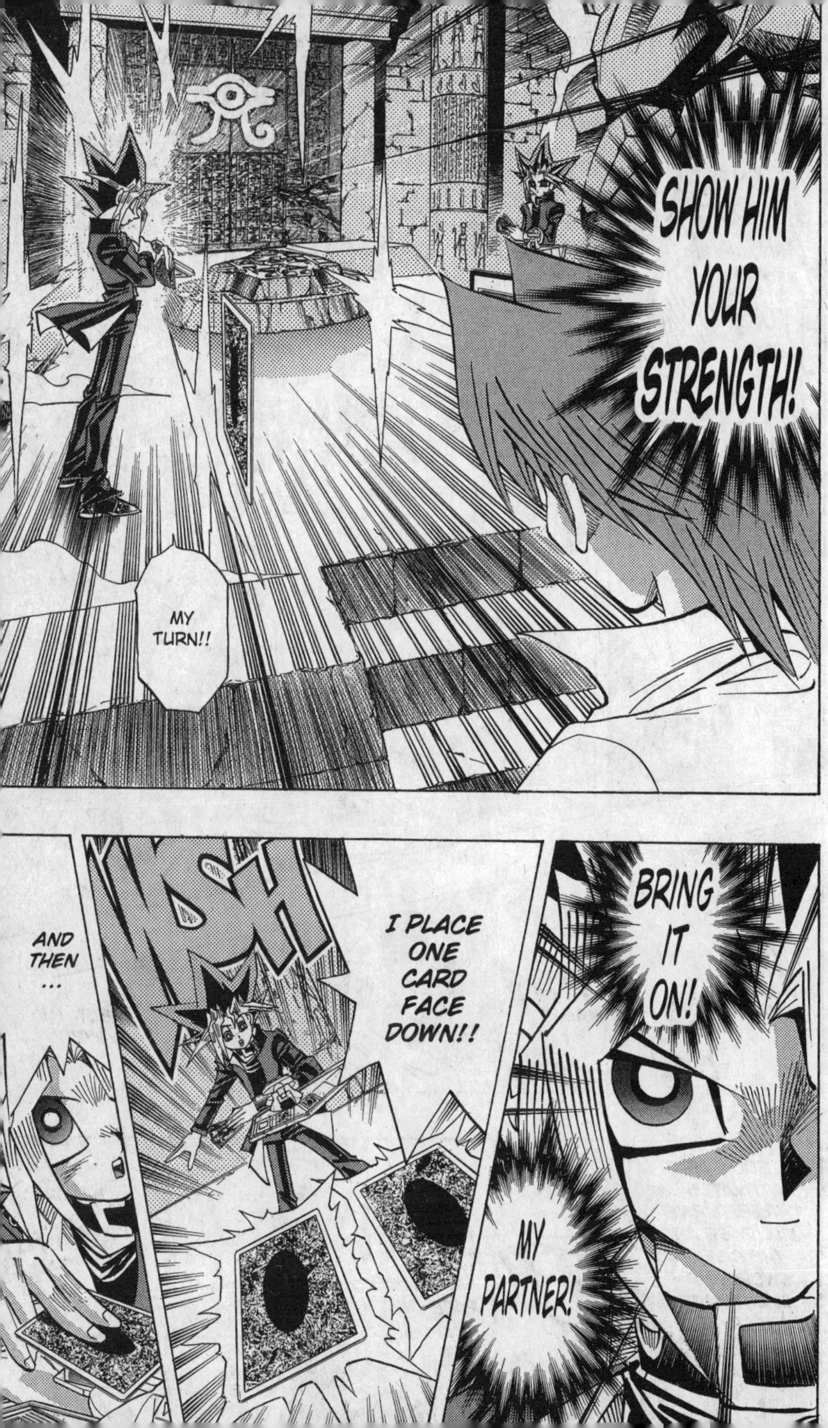
SHOW HIM YOUR STRENGTH!
MY TURN!!
BRING IT ON!
MY PARTNER!
I PLACE ONE CARD FACE DOWN!!
AND THEN ...

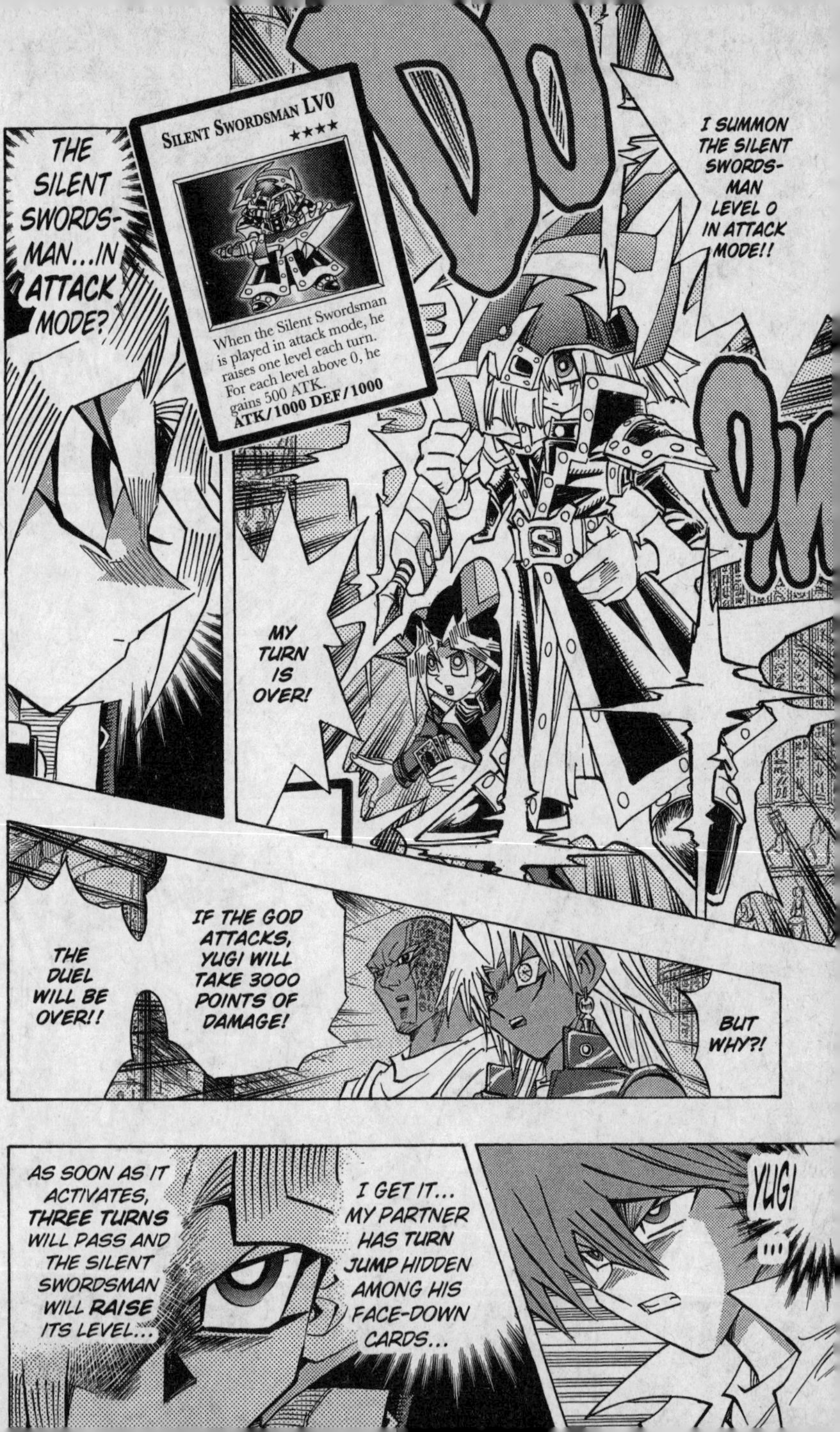
I SUMMON THE SILENT SWORDS-MAN LEVEL 0 IN ATTACK MODE!!
SILENT SWORDSMAN LV0
★★★★
When the Silent Swordsman is played in attack mode, he raises one level each turn. For each level above 0, he gains 500 ATK.
ATK/1000 DEF/1000
MY TURN IS OVER!
THE SILENT SWORDS-MAN...IN ATTACK MODE?
BUT WHY?!
IF THE GOD ATTACKS, YUGI WILL TAKE 3000 POINTS OF DAMAGE!
THE DUEL WILL BE OVER!!
YUGI ...
I GET IT... MY PARTNER HAS TURN JUMP HIDDEN AMONG HIS FACE-DOWN CARDS...
AS SOON AS IT ACTIVATES, THREE TURNS WILL PASS AND THE SILENT SWORDSMAN WILL RAISE ITS LEVEL...

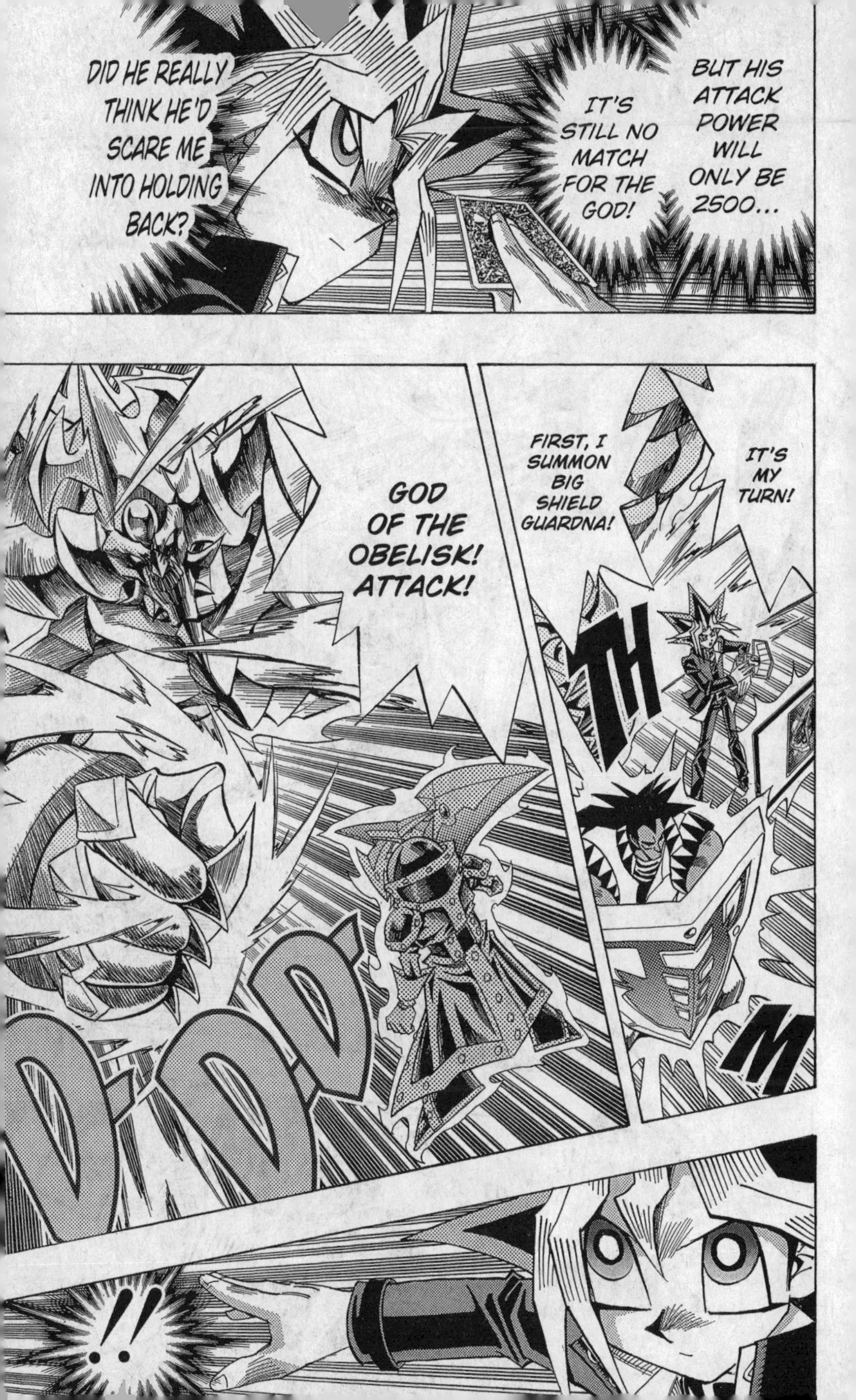
BUT HIS ATTACK POWER WILL ONLY BE 2500...
IT'S STILL NO MATCH FOR THE GOD!
DID HE REALLY THINK HE'D SCARE ME INTO HOLDING BACK?
IT'S MY TURN!
FIRST, I SUMMON BIG SHIELD GUARDNA!
TH
M
GOD OF THE OBELISK! ATTACK!
!!

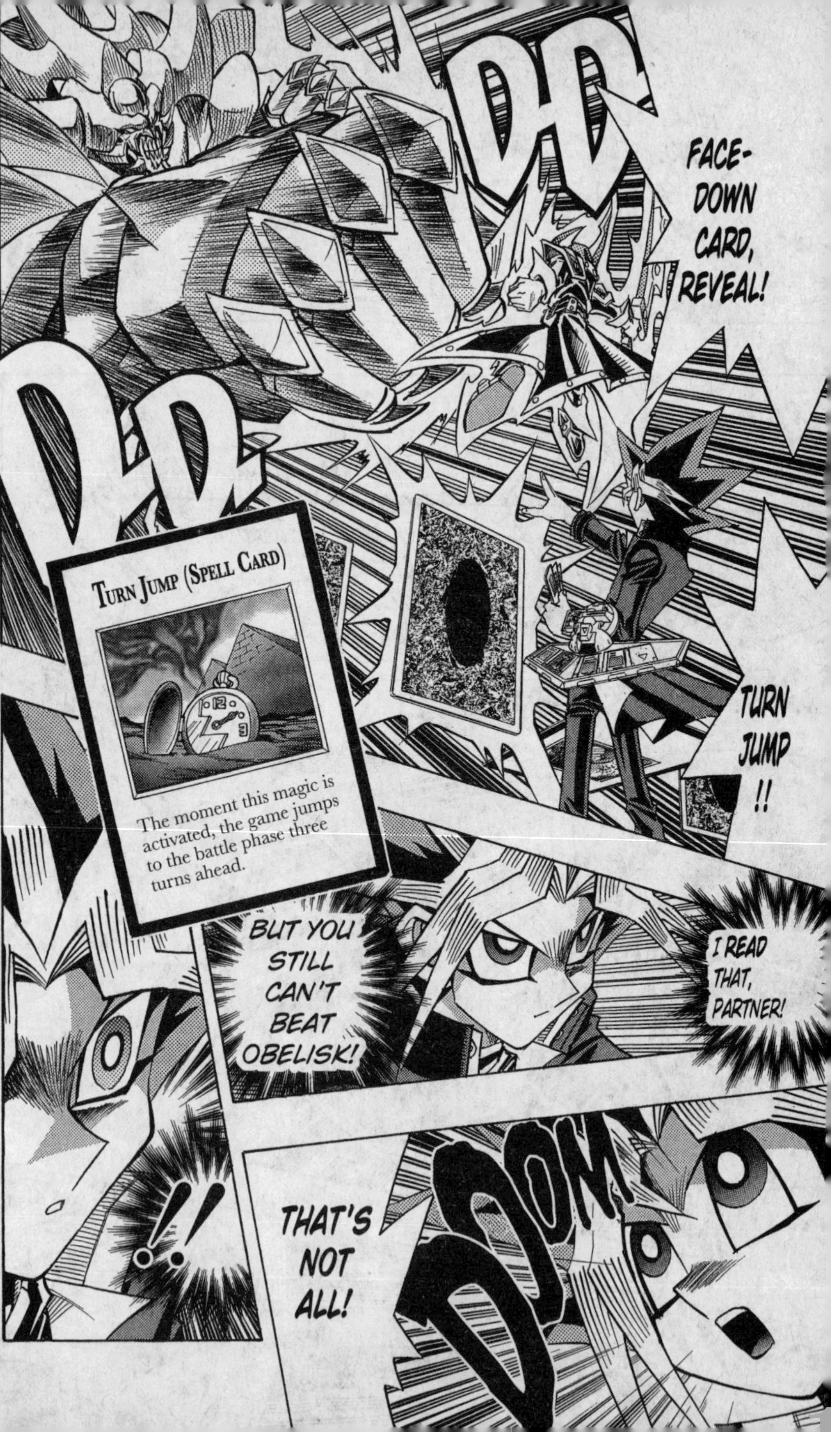
FACE-DOWN CARD, REVEAL!
TURN JUMP !!
TURN JUMP (SPELL CARD)
The moment this magic is activated, the game jumps to the battle phase three turns ahead.
I READ THAT, PARTNER!
BUT YOU STILL CAN'T BEAT OBELISK!
!!
THAT'S NOT ALL!

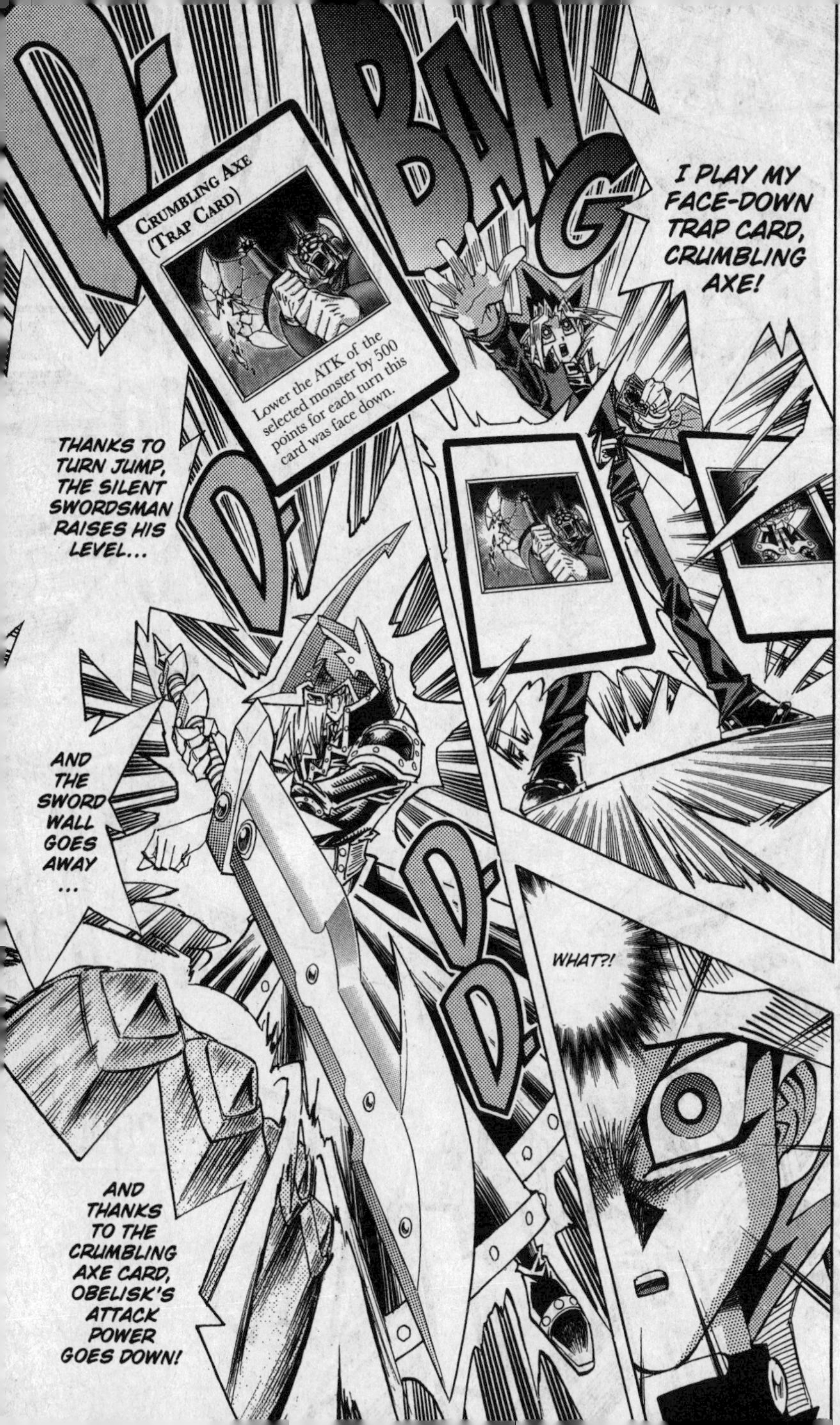
I PLAY MY FACE-DOWN TRAP CARD, CRUMBLING AXE!
Crumbling Axe (Trap Card)
Lower the ATK of the selected monster by 500 points for each turn this card was face down.
WHAT?!
THANKS TO TURN JUMP, THE SILENT SWORDSMAN RAISES HIS LEVEL...
AND THE SWORD WALL GOES AWAY...
AND THANKS TO THE CRUMBLING AXE CARD, OBELISK'S ATTACK POWER GOES DOWN!

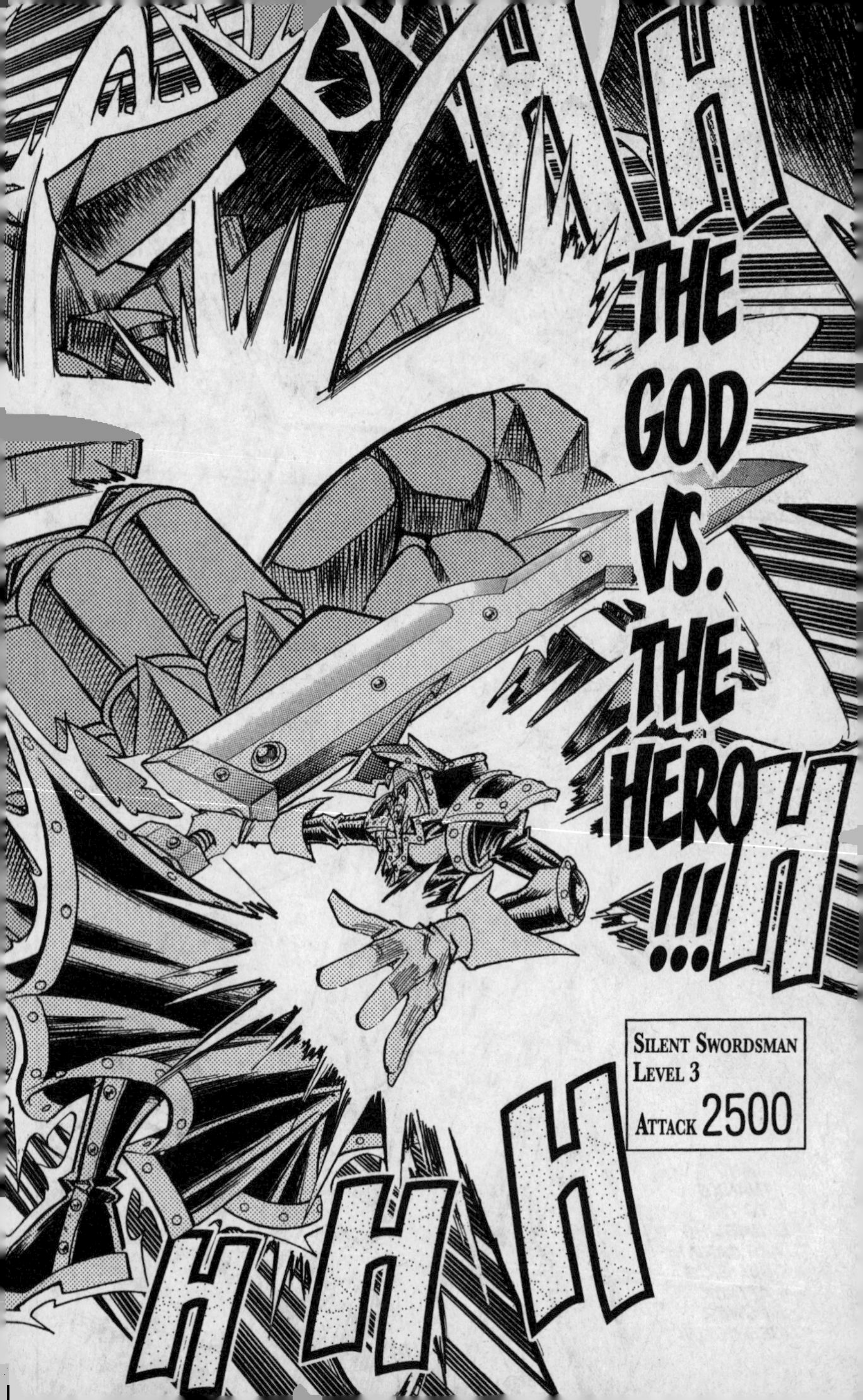

HHH
THE GOD VS. THE HERO!!!
HHHH
SILENT SWORDSMAN
LEVEL 3
ATTACK 2500

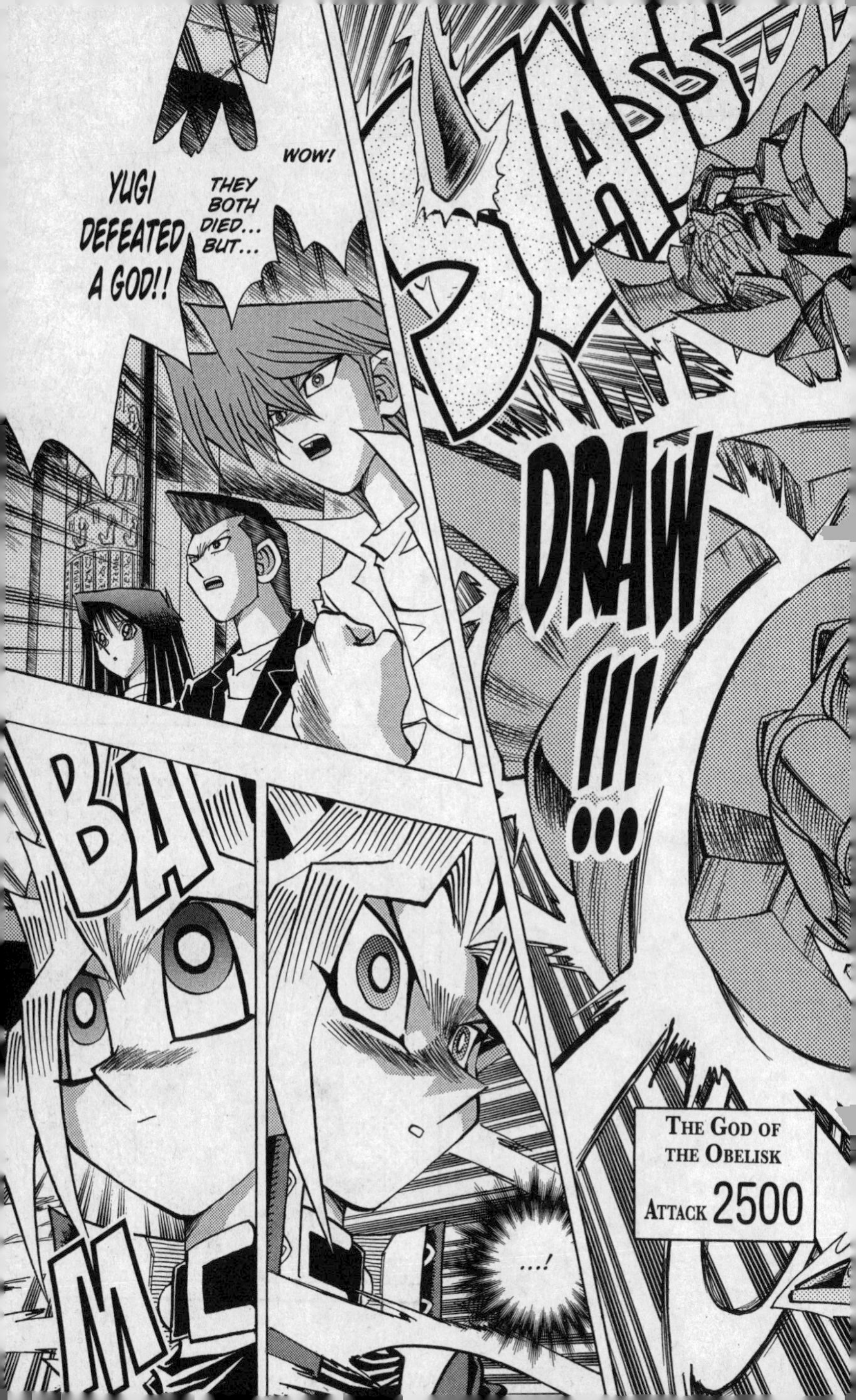
DRAW!!!...
THE GOD OF THE OBELISK
ATTACK 2500
WOW!
THEY BOTH DIED... BUT...
YUGI DEFEATED A GOD!!
...!
BA

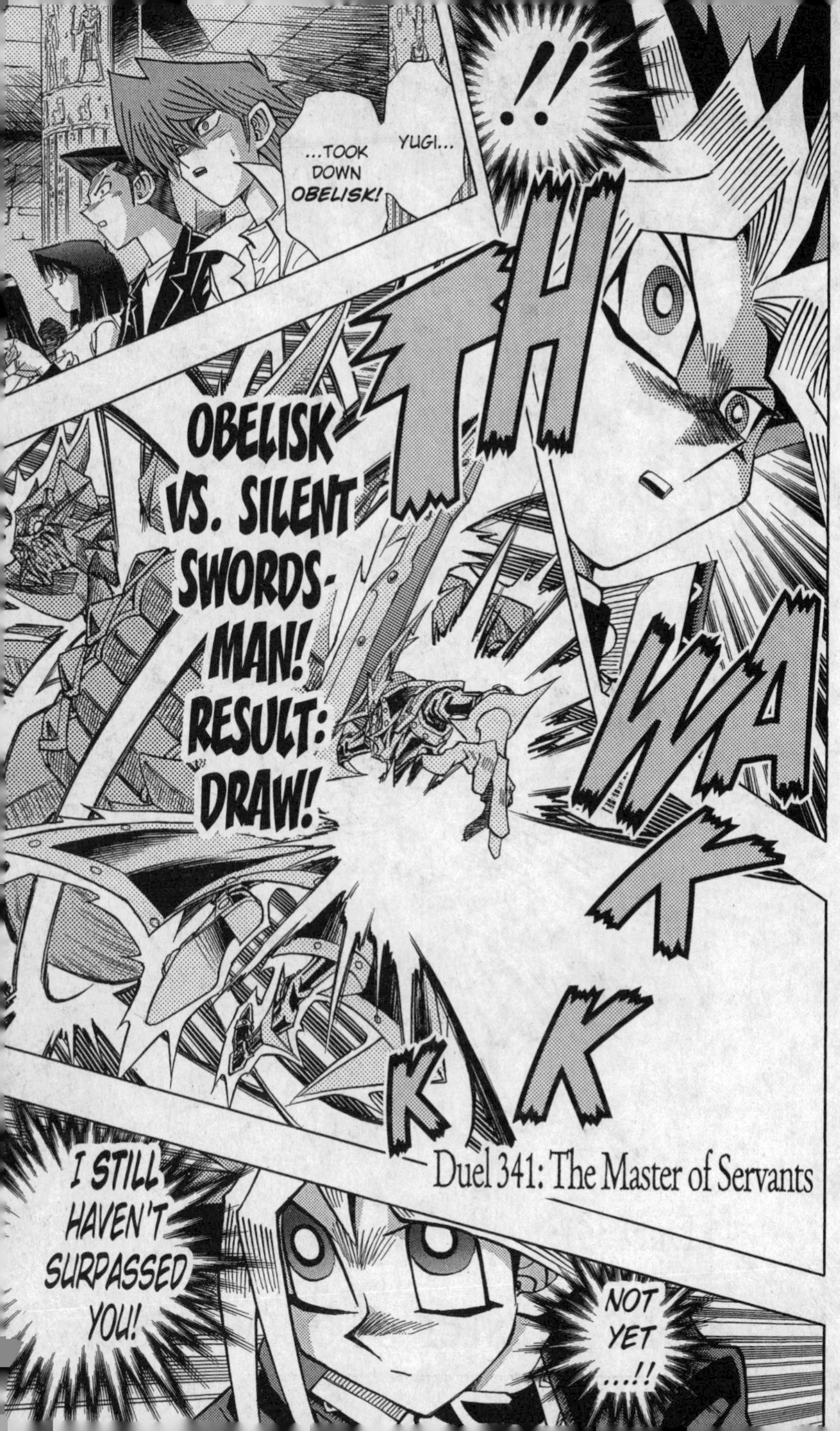
!!
YUGI...
...TOOK DOWN OBELISK!
THWAK
OBELISK VS. SILENT SWORDS-MAN! RESULT: DRAW!
K
K
K
Duel 341: The Master of Servants
NOT YET ...!!
I STILL HAVEN'T SURPASSED YOU!

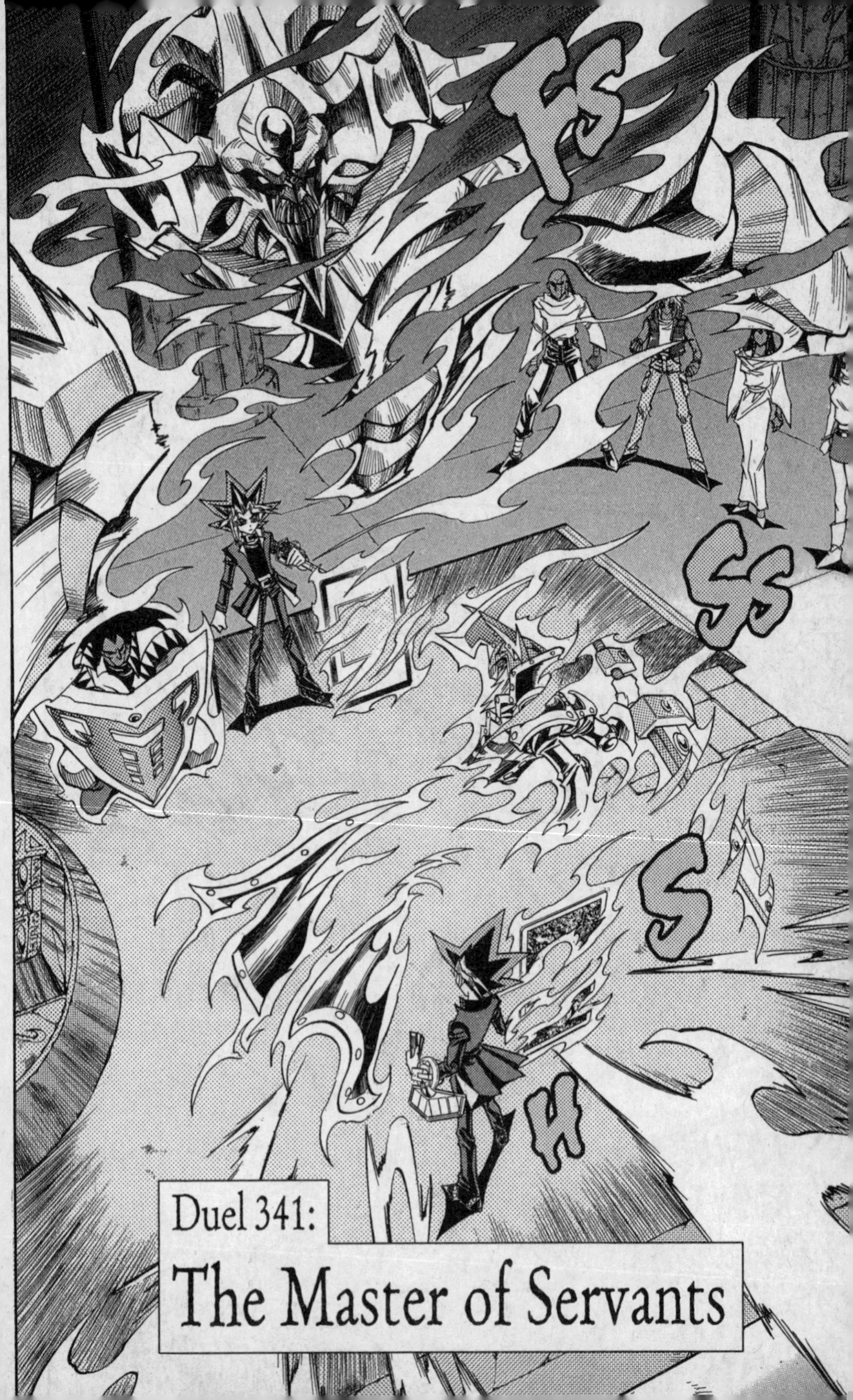
FS
SS
S
H
Duel 341:
The Master of Servants

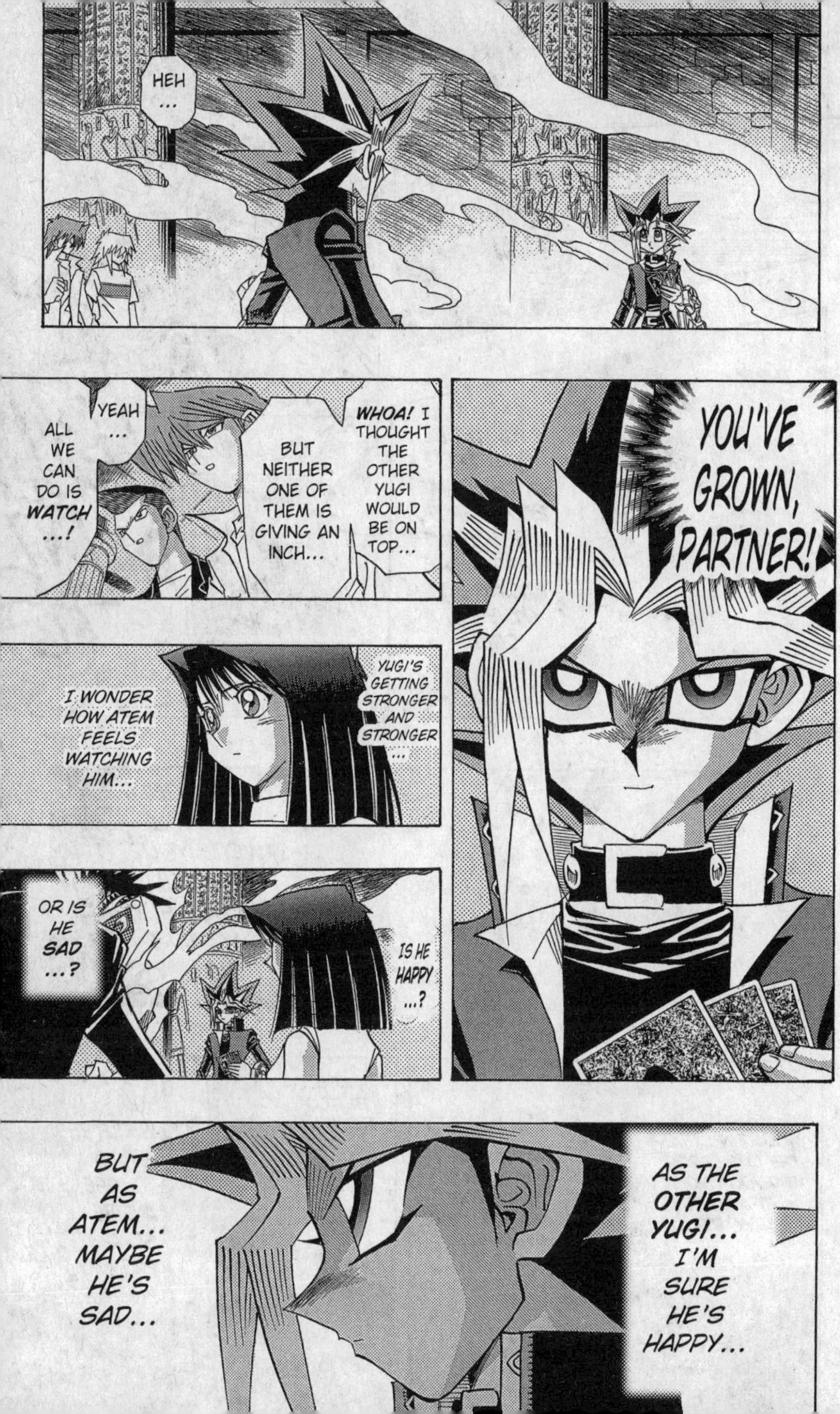
HEH ...
YOU'VE GROWN, PARTNER!
WHOA! I THOUGHT THE OTHER YUGI WOULD BE ON TOP...
BUT NEITHER ONE OF THEM IS GIVING AN INCH...
YEAH ...
ALL WE CAN DO IS WATCH ...!
YUGI'S GETTING STRONGER AND STRONGER ...
I WONDER HOW ATEM FEELS WATCHING HIM...
IS HE HAPPY ...?
OR IS HE SAD ...?
AS THE OTHER YUGI... I'M SURE HE'S HAPPY...
BUT AS ATEM... MAYBE HE'S SAD...

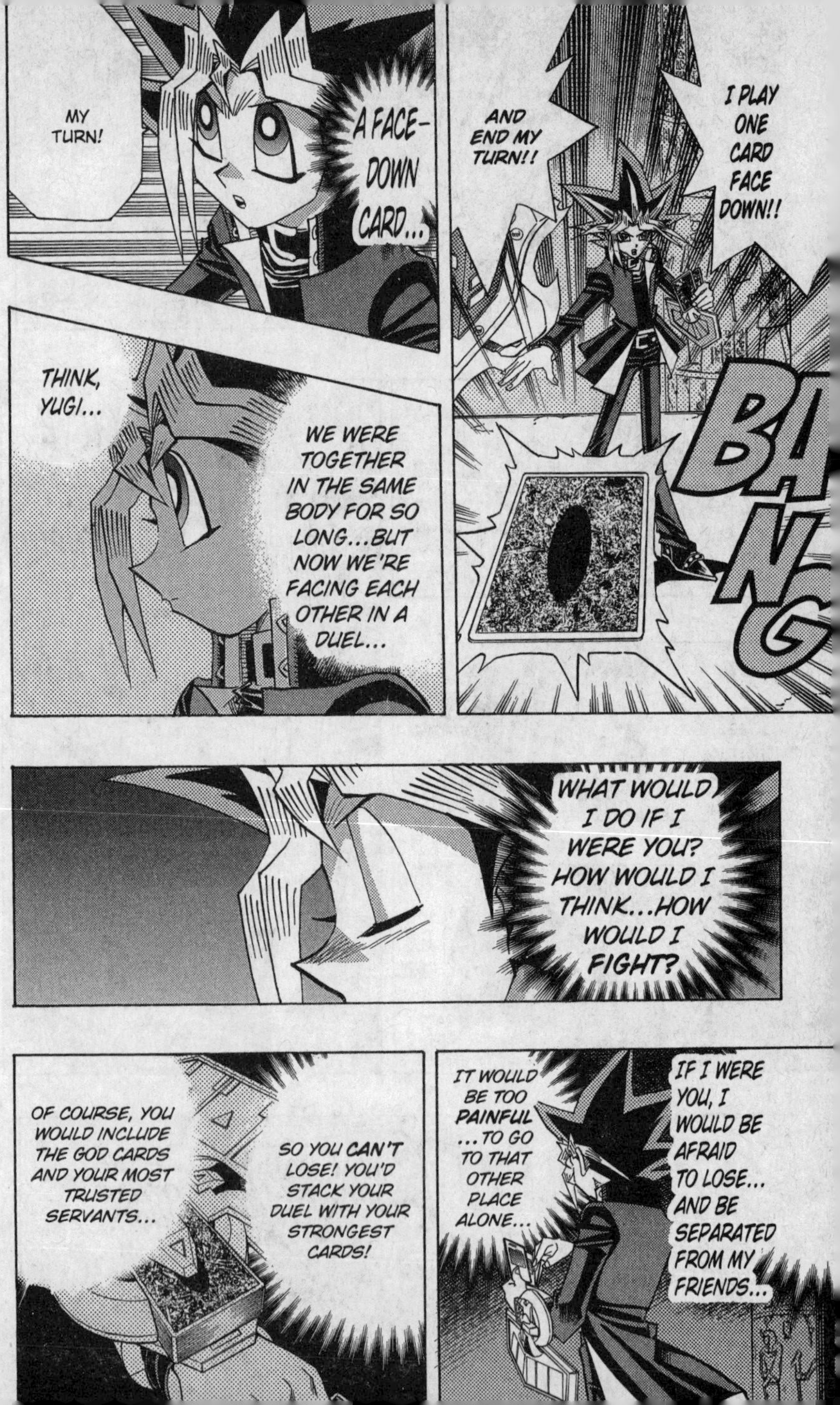
I PLAY ONE CARD FACE DOWN!!
AND END MY TURN!!
BANG
A FACE-DOWN CARD...
MY TURN!
WE WERE TOGETHER IN THE SAME BODY FOR SO LONG...BUT NOW WE'RE FACING EACH OTHER IN A DUEL...
THINK, YUGI...
WHAT WOULD I DO IF I WERE YOU? HOW WOULD I THINK...HOW WOULD I FIGHT?
IF I WERE YOU, I WOULD BE AFRAID TO LOSE... AND BE SEPARATED FROM MY FRIENDS...
IT WOULD BE TOO **PAINFUL** ...TO GO TO THAT OTHER PLACE ALONE...
SO YOU **CAN'T** LOSE! YOU'D STACK YOUR DUEL WITH YOUR STRONGEST CARDS!
OF COURSE, YOU WOULD INCLUDE THE GOD CARDS AND YOUR MOST TRUSTED SERVANTS...

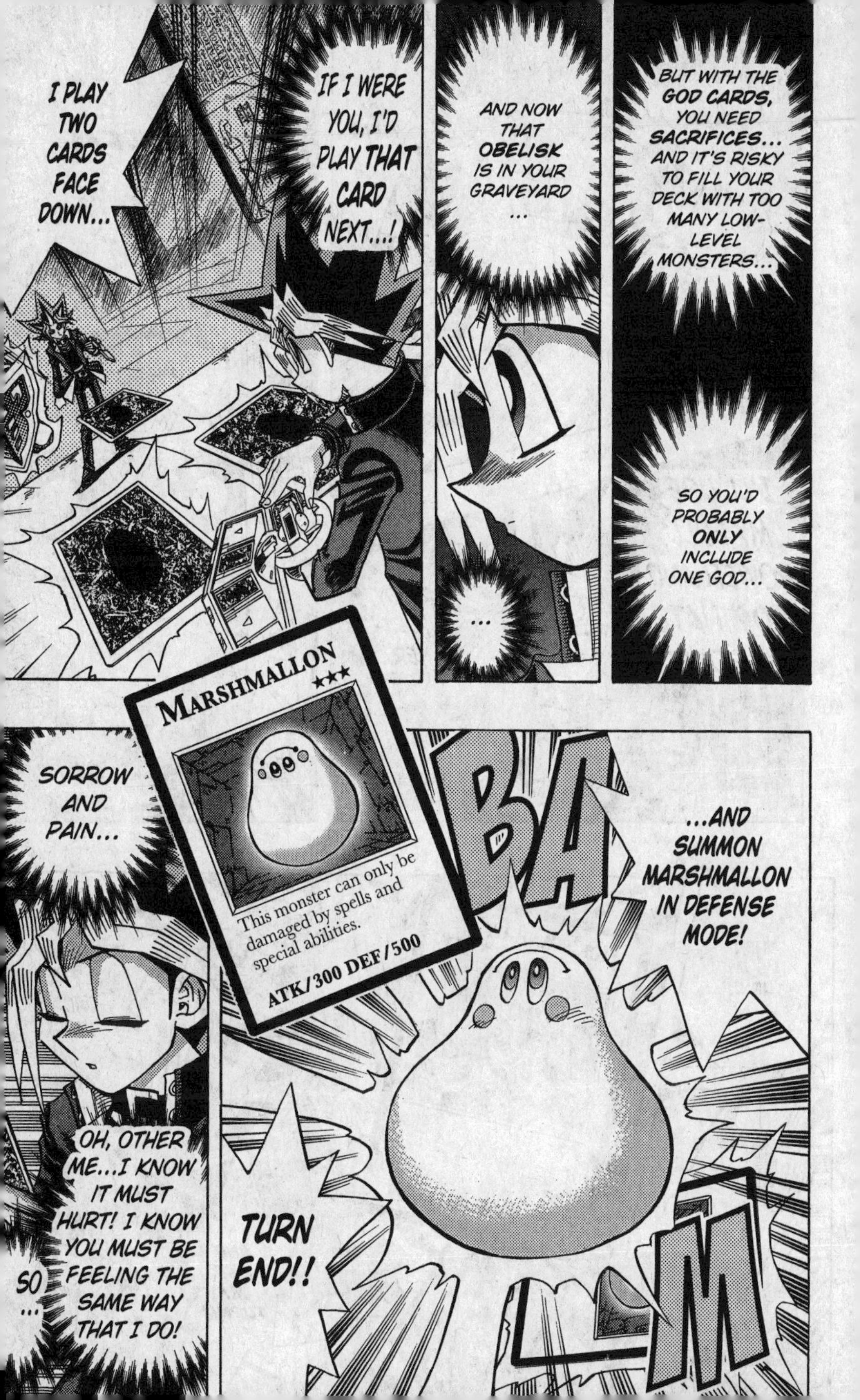
BUT WITH THE GOD CARDS, YOU NEED SACRIFICES... AND IT'S RISKY TO FILL YOUR DECK WITH TOO MANY LOW-LEVEL MONSTERS...
SO YOU'D PROBABLY ONLY INCLUDE ONE GOD...
AND NOW THAT OBELISK IS IN YOUR GRAVEYARD ...
...
IF I WERE YOU, I'D PLAY THAT CARD NEXT...!
I PLAY TWO CARDS FACE DOWN...
BA
...AND SUMMON MARSHMALLON IN DEFENSE MODE!
MARSHMALLON ★★★
This monster can only be damaged by spells and special abilities.
ATK/300 DEF/500
TURN END!!
M
SORROW AND PAIN...
OH, OTHER ME...I KNOW IT MUST HURT! I KNOW YOU MUST BE FEELING THE SAME WAY THAT I DO!
SO ...

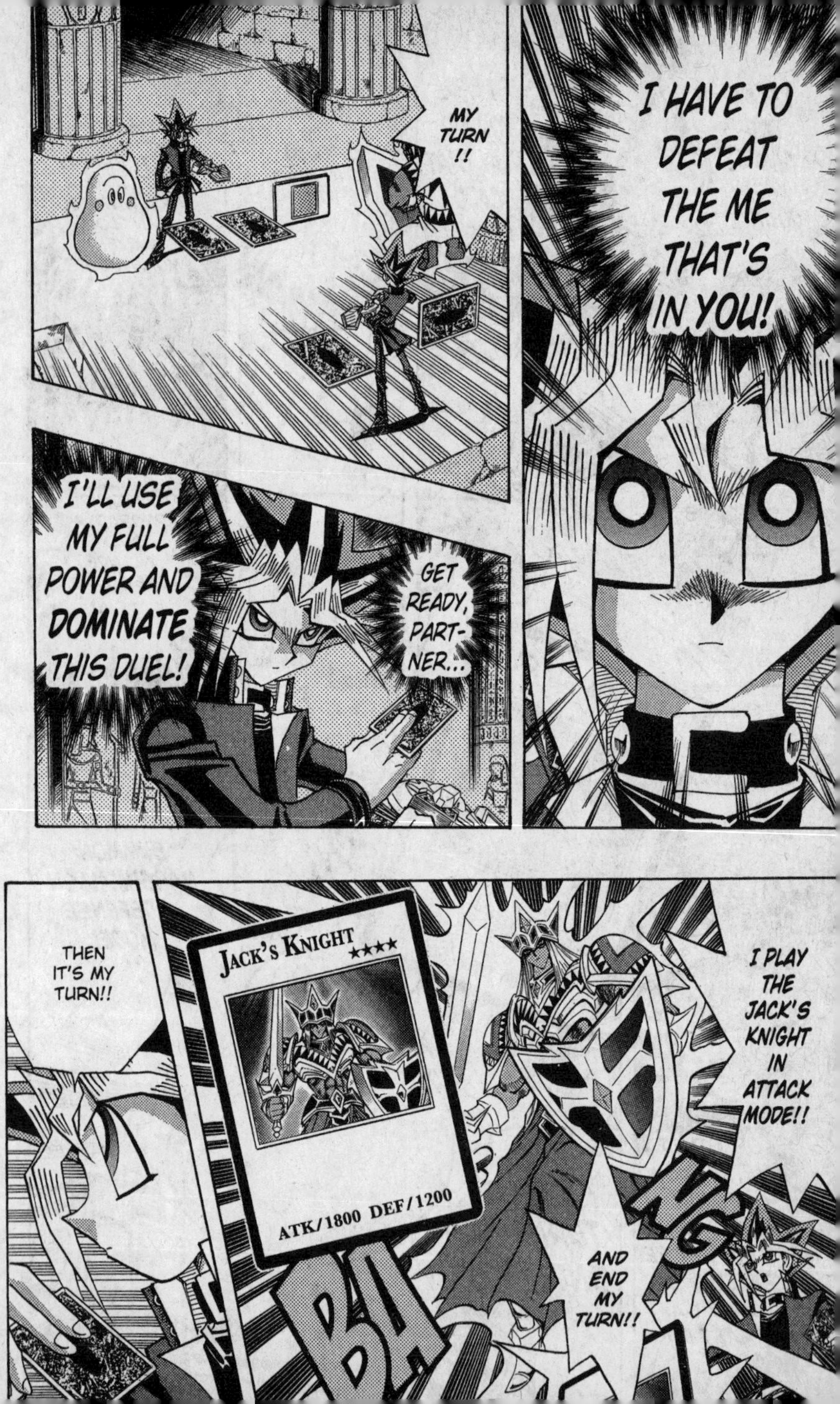
I HAVE TO DEFEAT THE ME THAT'S IN YOU!
MY TURN !!
I'LL USE MY FULL POWER AND DOMINATE THIS DUEL!
GET READY, PART-NER...
I PLAY THE JACK'S KNIGHT IN ATTACK MODE!!
AND END MY TURN!!
NG
JACK'S KNIGHT
ATK/1800 DEF/1200
BA
THEN IT'S MY TURN!!

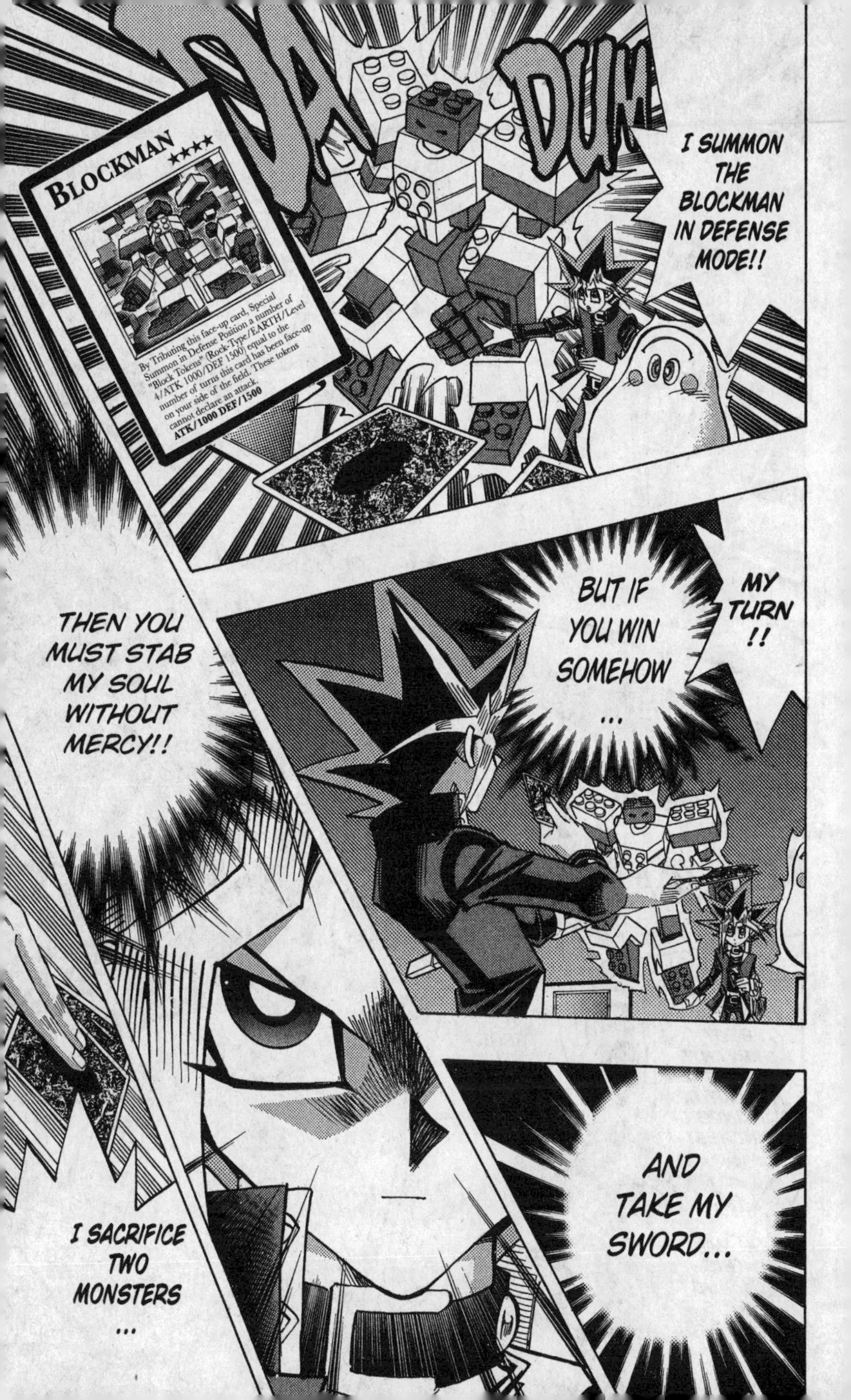
DA DUM
I SUMMON THE BLOCKMAN IN DEFENSE MODE!!
BLOCKMAN ★★★★
By Tributing this face-up card, Special Summon in Defense Position a number of "Block Tokens" (Rock-Type/EARTH/Level 4/ATK 1000/DEF 1500) equal to the number of turns this card has been face-up on your side of the field. These tokens cannot declare an attack.
ATK/1000 DEF/1500
MY TURN!!
BUT IF YOU WIN SOMEHOW...
THEN YOU MUST STAB MY SOUL WITHOUT MERCY!!
AND TAKE MY SWORD...
I SACRIFICE TWO MONSTERS...

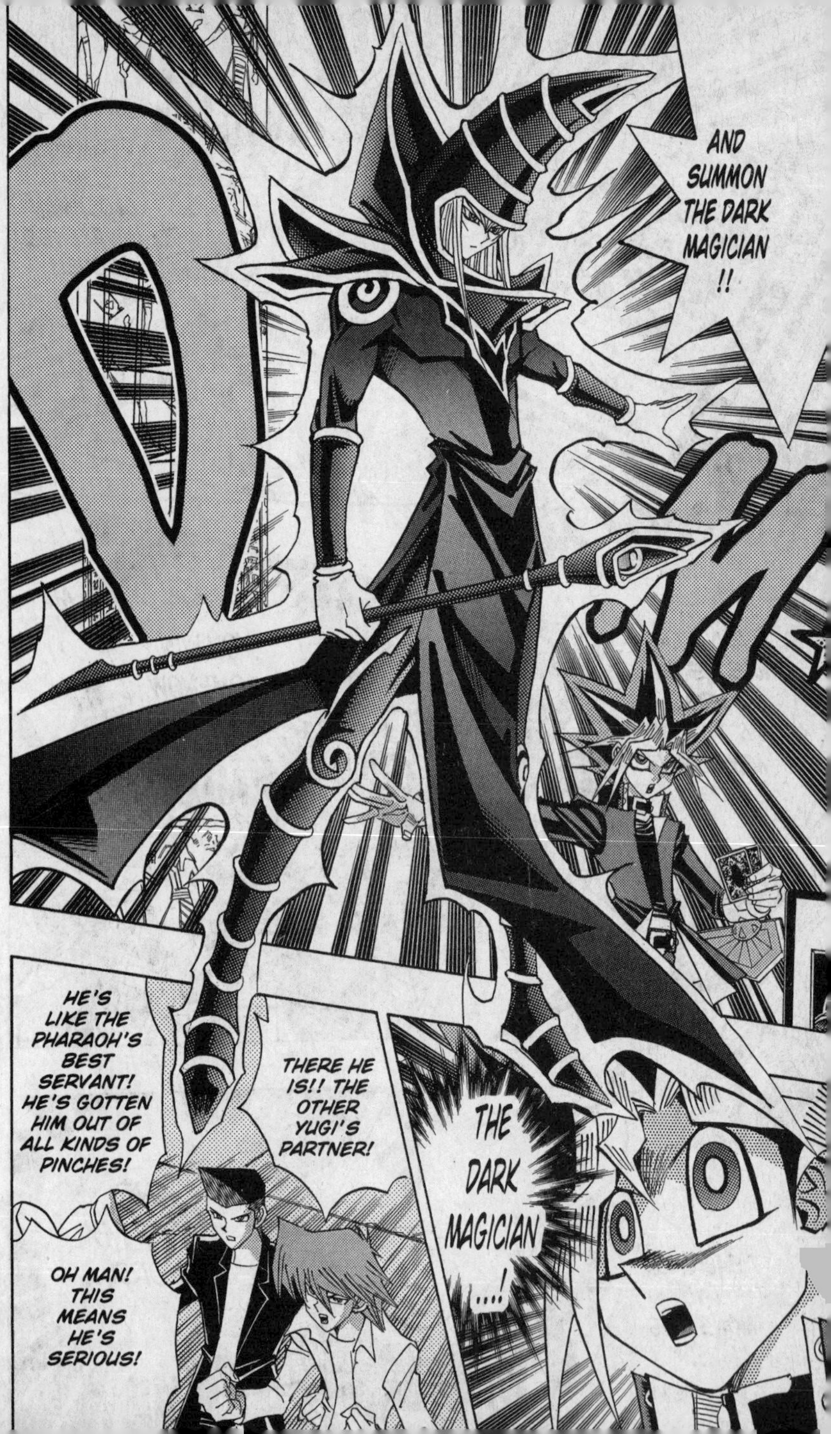
AND SUMMON THE DARK MAGICIAN !!
THE DARK MAGICIAN ...!
THERE HE IS!! THE OTHER YUGI'S PARTNER!
HE'S LIKE THE PHARAOH'S BEST SERVANT! HE'S GOTTEN HIM OUT OF ALL KINDS OF PINCHES!
OH MAN! THIS MEANS HE'S SERIOUS!

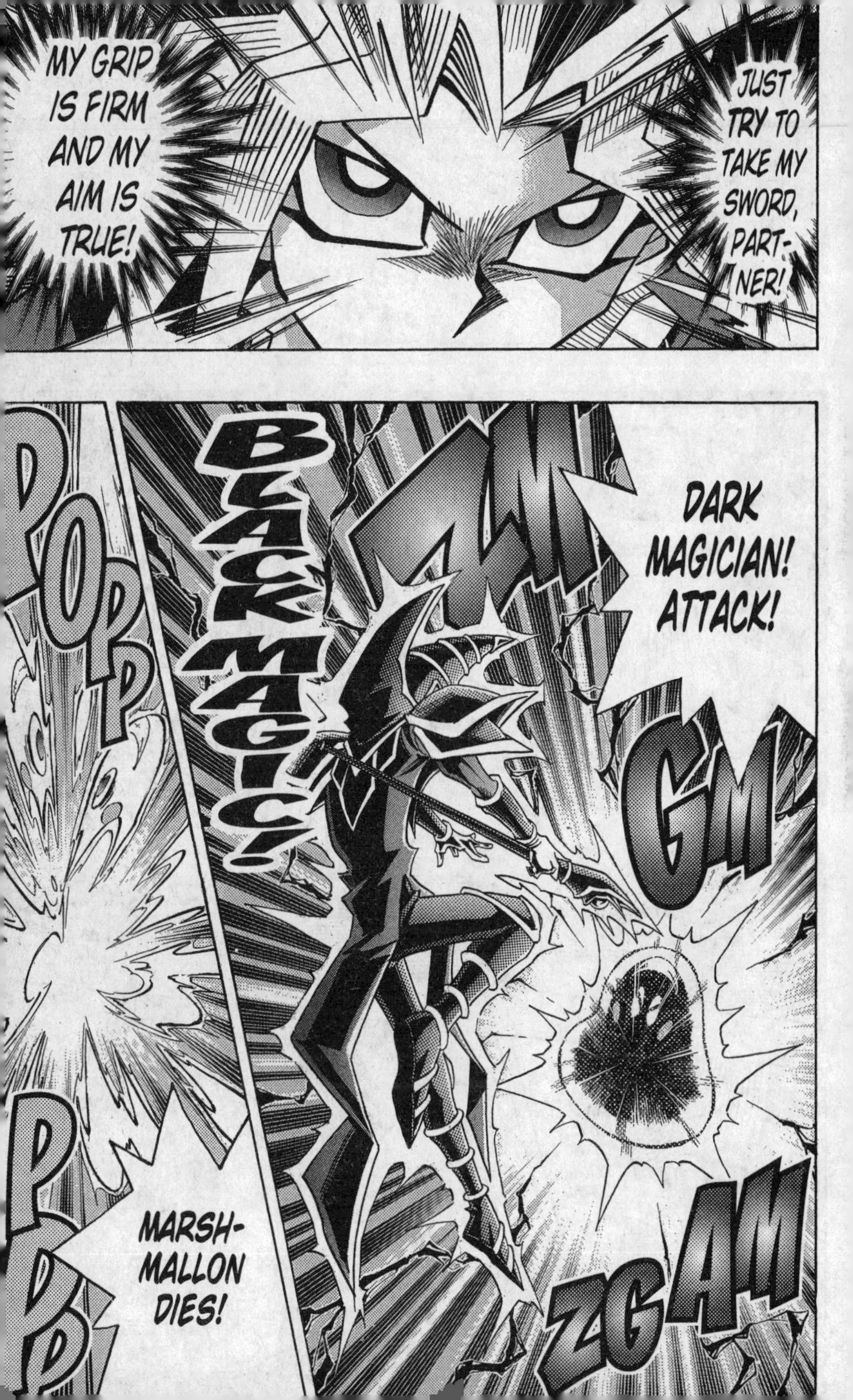
JUST TRY TO TAKE MY SWORD, PART-NER!
MY GRIP IS FIRM AND MY AIM IS TRUE!
DARK MAGICIAN! ATTACK!
BLACK MAGIC!
GM
ZGAM
POP
POP
MARSH-MALLON DIES!

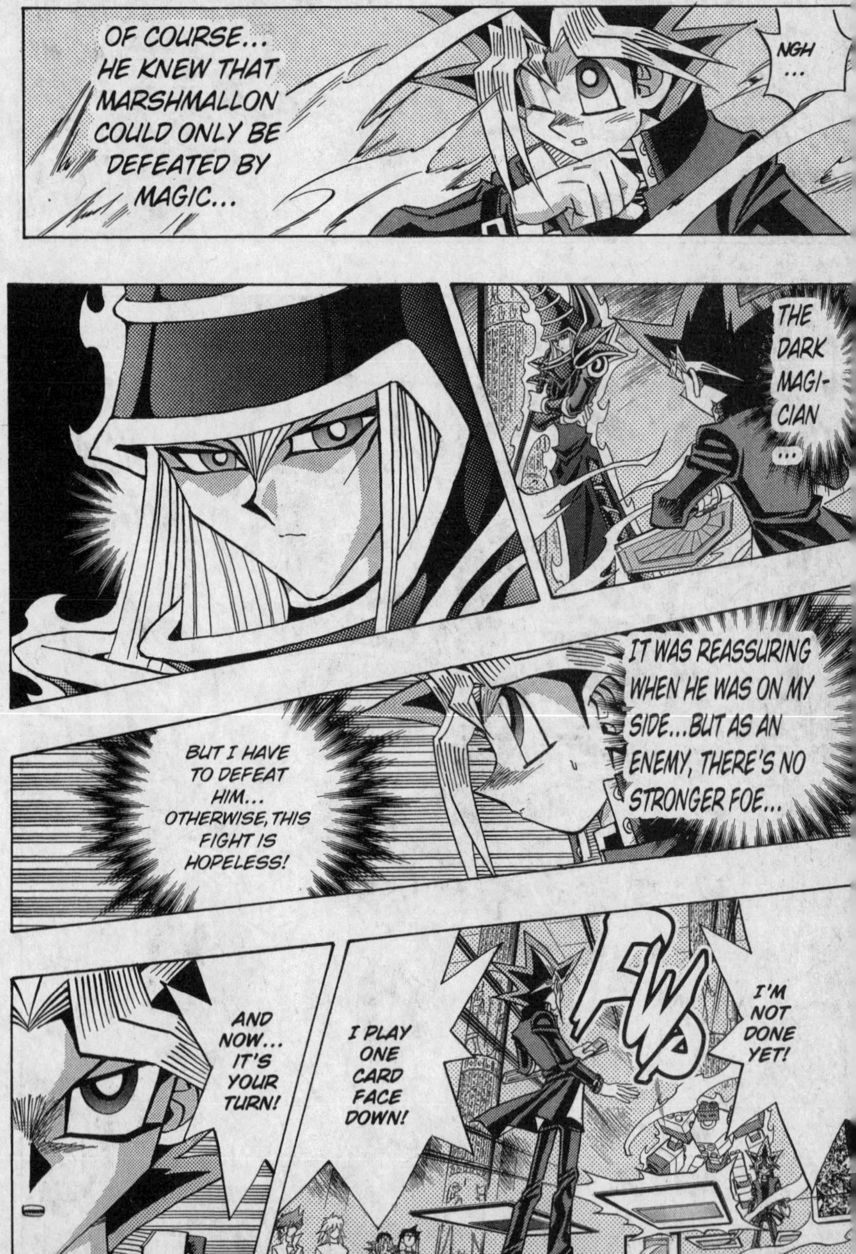
NGH...
OF COURSE... HE KNEW THAT MARSHMALLON COULD ONLY BE DEFEATED BY MAGIC...
THE DARK MAGICIAN...
IT WAS REASSURING WHEN HE WAS ON MY SIDE...BUT AS AN ENEMY, THERE'S NO STRONGER FOE...
BUT I HAVE TO DEFEAT HIM... OTHERWISE, THIS FIGHT IS HOPELESS!
I'M NOT DONE YET!
FWP
I PLAY ONE CARD FACE DOWN!
AND NOW... IT'S YOUR TURN!

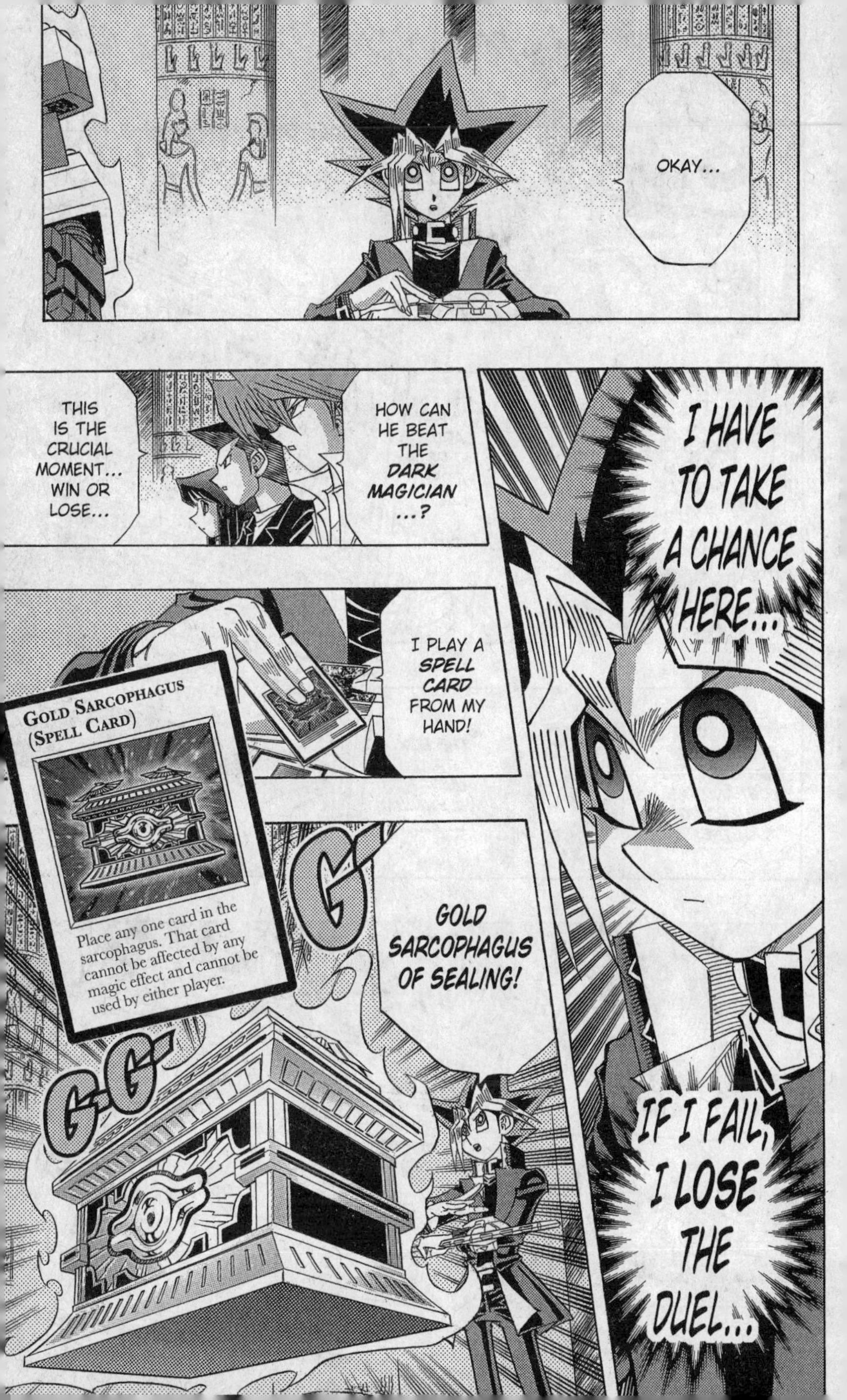

OKAY...
I HAVE TO TAKE A CHANCE HERE...
IF I FAIL, I LOSE THE DUEL...
HOW CAN HE BEAT THE DARK MAGICIAN...?
THIS IS THE CRUCIAL MOMENT... WIN OR LOSE...
I PLAY A SPELL CARD FROM MY HAND!
GOLD SARCOPHAGUS (SPELL CARD)
Place any one card in the sarcophagus. That card cannot be affected by any magic effect and cannot be used by either player.
G
GOLD SARCOPHAGUS OF SEALING!
G-G-

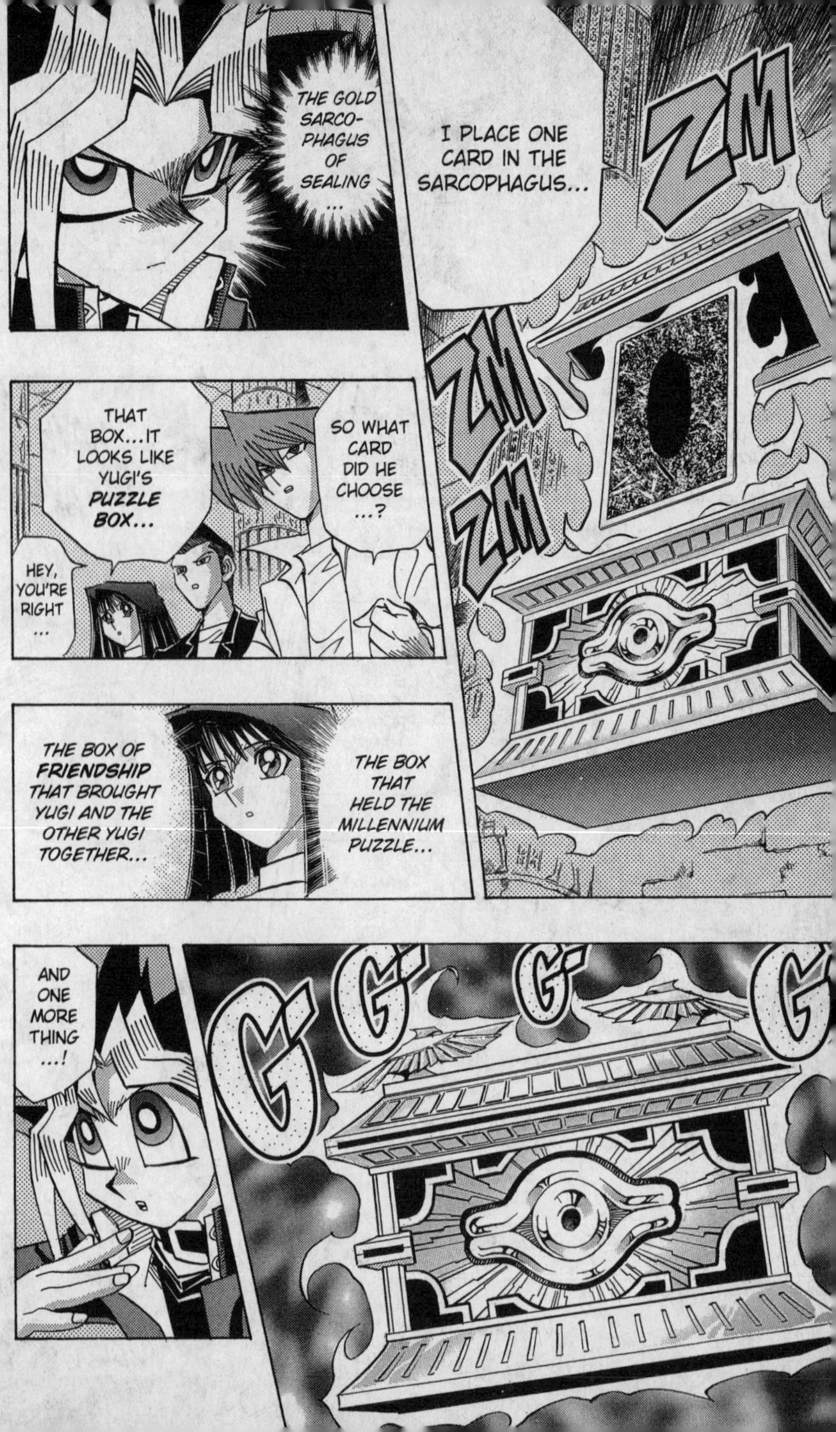
I PLACE ONE CARD IN THE SARCOPHAGUS...
ZM
ZM
ZM
THE GOLD SARCOPHAGUS OF SEALING...
SO WHAT CARD DID HE CHOOSE...?
THAT BOX...IT LOOKS LIKE YUGI'S PUZZLE BOX...
HEY, YOU'RE RIGHT...
THE BOX THAT HELD THE MILLENNIUM PUZZLE...
THE BOX OF FRIENDSHIP THAT BROUGHT YUGI AND THE OTHER YUGI TOGETHER...
G G G G
AND ONE MORE THING...!

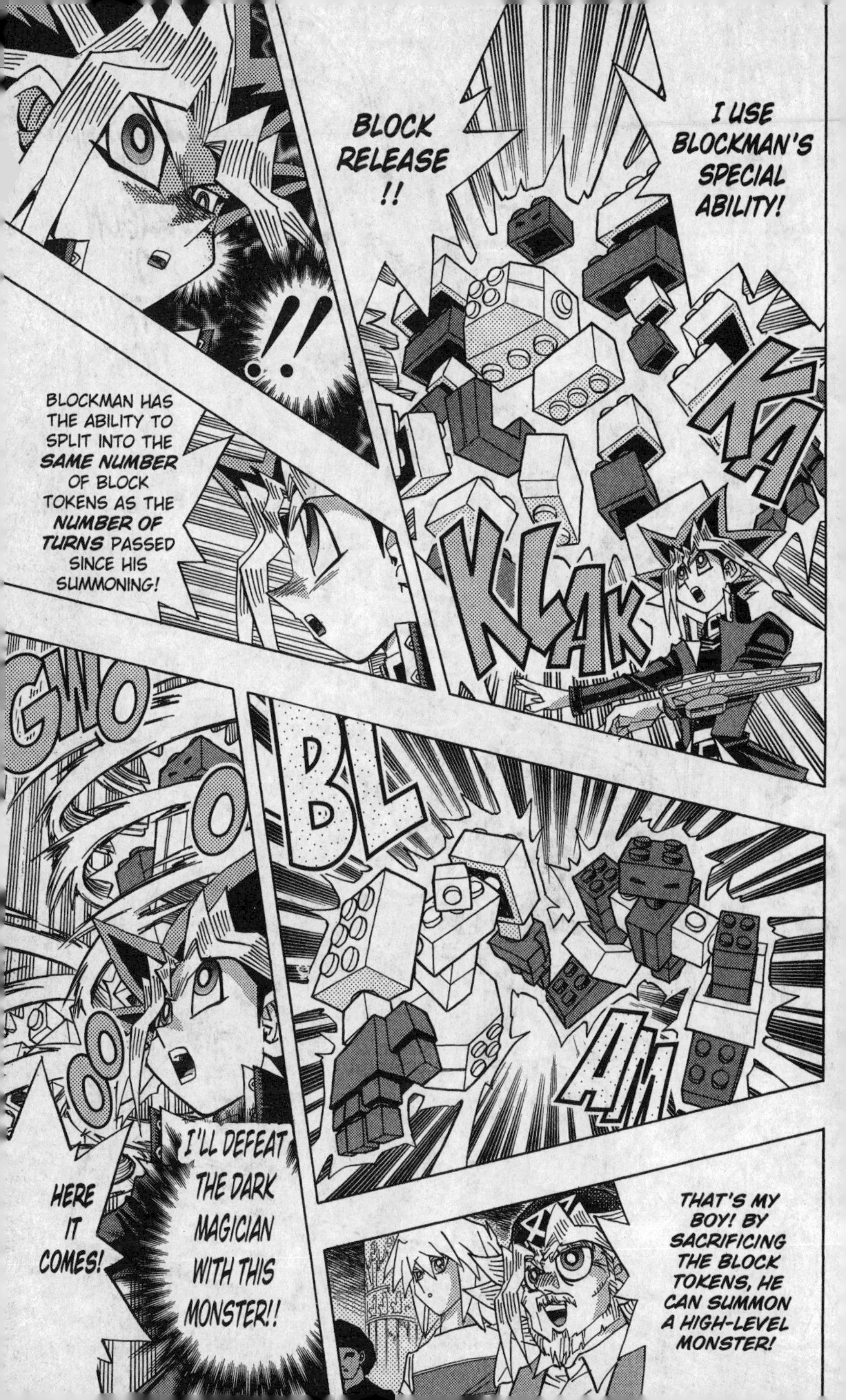
I USE BLOCKMAN'S SPECIAL ABILITY!
BLOCK RELEASE!!
KA
KLAK
!!
BLOCKMAN HAS THE ABILITY TO SPLIT INTO THE SAME NUMBER OF BLOCK TOKENS AS THE NUMBER OF TURNS PASSED SINCE HIS SUMMONING!
BL
AM
THAT'S MY BOY! BY SACRIFICING THE BLOCK TOKENS, HE CAN SUMMON A HIGH-LEVEL MONSTER!
GWO
O
OOO
I'LL DEFEAT THE DARK MAGICIAN WITH THIS MONSTER!!
HERE IT COMES!

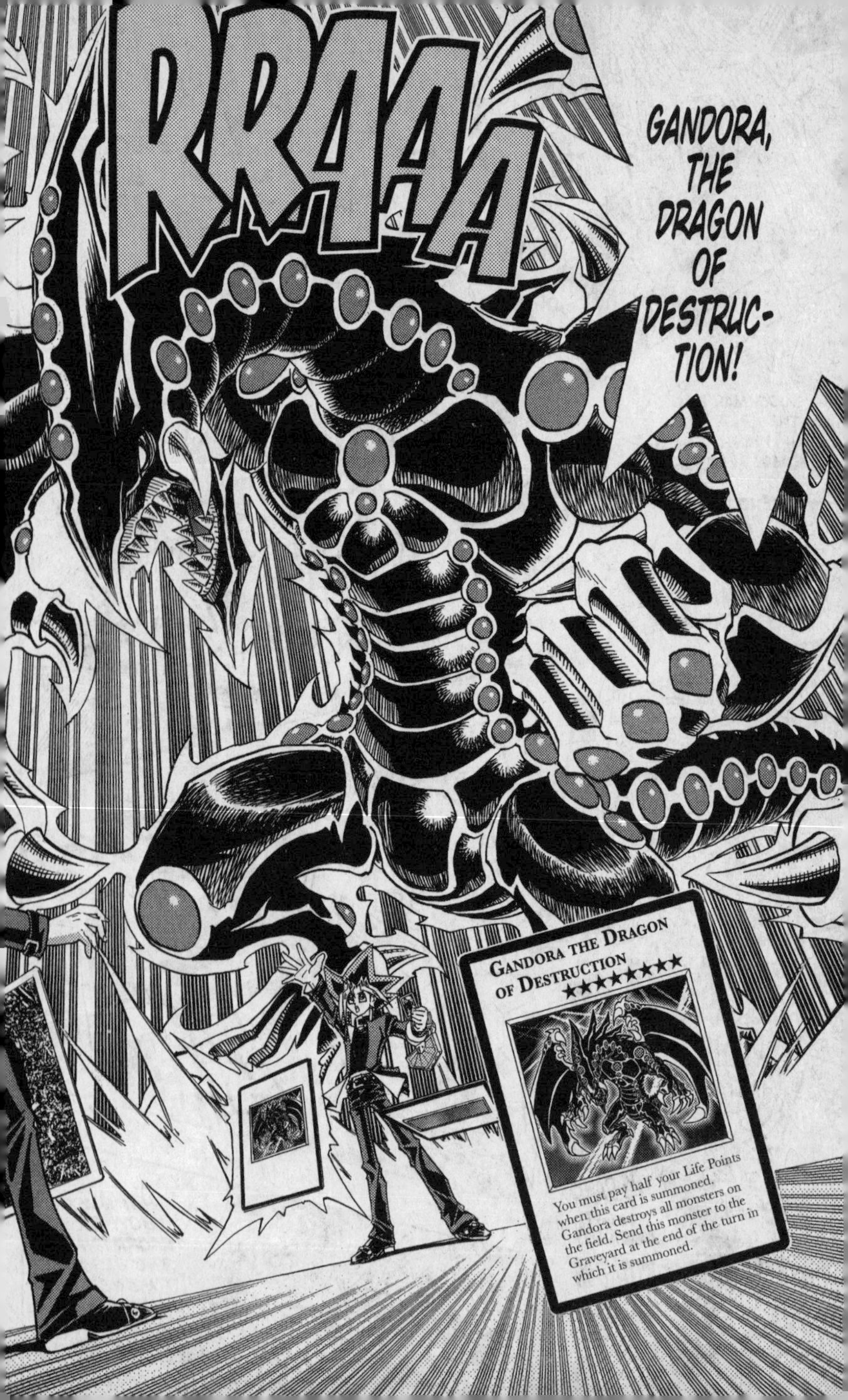
RRAAAA
GANDORA, THE DRAGON OF DESTRUC-TION!
GANDORA THE DRAGON OF DESTRUCTION
★★★★★★★★
You must pay half your Life Points when this card is summoned. Gandora destroys all monsters on the field. Send this monster to the Graveyard at the end of the turn in which it is summoned.

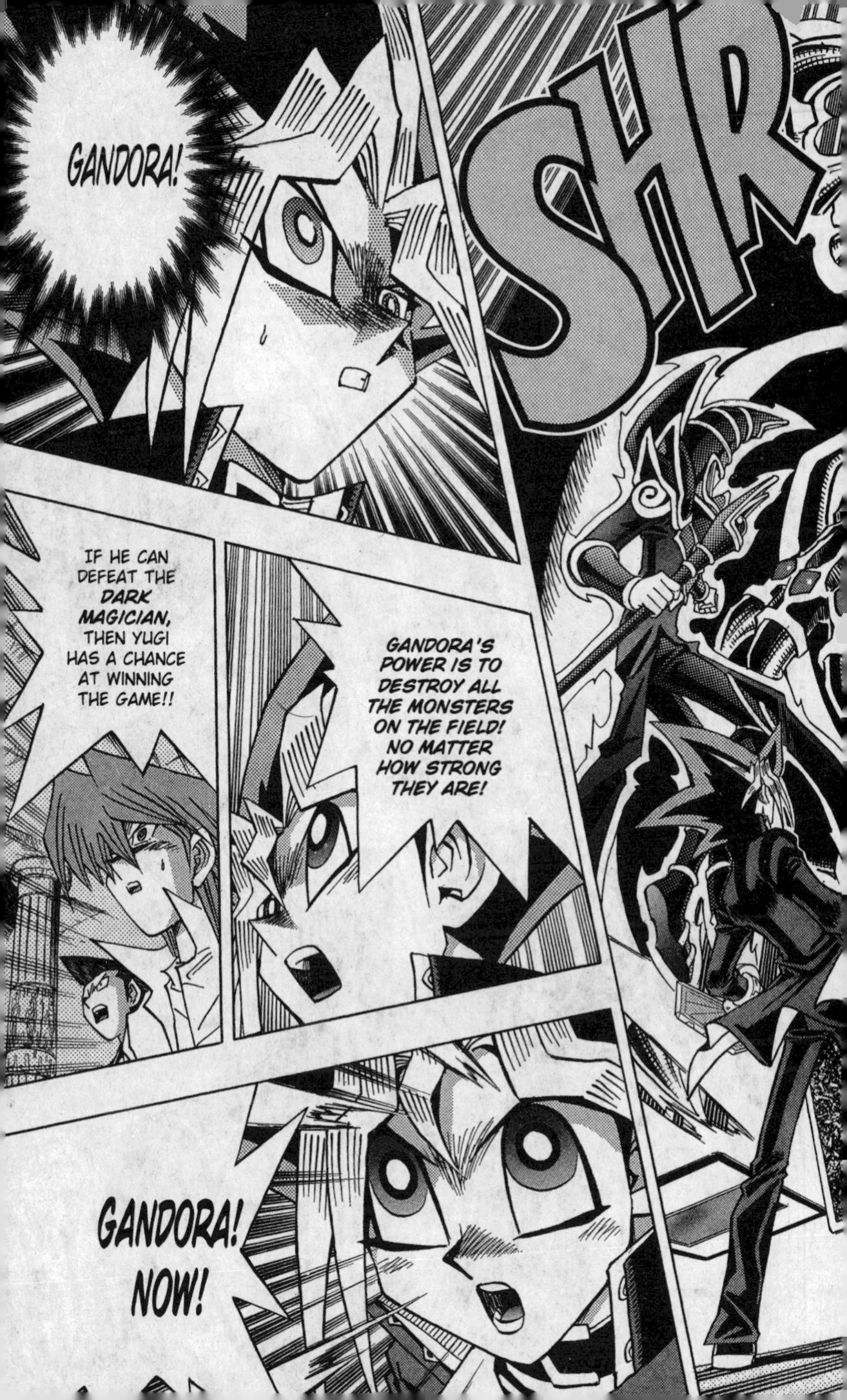
SHR
GANDORA!
GANDORA'S POWER IS TO DESTROY ALL THE MONSTERS ON THE FIELD! NO MATTER HOW STRONG THEY ARE!
IF HE CAN DEFEAT THE *DARK MAGICIAN*, THEN YUGI HAS A CHANCE AT WINNING THE GAME!!
GANDORA! NOW!

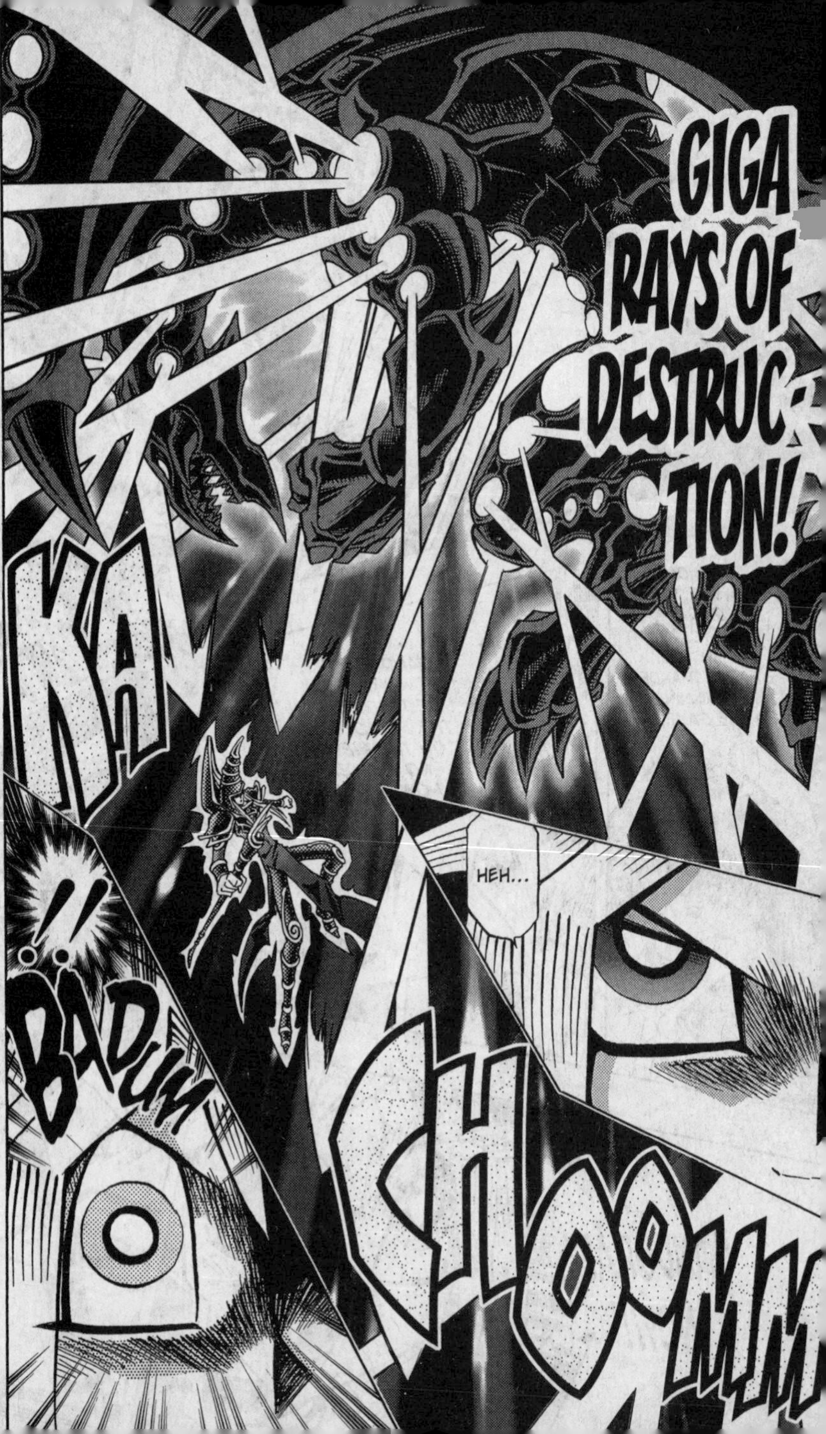
GIGA RAYS OF DESTRUC-TION!
KA
HEH...
CHOOMM
!!
BADUM

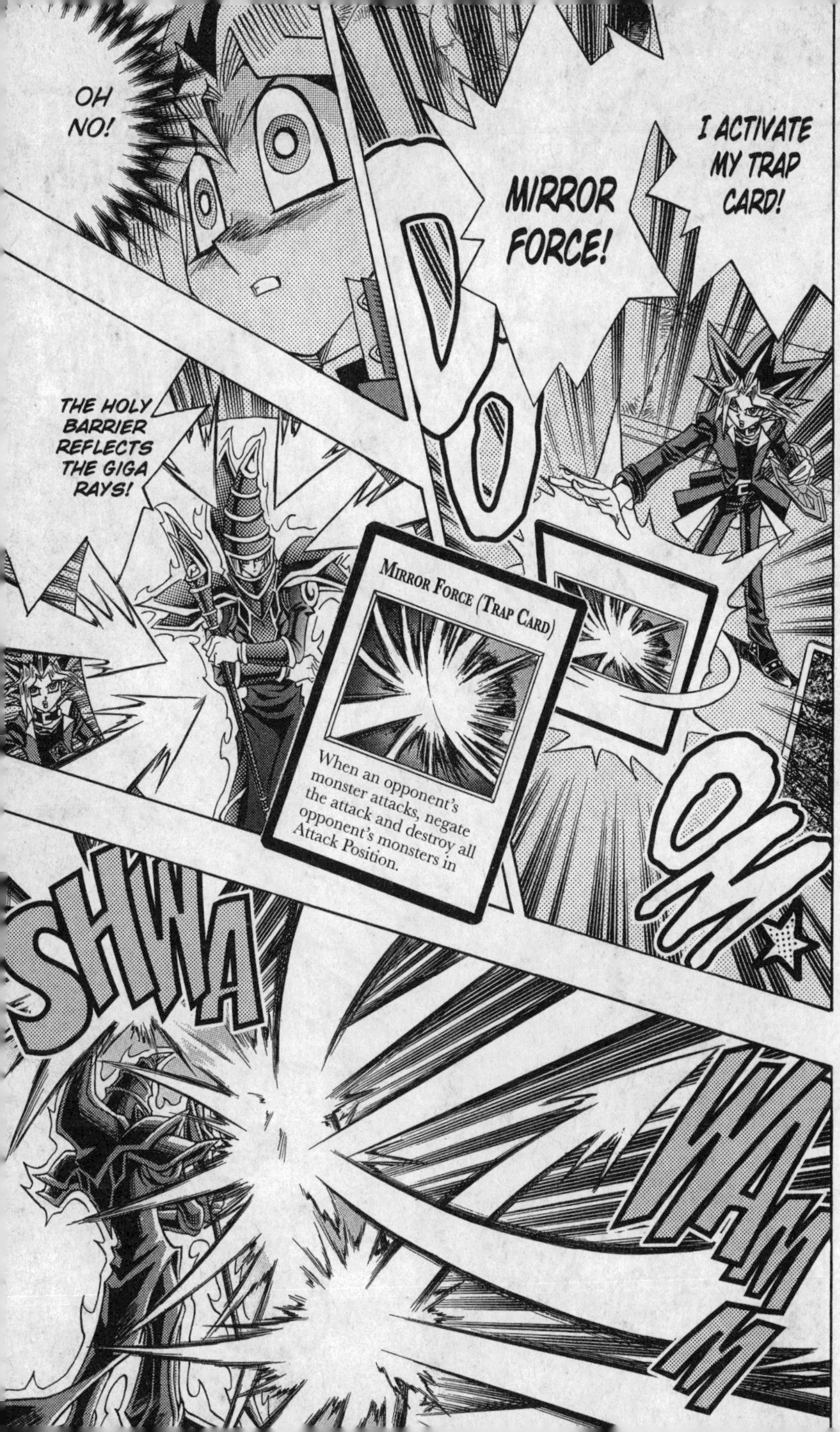
I ACTIVATE MY TRAP CARD!
MIRROR FORCE!
OH NO!
THE HOLY BARRIER REFLECTS THE GIGA RAYS!
MIRROR FORCE (TRAP CARD)
When an opponent's monster attacks, negate the attack and destroy all opponent's monsters in Attack Position.
SHWA

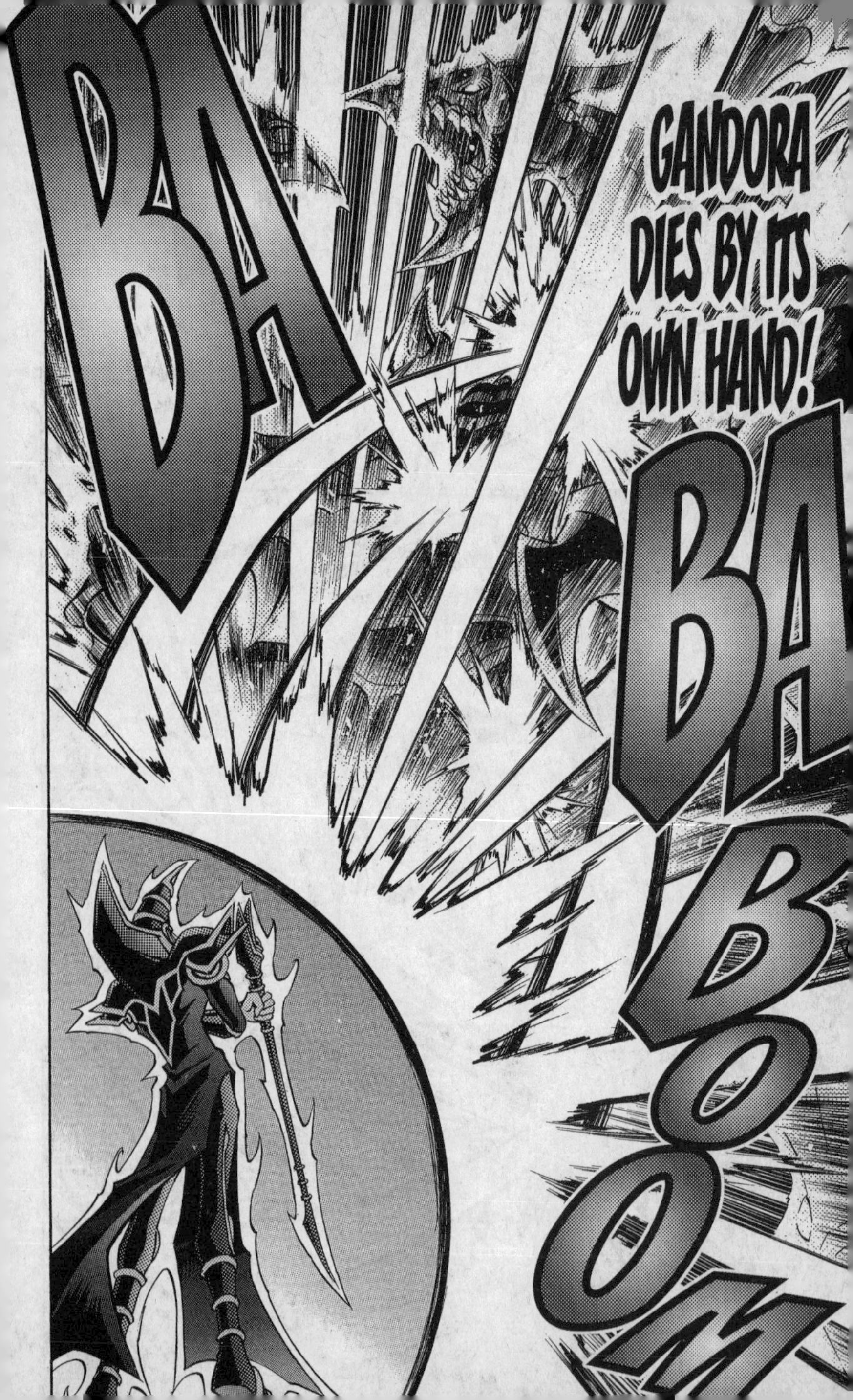
GANDORA DIES BY ITS OWN HAND!
BA
BA
BABOOM

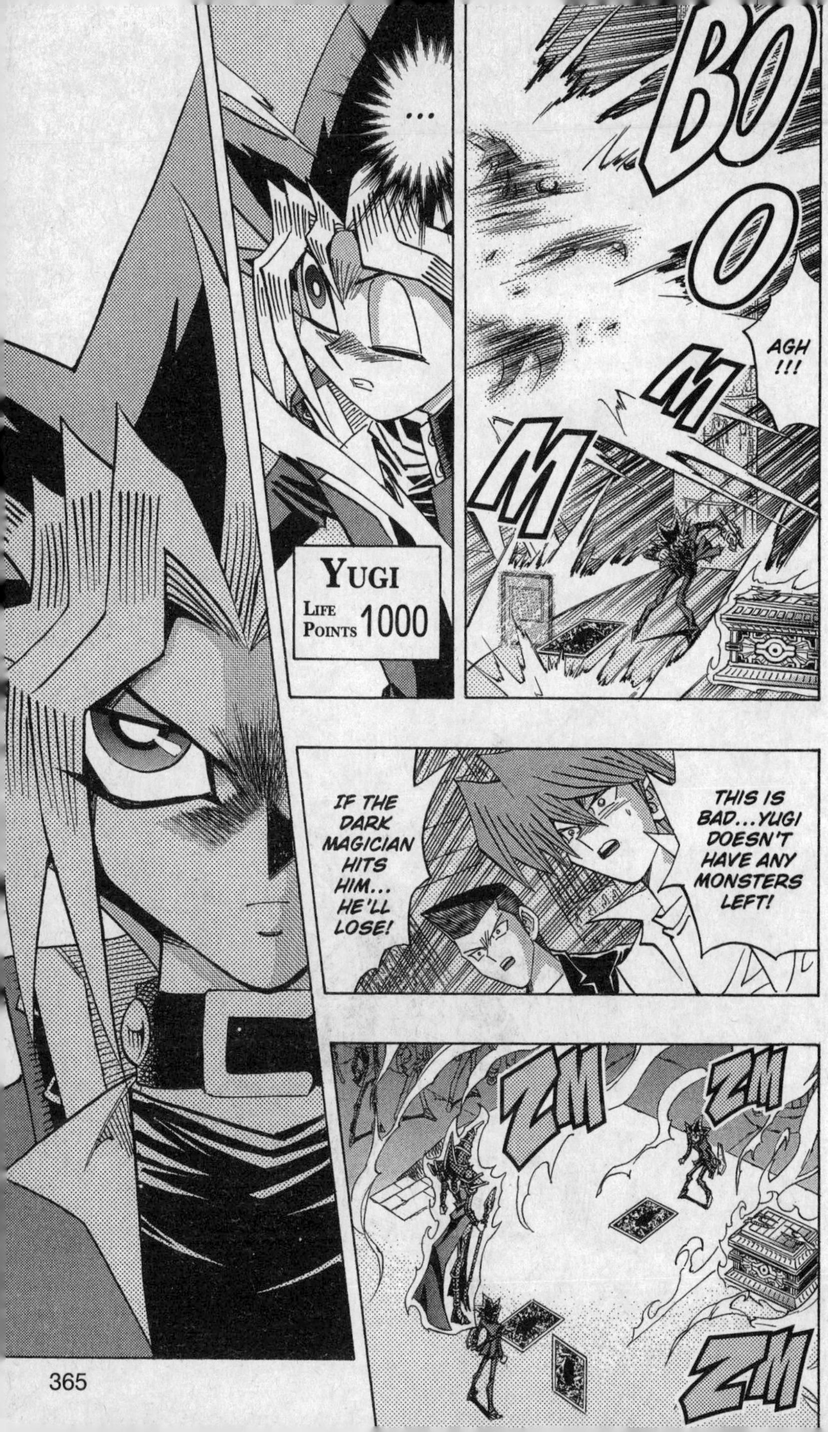
BOOM
AGH!!!
...
YUGI
LIFE POINTS 1000
THIS IS BAD...YUGI DOESN'T HAVE ANY MONSTERS LEFT!
IF THE DARK MAGICIAN HITS HIM... HE'LL LOSE!
ZM ZM
ZM

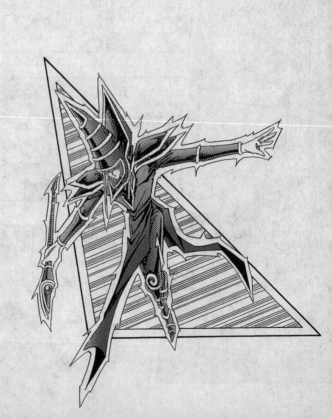

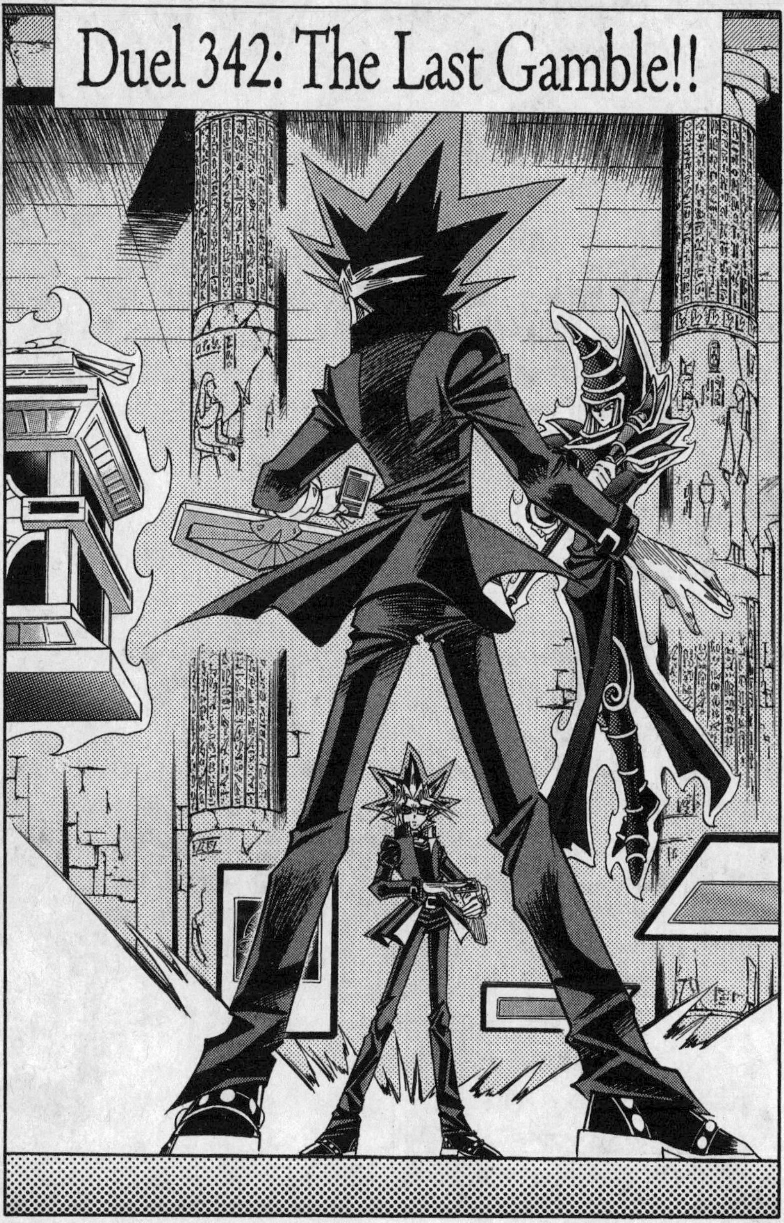
Duel 342: The Last Gamble!!

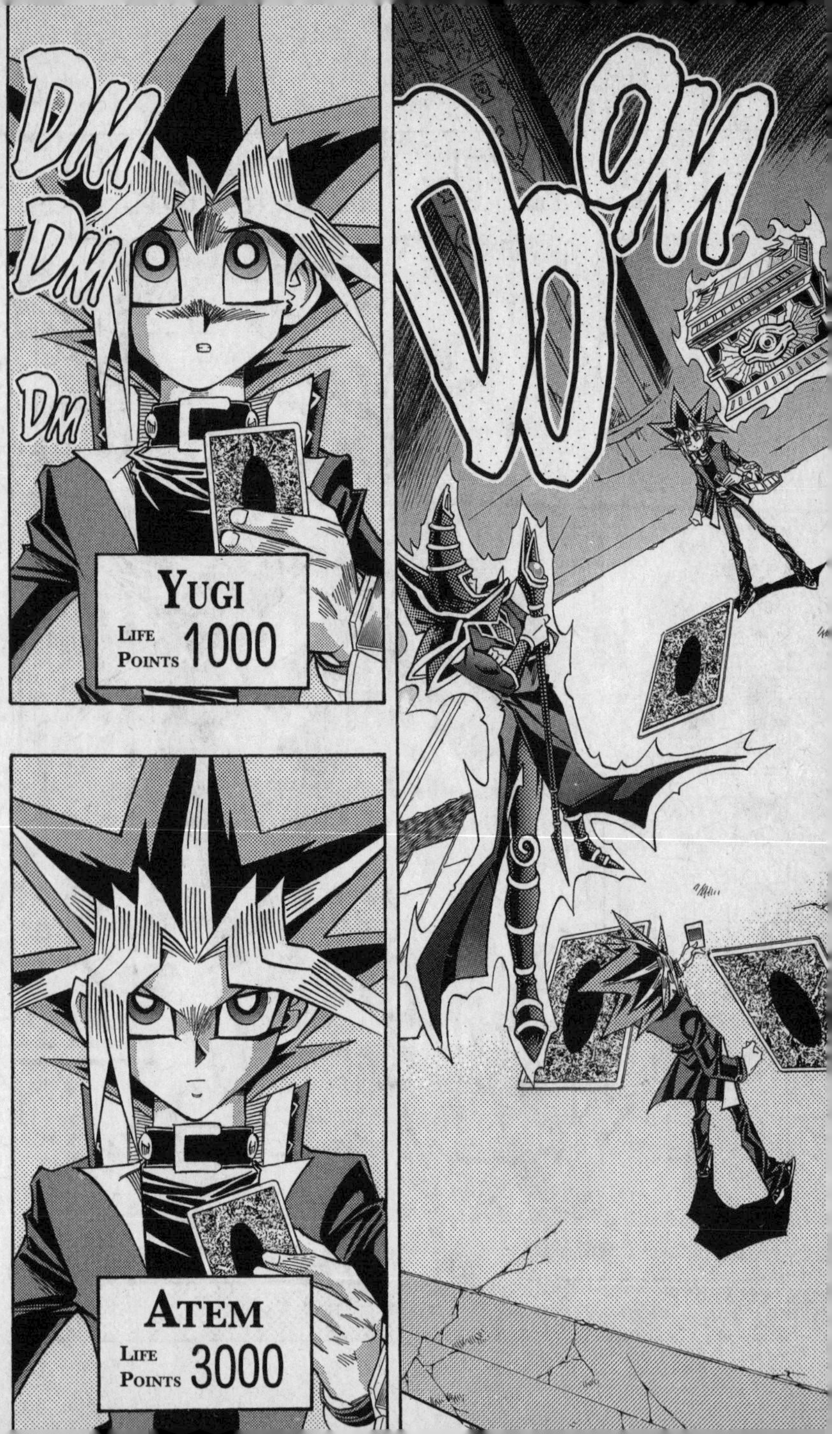
DOOM
DM
DM
DM
YUGI
LIFE POINTS 1000
ATEM
LIFE POINTS 3000

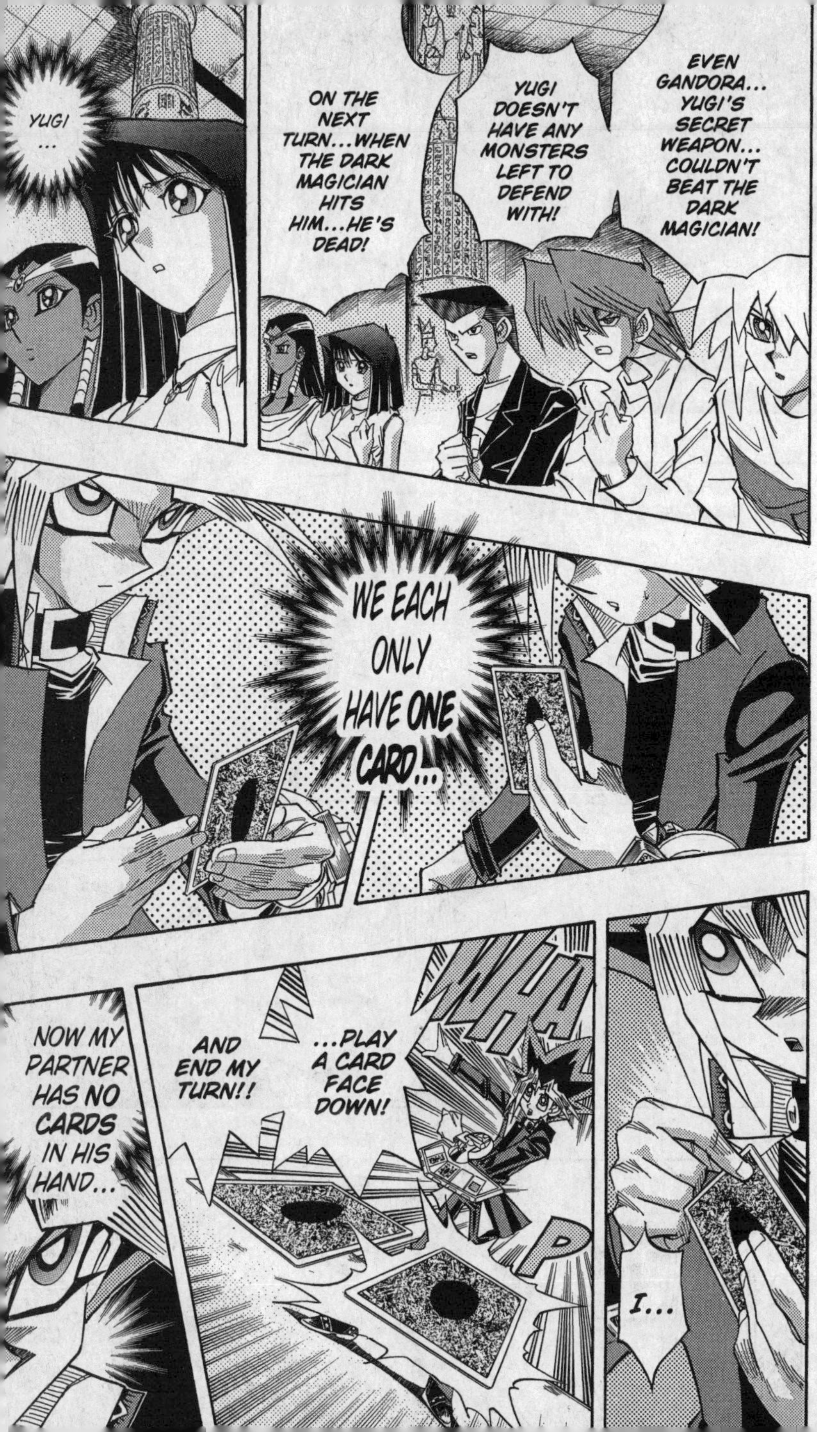
EVEN GANDORA... YUGI'S SECRET WEAPON... COULDN'T BEAT THE DARK MAGICIAN!
YUGI DOESN'T HAVE ANY MONSTERS LEFT TO DEFEND WITH!
ON THE NEXT TURN...WHEN THE DARK MAGICIAN HITS HIM...HE'S DEAD!
YUGI ...
WE EACH ONLY HAVE ONE CARD...
I...
WHAP
...PLAY A CARD FACE DOWN!
AND END MY TURN!!
NOW MY PARTNER HAS NO CARDS IN HIS HAND...

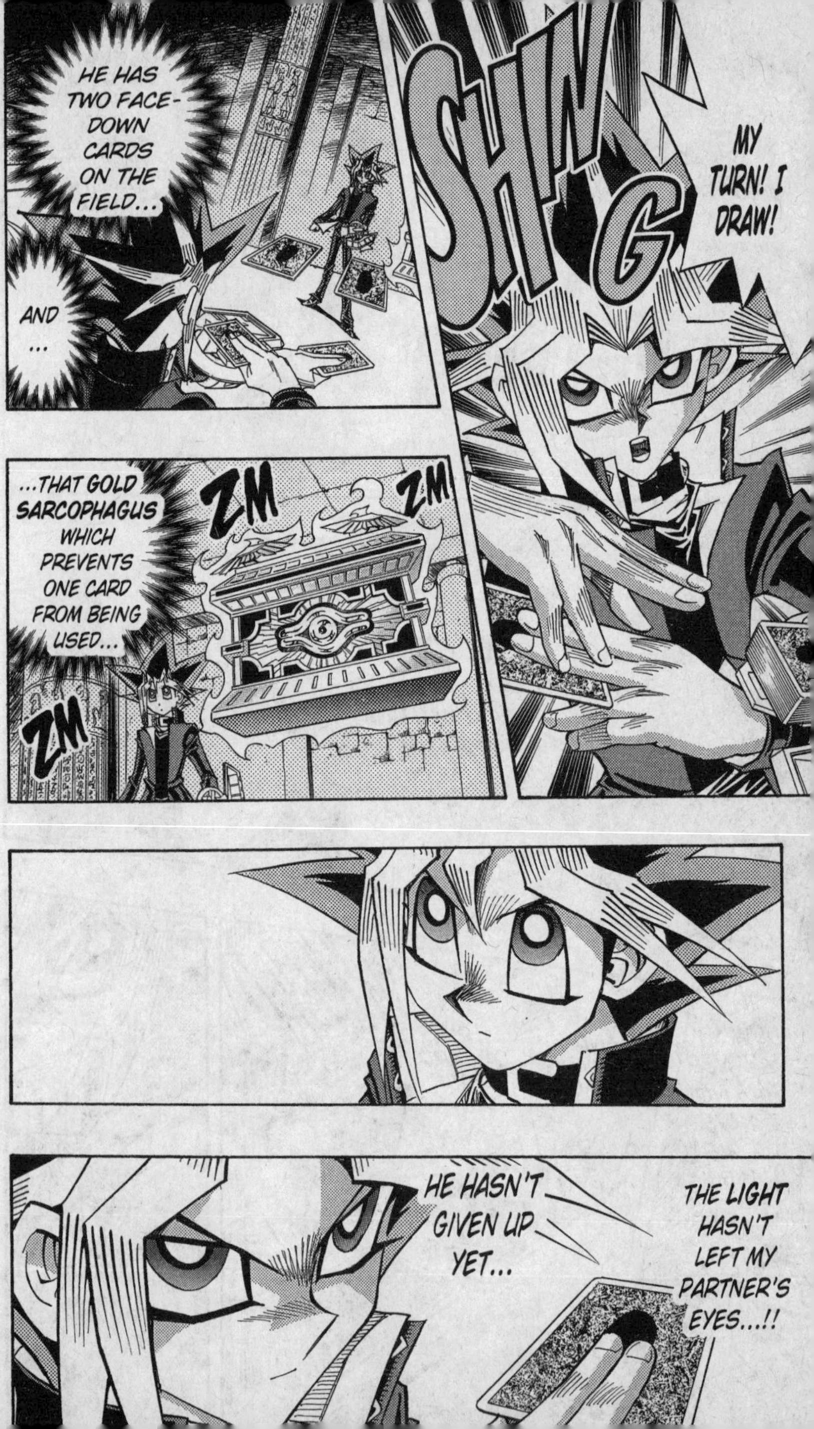
SHING
MY TURN! I DRAW!
HE HAS TWO FACE-DOWN CARDS ON THE FIELD...
AND ...
...THAT GOLD SARCOPHAGUS WHICH PREVENTS ONE CARD FROM BEING USED...
ZM
ZM
ZM
THE LIGHT HASN'T LEFT MY PARTNER'S EYES...!!
HE HASN'T GIVEN UP YET...

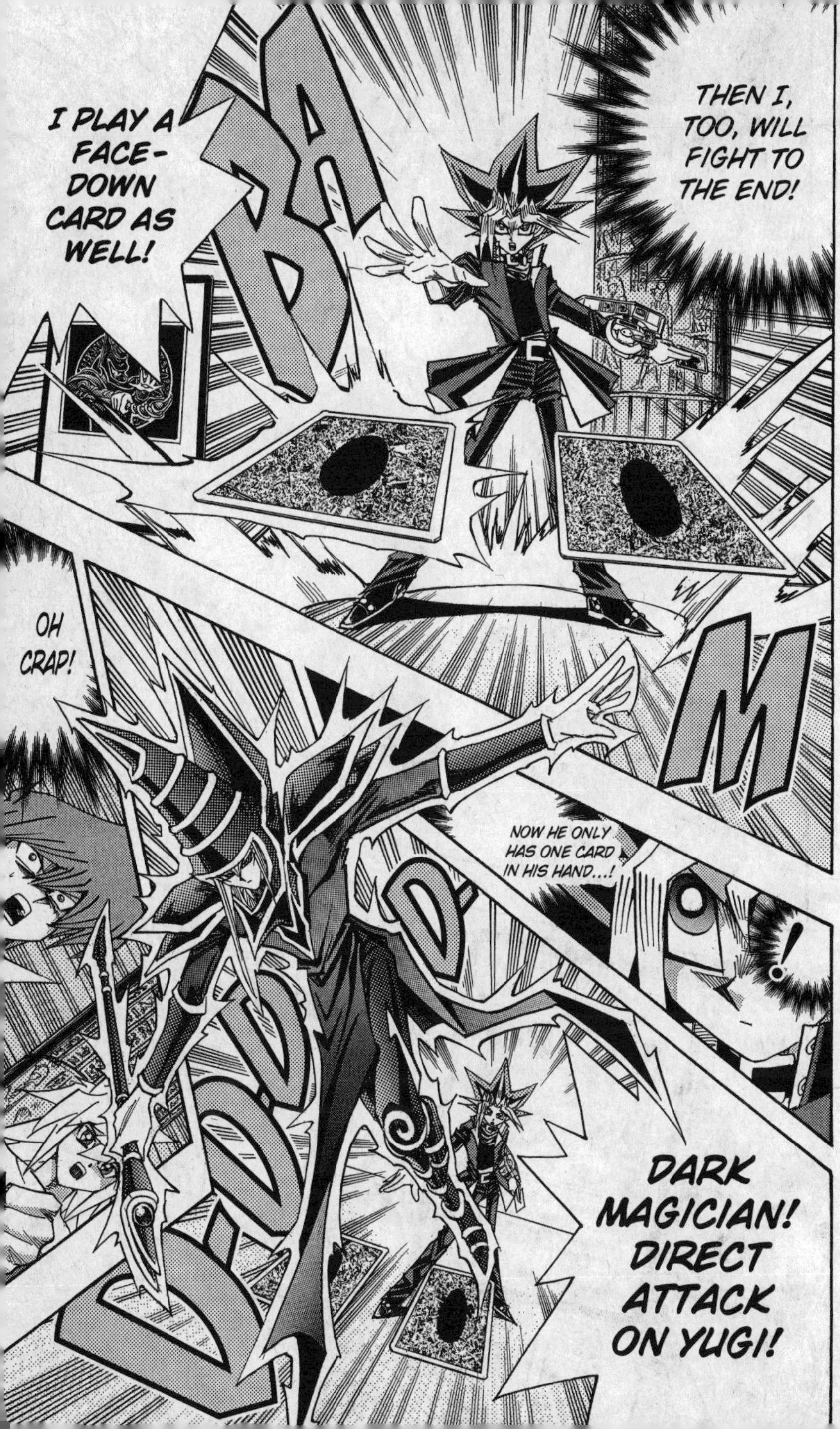
THEN I, TOO, WILL FIGHT TO THE END!
I PLAY A FACE-DOWN CARD AS WELL!
NOW HE ONLY HAS ONE CARD IN HIS HAND...!
!
OH CRAP!
DARK MAGICIAN! DIRECT ATTACK ON YUGI!

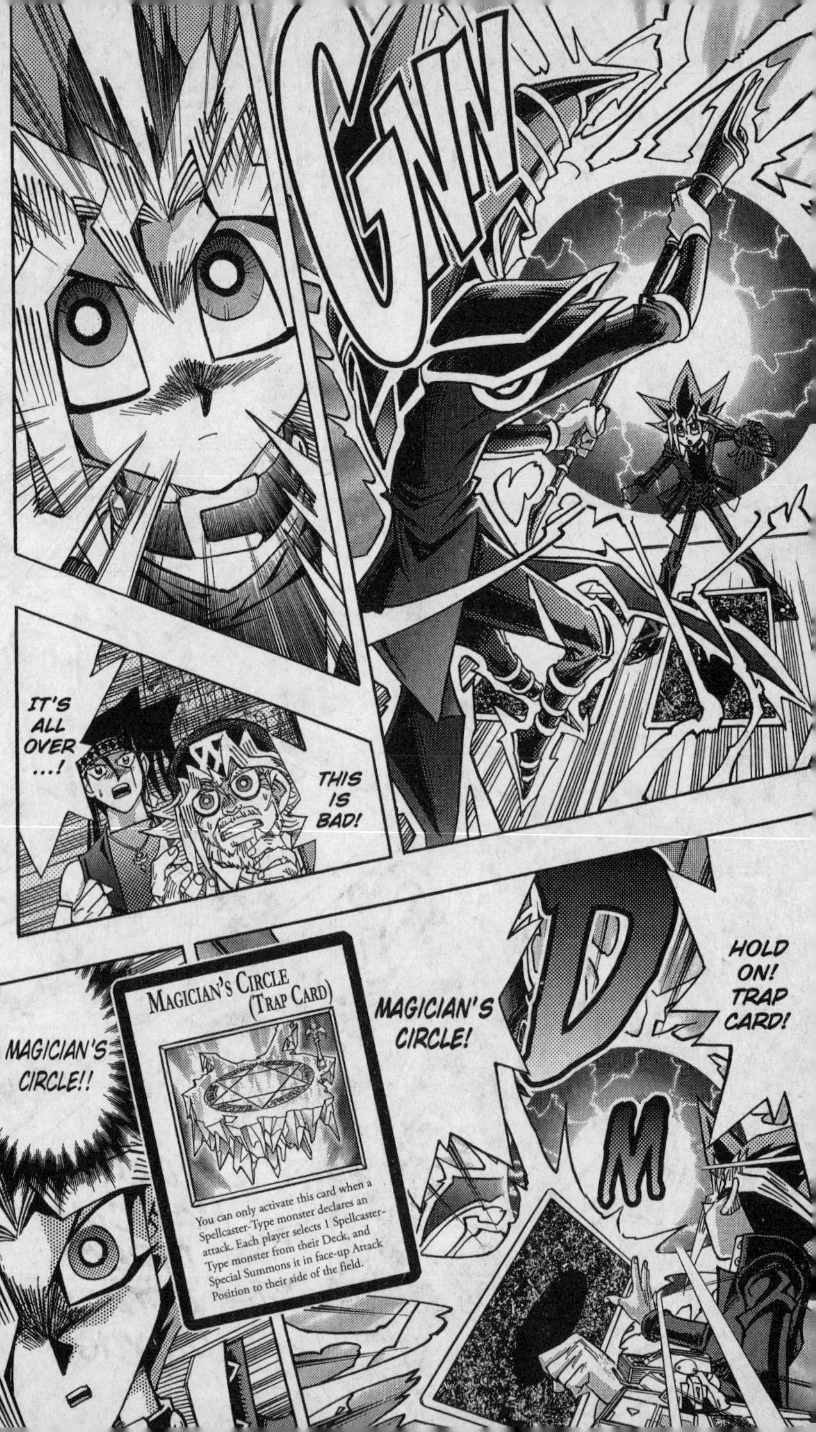
GWN
THIS IS BAD!
IT'S ALL OVER ...!
HOLD ON! TRAP CARD!
D
MAGICIAN'S CIRCLE!
M
MAGICIAN'S CIRCLE (TRAP CARD)
You can only activate this card when a Spellcaster-Type monster declares an attack. Each player selects 1 Spellcaster-Type monster from their Deck, and Special Summons it in face-up Attack Position to their side of the field.
MAGICIAN'S CIRCLE!!

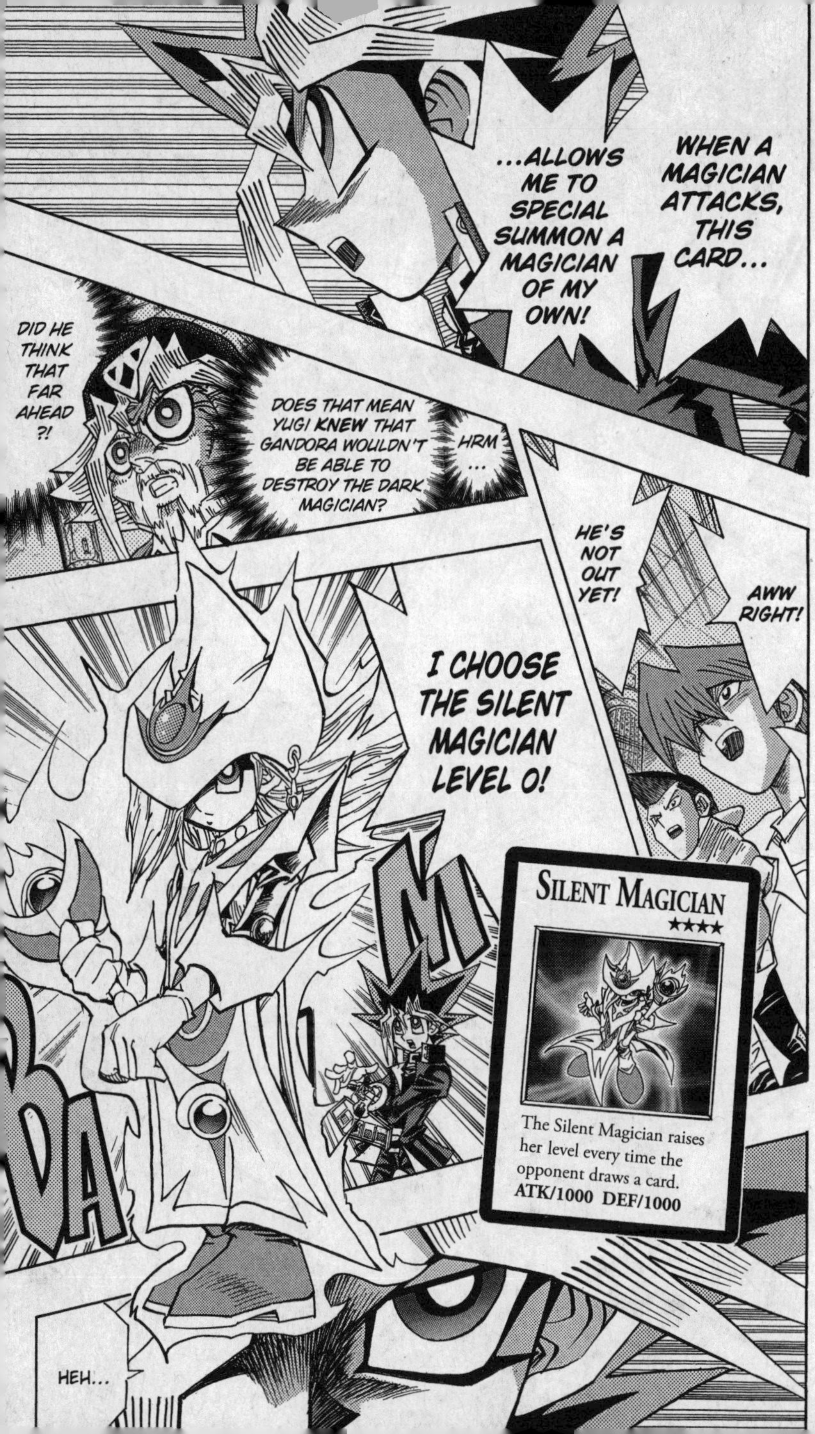
WHEN A MAGICIAN ATTACKS, THIS CARD...
...ALLOWS ME TO SPECIAL SUMMON A MAGICIAN OF MY OWN!
HRM...
DOES THAT MEAN YUGI KNEW THAT GANDORA WOULDN'T BE ABLE TO DESTROY THE DARK MAGICIAN?
DID HE THINK THAT FAR AHEAD?!
AWW RIGHT!
HE'S NOT OUT YET!
I CHOOSE THE SILENT MAGICIAN LEVEL 0!
SILENT MAGICIAN
★★★★
The Silent Magician raises her level every time the opponent draws a card.
ATK/1000 DEF/1000
HEH...

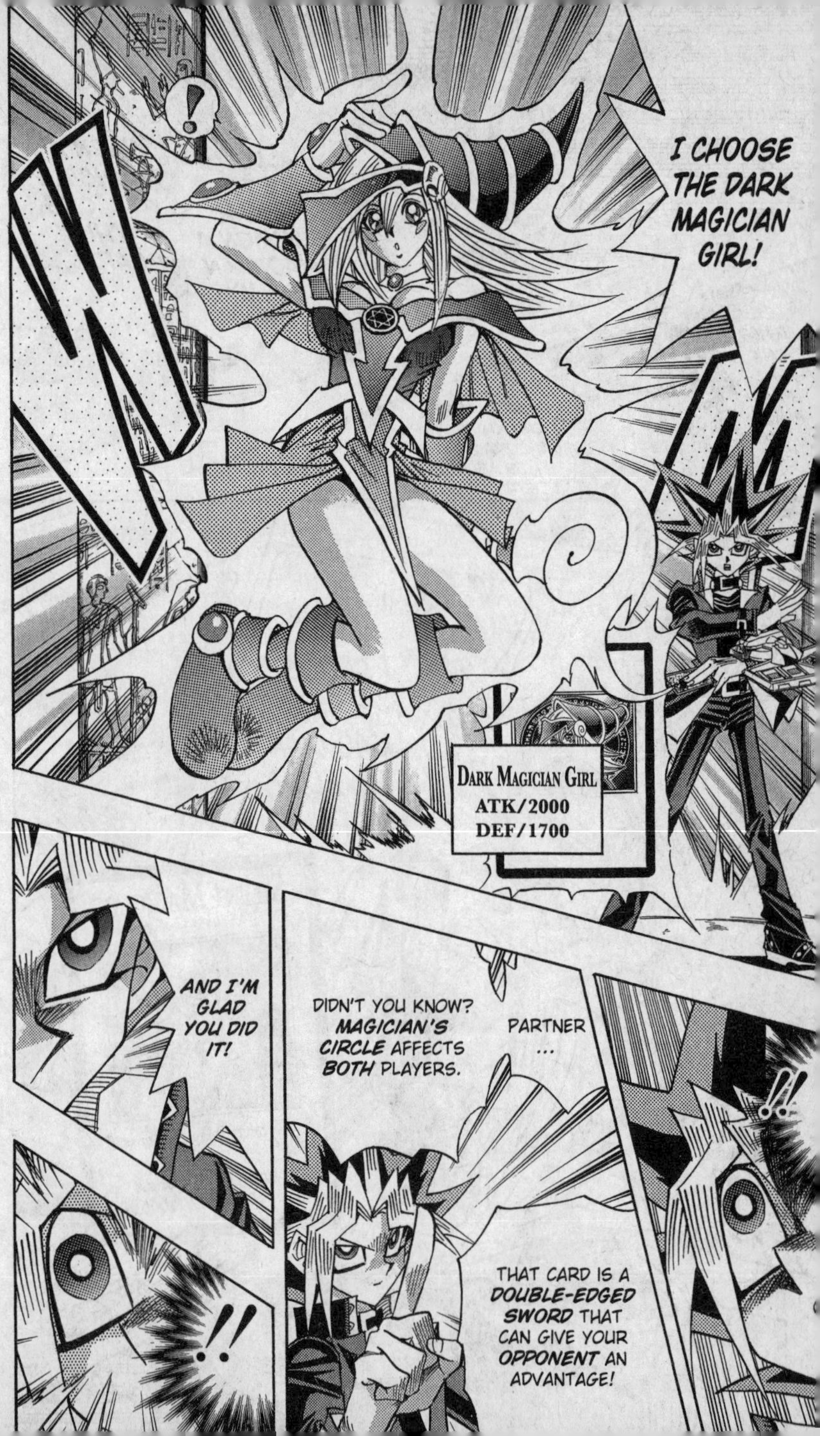
I CHOOSE THE DARK MAGICIAN GIRL!
!
DARK MAGICIAN GIRL ATK/2000 DEF/1700
!!
PARTNER ...
DIDN'T YOU KNOW? MAGICIAN'S CIRCLE AFFECTS BOTH PLAYERS.
THAT CARD IS A DOUBLE-EDGED SWORD THAT CAN GIVE YOUR OPPONENT AN ADVANTAGE!
AND I'M GLAD YOU DID IT!
!!

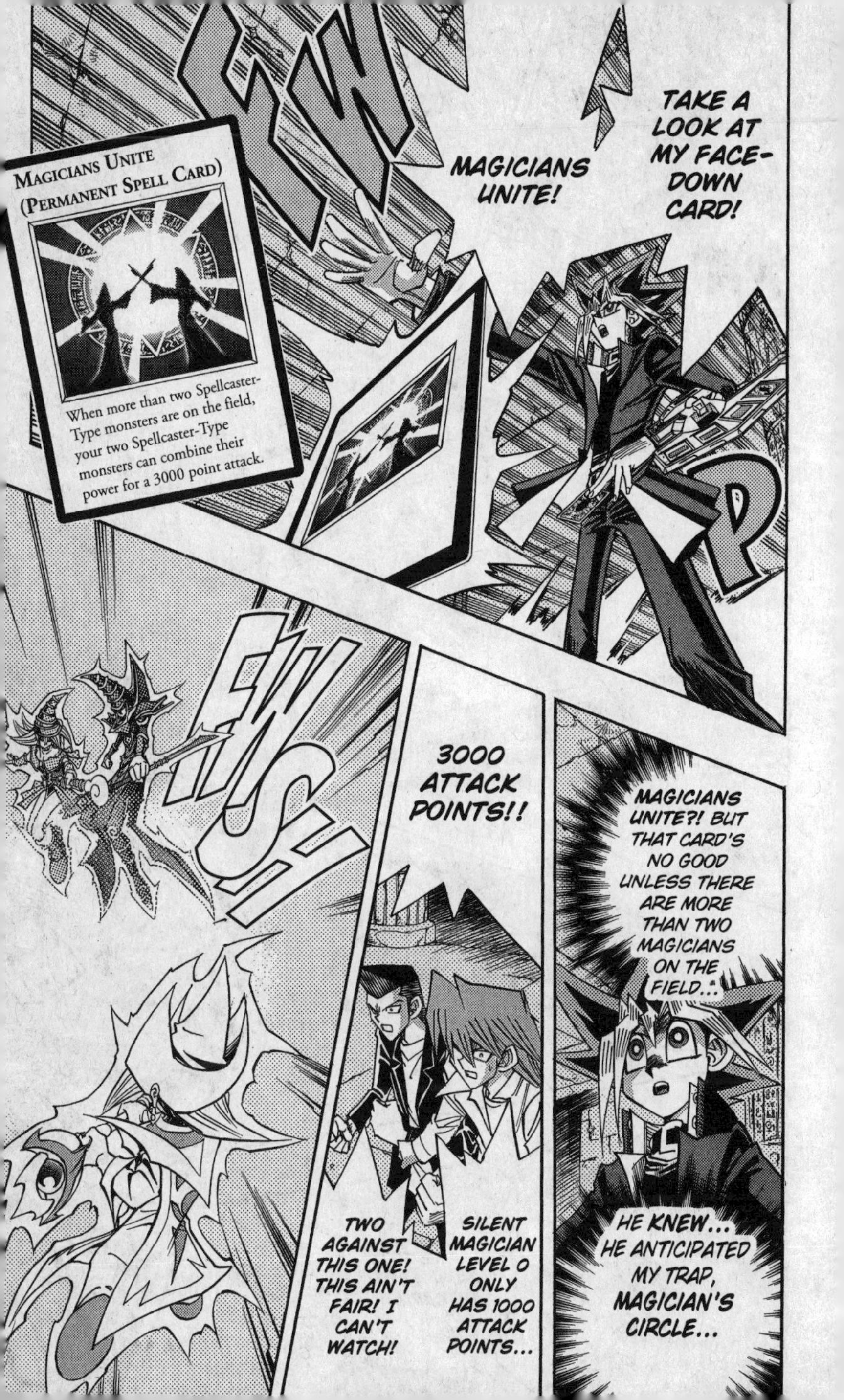
TAKE A LOOK AT MY FACE-DOWN CARD!
MAGICIANS UNITE!
MAGICIANS UNITE
(PERMANENT SPELL CARD)
When more than two Spellcaster-Type monsters are on the field, your two Spellcaster-Type monsters can combine their power for a 3000 point attack.
MAGICIANS UNITE?! BUT THAT CARD'S NO GOOD UNLESS THERE ARE MORE THAN TWO MAGICIANS ON THE FIELD...
HE KNEW... HE ANTICIPATED MY TRAP, MAGICIAN'S CIRCLE...
3000 ATTACK POINTS!!
SILENT MAGICIAN LEVEL 0 ONLY HAS 1000 ATTACK POINTS...
TWO AGAINST THIS ONE! THIS AIN'T FAIR! I CAN'T WATCH!

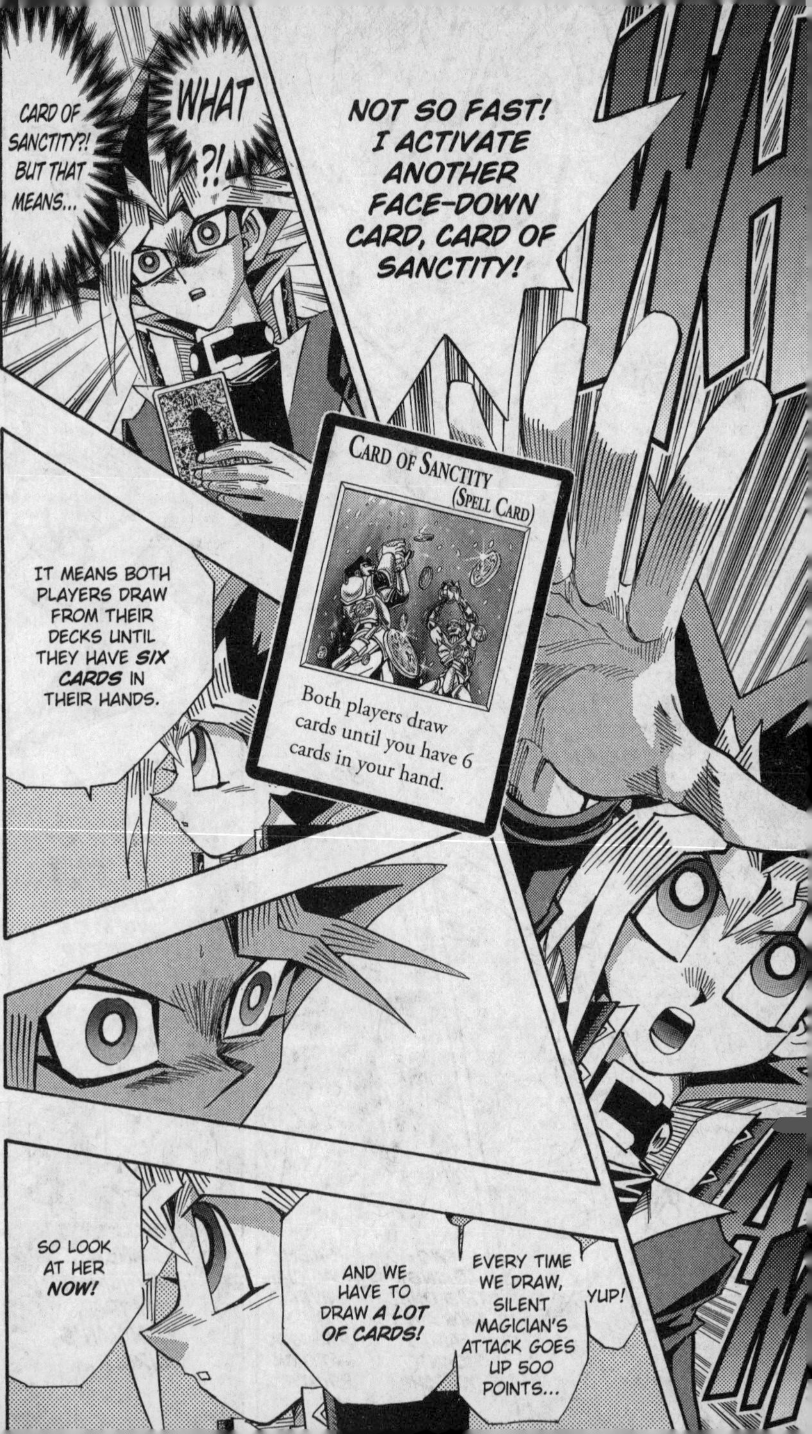
NOT SO FAST! I ACTIVATE ANOTHER FACE-DOWN CARD, CARD OF SANCTITY!
CARD OF SANCTITY
(SPELL CARD)
Both players draw cards until you have 6 cards in your hand.
WHAT ?!
CARD OF SANCTITY?! BUT THAT MEANS...
IT MEANS BOTH PLAYERS DRAW FROM THEIR DECKS UNTIL THEY HAVE *SIX CARDS* IN THEIR HANDS.
YUP!
EVERY TIME WE DRAW, SILENT MAGICIAN'S ATTACK GOES UP 500 POINTS...
AND WE HAVE TO DRAW *A LOT OF CARDS!*
SO LOOK AT HER *NOW!*

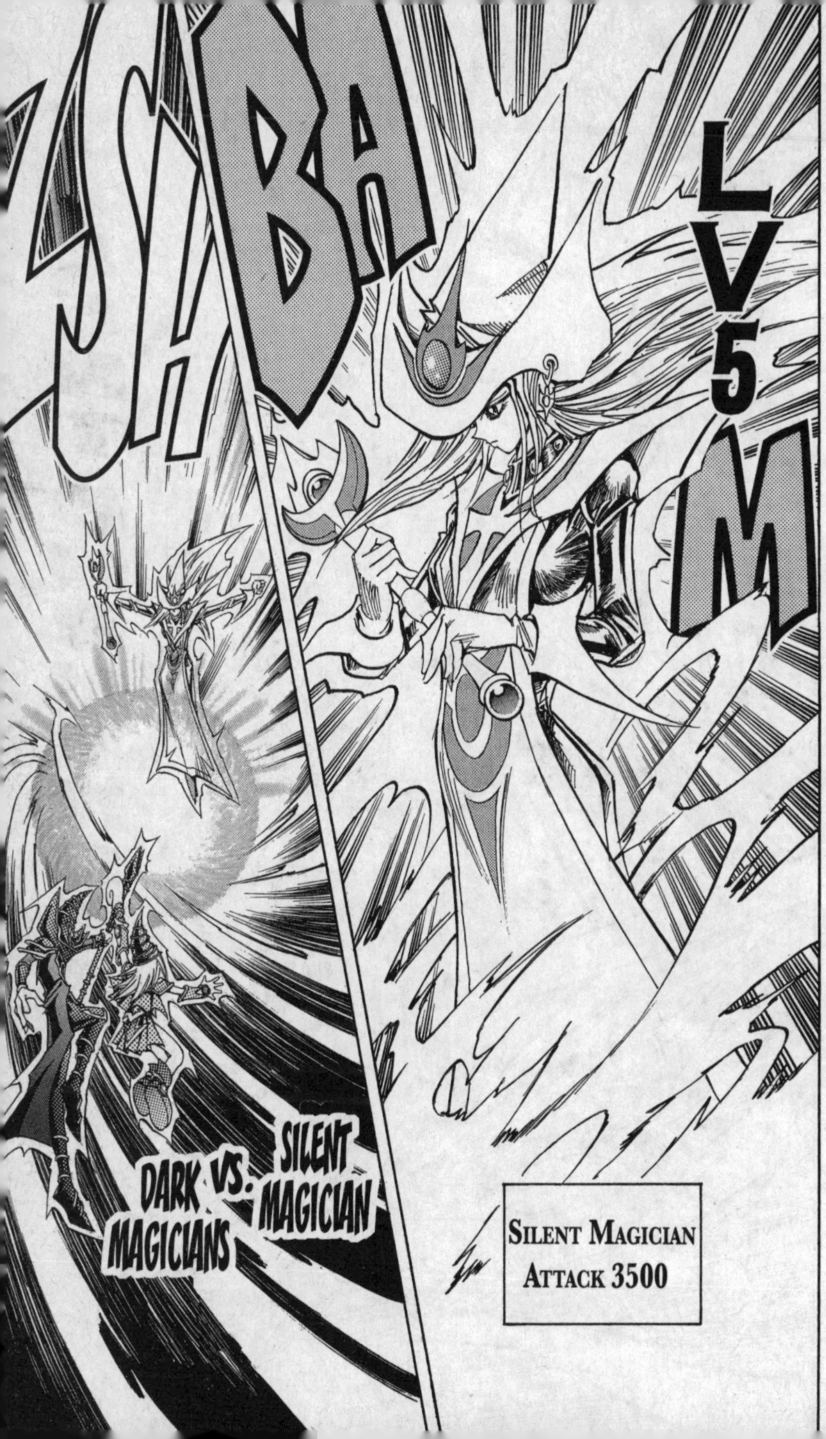
LV5
M
SILENT MAGICIAN
ATTACK 3500
SHABA
DARK MAGICIANS VS. SILENT MAGICIAN

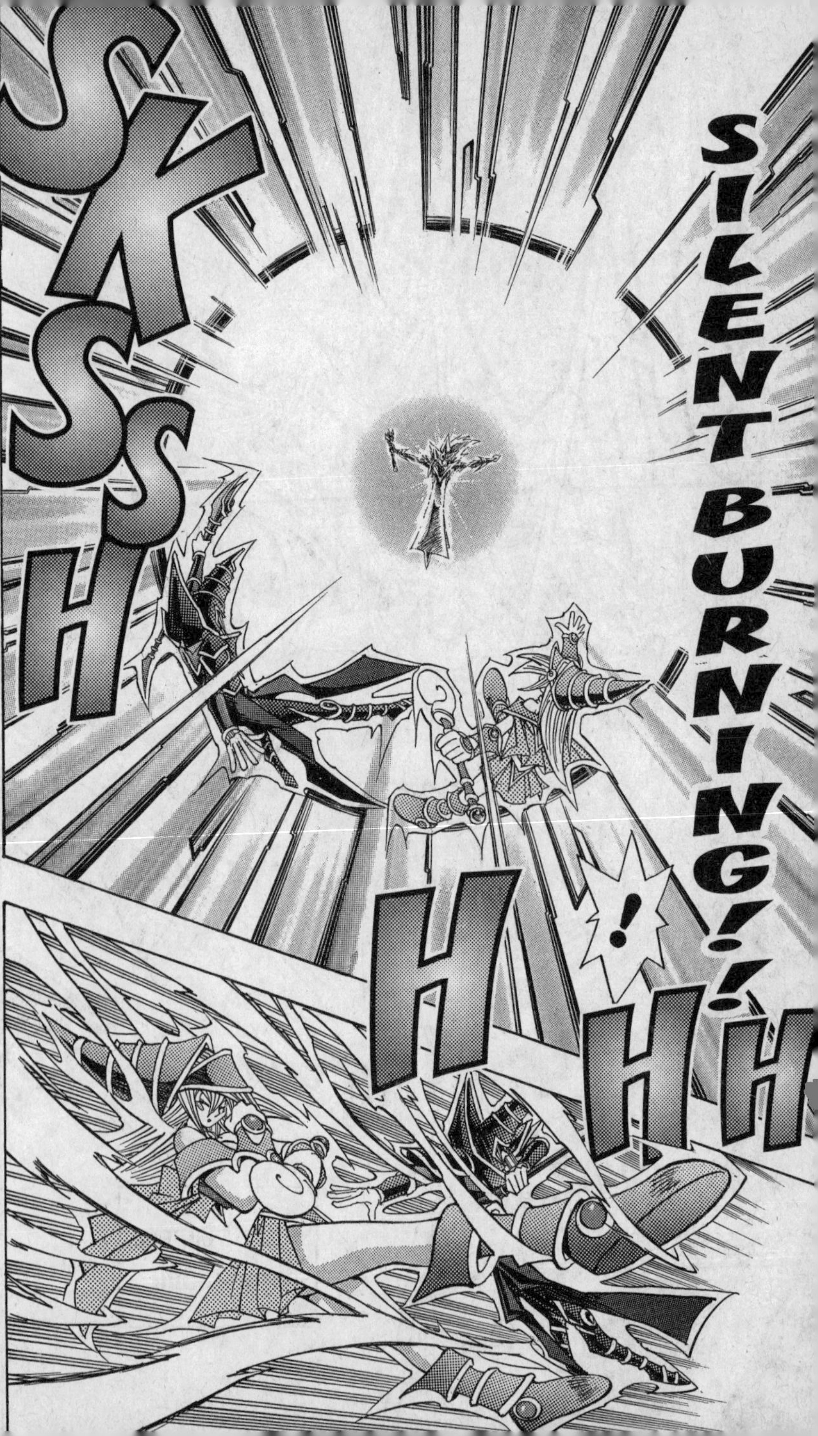
SILENT BURNING!!
SXSSH
!
HHH

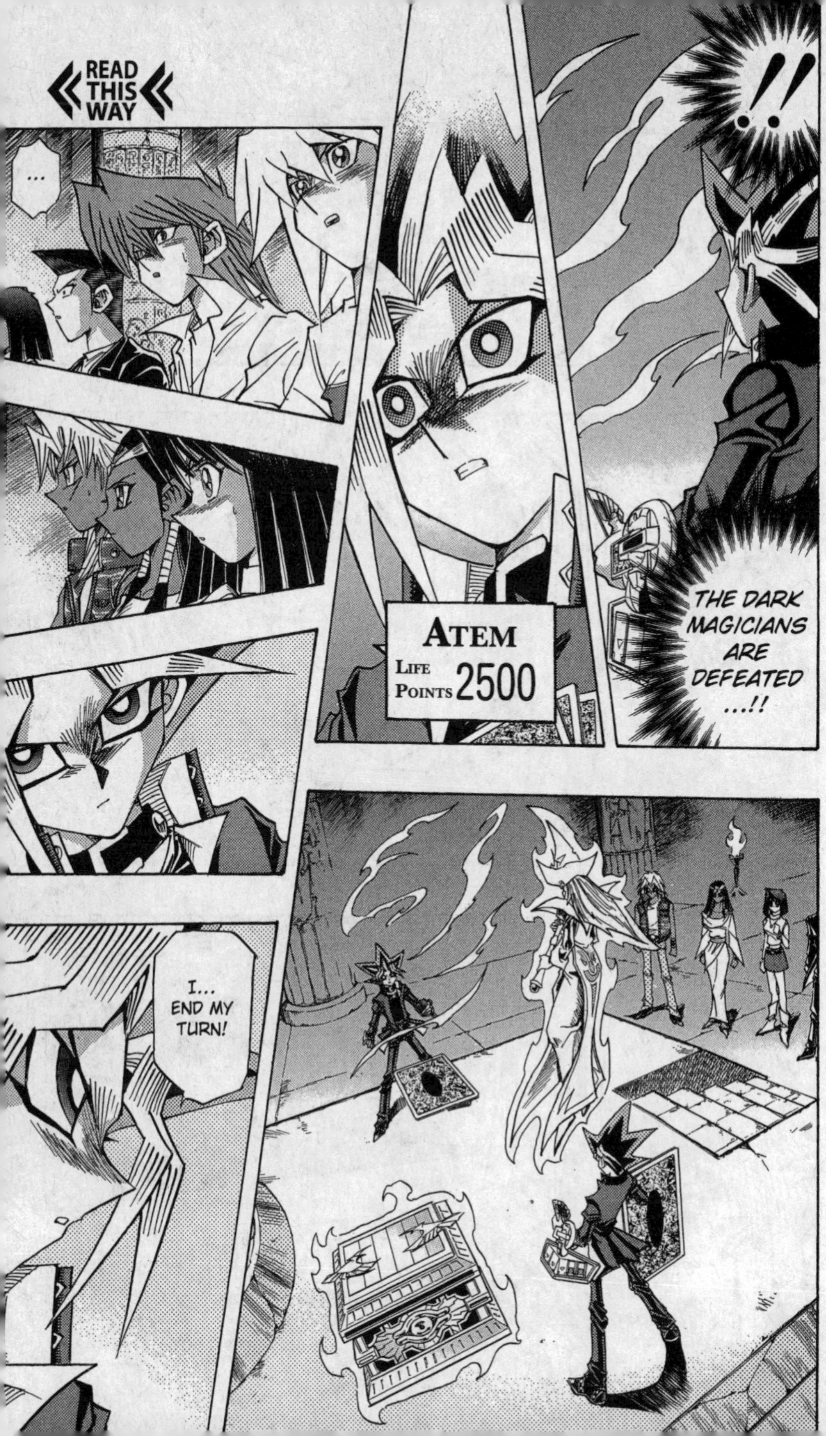
READ THIS WAY
!!
THE DARK MAGICIANS ARE DEFEATED ...!!
ATEM
LIFE POINTS 2500
...
I... END MY TURN!

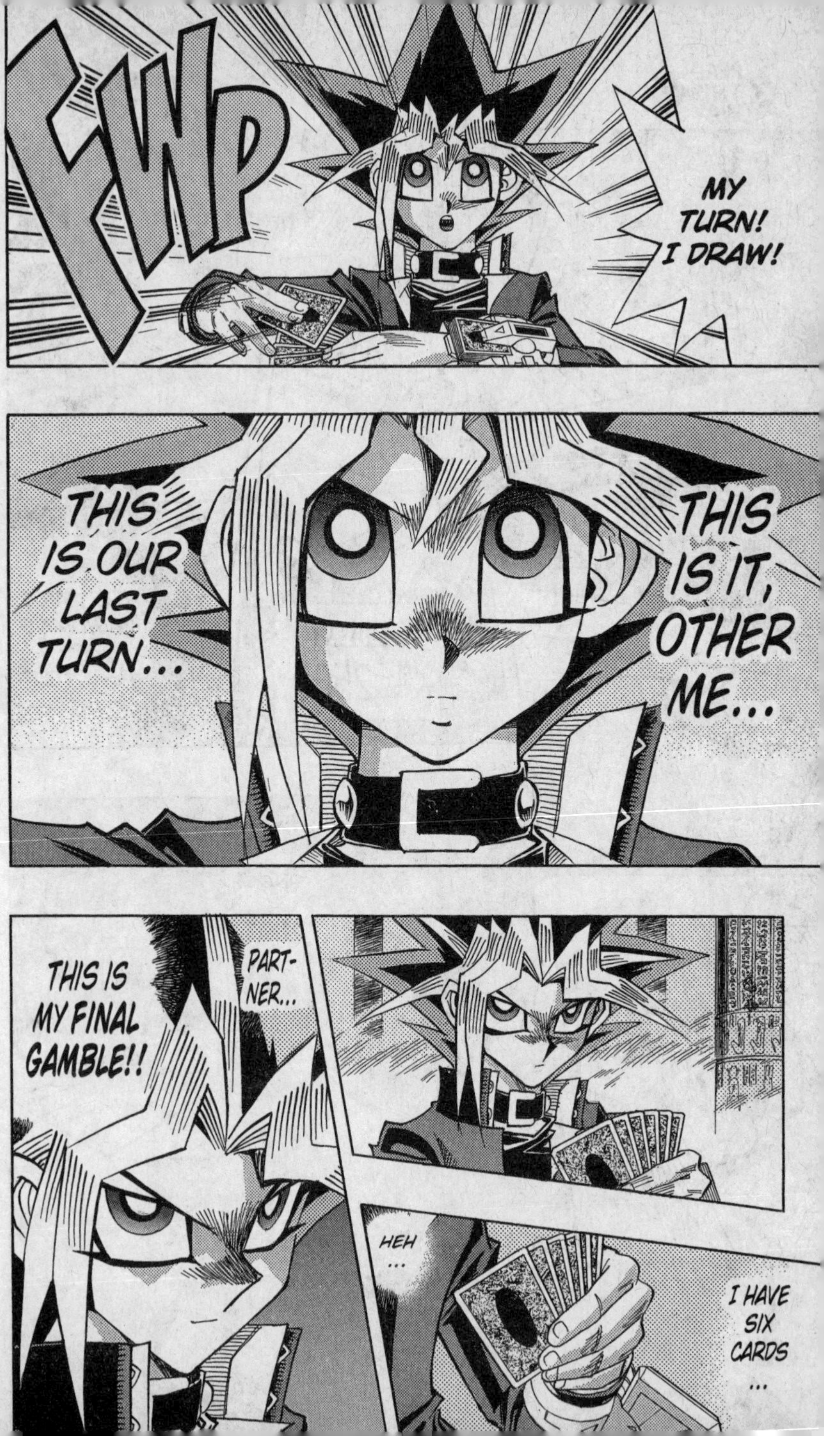
MY TURN! I DRAW!
FWP
THIS IS IT, OTHER ME...
THIS IS OUR LAST TURN...
I HAVE SIX CARDS ...
HEH ...
PART-NER...
THIS IS MY FINAL GAMBLE!!

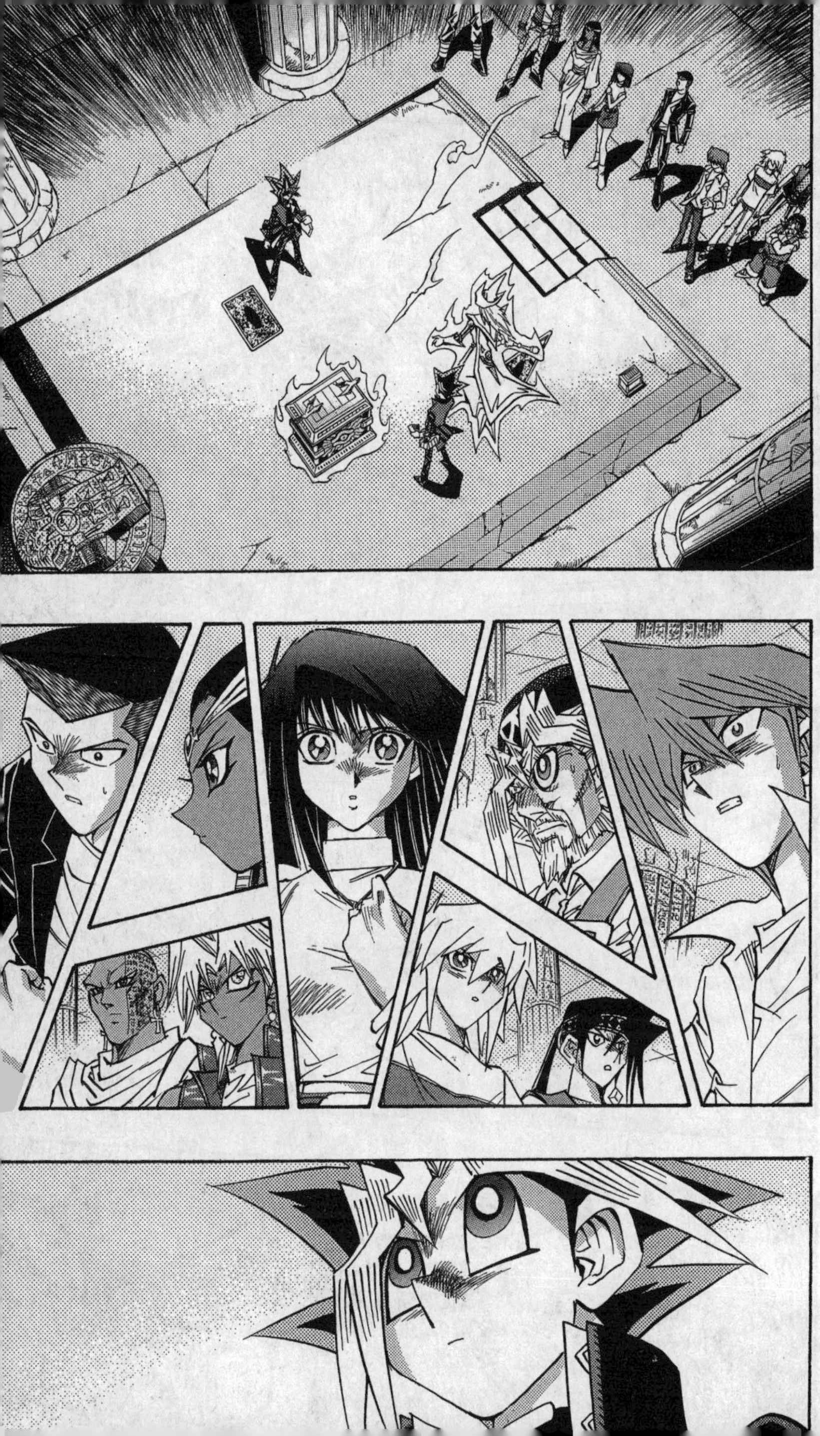

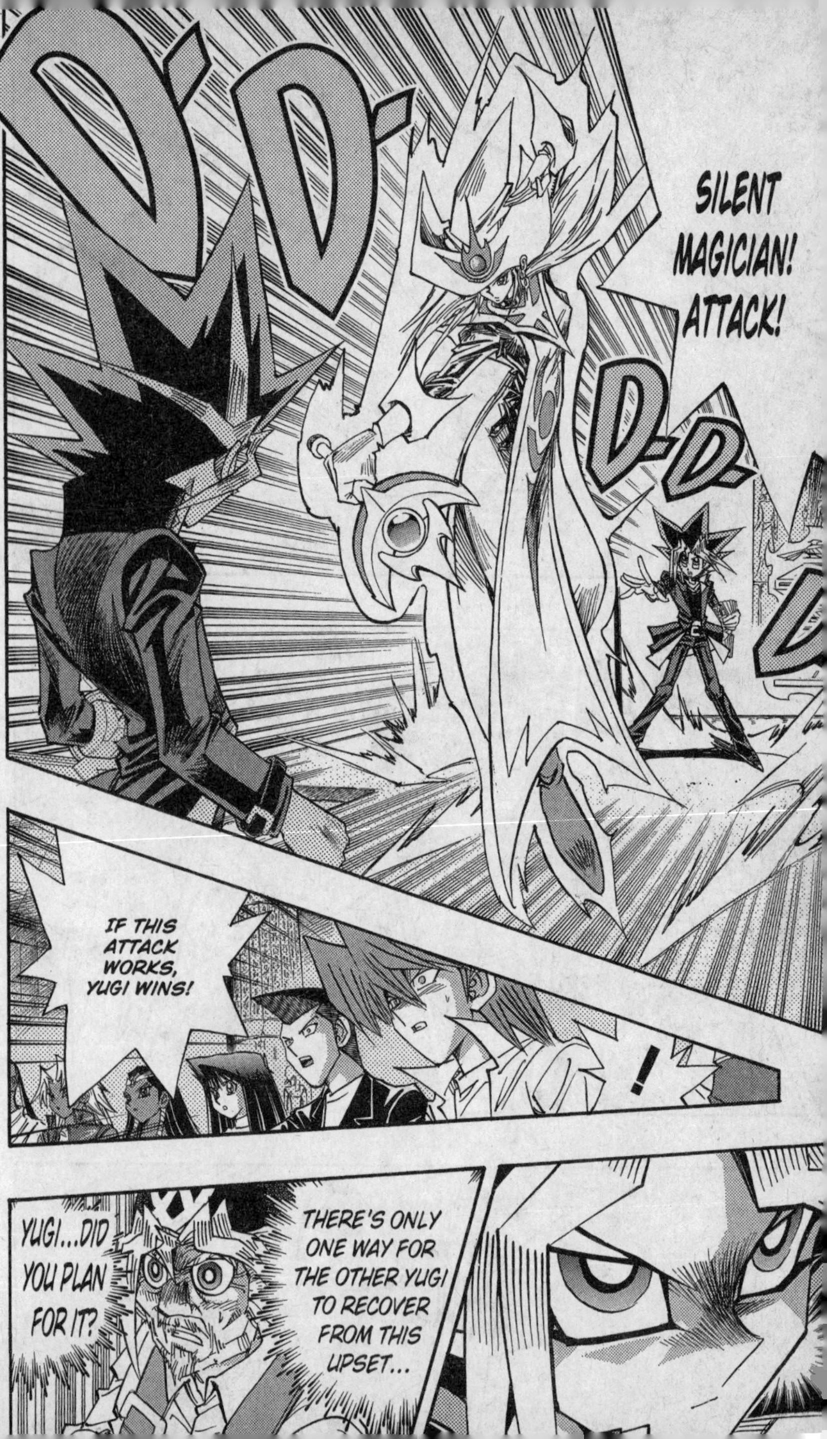
D-D-
SILENT MAGICIAN! ATTACK!
D-D-
IF THIS ATTACK WORKS, YUGI WINS!
!
THERE'S ONLY ONE WAY FOR THE OTHER YUGI TO RECOVER FROM THIS UPSET...
YUGI...DID YOU PLAN FOR IT?

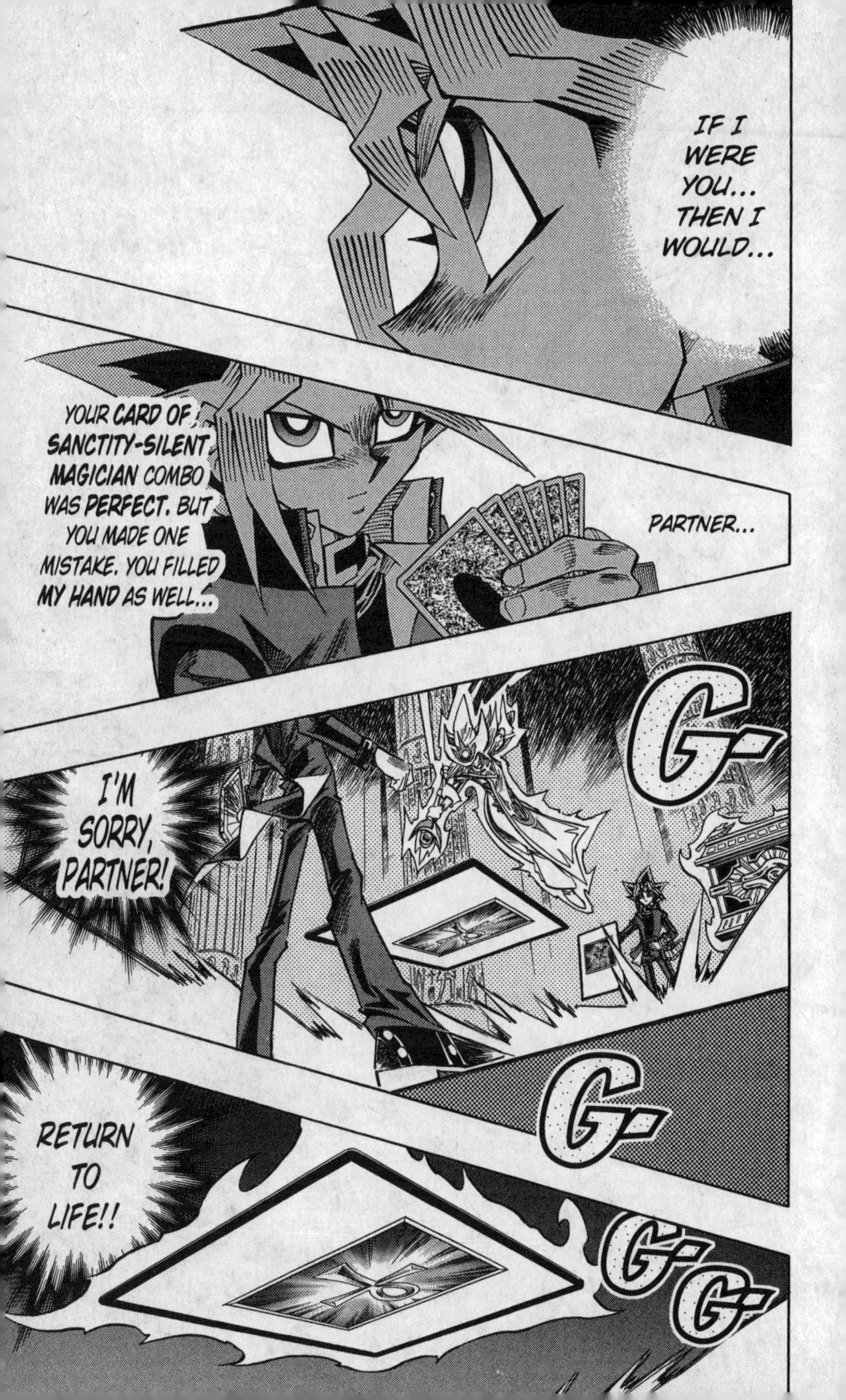
IF I WERE YOU... THEN I WOULD...
PARTNER...
YOUR CARD OF SANCTITY-SILENT MAGICIAN COMBO WAS PERFECT. BUT YOU MADE ONE MISTAKE. YOU FILLED MY HAND AS WELL...
G-
I'M SORRY, PARTNER!
G-
RETURN TO LIFE!!
G-G-

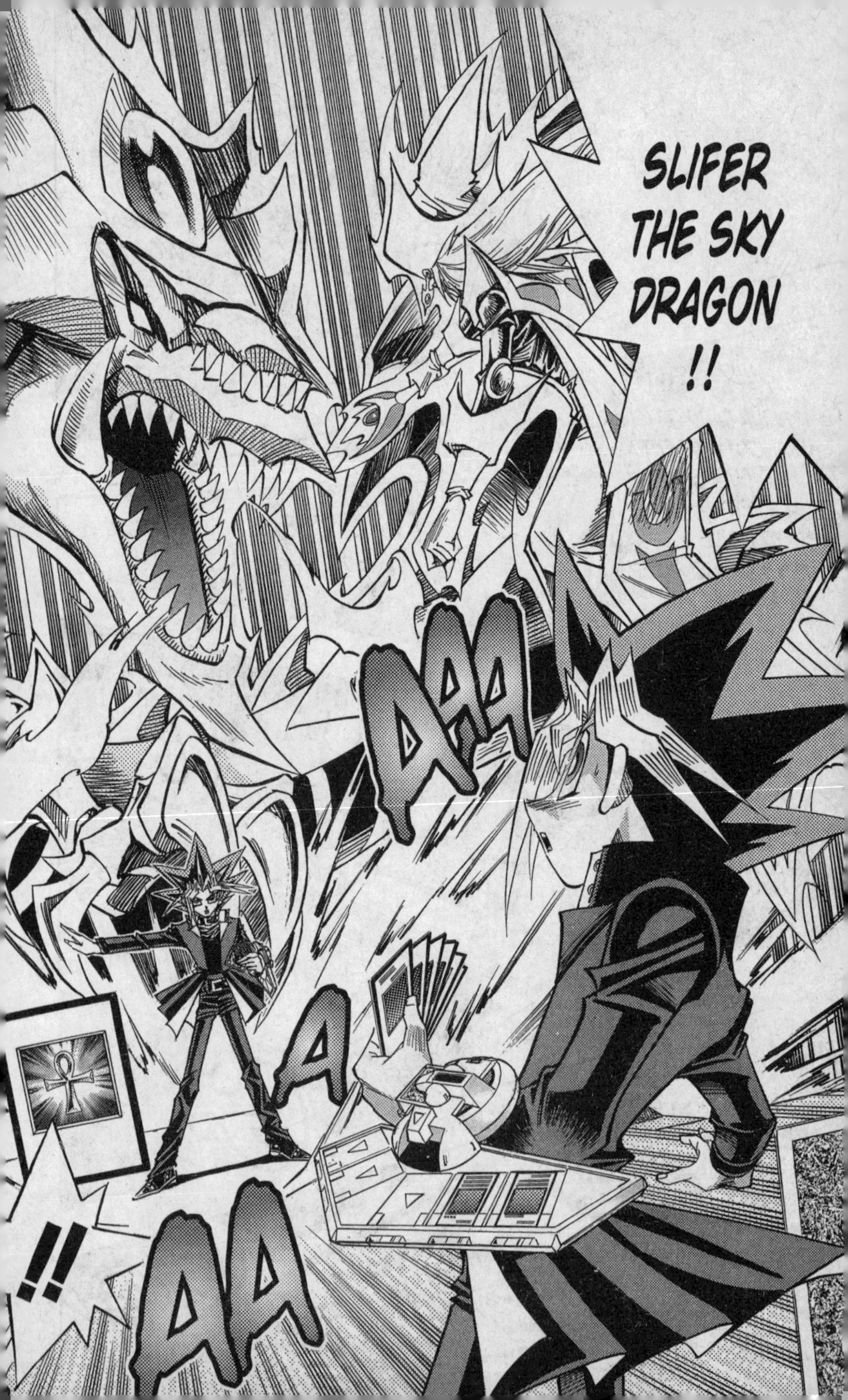
SLIFER THE SKY DRAGON !!
AAAAAA !!

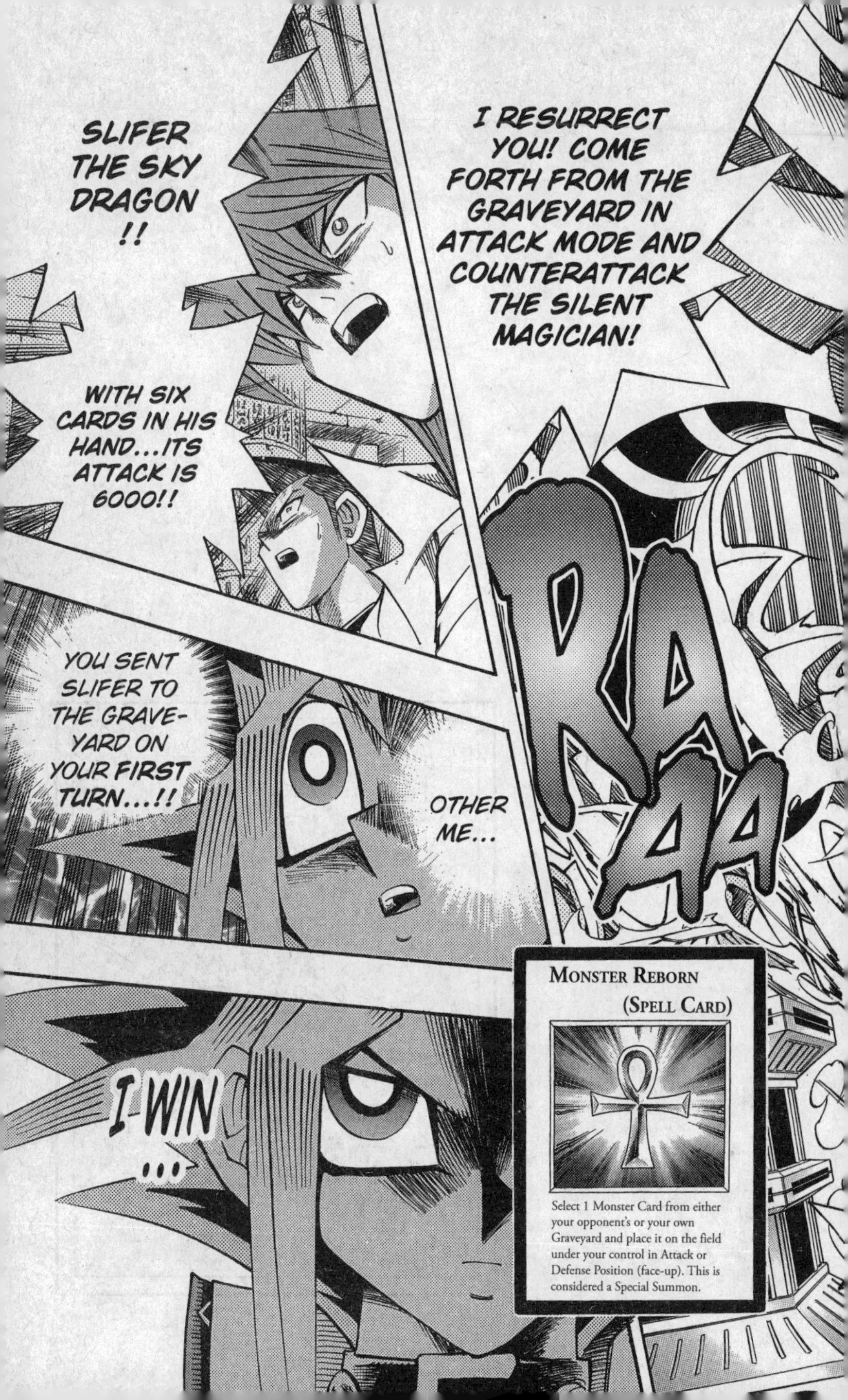
I RESURRECT YOU! COME FORTH FROM THE GRAVEYARD IN ATTACK MODE AND COUNTERATTACK THE SILENT MAGICIAN!
RAAA
MONSTER REBORN
(SPELL CARD)
Select 1 Monster Card from either your opponent's or your own Graveyard and place it on the field under your control in Attack or Defense Position (face-up). This is considered a Special Summon.
SLIFER THE SKY DRAGON !!
WITH SIX CARDS IN HIS HAND...ITS ATTACK IS 6000!!
OTHER ME...
YOU SENT SLIFER TO THE GRAVE-YARD ON YOUR FIRST TURN...!!
I WIN ...

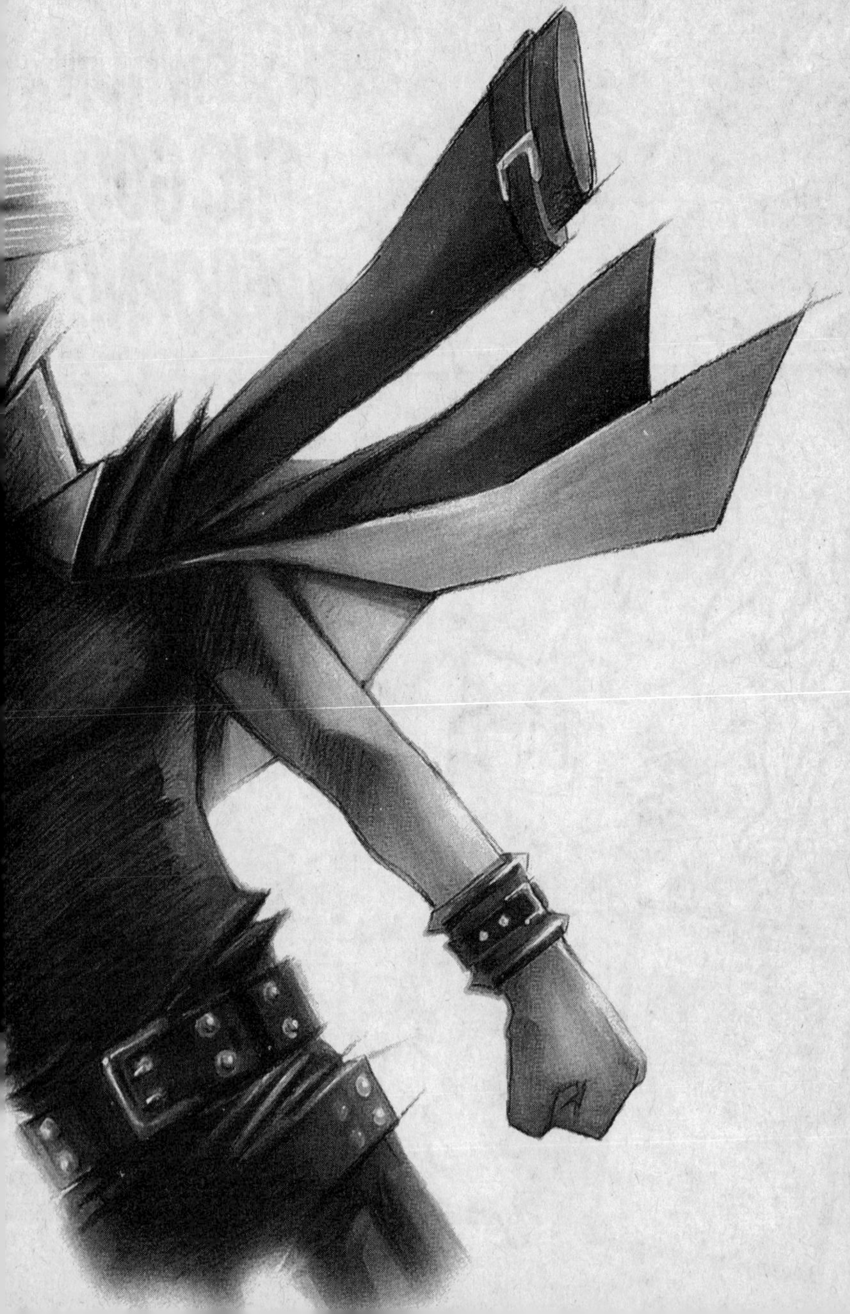

Last Duel:
The Journey of the King

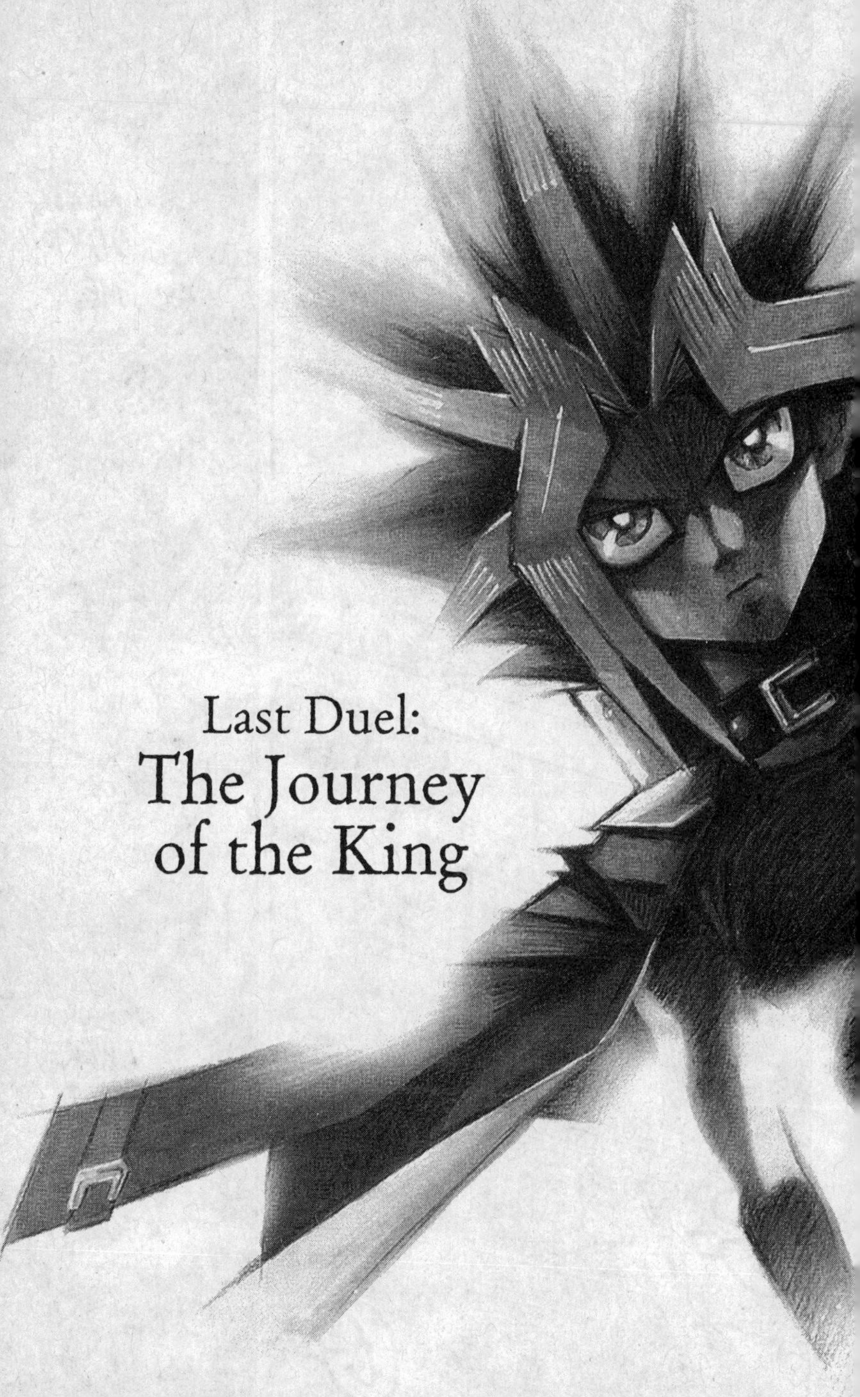

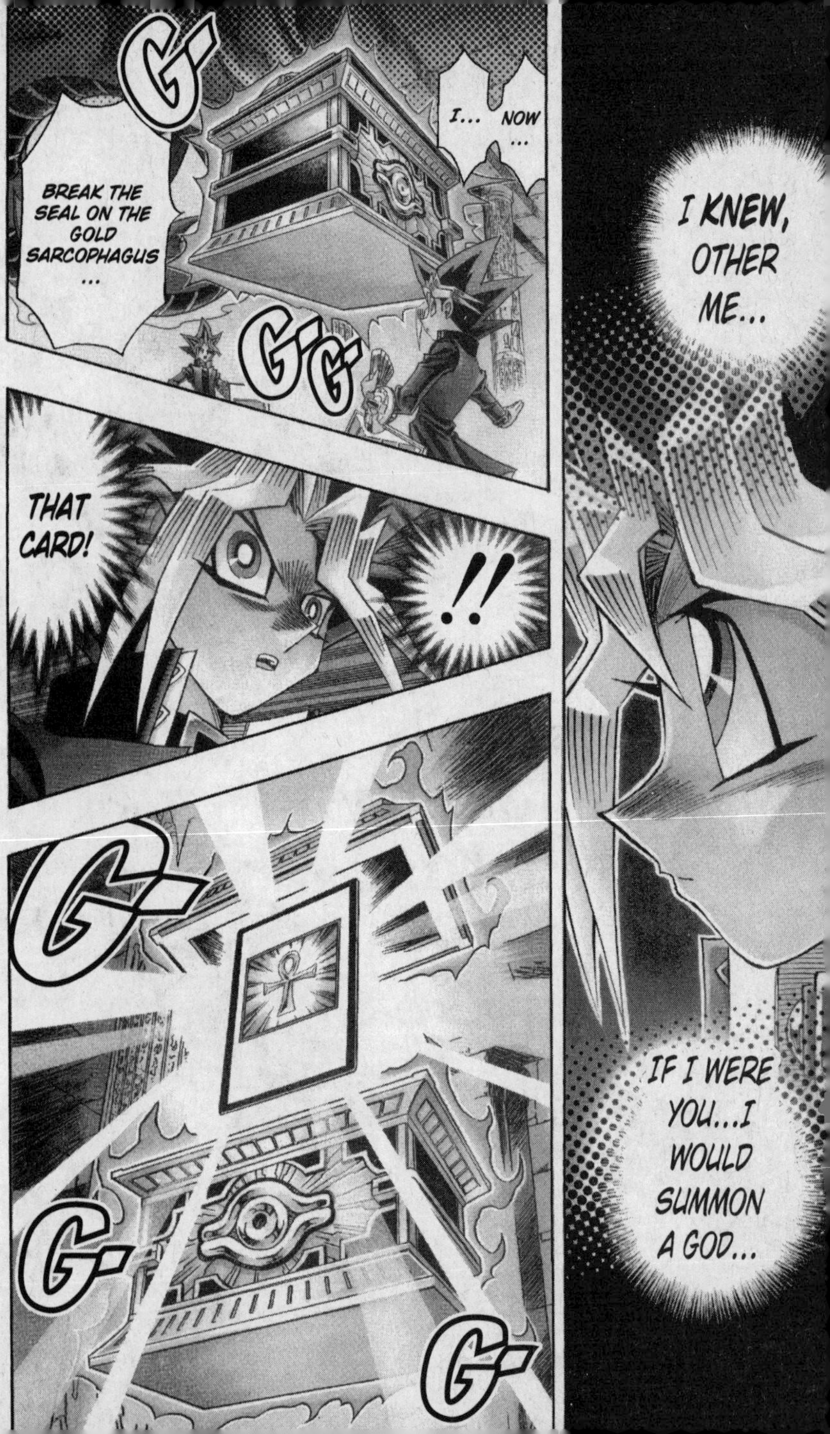
I KNEW, OTHER ME...
IF I WERE YOU...I WOULD SUMMON A GOD...
I... NOW ...
G-
BREAK THE SEAL ON THE GOLD SARCOPHAGUS ...
G-G-
THAT CARD!
!!
G-
G-
G-

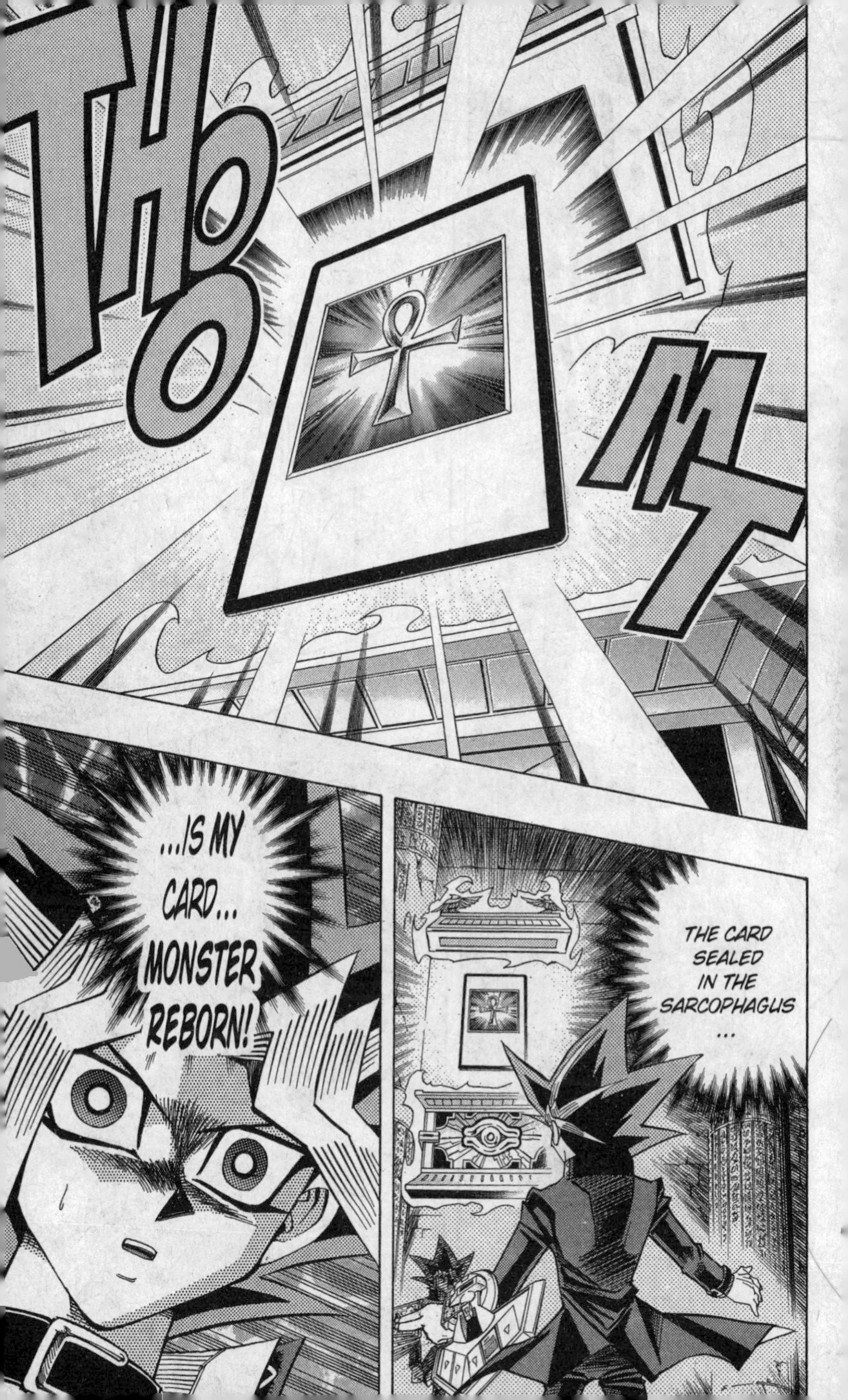
THOOMT
THE CARD SEALED IN THE SARCOPHAGUS ...
...IS MY CARD... MONSTER REBORN!

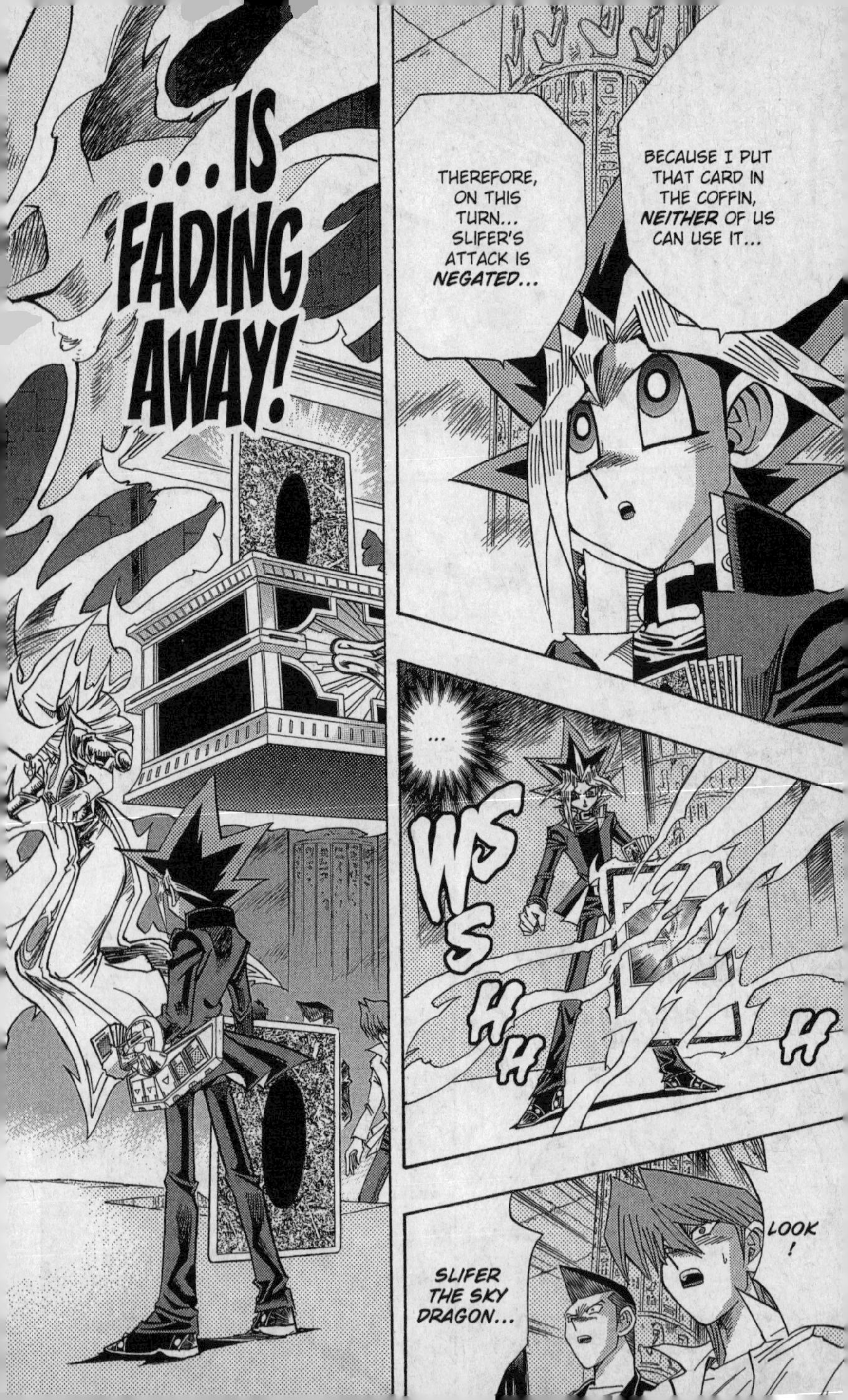
BECAUSE I PUT THAT CARD IN THE COFFIN, NEITHER OF US CAN USE IT...
THEREFORE, ON THIS TURN... SLIFER'S ATTACK IS NEGATED...
...
WSSHHH
LOOK!
SLIFER THE SKY DRAGON...
...IS FADING AWAY!

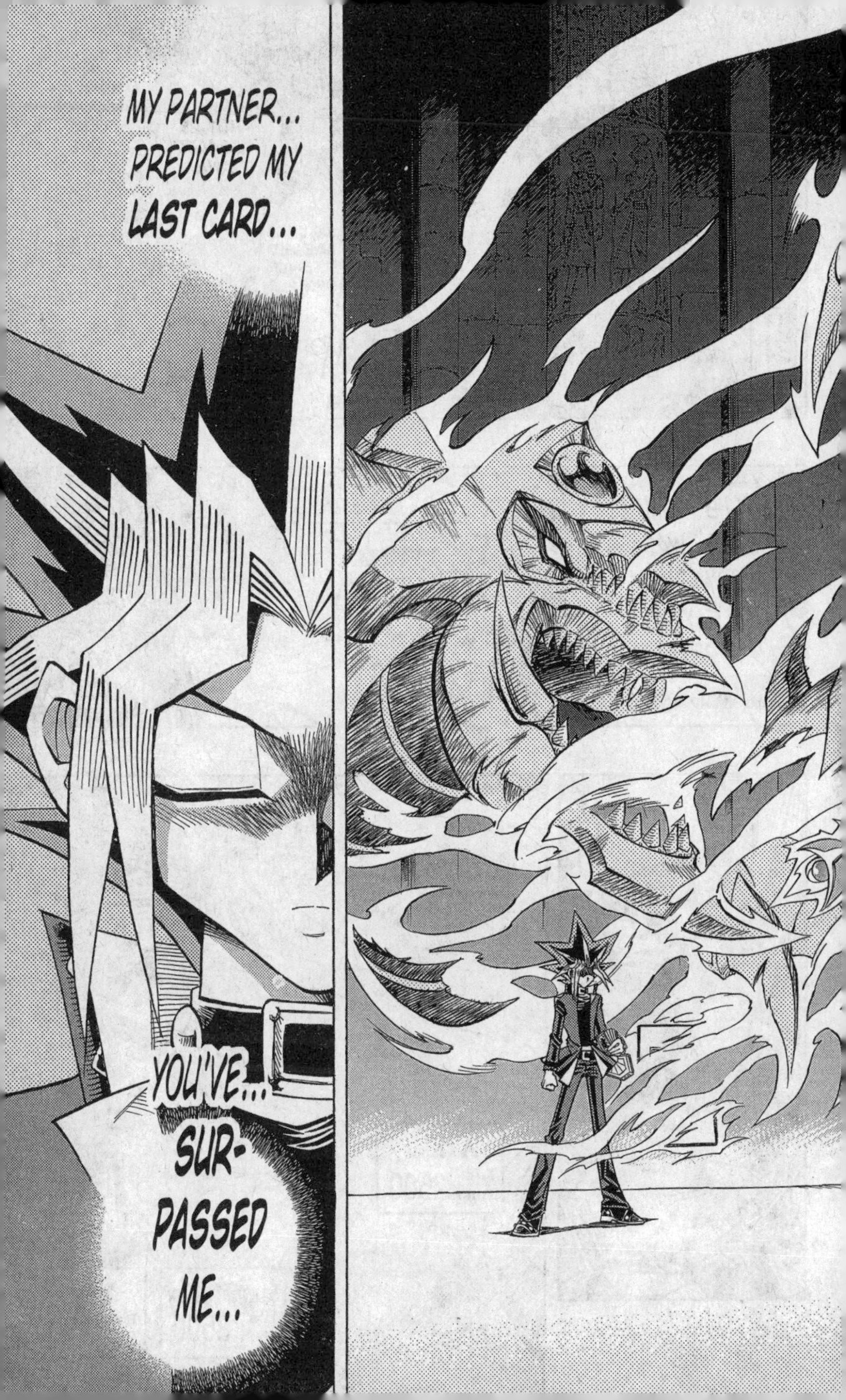
MY PARTNER... PREDICTED MY LAST CARD...
YOU'VE... SUR-PASSED ME...

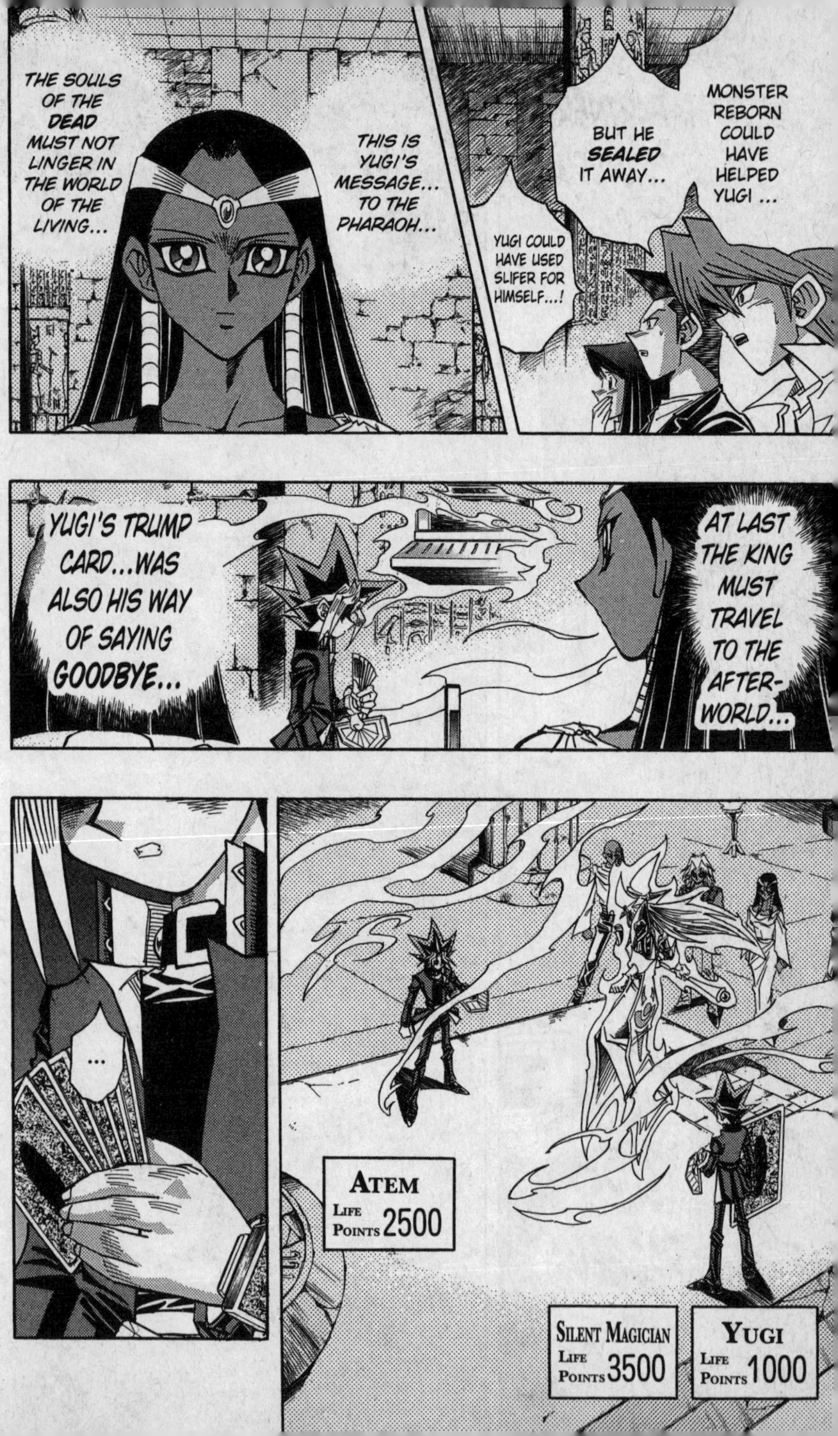
MONSTER REBORN COULD HAVE HELPED YUGI ...
BUT HE SEALED IT AWAY...
YUGI COULD HAVE USED SLIFER FOR HIMSELF...!
THIS IS YUGI'S MESSAGE... TO THE PHARAOH...
THE SOULS OF THE DEAD MUST NOT LINGER IN THE WORLD OF THE LIVING...
AT LAST THE KING MUST TRAVEL TO THE AFTER-WORLD...
YUGI'S TRUMP CARD...WAS ALSO HIS WAY OF SAYING GOODBYE...
ATEM LIFE POINTS 2500
YUGI LIFE POINTS 1000
SILENT MAGICIAN LIFE POINTS 3500
...

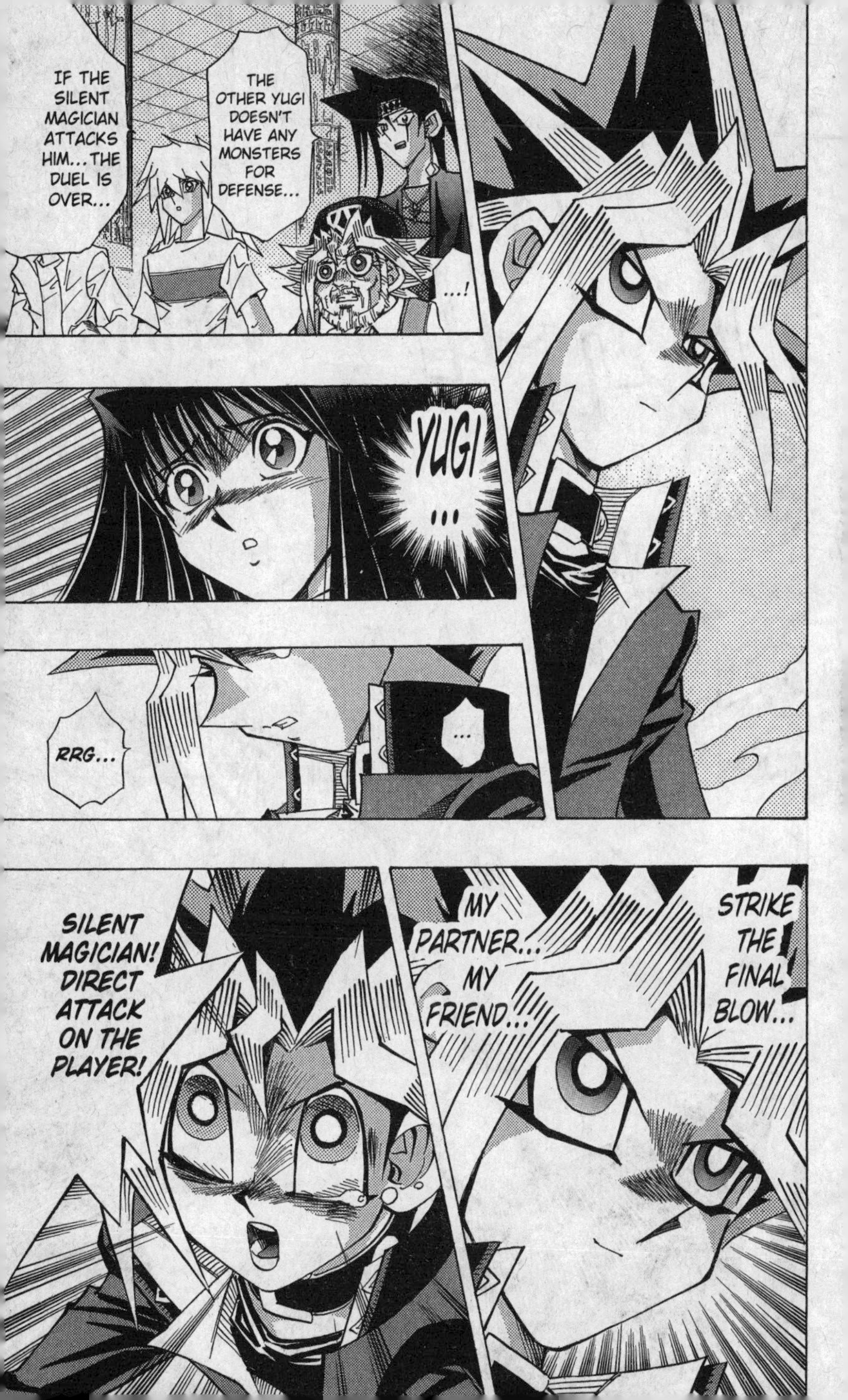
THE OTHER YUGI DOESN'T HAVE ANY MONSTERS FOR DEFENSE...
IF THE SILENT MAGICIAN ATTACKS HIM...THE DUEL IS OVER...
...!
YUGI ...
...
RRG...
STRIKE THE FINAL BLOW...
MY PARTNER... MY FRIEND...
SILENT MAGICIAN! DIRECT ATTACK ON THE PLAYER!

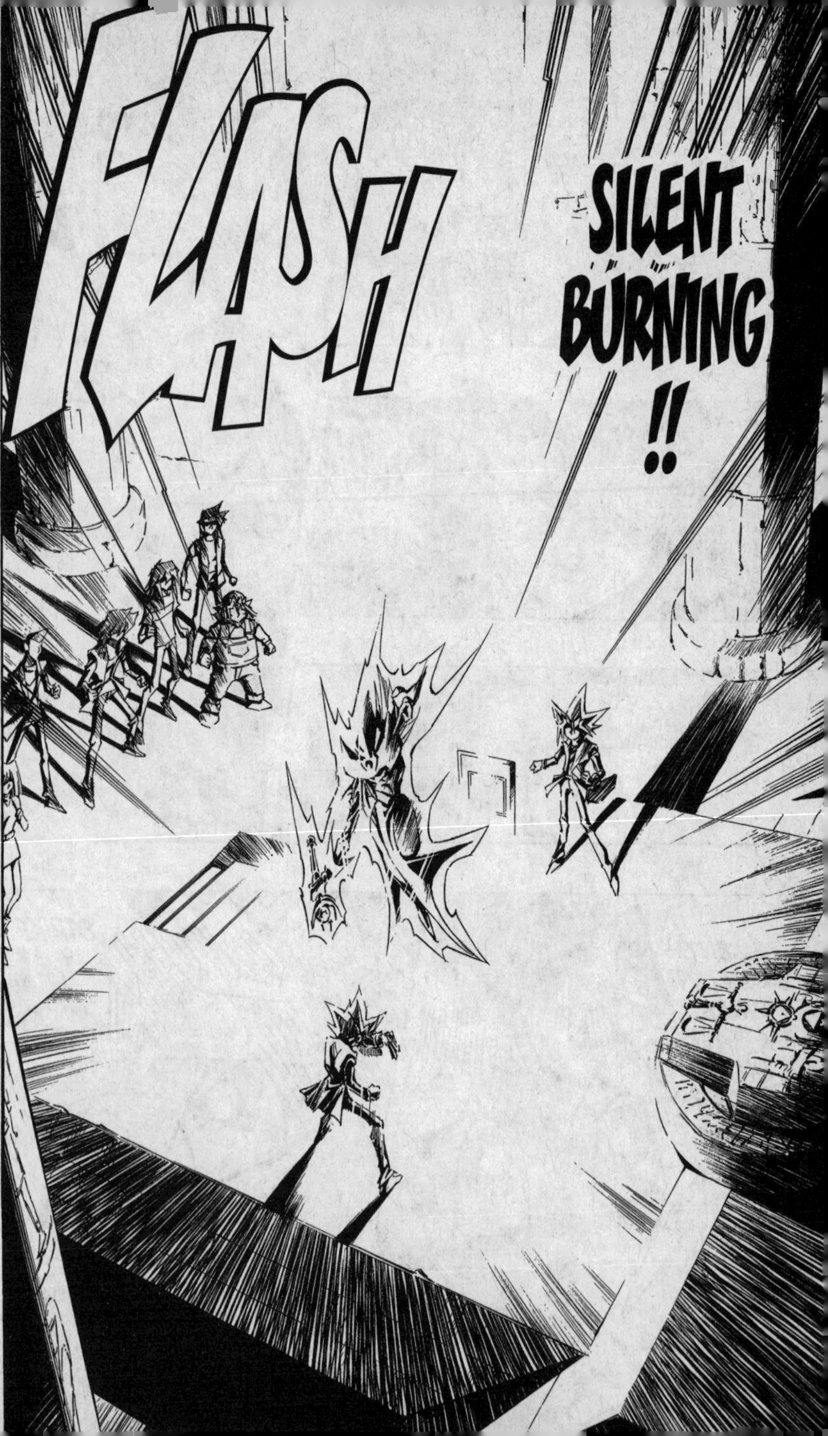
SILENT BURNING!!
FLASH

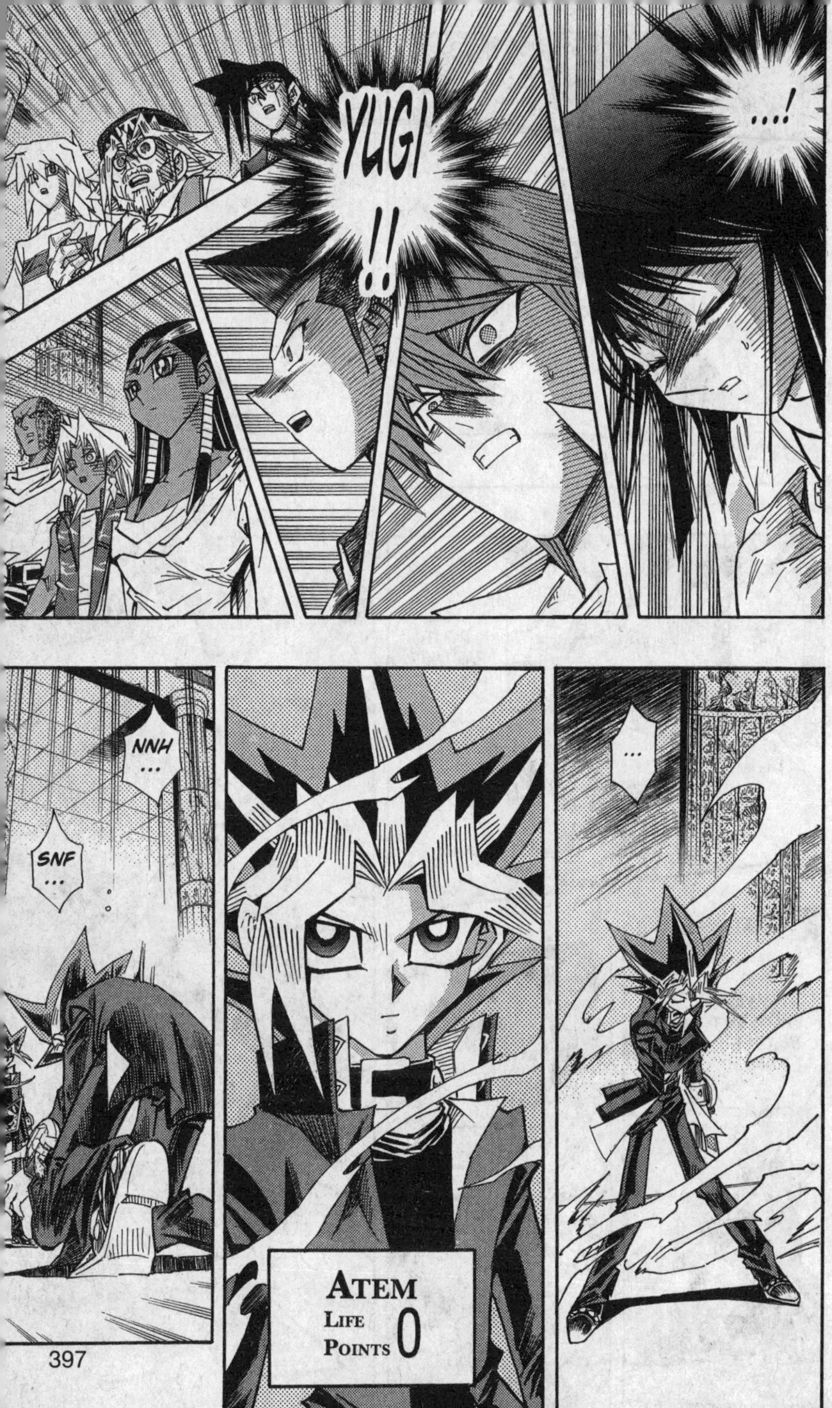
...!
YUGI !!
...
NNH ...
SNF ...
ATEM
LIFE POINTS 0

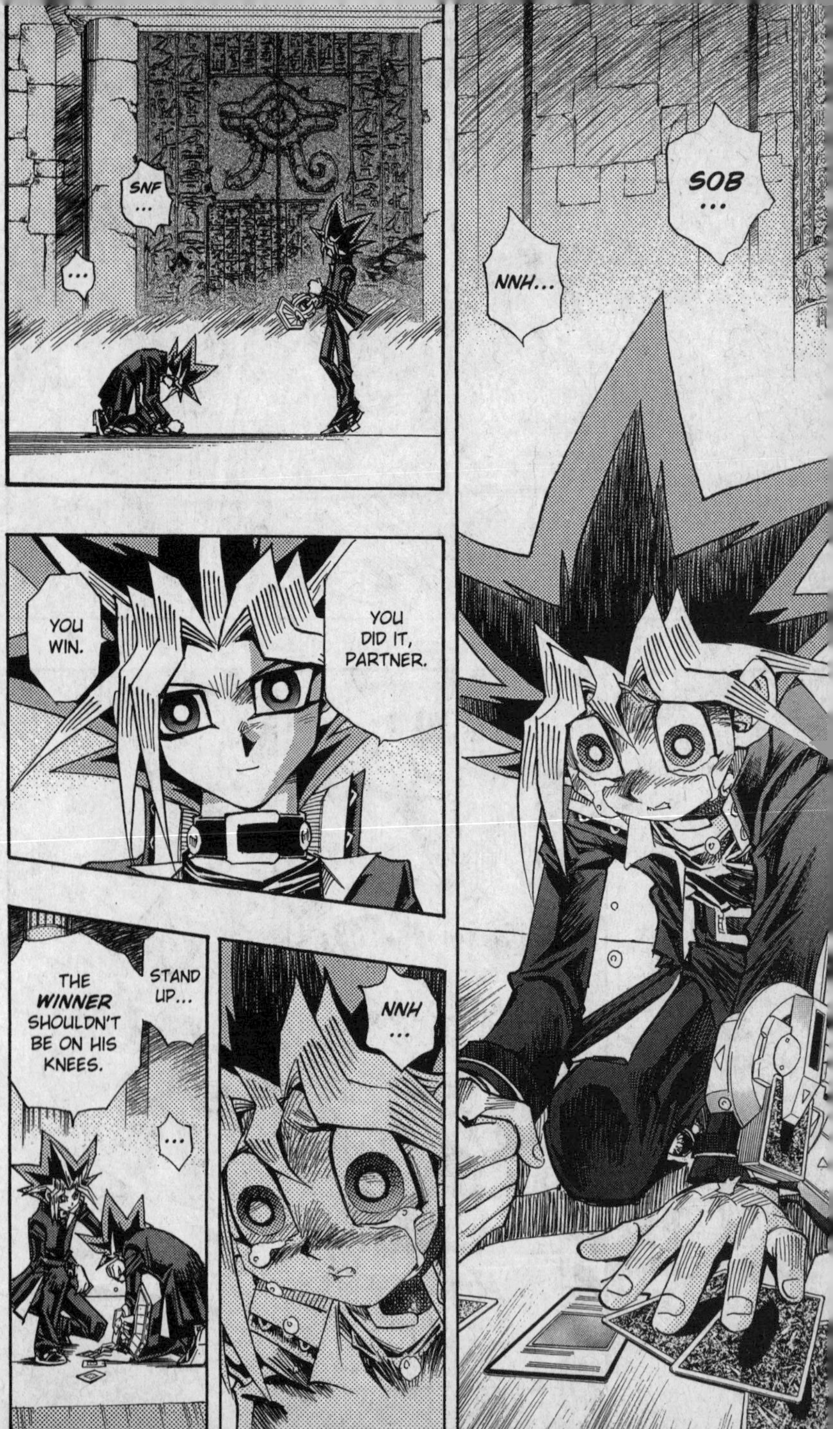
SOB ...
NNH...
SNF ...
...
YOU DID IT, PARTNER.
YOU WIN.
NNH ...
STAND UP...
THE WINNER SHOULDN'T BE ON HIS KNEES.
...

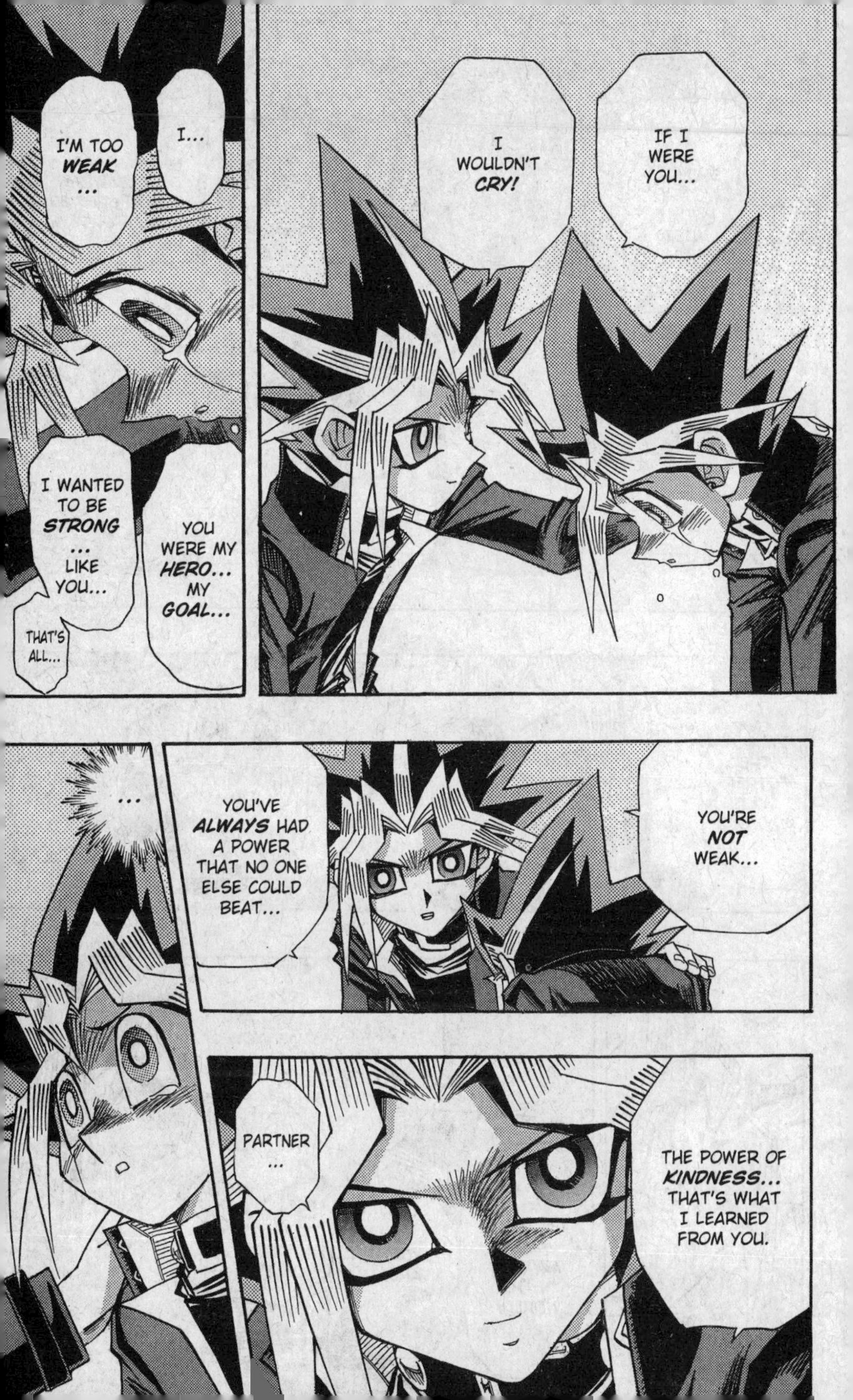
IF I WERE YOU...
I WOULDN'T CRY!
I...
I'M TOO WEAK ...
YOU WERE MY HERO... MY GOAL...
I WANTED TO BE STRONG ... LIKE YOU...
THAT'S ALL...
YOU'RE NOT WEAK...
YOU'VE ALWAYS HAD A POWER THAT NO ONE ELSE COULD BEAT...
THE POWER OF KINDNESS... THAT'S WHAT I LEARNED FROM YOU.
PARTNER ...
...

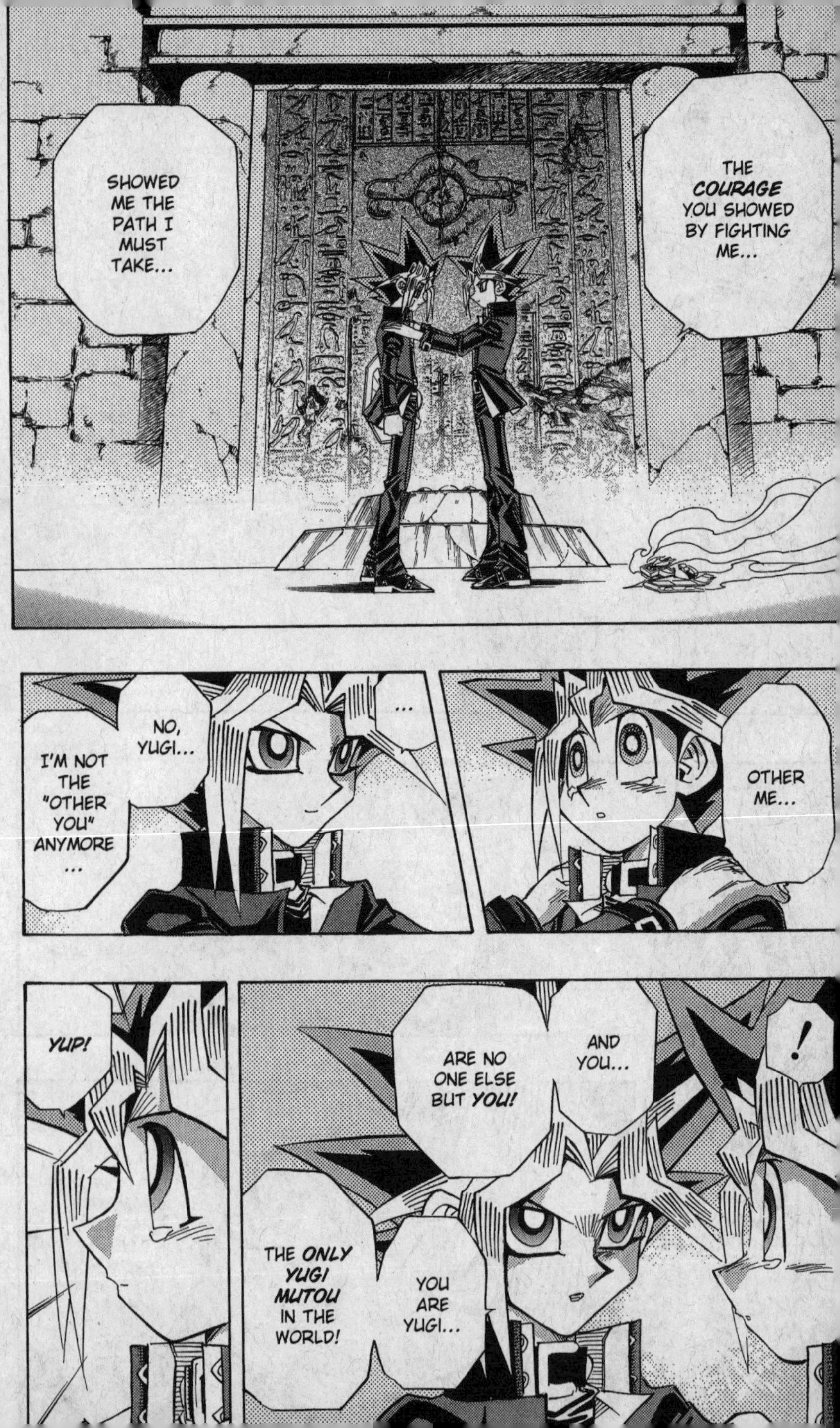
THE COURAGE YOU SHOWED BY FIGHTING ME...
SHOWED ME THE PATH I MUST TAKE...
OTHER ME...
...
NO, YUGI...
I'M NOT THE "OTHER YOU" ANYMORE ...
!
AND YOU...
ARE NO ONE ELSE BUT YOU!
YOU ARE YUGI...
THE ONLY YUGI MUTOU IN THE WORLD!
YUP!

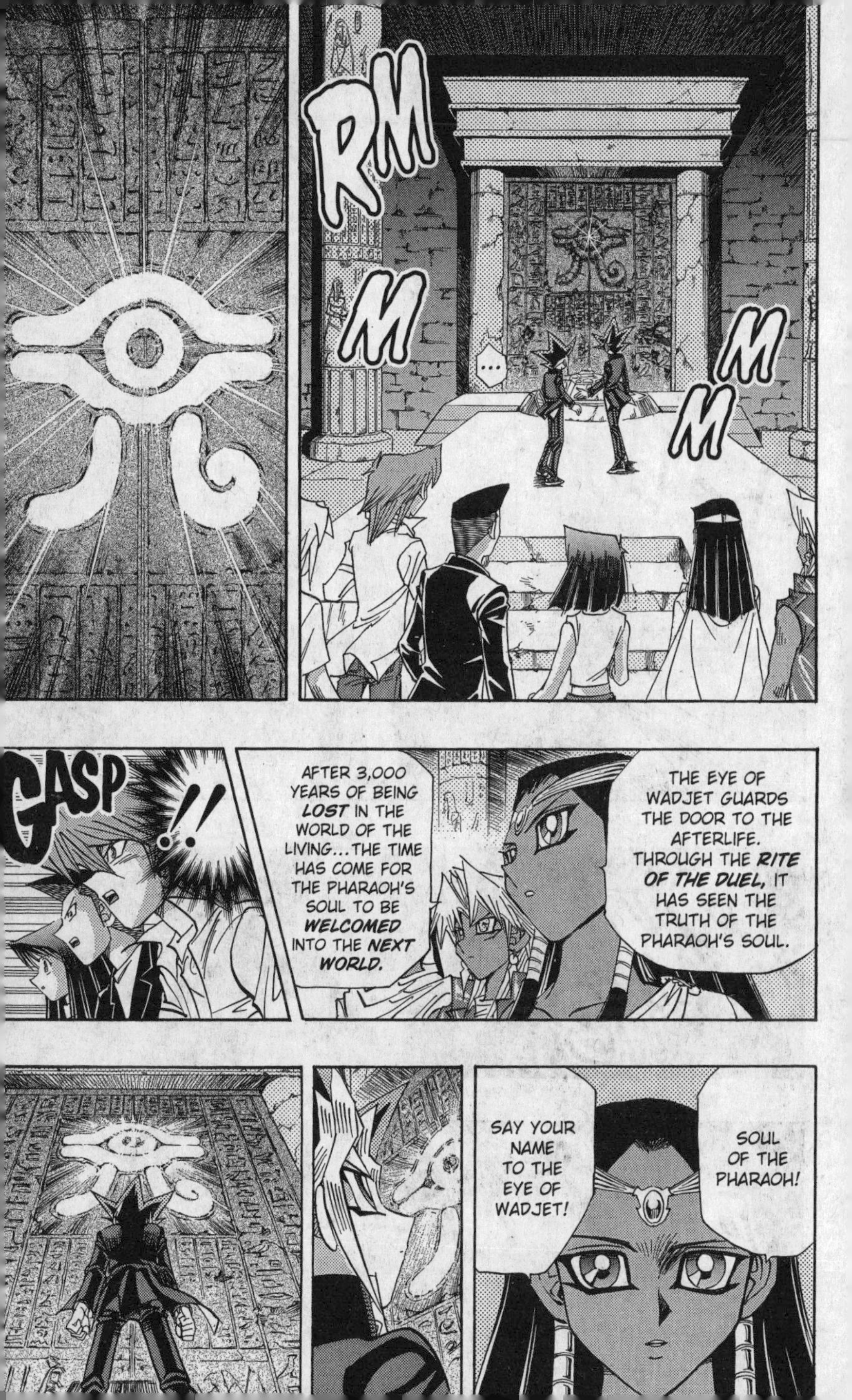
RM
M
...
M
M
THE EYE OF WADJET GUARDS THE DOOR TO THE AFTERLIFE. THROUGH THE ***RITE OF THE DUEL,*** IT HAS SEEN THE TRUTH OF THE PHARAOH'S SOUL.
AFTER 3,000 YEARS OF BEING ***LOST*** IN THE WORLD OF THE LIVING... THE TIME HAS COME FOR THE PHARAOH'S SOUL TO BE ***WELCOMED*** INTO THE ***NEXT WORLD.***
GASP
!!
SOUL OF THE PHARAOH!
SAY YOUR NAME TO THE EYE OF WADJET!

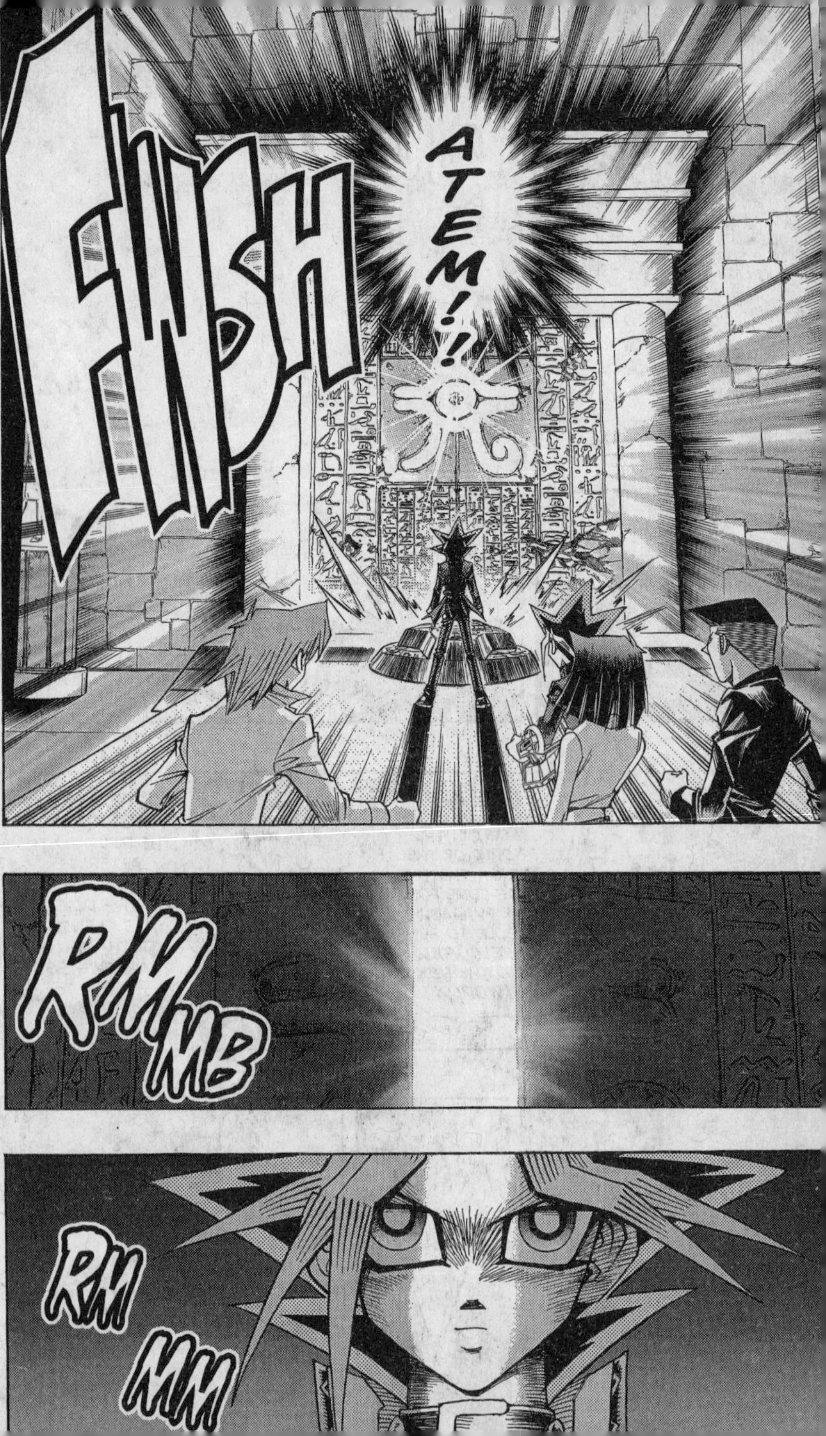
ATEM!!
FLASH
RMMB
RMMM

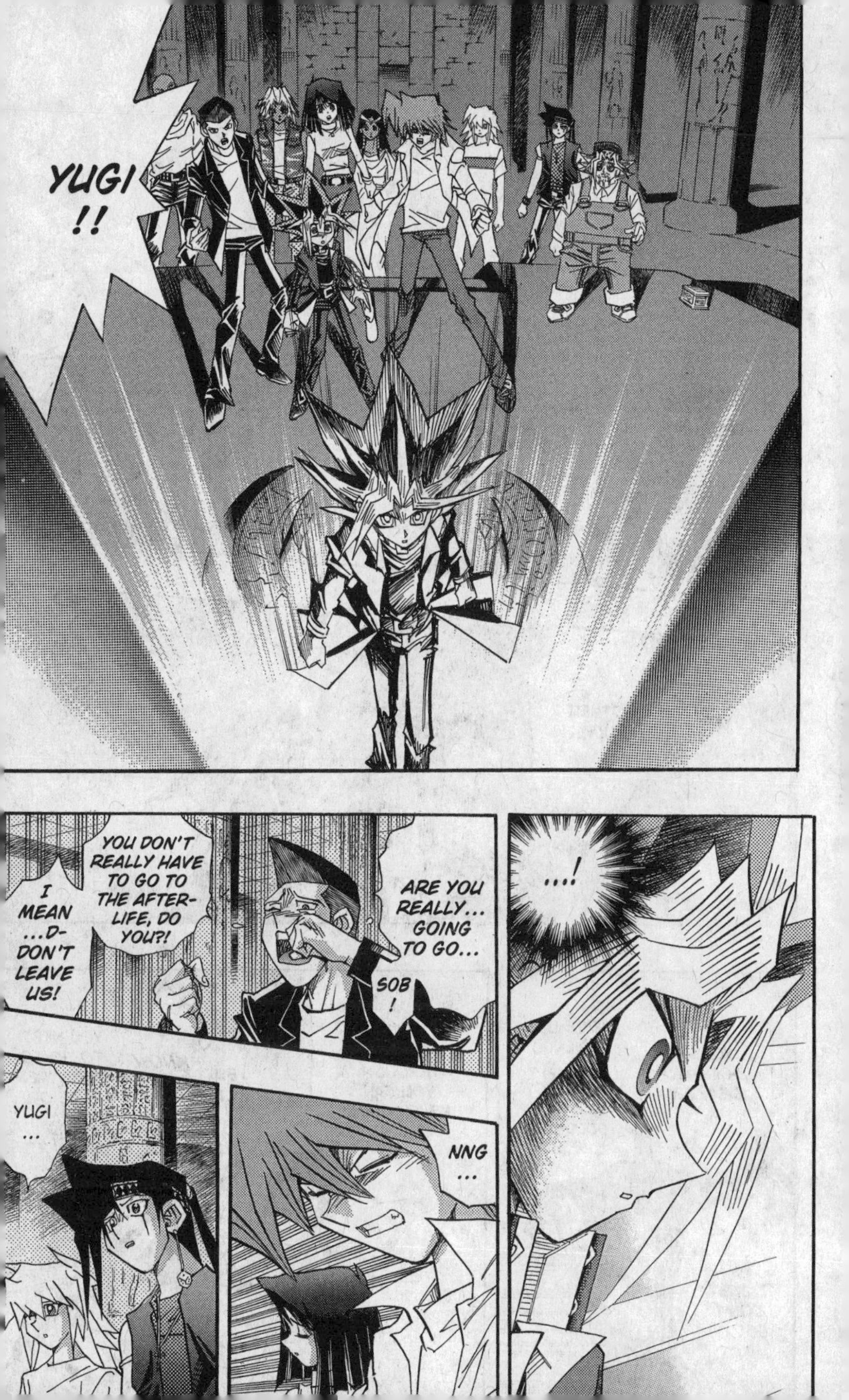
YUGI !!
...!
ARE YOU REALLY... GOING TO GO...
SOB!
YOU DON'T REALLY HAVE TO GO TO THE AFTER-LIFE, DO YOU?!
I MEAN ...D-DON'T LEAVE US!
NNG...
YUGI...

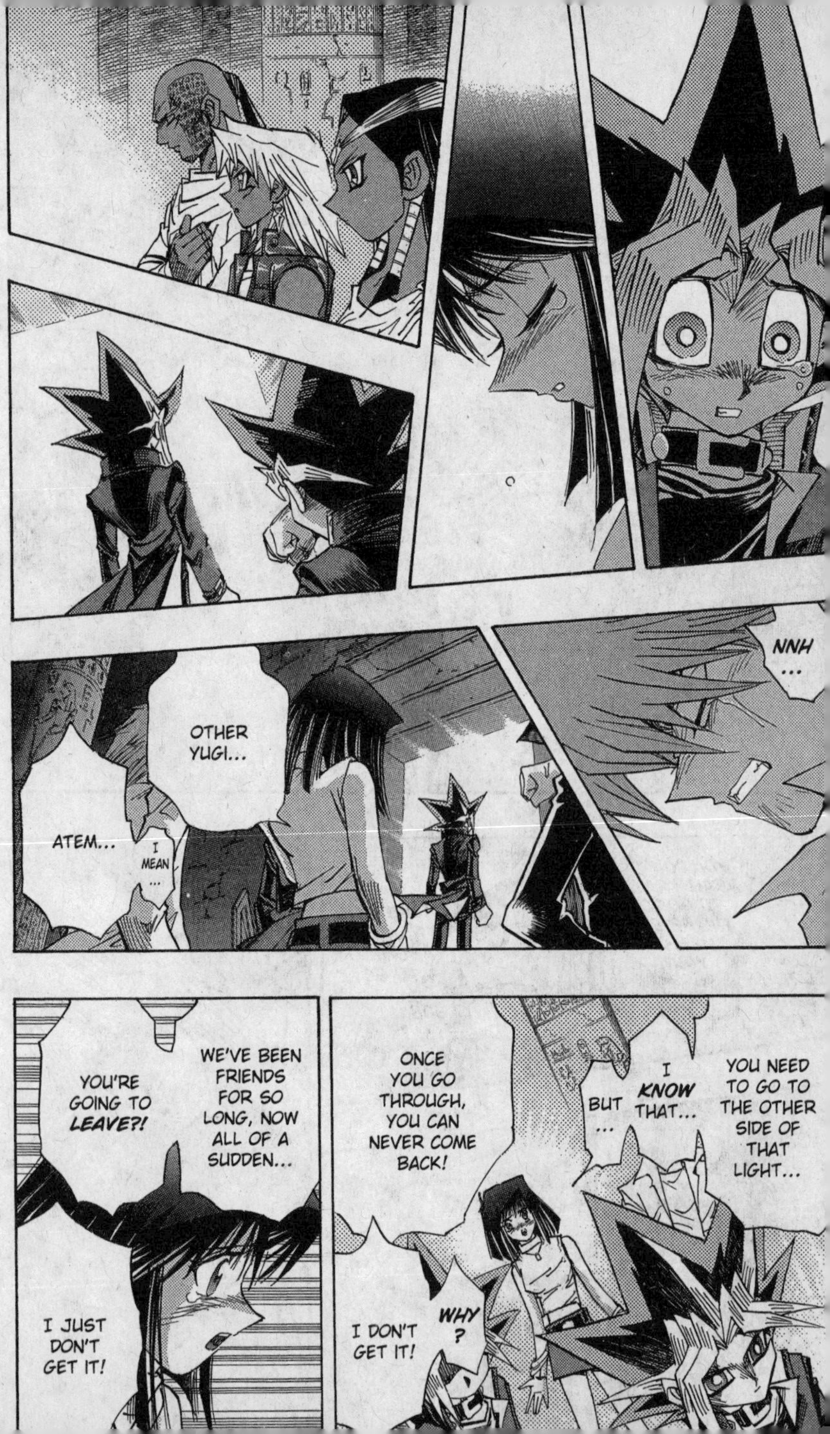
NNH...
OTHER YUGI...
I MEAN...
ATEM...
YOU NEED TO GO TO THE OTHER SIDE OF THAT LIGHT...
I ***KNOW*** THAT...
BUT...
ONCE YOU GO THROUGH, YOU CAN NEVER COME BACK!
WHY?
I DON'T GET IT!
WE'VE BEEN FRIENDS FOR SO LONG, NOW ALL OF A SUDDEN...
YOU'RE GOING TO ***LEAVE?!***
I JUST DON'T GET IT!

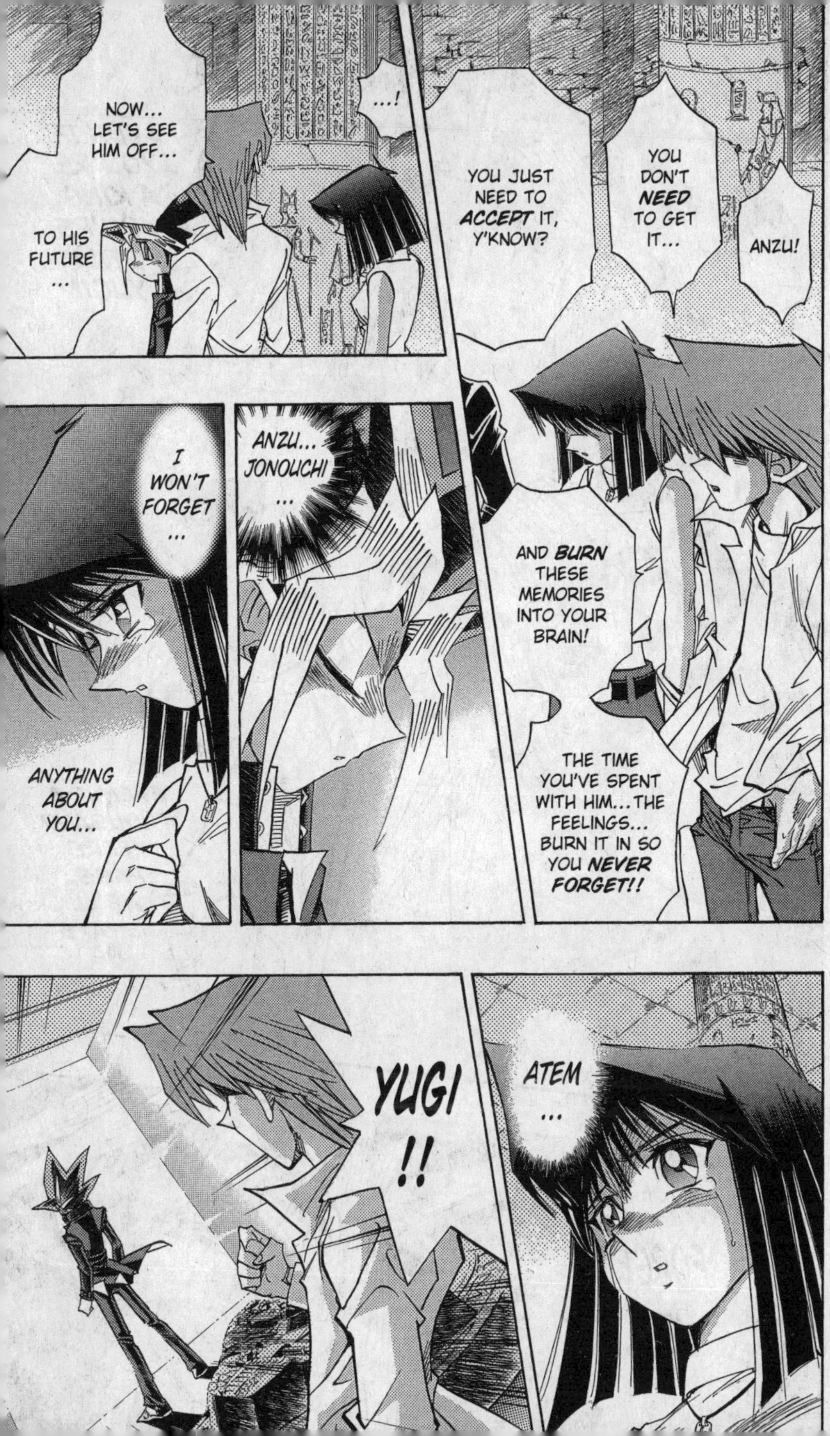
ANZU!
YOU DON'T NEED TO GET IT...
YOU JUST NEED TO ACCEPT IT, Y'KNOW?
AND BURN THESE MEMORIES INTO YOUR BRAIN!
THE TIME YOU'VE SPENT WITH HIM... THE FEELINGS... BURN IT IN SO YOU NEVER FORGET!!
...!
NOW... LET'S SEE HIM OFF...
TO HIS FUTURE ...
ANZU... JONOUCHI ...
I WON'T FORGET ...
ANYTHING ABOUT YOU...
ATEM ...
YUGI !!

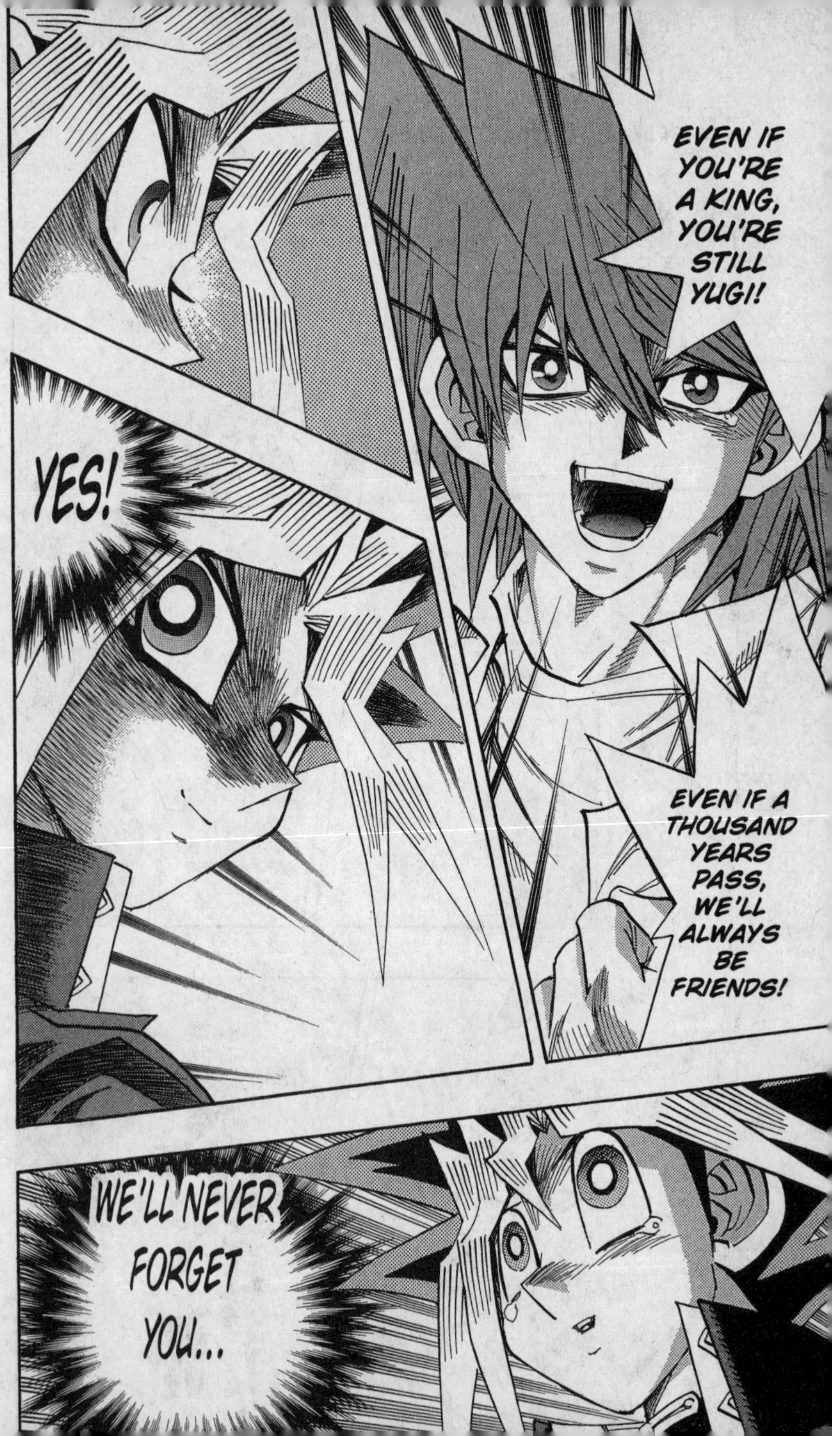
EVEN IF YOU'RE A KING, YOU'RE STILL YUGI!
EVEN IF A THOUSAND YEARS PASS, WE'LL ALWAYS BE FRIENDS!
YES!
WE'LL NEVER FORGET YOU...

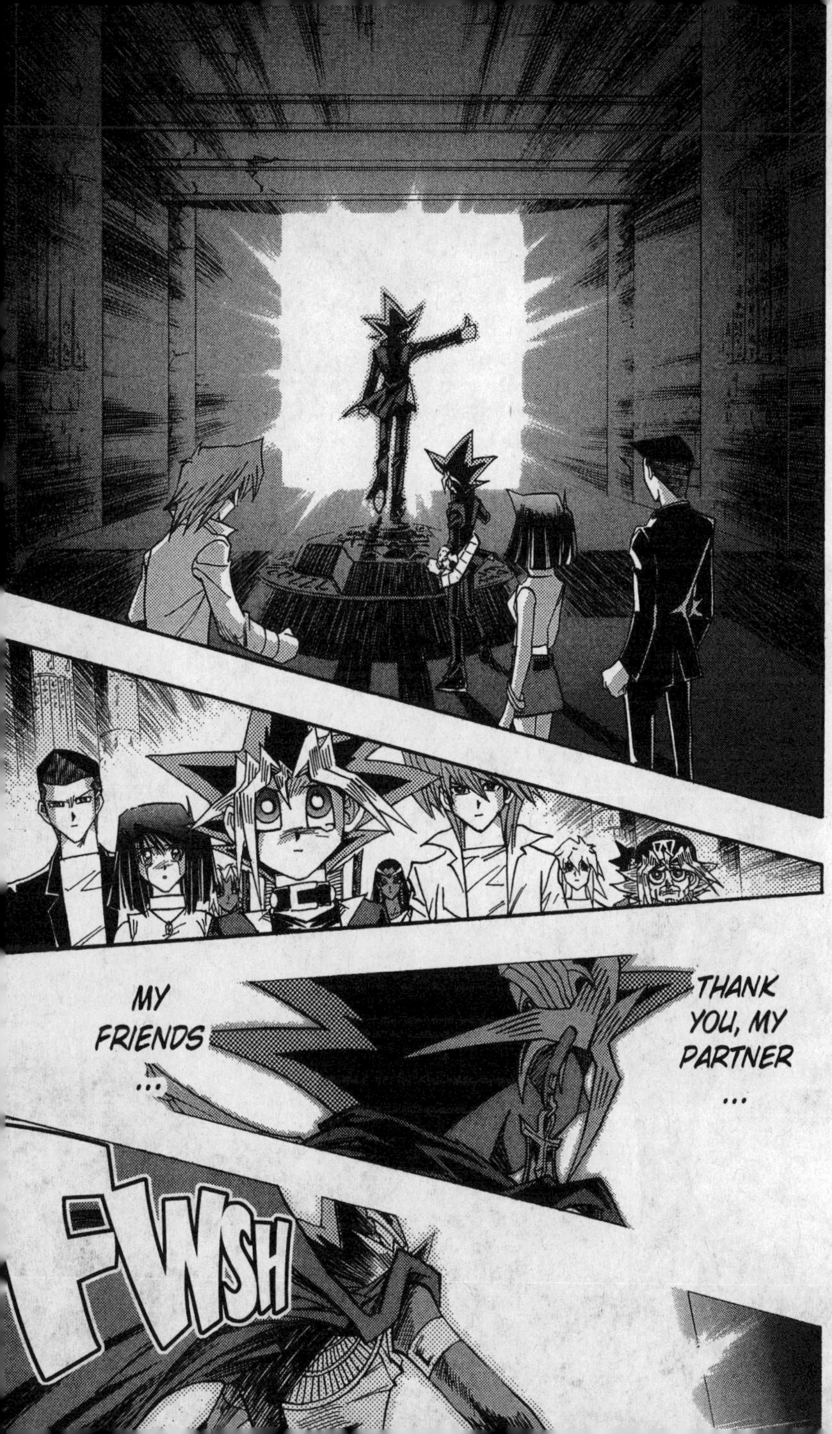
THANK YOU, MY PARTNER ...
MY FRIENDS ...
F-WSH

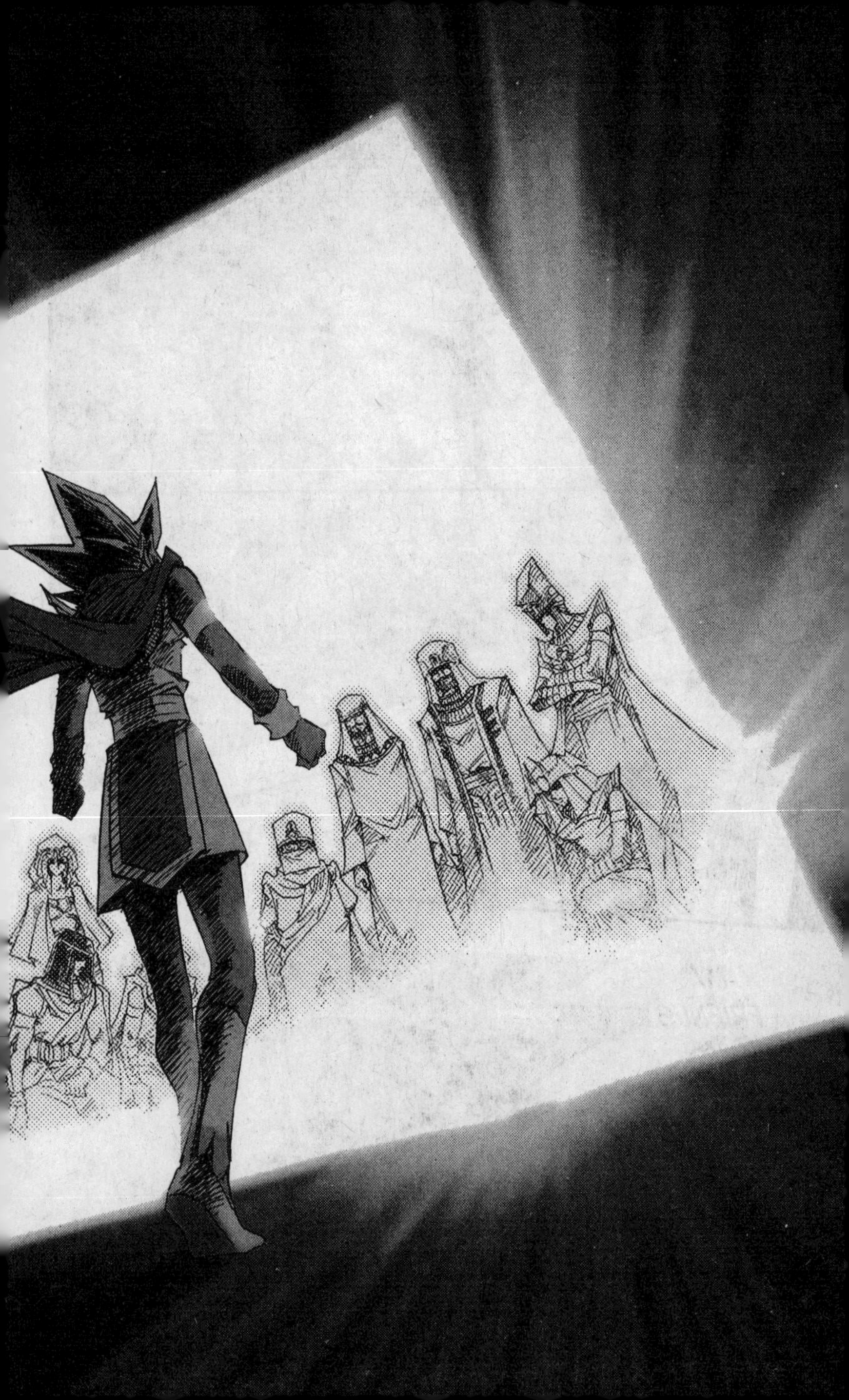

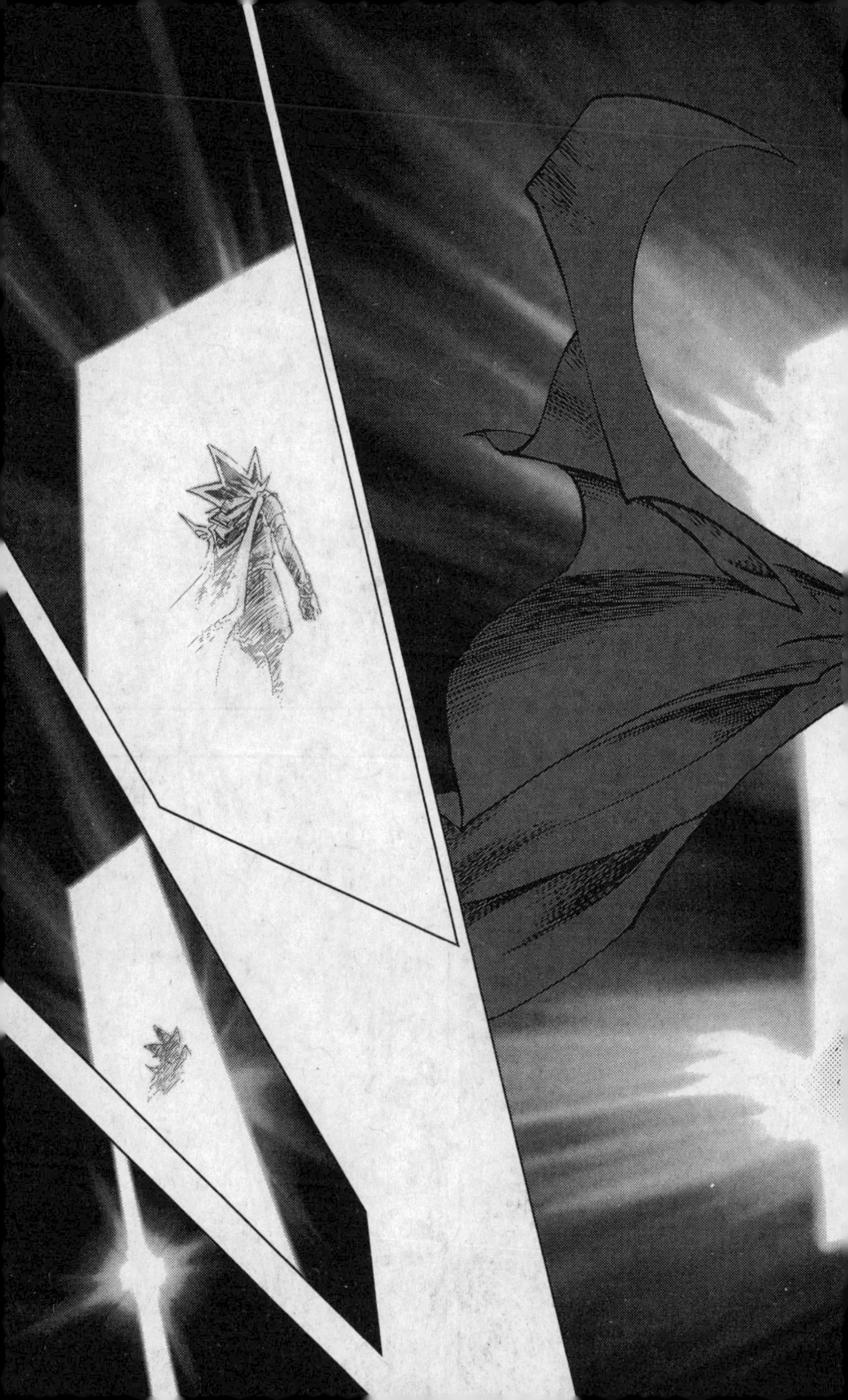

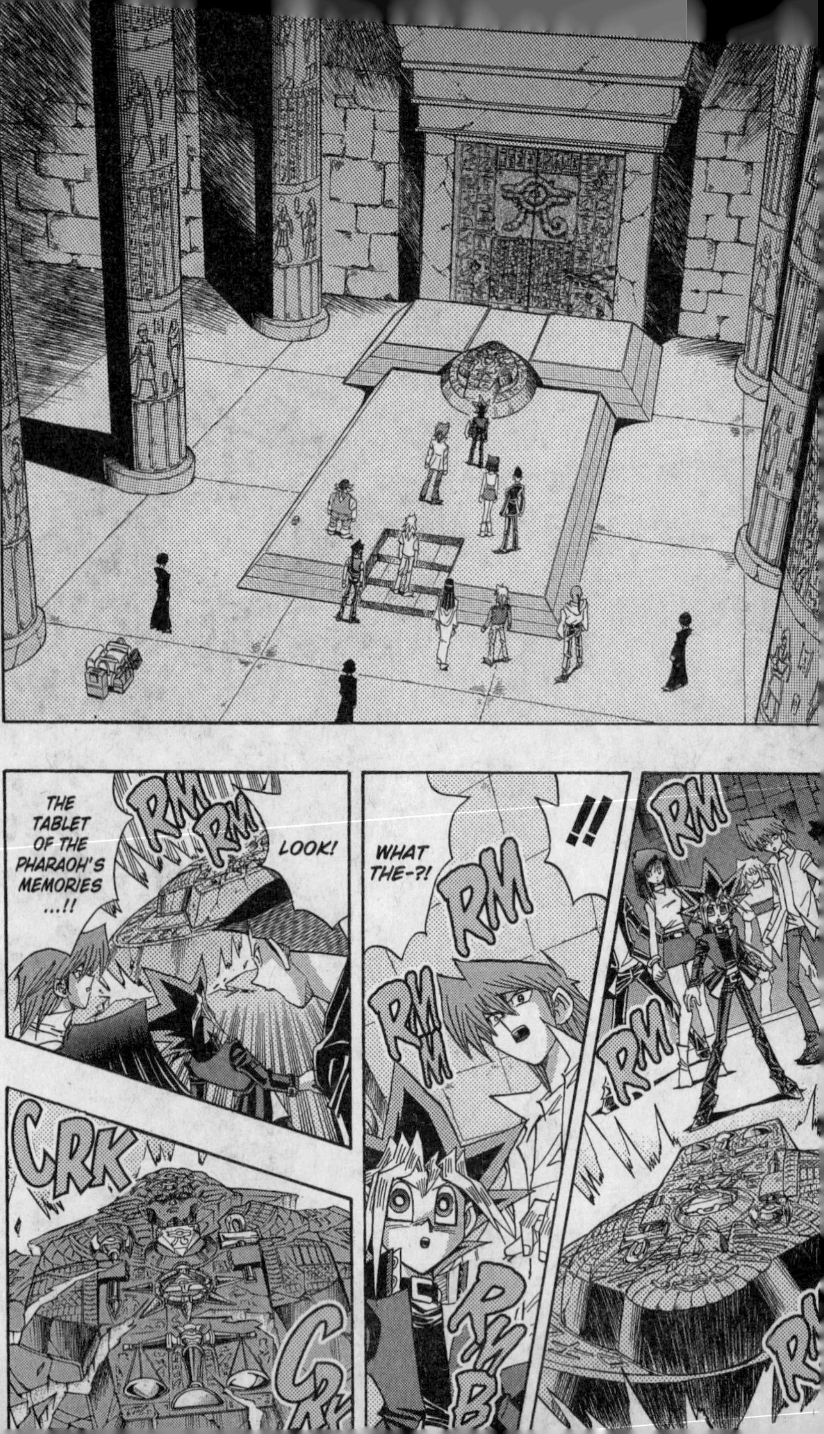
RM
RM
!!
WHAT THE-?!
RM
RM
LOOK!
RM
RM
THE TABLET OF THE PHARAOH'S MEMORIES ...!!
CRK

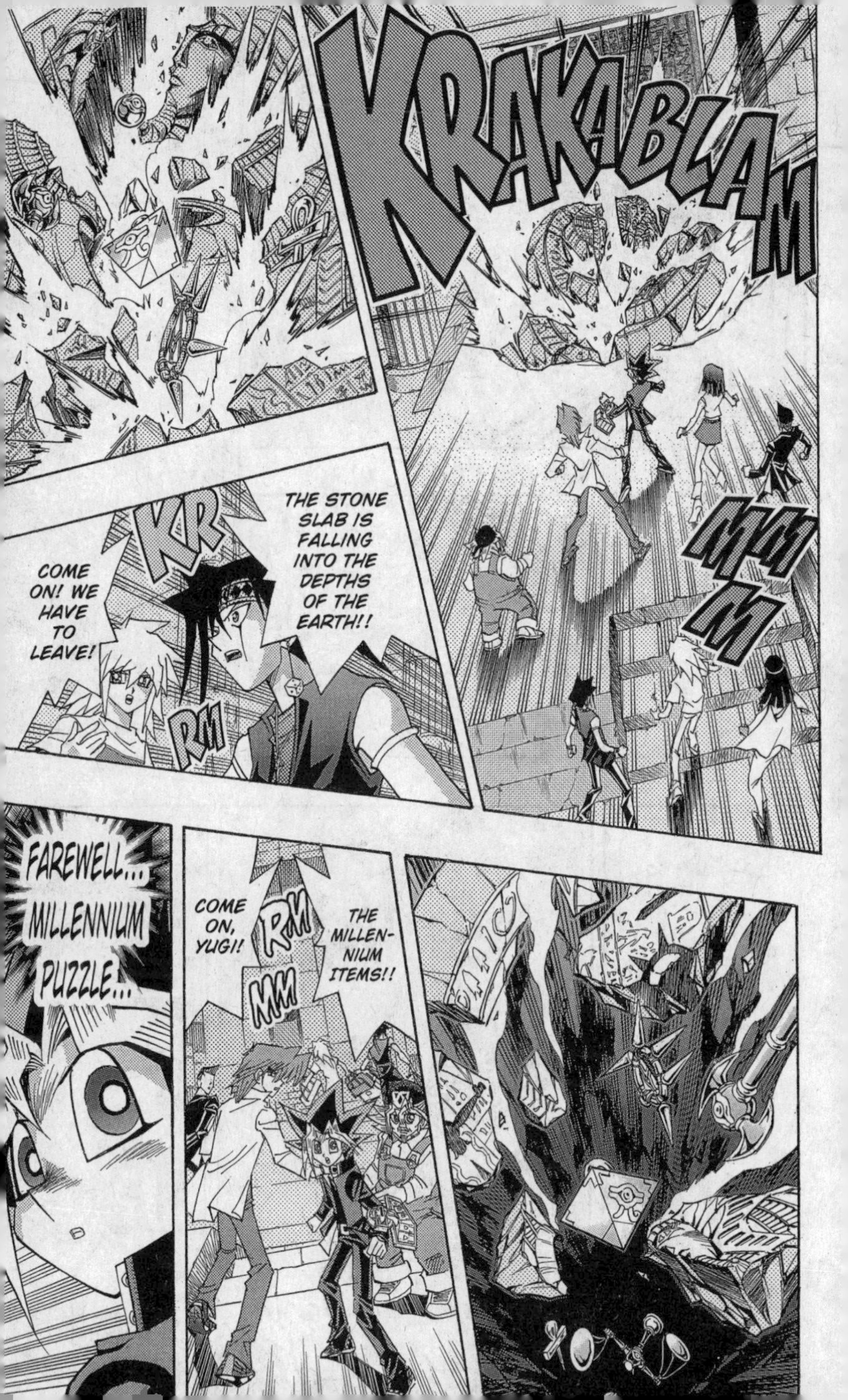
KRAKABLAM
MMMM
THE STONE SLAB IS FALLING INTO THE DEPTHS OF THE EARTH!!
KR
COME ON! WE HAVE TO LEAVE!
RM
THE MILLENNIUM ITEMS!!
RM
COME ON, YUGI!
MM
FAREWELL... MILLENNIUM PUZZLE...

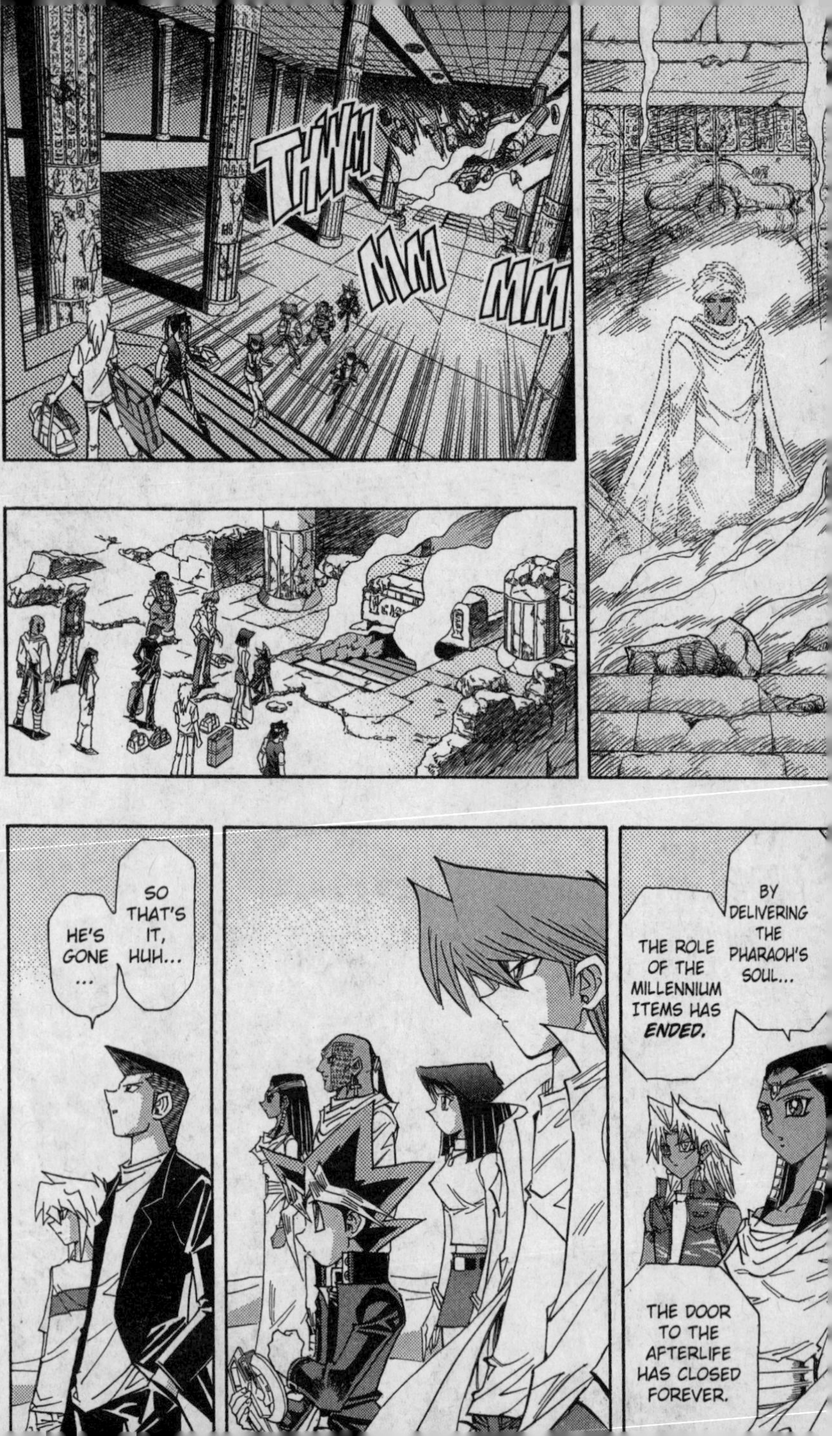
THWMMMMM
BY DELIVERING THE PHARAOH'S SOUL...
THE ROLE OF THE MILLENNIUM ITEMS HAS *ENDED.*
THE DOOR TO THE AFTERLIFE HAS CLOSED FOREVER.
SO THAT'S IT, HUH...
HE'S GONE...

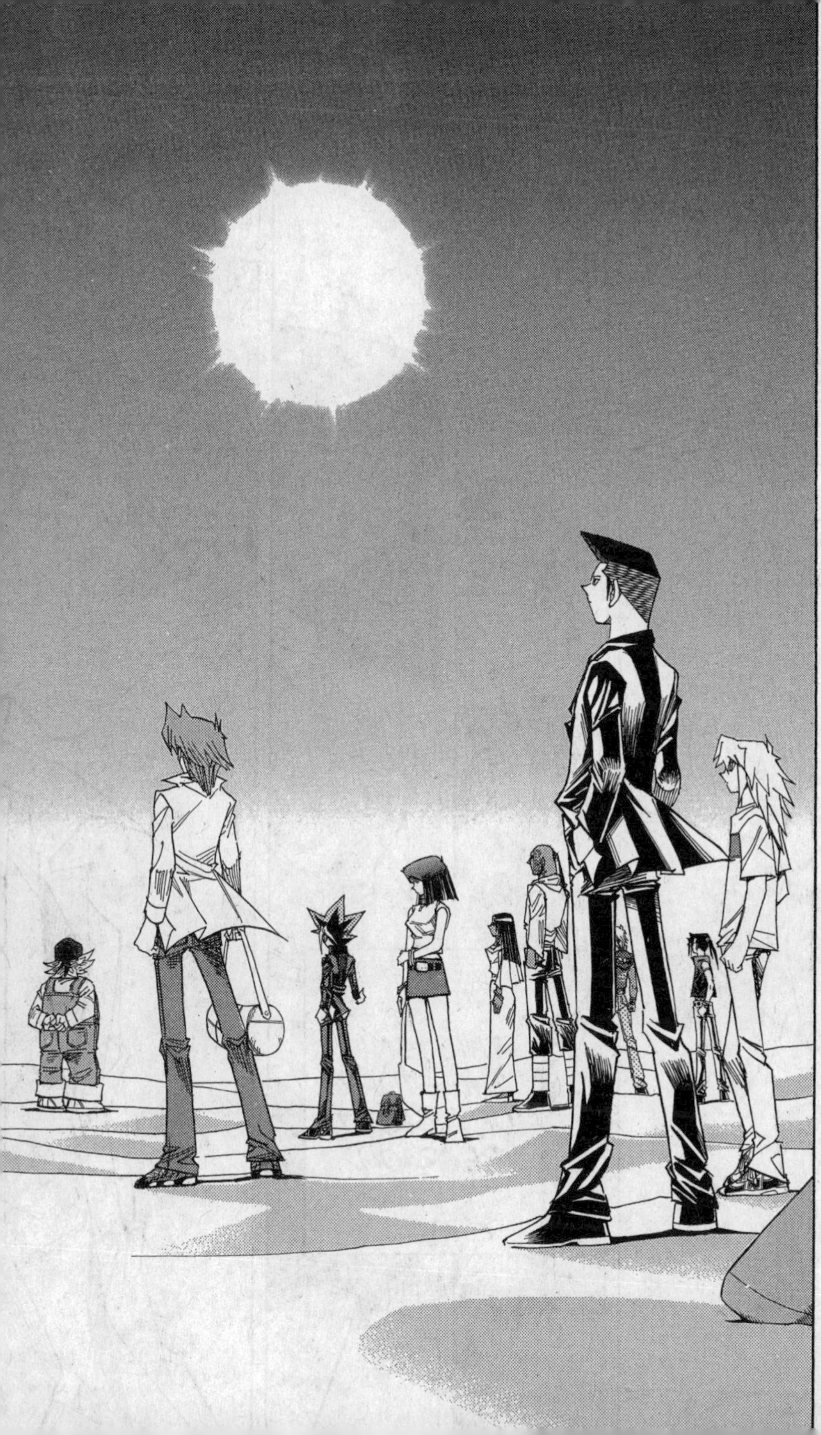

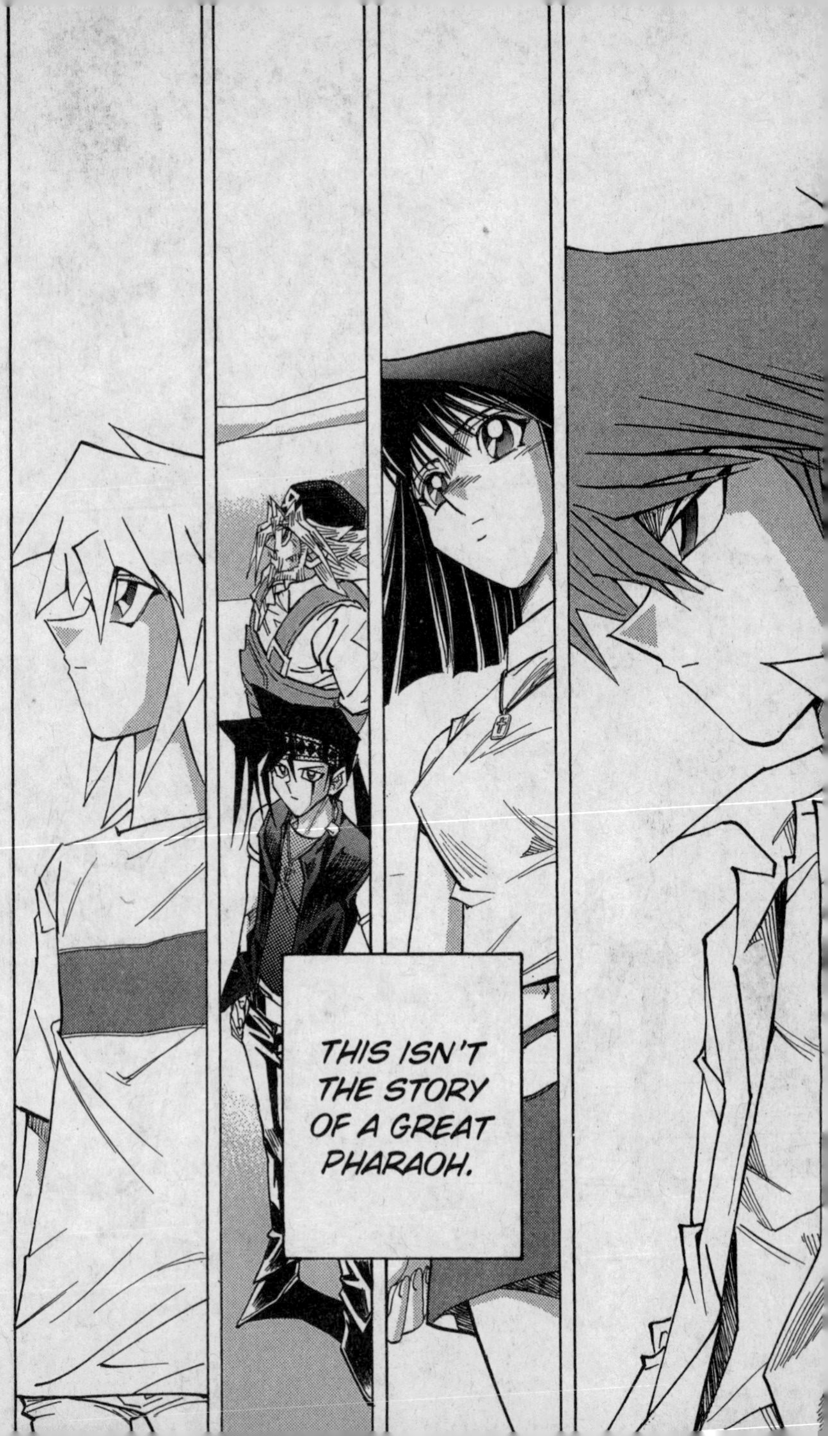
THIS ISN'T THE STORY OF A GREAT PHARAOH.

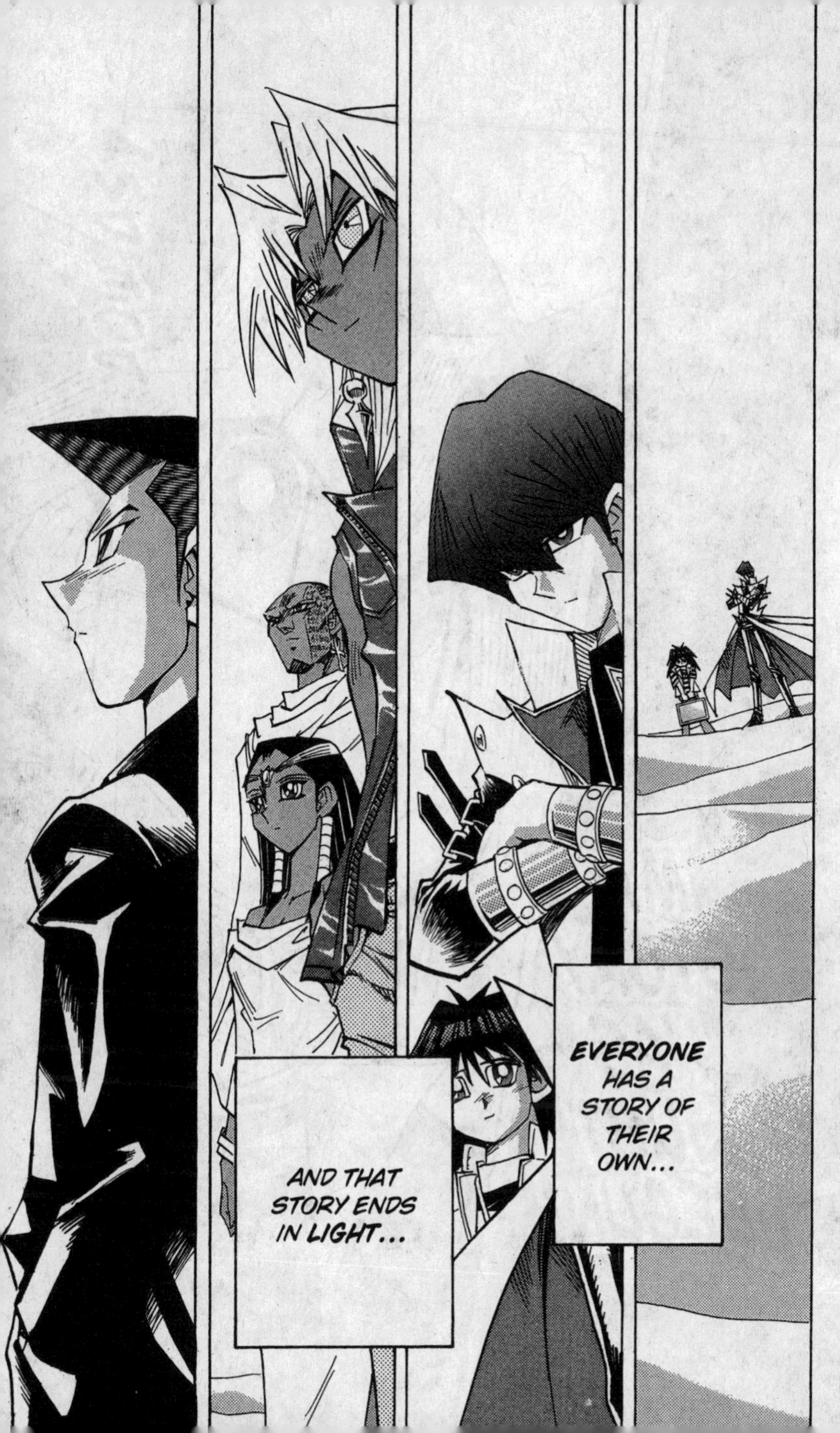
EVERYONE HAS A STORY OF THEIR OWN...
AND THAT STORY ENDS IN LIGHT...

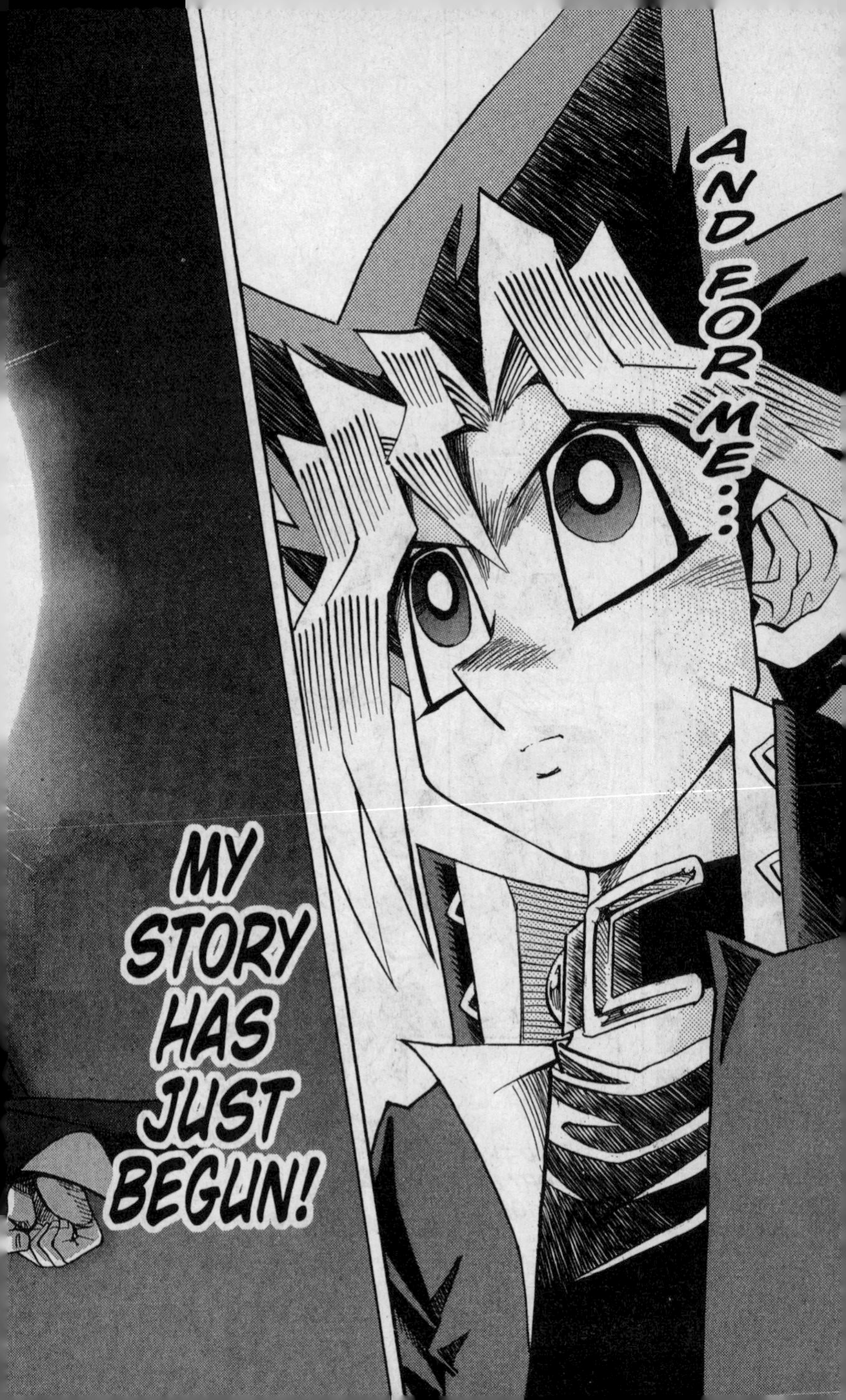
AND FOR ME...
MY STORY HAS JUST BEGUN!

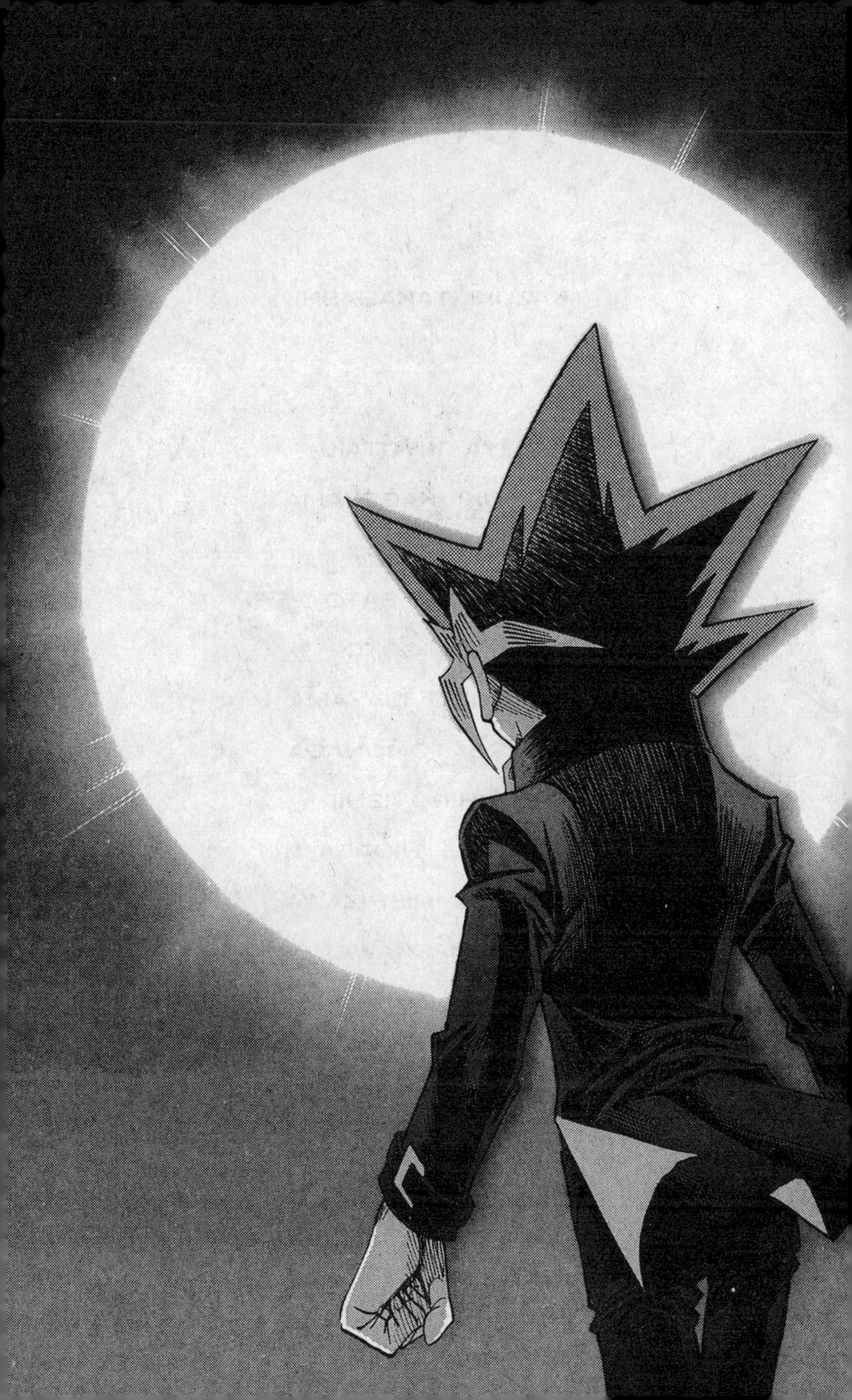

YU-GI-OH!

Presented by

KAZUKI TAKAHASHI

Staff

KEIYA KIYOTAKI

NAOYUKI KAGEYAMA

AKIRA ITO

MASASHI SATO

RYUJI GOTO

HIDENOBU ISAYAMA

AKIHIRO TOMONAGA

TOSHIRO ISHII

YOSHIO HIGASA

YOSHIAKI NISHIZAWA

YU MAEKAWA

Editor

YOSHIHISA HEISHI

HISAO SHIMADA

Special Thanks

TOSHIMASA TAKAHASHI

YU-GI-OH!

遊戯王

完

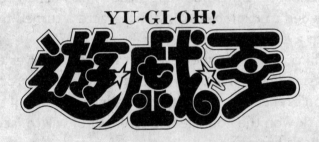

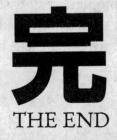

THE END

AFTERWORD

For seven long years, I've traveled with *Yu-Gi-Oh!* I think I've been able to draw the themes I've wanted to express, but as I end the series, my main concern is whether I've transmitted my message to my readers.

From the moment Yugi put together the Millennium Puzzle, the "other self" appeared in his heart. The time needed to explore two main characters turned this into a long series.

In our daily life, we never get to see ourselves except by standing in front of a mirror. But even a mirror won't reflect our hearts. The main characters of this work won the courage and strength of will to face each other's hearts.

****

As we go about our lives, we touch people, we see people, and interact with them; and in doing so we feel and think many things. Sometimes we make others happy, sometimes we hurt them, we sympathize, and we disagree. In the midst of this, we learn that people's thoughts and feelings are not a one-way street. You may say that's something very basic and natural, but what I wanted to draw and write in this work was just that interaction between people, and in order to do that, I used "games."

The games that the characters played were not played facing monitors, but facing other people. The opponents they played were the mirrors that reflected their hearts. In a basic sense, they fought each other's spirits. Because this was a manga, it was deeply colored by the battle between good and evil, but I think the basis of the "game" was to clarify what lies between people. I think this was the reason that the *Yu-Gi-Oh!* card game became so successful all over the world.

****

In my mind, *Yu-Gi-Oh!* has been completed. But throughout the world, many people are taking my work and the cards in their hands. In gratitude for that, I would like to prolong the world of *Yu-Gi-Oh!* for just a little while longer.

****

I borrow the end of this book to thank all of those who have participated in this world. Thank you from the bottom of my heart.

Kazuki Takahashi
April 14, 2004

ON SALE NOW
YU-GI-OH!
ARC-V

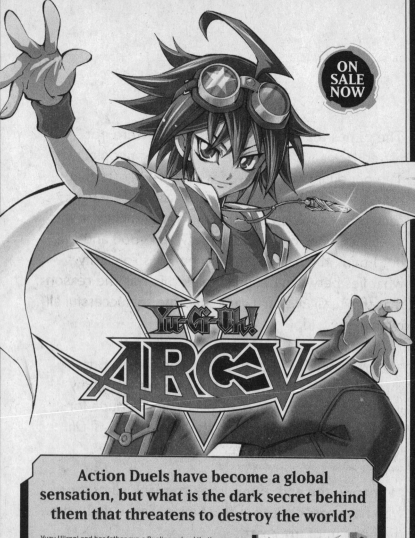

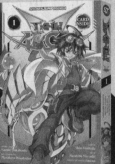

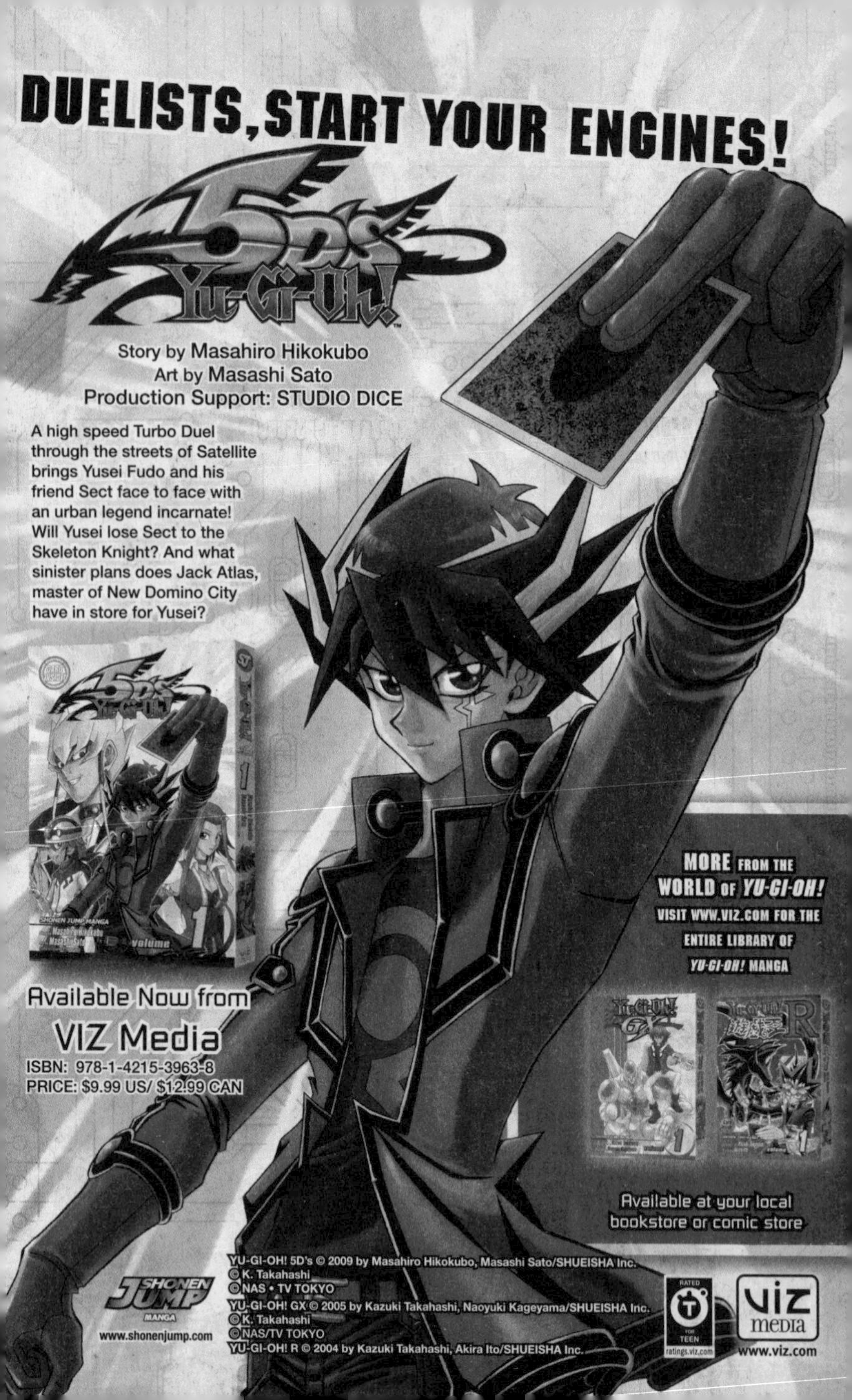
DUELISTS, START YOUR ENGINES!
5D's Yu-Gi-Oh!
Story by Masahiro Hikokubo
Art by Masashi Sato
Production Support: STUDIO DICE
A high speed Turbo Duel through the streets of Satellite brings Yusei Fudo and his friend Sect face to face with an urban legend incarnate! Will Yusei lose Sect to the Skeleton Knight? And what sinister plans does Jack Atlas, master of New Domino City have in store for Yusei?
Available Now from
VIZ Media
ISBN: 978-1-4215-3963-8
PRICE: $9.99 US/ $12.99 CAN
MORE FROM THE WORLD OF YU-GI-OH!
VISIT WWW.VIZ.COM FOR THE ENTIRE LIBRARY OF YU-GI-OH! MANGA
Available at your local bookstore or comic store
YU-GI-OH! 5D's © 2009 by Masahiro Hikokubo, Masashi Sato/SHUEISHA Inc.
© K. Takahashi
© NAS • TV TOKYO
YU-GI-OH! GX © 2005 by Kazuki Takahashi, Naoyuki Kageyama/SHUEISHA Inc.
© K. Takahashi
© NAS/TV TOKYO
YU-GI-OH! R © 2004 by Kazuki Takahashi, Akira Ito/SHUEISHA Inc.
SHONEN JUMP MANGA
www.shonenjump.com
RATED T FOR TEEN
ratings.viz.com
viz media
www.viz.com

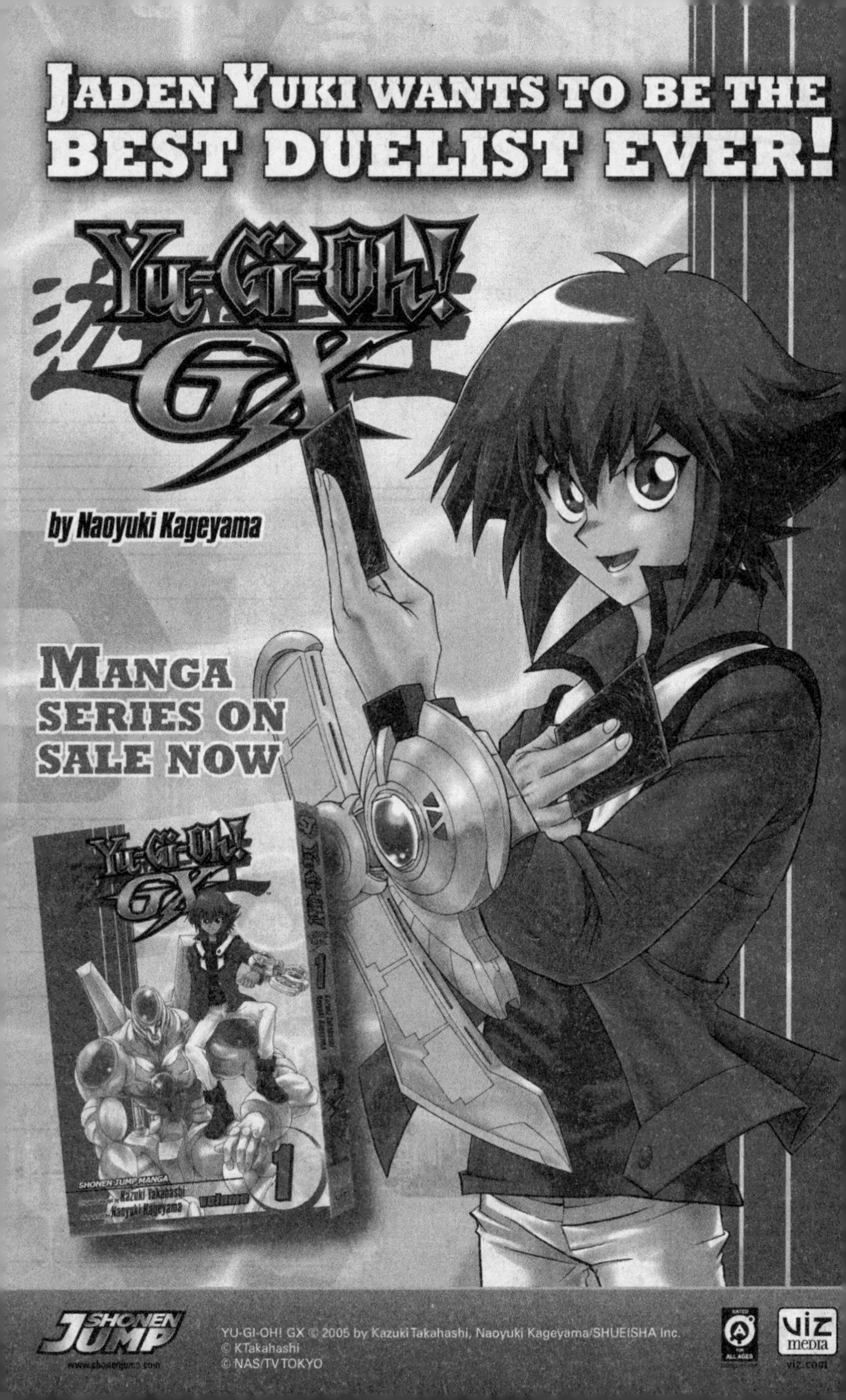
JADEN YUKI WANTS TO BE THE
BEST DUELIST EVER!
YU-GI-OH! GX
by Naoyuki Kageyama
MANGA
SERIES ON
SALE NOW
YU-GI-OH! GX
SHONEN JUMP MANGA
Kazuki Takahashi
Naoyuki Kageyama
1
SHONEN JUMP
YU-GI-OH! GX © 2005 by Kazuki Takahashi, Naoyuki Kageyama/SHUEISHA Inc.
© KTakahashi
© NAS/TV TOKYO
ALL AGES
VIZ media
viz.com

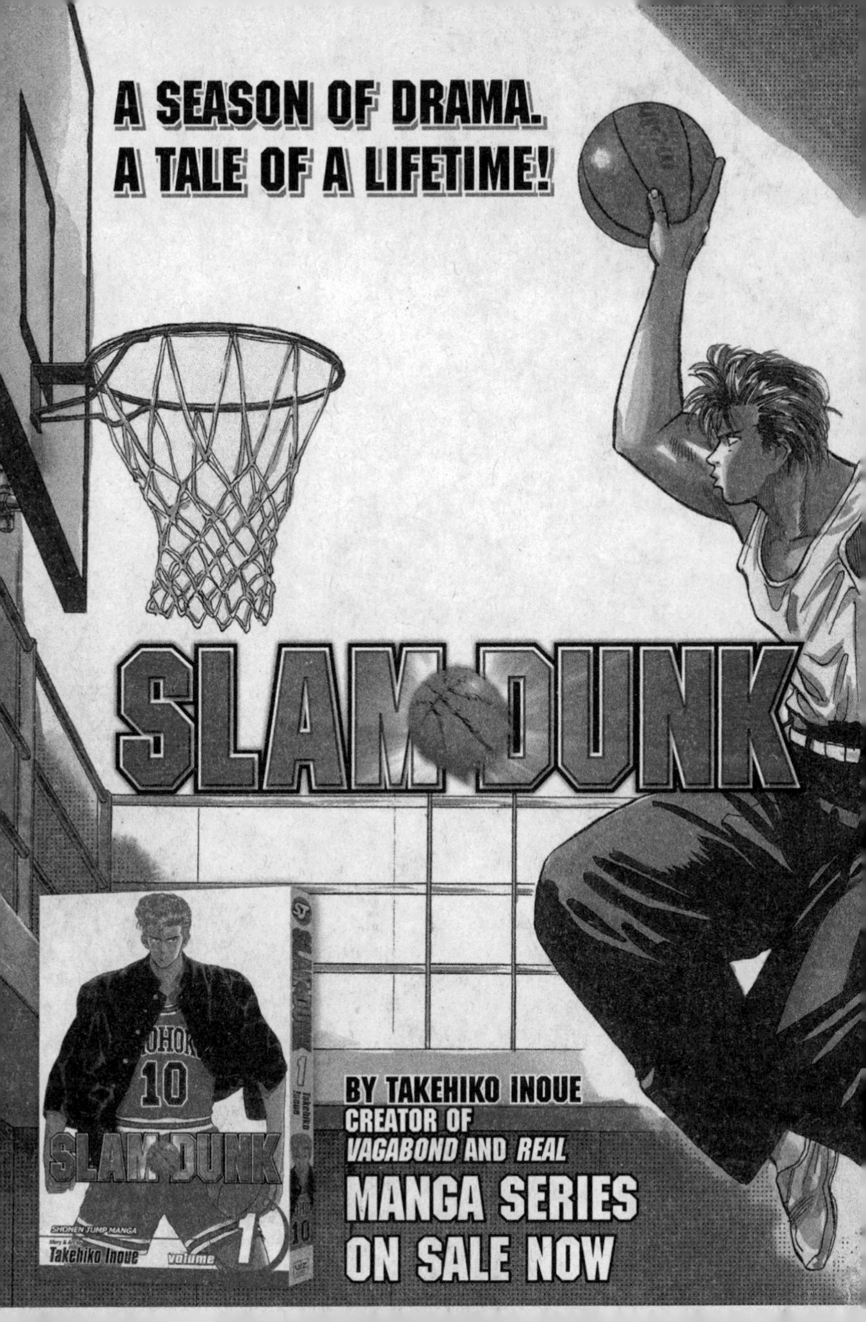
A SEASON OF DRAMA.
A TALE OF A LIFETIME!
SLAM DUNK
SLAM DUNK
SHONEN JUMP MANGA
Takehiko Inoue
volume 1
BY TAKEHIKO INOUE
CREATOR OF
VAGABOND AND REAL
MANGA SERIES
ON SALE NOW

A PREMIUM BOX SET OF THE FIRST TWO STORY ARCS OF ONE PIECE!

A PIRATE'S TREASURE FOR ANY MANGA FAN!

STORY AND ART BY EIICHIRO ODA

Comes with **EXCLUSIVE POSTER** and the **ROMANCE DAWN** mini-comic!

As a child, Monkey D. Luffy dreamed of becoming King of the Pirates. But his life changed when he accidentally gained the power to stretch like rubber...at the cost of never being able to swim again! Years later, Luffy sets off in search of the "One Piece," said to be the greatest treasure in the world...

This box set includes VOLUMES 1-23, which comprise the EAST BLUE and BAROQUE WORKS story arcs.

EXCLUSIVE PREMIUMS and GREAT SAVINGS
over buying the individual volumes!

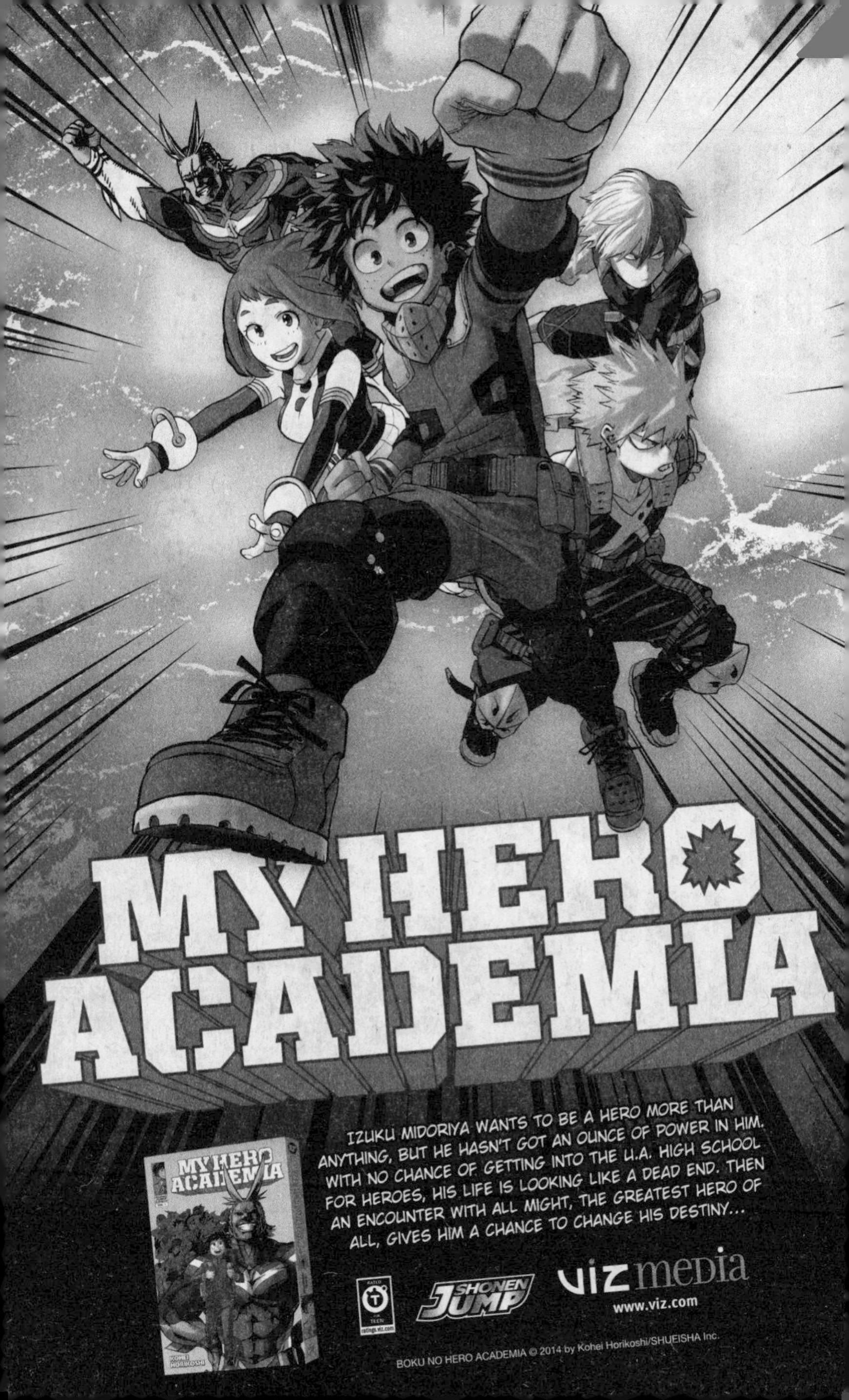
MY HERO ACADEMIA
IZUKU MIDORIYA WANTS TO BE A HERO MORE THAN ANYTHING, BUT HE HASN'T GOT AN OUNCE OF POWER IN HIM. WITH NO CHANCE OF GETTING INTO THE U.A. HIGH SCHOOL FOR HEROES, HIS LIFE IS LOOKING LIKE A DEAD END. THEN AN ENCOUNTER WITH ALL MIGHT, THE GREATEST HERO OF ALL, GIVES HIM A CHANCE TO CHANGE HIS DESTINY…
MY HERO ACADEMIA
KOHEI HORIKOSHI
SHONEN JUMP
viz media
www.viz.com
BOKU NO HERO ACADEMIA © 2014 by Kohei Horikoshi/SHUEISHA Inc.

THE ACTION-PACKED SUPERHERO COMEDY ABOUT ONE MAN'S AMBITION TO BE A HERO FOR FUN!

ONE-PUNCH MAN

STORY BY
ONE | ART BY
YUSUKE MURATA

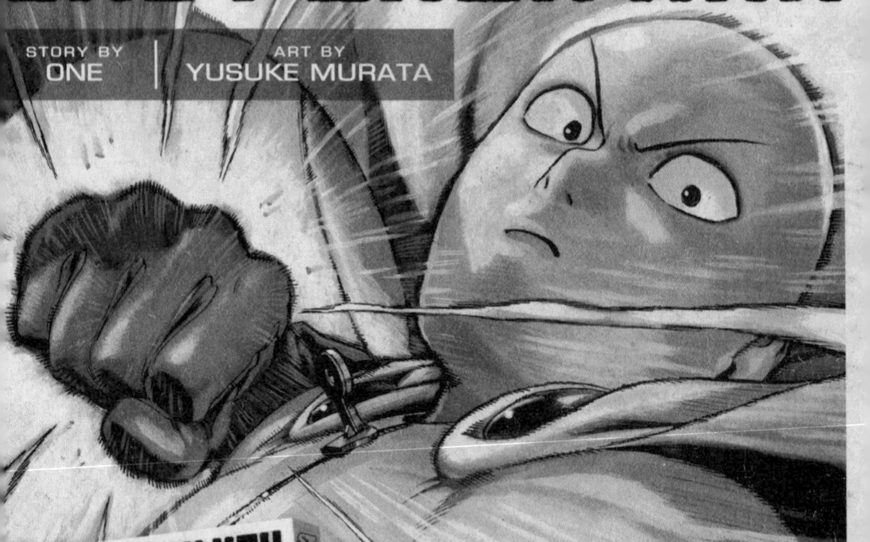

Nothing about Saitama passes the eyeball test when it comes to superheroes, from his lifeless expression to his bald head to his unimpressive physique. However, this average-looking guy has a not-so-average problem—he just can't seem to find an opponent strong enough to take on!

Can he finally find an opponent who can go toe-to-toe with him and give his life some meaning? Or is he doomed to a life of superpowered boredom?

RATED **T** TEEN
ratings.viz.com

SHONEN **JUMP**

VIZ media
www.viz.com